PERSPECTIVES ON WRITING
Series Editor, Susan H. McLeod

PERSPECTIVES ON WRITING
Series Editor, Susan H. McLeod

The Perspectives on Writing series addresses writing studies in a broad sense. Consistent with the wide ranging approaches characteristic of teaching and scholarship in writing across the curriculum, the series presents works that take divergent perspectives on working as a writer, teaching writing, administering writing programs, and studying writing in its various forms.

The WAC Clearinghouse and Parlor Press are collaborating so that these books will be widely available through free digital distribution and low-cost print editions. The publishers and the Series editor are teachers and researchers of writing, committed to the principle that knowledge should freely circulate. We see the opportunities that new technologies have for further democratizing knowledge. And we see that to share the power of writing is to share the means for all to articulate their needs, interest, and learning into the great experiment of literacy.

Other Books in the Series

Charles Bazerman and David R. Russell (Eds.), *Writing Selves/Writing Societies* (2003)

Gerald P. Delahunty and James Garvey, *The English Language: From Sound to Sense* (2009)

Charles Bazerman, Adair Bonini, and Débora Figueiredo (Eds.), *Genre in a Changing World* (2009)

David Franke, Alex Reid, and Anthony Di Renzo (Eds.), *Design Discourse: Composing and Revising Programs in Professional and Technical Writing* (2010)

Martine Courant Rife, Shaun Slattery, and Dànielle Nicole DeVoss (Eds.), *Copy(write): Intellectual Property in the Writing Classroom* (2011)

Doreen Starke-Meyerring, Anthony Paré, Natasha Artemeva, Miriam Horne, and Larissa Yousoubova, *Writing in Knowledge Societies* (2011)

Andy Kirkpatrick and Zhichang Xu, *Chinese Rhetoric and Writing: An Introduction for Language Teachers* (2012)

Chris Thaiss, Gerd Bräuer, Paula Carlino, Lisa Ganobcsik-Williams, and Aparna Sinha (Eds.), *Writing Programs Worldwide: Profiles of Academic Writing in Many Places* (2012).

INTERNATIONAL ADVANCES IN WRITING RESEARCH: CULTURES, PLACES, MEASURES

Edited by

Charles Bazerman
Chris Dean
Jessica Early
Karen Lunsford
Suzie Null
Paul Rogers
Amanda Stansell

The WAC Clearinghouse
wac.colostate.edu
Fort Collins, Colorado

Parlor Press
www.parlorpress.com
Anderson, South Carolina

The WAC Clearinghouse, Fort Collins, Colorado 80523-1052
Parlor Press, 3015 Brackenberry Drive, Anderson, South Carolina 29621

© 2012 by Charles Bazerman, Chris Dean, Jessica Early, Karen Lunsford, Suzie Null, Paul Rogers, and Amanda Stansell. This work is licensed under a Creative Commons Attribution-Noncommercial-No Derivative Works 3.0 United States License.

Printed in the United States of America

Library of Congress Cataloging-in-Publication Data

International advances in writing research : cultures, places, measures / edited by Charles Bazerman ... [et al.].
   p. cm. -- (Perspectives on writing)
 Papers presented at the 2011 WRAB conference.
 Includes bibliographical references.
  ISBN 978-1-60235-352-7 (pbk. : alk. paper) -- ISBN 978-1-60235-353-4 (hardcover : alk. paper) -- ISBN 978-1-60235-354-1 (adobe ebook) -- ISBN 978-1-60235-355-8 (epub)
  1. Rhetoric--Study and teaching--Congresses. 2. Rhetoric--Research--Congresses. 3. Composition (Language arts)--Study and teaching--Research--Congresses. 4. Written communication--Research--Congresses. I. Bazerman, Charles.
 P53.27.I57 2012
 808.007--dc23
                        2012033060

Copyeditor: Don Donahue
Designers: Mike Palmquist
Series Editor: Susan H. McLeod

This book is printed on acid-free paper.

The WAC Clearinghouse supports teachers of writing across the disciplines. Hosted by Colorado State University, it brings together scholarly journals and book series as well as resources for teachers who use writing in their courses. This book is available in digital format for free download at http://wac.colostate.edu.

Parlor Press, LLC is an independent publisher of scholarly and trade titles in print and multimedia formats. This book is available in paperback, cloth, and Adobe eBook formats from Parlor Press at http://www.parlorpress.com. For submission information or to find out about Parlor Press publications, write to Parlor Press, 3015 Brackenberry Drive, Anderson, South Carolina 29621, or email editor@parlorpress.com.

Acknowledgments

We would like to thank the many people who made possible the Writing Research Across Borders II Conference at George Mason University and who made possible this volume. We would especially like to thank the George Mason University Office of Research and Economic Development, which provided support for the production of this volume.

CONTENTS

Introduction 3

Section 1. Pedagogical Approaches 5

Chapter 1. Academic Writing Instruction in Australian Tertiary Education: The Early Years 7
    Kate Chanock

Chapter 2. Teacher's Perceptions of English Language Writing Instruction in China 23
    Danling Fu and Marylou Matoush

Chapter 3. Access and Teachers' Perceptions of Professional Development in Writing 41
    Sarah J. McCarthey, Rebecca L. Woodard, and Grace Kang

Chapter 4. Multimodality in Subtitling for the Deaf and the Hard-of-Hearing Education in Brazil 61
    Vera Lúcia Santiago Araújo

Section 2. Assessment 81

Chapter 5. Rethinking K-12 Writing Assessment to Support Best Instructional Practices 83
    Paul Deane, John Sabatini, and Mary Fowles

Chapter 6. Automated Essay Scoring and The Search for Valid Writing Assessment 103
    Andrew Klobucar, Paul Deane, Norbert Elliot, Chaitanya Ramineni, Perry Deess, and Alex Rudniy

Chapter 7. Construct Validity, Length, Score, and Time in Holistically Graded Writing Assessments: The Case against Automated Essay Scoring (AES) 121
    Les Perelman

Chapter 8. The Politics of Research and Assessment in Writing 133
    Peggy O'Neill, Sandy Murphy, and Linda Adler-Kassner

Chapter 9. Prominent Feature Analysis: Linking Assessment
and Instruction *151*
    Sherry S. Swain, Richard L. Graves, David T. Morse, and Kimberly J.
    Patterson

Chapter 10. "A Matter of Personal Taste": Teachers' Constructs of Writing
Quality in the Secondary School English Classroom *167*
    Helen Lines

Section 3. Writing at the Borders of School and the World *189*

Chapter 11. The Reality of Fiction-writing in Situations of
Political Violence. *191*
    Colette Daiute

Chapter 12. Naming in Pupil Writings (9 to 14 Years Old) *211*
    Christina Romain and Marie-Noëlle Roubaud

Chapter 13. Does the Internet Connect Writing in and out of Educational
Settings? Views of Norwegian students on the Threshold of Higher
Education *233*
    Håvard Skaar

Chapter 14. Sponsoring "Green" Subjects: The World Bank's 2009 Youth Essay
Contest *251*
    Anne E. Porter

Chapter 15. Metaphors of Writing and Intersections with Jamaican Male
Identity *267*
    Carmeneta Jones and Vivette Milson-Whyte

Section 4. Writing the borders of school and professional practice *285*

Chapter 16. Transcending the Border between Classroom and Newsroom: An
Inquiry into the Efficacy of Newspaper Editing Practices. *287*
    Yvonne Stephens

Chapter 17. Teachers as Editors, Editors as Teachers. *303*
    Angela M. Kohnen

Chapter 18. Academic Genres in University Contexts: An Investigation of
Students' Book Reviews Writing as Classroom Assignments. *319*
    Antonia Dilamar Araújo

Chapter 19. Learning Careers and Enculturation: Production of Scientific Papers by PhD Students in a Mexican Physiology Laboratory: An Exploratory Case Study *335*
Alma Carrasco, Rollin Kent, and Nancy Keranen

**Section 5. Scientific and Academic Practice. *353*

Chapter 20. The Life Cycle of the Scientific Writer: An Investigation of the Senior Academic Scientist as Writer in Australasian Universities *355*
Lisa Emerson

Chapter 21. Publication Practices and Multilingual Professionals in US Universities: Towards Critical Perspectives on Administration and Pedagogy *373*
Missy Watson

Chapter 22. Immersed in the Game of Science: Beliefs, Emotions, and Strategies of NNES Scientists who Regularly Publish in English *387*
Nancy Keranen, Fatima Encinas, and Charles Bazerman

Chapter 23. Critical Acts in Published and Unpublished Research Article Introductions in English: A Look into the Writing for Publication Process *403*
Pilar Mur-Dueñas

Chapter 24. Towards an Integrative Unit of Analysis: Regulation Episodes in Expert Research Article Writing. *421*
Anna Iñesta and Montserrat Castelló

Chapter 25. Producing Scholarly Texts: Writing in English in a Politically Stigmatized Country *449*
Mehdi Riazi

Chapter 26. The Evaluation of Conference Paper Proposals in Linguistics . *467*
Françoise Boch, Fanny Rinck, and Aurélie Nardy

**Section 6. Cultures of Writing in the Workplace. *485*

Chapter 27. Genre and Generic Labor *487*
Clay Spinuzzi

Chapter 28. Construction of Caring Identities in the New Work Order. . . *507*
Zoe Nikolaidou and Anna-Malin Karlsson

Chapter 29. Online Book Reviews and Emerging Generic Conventions: A Situated Study of Authorship, Publishing, and Peer Review.........*521*
    Tim Laquintano

Chapter 30. Coming to Grips with Complexity: Dynamic Systems Theory in the Research of Newswriting................................*539*
    Daniel Perrin

INTERNATIONAL ADVANCES IN WRITING RESEARCH: CULTURES, PLACES, MEASURES

INTRODUCTION

Although research on writing has developed along many lines and in many regions over the past 30 years, the researchers who conduct that work have been in most instances divided along national, disciplinary, and theoretical lines. The Writing Research Across Borders (WRAB) conference series has attempted to bring together the many different disciplines and subfields that study writing in an open forum where researchers of all career stages can share the results of their studies and provide updates on works in progress. The expanded research networks that have emerged from these conferences have led to the formation of the International Society for the Advancement of Writing Research (ISAWR), whose mission is to advance writing research globally.

The fourth iteration of the conference series, Writing Research Across Borders II, took place in February of 2011 at George Mason University in northern Virginia near Washington, DC. At the conference, over 625 participants gathered from 40 countries to meet with colleagues, share works in progress, and hear the latest writing research from across a wide range of disciplines including psychology, linguistics, education, composition, and sociology. The 30 chapters in this volume were selected through a careful review process from the over 500 presentations and then developed through rigorous editing and revision.

Representing the forefront of work at this broad-ranging conference, the chapters are a strong indicator of some of the leading edges of current writing research. The chapters selected for their individual merit, nonetheless thematically cluster, as the editors discovered when organizing the table of contents. Instruction and learning in school contexts, from early childhood through higher education, remain central concerns of research, as the chapters in Section 1. Pedagogical Approaches elaborate. Recently in the US and elsewhere we have seen a dramatically increased emphasis on assessing writing at an institutional level. This pressure and the digital tools being used to facilitate assessment have served to focus and narrow the teaching and learning of writing. While this may seem to be a concern particular to the US, interest in assessment and accountability is influencing educational policy discussions in many regions internationally. To ensure that the contentious debate over assessment tools is grounded in careful research we present a series of studies from leading voices on all sides of the issue in Section 2. Assessment.

Despite the effect of assessments to constrain instruction to meet school-based requirements, researchers and practitioners have shown increasing concern for how school learning is situated in broader social issues (the theme of Section 3. Writing at the Borders of School and World) and how instruction relates to writing practices outside the school (the theme of Section 4. Writing the Orders of School and Professional Practice.) Further attention to writing development extends to the upper reaches of the academy with examination of post-graduate education and scientific publication throughout the career in Section 5. Scientific and Academic Practice. Further, research has continued to grow on writing practices in the workplace, as examined in the closing Section 6. Cultures of Writing in the Workplace.

In brief introductions to each of the sections of this book, we elaborate on the contents and connections of the articles that comprise each. Looking at these clusters of research, we can see overall an interest in the many places writing occurs and the school, disciplinary and workplace cultures that shape writing situations. In that context, assessment itself can be seen as defining a place and shaping a culture of writing. From this orientation toward the contexts of writing we have developed the subtitle of this volume: *Cultures, Places, Measures*.

Early on in our planning process we determined to publish this present volume in an open access format knowing that the free electronic distribution of this research will provide wider and easier access to scholars around the world. This volume indicates growth and development from the volume *Traditions of Writing Research*, which arose out of the first Writing Research Across Borders conference in 2008. Much of that conference and volume served to introduce the great variety of work globally, the varying methodological and theoretical traditions, and the different national and historical contexts which have focused work. This volume evidences the rise of common themes of inquiry across regions, theories, and methods. We look forward to seeing what emerges over coming years and future volumes.

—CB, KL, & PR

SECTION 1.
PEDAGOGICAL APPROACHES

Around the world, students' first hand experiences in learning to write and the pedagogical practices of teachers in classrooms are deeply influenced by educational policy. These policies are situated within rich and layered contexts that include a wide variety of stakeholders including many not directly involved in working with students, such as policy makers, employers, institutional administrators, and various public audiences. What students experience in classrooms and how teachers teach can thus be seen in relation to legal mandates, institutional arrangements (regarding personnel, curriculum, and assessments), as well as conflicting and competing theoretical positions on the nature of learning and appropriate methods for teaching.

To understand and speak to the complexities of actualities of educational practice associated with writing, researchers must investigate a variety of activity systems. This section includes a sampling of work that point towards the pedagogical complexities of instruction in writing at a variety of levels and in specific contexts. We begin with Chanock's overview of education policy and practice related to tertiary writing in Australia, in which the author examines why rich perspectives on writing development drawn from researchers, theorists, and practitioners failed to become the dominant influence on writing instruction. Her work underscores the challenges researchers and teachers face in guiding literacy instruction and curriculum design.

In a contemporary examination of the teaching of English in China today, Fu and Moutash provide a snapshot of educational policy in action across much of China where English language instruction is a required component of education beginning in the third grade. Their work shows, however, that instructional practices in English suffer from a narrow, mechanical approach that ignores both the long history of Chinese writing instruction and the advances in the understanding of the effective learning and teaching of writing across the rest of the world.

As national contexts for schooling, discursive practices, and educational policy continue to change and exert influence on teachers and students in classrooms, the need for teachers to take part in professional development to continuously adapt and respond to the needs of their students is essential. In their study of professional development for teachers in K-12 in the US, McCarthey, Woodard, and Kang show that professional development is also a highly situated activity. Those responsible for designing and delivering professional development must take a number of factors into consideration, and in particular the geographical setting in which the teachers teach, as well as the quality and type of relationships embedded in the professional development experience.

In addition to informing our understanding of the global and policy context for writing instruction, writing research helps inform our understanding of how advances in technology enable and constrain literate practices and new methods of literacy learning. Santiago Araújo's chapter presentes an update of work in progress focused on how multimodal transcription methods are being applied in tackling the constraints of the the subtitling process for films, and how best to enable learners to make choices in learning these processes.

—PR

CHAPTER 1.

ACADEMIC WRITING INSTRUCTION IN AUSTRALIAN TERTIARY EDUCATION: THE EARLY YEARS

Kate Chanock
La Trobe University

This chapter arises out of a historical review of the literature of the first decade of tertiary writing instruction in Australia, the nineteen eighties (for a fuller discussion, see Chanock, 2011a, 2011b).[1] In that study, I sought to discover how the people who shaped the early development of writing instruction understood their role and the difficulties experienced by their students, and what sort of practice they developed to address these. To this end, I read every publication in this field that I could obtain from the eighties, often in the form of non-refereed conference papers. I looked at how the conversation flowed and eddied, the points of convergence and divergence, and the social-professional constellations involved in academic language and learning.

What emerged was a picture in many ways like our present situation in Australia, which will resonate, I think, with readers in the United Kingdom and North America. The framing of education for economic productivity requires "wider participation" in higher education (Bradley, 2008; Department of Employment, Education and Training, 1990; Nelson, 2003; UK National Committee of Enquiry into Higher Education, 1997), and this planned expansion has intensified anxiety about students' (lack of) preparedness for university study (e.g., Department of Education, Training and Youth Affairs (DETYA), 2000). Particular cohorts are targeted for remedial instruction, while plans are made to reform whole course curricula to accommodate the development of transferable skills in every graduating student (Bowden, Hart, King, Trigwell, & Watts, 2002; Hager, Holland, & Beckett, 2002; La Trobe University, 2009; for the UK, see Burke, 2002). All of this might seem to afford opportunities for the learning advisers responsible for writing instruction to shape their universities' responses; it should be instructive, therefore, to look back to an earlier time when similar pressures were felt. What my study suggests, however, is that universities in the eighties largely ignored what their learning advisers knew about supporting students. The literature of that decade manifests an approach that was intellectually persuasive—with ideas similar to those of the Writing Across the Curriculum movement in the US and to the later "tertiary literacies" approach in the UK (Russell, Lea, Parker, Street, & Donahue, 2009) —but not institutionally powerful. In the larger context of Australian universities' efforts to improve teaching and learning, little attention has been given, then or now, to the nature of writing, even though it is the medium by which students' learning is most commonly assessed in many courses. The puzzle of why writing development has received so little institutional attention is the focus of this chapter.

AN OVERVIEW

For most of its thirty-year history, academic writing instruction in Australian colleges and universities has been the responsibility of a small group of specialists in academic language and learning. Initially, conversations around tertiary students' learning included academic developers, who worked with faculty, as well as learning advisers, who worked with students. As the decade progressed, however, these groups diverged into largely separate communities of practice, owing to differences in their theories, methods, and missions. This split had implications for the teaching of writing, because the group that was better positioned to influence institutional policy around teaching and learning—the academic developers—were not concerned with writing but with students' "approaches to learning (deep or surface)" more generally. Learning advisers were more inclined to locate the problems of learning in the discourses their students struggled to appropriate. Though tasked with helping students who were thought deficient for reasons of language, culture, or prior educational experience, they came to challenge the institutional view that cultural adjustment was a problem for a minority of (mainly "non-traditional") students. Instead, they saw all students as confronting unfamiliar cultures of enquiry, and saw their own role as guiding students into the cultures of their disciplines and explicating their discourses. While this enabled them to help students towards often dramatic improvements in their academic writing, the specialised nature of learning advisers' knowledge about discourse—informed by theories about language, rhetoric(s) and culture(s) —was not easy to communicate beyond the borders of their community of practice.

REMEDIAL ORIGINS OF LEARNING SUPPORT

The institutional division of labour between learning advisers and academic developers in Australia goes back to the circumstances in which their roles were separately established. Although the challenges of teaching "non-traditional" students are commonly traced to a "massification" of higher education, it is clear from the literature of the nineteen eighties that this assumption belongs to a "myth of transience" (Rose, 1985; Russell, 1991) in Australia as elsewhere. While "massification" is supposed to have begun with the government-mandated amalgamation of vocational and higher education institutions in 1988 (Dawkins, 1998), we find that well before that time, university administrations were concerned about student success and retention (Anderson & Eaton, 1982). Counselling services were founded from the nineteen fifties in response to intractable problems of failure and attrition, and were given responsibility for improving students' study skills (Quintrell & Robertson, 1995; Stevenson & Kokkinn, 2007). However, as Higher Education research tried and failed to identify deficiencies in particular categories of students, questions began to be asked about teaching as well, and academic development units developed from the late nineteen-sixties (Anderson & Eaton, 1982).

REFRAMING THE ROLE

While academic skills development in Australia was initially located in counselling services, the work required more specialised knowledge about language, and increasingly learning advisers, many with backgrounds in applied linguistics, were employed to remediate under-preparedness in growing cohorts of tertiary students, and to mediate the problems of non-traditional students in particular. However, many soon reframed their role to provide "initiation, not remediation," as Beasley (1988, p. 50) put it. They saw themselves as interpreters between the cultures of their students and the cultures of their institutions (Clerehan, 1990). Ballard (1982), working in the Study Skills centre at the Australian National University, wrote,

> Australian universities are ... bound within the Western cultural traditions of approaches to knowledge and learning. Academic staff can be as culturally blinkered as any overseas undergraduate, and ... the skill I need here is two-fold: to make explicit for the student the cultural values that are deeply implicit in each academic system, and to interpret for both the students and the academic staff member across this cultural divide. (p. 119)

Advisers identified what these cultural values and assumptions were by close reading of the texts that students were asked to read and write for their disciplines, which revealed not only broad differences in national traditions of enquiry, but differences between school and university literacies and between the literacies of different disciplines. And when advisers looked closely at students' use of language, they found that students did not make the same errors consistently, either within an essay or in their writing for different disciplines, and found also that new "expression" problems could appear in later years (Taylor, 1988). This challenged the common view that students were bringing unsuitable dialects to the university, but suggested instead that they had to learn new academic dialects on arrival. Learning advisers also found that students were successful if their work addressed the lecturers' reasons for assigning a question, and used Anglo-western conventions of argument, regardless of whether their actual English usage improved. Ballard (1987) described examples of students' improvement

> .... which display a similar pattern: academic success in the home culture, failure in the new context of a western university, intervention by an adviser who identified the problem as one of cultural dislocation rather than linguistic incompetence, and thereafter a rapid—sometimes spectacular—regaining of competence. (p. 51)

Although the students referred to here were foreign, Ballard went on to point out that domestic students, too, were faced with "cultural dislocation" on entering the university, and that the way her group of colleagues worked with students from overseas was

> only a further development of the way we work with our Australian students. With these students too we move as quickly as possible from the initial "My lecturer sent me because of my poor expression" or "This essay is illiterate" to a consideration of the thinking underlying the piece of writing—the terms of the topic, the appropriate questions to be raised, the evidence and methods of analysis particular to the discipline or the course, the most effective organisation and presentation of the whole argument. We are always, in our work, consciously moving the student towards a clearer recognition of the different styles of thinking appropriate to the sub-cultures of the different disciplines he is studying. With overseas students I am only adding a further cultural

dimension —the habits of thought and exposition peculiar to Western academic culture. (Ballard, 1982, p. 127)

Learning advisers, therefore, were often working against the remedial assumptions on which their employment had been based for, as Ballard (1984) found, "instruction in grammar or ideal structures for essays ... seems to be of marginal value ... . if [students] are approaching their materials in a manner inappropriate to the academic culture of which they are a part" (p. 52). Therefore,

> assistance in the fundamental reorientation of intellectual behaviour cannot be achieved in a short preliminary course divorced from academic content; just as with language skills, we have found it can best be achieved through concurrent assistance, in close relation to the actual demands of the student's course. (Ballard, 1987, p. 117; cf. Buckingham, 1990)

DIVERGENT PARADIGMS

In this respect, there was a good deal of common ground between learning advisers and academic developers, in that both thought it was time to shift focus from what was wrong with students to look at the curriculum and try to understand the students' encounter with what they were taught and how they were taught it. The two groups had very different ways, however, of conceptualising this encounter. Academic developers were drawing on a body of theory coming out of Sweden and the UK, based on a phenomenographic method of researching how students experienced their learning of particular subject matters (Marton, Hounsell, & Entwistle, 1984). Phenomenographers identified three contrasting ways in which students approached their studies: surface learning, aimed at giving the examiner what s/he wanted on assessments in order to survive the course; deep learning, aimed at understanding for the students' own intellectual satisfaction; and instrumental learning, which might use either of these approaches depending on what the student perceived the subject to call for, and which was aimed at optimising grades (Biggs, 1989). At first these approaches were thought to be traits of the individual student, but the theory developed to see them more as responses to the design of subjects, depending on whether students thought a subject was designed to elicit memorisation of facts or understanding of concepts. Out of this theory came the idea of constructive alignment, which is the dominant paradigm today—the idea that teaching should be designed to encourage understanding, and that intended learning outcomes, learning activities, and assessments should all support deep learning (Biggs, 1996,1999).

Learning advisers did not disagree with any of this; it just seemed obvious to many of them, as far as it went, and also in the view of many it did not go far enough. What they felt was missing was any emphasis on culture, either the differences in the cultures that students came from, or the differences in the cultures of enquiry that they encountered at university. Phenomenography was not about culture, and it is possible to suggest reasons for this. First, it developed initially in Sweden, which is not a very multicultural context, and secondly many of its theorists came from scientific backgrounds. This seems to be reflected in Saljo's (1979) characterisation of "deep learning as 'an interpretative process aimed at understanding reality'" (as cited in Taylor, 1990, p. 56).

The learning advisers' insights had no place in a worldview in which "construction of knowledge" referred solely to a cognitive, not a cultural, operation. In this view, student learning constituted a progression from misconceiving reality to understanding it correctly. In many fields, however, different perspectives can produce different, competing or coexisting interpretations, and Bock (1986) objected that the phenomenographers' definition of "learning as the integration of complex wholes leading to a personal change in the student's conception of reality ... leaves little space for exploring the process through which a student learns to reject, knowingly, in total or part, the conception of reality offered by a particular writer" (Bock, 1986, p. 99). As learning advisers saw it, what students needed to understand was not a single, objectively accessible reality, but the ways that people in different disciplines or intellectual traditions construct their distinctive accounts of reality.

The relevance of this perspective is clear from the few examples offered in the literature. For example, Ballard and Clanchy (1988) had a student who received very high grades in anthropology, but a low grade for an English essay because of the "intrusion, into what should be a literary critical analysis, of anthropological concerns and perspectives," when the student called the gravedigger in Hamlet a "non-aligned source of objective social criticism" (Ballard & Clanchy, 1988, p. 16). After talking with a learning adviser, the student rewrote her essay to focus on how the gravedigger scene functions in the dramatic structure of the play, and her grade improved. This was a very different problem from the one that concerned phenomenographers, that is, whether students aim to understand their reading, or just to reproduce it. This student was reading to understand, but what she wanted to understand was the gravedigger's social role—and indeed, she was making those connections between different ways of thinking that we claim we want students to make—when all that was appropriate to the discourse was to comment on the way that drama works.

LOSING THE ARGUMENT

Now, both approaches, whether from learning theory or from discourse, produced insights that could support teaching and learning, but only one of them came to have much influence. Instead of drawing on both, universities have tended to embrace deep and surface learning theory, while culture and language have continued to be seen as problems that some students have rather than as something fundamental to learning. Why, then, did the focus on discourses not gain more traction? It seems that this was partly because many academic developers, who were given the job of improving teaching, regarded the work of learning skills advisers as irrelevant to students' success. In their paradigm, the only role for learning advisers was to support the instrumental approach by teaching generic skills of time and task management and note taking to help students develop the habits that would maximise their chances of coping with their studies. But "the key to improving learning in higher education is not the provision of skills," Ramsden (1987) wrote,

> but the provision of teaching and assessment that will permit able students to realise their demonstrated potential. By studying how and what students learn, academics can improve their teaching, maximising the chances of students engaging with content in the ways they wish them to engage with it, and identifying misconceptions that require special attention. (p. 151)

BARRIERS TO COMMUNICATION

The irony here, of course, is that many learning advisers agreed that generic recipes for study were not what students needed, but the things they thought were needed were not widely heard, outside of their own circles. One reason for this seems to have been that the academic developers who represented the work of learning advisers in the terms above ignored the body of work by learning advisers that demonstrated their interest in questions of culture and epistemology, representing them instead as narrowly focused on a "technification" of study through imparting a repertoire of strategies to struggling students (Biggs, 1989). While academic developers had to work hard to get the ear of institutional management, they were seen to have more academic authority than learning advisers, and more opportunity, therefore, to promote their preferred approach. However, there may be other reasons for the lesser success of learning advisers' insistence on the importance of written academic discourse. For one thing, although working one-to-one—as Taylor (1990, p. 70) put it, "engag[ing] seriously," along with our students, in the problems of the disciplines—was a very effective method of helping students, it limited advisers' influence on wider institutional policies and practices. Academic developers could suggest curriculum reforms designed to improve all students' learning in ways that were replicable and, crucially, measurable, which the dialogue between advisers and individual students was not. From these dialogues, learning advisers gained valuable insights into students' experience, with potential implications for teaching; but their evidence could always be dismissed as "anecdotal".

Another problem may have been the specialised language of their discussions. The analytical methods that learning advisers used came from applied linguistics, contrastive rhetoric, and sometimes systemic functional linguistics. And here particularly, the grammatical metalanguage of "field, tenor, mode, participants and processes, lexical density and grammatical metaphor" was different from any that discipline lecturers might already have (for examples in use, see e.g., Jones, Gollin, Drury & Economou, 1989). Where academic developers found it easy to talk about deep or surface learning in their meetings with faculty, learning advisers lacked a common language to talk with managers and discipline teaching staff.

WHAT NEXT?

My focus here has been on the territorial and epistemological divide, in Australia, between the professional groups responsible for students' learning, as a way of explaining how writing got left out of this picture. Where phenomenographers were interested in how knowledge about reality is cognitively constructed in the mind, learning advisers were interested in how knowledge about interpretation is rhetorically constructed on the page (Chanock, 2011b). The more accessible theory of deep and surface learning, and the resulting paradigm of "constructive alignment" may be useful for improving curriculum design. But they do not address the complexity that learning advisers recognised in students' encounters with academic cultures, because the phenomenographical theory of approaches to learning was not about culture.

Two and a half decades later, moreover, this complexity is still not adequately addressed, with academic skills commonly provided as a remedial service for "underprepared" students (Baik & Greig 2009). There is, concurrently, a move afoot in Australia and the UK to locate the development of learning skills, in the form of "Graduate Attributes (Skills/Capabilities)," in discipline curricula, and this could provide a space for focussing on the discourses of those disciplines as expressions of their cultures. However, the persistent view that graduate skills are generic and transferable does nothing to encourage such a focus, and there is still the risk that insights from linguistics and from working intensively with students may be lost.

The push to teach generic skills comes from employers and the government, rather than from academics (Commonwealth of Australia, 1998; DETYA, 2000; Hager, Holland, & Beckett, 2002; Nelson, 2003; for the UK, see NAB/UGC, 1984; for Canada, see Metcalfe & Fenwick, 2009). Among scholars of writing in the disciplines, a consensus has been building that little of value can be said about writing at a generic level. The writing of the disciplines reflects their various epistemologies and ways of working, which can differ considerably despite appearances of commonality (Baik & Greig, 2009; Bazerman, 1981; Durkin & Main, 2002; Elton, 2010; Hyland, 2002; Jones, 2009; Magyar, McAvoy, & Forstner, 2011; Parry, 1998; Reid & Parker, 2002; Wingate, 2007). For this reason, "[t]erminology widely used by tutors and/or guidelines to name academic writing conventions .... [such as] argument and structure. ... ha[s] been signalled ... as being hugely problematic by a number of researchers" (Lillis & Turner, 2001, p. 58).

The variety of disciplinary discourses has led scholars to question the assumption that expertise in these discourses is transferable, or at least, that transfer can occur from generic instruction to discipline practice (e.g., Baik & Greig, 2009; Gibbs, 2009; Gimenez, in press; Griffin, 1994; Hyland, 2002; Jones, 2009; Kift & Moody, 2009; Neumann, Parry, & Becher, 2002). It seems to follow that explicit instruction in, and development of, academic literacies should be integrated into the curriculum of each discipline. This is a development consistent with the views of learning advisers going back to the nineteen eighties, as we have seen, and with the current view of our peak body, the Association for Academic Language and Learning (AALL), on "best practice." In its submission to the Good practice principles for English language proficiency for international students in Australian universities, AALL calls for "an integrated approach, [in which] the literacy demands of the discipline become an explicit part of the subjects that students study" (Australian Universities Quality Agency, 2009, Appendix 2, p. 9).

But will such a shift bring opportunities for learning advisers to collaborate with discipline lecturers in reworking their subjects to include a focus on the discourses with which students must engage? Or will they once again be excluded, as suggested by Wingate's view that "[b]ecause of the disciplinary differences in the construction of knowledge, the support of subject tutors rather than that of external 'learning experts' is needed" (2007, p. 395; cf. Gibbs, 2009, p. 5)? This is more than an industrial question (though it is that too). Scholars (including Wingate) point to the problem that discipline lecturers often lack the interest and knowledge required to do this kind of work (Bailey, 2010; Donahue, 2010; Fallows & Steven, 2000; Ganobcsik-Williams, 2004; Jones, 2009; Star & Hammer, 2008; Wingate, 2006, 2007). This is why collaboration is vital: as Elton (2010) puts it, because "[t]he genre of academic writing is discipline dependent, ... neither specialists in academic writing nor practising academics in a discipline can, independently of each other, provide students with the necessary help to develop the ability to write in their academic disciplines" (p. 151; cf. Magyar et al., 2011). He is concerned, however, that the disparity in academic status between learning advisers and discipline lecturers means that "[s]eldom is there a constructive collaboration between equals—discipline specialists and writing specialists—in the interests of students" (Elton, 2010, p. 151).

Even as "best practice" is seen to consist of collaboratively embedding the development of academic writing and other skills into discipline curricula, the actual practice falls well short of this. We must hope that, with the current enthusiasm for returning responsibility for development of academic literacies to the disciplines, learning advisers with their considerable knowledge of these literacies will be called upon to inform effective curriculum renewal.

NOTE

1. This study is associated with a project by the national Association for Academic Language and Learning (AALL) to develop a searchable database of publications by teachers of academic skills in Australian tertiary institutions. Interested readers can find this soon at http://www.aall.org.au.

REFERENCES

Anderson, D., & Eaton, E. (1982). Australian higher education research and society part I: Post-war reconstruction and expansion: 1940-1965. *Higher Education Research and Development, 1*(1), 5-32.

Australian Universities Quality Agency (AUQA) (2009). *Good practice principles for English language proficiency for international students in Australian universities.* (Report to the Department of Education, Employment and

Workplace Relations, Canberra). Retrieved from http://www.deewr.gov.au/HigherEducation/Publications/Pages/GoodPracticePrinciples.aspx

Baik, C., & Greig, J. (2009). Improving the academic outcomes of undergraduate ESL students: The case for discipline-based academic skills programs. *Higher Education Research and Development, 28*(4), 401-416.

Bailey, R. (2010). The role and efficacy of generic learning and study support: What is the experience and perspective of academic teaching staff? *Journal of Learning Development in Higher Education, 2*, 1-13. Retrieved from http://www.aldinhe.ac.uk/ojs/index.php?journal=jldhe&page=issue&op=view&path%5B%5D=9

Ballard, B. (1982). Language is not enough: Responses to the difficulties of overseas students. In H. Bock & J. Gassin (Eds.), *Papers from the Conference, Communication at University: Purpose, Process and Product* (pp. 116-128). Melbourne: La Trobe University. Retrieved from http://www.aall.org.au/conferences.

Ballard, B. (1984). Improving student writing: An integrated approach to cultural adjustment. In R. Williams, J. Swales, and J. Kirkman (Eds.), *Common ground: Shared interests in ESP and communication studies* (pp. 43-54). Oxford: Pergamon Press.

Ballard, B. (1987). Academic adjustment: The other side of the export dollar. *Higher Education Research and Development, 6*(2), 109-119.

Ballard, B., & Clanchy, J. (1988). Literacy in the university: An "anthropological" approach. In G. Taylor, B. Ballard, V. Beasley, H. Bock, J. Clanchy & P. Nightingale. *Literacy by degrees* (pp. 7-23). Buckingham, UK, & Philadelphia: SRHE & Open University Press.

Bazerman, C. (1981). What written knowledge does: Three examples of academic discourse. *Philosophy of the Social Sciences, 11*(3), 361-388.

Beasley, V. (1988). Developing academic literacy: The Flinders experience. In G. Taylor, B. Ballard, V. Beasley, H. Bock, J. Clanchy & P. Nightingale. *Literacy by degrees* (pp. 42-52). Buckingham, UK, & Philadelphia: SRHE & Open University Press.

Biggs, J. (1989). Approaches to the enhancement of tertiary learning. *Higher Education Research and Development, 8*(1), 7-25.

Biggs, J. (1996). Enhancing teaching through constructive alignment. *Higher Education 32*, 347-364.

Biggs, J. (1999). *Teaching for quality learning at university*. Buckingham, UK: SRHE and Open University Press.

Bock, H. (1986). Phenomenography: Orthodoxy and innovation or innovation and orthodoxy? In J. Bowden (Ed.), *Student learning: Research into practice. The Marysville Symposium* (pp. 95-114). Parkville, Melbourne: Centre for the Study of Higher Education, The University of Melbourne.

Bowden, J., Hart, G., King, B., Trigwell, K., & Watts, O. (2002). *Generic capabilities of ATN university graduates.* Teaching and Learning Committee, Australian Technology Network (RMIT, QUT, UTS, Curtin, & UNISA). Retrieved from http://www.clt.uts.edu.au/ATN.grad.cap.project.index.html

Buckingham, J. (1990). Learning styles and processes characteristic of Japanese and Australian education: The cultural divide. In M. Kratzing (Ed.), *Eighth Australasian learning and language skills conference 11-13 July 1990* (pp. 199-215). Brisbane: QUT Counselling Services.

Burke, P. (2002). Resource Guide: *The development of key skills in higher education.* LTSN Hospitality, Leisure, Sport and Tourism. Retrieved from http://www.heacademy.ac.uk/assets/hlst/documents/resource_guides/development_of_keyskills_in_higher_education.pdf

Chanock, K. (2011a). A historical literature review of Australian publications in the field of academic language and learning in the 1980s: Themes, schemes, and schisms: Part One. *Journal of Academic Language and Learning, 5*(1), A-36 – A-58. Retrieved from http://journal.aall.org.au/index.php/jall/article/view/119

Chanock, K. (2011b). A historical literature review of Australian publications in the field of academic language and learning in the 1980s: Themes, schemes, and schisms: Part Two. *Journal of Academic Language and Learning, 5*(1), A-59 – A-87. from http://journal.aall.org.au/index.php/jall/article/view/120

Clerehan, R. (1990). Learning needs of fee-paying overseas students at Chisholm Institute of Technology. In M. Kratzing (Ed.), *Eighth Australasian Learning and Language Skills Conference 11-13 July 1990* (pp. 217-226). Brisbane: QUT Counselling Services.

Commonwealth of Australia (1998). *Learning for Life: Final Report. Review of Higher Education Financing and Policy (The West Review).* Department of Employment, Education, Training and Youth Affairs. Retrieved from http://www.dest.gov.au/archive/highered/hereview/toc.htm

Commonwealth of Australia (2008). *Review of Australian Higher Education Final Report December 2008.* Canberra: Commonwealth of Australia. Retrieved from http://www.deewr.gov.au/HigherEducation/Review/Documents/PDF/Higher%20Education%20Review_Title%20page%20to%20chapter%202.pdf

Dawkins, The Hon. J. S. (1988). *Higher education: A policy statement.* Canberra: Australian Government Publishing Service.

Department of Employment, Education and Training (DEET) (1990). *A Fair Chance for All: Higher education that's within everyone's reach.* Canberra: Australian Government Publishing Service. Retrieved from http://www.dest.gov.au/NR/rdonlyres/37BDE622-FA72-4C9C-9A01-10AAC68FD90C/3740/90_06.pdf

Department of Education, Training and Youth Affairs (2000). *Employer Satisfaction with Graduate Skills: Research Report.* Commonwealth of Australia. Retrieved from http://www.dest.gov.au/archive/highered/eippubs/eip99-7/eip99_7pdf.pdf

Donahue, C. (2010). Writing, speaking and the disciplines at Dartmouth's Institute for Writing and Rhetoric. *Arts and Humanities in Higher Education, 9*(2), 223-226.

Durkin, K., & Main, A. (2002). Discipline-based study skills support for first-year undergraduate students. *Active Learning in Higher Education, 3*, 24-39.

Elton, L. (2010). Academic writing and tacit knowledge. *Teaching in Higher Education, 15*(2), 151-160.

Fallows, S., & Steven, C. (2000). Embedding a skills program for all students. In S. Fallows & C. Steven (Eds.), *Integrating key skills in higher education* (pp. 17-31). London: Kogan Page.

Ganobcsik-Williams, L. (2004). *A report on the teaching of academic writing in UK higher education.* The Royal Literary Fund. Retrieved from http://www.rlf.org.uk/FELLOWSHIPSCHEME/DOCUMENTS/tEACHINGwRITINGukhe.PDF

Gibbs, G. (2009). Developing students as learners: Varied phenomena, varied contexts and a developmental trajectory for the whole endeavour. *Journal of Learning Development in Higher Education, 1*, 1-12. Retrieved from http://www.aldinhe.ac.uk/ojs/index.php?journal=jldhe&page=article&op=view&path%5B%5D=30&path%5B%5D=14

Gimenez, J. (2011). Disciplinary epistemologies, generic attributes and undergraduate academic writing in nursing and midwifery. *Higher Education. Online First*, 16 June, 2011. DOI10.1007/s10734-011-9447-6

Griffin, A. (1994). Transferring learning in higher education: Problems and possibilities. In R. Barnett (Ed.), *Academic community: Discourse or disorder?* London: Jessica Kingsley

Hager, P., Holland, S., & Beckett, D. (2002). Enhancing the learning and employability of graduates: The role of generic skills. Position Paper No. 9. Melbourne: Business/Higher Education Round Table.

Hyland, K. (2002). Specificity revisited: How far should we go now? *English for Specific Purposes, 21*(3), 385-395.

Jones, A. (2009). Redisciplining generic attributes: The disciplinary context in focus. *Studies in Higher Education, 34*(1), 85-100.

Jones, J., Gollin, S., Drury, H., & Economou, D. (1989). Systemic-Functional Linguistics and its application to the TESOL curriculum. In R. Hasan & J. R. Martin (Eds.), *Language development: Learning language, learning culture* (pp. 257-328). Norwood, NJ: Ablex.

Kift, S., & Moody, K. (2009 November). Harnessing assessment and feedback in the first year to support learning success, engagement and retention. Paper presented at the ATN Assessment Conference 2009: Assessment in Different Dimensions, held November 19-20, 2009 at RMIT University, Melbourne. Abstract retrieved from http://emedia.rmit.edu.au/conferences/index.php/ATNAC/ATNAC09; follow link to http://emedia.rmit.edu.au/conferences/index.php/ATNAC/ATNAC09/paper/viewFile/96/15

La Trobe University (2009). *Design for Learning: Curriculum review and renewal at La Trobe University.* Retrieved from University of LaTrobe website http://www.latrobe.edu.au/ctlc/assets/downloads/dfl/DFL-booklet.pdf

Lillis, T., & Turner, J. (2001). Student writing in higher education: Contemporary confusion, traditional concerns. *Teaching in Higher Education, 6*(1), 57-68.

Magyar, A., McAvoy, D., & Forstner, K. (2011). "If only we knew what they wanted": Bridging the gap between student uncertainty and lecturers' expectations. *Journal of Learning Development in Higher Education, 3*, 1-18. Retrieved from http://www.aldinhe.ac.uk/ojs/index.php?journal=jldhe&page=article&op=view&path%5B%5D=68

Marton, F., Hounsell, D., & Entwistle, N. (Eds.). (1984). *The experience of learning.* Edinburgh: Scottish Academic Press.

Metcalfe, A., & Fenwick, T. (2009). Knowledge for whose society? Knowledge production, higher education, and federal policy in Canada. *Higher Education, 57*(2), 209-225.

National Advisory Board for Public Sector Education/University Grants Committee (NAB/UGC) (1984). Higher education and the needs of society. London: National Advisory Board for Public Sector Education/University Grants Committee.

Nelson, B. (2003). *Our universities: Backing Australia's future.* Canberra: Commonwealth of Australia. Retrieved from http://www.cdu.edu.au/newsroom/stories/2003/may/fedbudget/policy_paper.pdf

Neumann, R., Parry, S., & Becher, T. (2002). Teaching and learning in their disciplinary contexts: A conceptual analysis. *Studies in Higher Education, 27*(4), 405-417.

Parry, S. (1998). Disciplinary discourse in doctoral theses. Higher Education, 36(2), 273-299.

Quintrell, N., & Robertson, M. (1995). Student counselling in Australian universities: Forty years of development. *International Journal for the Advancement of Counselling, 18*(4), 203-221.

Ramsden, P. (1987). Why and how to study student learning. In A. Miller & G. Sachse-Akerlind (Eds.), *Research and development in higher education volume*

9: The learner in higher education: A forgotten species?* (pp. 141-154). Sydney: HERDSA.

Reid, I., & Parker, L. (2002). Framing institutional policies on literacies. *Australian Review of Applied Linguistics, 25*(2), 19-27.

Rose, M. (1985). The language of exclusion: Writing instruction at the university. *College English, 47*, 341-359.

Russell, D. (1991). *Writing in the academic disciplines, 1870-1990: A curricular history.* Carbondale Il: Southern Illinois University Press.

Russell, D., Lea, M., Parker, J., Street, B., & Donahue, T. (2009). Exploring notions of genre in "academic literacies" and "writing in the disciplines": Approaches across countries and contexts. In C. Bazerman, A. Bonini, & D. Figueiredo (Eds.), *Genre in a changing world.* Perspectives on writing. Fort Collins, CO: The WAC Clearinghouse and Parlor Press. Retrieved from http://wac.colostate.edu/books/genre

Star, C., & Hammer, S. (2008). Teaching generic skills: Eroding the higher purpose of universities, or an opportunity for renewal? *Oxford Review of Education, 34*(2), 237-251.

Stevenson, M., & Kokkinn, B. (2007). Pinned to the margins? The contextual shaping of academic language and learning practice. *Journal of Academic Language and Learning, 1*(1), A-44 – A-54. Retrieved from http://journal.aall.org.au/index.php/jall/issue/view/2

Taylor, G. (1988). The literacy of knowing: Content and form in students' English. In G. Taylor, B. Ballard, V. Beasley, H. Bock, J. Clanchy, & P. Nightingale (Eds.), *Literacy by degrees* (pp. 53-64). Buckingham, UK, & Philadelphia: SRHE & Open University Press.

Taylor, G. (1990). The notion of skill: An hermeneutical perspective. In M. Kratzing (Ed.), *Eighth Australasian learning and language skills conference 11-13 July 1990* (pp. 52-74). Brisbane: QUT Counselling Service.

Taylor, G., Ballard, B., Beasley, V., Bock, H., Clanchy, J., & Nightingale, P. (1988). *Literacy by degrees.* Buckingham, UK, & Philadelphia: SRHE & Open University Press.

UK National Committee of Enquiry into Higher Education (the Dearing Committee) (1997). *Higher education in the learning society: Report of the national committee.* London: HMSO. Retrieved from http://www.leeds.ac.uk/educol/ncihe

Wingate, U. (2006). Doing away with "study skills." *Teaching in Higher Education, 11*(4), 457-469.

Wingate, U. (2007). A framework for transition: Supporting "learning to learn" in higher education. *Higher Education Quarterly, 61*(3), 391-405.

CHAPTER 2.

TEACHER'S PERCEPTIONS OF ENGLISH LANGUAGE WRITING INSTRUCTION IN CHINA

Danling Fu and Marylou Matoush
University of Florida and Western Carolina University

English is taught in every school throughout the People's Republic of China (PRC). It is estimated that there are more teachers of English in China than in the United States, and that by year 2016, China will have the largest English speaking population in the world. While English learning is widespread in China, indigenous English language teacher's perceptions regarding the teaching of English writing have led us to believe that English, although popular, may be seen as a tool meant for limited functional mimetic use rather than as a vehicle for enabling full fledged empowered bilingual communicative competence in a globalized world. We found a heavy focus on linguistically controlled language instruction rather than literacy instruction embedded in the humanities complemented by socially complex pragmatics. That focus, plus a lack of teacher preparation and a test-driven orientation may contribute to English writing instruction that pales in comparison to Chinese writing instruction. It is possible that the two forms of instruction differ to the point that Chinese students fail to transfer strategies from one to another and that the difference contributes to poor national scores on tests of writing in English and positions them as mere linguistic manipulators rather than as biliterate bilinguals.

BACKGROUND

HUMANITIES-BASED TRADITIONAL L1 WRITING INSTRUCTION

China has a rich history of valuing writing dating back to early Confucian age. Like traditional native language writing instruction in Europe, traditional writing instruction in China was deeply rooted in a classical vision of the humanities and a desire to perpetuate the wisdom of the ages via the development of an academically elite class. Instruction in the two hemispheres, although different in content and emphasis, bore many similarities. Both traditions focused on the education of the affluent, yet allowed a degree of advancement through education. Both emphasized canonical texts. Student writing was evaluated in both by canonical standards of genre, style, grammar, spelling, and handwriting or calligraphy. Although, Europeans appear to have been more inclined to judge simple literacy by the ability to read the Bible and advanced literacy through close reading, the Chinese placed a greater emphasis on writing as evidenced by the elevation of calligraphy to an artistic form and the institutionalization of civil service writing exams.

These humanities-based approaches dominated writing instruction until and throughout the twentieth century despite the egalitarian turn associated with Maoism. Indeed, in China, according to Li (1996), writing teachers "perceive of themselves and act like a link between the past and student to form an unbroken link that stretches as far back as three thousand years" (p. 96). One of Li's interviewees stated: "… tradition is still alive. Teachers still prefer writing that demonstrates a good grasp of vocabulary, history, and classic works, uses vivid imagery, and employs a variety of rhetorical devices. The use of the colloquial and vulgar is considered a lack of elegance and beauty and is looked down upon" (p. 65). While steeping students in a culture-bound historical perspective, such instruction situates writing as literate activity or as a fully developed tool for thinking and communicating within Chinese culture, but may not adequately prepare any but the most advanced students to manage the "interpretive ambiguity" (Bhabha, 1997) necessary to navigate the multiple perspectives they are apt to encounter in a globalized world where culture may be viewed as something other than nation-bound or static. The problem is magnified when second language writing education takes on a narrow, linguistically controlled approach drawing neither on the rich culture-bound Chinese literacy tradition nor on any of the multiple meaning and composition based approaches from the West.

LINGUISTICALLY CONTROLLED L2 WRITING INSTRUCTION

Hu's studies (2002 and 2005) indicated a linguistically controlled approach to L2 English language and writing instruction appears to dominate in China. According to Silva's (1991) review of second language writing instruction between 1945 and 1990, Charles Fries (1945) was first credited with using principles of behaviorism and structural linguistics to develop an "oral approach" to second language instruction, thereby deemphasizing written language. Although Erazmus (1960) and Briere (1966) recommended the use of written language as a means to extend control and promote fluency, others, notably Pincas (1962) scorned the humanities approach in favor of the "manipulation of fixed patterns" (p. 186), an approach which begins with systematic habit formation via language patterning focused on listening and speaking supported by reading and writing frames which eventually achieve dominance over aural and oral patterning. Repetition, patterning, and predictability across language activities are stressed. Writing instruction exists as a form of linguistic exercise focused on formal accuracy and grammatical correctness, consisting primarily of reproducing language frames, usually at the sentence level, followed by substitutions, transformations, expansions, completions of linguistic patterns using a controlled, but cumulative vocabulary and increasingly complex grammar. Concern for content beyond the acquisition of increased vocabulary, communicative intent, audience, purpose, or style is rare (Silva, 1991). The writer is positioned as a manipulator of grammatically correct sentence patterns. Studies of the effectiveness of language learning from this perspective abound including Ellis (1984), Myles, Mitchell, and Hooper (1999), and Schmidt (2001).

Kaplan (1967) and Hinds (1983) addressed the inadequacies of this sentence level focus by suggesting a contrastive rhetoric approach, which was characterized as "more a pattern drill at the rhetorical level than at the syntactic level" (Kaplan, 1967), promoting writing instruction as organizing content into patterned forms of traditional academic writing (Connor, 1996). Despite this strict structural emphasis, instruction is largely compatible with, but lacks the sociocultural depth associated with traditional humanities-based approaches and is apt to impose structures that are culturally related to the non-native language in an expectation of the development of nativeness in second language usage. The writer is positioned as a manipulator of text patterns and linguistic forms. Expository and persuasive writing amount to organizing a cohesive main idea with supportive details into topic, supporting, and concluding sentences; introductory, supportive, and concluding paragraphs; and the subsequent arrangement of those paragraphs into sections. The use of rhetorical devices such as precise definitions and evidentiary examples, classification or compare and contrast, and cause and effect are also taught. Narrative structures, when introduced, are similarly structured. Formal accuracy and grammatical correctness is emphasized. Matsuda (1997) objected to this "mechanical" view of the writer, recommending that writers be equipped with the ability to mobilize a repertoire of discursive strategies.

In China this approach has led to the observation that, "writing in English, when taught at all, has primarily been seen as a matter of filling in blanks, following pattern drills, and producing error-free text of the type associated with linguistically controlled writing and that the present teaching force in China is ill-prepared to teach English writing" (Spalding, Wang, Lin & Hu, 2009, p. 25). Further, despite a long history of Chinese writing instruction and current widespread commitment to English language teaching, the PRC was ranked lowest in English writing ability internationally in 2008 (Beijing New Oriental School, 2010), though reasonably high scores were attained in reading and listening. There is research demonstrating that native language literacy skills transfer to and support the development of ESL literacy (Cummins, 1981, 2003; Kenner & Kress, 2003). However, Zhaohui Wang (http://CELEA.org) asserted that "Chinese students have sufficient opportunities to express themselves in Chinese," but, that the gap between Chinese literacy instruction and EFL language instruction may be too great to accommodate the transfer of understandings from Chinese writing to English writing.

A SURVEY STUDY ON ENGLISH WRITING INSTRUCTION AT K-12 LEVEL IN CHINA

To identify the challenges that Chinese teachers of English face when teaching L2 writing, we designed a twenty question survey study requesting information about the nature of English writing instruction at the K-12 level as well as the preparation and support for teachers to deliver L2 writing instruction.

DATA COLLECTION

The Chinese education system has a unified curriculum in place nationwide (People's Republic of China-Ministry of Education Website), but there may be differences in implementation between metropolitan and rural areas or rich and poor regions. Because we wanted to understand how English writing is taught at K-12 level across China, we chose to survey a substantial number of teachers, reflecting Babbie's (1990) view that "survey methods ... provide a 'search device' when you are just beginning your inquiry into a particular topic" (p. 53). Before we contacted research collaborators in China, we asked visiting scholars from China for their review, feedback, and written translation of the survey. Then, in collaboration with the current visiting Chinese scholars, we sent a dual language survey, via email, to a dozen English language educators across China, most of these "research partners" had also been visiting scholars in previous years. We relied upon them, as our research partners, to distribute the survey to teachers of English at K-12 level.

Three months later we had achieved a 60% response rate, a follow-up reminder yielded a total of 123 responses from teachers representing 30 schools in 13 cities and districts. Except for Tibet, Uygur, Inner Mongolia and the Northeast regions, populated areas across China were represented. The number of responses from each place varied from five to 25. Our Chinese research partners reported that it was easy to elicit responses through the social network in China, but those who attempted formal channels such as contacting the local school principals or the district board of education, received rejections or got no response. Two of our research partners generated no data, but quite a few made an effort to send the survey beyond their local areas. Of 123 responses, most were written in Chinese, some in English, and some in both languages. Most lengthy narrative responses were written in Chinese.

DATA ANALYSIS

Data analysis began with open coding. We read all responses multiple times, highlighting commonalities and raising questions while "memoing." We then categorized and attempted to chart data, making note of representative responses. Our memos included "code notes," "theoretical notes," and "operational notes" as per Strauss and Corbin (1998). However, we found that determining intended meanings from the written responses of distant respondents in another country/culture who variously responded in two languages was far from a straightforward task. The ambiguity of interpretation that Bhabha (1997) characterizes in terms of the "Third Space" was clearly apparent.

A number of our memos perhaps should be distinguished from Strauss and Corbin's three types as "cross-cultural interpretative memos," a term which more accurately reflects our pursuit of negotiation of ambiguous meanings between languages and educational cultures. Data was discussed with current Chinese visiting scholars in meetings designed to facilitate this cross-cultural data analysis. The three current Chinese visiting scholars, who worked closely with us on the data analysis, are all English instructors at university level in China; one serves as the associate dean of the foreign language department at a university, one is the associate chair of the English department in a foreign language institute who has been heavily involved with teacher training programs in China, and the third had almost 15 years of teaching experience in higher education. We relied upon these scholars to provide contextual/cultural-specific background knowledge and sometimes to get the actual meaning of certain expressions. For example, a data discussion meeting with these scholars began with the following memo and a tentative chart enumerating types of writing mentioned in response to a question about the types of writing their students were required to do:

- It seems that respondents had hard time in their response to this question confusing writing genre, writing content, or test format.

The current visiting scholars responded with the following comments:

- We may have different terms when we talk about genres. There are three genres we usually talk about: narrative writing which include personal narrative and story telling, functional writing which include letters, memos, announcement, and essay writing which includes argumentative and persuasive writing.

- English writing is very rarely taught at elementary level, where language learning is the focus. Children are taught to make sentences with vocabulary and sentence structure they have learned. Some teachers may consider this is English writing.

- Mostly students start to learn to write narrative to functional and then essay writing in English at the 7th grade. Commonly, teachers give writing models, and students write accordingly, like a template.

- We have a very test-driven culture. Teachers and students tend to pay more attention to what counts more in the tests. Correctness is the focus for assessment. Writing counts only 10-15 percent in the English exams and only narrative or functional writing is required.

This process inevitably generated not only code memos but also a substantial number of additional memos of all types which became part of the data. It also led to further questions: How do the teachers get their writing models? Do they write them themselves or get them from a textbook? Is an English writing test tied to curriculum standards? And, how are the teachers informed of these standards?

We went through the responses to each question one by one in this manner during multiple meetings with current visiting scholars. We then cross-analyzed the results from varying questions finding redundant responses in the course of axial coding. For instance, embedded in responses to one or more questions we found that 80% responders stated that they never had any professional development; 78% said there were no resources on how to teach English writing provided to them; and 69% reported that they had little idea of English writing curriculum, but had to teach based on textbooks which focused on language learning. Triangulation to avoid misrepresentation involved asking the current visiting scholars to review our data summary and analyses before sending them to the research partners in China for member-checks.

FINDINGS

LANGUAGE FOCUS IN ENGLISH WRITING INSTRUCTION

Twenty-first century policy makers in China decided that formal English language education should begin at third grade nationwide. Our research data strongly indicates that the Chinese adopted this policy wholeheartedly and have gone beyond. Eighty percent of our respondents stated that students start to learn English in third grade, 11% indicated that schools start to teach English in first grade, and another 9% stated that many children actually start to learn English at the pre-school age. In addition, multimillion-dollar business ventures based on English test-preparation like the New Oriental Enterprise, bilingual preschools, and private tutoring are common.

However, English writing instruction appears to confront English language educators with many challenges. The majority of responses indicated that students at elementary level have three to five periods (45 minutes) of English class weekly and those at secondary level have five to seven (50 minutes) periods weekly. Time devoted to writing varied: 55% of the responses indicated that beginning in seventh grade, one period is devoted to writing weekly; 20% stated that they didn't teach writing at all; 16% said that writing was part of language learning or reading unit; and 9% expressed confusion about what we meant by writing. For instance, one asked:

> Is sentence making or copying or answering questions considered as writing? If so, our students wrote all the time, as long as they started to learn English (from Zhengzhou, English).

While Hu's (2005a, 2005b) assertion that English writing consists mostly of language exercises may not be entirely accurate, our data, in general, seems to support Hu's characterization. Many responses emphasized "copying" as a key strategy:

> Copying and correcting, copying and writing, translation

and back-translation, expanding outlines, organizing materials, summary, picture description, ... through copying how good writing should be, they learn how to write their own (from Nanjing, English).

Certainly, there is an emphasis on surface level correctness. Two teachers wrote,

In teaching writing, we guide students to some formal aspects: neat handwriting, correct spelling and punctuation, more careful constructions, more precise and varied vocabulary, more correctness of expression in general as well as acceptable grammar (from Shanghai, English).

Generally, [in writing] students are required to translate the Chinese sentences into English using some vocabulary or sentence patterns they have learned, or use some sentences to describe a subject/ topic. Skills are learned accordingly. Let the students practice the language, get familiar with the expression in English, consolidate the English words, promote their writing skills, support their listening, speaking and reading ability (from Nanjing, English).

Further, it seems that weekly writing periods are primarily spent talking about the language, vocabulary, and format needed for the day's writing topic, leaving only 10 minutes for actual writing. Usually a writing model such as a sample invitation letter was provided and the students would write strictly according to that model.

Also, because most teachers at K-12 level in China have to teach 50-60 students per class and feel that they have to cover as many "language points" as possible in each lesson, they reported that they often didn't get to writing exercises at the end of the reading units. One respondent commented,

We integrated writing into other language learning. For instance in a 40 minute class, we have 10 min. for reading, 10 min. for listening, 10 min. for speaking and 10 min. for writing. Students write their answers to the questions to the reading. In each reading unit, there is a writing exercise required at the end, but often we don't have time to get there (from Chongqing, translation).

Table 1 was developed from the responses the teachers made. Taken together, their responses point to significant differences between Chinese and English writing instruction.

Table 1. Comparison of junior high L1 and L2 writing instruction

	Chinese Writing	English Writing
Length	800-1000 words	50-80 words
Language	Variety and beauty	Correctness
Style	Unique and artistic	Simple and clear
Teaching focus	Model texts, variety of genres and styles, and rhetorical tradition	Words, phrases and sentence structure and grammar
Time for instruction	90 minutes weekly	20 minutes weekly
Teacher training	Focused on composition	Focused on language

Our respondents suggested that English writing is not linked to Chinese writing in the minds of students. Yet, studies by Spack (1997) and Kobayashi and Rinnert (2002) confirm that instructional approaches to language learning influence the student expectations about writing. 63% of our respondents indicated that:

- Students hope to know how to write correct sentences with complicated sentence structures and few spelling mistakes;
- Students can't spell some words they want. They also find it hard to arrange the order of the words in a sentence. When finished, they are anxious to know whether they are right or wrong.
- Students would like to have more chances to read/copy/learn from written work by students from English-speaking countries;
- Students want to know how to write beautifully by using words correctly and precisely.

In comparison to Chinese writing instruction, the English writing instruction not only has a strong language-focus but also is less valued as the native language writing.

LACK OF PREPARATION AND SUPPORT FOR ENGLISH WRITING TEACHERS

The data gave clear evidence that these teachers are not academically prepared to bridge the gap between Chinese literacy and EFL language instruction or to teach writing. 50% of respondents claimed that they never had any training in teaching of writing; 26% said that they had one course on English writing in college, in which they were introduced to the five-paragraph format associated with the contrastive rhetoric approach, but never had any inservice training after they graduated from college; 17% stated that they learned how to teach writing from the veteran teachers in their schools; and 8% said they self-taught via their own practice, or through searching the Internet or reference books. A representative response read:

> We never had any training in teaching English writing. Usually we go to observe other teachers in the school, but few English teachers teach writing, but only teach reading and language skills. So we have to learn how to teach writing on our own: for instance, let students look at a writing model, and ask them imitate how to write according to the model(from Hangzhou, translation).

Our current visiting scholars explained that when they majored in English in college, they learned English language grammar and other related linguistic skills, read British and American classics, and wrote a few reading reports and essays each year. After graduation, if they got a job teaching in a college, they would teach exactly as they were taught. Those who got jobs teaching at K-12 level taught according to textbooks, which mostly seek systematic habit formation via language patterning. It appears that teaching English writing in China is a brand new field in which few teachers have either much knowledge or experience.

While there is unified curriculum and set of standards for English writing instruction at secondary education (People's Republic of China—Ministry of Education Website), most of the teachers surveyed were not informed about its existence. The current scholars indicated that those who have a clear knowledge of the curriculum probably are either master teachers at the district level or leaders of English departments in schools. They asserted that teachers have little to say in what and how to teach, and are not prepared or supported in teaching English writing. Upon reading the survey responses, they chose the following response to represent the plight of English teachers:

> We all know writing is important as it demonstrates the students' comprehensive competency in English proficiency. But there is no textbook or English writing curriculum; writing instruction became the weakest part of our English instruction (from Xi-an, translation).

Indeed, 51% of the teachers surveyed responded they didn't know if there was a curriculum for English writing; 31% said that they knew something about different levels of English writing for junior and senior high school students, but never connected those to their instruction; and 18 % gave no response, which might indicate they either didn't how to respond or had no ideas about the curriculum. Our current visiting scholars explained that textbooks serve as curriculum. Teachers move from one lesson or one unit to the next without needing to know or ask about the curriculum for the grade they teach. EFL writing instruction is not prominent in those textbooks. Ninety-five percent of the respondents stated that they have never seen or been provided with any textbooks specifically on teaching writing in English. In addition, 35% expressed that they didn't like the textbooks they were provided for their teaching, stating that the textbooks were: "too boring," "not appropriate for our students," or "irrelevant to our students' interest," and "wish our students can read something written by or about the children of their age." When asked about who chose the textbooks 77% responded they were not sure, the remainder responded: "the Board of Education in our province," "the leaders of the school district," and "probably a group of people formed by lead teachers, education experts and leaders at the school board."

TEST-CENTERED INSTRUCTION

At first we were puzzled about how most teachers could remain uninformed about the curriculum and standards and how learning outcomes could be assessed if grade level standards were not clearly presented to the teachers. We soon realized that China has been test-driven for centuries and that tests, not curriculum standards or even the textbooks, may drive instruction.

When asked about the importance of K-12 English writing instruction in the eyes of educators, policy makers and parents almost all of the respondents stated that, as educators, they think that English writing instruction is important at all levels. However, 83% stated that high-school and college entrance exams were key to making teaching of English writing necessary at middle and high schools:

> As a communication tool, writing should be an essential goal for English learners. And the most important reason is that the high school students have to take college entrance exam. Writing counts for 16% of the total score, that is very important part (from Zhengzhou, translation)

> Probably because we are in a poverty region, we only consider what is in the exam important (from Hunan, translation)
>
> We all think that writing is one of important areas that can show students' language competence. But it is easy to neglect, since it counts only for 10% of the total test score (from Nanjing, translation).

The test also drives the attitude of students and parents toward English writing. Quite a few teachers stated that parents didn't know what English skills their children should learn, but paid close attention to the test scores their children get on their exams, because scores determine the high school or college they can enter, and so signify the future their children may have. Since writing only counts 10 to 16 % of the English exam (compared to 42% in the Chinese exam), parents and students don't feel they should put much time or effort into English writing. One teacher wrote:

> Since English writing only counts a small portion in the English test, the students didn't have any incentive to study hard in English writing, and often what they wrote makes them feel and look stupid, and even uneducated (from Kunming, translation).

Another wrote:

> Why waste your energy for something no one cares? (from Jinan, English)

When we compared the English writing curriculum and standards with the writing test prompts in the English test for high school and college entrance exam over the past five years found online, a discrepancy emerged. According to a teacher in Hangzhou, the standards state:

> Based on new standard of high school English writing curriculum, students should be able to write brief description of a specific event or incident:
> - With focus and sufficient examples
> - With variety of sentence structures and word usages
> - With precise language expressions
> - With proper transition
> - With clear paragraphs and format

- With a strong sense of audience and purpose
(from Hangzhou, translation)

An exam-related English writing prompt seems less demanding (Die, 2009):

Context for the essay: Your name is Li Hua, the president of Student Council in Yucai High School. Your school is going to hold an English Speech Contest. You want to invite a foreign instructor, Ms. Smith, to be a judge at the contest. Please write an invitation to Ms. Smith based on the following event notice.

English Speech Contest
- Topic: Human and Nature
- Place: Classroom 501
- Time: 2:00 to 5:00 pm, June 15
- Participants: 10 students
- Contact person: Li Hua (tele: 44876655)
- Word limit: about 100 words in the following format:

Dear Ms. Smith

With best wishes,

This test question only requires test takers to restate the information with vocabulary provided. This demonstrates how a test-driven focus can contrive to lead teachers and learners to mediocrity by limiting expectations. Despite a test-driven culture, many teachers cried out for change. When asked "What would be your suggestions and recommendations in English writing instruction?" many uttered things like "Making teaching interesting and meaningful to students;" "Making teaching relevant to students' life experience and interest;" and "Don't just teach for test, but for real world purposes."

DISCUSSION

It is worrisome that students apparently expect English writing to be different from the writing they've experienced in Chinese classrooms. While a newer, more communicative view of contrastive rhetoric is emerging according Connor (1996) and Kobayashi and Rinnert (2002), it is doubtful that flexible communicative competence can be attained by situating English language learning in years of exposure to instructional techniques focused on the adoption of forms and structures developed in the Western world. Such a focus positions non-native language users to think of themselves as mimics who seek a surface level resemblance to nativeness rather than as empowered biliterate bilinguals. Empowering communicatively competent actors on the world stage requires preparing students to actively inquire into the affordances and challenges of various structural frameworks and modes of representation that can be mindfully selected, combined, or modified according to intended purposes and audiences. This would require teachers who appreciate the potential benefits of consciously using native language knowledge of writing during EFL writing and who demonstrate an ability to do so themselves.

CONCLUSION

There appears to be a significant gap that separates English language learning with its weak or nonexistent focus on English writing from writing instruction in Chinese; however, it is important to note that China is certainly not alone in perpetuating such a gap. In so far as language learning is conceived of as systematic habit formation via language patterning augmented by comparative rhetoric with the goal of inculcating resemblance to native language users, but not as literacy learning aimed at negotiating meanings and navigating multiple perspectives, this gap is perpetuated the world over.

Such an approach may be effective in terms of acquiring a new language's vocabulary and form, but treats the new language as something that is isolated from prior learning, thereby obliterating the possibilities for transfer of native language literacy, traditions, or perspectives. This separation between language learning and first language literacy is limiting for those who wish to pursue advanced study in English speaking countries and/or position themselves as biliterate, but also presents problems for those who simply negotiate meaning in a globalized world where nuanced multiple perspectives presented in English abound.

If China sincerely wants students to achieve communicative competence in a globalized, English-dominated world there is a need to move beyond the systematic habit formation approach. If English is to serve the multiple perspectives of an increasingly international community, educational focus on "erroneous, fossilized, inter-language versions of 'proper' English" (Nayar, 1997, p. 31) needs to be reconceptualized. There is a need for the development of theorized interdisciplinary (Chinese literacy combined with English language) education that is specifically aimed at adequately acknowledging the depth of knowledge associated with native language literacy, while positioning students to grow into consciously flexible biliterate bilinguals who, equipped with a repertoire of discursive strategies, are able to demonstrate deeply structured, empowered discourse.

REFERENCES

Babbie, E. R. (1990). *Survey research methods* (2nd ed.). Belmont, CA: Wadsworth.

Briere, E. J. (1966). Quantity before quality in second language composition. *Language Learning, 16*, 141-151.

Beijing New Oriental School. (2001). *Why Are the Chinese Students' Oral English Abilities Ranked the Worst Internationally?* Retrieved from http://news.koolearn.com/t_0_10447_0_367880.html

Connor, U. (1996). *Contrastive rhetoric: Cross-cultural aspects of second-language writing*. New York: Cambridge University Press.

Cummins, J. (1981). The role of primary language development in preventing education success for language minority students. In Charles F. Leyba (Ed.), *Schooling and language minority students: A theoretical framework* (pp. 3-49). Los Angeles: California State University, Evaluation, Dissemination and Assessment Center.

Cummins, J. (2003). Bilingual education: Basic principles. In J. M. Daelewe, A. Housen, & L. Wei (Eds.), *Bilingualism: Beyond basic principles. Festschrift in honour of Hugo Baetens Beardsmore* (pp. 56-66). Clevedon, UK: Multilingual Matters.

Die, M. (2009). *2008 100 English Writing Prompts and Samples*. Retrieved from http://www.hrexam.com/standard.htm

Ellis, R. (1984). *Classroom second language development*. Oxford, UK: Pergamon.

Erazmus, E, T. (1960). Second language practice in writing. *English Language Teaching, 19*, 23-26.

Freies, C. (1945). *Teaching and learning English as a second language*. Ann Arbor, MI: University of Michigan Press.

Graves, D. H. (1983). *Writing: Teachers and children at work*. Portsmouth, NH: Heinemann.

Hinds, J. (1983). Contrastive rhetoric: Japanese and English Text. *Interdisciplinary Journal for the Study of Discourse, 3*(2), 183-196.

Horowitz, D. M. (1983). Process not product: Less than meets the eye. *TESOL Quarterly, 20*, 141-144.

Hu, G. (2002). Potential cultural resistance to pedagogical imports: The case of communicative language teaching in China. *Language, Culture, and Curriculum, 15*(2), 93-105.

Hu, G. (2005a). Contextual influences on instructional practices: A Chinese case for an ecological approach to English language teaching. *TESOL Quarterly, 39*, 635-660.

Hu, G. (2005b). Professional development of secondary EFL teachers: Lessons from China. *Teachers College Record, 107*, 654-705.

Kaplan, R. B. (1967). Contrastive rhetoric and the teaching of composition. *TESOL Quarterly, 1*, 10-16.

Kenner, C., & Kress, G. (2003). The multisemiotic resources of biliterate children. *Journal of Childhood Literacy, 3*(2), 179-202.

Kobayashi, H., & Rinnert, C. (2002). High school student perceptions of first language literacy instruction: Implications for second language writing. *Journal of Second Language Writing, 11*, 91-116.

Li, X. (1996). *"Good writing" in cross cultural context.* Albany, New York: State University of New York Press.

Matsuda, P. K. (1997). Contrastive rhetoric in context: A dynamic model of L2 writing. *Journal of Second language Writing, 1*(2), 141-165.

Myles, F., Mitchell, R., & Hooper, J. (1999). Interrogative chunks in French L2: A basis for creative construction? *Studies in Second Language Acquisition, 21*, 49-80.

Nayer, P. B. (1997). ESL/EFL dichotomy today: Language politics or pragmatics? *TESOL Quarterly, 31*(1), 9-37.

People's Republic of China—Ministry of Education Website (2011). *National Curriculum and Standards: English Curriculum and Standards.* Retrieved from http://www.tl100.com/zhongkao/200902/35170.shtml

Pincas, A. (1962). Structural linguistics and systematic composition teaching to students of English as a second language. *Language Learning, 12*, 185-194.

Schmidt, R. (2001). Attention. In P. Robinson (Ed.), *Cognition and second language instruction* (pp. 3-32). Cambridge, UK: Cambridge University Press.

Silva, T. (1991). Second language composition instruction: Developments, issues and directions in ESL. In B. Kroll (Ed.), *Second language writing: Research insights for the classroom* (pp. 7-21). Cambridge, UK: University of Cambridge Press.

Spack, R. (1997). The acquisition of academic literacy in a second language: A longinitudinal study. *Written Communication, 14*(1), 3-62.

Strauss, A., & Corbin, J. (1998). *Basics of qualitative research: Techniques and procedures for developing grounded theory.* Thousand Oaks, CA: Sage.

Spaulding, E., Wang, J., Lin, E., & Hu, G. (2009) Analyzing voice in the writing of Chinese teachers. *Research in the Teaching of English, 44*(1), 23-50.

Wang, Z. (2011). *Chinese high school students' L2 writing instruction: Implications for EFL writing in college: A qualitative study.* Chinese English Language Education Association. Retrieved from http://www.celea.org.cn/pastversion/lw/pdf/wangzhaohui.pdf

CHAPTER 3.

ACCESS AND TEACHERS' PERCEPTIONS OF PROFESSIONAL DEVELOPMENT IN WRITING

Sarah J. McCarthey, Rebecca L. Woodard, and Grace Kang
University of Illinois at Urbana-Champaign

Dana and Beth are both early childhood educators with over twenty years of teaching experience. In the year this study took place (2009-2010) and the three years prior to this study (2006-2010), however, they had very different professional development (PD) experiences in writing. On the one hand, Dana participated in two long-term university school partnerships, collaborated with her literacy coach, attended multiple district workshops, and worked on a master's degree program in language and literacy studies. On the other hand, Beth's only PD experiences in writing were district workshops (about one per year), and getting materials from her literacy coach. Dana perceived both of the writing-focused university-school partnerships as highly influential on her writing instruction, whereas Beth perceived a half-day workshop focused on writing as the most influential PD she engaged in. Their experiences with PD in writing as a small urban (Dana) and rural (Beth) teacher are representative of our findings in this study.

The purpose of this study was to understand urban and rural teachers' access to and perceptions of professional development in writing. Particularly in the No Child Left Behind (NCLB) era focused on improving reading and math achievement,[1] PD in writing has often been neglected in elementary settings (McCarthey, 2008). Recently, though, the National Commission on Writing (2003) recommended PD for teachers as part of a "writing revolution" (p. 3).[2] Additionally, efforts such as the National Writing Project (2011) have focused on providing PD through its Summer Institute bringing teachers together to "improve writing and learning for all learners."[3]

Perhaps in response to this reform culture, much current research is focused on identifying the features of effective PD that ultimately increase student achievement (e.g., Desimone, 2009; Troia, Lin, Cohen & Monroe, 2011). For example, Desimone (2009) identified five critical features for effective PD: (a) a content focus (i.e., activities that focus on subject matter content and how students learn); (b) active learning (i.e., how teachers engage in knowledge instruction); (c) coherence (i.e., the extent to which teacher learning is consistent with teacher's knowledge and beliefs); (d) duration (i.e., span of time spent on activity), and (e) collective participation (i.e., arrangements that encourage interaction and discourse). She argued that researchers need to move past teacher satisfaction and attitude studies towards more "empirically valid methods of professional development," and that "the myriad of experiences that count as teacher learning pose a challenge for measuring professional development in causal studies ... measuring the core features of teachers' learning experiences is a way to address this challenge" (p. 181). While the twenty teachers in our study did tend to have particularly positive experiences with PD that had these critical features, their physical locations limited or expanded their access, and the relationships they formed with colleagues and professional development providers greatly informed their perceptions. We argue that context and teachers' perceptions must be central to our studies, not peripheral, if we are to better understand the messy work of teaching and learning. Sociocultural theories, then, deserve attention in studies of professional development in writing (e.g., Grossman, Smagorinsky, & Valencia, 1999).

CATEGORIZING PROFESSIONAL DEVELOPMENT IN LITERACY

While we realize that categorization can be limiting, during teacher interviews, we realized that the teachers' PD in writing fit into four distinct categories: (a) university/school partnerships, (b) district-level PD, (c) school-based PD, and (d) self-directed PD. We became interested in how teachers perceived these different kinds of PD, and in their access to the kinds of PD they found most influential on their instruction.

UNIVERSITY-SCHOOL PARTNERSHIPS

University-school partnerships focused on school-wide reform are increasingly common. Research on university-partnership projects such as the National Writing Project (National Writing Project & Nagin, 2006; Whitney, 2008), the School-Based Change approach (Au, Raphael, & Mooney, 2008), and the Master Teacher Program (Crawford, Roberts, & Hickman, 2008), are overwhelmingly in favor of such pairings. They cite benefits such as changing the mindsets of teachers (Crawford et al., 2008), increasing teacher confidence

(Godt, 2007; Whitney, 2008), and creating on-going professional networks for teachers (Au et al., 2008).

The National Writing Project has received much attention for its PD networks embedded in school-university partnerships (Lieberman & Wood, 2002). Whitney (2008) found that participants in the NWP described their experiences as "transformative." A key feature of all 200 sites is the 20-day Summer Institute in which teachers conduct PD activities for peers.

District-Level Professional Development

Traditional district-level PD structures have received extensive criticism (Crawford et al., 2008; Hawley & Valli, 1999). These short-term workshops where outside experts come in to train teachers on administrative-chosen topics usually emphasize individual activity, passivity, and immediate results. In contrast, Elmore's (1997) study of Community School District 2 in New York City documents the exemplary use of PD to mobilize knowledge in system-wide reform. He concluded that it is essential for districts to engage in problem solving through sustained efforts that focus on instructional improvement.

School-Based Professional Development

School-level professional development in literacy has become a focus in recent years, as many states, districts, and schools are moving toward the literacy coach position (Dole, 2004). The strength of literacy coaching is the accessibility of change agents who have relationships with school staff (Desimone, Porter, Garet, Yoon, & Birman, 2002; Parise & Spillane, 2010). Literacy coaching has contributed to improvements in students' literacy learning (Biancarosa, Bryk, & Dexter, 2010), as well as teachers' knowledge and quality of their practices (Neuman & Wright, 2010). However, variability in the amount of time coaches spend with teachers can affect students' proficiency (Bean, Draper, Vandermolen, & Zigmond, 2010). Teachers value collaboration with coaches, on-going support, and instructional strategies they learned through the coaches' work in classrooms and study groups (Vanderburg & Stephens, 2010). In Walpole and Blamey's (2008) two-year study of a staff development program, coaches identified having multiple roles, whereas the participants identified coaches as either directors or mentors.

Self-Directed Professional Development

Technology has created unprecedented access to knowledge and PD, particularly for isolated teachers. Professional organizations are beginning to offer self-directed professional development for teachers online (e.g., NCTE Pathways, 2011), but little research has documented the results of organized online programs. Participation in professional organizations is another type of self-directed professional development that provides teachers with an independent professional community, the capacity to advance and disseminate specialized knowledge, opportunities for ongoing PD, and advocacy for members (Bauman, 2008; Hargreaves, 2000; Roen, Goggins, & Clary-Lemon, 2008); yet, few empirical studies have focused on the effects of professional membership on teacher beliefs and practices (Little, 1993).

With this framework for categorizing PD in mind, our guiding questions were: (a) What access to professional development about writing do teachers have? (b) What are teachers' perceptions of the impact of PD on their writing instruction? And (c) How does access influence teachers' perceptions?

METHODS

PARTICIPANTS AND SELECTION

The study focused on 20 teachers from four districts: two districts from a small urban community located near a large state university, and two schools from rural districts.

District 1 has a diverse student population: 45.7% are White, 37.3% are Black, 6.8% are Hispanic, 9.8% are Asian, .3% are Native American, .1% are multi-racial, and 47.1% qualify for free or reduced lunch. The district writing curriculum consisted of the Units of Study (Calkins, 2003, 2006), and was mandated for all elementary teachers. The teachers who participated were: six white, three African American, one Asian American; eight female and two male.

District 2 has the following demographics: 42.8% White, 33.8% Black, 8.2% Hispanic, 6.1% Asian, .2% Native American and 8.9% multi-racial, and 63% are low-income. The district recently adopted the Write Traits (Spandel & Hicks, 2009) curriculum. The teachers who participated were: three white, one African American; four females.

District 3 is a rural district: 97.6% White, 0% Black, 0.4% Hispanic, 0.8% Asian, 0% Native American, 1.2% multi-racial, and 16% are low-income. The writing curriculum is a Harcourt basal series. The participants were two white females.

District 4 is a rural district: 95.1% White, 1.3% Black, 0.4% Hispanic, 0.1% Asian, 0.1% Native American, 3% multi-racial, and 32% are low-income. The district uses the Trophies (2003) basal curriculum. The participants were four white females.

To select participants, districts were contacted by the university-schools relationships coordinator; then schools were nominated by educators familiar with PD opportunities; school principals were contacted; finally, all K-6 teachers at the schools were invited to participate and offered a small stipend.

Data Collection/Analysis

Three researchers conducted three interviews and observations of each teacher over the course of one school year. Data collection occurred throughout the school year (e.g., Round 1: September/October; Round 2: January-March; Round 3: April/May) to capture changes in perceptions of PD and writing practices. The semi-structured interviews focused on curriculum, student work, and professional development. For this analysis, the researchers focused on the professional development section of each of the protocols, which included questions with specific probes about opportunities and teachers' perceptions of their effectiveness and impact on writing practices.

We interviewed two University Curriculum Specialist (UCS), who worked extensively with two of the school districts, about their roles and perceptions of the districts' writing curriculum; two elementary language arts specialists from District 1 about the role of coaches and the curriculum selection; and one curriculum specialist from District 4.

Interviews were transcribed by the researchers or verbatim by a professional transcriber. Data analysis began by combining the responses related to professional development from all three interviews for each of the 20 teachers and placing them into one document. The team summarized each teacher's responses and created charts to represent the opportunities to participate in different types of PD within the last three years. The charts included four main categories of PD taken from the literature: (a) university-school partnerships, (b) district-level workshops, (c) school-level opportunities, and (d) self-initiated activities.

Once we established the opportunities each teacher had, we categorized their perceptions into: (a) benefits and (b) disadvantages of each type of PD. We used their responses to questions about major influences on their writing instruction to understand the potential impact of PD on their instruction. Interviews from the district-level coordinators and UCSs were used to provide context for the writing programs, role of the coaches in buildings, and perceptions of effectiveness of implementation.

FINDINGS

Our findings suggested that access to K-12 professional development opportunities varied by location. The two small urban districts (1 and 2) had the following, (a) seven University Curriculum Specialists (UCS) who work in local schools modeling in classrooms and collaborating with teams of teachers on either math or literacy; (b) the Summer Academy (SA) a week-long, intensive experience on the university campus involving keynote speakers and school-based teams who plan curricular implementations; (c) the local site for the National Writing Project with a 20 day Summer Institute focused on writing with technology; (d) district literacy coaches who had variable roles (e.g., working with children, providing resources, or acting as mentors) in elementary buildings; (e) district-run workshops with release time for all teachers to attend. In addition, some of teachers were in the master's program at the university; several discussed self-initiated professional development such as National Board Certification.

The rural districts (3 and 4) both had district-run workshops and in-service professional development, but they did not focus on writing. The in-service at both schools primarily focused on school-wide Response To Intervention (RTI) training (Illinois State, 2008). District 4 had a literacy coach and curriculum specialist in the elementary building, whereas District 3 only had an RTI coordinator.

Table 1 presents an overview of the professional development activities in which the 20 teachers participated. All teachers were involved in some type of professional development; however, not all types of PD were available to all teachers. The teachers in small urban districts had substantially more opportunities to work with the university in three different types of PD focused on writing—working with a UCS, participating in a Summer Academy, and participating in the local NWP. By contrast, the rural districts did not have any teachers participating in the university-school partnerships, but they did have literacy coaches in their buildings.

Below, we (a) describe the types of PD, (b) indicate the numbers of teachers who had access to that type of PD, and (c) communicate teachers' perceptions of the impact of various types of PD on their teaching of writing.

University School Partnerships

Three different types of university-school partnerships were available to teachers in the two small urban districts. Teachers who participated in these activities reported having positive experiences with the PD offered.

Table 1. Participation in professional development

Teacher (District)	University-school Partnerships			School-based		District-level	Self-directed			
	Summer Academy	University Curric. Specialists	NWP Summer Institute	Literacy Coach	Colleagues	District Workshops	Professional Literature	Master's Program	Professional Membership	National Board Certified
Tamara (D1)			X	x		x				
Mandy (D1)	x			X	X	x				x
Jocelyn (D1)	x			x	X	x		x		
Vicky (D1)	x	X		x	X	x		x		
Dana (D1)		X	X	x		x		x		
Ellen (D1)	x	X		x	x	x				
Wanda (D1)	x	X		x			x	x		
Mike (D1)	x	X		x		x				
Tara (D1)	x	X		x		X				
Jackson (D1)		X		x		x		x		
Elana (D2)		X	X	x	x	x				
Natasha (D2)	x			x	X	X				
Amber (D2)	x	x			X	X				
Melanie (D2)	X	x		X	X	X		x		
Kerry (D3)					X				x	
Rebecca (D3)					X		x			
Beth (D4)				x		X				
Cora (D4)				x	X	X				
Katie (D4)				x		x		X		
Kendra (D4)				x	X	x				
TOTAL	10	10	3	17	12	17	2	7	1	1

Note. Lower case x=PD in which teachers participated. Upper case X=PD that was most influential on teachers' writing instruction.

University Curriculum Specialists

Of the seven UCSs, two (Claire and Elizabeth) worked with elementary schools in the urban districts on literacy. Claire worked with groups of teachers at individual schools on their literacy curriculum in four to six week cycles. She had been in this role for three years, and described her work as a combination of co-teaching, modeling, planning and debriefing. She believed the major benefits of her work were providing support for teachers and working with children in the classroom context. Claire described an evolving model, "primarily, I meet with groups of teachers or individual teachers. They identify something that they struggle with. [In this last semester, it's been all writing related.] Then, we set up time to plan together and then usually what ensues from that is a lot of co teaching, a lot of modeling, a lot of them talking about things afterward, and then we have student work."

All of the teachers (10) who had the opportunity to work with Claire or Elizabeth in their classrooms reported that the UCS had an impact on their curriculum. They commented on the importance of their being in the classroom to model lessons and discuss writing. District 1 teachers were particularly enthusiastic. Ellen described how the UCS met with teachers by grade level, then modeled with students, and finally debriefed. Vicky had the opportunity to have Claire twice the year before, "it was so helpful to watch her with kids," and stated that Claire "is like a master at teaching writing." Mike reported that the partnership serves as a "liaison between public schools" and "the university can really bridge that divide."

In District 2, Amber had worked a bit with the UCS (Claire) and found that she was "phenomenal and the kids responded to her. She is fabulous and so intelligent, a pleasure to work with." Elana noted the effectiveness of modeling lessons to see how Claire worked with her students on various writing activities and decided to make some changes in her instruction. The key element for the success of the UCSs with teachers was the relationships they established with individual teachers who encouraged them to come into classrooms, model, and debrief about writing instruction.

Summer Academy

The Summer Academy (SA) had been supported by the university administration for five years to bring teachers to campus in an effort to improve local schools. The SA then became a part of a larger initiative to bring the university and schools together with the seven UCSs playing roles in leading it. The initial effort was to make major changes in instruction in each participating building, but evolved to focus on assessment, student work, and reflective practice.

Many teachers who had been part of the SA (seven of 10) also reported gaining confidence in their writing instruction. Most important was the opportunity to work with colleagues from their school to differentiate their writing curriculum for students of varying abilities. The teachers who were critical of the SA were new teachers who had few opportunities to follow up with leaders or colleagues. Although the focus was not specifically on writing, most teachers from District 1 reported gaining confidence in their writing instruction due to the emphasis on differentiated instruction (DI). Vicky found that the SA helped her become, "More aware that I have 34 students with varying abilities. ... It is going to change the way I am going to assess. I am looking more for growth in my students than I ever was." Ellen said, "I look at learners as individuals instead of everybody needs to write a paragraph." However, Wanda was not enthusiastic about the SA because the curriculum was "idealized" and she could not always use it.

In District 2 teachers had more mixed responses. Melanie stated, "That was my first taste of differentiation ... so it was a huge learning time to bring back to my classroom. I still use the things I learned at the SA and how each kid could learn and how I know what they are learning, that was huge." Amber participated for two years in a row and said, "This year I did not feel it was as worthwhile as the previous year. The reason being, in 2008 they had phenomenal speakers and got you excited about DI. This year it was more do what you want to do… There was not enough instruction given to explain exactly what to do." Natasha participated in the SA, but did not find it very helpful because there were not enough classroom curriculum materials presented. She preferred PD that she could apply the next day with her students, and the SA did not provide that. Most teachers in both districts found the SA valuable, but it depended on the focus of instruction, the speakers, and the perceived applicability to their contexts. In addition, the teachers who valued the SA the most also had the opportunity to develop relationships with the UCS who integrated the SA with one-to-one modeling in the classrooms.

Summer Institute of NWP.

The local site of the NWP was established in 2008 with the following components: individual writing time, peer writing groups, demonstrations of teaching lessons, literature discussion groups, and a focus on technology where teachers each had their own laptops to create digital compositions. The three teachers who had participated in the local NWP noted their involvement enhanced their own writing and instruction, especially the focus on technology. Dana found the experience, "Life changing... you come back at the top of your game, using everything you learned." Tamara gained many ideas for writing including writer's notebooks, and considering technology outside of the computer lab. Elana felt that the NWP changed her perspective on the teaching of writing, but she noted that she was not able to use the projects related to technology at the kindergarten level. Although the teachers valued their experiences at NWP, they did not teach in the same schools and did not have many opportunities to sustain relationships they had built during the NWP.

DISTRICT-LEVEL PROFESSIONAL DEVELOPMENT

Both the urban and rural school districts offered "School Improvement" days (four to six days) in which students were released from school and teachers participated in mandatory PD activities. In the urban districts teachers had choices about which district-sponsored activities they wanted to attend, whereas teachers from rural districts were mandated to participate in particular activities. In District 1 the programs were not content-specific; the teachers found these to be somewhat valuable, but only loosely related to their writing instruction. In District 2, teachers met in grade level teams and presented to peers what they had done in their classrooms in writing. Melanie found it valuable to work with, "other teachers to bounce ideas off ... it was all about *Write Traits* and being able to dig into the materials and share our fears with our co workers." Amber found it was helpful to meet on those in-service days, "We talked about the Write Traits and how to teach each one to the class. We looked at student work and talked about it. We had a great presenter for the workshop." Natasha valued the grade level meeting times that the kindergarten teachers had, "Hearing what works for other teachers is meaningful and ... seeing one teacher using these journals, that at one point I thought it was great to show that at parent-teacher conferences." Teachers who found the district-level workshops helpful noted the importance of the collegiality that was formed among peers.

In districts 3 and 4, teachers reported that the focus of most in-service PD days was Response To Intervention, a state-mandated program with "three essential components: 1) using a three tier model of school supports, 2) utilizing a problem-solving method for decision-making, and 3) having an integrated data system that informs instruction" (Illinois State, 2008). The school in district 4 was particularly focused on their school improvement plan and improving test scores. All four district 4 teachers reported feeling frustrated with their in-service professional development. Katie said, "[Our PD has been about] RTI, MAP, ISAT, data-driven this whole year. Not really how we can fix the problem, just look at these scores and figure out what we need to do, but we haven't really been taught how to." Cora said, "Unfortunately I could say that overall I find it to be a waste of time. I know it's all politics, but I feel like sometimes people forget we're here for these kids. And so spending a day going over a plan that evaluates the leadership in my building … is not helping me be a better teacher." The district 3 teachers reported similar perceptions that their in-service PD time was not helpful. Kerry wished that their PD was about content "that I could just use more directly. Instead of more philosophy sort of things, like more things I could actually take back to the classroom and incorporate into what we already do." These findings suggest that there was major variability in the types of PD provided at the district level and that much of it was not consistent with teachers' desire for practical applications to their classrooms. Teachers had the most positive perceptions of PD that was content-focused and provided them with opportunities to develop collegiality with peers and relationships with PD providers.

School-Level Professional Development

School-level professional development had two inter-related aspects: coaching and working with colleagues. In District 1, the coordinators described the coaching model at the elementary schools as "evolving" over the last several years. A coach split his or her day between working with students for half of the day and "providing job-embedded professional development for teachers" for the other half. The district leaders found that the implementation depended on the building, "there is not a single model." They found that the coach "can wear many hats, providing resources, helping a teacher to plan, facilitating a discussion about data, co-teaching in the classroom." In District 2 the coaches had similar roles where they worked half day with students and the other half with teachers in the buildings. District 3 did not have literacy coaches, but they did have an RTI coordinator who led in-service sessions. In District 4, the school had both a curriculum coordinator and a literacy coach.

In all four districts, there was variation in how literacy coaches interacted with teachers. Teachers were somewhere along the continuum from simply receiving resources from their coach, to meeting often for co-planning sessions, to having lessons modeled by their coach. Many teachers indicated that if they initiated working with the coach, she was always responsive, but it usually required the teacher to be proactive. All 10 teachers in District 1 had literacy coaches in their buildings; however, some teachers worked with the coach primarily on reading and some teachers never worked with the coach. Seven of the ten teachers had positive perceptions of working with the coach because it was collaborative and contextualized. For example, Mandy valued working with her coach and wanted more opportunities to co-plan and co-teach with her. She found these coaching sessions to be the significant, "It is the most meaningful form of professional development because it's a long term relationship and it's ongoing." Ellen commented that the coach came into her classroom twice a week and they both conferred with students. Jackson found his literacy coach an invaluable resource, "It's a mutual trusting relationship. Anything you need she provides you, any support you need, she'll come in and do a mini-lesson, do it with you." However, implementation was inconsistent across buildings. Three teachers indicated that they did not have opportunities to work with the coach on writing because the coach pulled students out to work on reading skills or had not responded to requests for help.

District 2 also had building literacy coaches with varied roles. Melanie stated that the literacy coach helped her with assessment and organization. One of the important features was that they had a personal relationship, "We are good friends; we see each other in the hall and she will say, 'I have this great thing. Can I make copies for you?'" In contrast, Amber did not have access to the building coach, "I have not worked with her. She hasn't been into my classroom, unfortunately. I know she has worked with other teachers, but not at the intermediate level." Both Elana and Natasha commented that there was a building literacy coach, but they did not have much interaction with her.

In District 4 the teachers' perceptions of their coach's role and work differed, as evidenced by Cora and Katie. On the one hand, Cora said:

> Well I think the position of literacy coach in this building is a joke. It is not what a literacy coach is. I see her ordering supplies and pushing papers and… she's done nothing with my room. … My idea of a literacy coach is someone that's not only helping the teacher but is also working with students too. I mean that's another pair of hands that should be helping us.

On the other hand, Katie said the literacy coach helped her with RTI, helped her find activities, and pulled students to work with them every week. She said that the coach helped teachers if they used her but, "I don't think everybody uses her." Both Beth and Kendra agreed that the coach would find them materials when they asked her, but wished the coach supported them more in their classrooms.

The majority of the small urban district teachers did not mention working with colleagues as a form of PD; however, those who did found it to be significant. Two teachers from District 1 who were on the same grade level team at their school reported it as one of the most influential forms of PD. Mandy noted that she met often with Jocelyn for team planning and that she found "tons and tons of collaboration" extremely meaningful. She also continued, "I mean you can get ideas from the conferences, but if you don't come back and talk about how to implement those ideas, the ideas will work (only) for a particular group of students." Jocelyn realized that teaching writing was a weakness, "[meeting with colleagues] helped me to become better at it." In District 2, Natasha wanted PD that she could directly apply to her classroom. She felt that the best means for this was collaborating with her teammate, Elana, where they would brainstorm ideas together that were applicable to kindergarten.

Teachers in the rural districts, who had less access to structured professional development in writing, were more likely to mention colleagues as a significant influence on their writing instruction. Four of the six rural teachers described their colleagues as highly influential. Kerry said that observing and talking to other teachers has been her most significant PD. Rebecca planned writing with the third and fifth grade teachers based on ISAT needs. Kendra described the teacher next door, who taught the same grade, as a significant influence on her writing instruction. What was clear from teachers' responses was the importance of developing strong professional relationships with coaches or with colleagues in the schools and working collaboratively on instruction.

SELF-INITIATED PROFESSIONAL DEVELOPMENT

Teachers were involved in a variety of self-initiated professional development activities from being a part of master's degree programs at the university to reading professional literature or writing on their own. Seven teachers were in a master's degree program; only one of these teachers found it to be a major part of her growth as a teacher. Dana (District 1) integrated her work with the UCS, the NWP, and her coursework. She said, "There's just been a lot of wonderful input, theory, practice—I can't advocate for that enough. You feel like you're very theory grounded. You feel like you're current." However, the other teachers did not find that their coursework related to writing or was a factor in their attitudes toward writing. In District 2, Melanie had graduated with a master's in administration and felt that would have more of an impact when she became an administrator. Katie (District 4), who was a confident writing teacher, got her master's degree in 2003 at a nearby university where they focused on writing in the classroom.

Individual teachers had gained National Board Certification (1), mentioned professional literature that had made an impact on their writing practices (1), or discussed the workshops at Teachers College in New York City they had attended on their own (1). Most surprising, was that the teachers did not cite involvement in professional organizations even when specifically asked, and many were not connected to the local or national organizations available in the community. Only Kerry cited her involvement in the State Reading Council as a form or PD. What is striking about teachers' reports about self-initiated PD is the lack of opportunities to interact with colleagues or peers. Only Dana found self-initiated PD helpful, and she had developed ongoing relationships with the UCS and the professors who taught courses and directed the NWP.

DISCUSSION AND IMPLICATIONS

This study of 20 teachers from four districts demonstrates that access to high-quality professional development is varied in urban and rural districts, and that access to such PD plays a major role in teachers' perceptions of its impact on their writing instruction. While we found the Desimone (2009) model helpful for framing effective PD (i.e., coherent, content-focused, ongoing, collaborative), it failed to highlight context such as differences between urban and rural schools and the role of relationships in teachers' perceptions of PD. Thus, our work, like that of Grossman, Smagorinsky, and Valencia (1999), suggests a need for reframing PD models to consider sociocultural contexts. We need a more nuanced model that highlights how context shapes the differential opportunities Dana (from a small, urban community) had versus Beth (from a rural community).

While the small urban districts had collaborative relationships with the local university, neither rural district was connected to it. The consequences of this were that the urban teachers had more opportunities to engage in PD that was more consistent with the Desimone (2009) model—the university-school partnerships had a content focus (often writing), active learning components (teachers engaged in writing in the National Writing Project or reviewed student work with University Curriculum Specialist), coherence (NWP & UCS connected beliefs and practices), duration (lasted more than 1 day workshops), and collective participation (teachers and PD providers collaborated).

By contrast, rural teachers experienced mandated, test-driven activities provided by the district. Building-level coaches did not focus on writing, did not alleviate isolation nor help teachers improve their writing instruction. Without access to ongoing, embedded, discipline-specific writing PD, rural teachers relied on their building colleagues as their primary sources of information and support. An implication of our study is that rural teachers need to have access to high-quality PD that is ongoing, coherent and linked to classroom instruction (Desimone, 2009).

Most of the urban teachers who participated in the university-school partnerships found them to have a positive impact on their writing instruction. Working with the University Curriculum Specialists, who modeled writing in classrooms and met with small groups of teachers, was cited as the most significant influence on teachers' writing instruction. Teachers reported the other university-school partnerships such as the Summer Academy and local NWP also influenced their writing instruction. Thus, we recommend that universities extend partnerships from small urban schools to include rural districts. In addition, efforts need to be more bidirectional: rural administrators need to offer support for teachers to participate in high-quality PD.

However, merely forming these partnerships may not be enough. Our research found that university-school partnerships had an impact on teachers' perceptions, yet teachers were left to make their own links among them. Thus, we suggest that university-school partnerships (e.g., UCS, NWP, and SA) as well as district-run workshops become more coordinated, with explicit links to one another to improve writing instruction. For example, Troia et al. (2011) described a set of well-coordinated PD including weekly coaching sessions, classroom demonstrations, and curriculum planning, as well as resident authors who shared lessons and publishing opportunities with teachers and students. A more coordinated set of services that includes frequent opportunities to plan together, observe peers teaching writing, and talk about student work has the potential to make a greater impact on writing instruction. These collaborative, on-site features of PD could help build and maintain relationships at the same time that they focus on students' learning within school contexts.

Understanding school contexts and the relationships within them is essential to the success of professional development. Our research found that teachers had varied experiences with literacy coaches in different buildings depending on their roles, which varied from working with students to only providing resources (Walpole & Blamey, 2008), and teachers' relationships with them. Some teachers reported collaborating with the coaches and developed close professional/personal relationships with them, while others had little access to or did not take advantage of their building coaches. We recommend that the roles of coaches should be adapted to the school context, and that administrators and coaches communicate more clearly with classroom teachers about those roles, encouraging teachers to take full advantage of the building coaches.

Encouraging more collegial relationships between coaches and teachers can lead to the type of sustained change described by Parise and Spillane (2010) that has an impact on students. Our data suggest that developing close professional/

personal relations (even beyond collegiality) was a factor in teachers' reports about the influence of the UCS or literacy coaches on their instruction—those who had close relations with the individual providing the PD found it influential. This finding expands the research on coaching by identifying developing close relationships between coaches and teachers as a major factor in teachers' willingness to engage in reflective practice (Bean et. al., 2010; Walpole, McKenna, Uribe-Zarain, & Lamitina, 2010). Future studies should investigate the influence of personal relationships on changes in instruction in more contexts. Most importantly, we hope this research points to the need to develop PD opportunities in writing that are as rich, connected, and relational for rural teachers as they are for urban teachers.

NOTES

1. No Child Left Behind refers to the federal law that was passed in 2001 requiring states to comply with the following to receive federal funding: implementing academic context standards, administering standards-based assessments in grades 3-8 in reading and mathematics, employing a single statewide accountability system that measures adequate yearly progress of all schools, identifying schools for improvement, and requiring teachers to be highly qualified in their subject areas.

2. The College Board founded the National Commission on Writing in 2002 to focus national attention on the teaching and learning of writing, and respond to the growing concern within the education, business and policymaking communities that the level of writing in the United States is not what it should be. The commission uses multiple strategies to promote the teaching and learning of writing including issuing regular reports on the state of writing in the US.

3. The National Writing Project was founded by James Gray in 1974 to promote writing in K-12 schools with the belief that teachers should teach teachers. Prior to spring 2011 (when funding was suspended) there were over 200 local sites that received federal funding. The Summer Institute brought together teachers for 20 days to participate in demonstrations, writing, and responding to writing. Beyond these required components, sites may have a particular focus such as technology or English language learners.

REFERENCES

Au, K. H., Raphael, T. E., & Mooney, K. C. (2008). What we have learned about teacher education to improve literacy achievement in urban schools.

In L. Wilkinson, L. Morrow & V. Chou (Eds.), *Improving literacy achievement in urban schools: Critical elements in teacher preparation* (pp. 159-184). Newark, DE: International Reading Association.

Bauman, S. (2008). To join or not to join: School counselors as a case study in professional membership. *Journal of Counseling and Development, 86*, 164-177.

Bean, R. M., Draper, J. A., Vandermolen, J., & Zigmond, N. (2010). *Coaches and coaching in Reading First schools: A reality check.* Elementary School Journal, 111(1), 87-114.

Biancarosa, G., Bryk, A. S., & Dexter, E. R. (2010). Assessing the value-added effects of literacy collaborative professional development on student learning. *Elementary School Journal, 111(1)*, 7-34.

Crawford, P. A., Roberts, S. K., & Hickman, R. (2008). All together now: Authentic university-school partnerships for professional development. *Childhood Education, 85*, 91-95.

Desimone, L. M. (2009). Improving impact studies of teachers' professional development: Toward better conceptualizations and measures. *Educational Researcher, 38*, 181-199.

Desimone, L. M., Porter, A. C., Garet, M. S., Yoon, K. S., & Birman, B. F. (2002). Effects of professional development on teachers' instruction: Results from a three-year longitudinal study. *Educational Evaluation and Policy Analysis, 24*, 81-112.

Dole, J. A. (2004). The changing role of the reading specialist in school reform. *The Reading Teacher, 57*, 462-471.

Elmore, R. F. (1997). Investing in teacher learning: Staff development and instructional improvement in community school district #2, New York City (Report). New York: National Commission on Teaching and America's Future.

Godt, P. T. (2007). Leadership in reading. *Illinois Reading Council Journal, 35(4)*, 60-66.

Grossman, P. L., Smagorinsky, P., & Valencia, S. (1999). Appropriating tools for teaching English: A theoretical framework for research on learning to teach. *American Journal of Education, 108*, 1-29.

Harcourt (2003). *Trophies: Grade 3 teacher edition collection themes 1-6.* Orlando: Harcourt.

Hargreaves, A. (2000). Four ages of professionalism and professional learning. *Teachers and Teaching: History and Practice, 6*, 151-182.

Hawley, D. W., & Valli, L. (1999). The essentials of effective professional development. In L. Darling-Hammond & G. Sykes (Eds.), *Teaching as the learning profession: Handbook of policy and practice* (pp. 127-150). San Francisco, CA: Jossey-Bass.

Lieberman, A., & Wood, D. R. (2002). The National Writing Project. *Educational Leadership, 59*(6), 40-43.

Little, J. W. (1993). Teachers' professional development in a climate of educational reform. *Educational Evaluation and Policy Analysis, 15*, 129-151.

McCarthey, S. J. (2008). The impact of No Child Left Behind on teachers' writing instruction. *Written Communication, 25*(4), 462-505.

National Commission on Writing for America's Families, Schools, and Colleges. (2003). *The neglected "R": The need for a writing revolution.* New York: College Board.

National Writing Project. (2011). *National Writing Project.* Retrieved from http://www.nwp.org

National Writing Project, & Nagin, C. (2006). *Because writing matters: Improving student writing in our schools.* San Francisco, CA: Jossey-Bass.

National Council of Teachers of English. (2011). Pathways professional development program. http://www.ncte.org/pathways

Neuman, S. B., & Wright, T. S. (2010). Promoting language and literacy development for early childhood educators: A mixed-methods study of coursework and coaching. *Elementary School Journal, 111*(1), 63-86.

Parise, M., L., & Spillane, P., J. (2010). Teacher learning and instructional change: How formal and on-the-job learning opportunities predict change in elementary school teachers' practice. *The Elementary School Journal, 110,* 323-346.

Roen, D., Goggins, M. D., & Clary-Lemon, J. (2008). Teaching of writing and writing teachers through the ages. In C. Bazerman (Ed.), *Handbook of research on writing: History, society, school, individual, text* (pp. 347-364). New York: Erlbaum.

Spandel, V., & Hicks, J. (2004). *Write traits classroom kit.* Boston: Houghton Mifflin.

State of Illinois (2008) *The Illinois State Response to Intervention (RtI) Plan. (2008).* Springfield, IL: Illinois State Board of Education.

Troia, G. A., Lin, S. C., Cohen, S., & Monroe, B. W. (2011). A year in the writing workshop: Linking writing instruction practices and teachers' epistemologies and beliefs about writing instructions. *The Elementary School Journal, 112*(1), 155-182.

Vanderburg, M., & Stephens, D. (2010). The impact of literacy coaches: What teachers value and how teachers change. *Elementary School Journal, 111*(1), 141-163.

Walpole, S., & Blamey, K. L. (2008). Elementary literacy coaches: The reality of dual roles. *Reading Teacher, 62*(3), 222-231.

Walpole, S., McKenna, M. C., Uribe-Zarain, X., & Lamitina, D. (2010). The relationships between coaching and instruction in the primary grades: Evidence from high-poverty schools. *Elementary School Journal, 111*(1), 115-140.

Whitney, A. (2008). Teacher transformation in the National Writing Project. *Research in the Teaching of English, 43*(2), 144-187.

CHAPTER 4.
MULTIMODALITY IN SUBTITLING FOR THE DEAF AND THE HARD-OF-HEARING EDUCATION IN BRAZIL

Vera Lúcia Santiago Araújo
Universidade Estadual do Ceará

Since the pioneer work of the 90s, research on multimodality has been developing so as to include analysis of web page and film texts and genres, along with printed pages and static images.[1] Multimodal transcription (MT) is one of the methodologies devised for the examination of film texts and genres, and it has been applied successfully in much of the research on multimodality. Audiovisual translation (AVT), also known as Screen Translation, is the area in Translation Studies which deals with the translation meant for the mass media, with five different modes: subtitling, dubbing, voice-over, interpreting, and audiodescription. An outstanding sub-field in AVT is audiovisual accessibility, which deals with the translation of audiovisual products aimed at those with sensory disability: the blind (audiodescription), and the deaf (subtitling for the deaf and the hard-of-hearing—SDH).

Despite the obvious interface between multimodality and AVT, little has been done in terms of methodology to join the two approaches. So far we are aware of only one investigation that uses MT of films in order to find a better way through novice subtitlers' training. Taylor (2003) proposed a model which joins MT and subtitling studies. MT involves "the breaking down of a film into single frames/shots/ phases," and the analysis "of all the semiotic modalities operating in each frame/shot/phase." (Taylor, 2003: 191)

The present work-in-progress aims at replicating Taylor's study with novice subtitlers for the deaf and the hard-of-hearing in Brazil. Research on SDH has been done at the State University of Ceara (Brazil) since 2000. Three studies were carried out in order to find parameters that meet the needs of the Brazilian deaf audience. Now that these parameters are being tested in Brazil's five regions, we felt it was time to train future subtitlers. This action is justified because the SDH produced in the country does not follow the ordinary procedures used for the hearing audience. The first procedure is the use of a subtitle rate of 145, 160 or 180 words per minute (wpm). According to D'Ydewalle et al. (1987), these rates are the ones that allow viewers to have a good reception, because they harmonize subtitle, speech and image. The second is the number of lines. Readability is guaranteed if the subtitle has two lines at maximum. The third is the subdivision of the speech into one or more subtitles (segmentation or line breaks). In order to achieve this, there are some criteria to be followed for the subtitle to be read comfortably. Finally, condensation of the speech is sometimes needed, because of the subtitle rates mentioned previously. The three studies suggest that these parameters plus the provision of additional information, such as identification of speaker and sound effects, are also to be used in SDH.

This chapter reports on an ongoing research project about the use of multimodal transcription in translators' training on SDH. The idea came out, after Fronteira (Frontier), a feature film, was subtitled by students from the Federal University of Minas Gerais and the State University of Ceará. At the time, it was hard to explain to the team members in which situations we should identify the speaker and how we should translate a sound into words. This explanation could have been easier to do if we had used MT. Our hypothesis is that MT can be a tool to teach future expert translators to handle text analysis and multimedia technology for successful SDH.

This chapter describes this training research in two steps. The first focuses on describing characteristics of Subtitling for the Deaf and the Hard-of-Hearing (SDH), following the parameters proposed by research on the topic carried out at the State University (cf. Araújo, 2004a, 2005, 2007; Franco & Araújo, 2003), and the patterns aimed at a hearing audience (cf. Araújo, 2004b; Diaz Cintas & Remael, 2007; D'Ydewalle et al., 1987; Ivarsson & Carol 1998; and Perego, 2003, 2008, 2009). The second step provides a multimodal transcription of an excerpt of Frontier in order to analyse its SDH as an element of a multimodal text. The final purpose is to devise a model to be used in SDH education that combines multimodality and AVT.

Besides the introduction, this chapter is divided into three parts. It starts with a brief account of our theoretical framework, which draws on multimodal transcription and AVT. Then the methodology used is outlined, and the analysis of the subtitling of an excerpt of the *Frontier* is presented and discussed. Finally, some conclusions are drawn and avenues for further research are pointed out.

THEORETICAL FRAMEWORK: SDH IN BRAZIL

Subtitling aimed at hearing viewers and subtitling produced for deaf and hard-of-hearing audiences seem to be viewed differently by Brazilian audiovisual producers and by the government because the production of both types of subtitles is different. The first type is regarded as a translation activity and follows the norms described by AVT researchers (cf. Diaz Cintas & Remael 2007; D'Ydewalle et al., 1987; Ivarsson & Carol 1998; and Perego, 2008). The second is seen as a transcription of speech and is not conceived as translation. The law itself corroborates this view, as Bill 310, which regulates the use of SDH, audiodescription and Sign Language Interpreting on TV, by defining SDH as the "transcription in Portuguese of dialogues, sound effects and other information which could not be perceived or understood by the hearing impaired."[2] Intralingual subtitling is included in translation studies because the field recognizes three types of translation: intralingual (within the same language), interlingual (between two different languages) and intersemiotic (between two different semiotic modes, for example, from the visual to the verbal and vice versa)

Subtitles for hearing viewers are made with the aid of software that allows spotting[3], translation, revision, and preview. The parameters followed by Brazilian subtitling companies are similar when creating this kind of subtitle in many aspects to those used in Europe. According to these parameters, subtitles normally have no more than two lines containing approximately 145 or 150 words per minute, with a screening duration of four seconds to 64 characters. Although Brazilians do not follow the European six-second rule (cf. Diaz Cintas & Remael 2007; D'Ydewalle et al., 1987; Ivarsson & Carrol 1998), the maximum number of spaces available for four seconds, the Brazilian standard, is very close to the spaces provided by Diaz Cintas and Remael (2007, p. 97). Table 1 summarizes the number of characters per line for the subtitle rate of 145wpm, as higher reading speeds (160 and 180 wpm) are not common here.

Brazilian subtitles for hearing audiences also tend to be condensed to make subtitles readable in the time available. This shortening allows synchrony across subtitle, speech, and image, which is essential in order to facilitate the viewer's reception. A viewer must have enough time to read the subtitles, see the images, hear the source audio, and enjoy the programme comfortably. Condensing the content can be achieved through the elimination of redundant and non-relevant ideas and by the omission of some source text words. These deletions are important in order to achieve subtitle-speech-image synchronism. Words frequently omitted are: (i) repeated words; (ii) conversational markers such, as "you know," "I mean," "right," etc.; (iii) interjections; (iv) tag questions; (v) clichés or routine formulae; (vi) cognate words; (vii) words related to people or things visible on the screen (Diaz Cintas, 2003, pp. 209-211).

Spotting or line breaking refers to the breaking down of dialogues into one or more units. Gottlieb (1994, pp. 109-110), quoting Helene Reid (1990), points out three criteria to be adopted when spotting: the visual (whenever a cut or a camera movement is present, a different subtitle is advisable); the rhetorical, (subtitles should follow speech rhythm: when speakers pause to breathe, subtitles should end); and the grammatical, (in the absence of cuts and breathing pauses, the grammatical parameter is adopted). Every subtitle must be a coherent whole, that is, semantic units should remain in the same subtitle.

Subtitle legibility is very important and for this reason, formatting is a key issue in the production and analysis of a subtitle. Apart from the number of lines, subtitle rate, condensing of information, spotting and subtitle duration (four or six seconds), there are a number of other elements relevant to subtitle readability: location, font type, and position. Subtitles are normally located at the bottom of the screen. Fonts with varied sizes and without serif are preferred, because they solve legibility problems. As to the position, subtitles are normally centre or left-aligned, but the centre-aligned form is regarded by most analysts as the best choice (Diaz Cintas & Remael, 2007, p. 84).

The same procedure is not adopted to create SDH. The professionals involved are not subtitlers, but stenocaptioners who operate a special keyboard—stenotype—linked to a computerised machine called a stenograph. The stenotype allows for very fast typing speeds and it is normally used to transcribe congressional and business meetings as well as courtroom sessions. Now it is also being used to subtitle pre-recorded and live TV programmes. Table 2 shows one example of these differences of subtitling (Araújo, 2009:166):

The subtitle exhibited on TV does not have a complete thought, as some word groups are separated ("the figures" and "of," for example), the number of

Table 1. Maximum of spaces for a 145-word-per-minute reading speed

Seconds: frames	Characters	Seconds: frames	Characters
01:00	16	02:20	40
01:04	17	03:00	44
01:08	18	03:04	46
01:12	20	03:08	48
01:16	23	03:12	50
01:20	25	03:16	52
02:00	29	03:20	54
02:04	32	04:00	58
02:08	34	04:04	60
02:12	36	04:08	62
02:16	38	04:12	64

Source: Diaz Cintas and Remael, 2007, p. 97

characters exceed the 145-wpm-subtitle rate (see Table 1). Because of the above mentioned parameters, the four subtitles were transformed into three in order to meet the number-of-character, condensation, and segmentation criteria.

Apart from these parameters, SDH will also be approached by means of an ongoing research project which aims at designing a model of SDH for Brazilian deaf and hard-of-hearing audiences. This model was developed by the State University research team with twelve deaf people from the Ceara Institute of Education for the Deaf. This project has its basis in the standards outlined in Table 1, and three studies were carried out at the university. Although more conclusive results are required in order to consider the model as capable of meeting the needs of Brazilian deaf and hard-of-hearing viewers, it may indicate the elements considered relevant to produce an efficient SDH service across Brazil. This preliminary model is being tested in Brazil's five regions (North, South, Southeast, Northeast, and Centre East). From each region, five deaf people from two states will test the model by watching four subtitled short-feature films. This study will not be described here, but some insights of the data collected so far will be referred to for the sake of clarification of some aspects of the third study.

The first study we carried out analysed SDH provided by the Globo TV network, the most popular in the country. At the time (2002), it was the only network offering SDH in Brazil. The participants (15 deaf-born students from the Ceara Institute of Education for the Deaf, based in Fortaleza, and a control group of 13 hearing students) were exposed to different genres of TV programming. Four hypotheses were formulated: (1) Whenever speech comprehension did not depend on images, lack of speech-subtitle-image synchronism would not impair the reception of the subtitles and the understanding of their content; (2) Whenever speech comprehension depended on images, lack of speech-

Table 2. Closed caption versus SDH parameters

Speech	Closed Caption	Proposed SDH
Only this year, eighty five women were murdered in the state of Ceará. Nonetheless, only three murderers were convicted. This impunity helps to increase the figures of sexual and domestic violence against women.	Only this year, eighty five women were murdered	In 2006, 85 women were murdered in Ceará
	in the state of Ceará. Nonetheless, only three murderers	but only 3 murderers convicted.
	were convicted. This impunity helps to increase the figures	Impunity rises sexual and home violence against women.
	of sexual and domestic violence against women.	

subtitle-image synchronism would impair reception; (3) Whenever there was speech-subtitle-image synchronism, reception would be facilitated; (4) When orality and acoustic markers considered to be (in)dispensable by the deaf participants were present (or lacking, as the case may be), reception would be compromised.

Hypotheses 1, 2 and 4 were confirmed, suggesting that speech-image synchronized subtitles facilitate reception on the part of the viewer (Franco and Araújo, 2003). However, hypothesis 3 was found unsustainable and this signals that perhaps speech-subtitle-image synchronism and condensing of content are not sufficient to facilitate efficient reception. The films shown had synchronisation of speech and image as well as condensed subtitles, but these proved challenging for participants. One possible explanation is that the subtitles used were less condensed than the subtitles directed at hearing viewers—as the editing did not follow parameters outlined earlier and was carried out only for image-subtitle synchronisation (Araújo, 2004a). Because deaf participants reported that they did not understand film content, we assumed that maybe the subtitles should be further condensed to reduce the time required to read them (Franco & Araújo, 2003). We are aware that further research is needed to test this assumption. Bearing in mind these results, we decided to re-subtitle the same programs for our second study in which we used only pop-on subtitles that adopted the most common parameter employed by subtitling companies in Brazil. As the 160-wpm-parameter was suitable for hearing viewers, we thought that it would also be efficient for deaf viewers.

The second study tested the condensed pop-on subtitles with the same group of deaf and hearing participants. After they watched the same programmes on a TV set, the participants answered written questionnaires, composed of open and closed questions,[4] a more efficient tool than the multiple choice questionnaires we had previously used. The new questionnaire consisted of "concept," "detail," and "picture" questions that related to the understanding of the content and the integration of images and subtitles. This time the participants' performance was better, but the results were still inconclusive (Araújo, 2004a). Sometimes the participants succeeded in understanding the main subject, but could not comment on the image and/or the clip's secondary ideas. As far as editing is concerned, the amount of condensing of information that occurred was regarded as uncomfortable (Araújo, 2004a). For this reason, condensing and editing were the focus of the third study.

The third study tried to find out what level of condensing would satisfy Brazilian deaf people's needs (Araújo, 2007). Moreover, we investigated what the ideal format would be, taking into account technical considerations as well as style, conventions and punctuation used. A group of twelve deaf students, comprising university (nine) and high school students (three), had monthly meetings with the research team during eight months. They watched different clips of the same programme with two different sets of SDH: the pre-existing content and the research team's proposal. The latter was based on the standards outlined in Table 1 which are directed at hearing viewers plus bracketing to provide additional information. After each viewing, participants were asked to talk about the content of the programme and to access the SDH. These recall protocols occurred in Brazilian Sign Language (LIBRAS) with the interpretation in Brazilian Portuguese filmed for further analysis.

The clips were subtitled with different reading speeds: 145 (see Table 1), 160, and 180wpm. Although there was not much difference between the three speeds, the deaf participants preferred the 145 word-per-minute rate, as this proved to be more comfortable to watch. This suggests that for Brazilian deaf people, a greater degree of editing is needed to facilitate the enjoyment of a TV programme.

The suggestions regarding format were for the use of brackets when signalling identification of speakers and sound effects. They rejected the European color system. Figure 1 displays the two parameters.

There is another interesting aspect related to speaker identification we would like to point out. Deaf participants said it was very difficult to distinguish who speaks in a scene. At first, they suggested the speakers should be named in every subtitle. When argued that a great deal of space would be lost on screen, they agreed that speaker identification should be present every time a different person speaks. These changes continue to be discussed in the current study, as some deaf people from other parts of Brazil are not identifying the characters properly, because it was our choice not to name the speaker when there was no other visible character on the screen. A good example can be seen in Figure 1. The character's name Romanza was not recognized by most deaf participants in the current research. She was always referred to as 'the little girl" and "the granddaughter."

We are beginning to realize that we should pay more attention to this issue. Therefore, we think we should try to address this subject in our subtitlers' training. The description of all multimodal elements by means of MT may help them decide in which situation this identification is needed.

MT may also be useful when we translate the sound track of a film. The current research has shown that translating all the sounds may not be an efficient strategy. Nearly all participants who have been exposed to the subtitles so far only seem to recognize the sound if it is linked to the film plot. For example, the deaf were able to recognize the sound: [Sad song]. This sound effect announced a dead character. The effect could be described as [sound of a bell]. This proved to be a good strategy, as the deaf did not recognize other songs in which we tried to characterize the sound like [Instrumental music] and [Drums], for example.

MULTIMODAL TRANSCRIPTION

Baldry and Thibault (2000), cited in Taylor (2003), are the authors of *multimodal transcription* (MT), a tool to describe and analyze film texts. Baldry and Thibault's MT is a grid with six columns that breaks down and thoroughly describes an audiovisual film text in terms of each semiotic mode it is made of. The grid contains six columns: (1) TIME in seconds; (2) visual frame—the static image; (3) visual image—description of scenario and participants displayed according to the camera position using the components described in

Figure 1. Identification of speaker: Brazil and Europe

Figure 2; (4) KINESIC ACTION of the participants; (5) SOUNDTRACK—dialogues, ambient sounds, music; and (6) METAFUNCTIONAL INTERPRETATION, where the movie is divided in phases and subphases defined by the identification of a pattern of semiotic modes in action, that will temporally make the transition into a distinct pattern of semiotic modes.

Taylor (2003) adapted Bladry and Thibaut's grid in his subtitling studies, claiming that it may be used as a tool for novice subtitlers to learn how to use the image to decide which information will be prioritized when adding or deleting, and which strategies will be needed to condense or edit a subtitle. The author claims that:

> (MT) As a tool for the professional it is, as so far developed, time-consuming and not commercially viable on a cost-benefit basis, but this article attempts to show that as an instrument for sensitizing translation students to the particular demands of multimodal translation, it takes us a step further along the road to optimizing subtitling strategies. (Taylor, 2003, p. 191)

Taylor made three considerable changes in Bauldry and Tibaut's model, because he considered the original table over detailed and refined it for the design of subtitles (Taylor, 2004). The author thus fused the third column with the fourth, deleted the last column disregarding the breakdown in phases and subphases, and then inserted a column with subtitles, as illustrated by Figure 3.

In accordance with Taylor's (2004) opinion, two other important alterations had to be made. The first change is that column (1) —TIME in seconds—was replaced with Time Code Reading (TCR), which is a method of accounting for vid-

CP	Camera Position (stationary/ moving)
HP	Horizontal Perspective (frontal/oblique)
VP	Vertical Perspective (short/median/long)
D	virtual Distance (close/median/far)
VS	Visually Salient items
VF	Visual Focus
VC	Visual Collocation – secondary items that provide meaningful content
CR	Colors
CO	Coding Orientation – from natural to surreal

Figure 2. Components of the multimodal transcription table

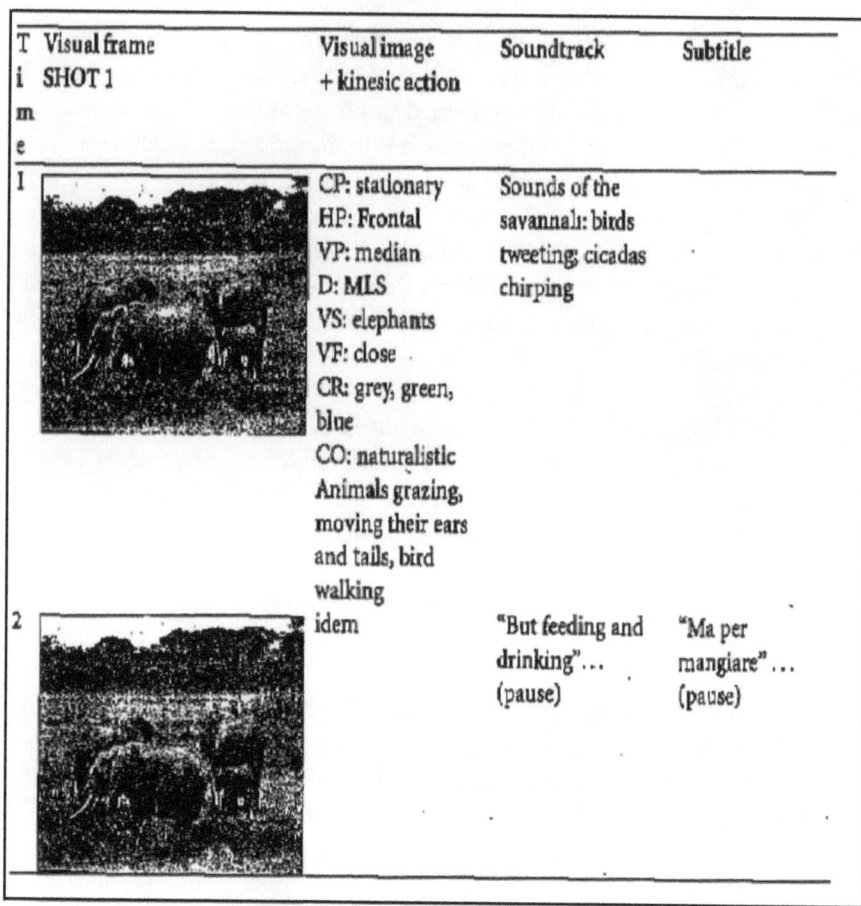

Figure 3. Taylor's multimodal transcription of an episode of a BBC comedy series. Source: TAYLOR, 2003, p. 162

eo footage and frames that reads HOURS: MINUTES: SECONDS: FRAMES (00:00:12:20). This was done because the duration of the scene, to which the titles must be inserted, is of crucial importance, for it determines the number of characters per second that should be on screen, to ensure readability. Each TCR presented on this chapter's MT table, was retrieved from the subtitling software Subtitle Workshop©, which will be explained in the next part of this chapter.

TCR	Visual Frame	Visual Image + Kinesic Action	Soundtrack	SDH

Figure 4. Multimodal transcription used here.

The other change is that the subtitle column became the SDH column where this chapter's final subtitling suggestion will be inserted. Figure 4 shows the complete MT structure.

THE TRAINING COURSE

As part of the two universities' cooperation project, subtitlers engaged in research and in audiovisual accessibility are taught subtitling procedures by means of a training course. As it was said previously, it was very difficult for the students to decide when a speaker should be identified and how to translate a sound into words. To facilitate student's choices, we thought the description of all semiotic elements involved in a scene provided by MT would be helpful. So, we are beginning to introduce this tool in the course.

The course outline is the following: a) theoretical issues related to subtitling; b) presentation of the subtitling software *Subtitle Workshop©*; c) subtitling practice. The freeware *Subtitle Workshop (SW), developed by URUsoft*—http://www.urusoft.net, enables us to work out all phases of the subtitling process: 1) SPOTTING OR CUEING; 2) TRANSLATION; 3 REVIEW (see Figure 5).

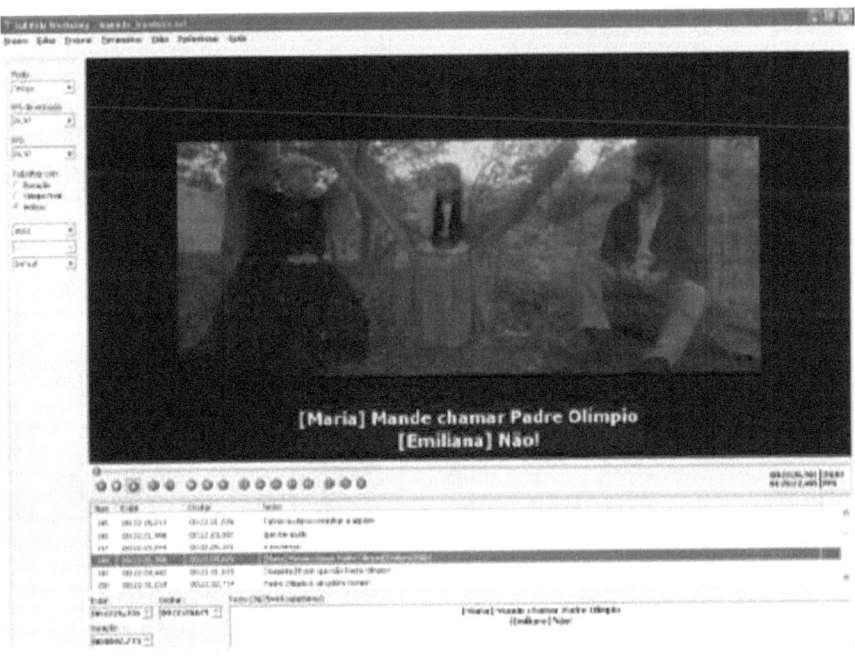

Figure 5. Subtitle Workshop

In the menu MOVIE we can load the film and in the menu FILE we can load preexisting subtitles or create new ones. The subtitled film can be viewed while the subtitles are being prepared, and we can choose the subtitles' format (color, font, size, etc.) in the menu EDIT. Besides, in and out times and duration can be visualized on the left side of SW. The subtitle text is written at the bottom of the screen.

In the following pages, we provide an example of how MT will be used in the training of novice subtitlers, and it will discuss the subtitling of an excerpt of *Frontier*. This movie was chosen to be our focus because it is an author film with limited dialogue and many sounds that helped to create the mysterious atmosphere.

SUBTITLING OF FRONTIER

Frontier (2008) was directed by Rafael Conde, who works for the Federal University. The DVD version, subtitled and audiodescribed by members of the project was out last year. It tells a love story, full of faith and mystery. It was shot in an old house where a young lady (Maria Santa), considered saint by the people from Minas Gerais, lives. The arrival of the Traveller, Maria Santa's lover, and Aunt Emiliana (an old lady), who is preparing the great miracle, will change Maria Santa's life forever.

As it has been said, the movie does not have a lot of dialogue, but a sound track that is necessary to create the mysterious atmosphere. Thus, identifying the speaker and the sound effects are essential to follow the plot. For this reason, we had students to pay close attention to what the images reveal so that they knew when to translate the two features.

On the scene focused here, Maria Santa and the Traveller are talking about a secret they share. The subtitling of this two-second scene requires that 29 spaces are used to achieve the rate of 145wpm (see Table 1). Although there was enough space for the translation of the sound (crying), the analysis of the

Figure 6. Front cover of the DVD

TCR	Visual Frame	Visual Image + Kinesic Action	Soundtrack	SDH
18:46:15- 18:49:10		CP: still HP: frontal VP: short VS: Maria Santa crying, hands on her mouth, eyes closed VC: sitting on a hammock outside the house, some trees, daylight CR: green, beige, white. CO: Naturalistic	Birds singing and Maria Santa crying	-
18:55:12- 18:57:10		CP: still HP: frontal VP: Short VS: Maria Santa crying, hands folded, eyes closed, VC: She is sitting on a hammock outside the house. There are some trees. It's daylight CR: green, beige, white. CO: Naturalistic	Birds singing and Maria Santa crying and saying: "Tenho pena de nós" [I'm sorry for us]	Tenho pena de nós. [I'm sorry for us]

Figure 7. Multimodal transcription 1

shot by means of MT shows that Maria Santa was crying before she said "I am sorry for us." The first frame in Figure 7 displays clearly that the character is crying. So the decision was not to subtitle this information because the image tells that to the audience. The previous shot, which lasted more than three seconds shows that Maria Santa was very sad and that her crying expressed her sorrow. In this case, it was an easy decision because there was no need to condense the text. However, in the other examples, MT proved to be an efficient aid to novice subtitlers.

The shot brings Maria Santa, the Traveler, and Aunt Emiliana. When the old lady joins the couple, it is necessary to identify her, because from a median distance, it is hard to realize which person is talking (see Figure 8). That is why the subtitle with the name EMILIANA was produced. The scene lasts two seconds and four frames and the translation should have 32 characters at the maximum (see Table 1). So, apart from EMILIANA in brackets (10 characters), the sentence *Estive rezando minhas ladainhas* (32 characters) also has to be included in the subtitle. Therefore, a shortened version was written, Rezei minhas ladainhas (23 characters). At the time, it took students a long time to subtitle the film, as it had many situations like that. We presume that if MT had been used, subtitling would have been easier.

The same kind of difficulty did not happen in the next subtitle pointed out in Figure 8, because, as one can see in the MT, the situation remains the same and the viewer can see that the old lady continues her speech. So it was not necessary to name her, and her speech, E agora vou descansar um pouco (1:18, 25 characters), could be fully subtitled and did not have to be edited to meet the 145wpm parameter (see Table 1).

The last subtitles to be discussed here are related to two situations involving Aunt Emiliana's anger, an anger perceived because she shouts while she is speaking. In both subtitles, it was not necessary to translate the information by adding [shouting] to the subtitle, as the images showed clearly the old lady's emotional reactions (see Figure 9).

This strategy was helpful in the second subtitle because it had to be edited. Without the inclusion of the sound effect, only the message's addressee (*você*) had to be removed. If [shouting] had been included, the subtitle would have to be more condensed, as only 40 characters were allowed in order to meet the convenient subtitle rate (see Table 1).

TCR	Visual Frame	Visual Image + Kinesic Action	Soundtrack	SDH
19:24:04 -19:26:08		CP: still HP: frontal VP: Median VS: Emiliana, the Traveller and Maria Santa are sitting outdoors. VC: Emiliana is sitting on a bench, Maria Santa, on a hammock and the Traveler on a trunk. There are some trees a mountain behind them. It's daylight CR: green, beige, white. CO: Naturalistic	Emiliana says: "Estive rezando as minhas ladainhas" [I have been saying my prayers …]	Rezei minhas ladainhas [I said my prayers]
19:26:09- 19:27:27		CP: still HP: frontal VP: Median VS: Emiliana, the Traveller and Maria Santa are sitting outdoors. VC: Emiliana is sitting on a bench, Maria Santa, on a hammock and the Traveler on a trunk. There are some trees and a mountain behind them. It's daylight CR: green, beige, white. CO: Naturalistic	Emiliana says: "E agora vou descansar um pouco" [And Now I'll rest a little bit]	E agora vou descansar um pouco [And Now I'll rest a little bit]

Figure 8. Multimodal transcription 2

TCR	Visual Frame	Visual Image + Kinesic Action	Soundtrack	SDH
20:44:08 -20:46:01		CP: still HP: frontal VP: Median VS: VS: Emiliana, the Traveller and Maria Santa are sitting outdoors. VC: Emiliana is sitting on a bench, Maria Santa, on a hammock and the Traveler on a trunk. There are some trees a mountain behind them. It's daylight. Emiliana is holding a paper CR: green, beige, white. CO: Naturalistic	Maria Santa says; "Mas o juiz disse que ..." [But the Judge said that...]	Mas o juiz disse que ... [But the Judge said that...]
20:46:01- 20:48:22		CP: still HP: frontal VP: Median VS: VS: Emiliana, the traveller and Maria Santa are sitting outdoors. VC: Emiliana is sitting on a bench, Maria Santa, on a hammock and the Traveler on a trunk. There are some trees a mountain behind them. It's daylight. Emiliana is holding a paper. She frowns at the camera and raises and clenches her fist. She looks angry. CR: green, beige, white. CO: Naturalistic	Emiliana interrupts Maria Santa shouting: "O juiz não aconselharia você a fazer uma coisa destas... ." [The Judge wouldn't advise you to do such a thing]	O juiz não aconselharia uma coisa dessas [The Judge wouldn't advise such a thing...]

22:56:09-22:58:17		CP: still HP: frontal VP: short VS: Close-up of Emiliana's face shown from chest up. She is shouting with her mouth wide open. VC: A big trunk and some branches can be seen behind her. Daylight can barely be seen. CR: green, beige, white. CO: Naturalistic	Emiliana shouts: "Padre Olímpio é o filho do demônio". [Father Olímpio is the Devil's son.]	"Padre Olímpio é o filho do demônio". [Father Olímpio is the Devil's son.]

Figure 9. Multimodal transcription 3

FINAL REMARKS

Although we have used MT to produce and to analyse SDH and audiodescription, it has not been tested yet. It is our aim to carry out a research study in which two groups of trainees will be formed. MT will only be used in the experimental group in order to find out whether MT really makes a difference.

Another aspect that came out in our observations related to the use of MT in subtitling is that transcription focusing only on salient items (VS) will be especially helpful in the condensation of long speech. It is our presupposition that it can be used in professional subtitling.

NOTES

1. The author wishes to thank the Brazilian Government Agency FUNCAP for financial support.

2. Bill 310 (http://www.mc.gov.br/o-ministerio/legislacao/portarias/portaria-310.pdf) regulates audiovisual accessibility on television, complementing bill 5296 from December 2, 2004 (http://www.planalto.gov.br/ccivil_03/_Ato2004-2006/2004/De-

creto/D5296.htm) which rules over the rights of people with any kind of physical, auditorial, mental, or visual impairment.

3. Spotting is the action to define at which moment of the film a subtitle starts and ends.

4. The communication with the team was mediated by a sign language interpreter.

REFERENCES

Araújo, V. L. S. (2004a). Closed subtitling in Brazil. In P. Orero (Ed.), *Topics in audiovisual translation* (pp. 199-212). Amsterdam/Philadelphia: John Benjamins.

Araújo, V. L. S. (2004b) To be or not to be natural: Clichés of emotion in screen translation. *Meta, 49*(1), 161-171.

Araújo, V. L. S. (2005). A legendagem para surdos no Brasil. In *Questões de Lingüística Aplicada: Miscelânea*. Fortaleza, Brazil:EdUECE,.

Araújo, V. L. S. (2007). Subtitling for the deaf and hard-of-hearing in Brazil. In J. D. Cintas, P. Orero, A. Remael (Eds.), *Media for All: Subtitling for the Deaf, Audio Description, and Sign Language* (pp. 99-107). Amsterdam; New York: Rodopi.

Araújo, V. L. S. (2009). In search of SDH parameters for Brazilian party political broadcasts *The Sign Language Translator and Interpreter, 3*(2). 157-167

Baldry, A. (2000). *Multimodality and Multimediality in the distance learning age*. J. Diaz Cintas (Ed.). Campobasso: Palladino.

D'ydewalle, G. et al. (1987). Reading a message when the same message is available auditorily in another language: The case of subtitling". In: K. K. O'Regan, & A. Lévy-Schoen (Eds.), *Eye movements: From physiology to Cognition* (pp. 313-321). Amsterdam and New York: Elsevier.

Franco, E., & Araújo, V. L. S. (2003). Reading Television: Checking deaf people›s Reactions to Closed Subtitling in Fortaleza, Brazil. *The Translator, 9*(2), 249-267.

Ivarsson, J., & Carrol, M. (1998). *Subtitling*. Simrishamn, Sweden: Grapho-Tryck AB.

Perego, E. (2003). Evidence of explicitation in subtitling: Towards a characterization. *Across Languages and Cultures, 4(1), 63-88*.

Perego, E. (2008). What would we read best? Hypotheses and suggestions for the location of line breaks in film subtitles. The Sign Language Translator and Interpreter, 2(1), 35-63.

Perego, E. (2009). The codification of non-verbal information in subtitled texts. In J. D. Cintas (Ed.), *New trends in audiovisual translation (pp. 58-69)*. Bristol, UK; Multilingual Matters.

Remael, A. (2007). *Audiovisual translation: Subtitling*. Manchester: St. Jerome.

Taylor, C. J. (2003). Multimodal transcription in the analysis, translation and subtitling of Italian films. *The Translator, 9*(2), 249-267.

Taylor, C. J. (2004). Multimodal Text Analysis and Subtitling. In E. Ventola, C. Charles, & M. Kaltenbacher (Eds.), *Perspectives on Multimodality* (pp. 153-172). Amsterdam; New York: John Benjamins.

Taylor, C. J. (2003). Multimodal Transcription in the Analysis, Translation and Subtitling of Italian Films. *The Translator, 9*(2), 249-267.

SECTION 2.
ASSESSMENT

Every time we write, we assess our plans and the words we produce to see whether we can improve them. Every time we provide feedback to students, we assess what they have done and suggest what they could do better. Every time we assign grades for writing assignments, we assess. However, in the United States, large institutional and policy pressures have driven assessment and the conflicts surrounding it to a very different level.

The establishment of remedial writing at US universities in the late nineteenth century led to assessments of writing skills of entering students to see who would be required to take such courses. The expansion of universities and increasingly democratic intake of students throughout the twentieth century made institutional assessment of writing an increasing institutional presence. Further, as state and urban systems of higher education became centralized, in the 1970s placement exams became standardized across campuses, led by system-wide exams in the California State University of then nineteen campuses, and the City University of New York of seventeen campuses. To maximize uniformity of evaluation and to limit costs, timed essays on general topics, graded through a four to six point holistic scale soon became the standard. Such tests were initially seen as an improvement on multiple choice examinations, in that students at least were required to produce extended coherent prose, although from the beginning the authenticity and validity of such writing was questioned.

These assessments in some systems then became not only placements but graduation requirements, as did the CUNY Writing Assessment Test. At the same time, external providers such as the Educational Testing Service developed timed essay writing tests, and strong pressures emerged to tailor writing instruction towards passing these high-stakes tests. Eventually in 2006 the ETS and the College Board were to introduce a writing component in the SAT college entrance exams. Writing educationists, however, over the years increasingly advocated for writing portfolios as more authentic and more supportive of good pedagogy, with a few systems moving in that direction despite the increased costs in time and human resources.

State and federal policies for accountability in secondary and primary schools then brought these timed examinations to the public primary and secondary education system, along with examinations in reading and math. At first such assessments were carried out only through selected samples aimed at evaluating school districts and states, as through the National Assessment of Educational progress initiated in 1969 and adding a writing exam in 1984. With the stricter standards for individual student accountability at the state level throughout the 1990s and accountability at the school level brought on by the No Child Left Behind Legislation, these examinations became increasingly endemic and with higher stakes, even though NCLB required only reading and mathematics examinations. With such large numbers of students taking such exams, it became increasingly attractive to external providers both to administer the exams and to provide educational support to assist students. Again the pedagogical consequences of the increasing reliance on these exams was highly controversial, with many seeing them as destructive of authentic, motivated writing that develops through an extended process within a meaningful situation in dialog with other writers and in engagement with information and subject area learning.

The development of digital writing assessment technologies brings the last piece to the controversies. While such technologies provide cost efficiencies for both large institutional testing and providing feedback for extended student practice, the lack of authentic situation, the effect of standardization of task and criteria, and the lack of meaning-making in the assessment have made such technologies highly controversial. Nonetheless, advocates argue that these technologies have a place within writing education at all levels from elementary through higher education.

In this section, we provide a cross-section of the current research addressing these controversies, providing different directions for the future of writing assessment at all levels, both from institutional and pedagogic perspectives. Deane et al. present the results of initial testing of new automated assessment tools built within a larger model of writing instruction and assessment. Klobucar et al. present the results of a collaboration between ETS and one university to integrate automated assessment into a wider suite of educational practices. Perelman provides a critiqe of the limitations of these technologies in providing meaningful assessment and feedback. O'Niell et al. analyze the political context of the assessment practices and technologies. Swain et al. and Lines provide alternative models for developing assessments.

—CB

CHAPTER 5.
RETHINKING K-12 WRITING ASSESSMENT TO SUPPORT BEST INSTRUCTIONAL PRACTICES

Paul Deane, John Sabatini, and Mary Fowles
Educational Testing Service

The work described in this chapter arises in a specific current United States context: one in which there is tension between best practices in writing instruction and standard approaches to writing assessment, particularly in the context of standardized tests, such as state accountability examinations. On the one hand, the instructional literature emphasizes the importance of teaching deliberate, well-developed writing processes; indicates the value of peer review; and strongly supports an instructional approach in which explicit strategies are taught in meaningful contexts where content matters (Perin, 2009). On the other hand, the requirements of standardized testing often favor creation of relatively decontextualized writing tasks in which students produce essays under timed conditions with little access to external sources of information—a state of affairs that may have deleterious effects on writing instruction, since the predominance of high-stakes assessments often forces instructors to focus on test preparation (Hillocks, 2002, 2008).

Not surprisingly, current reform efforts such as the Race to the Top program partially conceive of assessments as interventions, and various scholars have argued that such reforms should be guided by modern theories of learning and cognition (Pellegrino, 2009). This point has been advanced in particular by Bennett and Gitomer (2009), who propose a research program that they term CBAL (Cognitively-Based Assessment of, for and as Learning). The goal of this research program is to conceptualize and try out the components of an integrated system in which summative assessments, formative assessments, and teacher professional support combine to encourage and enhance effective teaching and learning.

This chapter presents some initial results from the CBAL program of research as it applies to writing. In particular, we have developed a framework that draws upon an extensive review of the literature on writing and related literacy skills; developed methods for designing summative and formative assessments to measure writing skill while modeling best practices in writing pedagogy; and begun analyzing results of preliminary (but in many cases, large-scale) pilots.

Our work is still in its early stages (though see Deane, 2011; Deane, Fowles, Baldwin, & Persky, 2011; Deane, Quinlan & Kostin, 2011; Deane, Quinlan, Odendahl, Welsh & Bivens-Tatum, 2008), but one central theme has begun to emerge: that writing must be conceptualized within an integrated system of socially-embedded literacy skills.

Effective assessment design requires us to construct an interpretive argument that connects construct theory to task demands through a chain of evidence elicited by those tasks (Kane, 2006; Mislevy & Haertel, 2006). Reading science has documented a developmental trajectory in which certain skills, such as decoding and verbal comprehension, start relatively independent, and gradually become integrated and interwined as expertise develops (Hoover & Gough, 1990; Vellutino, Tunmer, & Jaccard, 2007). Over time, some cognitive processes become increasingly fluent and automatized, while others become increasingly strategic and more finely sensitive to details of the situation in which communication or understanding must take place (Scarborough, 2001). It thus becomes necessary to consider skills both as stand-alone capabilities and as capacities invoked as part of a larger, more complex skill-set. Similar, parallel considerations apply to the description of the development of writing expertise. Developing writing expertise involves both skill development and their attachment as strategic resources within an activity system. The problem is that we must measure both the fluency and accuracy of skills as stand-alone tasks and the effectiveness with which readers/writers/thinkers can employ those skills flexibly to accomplish specific literacy goals; thus, we must conceptualize reading and writing not merely as individual skills, but also as interdependent and mutually supporting tools for social interaction.

The literacy framework developed for the CBAL project is based upon this kind of developmental trajectory and predicts that parallel expressive, interpretive, and deliberative skills invoke common, shared mental representations. A reader may start with letters on the page, and end up with ideas. A writer may start with ideas, and end up with letters on the page. A thinker may deal simultaneously with letters and words, sentences, paragraphs, documents, ideas, and rhetorical goals. One of the advantages and contributions of a combined reading/writing (English Language Arts) model is that it helps us to focus on the presence of common, shared cognitive resources deployed in literacy activity systems, whether the channel/modality itself is primarily reading, writing, or thinking. But in actual educational practice, reading and writing are typically treated separately, particularly in middle and upper grades, though both are taught by

English Language Arts (ELA) teachers. While classroom practice often integrates reading and writing, there are only scattered attempts to integrate theoretical models of reading and writing development, and even less effort to build an assessment system sensitive to an integrated literacy model. Ironically, reading and writing are frequently combined in high stakes assessments; on reading tests, students are asked to write to show they understand what they have read; on some writing tests, students are not even asked to produce writing, but only to edit, revise, or identify errors in sentences or simulated written compositions.

Treating reading and writing separately seems a missed opportunity with potentially negative learning consequences. If reading literacy is privileged in school at the expense of writing skill development, students may be ill-prepared for secondary and post-secondary academic learning which puts increasingly higher demands on the ability to express one's thinking (about what one reads) in written forms. Building more complex, integrated literacy assessments aligns well with best instructional practice and may assist learners in developing the full range of literacy skills.

In general, the community of reading researchers tends to acknowledge that writing instruction supports reading development, but relatively few researchers cross the precipice and see them as jointly determined. Often, writing instruction has been the historical runt of the reading, writing, and 'rithmetic litter. When state accountability scores drop, explicit reading and math interventions often squeeze out time for writing instruction. Yet reading scores continue stagnating nationally, which means that millions of children, adolescents, and adults have inadequate reading, writing, and likely, thinking skills. An integrated approach that emphasizes learning to write fluently and thoughtfully may also provide the most effective and efficient pathway to thoughtful reading, if only because cognitive reading processes are mostly invisible, whereas the processes of written composition can be made visible, transparent, and an object of metalinguistic reflection (Olson, 1991; Olson & Hildyard, 1985). The model described here is the starting point for mapping out the interdependencies we want to foster, even as the assessment challenge of separating them remains the target of most standards statements and external testing programs. We must first reform the social construct in order to assess the cognitive construct more productively.

MAJOR THEMES

Our perspective treats reading, writing, and critical thinking as integrated activity systems in the Vygotskian sense (Vygotsky & Luria, 1994) and along lines discussed in Bazerman (2004). We envisage writing (and, in particular, specific genres of writing) as forming part of an integrated set of tools for social communication. Thus, as Deane (2011) outlines in greater detail, writing skill is inherently intertextual, involving an interplay of skills that might, in isolation, be considered reading or critical thinking (Bloome, 1993). This point can be supported in part by considering the many shared elements that play roles not only in theories of writing but also in in theories of reading comprehension, such as verbal comprehension (Hoover & Gough, 1990) and text macrostructure (Graesser, Singer, & Trabasso, 1994). It can be reinforced by observing the key role that reading, deliberation, and reflection skills play in classical models of writing (Alamargot & Chanquoy, 2001; Bereiter & Scardamalia, 1987; Hayes, 1996; Hayes & Flower, 1980). But the importance of intertextuality emerges most strongly when we consider particular genres of writing and analyze the specific configurations of skills that are required in particular genres, along lines exemplified by Coirier, Andriessen and Chanquoy (1999).

In addition, we have found that it is useful to think of writing skill as involving the acquisition of specific skill bundles (only some of which are writing-specific) and their progressive elaboration and generalization. Beyond general fluency and accuracy of written production, there is specific evidence that progress in writing in particular genres is tied to the developmental sequence observed for specific skills.[1] For instance, progress in writing narratives seems to depend critically upon acquiring the ability first to represent event sequences causally in terms of character motivations and goals; and second, in acquiring the ability to represent narratives metacognitively as interpretive acts enacted by the author (McKeough, 2007; Nicolopoulou & Bamberg, 1997; Nicolopoulou, Blum-Kulka, & Snow, 2002). Similarly, the development of skill in argumentative writing partially reflects the underlying development of argumentation skills (Felton & Kuhn, 2001; Kuhn, 1999; Kuhn & Udell, 2003). When we analyze particular genres in this fashion, intertextual dependencies also emerge from the ecology of the activity system. For example, argumentative writing critically depends upon summary skills and not just the ability to create arguments, since participation in argument nearly always entails a response to prior and opposing points of view. Similarly, literary analysis critically depends upon the ability to find and explain evidence for interpretations in a text, and more generally upon the ability to evaluate and respond to such interpretations. Many of these dependencies are recognized in educational standards, at least implicitly. For instance, in the Common Core State Standards that have been adopted by 44 of the 50 US states (http://www.corestandards.org/the-standards/english-language-arts-standards), many of the language arts standards specifically address such skills as building a mental model of the events in a narrative, creating arguments, or finding evidence in a source text.

The considerations sketched thus far lead in specific directions: (i) toward assessment design strategies that borrow many features of performance assessments, (ii) by assessment designs that incorporate a (relatively) meaningful context and arrange task sequences so that their application outside the assessment context is transparent to students and teachers.

DESIGNING WRITING ASSESSMENTS TO SUPPORT INSTRUCTION

DESIGN CONSIDERATIONS

Any kind of formal assessment creates tradeoffs. The more we seek to standardize tests, to make tests equivalent and generalizable, the harder it is to capture interdependencies among tasks, to communicate why one task supports another, or to communicate the social context that motivates particular skills. On the other hand, pure performance tasks may create measurement and scoring difficulties. Within the overall CBAL research framework, we are researching both high-stakes assessments (where the pressures for standardization are greatest), and formative, classroom assessments (where performance tasks are often favored, yet must still be reliable enough to support instructional decisions based upon student performance).

In this chapter we primarily discuss our designs for high-stakes tests, with an emphasis on features intended to make high-stakes testing more supportive of instruction. We emphasize, in particular, features that make the high-stakes assessments more transparent—in the sense that each test exemplifies appropriate reading and writing practices and provides instructionally actionable results. Some of these considerations are not specific to writing but are particularly problematic for writing because of the time required to collect a single written response of any length. For instance, reliable estimates of ability require multiple measurements; and in the case of writing, that means a valid writing assessment will collect multiple writing samples on multiple occasions. Solving this problem is fundamental to the CBAL approach, which is focused on exploring the consequences of distributing assessments throughout the year (which makes it easier to collect multiple samples, but is likely to be feasible only if the high-stakes assessments are valuable educational experiences in their own right.)

Our goal is to develop a series of assessments that might be given at intervals, sampling both reading and writing skills, over the course of the school year. One logical way to do this is to focus each individual test on a different genre (but to sample systematically from all the reading, writing, and thinking skills necessary for success at each genre.) Having taken this first step, it becomes possible to introduce many of the features of a performance task into a summative design without sacrificing features necessary to produce a reliable instrument under high-stakes conditions.

STRUCTURE OF INDIVIDUAL ASSESSMENTS.

Certain design decisions are well-motivated if we conceive of individual writing assessments as occasions to practice the skills needed for success in particular genres, and plan from the beginning to provide multiple assessments during the course of the school year. In particular, the CBAL writing assessments have a common structure, involving:

- A unifying scenario
- Built-in scaffolding
- Texts and other sources designed to provide students with rich materials to write about
- Lead-in tasks designed to engage students with the subject and measure important related skills
- A culminating extended writing task

The Scenario

Rather than presenting a single, undifferentiated writing task, each test contains a series of related tasks that unfold within an appropriate social context. The scenario is intended to provide a clear representation of the intended genre and social mode being assessed, to communicate how the writing task fits into a larger social activity system, and to make each task meaningful within a realistic context. By their nature, such scenarios are simulations, and may not capture the ultimate social context perfectly; but to the extent that they transparently represent socially meaningful situations within which students may later be required to write (either inside or outside of school), the scenario helps to make explicit connections between items that (i) communicate why each item has been included on the test; (ii) help teachers connect the testing situation to best instructional practices; and (iii) support the goal of making the assessment experience an opportunity for learning.

Scaffolding

Building scaffolding elements into the test helps the assessment model best practices in instruction. Such elements include:

- Lead-In Tasks, which may involve reading or critical thinking activities and consist of selected-response as well as sentence- or paragraph-length writing tasks. Lead-in tasks are intended to satisfy several goals at once, to prepare students to write, to measure skills not easily measured in an extended writing task, and to exercise prerequisite skills.
- Task supports such as rubrics that provide explicit information about how student work will be judged, tips and checklists that indicate what kinds of strategies will be successful, and appropriate reference materials and tools to support reading comprehension and thinking. These materials are included to minimize irrelevant variation in student preparation that could obscure targeted skills.

Supporting Texts

Rather than asking students to write about generic subjects, we provide supporting texts intended to inform students about a topic and stimulate their thinking before they undertake the final, extended writing task. The goal is to require students to engage in the kinds of intertextual practices that underlie each written genre.

The Extended Culminating Writing Task

In each test, we vary purpose and audience, and hence examine different social, conceptual and discourse skills, while requiring writers to demonstrate the ability to coordinate these skills to produce an extended written text.

This general design is instantiated differently depending on what genre is selected for the culminating extended writing task. Each genre has a well-defined social purpose, which defines (in turn) a specific subset of focal skills. For the classic argumentative essay, for example, focal skills include argument-building and summarization. Given this choice, the problem is to create a sequence of lead-in tasks that exercise the right foci and thus scaffold and measure critical prerequisite skills. For a different, paradigmatic writing task, such as literary analysis, focal skills include the ability to identify specific support for an interpretation in a text, and to marshal that evidence to support and justify one's own interpretations. These are different kinds of intertextuality, supporting very different literacy practices. The final writing task is meaningful only to the extent that writers are able to engage in the entire array of reading and writing practices associated with each genre.

An Example: Two Middle School Writing/Reading Tests

Tables 1 and 2 show the structure of two designs that might be part of a single year's sequence of reading/writing tests: one focuses on the classic argumentative essay; the other, on literary analysis. The argumentation design contains a series of lead-in tasks designed, among other things, to measure whether students have mastered the skills of summarizing a source text and building an argument, while simultaneously familiarizing students with the topic about which they will write in the final, extended writing task. The literary analysis design contains a series of lead-in tasks intended to measure whether students have the ability to find textual evidence that supports an interpretation, can assess the plausibility of global interpretations, or can participate in an interpretive discussion.

An important feature of this design is that the lead-in tasks straddle key points in critical developmental sequences. Thus, the test contains a task focused on classifying arguments as pro or con—a relatively simple task that should be straightforward even at relatively low levels of argument skill. It also contains a rather more difficult task—identifying whether evidence strengthens or weakens an argument—and a highly challenging task, one that appears to develop relatively late, namely the ability to critique or rebut someone else's argument.

Note that a key effect of this design is that it includes what are, from one point of view, reading or critical thinking tasks in a writing test, and thus enables us to gather information about how literacy skills vary or covary when applied within a shared scenario. In addition, since the tests are administered by computer, we are able to collect process data (e.g., keystroke logs) and can use this information to supplement the information we can obtain by scoring the written products. The CBAL writing test designs thus provide a natural laboratory for exploring how writing skills interact with, depend upon, or even facilitate reading and critical thinking skills.

Also note that the culminating task is not (by itself) particularly innovative. One could be viewed as a standard persuasive essay writing prompt; the other, as a fairly standard interpretive essay of the kind emphasized in literature classes. This is no accident; the genres are well-known, and exemplary tasks have been chosen as exemplars because of the importance of the activity system (i.e., the social practices) within which they play key roles. Our contribution is to examine how these complex, final performances relate to other activities, often far simpler, that encapsulate key abilities that a skilled reader/writer is able to deploy in preparation for successful performance on the culminating activity.

In other words, within the perspective we have developed, we characterize all of these skills as literacy skills, and treat writing as a sociocognitive construct.

We are currently developing a variety of materials—some of them designed for use in the classroom as formative assessments, and some designed as teacher professional support—as part of the CBAL language arts initiative. In collaboration with classroom teachers at several pilot sites, we have begun exploring a wide range of questions about writing and its relation to reading and thinking skills. As noted above, the literature contains considerable evidence that reading and writing share a large base of common skills. But there is relatively little evidence about how these skills interact in the course of complex literacy tasks. The designs we have been developing are intended in part to support research intended to construct a shared reading/writing literacy model.

Table 1. Design: Argumentation

(Lead-in tasks help prepare students to write an essay on a controversial issue. Task supports include summary guidelines, essay rubrics, and planning tools, embedded as tabs accessible from the same screen as each item.)		
Item Description	**Timing (min.)**	**Task Description**
Lead-in Section (Task 1, Part 1) (Five selected-response items)	15	Apply the points in a summarization rubric to someone else's summary of an article about the issue.
Lead-in Section (Task 1, Part 2) (Two short constructed-response items)		Read and summarize two articles about the issue. (One with a simple macrostructure, another with a more complex one.)
Lead-in Section (Task 2, Part 1) (Selected Responses, 10 binary-choice items)	15	Determine whether statements addressing the issue are presenting arguments pro or con.
Lead-in Section (Task 2, Part 2) (Six multiple-choice items)		Determine whether specific pieces of evidence will weaken or strengthen particular arguments.
Lead-in Section (Task 3) (One short constructed-response item)	15	Critique someone else's argument about the issue.
Culminating Task (One long constructed-response-item)	45	Write an argumentative essay taking a position on the issue.

Table 2. Design: Literary analysis

Note: Lead-in tasks help students prepare to write an essay on how an author develops ideas over several passages in a literary work. Task supports include essay rubrics and planning tools, embedded as tabs accessible from the same screen as each item.

Item Description	Timing (min.)	Task Description
Lead-in Section (Task 1) (Five selected-response items)	20	Choose evidence to support an inference about a literary text.
Lead-in Section (Task 2) (One short constructed-response item)	15	Contribute to an interpretive discussion about a literary text.
Lead-in Section (Task 3, Part 1) (Six selected-response items)	15	Decide on the best justification for a global interpretation of a literary text.
Lead-in Section (Task 3, Part 2) (One short constructed-response item)		Explain briefly what has been learned by reading and interpreting passages from a literary text (including interpretation of figurative language embedded in the text).
Culminating Task (One long constructed-response item)	45	Write a literary analysis describing the effects achieved by a combination of passages in a literary text and identifing evidence from the text that helps illustrate how these effects were achieved.

MEASURING RELATIONSHIPS AMONG READING, WRITING AND CRITICAL THINKING SKILLS IN A COGNITIVELY BASED ASSESSMENT

The assessments based on this framework have been designed systematically to probe reading, writing, and thinking interrelationships. Several such assessments have been field-tested, including the two described in preceding parts of this chapter. As part of the field testing, we collected various sources of evidence: not only the student responses, but also keystroke logs capturing timing data for the culminating, written response, and we subjected student responses to analysis using natural language processing techniques. The result is a rich dataset that enables us to address a variety of issues relating reading and writing skills. In this section of the chapter, we briefly explore some of the research questions that can be addressed as a result.

Field Test Design

In 2009 multi-state field tests, 2,606 eighth grade students were administered two test forms selected from four forms total, in a counterbalanced design (that is, randomly selected students took each ordered combination of tests, which allows us to verify that the order or specific choice of tests did not change our results). Two of these forms are discussed in this chapter.[2] A total of 1,054 students completed the first form analyzed here (the argumentation design), and 1,109 completed the second form (the literary analysis design), with 293 students completing both forms. The sample was about half female, with a range of ability levels, socioeconomic status (SES), and race/ethnicity. SES, race/ethnicity and English language proficiency information was collected by survey, and noncompletes ranged as high as 45% on some questions; but of the students that responded, about half were low-SES (on free and reduced lunch), less than five percent reported having English Language Learner (ELL) status, and a majority (62%) were white, with substantial African-American (22%) and Hispanic (12%) subpopulations. Each assessment was completed in two 45-minute sessions, and focused on a specific written genre. The lead-in tasks occupied the first 45 minutes. The essay was written in the second 45 minute session, which took place either immediately after the first session, or with a few days' gap in between. Test reliability was high (literary interpretation, $\alpha=.81$, 13 items; persuasive essays, $\alpha=.76$, 25 items[3]).

Relationship Between Reading and Writing Scores

If we conceptualize the lead-in tasks as basically reading/thinking tasks, and the culminating tasks as writing tasks, the correlations were moderate to high when all reading tasks were summed to give a total score, as shown in Table 3.[4] This level of correlation led us to ask whether these assessment task designs capture evidence of shared thoughtful (deliberative) cognitive processing deployed in reading (interpretive) and writing (expressive) tasks, and how they are interrelated. Specifically, we wondered:

1. Do the scores for each reading/thinking task set contribute unique variance to the prediction of holistic composition scores?
2. Do holistic written composition scores contribute unique variance to the prediction of scores on the reading/thinking tasks over and above that contributed by other reading/thinking task set scores?[5]

Table 3. Pearson correlations between human essay scores and total lead-in tasks within and across prompts (p<.001)

	Argumentative Lead-in Task Score	Literary Interpretation Lead-In Task Score
Ban Ads Essay Score	.684	.607
Mango Street Essay Score	.584	.705

To address these questions, we ran a series of regression models predicting Essay scores (Task 4) from Task Sets (1-3). In each case, the results were highly significant (R^2= .474 & R^2=.464 for Literary and Persuasive respectively). Each Task Set was a significant predictor and added unique variance when added stepwise to the model. A second series of regression models were run predicting each Task Set, with other Task Sets entered first and Essay scores last. Again, in most cases, essay score predicted additional, unique variance (see tables 4, 5, 6 and 7).[6]

Table 4. Predicting the argument essay score from lead-in tasks (Adj. R^2=.464)

DV	B	Standard Error	Beta	t	Significance	Correlation
(Constant)	-.046	.113		-.407	.684	
Task_1	.163	.022	.193	7.504	.000	.440
Task_2	.184	.021	.234	8.679	.000	.506
Task_3	.443	.028	.428	15.789	.000	.611

Table 5. Predicting the interpretative essay score from lead-in tasks (Adj. R^2=.474)

DV	B	Standard Error	Beta	t	Significance	Correlation
(Constant)	0.357	0.061		5.901	0	
Task_1	0.082	0.009	0.245	8.667	0	.545
Task_2	0.444	0.029	0.399	15.168	0	.605
Task_3	0.131	0.019	0.192	6.888	0	.514

Table 6. Predicting the lead-in tasks from argumentative essay score

Model	Adjusted R Square	R Square Change	Significance of R Square Change
Model 1: Task 1 predicted from Tasks 2 & 3	.186		.000
Model 2: Task 1 predicted from Tasks 2,3 and Essay	.229	.043	.000
Model 3: Task 2 predicted from Tasks 1 and 3	.260		.000
Model 4: Task 2 predicted from Tasks 1, Task 3 and the Essay	.311	.051	.000
Model 5: Task 3 predicted from Tasks 1 and 2	.268		.000
Model 6: Task 3 predicted from Task 1, Task2 and the Essay	.414	.146	.000

Table 7. Predicting the lead-in tasks from the interpretive essay score (Adj. R^2=.366)

Model	Adjusted R Square	R Square Change	Significance of R Square Change
Model 1: Task 1 predicted from Tasks 2 and 3	.379		.000
Model 2: Task 1 predicted from Tasks 2, 3, and Essay	.420	.041	.000
Model 3: Task 2 predicted from Tasks 1 and 3	0.281		.000
Model 4: Task 2 predicted from Tasks 1, 3, and Essay	0.409	0.128	.000
Model 5: Task 3 predicted from Tasks 1 and 2	.362		.000
Model 6: Task 3 predicted from Tasks 1, 2, and Essay	.389	.027	.000

As we can see in Tables 4 and 5, each reading task contributes separate variance to predicting the writing score; and, as Tables 6 and 7 indicate, the writing score contributes additional unique variance above and beyond that contributed by the other lead-in tasks. The pattern of performance is consistent with (though of course not sufficient to demonstrate) the kind of interpretation we would suggest—in which reading and writing draw upon a common base of shared skills, and typically are most efficiently acquired and exercised as an integrated skill-set.

These examples illustrate one kind of research strategy enabled by the CBAL assessment framework. This strategy provides a research-based justification for an integrated approach to ELA literacy instructional and assessment that views reading, writing, and thinking as mutually reinforcing skills that draw upon shared mental representations. This study and its results comprise promising first steps. The test forms demonstrated feasible implementation and scoring, acceptable psychometrics, and patterns of results in the directions predicted by the framework and design.

CONCLUSIONS AND FUTURE DIRECTIONS: FROM WRITING TO READING AND THINKING

This chapter represents collaboration between researchers who previously focused separately on writing and reading. In the parlance of visual art, we have taken a "one-point" perspective so far, focusing on the development of writing skills and assessments. We have not neglected reading (interpretive) and critical thinking (deliberative) skills, but they have been viewed through the writing lens. Once we commit to the idea that writing skill must be assessed within a larger context, then we may want to view this landscape from two- or three-point perspective. That is, once we recognize that the act of writing may incorporate a whole series of literacy acts that do not directly involve text production, it becomes necessary to give a much more detailed accounting of the relationship among skills that puts equal focus on reading and thinking as activities in their own right.

In fact, the kind of integrated model we have proposed leads naturally to a position in which a three-point perspective is viewed as the norm toward which educational practice should strive. Shared, mutually supportive cognitive representations do not necessarily emerge spontaneously in the untrained, developing reader/writer/thinker. The pedagogical literature suggests (Langer, 2001) that these kinds of skills are promoted and developed by classroom learning and instruction that take advantage of and foster their integrated construction and use in social literacy practice.

The relationship of reading to critical thinking, though often contentious, is well established in the literature of reading comprehension and assessment, including its more recent incarnation, *reading for understanding* (Kintsch, 1998; Pearson & Hamm, 2005). Nearly every reading comprehension assessment blueprint in the past several decades has some variation of a cross of text types (typically narrative vs. expository vs. persuasive) against Bloomian-derived critical thinking skill types (typically inference, analysis, synthesis, evaluation, explanation, application) (e.g., NAGB, 2005). The ongoing challenge for reading theorists has been to find a way to distinguish some "purified" construct of advanced reading from an equally "pure" construct focused on verbal reasoning/critical thinking/problem solving, recognizing that the latter could be assessed using non-language stimuli (e.g., matrix rotations), or logic problems that rely minimally on verbal understanding.

But we can ask ourselves, is not a scenario-based, scaffolded writing test as we have described in this chapter also a test of reading proficiency? Is it not also a test of critical-thinking skill? Put differently, do we not have considerable de facto evidence of reading and critical thinking proficiency when a writer produces a well-constructed essay or composition that cites evidence derived from foundational texts and articulates a well-thought-out position, claim, argument, interpretation, description, or explanation? Such a performance arguably provides evidence that an individual has the complete literacy package. There are other ways of assessing advanced reading comprehension and thinking skills that do not require a student to compose a written product (e.g., giving an oration, producing a multi-media or video, performing an experiment or other actions, selecting correct answers to questions on an exam), but perhaps permit individuals to express their understanding in a specified well-known genre—a sanctioned, conventionalized, and therefore accepted social literacy communication format—is also one of the cleanest and fairest ways to gather evidence of reading and thinking skill.

This view, which forces us to speak of tasks in a compound way, variously as reading-for-writing, writing-for-reading-comprehension, text-production-to-stimulate-reasoning, or reasoning-in-support-of-writing, creates significant measurement issues because it is incompatible with simple factorial models of skills and ability. The entire direction of literacy development is toward greater integration and mutual dependency among skills, so that (for instance) an expert writer, by employing a knowledge-transforming composition strategy, is far more dependent upon skilled reading (both for knowledge acquisition and self-evaluation) and upon verbal reasoning/critical thinking skills, than is a novice writer who relies almost exclusively upon knowledge-telling. Tracking the development of writing expertise thus requires a highly nuanced account, since expert writers are distinguished from novice writers not by the possession of any single skill, but by the ability to coordinate many skills strategically to achieve writing goals.

Conversely, building a complex mental representation or model of a text or the integration of several text (and non-text) sources, and connecting and integrating those sources by updating one's existing knowledge of the domain, often demands iterations of writing (notes, outlines, explanations) and concomitant deliberation and reflection. We can flex this Rubik's Cube in exponential permutations to form myriad patterns, but ultimately we always have three-dimensional consequences.

NOTES

1. Outside the English Language Arts, such progressions are often called "Learning Progressions" (Duncan & Hmelo-Silver, 2009). We avoid this term here primarily to avoid confusion, since it is not clear in the current stage of research whether the developmental sequences observed with general literacy skills follow the same kinds of principles that may govern the learning of mathematical or scientific concepts. In our work for the CBAL program, we have ended up hypothesizing specific "Skills Foci" that correspond to disciplinary and academic genres and well-established literacy practices, and then proposing "hypothesized developmental sequences" that might underlie student learning and the kinds of curricular goals expressed in the standards. The assessments presented in this chapter depend in part on such an analysis being performed, since (for instance) we seek to include items that measure different levels of performance (and possibly different points in a developmental sequences) for targeted skills.

2. The other two focused on (i) arguing for a choice among alternatives and (ii) writing pieces of an informational pamphlet. These involved very little reading from extended texts and are therefore excluded from the present analysis.

3. Alpha (α) is a standard statistical measure that indicates the reliability or internal consistency of a test; high alpha is consistent with the hypothesis that all the items are measuring performance on a common underlying construct.

4. This level of agreement between reading and writing scores is about at the level seen between nationally normed, standardized tests of reading comprehension and writing.

5. For the purpose of this analysis, we do not distinguish between reading and thinking items, since the items designed to probe such skills as argumentation were pitched specifically to measure performance on argument tasks that combined reading and thinking.

6. A regression analysis creates a predicted score by assigning a weight to each of the predicting variables and adding the weighted variables together with a constant to produce a predicted score. The weights are adjusted to make the predicted score match the actual scores as closely as possible. R Square is a measure of the quality of the model. When R Square is 1 the dependent variable is fully predicted by the predictors; when it is 0, the dependent variable is not dependent on the predictors. A mid-range score

like .474 or .464 corresponds to a model that predicts about half of the variance—it works reasonably well, but with a significant amount of noise. In a regression analysis, R is the positive square root of R Square, and indicates the level of correlation between the values predicted by the model and the observed values of the dependent variable. Significance levels near 0 indicate that the results would be very unlikely if the null hypothesis were true. In Tables 4 and 5, the Beta value is important, since it is a standardized weight—it indicates the relative importance of each of the variables used in the regression in terms of a standard unit of measure. The higher the Beta, the more effect that variable has on the final score. In Tables 6 and 7, the R Square change is the most important figure, since it shows us how much of the prediction provided by the model can be produced by the other two lead-in tasks and how much is added by including the writing score.

REFERENCES

Alamargot, D., & Chanquoy, L. (2001). Planning process. In G. Rijlaarsdam, D. Alamargot & L. Chanquoy (Eds.), *Through the models of writing* (Vol. 9, pp. 33-64). Dordrecht, Netherlands: Kluwer.

Bazerman, C. (2004). Speech acts, genres, and activity systems. In C. Bazerman & P. A. Prior (Eds.), *What writing does and how it does it* (pp. 309-340). Mahwah, NJ: Lawrence Erlbaum.

Bennett, R. E., & Gitomer, D. H. (2009). Transforming K-12 assessment: Integrating accountability testing, formative assessment and professional support. In C. Wyatt-Smith & J. J. Cumming (Eds.), *Educational assessment in the 21st Century.* Berlin: Springer.

Bereiter, C., & Scardamalia, M. (1987). *The psychology of written composition.* Hillsdale, NJ: Lawrence Erlbaum.

Bloome, D. (1993). The social construction of intertextuality in classroom reading and writing lessons. *Reading Research Quarterly, 28*(4), 305-333.

Coirier, P., Andriessen, J. E. B., & Chanquoy, L. (1999). From planning to translating: The specificity of argumentative writing. In P. Coirier & J. Andriessen (Eds.), *Foundations of argumentative text processing* (pp. 1–28). Amsterdam: Amsterdam University Press.

Deane, P. (2011). *Writing assessment and cognition.* (ETS Research Report RR-11-14). Princeton, NJ: Educational Testing Service.

Deane, P., Fowles, M., Baldwin, D., & Persky, H. (2011). *The CBAL summative writing assessment: A draft eighth-grade design. (ETS Research Memorandum RM-11-01).* Princeton, NJ: Educational Testing Service.

Deane, P., Quinlan, T., & Kostin, I. (2011). *Automated scoring within a developmental, cognitive model of writing proficiency.* (ETS Research Report RR-11-16). Princeton, NJ: Educational Testing Service.

Deane, P., Quinlan, T., Odendahl, N., Welsh, C., & Bivens-Tatum, J. (2008). *Cognitive models of writing: Writing proficiency as a complex integrated skill. CBAL literature review-writing* (ETS Research Report RR-08-55). Princeton, NJ: Educational Testing Service.

Duncan, R. G., & Hmelo-Silver, C. E. (2009). Learning progressions: Aligning curriculum, instruction, and assessment. *Journal of Research in Science Teaching, 46*(6), 606-609.

Felton, M., & Kuhn, D. (2001). The development of argumentive discourse skill. *Discourse Processes, 32*(2/3), 135-153.

Graesser, A. C., Singer, M., & Trabasso, T. (1994). Constructing inferences during narrative text comprehension. *Psychological Review, 101*(3), 371-395.

Hayes, J. R. (1996). A new framework for understanding cognition and affect in writing. In C. M. Levy, & S. Ransdell (Eds.), *The science of writing: Theories, methods, individual differences, and applications* (pp. 1-27). Mahwah, NJ: Lawrence Erlbaum.

Hayes, J. R., & Flower, L. (1980). Identifying the organization of writing processes. In L. Gregg & E. R. Steinberg (Eds.), *Cognitive processes in writing* (pp. 3-30). Hillsdale, NJ: Lawrence Erlbaum.

Hillocks, G., Jr. (2002). *The testing trap.* New York: Teachers College Press.

Hillocks, G., Jr. (2008). Writing in secondary schools. In C. Bazerman (Ed.), *Handbook of research on writing: History, society, school, individual, text* (pp. 311-330). Mahwah, NJ: Lawrence Earlbaum.

Hoover, W. A., & Gough, P. B. (1990). The simple view of reading. *Reading and Writing: An Interdisciplinary Journal, 2,* 127-160.

Kane, M. T. (2006). Validation. In R. L. Brennan (Ed.), *Educational measurement* (4th ed., pp. 17-64). Westport, CT: Praeger.

Kintsch, W. (1998). *Comprehension: A paradigm for cognition.* Cambridge, UK: Cambridge University Press.

Kuhn, D. (1999). A developmental model of critical thinking. *Educational Researcher, 28*(2), 16-46.

Kuhn, D., & Udell, W. (2003). The development of argument skills. *Child Development, 74*(5), 1245-1260.

Langer, J. A. (2001). Beating the odds: Teaching middle and high school students to read and write well. *American Educational Research Journal, 38*(4), 837-880.

McKeough, A. (2007). Best narrative writing practices when teaching from a developmental framework. In S. Graham, C. MacArthur, & J. Fitzgerald (Eds.), *Best practices in writing instruction* (pp. 50-73). New York: Guilford.

Mislevy, R. J., & Haertel, G. (2006). Implications for evidence-centered design for educational assessment. *Educational Measurement: Issues and Practice, 25,* 6-20.

National Assessment Governing Board. (2005). *Specifications for the 2009 NAEP reading assessment.* Washington, DC: National Assessment Governing Board, American Institutes for Research.

Nicolopoulou, A., & Bamberg, M. G. W. (1997). Children and narratives: Toward an interpretive and sociocultural approach. In M. Bamberg (Ed.), *Narrative development: Six approaches* (pp. 179-215). Mahwah, NJ: Lawrence Erlbaum.

Nicolopoulou, A., Blum-Kulka, S., & Snow, C. E. (2002). Peer-group culture and narrative development. In S. Blum-Kulka & C. E. Snow (Eds.), *Talking to adults* (pp. 117-152). Mahwah, NJ: Lawrence Erlbaum.

Olson, D. R. (1991). Literacy as a metalinguistic activity. In D. R. Olson & N. Torrance (Eds.), *Literacy and orality* (pp. 251-270). Cambridge, U.K.: Cambridge University Press.

Olson, D. R., & Hildyard, A. (1985). *Literacy, language, and learning: The nature and consequences of reading and writing.* Cambridge, U.K.: Cambridge University Press.

Pearson, P. D., & Hamm, D. N. (2005). The assessment of reading comprehension: A review of practices- past, present, and future. In S. G. Paris & S. A. Stahl (Eds.), *Children's reading comprehension and assessment* (pp. 17-30). Mahwah, NJ: Lawrence Earlbaum.

Pellegrino, J. W. (2009, December). The design of an assessment system for the Race to the Top: A learning sciences perspective on issues of growth and measurement. Paper presented at the Exploratory Seminar: Measurement Challenges Within the Race to the Top Agenda. Abstract retrieved from http://www.k12center.net/rsc/pdf/PellegrinoPresenterSession1.pdf.

Perin, D. (2009). Best practices in teaching writing to adolescents. In S. Graham, C. MacArthur, & J. Fitzgerald (Eds.), *Best Practices in writing instruction* (pp. 242-264). New York: Guilford.

Scarborough, H. S. (2001). Connecting early language and literacy to later reading (dis)abilities: Evidence, theory, and practice. In S. Neuman & D. Dickinson (Eds.), *Handbook for research in early literacy* (Vol 1., pp. 97-110). New York: Guilford.

Vellutino, F., Tunmer, W. E., & Jaccard, J. (2007). Components of reading ability: Multivariate evidence for a convergent skills model of reading development. *Scientific Studies of Reading, 11*(1), 3-32.

Vygotsky, L., & Luria, A. R. (1994). Tool and symbol in child development. In R. van der Veer & J. Valsiner (Eds.), *The Vygotsky reader* (pp. 99-174). Oxford, UK: Blackwell.

CHAPTER 6.

AUTOMATED ESSAY SCORING AND THE SEARCH FOR VALID WRITING ASSESSMENT

Andrew Klobucar, Paul Deane, Norbert Elliot, Chaitanya Ramineni, Perry Deess, and Alex Rudniy
New Jersey Institute of Technology and Educational Testing Service

In educational settings, assessment targets determine the need for local validation. Instructional improvement, for example, is validated by examining the relationship between curricular innovations and improvements in criterion measures such as course grades. In such cases, as both the educational measurement community (Cizek, 2008; Shepard, 2006) and the writing assessment community (Good, Osborne, and Birchfield, 2012; Huot, 1996; Lynne, 2004) recognize, assessments are most meaningful when they are site based, locally controlled, context sensitive, rhetorically informed, accountable, meaningful, and fair.

In the context of a first-year writing course, there are multiple reasons and occasions for measurement. Before a student enrolls, some information may be available and used for placement; but placement decisions are not perfect, and it is important to identify students who may require additional instructional support (Complete College America, 2012). At course completion, overall student performance must be assessed, both for the purposes of assigning course grades, and for purposes of program evaluation. Historically, New Jersey Institute of Technology (NJIT) has used measures such as the SAT Writing (SAT-W) for placement (Elliot, Deess, Rudniy, & Joshi, 2012). It has used human-scored writing samples allowing 48 hour completion to identify students for instructional support. Course grades are based upon teacher evaluation of student writing produced during the course. Student papers are also assembled into portfolios and human-scored on holistic and analytic rubrics for purposes of program evaluation. The availability of new technologies supports alternative approaches to scoring, such as Automated Essay Scoring (AES) systems, and alternative approaches to collecting samples of student work, such as the use of electronic portfolios (EPortfolios). Such innovations exemplify the 21st century emphasis on writing in digital environments.

Because digital environments provide occasions for experimentation in teaching and assessing writing, both AES and EPortfolios can be viewed, along with blogging and podcasting, as electronic tools. In fact, similar pedagogical aims in the development of these learning technologies are evident in an environment where students are encouraged to consider information organization, document design, and social networking as increasingly integral to writing processes, products, and the audiences they serve. Digital environments, it can be argued, present a much more complex framework for writing than print environments (Neal, 2011). Part of the change in intricacy derives from the technologies themselves. Electronic texts involve an ever expanding assortment of writing tools and programs, encapsulating nearly every stage of writing, from concept generation, through data organization, to the design, presentation and even distribution of the final document. Given these developments, it seems relatively easy to predict a deeper role for automated assessment technologies in both instruction and assessment. The key issue in such practices is to determine how to use such tools to develop skills and facilitate success for writers attempting increasingly challenging writing tasks that might, without the digital technologies, have been too difficult.

This chapter presents results from collaboration between NJIT and the Educational Testing Service (ETS). The focus of this collaboration is the Criterion® Online Writing Evaluation Service (Attali, 2004; Burstein, Chodorow, & Leacock, 2004), an integrated assessment and instructional system that collects writing samples and provides instant scores and annotated feedback focusing on grammar, usage and mechanics; style; and elements of essay structure.

Criterion exemplifies the trend toward writing in digital environments, and in particular, a movement toward making automated scoring and feedback available in such environments. Accordingly, systems have been developed for a variety of constructed-response tasks (Baldwin, Fowles & Livingston, 2005) including mathematical equations (Singley & Bennett, 1998), short written responses with well-defined correct answers (Leacock & Chodorow, 2003), and spoken responses (Xi, Higgins, Zechner, & Williamson, 2008). More than 12 different automated essay evaluation systems have been developed, including Project Essay Grade (Page, 1966, 1968, 2003), engine 5 (now available as Intelligent Essay Assessor from Pearson) from Knowledge Analysis Technologies™ (Landauer, Laham, & Foltz, 2003), Intelligent Essay Assessor (Rudner, Garcia, & Welch, 2006), and e-rater® (Attali & Burstein, 2006; Burstein, 2003). Each engine predicts human scores by modeling features of the written text and combining them using some statistical method (Shermis & Burstein, 2003). Automated scoring can reproduce many of the advantages of multiple-choice scoring, including speed, consistency, transparent scoring logic, constant availability, and lower per-unit costs; because automated scoring is based on productive samples of student writing, it provides detailed performance-specific feedback (Shermis & Hammer, 2012).

The design of Criterion, drawing upon the features built into the e-rater engine, is intended to help writers achieve writing competency, develop confidence, and ultimately achieve fluency by providing real-time evaluation of their work in terms of grammar, usage and mechanics, features of style, and elements of essay structure. If we recognize that there are many paths to literacy, especially in digital environments (Black, 2009), then AES can and arguably should be viewed as but one tool to help students and their instructors along the way. It is, however, important to note that the value of automated methods to score writing is contested in many contexts. Concerns range from the signaling effect AES use sends about the general nature of composition studies to the specific impact of the technology on writing instruction and student learning (Bowen, Chingos, & McPherson, 2009). The research reported here is not intended to address such controversies; rather, our focus is to explore ways in which automated essay scoring might fit within a larger ecology as one among a family of assessment techniques supporting the development of digitally enhanced literacy in its many forms. Viewed in this way, our work is responsive to a change in the nature of communication that is taking place within contemporary culture and which is certain to have profound ramifications for writing in academic environments.

With the rise of digital writing frameworks, first-year writing programs in institutions such as NJIT find themselves in what Rice (2007) has called choral moments, pedagogical events that call into question many of the conventions surrounding print-based logic. AES is strikingly continuous (and congruent) in the digital environment of NJIT in which the phrase "digital everyware" is part of a five-year strategic plan intended to unify the university. For NJIT students, digital communication is part of professionalization and thus an important emphasis for the first-year writing program. With the shift from print to digital environments, the digital medium, along with the tools and software needed to generate it, has become increasingly prominent. Transferred to digital media, the very concept of genre might be taught to students as both a form of response to exigence and as integral to design patterns that contribute to communication in complex contexts (Müller 2011).

Is it a bridge too far to advance writing assessment by suggesting that it have a new relationship to digital pedagogy? Customary perspectives on writing and its evaluation have followed print-based conceptualizations of the rhetorical arts (Downs and Wardle, 2007). Accordingly, assessment procedures attempt to control extraneous contextual factors as strictly as possible, an effort that begins in most writing programs with an explicit call for evaluation standards and universal scoring tactics. Such efforts to construct a stable scoring environment usually entail establishing well-defined, collectively accepted rubrics, as well as a shared understanding of different prose genres, number of assignments, and writing goals to be covered.

While AES technologies do not eradicate the role of controlled context, they tend to de-emphasize it when integrated with other forms of digital communication. In digital environments, students find themselves working with technologies that incorporate assessment into the writing process itself. The digital screen functions here less as a mode of individual authorial expression, as human reader scores on a rubric might; instead, as subsequent research is demonstrating at NJIT, students compose in an interactive medium in which an AES system such as Criterion becomes part of a fluid environment where a machine score is viewed as an invitation to revise instead of a judgment to be suffered. In a digital environment, terms such as rhetorical knowledge and writing assessment are re-imagined by students and instructors alike. As one first-year student recently noted in a writing course emphasizing digital frameworks, audiences are static but networks are dynamic. The mental models underlying such a statement suggest that our concepts of writing must be reconsidered.

THE RELATIONSHIP OF AUTOMATED ESSAY SCORING TO OTHER WRITING ASSESSMENT SYSTEMS

However, we view such expansive possibilities, the immediate goal of assessment is to respond to existing needs and to improve current practices, often incrementally, and it is to such goals that we now turn. As we have already noted, several methods of writing assessment are at use at NJIT, including standardized tests, writing samples, course grades, and portfolio assessment of student work. These assessments differ in scope and applicability. Each has benefits but also drawbacks that must be considered to determine the uses for which each tool may validly be used. While, for instance, portfolios address the fullest possible range of the target domain of writing that can be demonstrated in a first-year course, other assessments such as the SAT-W, the 48 hour essay, and Criterion address a subset of that target domain. While timed writing is not part of the portfolios, the command of construct coverage associated with the brief essay, especially knowledge of conventions, is significant in establishing course grades. Given the tradeoffs, there may be much to gain by combining methods to take advantage of their different strengths. This approach allows one method to offset the disadvantages of another. The best ways to combine multiple assessment methods, however, is not clear in advance. Since 2009, we have been experimenting with each of these methods, focusing on determining what kind of information they provide, working to determine what uses they best support.

In the case of existing measures, a great deal already is known. SAT-W as a measure of writing skill has been discussed extensively elsewhere (Bowen, Chingos, & McPherson, 2009), and need not be discussed in detail here. It is a useful, though partial, indicator of writing competency for purposes of admission or placement. The 48 hour human-scored writing samples are typical instances of the use of direct writing assessment in writing program assessment (Adler-Kassner & O'Neill, 2010; Huot, 2002). More attention should be focused on the two end-of-course measures: traditional, paper-based portfolios and course grades.

Traditional, paper-based portfolios are designed to provide cumulative demonstrations of student experiences with writing, reading, and critical analysis. At NJIT, writing portfolios are designed to yield information about program effectiveness (Middaugh, 2010) and are not intended to assess individual student performance. Portfolios are selected according to a sampling plan designed to yield a 95% confidence interval by using the smallest possible number of portfolios (Elliot, Briller, & Joshi, 2007). Following the writing, reading, and critical analysis experiences outlined in the *Framework for Success in Postsecondary Writing* (CWPA, NCTE, WPA, 2011), the scoring rubric is designed to capture the variables of rhetorical knowledge, critical thinking, writing process, and knowledge of conventions. Portfolios are scored by two readers, with scores that differ by more than one point referred to a third reader.

While course grades are not often thought of as writing assessment systems, grades are nevertheless the most consequential and enduring assessment system used by schools. Willingham, Pollack, and Lewis (2002) have proposed a framework for understanding possible sources of discrepancy in course-level grading, identifying such factors as content differences, specific skill assessment, components other than subject knowledge, individual differences, situational differences, and errors as sources of variance. Varying emphasis on any of these could result in differences between course grades and portfolios scores, especially at NJIT when portfolios are assessed independently (and often after) final grades are awarded.

There are two new measures we are currently exploring: use of EPortfolios and AES. In the study reported in this chapter, implementation of EPortfolios was in its first year, and too few electronic portfolios were available to support a meaningful comparison with existing measures or with AES. We therefore focused on AES, and in particular, on the use of Criterion to provide embedded assessment within the writing course.

In the case of AES, the usefulness of the assessment is judged by its ability to reliably assess student writing according to a defined construct model of writing (Shermis & Hamner, 2012). The scoring engine must base its score on a valid construct definition and handle unusual or bad-faith responses appropriately. Moreover, there must be a close match between the intended use of a system and key features of the scoring engine. At ETS, there are standard procedures and evaluation criteria for model building and validation: construct relevance and representation; association with human scores; association with other independent variables of interest; fairness of scores across subgroups; and impact and consequences of using automated scoring in operational settings. Because the specific features extracted by the e-rater engine are combined using a regression-based procedure, these models must also be validated. These kinds of validations have been done on general populations as part of the development of Criterion (Attali, 2004; Burstein, Chodorow & Leacock, 2004). However, the place of the construct that Criterion measures within a curriculum, in tandem with the role it plays within a local setting, requires validation within an institution. We are actively engaged in research to train and validate e-rater models specifically for the NJIT population, but in the study reported here, we use off-the-shelf Criterion prompts and e-rater scoring models. The results we report should therefore be viewed as establishing a baseline of Criterion performance in the context and use described, and not as establishing a ceiling.

DESIGN OF THE 2010 STUDY

In the fall of 2010, the research team invited the entering first-year class at NJIT (N=1006) to participate in a rapid assessment so that students who were weak in the writing features covered by Criterion could be identified and writing program administrators could direct them to the university writing center for tutoring. Since the two submitted Criterion essays (N = 603) were timed at 45 minutes per persuasive prompt with an 800 word limit, we also asked students to submit, along with these two essays, samples that they had 48 hours to complete (N = 300), also written to college-level persuasive prompts. During that time, the students could draft and revise as they pleased and seek peer and instructor review. Seasoned faculty and instructional staff assigned essays scores on a 6-point Likert scale; resource constraints precluded having the 48 hour essays read twice.

In addition to the writing samples, course grades were collected for all students, and a random sample of traditional paper portfolios was scored (N=135). A subset of these portfolios (n = 44) were read twice in order to infer reliability for the larger sample. Both trait scores and a holistic score were collected. The holistic score was selected as the most directly parallel for purposes of comparing the paper portfolios with other measures. As a follow-up measure, a second round of e-rater scores, was collected at the end of the semester, but the total number of students participating (N = 249) was relatively low, and the intersection between this group and the group of students for whom traditional portfolios were collected was even smaller (N = 57). We therefore excluded the December Criterion administration from the analysis presented below.

RESULTS AND DISCUSSION

The dataset we analyze thus contains SAT-W scores, scores on the two automatically-scored essays in Criterion, which we considered both separately and summed, scores on the 48 hour human-scored essays, course grades, and holistic traditional portfolio scores. Descriptive statistics for these measures can be found in Table 1.

Table 1. Descriptive statistics for all writing performance measures and end-of-course grades

Measure	N	M (SD)	(Min, Max)
Prior to the semester			
SAT Writing	735	526 (82)	300, 800
At the beginning of the semester			
Criterion essay 1	603	4.17 (0.85)	1,6
Criterion essay 2	603	4.08 (0.94)	1,6
Combined Criterion score	603	8.25 (1.64)	2,12
The 48 hour essay	300	3.85 (1.06)	1,6
At the end of the semester			
Combined Criterion score	273	8.03 (1.97)	2,12
Traditional Portfolio	135	8.13 (1.90)	2,12
EPortfolio	44	7.02 (2.86)	2,12
Grades	736	2.95 (1.04)	0,4

Traditional portfolio scoring was performed using standard NJIT methodology and rubrics. Due to the complexity of the task, the following weighted Kappa adjudicated ranges are lower than those found in timed essays: rhetorical knowledge ($K = .63$, $p < 0.01$); critical thinking ($K = .47$, $p < 0.01$); writing process ($K = .7$, $p < 0.01$); conventions (K = .63, $p < 0.01$); and holistic score ($K = .62$, $p < 0.01$). However, the relationship between the outcome variable (holistic portfolio score) and the predictor variables (rhetorical knowledge, critical thinking, writing process, and knowledge of conventions) is high: $R = .87$, $R^2 = .76$, $F(4,142) = 110.16$, $p < 0.01$. We therefore were confident in using the holistic portfolio scores as a criterion measure.

Correlations between portfolio trait scores and course grade were in the moderate range (.35-.5). The correlation between the holistic portfolio score and course grade was at the high end of that range (.43). Grades are subject to many additional influences above and beyond writing competency (Willingham, Pollack & Lewis, 2002), and so the size of these correlations is in the expected range, comparable to those observed in earlier years of portfolio assessment with NJIT students (Elliot, Briller, & Johsi, 2007; Elliot, Deess, Rudniy & Johsi, 2012).

Correlations between SAT Writing scores, Criterion essay scores, traditional portfolio scores, and course grades are shown in Table 2. Correlations between the timed writing prompts fall in the moderate range (.29-.41). Correlations between these measures and the end-of course measures fell in a similar range (.24-.43 for grades, .32-43 for traditional portfolios.) The e-rater correlations are slightly lower than the correlations for the 48 hour essay, but equal to or higher than correlations for SAT Writing.

As an embedded assessment, Criterion can be use as an early warning system for instructors and their students. While 10 to 15 percent of admitted students are traditionally placed in basic writing at NJIT, a combined criterion score of 6 (15.6 cumulative percent of score frequency) was used as an early warning score so instructors could identify potentially at-risk students for writing center and tutoring help. Of the 93 students earning scores of 6 or below early in the semester, only 12 students (13 percent) received a grade of D or F; that is, 16 percent received a grade of C, 17 percent received a grade of C+, 30 percent received a grade of B, 10 percent received a grade of B+, and 14 percent received a grade of A. Such student success suggests the value of Criterion for embedded assessment and early warning. Because Criterion was primarily at the beginning of the semester in the fall of 2010, decline in student use is clear as the number of submissions declined from 603 combined scores to 273 combined scores at the end of the semester. Emphasis on using Criterion throughout the semester remains a challenge.

Table 2 reveals the importance of having multiple measures in writing assessment—as well as the importance of demonstrating wide construct coverage with those measures. Different writing assessment systems may tap different construct domains and only partially capture information about overall student performance. The moderate, statistically significant relationship of the target domain of Criterion and that of the 48 hour essay provide convergent validity evidence that the two assessments—similar to the SAT-W—are different mea-

Table 2. Correlations between writing performance measures from prior to (or beginning-of) semester and end of semester portfolio measures and course grades, with number of student submissions

	SAT Writing	Criterion Essay 1	Criterion Essay 2	Combined Criterion score	The 48 hour Essay	Traditional Portfolio
SAT writing	1					
Criterion Essay 1	0.42 (591)	1				
Criterion Essay 2	0.34 (591)	0.68 (603)	1			
Combined Criterion Score	0.41 (591)	0.91 (603)	0.93 (603)	1		
The 48 hour Essay	0.41 (296)	0.31 (274)	0.23 (274)	0.29 (274)	1	
Traditional Portfolio	0.40 (135)	0.42 (116)	0.32 (116)	0.39 (116)	0.43 (56)	1
Grades	0.25 (720)	0.29 (595)	0.24 (595)	0.29 (595)	0.35 (296)	0.43 (135)

Note. All correlations significant at the $p < 0.01$ level. EPortfolio not included because of the small N. EPortfolio correlations with SAT-W and E-rater scores are > .25, but not significant since for N=45, only correlations > .288 will be significant at the .05 level.

sures of a related trait (Brennan, 2006). Indeed, the relatively slightly lower correlations between Criterion essay scores and the end-of-course measures may be related to the fact that the constructs directly measured by Criterion are a subset of the instructional goals of the course, designed to address the writing and critical analysis experiences of the *Framework for Success in Postsecondary Writing*, and so may be necessary, but not sufficient, to achieve success in the course.

Regression analyses shown in Table 3 provide further evidence of the relation among the timed essays and their ability to predict end-of-course scores. Since the intended use of e-rater scores was to substitute for the 48 hour essay in identification of students who might be in need of instructional support, we examine the effects of using the e-rater scores and the 48 hour essay scores both alone and in combination with SAT Writing scores. Corresponding to the moderate correlations observed in Table 2, we observe low R² values, but relatively small differences between the three predictors. The 48 hour essay performed better than the combined e-rater scores, which performed better than the SAT Writing prompt. However, the differences were relatively small. If we combine the SAT Writing score with the Criterion essay scores, the resulting model exceeds the performance of the 48 hour essay (R^2 = .20 vs. .17) in predicting traditional portfolio scores, and is only slightly less effective at predicting course grades (R^2=.10 vs. .12). Combining the 48 hour essay score with SAT Writing improves prediction of grades slightly (R^2 = .14 instead of .12), but when applied to traditional portfolio scores, fails to yield a model in which the 48 hour essay is a significant predictor.

Table 3. Prediction of end of semester portfolio scores and course grades using prior to (and/or beginning of) semester writing performance measures

Model	RSquare for the outcome	
	Traditional Portfolio	Grades
SAT Writing	0.15	0.06
Combined Criterion score	0.14	0.08
The 48 hour essay	0.17	0.12
SAT Writing + Combined Criterion score	0.20	0.10
SAT Writing + The 48 hour essay	- *	0.14

*RSquare = 0.31, but model rejected since regression coefficient for the 48 hour essay was not significant. The N=56 for this model is very small. All other predictors significant p < 0.01 level.

It is important to note that the highest correlation with the course grade is produced from a sample that allowed students the most time to compose their submission; in fact, the correlation between the 48 hour essay and the final grade is higher than the .2 correlation reported by Peckham (2010) in his study of iMOAT, a system that allows extended time for essay submission. These results suggest that although the 48 hour essay scores are a better predictor of end-of-course performance than 2 45-minute essay scores, they are only marginally better—and have the disadvantage of requiring human scoring of more than a thousand essays within a very short timeframe. Since the purpose of assessment is to identify students in need of instructional support, a purely formative use, the case for using e-rater scores instead of 48 hour essays is relatively strong based on grounds of practicality, subject to further validation and evaluation.

IMPLICATIONS FOR LOCAL PRACTICE

While it is important to have in place traditional measures that provide substantial construct coverage, such as portfolios, it is equally important to experiment with innovative ways of capturing and assessing student performance in order to encourage new forms of digital communication. For institutions such as NJIT, research located at the intersection of technology and assessment of student learning is appropriate. Indeed, mission fulfillment for NJIT—as judged by its regional accreditation agency, the Middle States Commission on Higher Education—relies on technological experimentation throughout the university, especially in student learning and its assessment. As part of New Jersey's science and technology university, all NJIT shareholders—alumni, administrators, instructors, students—embrace technology and are more than willing to entertain its applications. It is in this spirit that we have undertaken the work reported in this study. However, it would be a mistake to focus solely on the results of a single study, or even on the possibilities for using a particular AES tool such as Criterion, or to imagine that innovations will long be restricted in their scope. The possibilities for new forms of local practice are inherent in the spread of digital communications technology, and the most important role that local writing communities can play in this process is to help to shape it.

The availability of new tools such as Criterion creates new possibilities both for assessment and instruction, and it is advisable to consider how these tools can be put to effective use. Whithaus (2006) provides a way forward by noting that data-driven investigations of how these systems are presently being used in postsecondary writing courses will be beneficial. In a similar fashion, Neal (2011) has provided a direction for experimentation with digital frameworks for writing instruction and assessment by focusing on hypertext (connections in EPortfolios), hypermedia (multimodal composition), and hyperattention (information processing). Together, these two areas of development—digital communication technology and its theorization—are instrumental in transforming the study and practice of writing.

Nevertheless, a critical stance to any such brave, new world includes concerns, and ours are similar to those reported by Perelman (2005) in his critique of the SAT-W. First, at NJIT we wonder if our use of the 48 hour essay and Criterion will lead students to believe that knowledge of conventions is prerequisite to their experiments with print and digital exploration of rhetorical knowledge, critical thinking, experience with writing processes, and the ability to compose in multiple environments. In other words, we must be on guard against a 21st century surrogate of the error fixation that drove much of writing instruction in the early 20th century. Second, because the NJIT writing assessment system includes essays that are machine scored, we guard against the possibility that the machine will misjudge a writing feature and that students will be wrongly counseled. As ever, machines make good tools, but terrible masters. Third, we are alert to the possibility that declining state budgets may result in an efficiency-minded administrator concluding that the whole of writing assessment can be accomplished through machine scoring. The next step, of course, might be to withdraw funding for first-year portfolio assessment, the system offering the most robust construct representation. Fourth, we must never forget that surface features such as the length of an essay, heft of a portfolio, or design of a web site are not proof of rhetorical power. There is very little difference between an AES system that relies too heavily on word count and the instructor who gives high scores to a beautifully designed web portfolio that lacks critical thought in the documents uploaded to it. A system, no matter how technologically sophisticated or visually well-designed, may fail to justify anything beyond its own existence.

What we have seen thus far is a baseline study of the role that AES can play at a specific institutional site, based upon current technology and current assumptions about how it can be validated in local settings. It would be a mistake to assume that technology will remain constant, or that future technologies will only measure features captured in the present generation of AES systems. There is every reason to expect that future research will open up a wide range of features that provide much more direct information about many aspects of writing skill.

Consider some of the features for which automated measurement is currently available, such as plagiarism detection; detection of off-topic essays; detection of purely formulaic essay patterns; measurement of organizational complexity; measurement of sentence variety; measurement of vocabulary sophistication; and detection of repetitive or stylistically awkward prose. Such features may be useful for scoring. But if we imagine an environment designed to encourage student writing, with automated feedback driven by an analysis of student responses, such features may have additional value as cues for feedback that is fully integrated with the writing process. As technology advances, it may be possible to deploy features that that support effective writing shown in the non-shaded cells of Table 4, a representation that would yield more coverage of the writing and critical analysis experiences advocated in the *Framework for Success in Postsecondary Writing*. (See Deane, 2011, for a more detailed outline of these ideas.) In the future, as linguistic technologies become more refined, students

Table 4. A partial analysis of writing skills

	Expressive	Interpretive	Deliberative
	(Writing Quality)	(Ability to Evaluate Writing)	(Strategic control of the writing process)
Social Reasoning	Purpose, Voice, Tone	Sensitivity to Audience	Rhetorical strategies
Conceptual Reasoning	Evidence, Argumentation, Analysis	Critical stance toward content	Critical thinking strategies
Discourse Skills	Organization, Clarity, Relevance/Focus, Emphasis	Sensitivity to structural cues	Planning & revision strategies
Verbal Skills	Clarity, Precision of Wording, Sentence Variety, Style	Sensitivity to language	Strategies for word choice and editing
Print Skills		Sensitivity to print cues and conventions	Strategies for self-monitoring and copyediting

Note. Shaded cells represent skill types for which there are well-established methods of measurement using automated features.

will no doubt learn to reference an increasing number of tasks—improvement of sentence variety, for example—through software (Deane, Quinlan, & Kostin, 2011).

More generally, we would argue, it is very likely that current debates are responding to a moment in time—in which the limited range of features shown in the shaded area of Table 4 have been incorporated into automated scoring technology—and in so doing, may risk forming too narrow a view of possibilities. The roles that writing assessment systems play depend on how they are integrated into the practices of teachers and students. If automated scoring is informed by enlightened classroom practice—and if automated features are integrated into effective practice in a thoughtful way—we will obtain new, digital forms of writing in which automated analysis encourages the instructional values favored by the writing community. Though AES is in a relatively early stage, fostering these values is the goal of the research we have reported.

NOTES

1. Of particular interest in discussions of timed writing is the role of word count in AES systems. As Kobrin, Deng, and Shaw (2011) have noted, essay length has a significant, positive relationship to human-assigned essay scores. The association typically

involves correlations above .60 but at or below .70. This relationship is not surprising given that words are needed to express thoughts and support persuasive essays. Shorter, lower-scoring responses often lack key features, such as development of supporting points, which contribute both to writing quality and to document length. Arguably the association between document length and human scores reflects the ability of students to organize and regulate their writing processes efficiently. As long as an AES system measures features directly relevant to assessing writing quality, and does not rely on length as a proxy, an association with length is both unavoidable and expected.

2. While the work is in a fairly early stage, differences in instructor practice are already revealing, and underscore the importance of (re)centering rhetorical frameworks in digital environments (Neal, 2011). Analysis of the contents of the portfolios revealed that some instructors used the EPortfolios as electronic filing cabinets. Other instructors worked with their students to design web sites that required students to post documents, podcasts, and blogs to sections of Web sites they had designed to highlight their writing, reading, and critical thinking experiences, accompanied by the brief reflective statements advocated by White (2005). These EPortfolios (n = 17) received higher average scores than traditional portfolios when scored to the same rubric, though the number of cases is too small to draw any firm conclusions at the present time.

REFERENCES

Adler-Kassner, L., & O'Neill, P. (2010). *Reframing writing assessment to improve teaching and learning.* Logan, Utah: Utah State University Press.

Attali, Y. (April, 2004). *Exploring the feedback and revision features of Criterion.* Paper presented at the National Council on Measurement in Education conference, San Diego, CA.

Attali, Y., & Burstein, J. (2006). Automated essay scoring with e-rater® v.2. *Journal of Technology, Learning, and Assessment, 4*(3). Retrieved from http://www.jtla.org

Baldwin, D., Fowles, M., & Livingston, S. (2005). *Guidelines for constructed response and other performance assessments.* Princeton, NJ: Educational Testing Service.

Black, R. W. (2009). Online fan fiction, global identifies, and imagination. *Research in the Teaching of English, 43,* 397-425.

Bowen, W. G., Chingos, M. M., & McPherson, M. S. (2009). *Crossing the finish line: Completing college at America's public universities.* Princeton, NJ: Princeton University Press.

Brennan, R. L. (2006). Valditation. In R. L. Brennan (Ed.), *Educational measurement* (4th ed.) (pp. 17-64). Westport, CT: American Council on Education/Praeger.

Burstein, J. (2003). The e-rater® scoring engine: Automated essay scoring with natural language processing. In M. D. Shermis & J. C. Burstein (Eds.), *Automated essay scoring: A cross-disciplinary perspective* (pp. 113-121). Hillsdale, NJ: Lawrence Erlbaum.

Burstein, J., Chodorow, M., & Leacock C. (2004) Automated essay evaluation: The Criterion online writing service. *AI Magazine, 25,* 27–36.

Cizek, G. J. (2008). Assessing Educational measurement: Ovations, omissions, opportunities. [Review of *Educational measurement,* 4th ed., by R. L. Brennan (Ed.).] *Educational Researcher, 37,* 96-100.

Complete College America (2012). R*emediation: Higher education's bridge to nowhere.* Washington, DC: Complete College America. Retrieved from http://www.completecollege.org/docs/CCA-Remediation-final.pdf

Council of Writing Program Administrators, National Council of Teachers of English, & National Writing Project. (2011). *Framework for success in postsecondary writing.* Retrieved from http://wpacouncil.org

Deane, P. (2011). *Writing assessment and cognition.* (ETS Research Report RR-11-14). Princeton, NJ: Educational Testing Service.

Deane, P., Quinlan, T., & Kostin, I. (2011). *Automated scoring within a developmental, cognitive model of writing proficiency* (No. RR-11-16). Princeton, NJ: Educational Testing Service.

Downs, D., & Wardle, E. (2007). Teaching about writing, righting misconceptions: (Re)envisioning "first-year composition" as "introduction to writing studies." *College Composition and Communication, 58,* 552-584.

Elliot, N., Briller, V., & Joshi, K. (2007). Portfolio assessment: Quantification and community. *Journal of Writing Assessment, 3,* 5–30. Retrieved from http://www.journalofwritingassessment.org

Elliot, N., Deess, P., Rudniy, A., & Johsi, K. (2012). Placement of students into first-year writing courses. *Research in the Teaching of English, 46,* 285-313.

Good, J. M., Osborne, K., & Birchfield, K. (2012). Placing data in the hands of discipline-specific decision-makers: Campus-wide writing program assessment. *Assessing Writing, 17,* 140-149.

Huot, B. (1996). Towards a new theory of writing assessment. *College Composition and Communication, 47,* 549-566.

Huot, B (2002). *(Re)Articulating writing assessment for teaching and learning.* Logan, Utah: Utah State University Press.

Kobrin, J. L., Deng, H., & Shaw, E. J. (2011). The association between SAT prompt characteristics, response features, and essay scores. *Assessing Writing, 16,* 154-169.

Landauer, T. K., Laham, D., & Foltz, P. W. (2003). Automated scoring and annotation of essays with the Intelligent Essay Assessor. In M. D. Shermis & J. C. Burstein (Eds.), *Automated essay scoring: A cross-disciplinary perspective* (pp. 87-112). Hillsdale, NJ: Lawrence Erlbaum.

Leacock, C., & Chodorow, M. (2003). C-rater: Scoring of short-answer questions. *Computers and the Humanities, 37,* 389–405.

Lynne, P. (2004). *Coming to terms: A theory of writing assessment.* Logan, UT: Utah State University Press.

Middaugh, M. F. (2010). *Planning and assessment in higher education: Demonstrating institutional effectiveness.* San Francisco, CA: Jossey-Bass.

Müller, K. (2011). Genre in the design space. *Computers and Composition, 28,* 186-194.

Neal, M. R. (2011). *Writing assessment and the revolution in digital technologies.* New York, NY: Teachers College Press.

Page, E. B. (1966). The imminence of grading essays by computer. *Phi Delta Kappan, 48,* 238–243.

Page, E. B. (1968). The use of the computer in analyzing student essays. *International Review of Education, 14,* 210–225.

Page, E. B. (2003). Project essay grade: PEG. In M. D. Shermis & J. C. Burstein (Eds.), *Automated essay scoring: A cross-disciplinary perspective* (pp. 43-54). Hillsdale, NJ: Lawrence Erlbaum.

Peckham, I. (2010). Online challenge vs. offline ACT. *College Composition and Communication, 61,* 718-745.

Perelman, L. (2005, May 29). New SAT: Write long, badly and prosper. *Los Angeles Times.* Retrieved from http://articles.latimes.com/2005/may/29/opinion/oe-perelman29

Rice, J. (2007). *The rhetoric of cool: Composition studies and the new media.* Carbondale, IL: Southern Illinois University Press.

Rudner, L. M., Garcia, V., & Welch, C. (2006). An evaluation of IntelliMetric™ essay scoring system. *The Journal of Technology, Learning and Assessment, 4*(4). Retrieved from http://www.jtla.org

Shepard, L. A. (2006). Classroom assessment. In R. L. Brennan (Ed.), *Educational measurement* (4th ed., pp. 623-646). Westport, CT: American Council on Education and Praeger.

Shermis, M. D., & Burstein, J. C. (Eds.). (2003). *Automated essay scoring: A cross-disciplinary perspective.* Hillsdale, NJ: Lawrence Erlbaum.

Shermis, M. D., & Hammer, B. (2012). Contrasting state-of-the-art automated scoring of essays: Analysis. Paper presented at the annual meeting of the National Council of Measurement in Education, Vancouver, BC, Canada.

Singley, M. K., & Bennett, R. E. (1998). *Validation and extension of the mathematical expression response type: Applications of schema theory to automatic scoring and item generation in mathematics* (GRE Board Professional Report No. 93-24P). Princeton, NJ: Educational Testing Service.

White, E. M. (2005). The scoring of writing portfolios: Phase 2. *College Composition and Communication, 56,* 581-600.

Whithaus, C. (2006). Always already: Automated essay scoring and grammar checkers in college writing courses. In P. E. Ericsson & R. Haswell (Eds.), *Machine scoring of student essays: Truth and consequences* (pp. 166-176). Logan, UT: Utah State University Press.

Willingham, W. W., Pollack, J. M., & Lewis, C. (2002). Grades and test scores: Accounting for observed differences. *Journal of Educational Measurement, 39,* 1-97.

Xi, X., Higgins, D., Zechner, K., & Williamson, D. M. (2008). *Automated scoring of spontaneous speech using SpeechRater v1.0.* (ETS Research Report RR-08-62). Princeton, NJ: Educational Testing Service.

CHAPTER 7.

CONSTRUCT VALIDITY, LENGTH, SCORE, AND TIME IN HOLISTICALLY GRADED WRITING ASSESSMENTS: THE CASE AGAINST AUTOMATED ESSAY SCORING (AES)

Les Perelman
Massachusetts Institute of Technology

Automated Essay Scoring (AES), the use of computers to evaluate student writing, first appeared in 1966 with Project Essay Grade (Page, 1994). Since 1990, the three major products have been Vantage Technologies' Intellimetric, Pearson's Intelligent Essay Assessor, and the Educational Testing Service's e-rater. Advocates of Automated Essay Scoring originally justified the efficacy of their various algorithms by the ability of AES to replicate closely the scores of human graders. This concurrent validity proved, however, to be insufficient, because as Attali & Burstein note, "In the case of AES, the significance of comparable single-essay agreement rates should be evaluated against the common finding that the simplest form of automated scoring which considers only essay length could yield agreement rates that are almost as good as human rates. Clearly, such a system is not valid" (2006, p. 5). The various AES systems then developed constructs that their creators claimed, could make their assessments more valid and reliable than human graders.

This chapter argues that although the whole enterprise of automated essay scoring claims various kinds of construct validity, the measures it employs substantially fail to represent any reasonable real-world construct of writing ability. (The term *validity i*n psychological testing refers to the ability of assessment scale or instrument to measure what it claims to be measuring. The term, *construct validity,* refers to an assessment instrument's ability to measure a theorized scientific construct that cannot be directly measured, such as intelligence, creativity, critical thinking, or writing ability.) The metrics employed by AES are not relevant to effective writing in the twenty-first century and, in many cases, detrimental to it. Its main success has been in producing correlations with

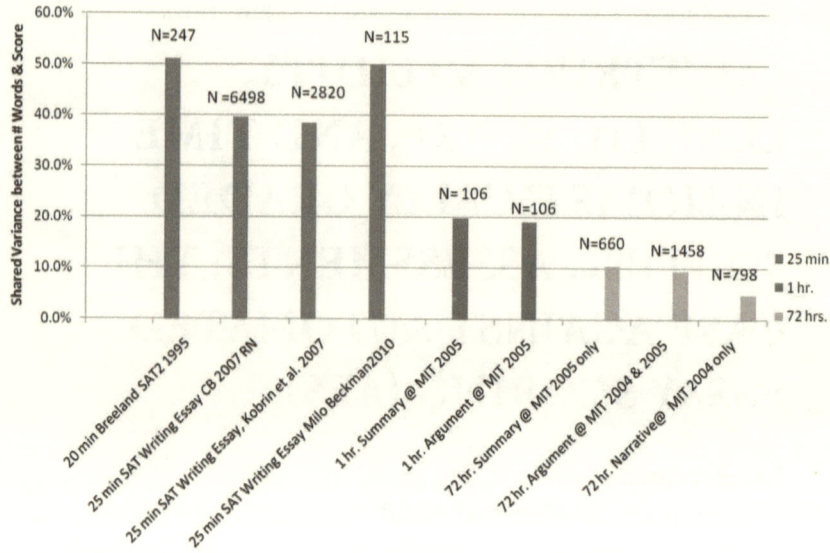

Figure 1. Shared Variance between Holistic Score and Length as a Function of Time Allowed

human grades based almost entirely on length of essays. More importantly, the importance of length in ranking essays is almost entirely an artifact of the type of artificial assessment used in most mass market writing assessments be they graded by humans or machines, the very short timed impromptu.

THE TIMED IMPROMPTU

Although White (1995) has made a case for the timed-impromptu for certain assessment decisions, it is a genre of writing that has no real analogue in real human communication and therefore is invalid as a measure. Indeed, the timed impromptu exists in no activity system except for mass-market writing assessments and education geared towards mass-market writing assessments. Writing on demand occurs in numerous situations including the traditional college essay examination. Students study for examinations to anticipate the kind of questions they will be asked and the types of information and arguments they will be required to provide. In other contexts, as well, a request for a quick written response always assumes that the writer has prior knowledge of the topic. A supervisor may ask an employee to comment on some project he or she is working on and may even want a written answer within thirty minutes, but will never ask for a response to the type of general questions that populate mass-market writing assessments. A boss does not send an email to a subordinate stating, "'Failure is necessary for success.' Send me a well organized response to this statement in 25 minutes." People do not write on general topics on demand to no one.

In the early days of writing exams for admission or placement to American colleges and universities, the essay questions were always based on a list of set texts, almost always literary. The English Composition essay of 1874 entrance examination for Harvard College, for example, was based a reading list that included three plays of Shakespeare, and novels by Goldsmith and Scott (Elliot, 2005).

In the early twentieth century, psychologists such as Carl Brigham, the Secretary of the College Board and the subsequent developer of the Scholastic Aptitude Test, moved away from what Brigham classified as Restrictive Examinations based on specific knowledge toward what he classified as Comprehensive Examinations in English. These examinations had more open-ended questions than the earlier Restrictive Examinations and more closely resembled the kind of open-ended questions that exist now in the timed-impromptu "When you have a radio or victrola in your home, is it worthwhile to play a musical instrument?" (Elliot, 2005, p. 81). The essay assessment allowed students to choose from multiple prompts. These prompts set a relatively modest length of about 350 words and gave students one hour to complete them. Brigham, however, was unhappy with reader reliability, which was extremely low (Brigham, 1934). (Reliability refers to the consistency of measurement. All measurements contain some amount of error, but multiple measurements with high reliabilty have only very small and inconsequential differences among them, while the differences in multiple measurements with low reliability will vary substantially.)

As Huot notes (2002), the whole psychometric community was obsessed with reliability, especially, in the case of writing assessments, at the expense of validity. After World War II, inter-rater reliability was achieved by limiting students to a single essay prompt, scoring the essays on a rubric based holistic scale, and severely limiting the time allowed students to write the prompt (Diederich, 1974; Godshalk, Swineford, & Coffman, 1966)

SHORT TIME FOR WRITING ENABLES LENGTH TO BE MAIN PREDICTOR OF SCORE

The quotation from Attali & Burstein at the beginning of this chapter offers strong evidence that this reliability in grading short timed impromptu writing tests, be it inter-rater reliability or reliability between a machine and a human rater, is largely a function of length. This evidence is corroborated by the comparison of data from various College Board Research Reports (Breland, Bonner, & Kubota, 1995; Kobrin, Deng, & Shaw, 2007; Mattern, Camara, & Kobrin, 2007), a recent study by Milo Beckman (2010), and data I have collected from both online and timed writing assessments I have given at MIT. These data are displayed in Figure 1. Simply stated, when students are being asked to write an essay on a subject they may not have thought much about in a very short amount of time, length becomes the major determinant of the holistic score. However, the function is negative and exponential. Although length appears to predict 40-60% of the shared variance for essays written in 25 minutes, as the time allotted increases, the correlation between length and score decreases significantly. When students have one hour to write, the shared variance predicted by length decreases to approximately 20%, and when students are given 72 hours, length predicts 10% or less of the shared variance of the holistic score.

These findings are also supported by the review of studies of the effect of length and score by Powers (2005). In particular, the effect of length appears to diminish significantly when students are asked to write about something they know about. A study of untimed essays with a word limit of 1,250 words written for a first-year undergraduate psychology class displayed a shared variance between grade and length of only 1.7% (Norton, 1990). These results reflect both common sense and observations from years of evaluating student papers. Writing tasks, not only in composition classes but also in most academic and professional contexts are given with an explicit range of appropriate length (e.g., 250-300 words; 2000-2500 words; or five to seven pages). Almost all writing falls within the specified range, and more often than not, longer papers within the specified range are, in the aggregate, no better than shorter papers. Indeed, it is a fairly unique feature of the timed impromptu that there is no specified length, reinforcing the sense that the student does better who spews out the most words regardless of content or coherence. Moreover, it is similarly apparent that students writing on a subject they know in advance also reduces the influence of length on score.

AES AND CONSTRUCT VALIDITY

The inescapable fact that there is such a close correlation between length and holistic score has not prompted questioning by those involved in Automated Essay Scoring about the validity of the timed-impromptu as a measure of writing ability. Rather, it has prompted them to argue that Automated Essay Scoring can achieve better construct validity than human readers because human raters are unreliable and sometimes capricious evaluators (Attali & Burstein, 2006; Ben-Simon & Bennett, 2007). They do, however, admit that construct coverage still needs improvement (Quinlan, Higgins, & Wolff, 2009). This chapter will focus on the construct validity of e-rater 2.0 because the Educational Testing Service has been more transparent than the other developers of Automated Essay Scoring—Vantage Technologies and Pearson Education—in describing the specific features that constitute its scoring algorithm.

Although most of the publications by ETS define e-rater's score as *holistic*, the score is no sense the holistic score defined by White in his seminal article, "Holisticism" (1984). The "holistic" score derived by e-rater is, in reality, a weighted sum of analytic scores and sub-scores that fall into five broad categories: organization, development, lexical complexity, topic specific vocabulary usage, and grammar, usage, mechanics, and style. (Attali & Burstein, 2006; Ben-Simon & Bennett, 2007). Quinan, Higgins, and Wolff (2009) argue that these categories map onto the National Writing Project's 6 + 1 Analytic Writing Continuum that was originally based on the categories of 1) Ideas and Content; 2) Organization; 3) Voice; 4) Word choice; 5) Sentence Fluency; and 6) Conventions, but they offer no evidence to support such a claim. A closer analysis of the metrics used for each of the five e-rater categories highlights the basic limitation of all Automated Essay Scoring. They do not understand meaning, and they are not sentient. They do not react to language; they merely count it.

The organization and development metrics are based on the concept of the "discourse element," which derives from the structure of the traditional five-paragraph essay (Attali & Burstein, 2006). The sole metric for organization is the number of discrete discourse elements in the essay such as "thesis, main ideas, and conclusion" (Ben-Simon & Bennett, 2007, p. 10). Operationally, a discourse element is usually seen as a paragraph, with the introductory and concluding paragraphs having a slightly different structure than the middle supporting paragraphs.

It assumes a writing strategy that includes an introductory paragraph, at least a three-paragraph body with each paragraph in the body consisting of a pair of main point and supporting idea elements, and a concluding paragraph. The organization score measures the difference between this minimum five-paragraph essay and the actual discourse elements found in the essay. Missing elements could include supporting ideas for up to the three expected main points or a missing introduction, conclusion, or main point. On the other hand, identification of main points beyond the minimum three would not contribute to the score (Attali & Burstein, 2006, p. 10).

E-rater is so wedded to the structure of the five-paragraph essay that it intentionally will not recognize more than three "supporting points," which translates as the traditional three supporting paragraphs. While the feature *organization* is defined as the number of discourse elements, development is defined as average length of each discourse element in words. E-rater, and possibly, other machine scoring algorithms, equates length with development. It is not surprising then, that two ETS researchers, Attali and Powers (2008), found that the correlation between both organization and development and overall number of words was so strong, that they could just substitute length in words for both development and organization.

Yet common sense tells us that development and organization are much more complex features than mere verbiage. A horde of rambling unconnected sentences does not develop an idea. Development is the modern equivalent of *Inventio,* Invention, one of the five departments of Classical Rhetoric. However, AES does not know Aristotle, Cicero, or Quintilian. Again, all the machine can really do is count.

Similarly, the two metrics that constitute e-rater's notion of "lexical complexity" are not complex but entirely mechanical and reductive. The first metric simply judges the complexity of words by counting their letters. The longer the word, the more complex it is, replicating the same bizarre logic that determined that the longer a paragraph is, the more developed it is. The second metric is even more curious. It counts the number of words that are infrequently used in a large representative corpus of English prose. Consequently, e-rater rewards the use of jargon and obscure and pretentious language.

These constructs, however, directly contradict the most widely accepted standards for common English prose, although, of course, different discourse genres diverge on specific features. In most contexts, however, brevity is preferred to verbosity, and simplicity preferred to pretentious diction. As Gowers in Chapter 7 of the *Complete Plain Words* (1954) states, "If the choice is between two words that convey a writer's meaning equally well, one short and familiar and the other long and unusual, of course the short and familiar should be preferred." Similarly, the sixth principle of composition in Strunk and White is "Omit needless words" (Strunk & White, 1962, p. 26). Orwell in "Politics and the English Language" (1945) admonishes the reader to avoid pretentious diction and "never use a long word where a short one will do."

These three authors, of course, represent a notion of single standard style for acceptable writing. Recent work has shown that many of the common rules given by these authors, such as to avoid the passive voice, are in direct conflict with common genres of different discourse communities. Scientists and engineers, for example, often prefer the passive voice because it reinforces their activities as observers of objects. Scientific and engineering genres also prefer jargon particular to the specific genres and discourse communities as a shorthand for communication with audiences who are familiar with those particular concepts. In most, if not all modern genres of written English, however, brevity is preferred to verbosity and simplicity to polysyllabic words. In business discourse, for example, the one or two page memorandum is norm. Less is more. In addition, there are few, if any genres that would, like e-rater, prefer *plethora* and *myriad* to *many* and *egregious* to *bad*.

The last two vocabulary metrics measure "Prompt-specific Vocabulary Usage." This technique is similar to the "Bag of Words" algorithms used by Latent Semantic Analysis, Probabilistic Latent Semantic Analysis, and Naïve Bayes approaches (Rosé, Roque, Bhembe, & VanLehn, 2003). In essence, the machine goes through each sentence looking for specific vocabulary based on the assumption that similarly scoring essays will contain similar vocabulary. With e-rater, there are two distinct metrics. The first metric evaluates an essay, based on a graded sample set of essays, on which numerical score category contains essays with similar vocabulary. The second metric compares the vocabulary of the essay to those of highest scoring essays in the sample set (Attali & Burstein, 2006). These two features, however, ignore the crucial relationships among words that are crucial to meaning. They, in essence, are looking for certain "buzz" words without regard to whether they make any sense. Many six-point essays written to a specific prompt, for example, may contain the word entrepreneurship. However, training students to use such words without caring that they are using them properly, which is what e-rater does, is not improving students' writing skills; it is teaching them to value and write meaningless verbiage with little consideration of content.

GRAMMAR, USAGE, MECHANICS, AND STYLE

In addition to the features outlined above, e-rater evaluates grammar, usage, mechanics, and style by assessing sets of sub-features such as pronoun errors, sentence fragments, subject verb-agreement, article errors, spelling errors, punctuation errors, too many long sentences, too many short sentences, the repetition of words, and the use of the passive voice (Quinlan, Higgins, & Wolff, 2009). These abilities to identify these types of errors in English prose, of course, are not an innovation of e-rater, but rather, e-rater's grammar checking software is just a recent addition to a collection of software that goes back to Writer's Workbench, Grammatik, Correct Grammar, and Right Writer. In the early 1990s, the two leading word processing software packages, Microsoft Word and Word Perfect incorporated highly sophisticated grammar and style checking software that not only identifies problems in spelling, grammar, and style, but allows users to the option of having the system automatically correct obvious and unambiguous spelling errors. In addition, from 1995 onwards, MS Word not only offers possible corrections for some errors along with offering the user an explanation of the grammatical or stylistic rule.

Microsoft's Grammar Checker (MSGC) was developed and is maintained and improved by the Natural Language Processing Group of Microsoft Research, which consist of approximately fifty computational linguists. But although much more sophisticated than earlier grammar checkers and backed with enormous resources for continuing development, the MSGC is still often capable of giving very bad advice. The anomaly noted in Word 2000 by McGee and Ericsson (2002) still exists in MS Word 2007. If I write that Bill was left by the side of the road, MSGC still suggests to change it to "The side of the road left Bill." Recently, Herrington and Moran (2012), have demonstrated significant flaws in e-rater and Criterion. The system marks perfectly correct parts of sentences as grammatical errors.

This digression on Microsoft Word's grammar and style checker is meant to demonstrate that the grammar and style algorithms in specialized programs such as e-rater will never have the sophistication and continuing improvement of MSGC, which still possesses substantial limitations. The reason is simply a matter of scale. Millions of copies of MS Word are sold every year, more than enough to support a large team of computational linguists constantly improving the product. The combined customer base of all three major AES systems, Intellimetric, Intelligent Essay Assessor, and the Educational Testing Service's e-rater is a miniscule fraction by comparison.

CONCLUSION

There are, then, four interrelated points, that argue strongly against the use of AES both as an assessment tool and as an aid in instruction. First, the "holistic" score produced by AES is largely a function of the length of the essay. Second, the abnormal nature of the short timed impromptu writing test produces this strong correlation of length to score. This strong correlation does not appear in prose in which the student either knows the subject beforehand or has had sufficient time to write. Third, the metrics employed by programs like e-rater do not reflect the constructs they are supposed to measure. They are largely irrelevant at best, and sometimes counter-productive at worst. Finally, the grammar checking and instructional function of e-rater and Criterion are much more limited than the much more developed functions in standard software such as MS Word, which itself has major limitations.

E-rater, and probably the two other major AES engines Vantage Technologies' Intellimetric˚, and Pearson's Intelligent Essay Assessor primarily perform two actions: they imperfectly count errors and count words and characters with unerring precision. This counting is the real construct informing AES. Often the underlying, but unstated, motive in assigning timed impromptu writing test is to elicit errors from students and count them. A low density of error, that is, the longer the student text and the fewer errors in it quickly becomes the unstated but very real construct that underlies this kind of assessment. Yet the past thirty years of writing studies, beginning with Mina Shaughnessy (1979) reveal that command of grammar, mechanics, topic specific vocabulary, and sentence complexity are an integral part of a complex set of socio-cognitive processes.

For AES to be valid, it must incorporate valid constructs and accurate measures of those constructs. Developers of AES systems say that these constructs must come from writing teachers (Attali & Burstein, 2006; Ben-Simon & Bennett, 2007; Quinlan, Higgins, & Wolff, 2009). Yet AES systems measure a construct that bears no relation to the well-articulated abilities enumerated in the recent *Framework for Success in Postsecondary Writing jointly* developed by the Council of Writing Program Administrators, the National Council of Teachers of English, and National Writing Project (2011). This *Framework* clearly articulates the construct that needs be measured to assess writing ability: the rhetorical ability to integrate an understanding of audience, context, and purpose when both writing and reading texts; the ability to think and obtain information critically; the ability to effectively employ multiple writing strategies; the ability to learn and use the conventions appropriate to a specific genre of writing; and the ability to write in various and evolving media. There is no construct of AES that comes close to assessing these skills.

Portfolio evaluations clearly offer the most promising platform for assessing this complex construct. But there are other more limited platforms that, at least, come much closer than AES, and as technology advances there will be others. The iMOAT system and similar online systems, for example allow for a much greater construct validity in that they assess students' engagement with texts, their ability to think critically for more than five minutes, and their ability engage in all stages of the writing process (Peckham, 2006; Peckham, 2009; Peckham, 2010; Perelman, 2004). Other, more advanced platforms will evolve. It is almost certain, however, that the prose written on these platforms will not be amenable to grading by machine until several significant revolutions occur in both theoretical and applied linguistics, until there is a theoretical framework for semantics that will allow a computational implementation, until machines understand meaning. Until then, all AES will be is reductive counting.

NOTE

1. I want to thank Norbert Elliot, Suzanne Lane, Charles Bazerman, and the anonymous reviewers who helped me immensely in focusing this chapter and providing me helpful and crucial suggestions.

REFERENCES

Attali, Y. (2007). *Construct validity of e-rater in scoring TOEFL essays* (ETS Research Rep. No RR-07-21). Princeton, NJ: Educational Testing Service.

Attali, Y., & Burstein, J. (2006). Automated essay scoring with e-rater V.2. *The Journal of Technology, Learning, and Assessment*, 4(3). Retrieved from http://escholarship.bc.edu/jtla/vol4/3/

Attali, Y., & Powers, D. (2008). *A developmental writing scale* (ETS Research Report RR-08-19). Princeton, NJ: Educational Testing Service.

Beckman, M. (2010). Quality vs. quantity: How to score higher on the SAT essay component (Unpublished manuscript).

Ben-Simon, A., & Bennett, R. E. (2007). Toward more substantively meaningful automated essay scoring. *The Journal of Technology, Learning and Assessment*, 6(1), Retrieved from http://escholarship.bc.edu/jtla/vol6/1/

Biola, H. (1982). Time limits and topic assignments for essay tests. *Research in the Teaching of English, 16*, 97-98.

Breland, H., Bonner, M., & Kubota, M. (1995). *Factors in performance on brief, impromptu essay examinations* (Report 95-4). New York: College Board.

Brigham, C. C. (1934). *The reading of the comprehensive examination in English: An analyis of the procedures followed during the five reading periods from 1929-1933*. Princeton, NJ: Princeton University.

Chodorow, M., & Burstein, J. (2004). *Beyond essay length: Evaluating e-rater's performance on TOEFL essays* (Research Report 73). Princeton, NJ: Educational Testing Service.

Council of Writing Program Administrators, National Council of Teachers of English, and National Writing Project. (2011). *Framework for Sucess in Postsecondary Writing*. Retrieved from http://wpacouncil.org/files/framework-for-success-postsecondary-writing.pdf

Diederich, P. B. (1974). Measuring Growth in English. Urbana, IL: NCTE.

Elliot, N. (2005). *On a scale: A social history of writing assessment in America*. New York: Peter Lang.

Godshalk, F. I., Swineford, F., & Coffman, W. E. (1966). *The measurement of writing ability*. New York: College Entrance Examination Board.

Gowers, E. (1954). *The complete plain words.* Retrieved from http://www.ourcivilisation.com/smartboard/shop/gowerse/complete/index.htm

Herrington, A., & Moran, C. (2012). Writing to a machine is not writing at all. In N. Elliot & L. Perelman (Eds.), *Writing assessment in the 21st century: Essays in honor of Edward M. White.* New York: Hampton Press.

Huot, B. (2002). *(Re)articulating writing assessment.* Logan, UT: Utah State University Press.

Kobrin, J. L., Deng, H., & Shaw, E. (2007). Does quantity equal quality?: The relationship between length of response and scores on the SAT essay. *Journal of Applied Testing Technology, 8*(1), 1-15.

Mattern, K., Camara, W., & Kobrin, J. (2007). *SAT® writing: An overview of research and psychometrics to date.* New York: College Board.

McGTee, T., & Ericsson, P. (2002). The politics of the program: MS Word as the invisible grammarian. *Computers and Composition, 19,* 453-70.

Norton, L. S. (1990). Essay-writing: What really counts? *Higher Education,* 20, 411-442.

Orwell, G. (1945). P*olitics and the English language.* Retrieved from http://mla.stanford.edu/Politics_&_English_language.pdf

Page, E. B. (1994). Computer grading of student prose, using modern concepts and software. *Journal of Experimental Education, 61*(4), *127-142.*

Peckham, I. (2010). Online challenge versus offline ACT. *College Composition and Communication 61*(4), 718-745.

Peckham, I. (2009). Online Placement in First-Year Writing. *College Composition and Communication 60*(3), 517-540.

Peckham, I. (2006). Turning placement into practice. *WPA: Writing Program Administration, 29*(3) 65-83.

Perelman, L. (2004). *Assessment in cyberspace.* Retrieved from http://www.mhhe.com/socscience/english/tc/perelman/perelman_module.html

Powers, D. (2005). *"Wordiness": A selective review of its influence and suggestions for investigating its relevance in tests requiring extended written responses.* Princeton, NJ: Educational Testing Service.

Powers, D., & Fowles, M. (1997). *Effects of applying different time limits to a proposed GRE writing test* (Research Report 96-28). Princeton, NJ: Educational Testing Service.

Powers, D., Burstein, J., M., C., Fowles, M., & Kukich, K. (2001). *Stumping e-rater: Challenging the validity of automated essay scoring* (Research Report 01-03). Princeton, NJ: Educational Testing Service.

Quinlan, T., Higgins, D., & Wolff, S. (2009). *Evaluating the construct-coverage of the e-rater scoring engine.* Princeton, NJ: Educational Testing Service.

Rosé, C. P., Roque, A., Bhembe, D., & VanLehn, K. (2003). *A Hybrid Approach to Content Analysis for Automatic Essay Grading.* Retrieved from http://acl.ldc.upenn.edu/N/N03/N03-2030.pdf

Shaughnessy, M. P. (1979). *Errors and expectations.* New York: Oxford University.

Strunk, W., & White, E. B. (1962). *The elements of style* (2nd ed.). New York: Macmillan.

White, E. M. (1995). An apologia for the timed impromptu essay test. *College Composition and Communication*, 46(1), 30-45.

White, E. M. (1984). Holisticism. *College Composition and Communication,* 35(4), 400-409.

CHAPTER 8.

THE POLITICS OF RESEARCH AND ASSESSMENT IN WRITING

Peggy O'Neill, Sandy Murphy, and Linda Adler-Kassner
Loyola University, Maryland, University of California, Davis, and University of California, Santa Barbara

With the rise of social science research and the professionalization of education during the late nineteenth century, educational research and practice have been tightly entwined (Bender, 1993; Labaree, 2007). Since that time, researchers studying education —especially K-12 education—have investigated a series of related questions: What should students learn, and why those things? Through what methods? To what extent are students learning what they should? How can learning be improved? A consistent definition of research has informed work undertaken to investigate these questions: It is a systematic gathering and analysis of information. In academic contexts, research is considered a discipline-defining activity; definitions of research are informed by specific fields of study. Members of academic disciplines determine appropriate questions to explore, employ appropriate methods for addressing those questions and interpreting results, and identify means for disseminating the information (Smart, Feldman & Ethington, 2000, pp. 6-7). Moreover, in academic disciplines, research is traditionally understood to be context and content neutral. But this positioning elides the reality that the act of research—the construction of research methods, the shaping of research results—is influenced by social and political factors that extend from the individual (what a person is inclined to see or not see) to the social and contextual (such as what research is funded, what type is valued, and what role it plays in policy decisions) (e.g., West 1989).

Educational research is particularly controversial because education is a complex, highly contested, politicized activity. This reality is evident in contemporary education in the United States. Increasingly, this research comes in the form of multiple assessments—of students' learning in particular subject areas; of teacher performance; of schools' achievement of particular goals. As Barbara Walvoord (2004) notes, assessment is "action research" intended to "inform local practice" (pp. 2-3) a "systematic collection of information about student learning" (pp. 2-3). At the K-12 and, increasingly, the postsecondary level, a number of stakeholders and interested others—testing companies, policy think tanks, classroom teachers, university researchers—are engaged in this kind of research, which is often linked to the day-to-day work of teaching: classroom activities, curricula, school structure and design. Student performances on tests or assessments are frequently used as the primary means to determine the success of change or the new programs aimed at creating change. The results of assessment research, then, have become a significant component of educational research and reform. In this chapter, we examine several studies in which what is included in and excluded from research has, or has the potential to have, considerable consequences for the students and teachers whose learning experiences will be affected by the activities being investigated. We also consider these efforts within the broader context of educational policy and the push for evidence of success.

WHY NOW?

While discussions about literacy crises are ubiquitous throughout the history of literacy in the United States (Graff, 1987, p. 16), they seem particularly consequential in the early twenty-first century because they are intertwined with considerable economic and political turmoil. Educational historian Diane Ravitch (2010) points to the 2001 passage of No Child Left Behind (NCLB), which provides funding for US public schools, as a primary culprit.[1] Under this policy, schools are required to demonstrate proof of annual yearly progress (AYP); ultimately, this demonstration is linked to the school's continued eligibility for particular kinds of federal funding. It is the responsibility of individual states to create (or adopt) measures and methods by which students demonstrate AYP. But the passage of NCLB has coincided with a dramatic reduction in federal and state funding for education; as a result, states have moved toward developing standardized assessments. These tests are administered to students yearly; students' "progress" is marked by the improvement of scores year to year. While individual students are expected to improve, so are schools' overall scores. The problems with these kinds of assessments are multiple (see, for example, Bracey 2006; Kohn 2000; Ravitch 2010); yet, because of the high stakes associated with them, they have come to drive instructional practices in many K-12 schools. In keeping with the traditional academic view of research as content and context neutral, proponents assumed that the assessment regime mandated by NLCB would produce context and content neutral results.

DEFINING THE "GOLD STANDARD": THE NATIONAL READING PANEL AND THE PRIVILEGING OF CERTAIN KINDS OF RESEARCH

Some of the tangled roots of NCLB extend from the National Reading Panel (NRP), whose work in the late 1990s revealed just how significant the impact of research definitions could be. Convened by the US Department of Education in 1997, the Panel was charged with "assess[ing] the status of research based knowledge about reading acquisition in young children" (NRP, 2000). In reviewing and evaluating the research to determine the most effective methods for teaching reading, the NRP only considered research that met their "gold standard"—that is, research using experimental or quasi-experimental designs. This decision "completely eliminated correlational and other observational research, two other branches of scientific study long accepted by the educational research community as valid and productive" (Yatvin, Weaver, & Garan, 1998, n.p.). The NRP definition of "gold standard" research had direct effects on education policy, which in turn affected classroom practice. It was used for the Reading Excellence Act of 1998 and the Reading First Initiative, both of which explicitly connected the results of research with teaching by providing funding for schools to implement curriculum shown to be effective by experimental and quasi-experimental research, but did not fund curriculum that had been proven effective through other research methods. Elements of the definition also found their way into NCLB. The definition of "gold standard" work extending from the NRP study continues to be used (almost exclusively) by the US Department of Education. The What Works Clearinghouse (WWC) and the Investing in Innovation (i3) fund, both programs sponsored by the Department of Education under the auspices of the Institute of Educational Sciences that provide funding for educational innovation, privilege experimental and quasi-experimental studies for determining program effectiveness (Investing in Innovation, 2010). These criteria are also used to assess research included in the WWC, a "central and trusted source of scientific evidence for what works in education" (United States Department of Education Institute of Education Science What Works Clearinghouse, 2010). According to the WWC evidence standards, "only well-designed and well-implemented randomized controlled trials (RCTs) are considered strong evidence, while quasi-experimental designs (QEDs) with equating may only meet standards with reservations; evidence standards for regression discontinuity and single-case designs are under development" (United States Department of Education Institute of Education Science, 2008, n.p.). Thus, researchers looking for evidence of effective practice will find only "gold standard" studies in this Education Department site.

The ubiquity of experimental and quasi-experimental research in US Department of Education policy and practice might suggest that it has gone unchallenged since the late 1990s. But in fact, as soon as the NRP findings were published in 1998, the educational research community began to provide alternative definitions of "the best" and "appropriate" research that would enable inclusion of a greater range of research methodologies and evidence and thus allow for a wider range of educational practices extending from research conducted within those definitions. The National Research Council Committee on Scientific Principles for Education Research published a monograph suggesting that scientific research must pose significant questions that can be investigated empirically, link research to relevant theory, use methods that permit direct investigation of the question, provide a coherent and explicit chain of reasoning, replicate and generalize across studies, and disclose research to encourage professional scrutiny and critique (Shavelson & Towne, 2002, p. vii). The committee also supported the use of multiple types of research methods (Shavelson & Towne, 2002, p. 25). Other professional organizations also argued for multiple methods in response to the narrowly defined "gold standard" that made its way from the NRP to Reading First, and from NCLB to K-12 classrooms across the country. The American Evaluation Association noted that "[a]ctual practice and many published examples demonstrate that alternative and mixed methods are rigorous and scientific" (AEA, 2003). The American Educational Research Association also actively supported a more inclusive definition of scientifically-based research: "the term 'principles of scientific research' means the use of rigorous, systematic, and objective methodologies to obtain reliable and valid knowledge" (AERA, 2008).

Additionally, researchers examined the problems extending from narrow definitions of what research is appropriate that arise when research is used as the basis for policy decisions that, in turn, affect classroom teaching. The use of research to make such decisions is exceedingly complicated. Luke, Green and Kelly (2010) argue that teachers, students and schools do not function in neutral, universal, generalizable contexts (p. xiii). Furthermore, they contend that educational research cannot be transposed into policy that then becomes unexamined practice; instead, teachers must adapt policy research and policy so that they are appropriate for their specific classroom contexts.

Together, these researchers point to the issues associated with treating experimental and quasi-experimental research as the "gold standard." Limiting research to only experimental and quasi-experimental methods narrows the amount and kind of data that is collected, which in turn narrows the possibilities for interpreting those data and creating a variety of teaching practices appropriate for different classrooms and learners. Far from functioning as a neutral definition of what research is appropriate, this standard has marginalized researchers and narrowed research-based perspectives. Additionally, it has extended beyond the boundaries of classroom or institutional study to profoundly affect educational policy in the United States. In other words, "gold standard" research may not provide the kind of data that would lead to information needed to make effective decisions about teaching and learning in real contexts.

BROADENING PERSPECTIVES THROUGH RESEARCH

While the "gold standard" holds sway at the federal level, many educators and researchers have attempted to assert that rigorous evaluation of an educational program requires more than test scores or other metrics related to experimental and quasi-experimental research (e.g., Davies, 2009; Luke, Green & Kelly, 2010; Wiseman, 2010). Additionally, researchers have gone on to make the case that including teachers and others who are involved in teaching and learning (such as administrators, students, and or parents) as partners in assessment research contributes to the development of robust tools and capacities to enhance students' learning.

Two recent national efforts involving writing scholars and teachers illustrate how much can be accomplished through alternative conceptualizations of research that enable the application of different questions and methods and allow for engagement by a broader range of participants. One is a multi-state, multi-year research project focused on K-12 writing instruction orchestrated by the National Writing Project; the other is a multi-state research project focused on first-year composition supported by the Fund for the Improvement of Postsecondary Education. To illustrate the potential of research conducted beyond the rigid confines of standardized measures and randomized control groups, we examine five elements of these efforts: the purpose of research; how research is defined; who was involved in the development of the research; what role was played by instructors as part of the research; and what kind of evaluation instrument emerged from or was linked to the effort.

THE NATIONAL WRITING PROJECT: RESEARCH AND ENGAGEMENT

The National Writing Project (NWP) is a network of professional development sites anchored at colleges and universities that serve teachers across disciplines and grade levels. The core principles at the foundation of NWP's national program model stress the centrality of writing for students, and the expertise and agency of teachers to act as researchers and "agents of reform" for writing education. Through its local sites, NWP teacher consultants provide professional development, create resources, conduct research, and act on knowledge to improve the teaching of writing and student learning. As part of its work to improve the teaching of writing, NWP has conducted research projects at local sites to "examine professional development, teacher practices, and student writing achievement" (NWP, 2010, p. 1). The broad purpose of the research has been to learn about the effectiveness of particular approaches to writing instruction in *specific settings*.

While these studies purposefully used experimental or quasi-experimental designs, the methods employed in each study depended on the local participants. However, all collected samples of student writing and employed pre- and post- measures to compare the performance of students whose teachers had participated in NWP programs to that of students whose teachers had not. The samples of student writing were independently scored at a national scoring conference using the Analytic Writing Continuum (NWP, 2006, 2008), an instrument developed and tested over a period of years by a group of writing assessment specialists and teachers of writing affiliated with the NWP.

All told, the sixteen research projects included in the studies ranged across seven states with an average contribution of 42 hours per teacher. One hundred forty-one schools, 409 teachers, and 5,208 students from large and small schools, urban and rural, with learners from diverse language backgrounds were involved (NWP, 2010, p. 4).

The local teachers and researchers who participated were not objective, neutral outsiders, but well-informed participants who understood the contexts for writing. However, this insider view was balanced by the national component of the research that brought participants from various sites together with writing assessment experts to score writing samples collected through the local research studies with a standardized rubric. The research design thus brought a number of voices involved and invested in education into the projects. One study in California, for instance, examined a program designed to improve students' academic writing that included sustained partnerships with teams of teachers from low-performing schools in both urban and rural areas. Another examined the impact of a program focused on the teaching of writing in grades 3 through 8 on teachers' classroom practice and on students' performance and attitudes. A study in Mississippi examined the impact of Writing Project partnerships on the achievement of ninth-graders in two high schools with predominately African American populations.

One important difference between these studies and others that have employed experimental or quasi-experimental methods was the ability, as part of the overall study design itself, to consider relationships between context and achievement. Another difference concerned the individuals and groups involved in the projects and the collaborative nature of the project itself. Instead of research conducted by disinterested outsiders—neutral researchers—these studies were developed and carried out by teachers and a range of others interested in the results of the studies and knowledgeable about the classrooms and the contexts: parents, other teachers, students, and school administrators. Teachers at the scoring conference were positioned as co-researchers in a form of action research, an approach where teachers and researchers work together and data are used for continuous, extended program improvement (Gilmore, Krantz & Ramirez, 1986; O'Brien, 2001). Findings from a study of the scoring conference showed that participant/scorers gained skills and knowledge about writing, and writing assessment, instruction, and development, and they took what they learned into their professional roles (Swain et al., 2010).

The collaborative, participatory nature of this research also led to assessment instruments that were employed across a variety of local sites to assess writing. Because the instrument had been developed by and with teachers, cultivating additional "buy-in," use of the instrument to develop yet more data that could be used to improve education, was not difficult. Shared use led to the development of shared language for the evaluation of writing among the participants in the studies. Equally important, it enabled assessment that was locally contextualized yet linked to common standards of performance shared across multiple sites. The results of the research, including the assessments of student writing and investigations of the effects on teachers of participating in the scoring sessions, indicated that both teaching and learning improved through local research initiatives and the scoring sessions (NWP, 2010; Swain et al., 2010).

NWP's work provides an example of experimental and quasi-experimental research that was sensitive to local context and included contributions from interested parties. The work was "based upon the premise that writing assessment and writing instruction exert an influence on one another" and that they are "situated within the larger contextual dynamic of district, school, classroom, and other professional policies and practices" (Swain et al., 2010, p. 5). Researchers associated with NWP claimed that "teachers thinking together with writing assessment experts helped to create a technically sound and rigorous assessment, one that is useful in the classroom as well as in research" (Swain & LeMahieu, in press, p. 22). An important assumption guiding this research and assessment project was that teachers bring an important perspective about what is happening in their classrooms, schools and districts to both research and assessment. This approach, then, honored the local contexts while also meeting national standards.

POSTSECONDARY INTER-INSTITUTIONAL WRITING ASSESSMENT

While the NWP's work has largely focused on education prior to postsecondary study, American colleges and universities are beginning to face some of the same pressures for "accountability" that have led to the test-driven processes associated with No Child Left Behind (NCLB). This is a relatively new phenomenon, however, because the structures through which postsecondary education has developed in the United States vary from those surrounding K-12 education. The federal government has overseen K-12 education through a department (or part of a department) dedicated to education since the early twentieth century. Historically, there has been variation in the curriculum among schools, and local and state governments have had substantial influence. Addressing inequities perpetuated by some of this variation, in fact, is one of the motivations for legislative action such as NCLB.

An important difference between K-12 and postsecondary education in the US is that colleges and universities have intentionally differentiated themselves from one another, based on their missions. Particularly following the end of World War II, the United States has endorsed access to higher education for all citizens. As a result, a variety of different kinds of institutions have developed (two-year colleges focusing on vocational training and/or preparing students to transfer to four-year institutions; four year institutions of various types such as liberal arts colleges and technical institutes as well as comprehensive and research universities), each driven by its own individual mission (Bastedo & Gumport, 2003, p. 341). A second important difference is that as the American academy developed in the late nineteenth and early twentieth centuries, its professoriate relied heavily on peer review for everything from vetting research to determining standards. Thus, accreditation for postsecondary institutions, whose missions are specific to the institution, comes from private organizations (grounded in peer review), not the government.

Although the accreditation system has required postsecondary institutions to undergo program reviews and evaluations, until recently neither policymakers nor the public had questioned the autonomy or results of this system. However, in the last 10-15 years, calls for postsecondary educators to be "accountable" to public audiences and provide *comparable* data about their institutions have become ever-louder. As a result of the increasing emphasis on student achievement (and in an attempt to ward off the kind of top down, legislated assessments associated with K-12), the higher education community has intensified efforts to document student. But because US colleges and universities tend to be independent, mission driven institutions, serving different populations in different ways, most assessment programs operate at the level of the institution with little history of networking or collaboration among institutions (with some notable exceptions linked to basic competency testing at the state level, such as programs legislated in Georgia, Florida and Texas). Thus, recent interest in accountability that draws in part on comparability across institutions, and sometimes missions, means that building networks and partnerships such as the NWP are in the nascent stages.[2]

The largest of these cross-institutional postsecondary assessment efforts is the Voluntary System of Accountability, a collaboration of two postsecondary organizations that has been adopted by "over 520 public institutions that enroll 7.5 million students and award 70 percent of bachelor's degrees in [the] US each year" (VSA).[3] While the VSA does not explicitly mention "gold standard" research, it draws on similar conceptualizations of research as earlier projects mentioned here, and does not engage faculty in the process of assessment of learning that is presumed to be occurring in their classes and programs.

Through the VSA, institutions create "College Portraits," online pages that purport to present unbiased, neutral information about colleges and universities for comparison purposes (VSA College Portrait, 2008, n.p.). While writing is not the exclusive focus of assessment used for these portraits, institutions participating in the VSA are required to administer (yearly) one of three standardized exams that are "designed to measure student learning gains in critical thinking (including analytic reasoning) and written communication." These tests are said to "measure these broad cognitive skills ... at the institution level across all disciplines and are intended to be comparable across institution types" (VSA Background and Overview, 2008, n.p.). But this claim and the exams developed for it, like the claims underscoring the gold standard of experimental and quasi-experimental research extending from the NRP, reflect a particular perspective on the methods that should be used in research and assessment. Institutions participating in the VSA can choose from among three exams:

1. the Collegiate Assessment of Academic Proficiency (CAAP), developed by ACT, creators of one of two standardized exams taken by most American students who want to attend college or university;
2. the ETS Proficiency Profile, developed by ETS, creators of the SAT, the other standardized exam taken by most college-bound American students, as well as other tests taken by students wishing to enter postsecondary or graduate study; or

3. the Collegiate Learning Assessment, a product of the Council for Aid to Education.

The CAAP includes multiple choice questions intended to measure writing skills (broken down into "usage and mechanics" and "rhetorical skills") and a written portion that requires students to produce two, 20 minute responses to a prompt. The ETS Proficiency Profile includes multiple choice questions and an optional essay that is scored by eRater, a computer program that scores writing. The CLA asks students to produce written responses to case studies and has been scored with Pearson's Intelligent Essay Scorer since fall 2010, with some responses scored by human raters (Council for Aid to Education, n.d., p. 5).

The problem with these exams, as writing researcher Patricia Lynne (2004) has noted, and Chris Gallagher (2010) has reinforced, is that they do not assess writing in context, done for genuine audiences and purposes—three principles of effective assessment that have been reiterated time and again (e.g., CCCC 2009; NCTE-WPA 2008). Additionally, *institutions*—not faculty members—choose to participate in the VSA. The extent to which faculty are involved in any aspect of this decision depends on the institution; increasingly, writing researchers and instructors share stories about their exclusion from such decisions. This large effort to conduct cross-institutional assessment at the postsecondary level, then, reflects many of the issues associated with experimental and quasi-experimental research. It is a top-down mandate that does not engage participants; relies on artifacts created outside of the day-to-day contexts for student learning; and does not bring instructors into decisions about development, implementation, or interpretation of results.

A second approach to recent demands to create cross-institutional postsecondary assessments is the Valid Assessment of Learning in Undergraduate Education (VALUE) project from the Association of American Colleges and Universities (AACU).[4] While the VSA relies on standardized assessment results to generate information purported to attest to the development of students' abilities, institutions participating in the VALUE project use rubrics created by faculty from across different institutions and institutional types to assess portfolios of students' work from actual courses. The VALUE project also rejects the premises underscoring the "gold standard" of experimental and quasi-experimental research, stating that "that there are no standardized tests for many of the essential outcomes of an undergraduate education." Instead, it has "developed ways for students and institutions to collect convincing evidence of student learning" through the use of common rubrics ("Project Description"). The rubrics, according to the Project Outcomes, "reflect broadly shared criteria and performance levels for assessing student learning;" however, faculty are encouraged to "translate" the criteria "into the language of individual campuses." As with the VSA, the VALUE project includes written communication as one of several competencies students should develop across the curriculum and throughout their education. However, it differs from the VSA in significant ways: it does not use standardized exams, it encourages institutions and their faculty to accommodate their individual contexts, it uses authentic class work, and it involves local faculty in the scoring. Yet, it still allows for cross-institutional comparisons.

While both the VSA and VALUE projects include writing, they are not focused on writing exclusively or on writing programs. Writing assessments more narrowly focused on writing programs have remained, for the most part, concentrated on local issues and curriculum. A notable exception is an interinstitutional assessment effort developed by writing faculty members at six different institutions of higher education, each with its own mission and institutional identity. This partnership reflects a unique response to requests for data about student learning at the college level (Pagano, Bernhardt, Reynolds, Williams, & McCurrie, 2008). Like the NWP's ongoing work, it is sensitive to concerns about assessment of student learning across institutions and within the context of public concerns; at the same time, it is driven by and dependent upon faculty's engagement with student learning and their own teaching and subject matter expertise. The collaboration also arose out of discussions about accountability in higher education, taking into consideration the rapid adoption across institutions of the VSA and the standardized exams it specifies (Pagano et al., 2008). But rather than rely on assessment perspectives reflected in experimental or quasi-experimental research and standardized tests, here a group of postsecondary writing faculty came together to create an alternative assessment to speak to demands to "assess individual change and establish effectiveness relative to national norms" (Pagano et. al., 2008, p. 287). The researchers sought to create a process for "jointly assessing authentic, classroom-produced samples of student writing ... [and] create a public argument for the multiplicity of forces that shape an individual's writing and an institution's writing program" (Pagano et al., 2008, p. 287). Both this process and the assessment that resulted, then, were developed by and with the educators who would be affected by the assessment and, in turn, any effects resulting from it.

To undertake the investigation, each participating institution appointed a representative with expertise in composition studies to the project team. Team members worked together to develop the study and the mechanism used to evaluate data collected as a part of the research; at the same time, the "autonomy of individual programs" and "the goals of writing as taught within an institutional setting" were understood to be of primary importance (Pagano et al., 2008, pp. 290-291). This point highlights the productive tension between local missions and purposes and the desire for cross-institutional comparison and consistency. Ultimately, each institution in the study decided to collect writing that involved students' "response to a text," a frequent requirement of academic writing (e.g., Greene & Orr, 2007, p. 138; Thaiss & Zawacki, 2006). But while the parameters of the prompt were shared ("response to a text"), what "respond to a text" meant for the specific campus was shaped by individual programs in the context of their institution. Team members met, scored project, and revised the rubric used for scoring; as a result of repeated scoring meetings, the team also created a more thorough set of descriptors for each criterion and increased the rating scale from five points to six (Pagano et al., 2008, pp. 295; 315-317). In this research project, then, the teacher-researchers used their expertise as both writing instructors and researchers to develop the rubric and use it.

Ultimately, the inter-institutional study resulted in information that each of the participating programs used to contribute to the development of student learning and enhance the "value added" in their institutions—certainly, a desired outcome of any assessment. Because researchers were engaged in the process of creating the design and conducting the study, they also were able to raise important questions about their process, as well as their results. This degree of reflection on the very process used for the assessment is only occasionally included by researchers engaged in experimental and quasi-experimental work.[5] Two elements of this inter-institutional study, then, provide important models for postsecondary writing research moving forward. First, like the NWP's writing assessment research discussed above, it attempted to address national concerns about learning development across a broad range of institutional concepts, by using *locally determined* questions and the means for addressing those questions. Second, it turned a lens back on itself, continually examining not just the subject of its study (writing development among college students), but the *methods used for that study*. That is, it worked from the presumption that these methods are not neutral, not unbiased, and not distinct from the very process of investigation itself.

Like the NWP research, the inter-institutional assessment demonstrates the extent to which quality writing instruction must be responsive to the institution where the instruction is taking place, and the benefits of assessment grounded in the actual work of classroom instruction for student and faculty development. It also highlights the complexity in collaborating across postsecondary institutions that have very different missions, students, instructional personnel, and curricula. Balancing the commitment to the individual context with the desire for comparability is difficult as demonstrated by Pagano and his research partners and by the critiques of research into student learning that relies on standardized exams and is conducted only by outsiders.

LESSONS LEARNED

Both the inter-institutional college writing assessment and the NWP assessment were developed and led by teachers to determine effectiveness of particular writing programs and practices. Both involved low-stakes writing assessments. Both relied on voluntary participation and collaboration across institutions and states. Both honored local conditions, expertise, and curricula; they were responsive as the situations demanded. Both produced research results that were useful for the specific teachers and writing programs involved as well as for determining effectiveness, including cross-institutional comparative information. Yet, neither conformed strictly to the "gold standard" definition of research. In fact, participants in both initiatives identified engagement in the research projects—not just the results produced—as a key benefit. Thus, the projects included more than an assessment of student work. They encompassed professional and curricular development with teachers positioned as co-researchers and professionals with requisite knowledge and expertise, not as technicians delivering a program and curriculum.

These studies also illustrate challenges facing writing researchers who aim to develop evidenced-based research studies exploring program effectiveness. In this kind of research, tests should be just one piece of evidence used to determine program effectiveness, teacher quality or comparability. Unfortunately, in the current research and assessment climate, student test results are considered the primary—or only—evidence of success. Researchers need to use multiple methods, as professional disciplinary organizations and scholars advocate, if we are really concerned with promoting learning and teaching.

The two research projects we highlight here also demonstrate the complexity of developing evaluation systems that balance local context with the need for some degree of standardization. Because both the NWP and the inter-institutional projects relied on voluntary participation, translating the approach to a top-down, mandated evaluation system may be difficult. These projects also demonstrate the wealth of resources needed—especially in terms of teacher time—to carry out the projects. However, the needs of policymakers for cost effective assessment information must not outweigh the potential benefits to the educational system as a whole. Although the assessments and research studies described here may be time consuming and costly, they offer important benefits. Healthy educational systems create situations in which teachers profit from their experience with research and assessment development, and which promote the professionalization of teaching. Further, they accommodate diversity in the programs that teachers offer and in the ways that students, local districts and states can demonstrate accomplishment. The rubrics developed by

NWP and the inter-institutional group enable diversity at the local level, but comparable standards across diverse sites.

As these projects also illustrate, discussions about what research counts, how research will be used, and how program effectiveness is determined are not academic, abstract, or carried out only in scholarly journals and conferences. Everyday, K-12 researchers, teachers, and students experience the repercussions extending from the privileging of experimental research as evidenced through the NRP and ensuing policies. As educational reform continues to be championed through federal programs such as Race to the Top and the "voluntary" Common Core State Standards Initiative that it endorses, policymakers could look to research like that conducted through the NWP, VALUE and inter-institutional assessments to learn more about how to use research and assessment in ways that position teachers as professionals who take responsibility for student learning and who care about what students are learning and to what degree. Approaching research and assessment in this way recognizes teachers' expertise and promotes research and assessment as means of professional development. It values the knowledge and experience that teachers have, yet it still enforces research standards and allows comparability, providing information that helps educators and the public understand how students are performing. As US policymakers push to make the transition from K-12 and college education more seamless for students, encouraging research and assessment that goes beyond experimental and quasi-experimental methods will provide a richer and more complete understanding of both teaching and learning. Relying on a narrowly defined, top down approach will misrepresent not only what students know and can do but also what it means to write and to teach writing.

NOTES

1. NCLB was the name given to the reauthorization of the Elementary and Secondary Authorization Act of 2001. The original Elementary and Secondary Authorization Act was passed in 1965 during the administration of President Lyndon B. Johnson. (http://www.aect.org/about/history/esea.htm)

2. A significant exception is the collaboration among prestigious Northeastern colleges during the early to mid twentieth century that resulted in the College Board and the SAT (see Traschel, 1992; Lemann, 1999).

3. The Association of Public and Land Grant Universities and the American Association of State Colleges and Universities

4. In fact, the VALUE project and the VSA were created simultaneously as part of a grant shared by AAC&U and AASCU, and APLU to develop two different pilot frameworks for assessing student learning across institutions.

5. Education researchers have, of course, voiced multiple concerns about the methodologies associated with experimental and quasi-experimental work—however, these are published separately from the studies themselves (e.g., Lather, 2004; Altwerger, 2005.)

REFERENCES

Adler-Kassner, L., & O'Neill, P. (2010). *Reframing writing assessment to improve teaching and learning.* Logan, UT: Utah State University Press.

Altwerger, B. (2005). *Reading for profit: How the bottom line leaves kids behind.* Portsmouth, NH: Heinemann.

American Educational Research Association. (2008). *Definition of scientifically based research.* Retrieved from http://www.aera.net/Default.aspx?id=6790

American Evaluation Association. (2003). *Response to U. S. Department of Education notice of proposed priority, Federal Register RIN 1890-ZA00, November 4, 2003 "Scientifically Based Evaluation Methods."* Retrieved from http://www.eval.org/doestatement.htm

Association of American Colleges and Universities. (n.d.). *VALUE: Valid assessment of learning in undergraduate education.* Retrieved from http://www.aacu.org/value/index.cfm

Bastedo, M., & P. Gumport. (2003.) "Access to what? Mission differentiation and academic stratification in US public higher education. *Higher Education 46,* 341-359.

Bender, T. (1993.) *Intellect and public life.* Baltimore: Johns Hopkins University Press.

Bracey, G. (2006). *Reading educational research: How to avoid getting statistically snookered.* Portsmouth, NH: Heinemann.

Conference on College Composition and Communication. (2009). *Writing assessment: A position statement.* Retrieved from http://www.ncte.org/cccc/resources/positions/writingassessment123784.htm

Council for Aid to Education. (n.d.). *Architecture of the CLA tasks.* Retrieved from http://www.collegiatelearningassessment.org/files/Architecture_of_the_CLA_Tasks.pdf

Davies, R. (2009, November). Evaluating what works in education: Causation or context. Paper presented at the American Evaluation Association's annual conference, Orlando, FL.

Educational Testing Service. (2010). *ETS proficiency profile: User's guide.* Retrieved from http://www.ets.org/s/proficiencyprofile/pdf/Users_Guide.pdf

Gallagher, C. W. (2010). Opinion: At the precipice of speech: English studies, science, and policy (ir)relevancy. *College English 73,* 73-90.

Gilmore, T., Krantz, J., & Ramirez, R. (1986). Action based modes of inquiry and the host-researcher relationship. *Consultation, 5*(3), 160-176.

Graff, H. (1987). *Labyrinths of literacy: Reflections on literacy past and present.* Sussex: Falmer Press.

Greene, S., & Orr, A. J. (2007). First-year college students writing across the disciplines. In P. O'Neill (Ed.), *Blurring boundaries: Developing writers, researchers, and teachers* (pp. 123-156). Cresskill, NJ: Hampton,.

Hillocks, G., Jr. (2002). *Testing trap: How states' writing assessments control learning.* New York: Teachers College Press.

Johnson, T. S., Smagorinsky, P., Thompson, L., & Fry, P. G. (2003). Learning to teach the five-paragraph theme. *Research in the Teaching of English, 38,* 136–176.

Ketter, J., & Pool, J. (2001). Exploring the impact of a high-stakes direct writing assessment in two high school classrooms. *Research in the Teaching of English 35,* 344-393.

Kohn, A. (2000). *The case against standardized testing.* Portsmouth, NH: Heinemann.

Labaree, D. (2007.) *Education, markets, and the public good.* London: Routledge.

Lather, P. (2004.) Scientific research in education: A critical perspective. *British Educational Research Journal 30,* 759-772.

Lemann, N. (1999). *The big test: The secret history of the American meritocracy.* New York: Farrar, Straus and Giroux.

Loofbourrow, P. (1994). Composition in the context of the CAP: A case study of the interplay between composition assessment and classrooms. *Educational Assessment, 2*(1), 7–49.

Luke, A., Green, J., & Kelly, G. J. (2010) Introduction: What counts as evidence and equity? *Review of Research in Education 34,* vii-xvi.

Miller, C. et al. (2006). *A test of leadership: Charting the future of US higher education.* Washington, DC: US Department of Education.

National Council of Teachers of English. (2002). *Resolution on the reading first initiative.* Retrieved from http://www.ncte.org/positions/statements/readingfirst.

National Council of Teachers of English & Council of Writing Program Administrators. (2008) *NCTE-WPA White paper on writing assessment in colleges and universities.* Retrieved from http://wpacouncil.org/whitepaper

National Reading Panel. (2000). *Teaching children to read: An evidence-based assessment of the scientific research literature on reading and its implications for reading instruction.* National Institute of Child Health and Human Development/US Department of Education. Retrieved from http://www.nationalreadingpanel.org

National Writing Project. (2006, 2008). *Analytic Writing Continuum.* Berkeley, CA: National Writing Project.

National Writing Project. (2010). *Writing project professional development continues to yield gains in student writing achievement.* (Research Brief.) Retrieved from http://www.nwp.org/cs/public/download/nwp_file/14004/FINAL_2010_Research_Brief.pdf?x-r=pcfile_d

O'Brien, R. (2001). An overview of the methodological approach of action research. In R. Richardson (Ed.), *Theory and practice of action research.* Retrieved from http://www.web.net/~robrien/papers/arfinal.html#_Toc26184650

Pagano, N., Bernhardt, S. A., Reynolds, D., Williams, M., & McCurrie, M. K. (2008). An interinstitutional model for college writing assessment. *College Composition and Communication 60,* 285-320.

Ravitch, D. (2010). *The life and death of the great American school system.* New York: Basic Books.

Rudd, A., & Johnson, R. B. (2008). Lessons learned from the use of randomized and quasi-experimental field designs for the evaluation of educational programs. *Studies in Educational Evaluation 34,* 180-188.

Scherff, L., & Piazza, C. (2005.) The more things change, the more they stay the same: A survey of high school students' writing experiences. *Research in the Teaching of English, 39(3),* 271–304.

Shavelson, R. J., & Towne, L. (Eds.). (2002). *Scientific research in education.* Washington, DC: National Academy.

Smart, J. C., Feldman K. A., & Ethington, C. A. (2000). *Academic disciplines: Holland's theory and the study of college students and faculty.* Nashville, TN: Vanderbilt University Press.

Swain, S. S., & LeMahieu, P. (in press). Assessment in a culture of inquiry: The story of the National Writing Project's analytic writing contiuum. In N. Elliot & L. Perelman (Eds.), *Writing assessment in the 21st century: Essays in honor of Edward M. White.* Cresskill, NJ: Hampton.

Swain, S. S., LeMahieu, P., Sperling, M., Murphy, S., Fessahai, & Smith, M. (2010). Writing assessment and its impact on scorers. Paper presented and the Annual Conference of the American Educational Research Association, Denver, CO.

Thaiss, C., & T. Myers Zawacki. (2006). *Engaged writers and dynamic disciplines.* Portsmouth, NH: Heinemann.

Traschel, M. (1992). *Institutionalizing literacy: The historical role of the college entrance examinations in English.* Carbondale, IL: Southern Illinois University Press.

United States Department of Education. (1998). *Reading First funding guidelines.* Retrieved from http://www2.ed.gov/programs/readingfirst/index.html

United States Department of Education Institute of Education Science. What Works Clearinghouse. (2008). Procedures and Standards Handbook Version 2.0. Retrieved November 1, 2010, from http://ies.ed.gov/ncee/wwc/references/idocviewer/Doc.aspx?docId=19&tocId=4#design

United States Department of Education Institute of Education Science. (2010). *Investment in Innovation Fund.* Retrieved from http://www2.ed.gov/programs/innovation/index.html

United States Department of Education Institute of Education Science What Works Clearinghouse. (2011). *Welcome to WWC.* Retrieved from http://ies.ed.gov/ncee/wwc/

United States Department of Education Office of the Inspector General. (2006). *The Reading First Program's grant application process: Final inspection report.* Retrieved from www.ed.gov/about/offices/list/oig/aireports/i13f0017.pdf.

Voluntary System of Accountability. (n.d.). *VSA Online.* Retrieved from http://www.voluntarysystem.org/index.cfm?page=homePage.

Voluntary System of Accountability College Portraits. (2009). *College portraits of undergraduate education.* Retrieved from http://www.collegeportraits.org

Wallace, V. L. (2002). Administrative direction in schools of contrasting status: Two cases. In G. Hillocks Jr. (Ed.), *The testing trap: How state writing assessment control learning* (pp. 93–102). New York: Teachers College Press.

Walvoord, B., & Banta, T. (2004). *Assessment clear and simple: A practical guide.* San Francisco: Jossey-Bass.

West, C. (2009.) *The American evasion of philosophy: A geneology of pragmatism.* Madison, WI: University of Wisconsin Press.

Wiseman, A. W. (2010). Uses of evidence for educational policymaking: Global contexts and international trends. *Review of Research in Education 34,* 1-24.

Yatvin, J., Weaver, C., & Garan, E. (1998). *Reading First cautions and recommendations.* Retrieved from http://www.edresearch.info/reading_fir

CHAPTER 9.
PROMINENT FEATURE ANALYSIS: LINKING ASSESSMENT AND INSTRUCTION

Sherry S. Swain, Richard L. Graves, David T. Morse, and Kimberly J. Patterson
National Writing Project, Auburn University, and Mississippi State University

Prominent feature analysis grew out of our study of 464 papers from a statewide writing assessment of seventh graders (Swain, Graves, & Morse, 2011). The original purpose of the study was to identify the characteristics of student writing at the four scoring points of the assessment (1–4, with 4 as highest), hoping that such information would assist teachers in linking their writing instruction to writing assessment.

We began by assembling a team of exemplary English language arts teachers, all with advanced certifications or degrees. The plan was to bring expert eyes to the papers, asking, "What stands out here? What is prominent?" We hypothesized that identifying the prominent features in papers at each scoring level could guide instruction. As part of the training, we read common papers and discussed what constitutes prominence at the seventh grade. Though we had no predetermined rubrics or guidelines, relying instead on the educated wisdom of team members, we sought to make our terminology as standard as possible; for example, all metaphoric language was classified as metaphor rather than simile, personification, or metaphor. We needed to achieve consistency while maintaining a keen professional insight into student writing (Swain, et al., 2011).

Prior to the analysis, team members discussed features that required clarification: cumulative sentences and final free modifiers, voice, and certain intersentential connections, among others. The cumulative sentence and final free modifiers were first described by Francis Christensen (1963), who asserted that the form of the sentence itself led writers to generate ideas. The sentence form has been examined by Faigley (1979, 1980) and Swain, Graves & Morse (2010) for its impact on writing quality. Voice has been presented as socially and culturally embedded in both the writer and the reader by Sperling (1995, 1998),

Sperling and Freedman (2001), and Cazden (1993). Elbow (1994), Palacas (1989) and others have offered theories about voice. The present study defines voice in terms of its correlation with other more concrete features rather than in a formal statement. Flawed sentences were characterized by Krishna (1975) as having a "weak structural core." Features that touch on larger aspects of writing, organization, paragraph structure, coherence and cohesion, have been described by Christensen (1965), Becker (1965), Witte and Faigley (1981), and Corbett (1991).

In the analysis, 32 prominent features, 22 positive and 10 negative, were identified and are shown in Appendix A. All 464 pieces of writing were read twice for accuracy and consistency and reviewed by the authors. To establish the level of classification consistency, we examined the individual score sheets for each of the 464 papers, determining how many changes were made from the initial analysis through the final reading. There were 484 changes assigned to the entire set of 464 papers across the multiple readings. There was a possibility of 14,848 changes, considering that there were 32 features, and that each of the features originally assigned to each paper could have been deleted and each feature not assigned could have been added. The percentage of agreement in this case is 97%. The judgments of presence or absence of prominent features are therefore considered to be both highly consistent across independent readers and to have yielded credible data for the analyses.

Correlational analyses were conducted to examine the relationship between the prominent features and the statewide assessment scores; however, this task proved problematic. The state score distribution was severely restricted, tending to attenuate the correlations between these scores and the prominent features. For example, of the 464 papers, only 7 students scored "1," the lowest score, and 28 scored "4," the highest score. Thus roughly 91% of the students scored at level 3 or level 2. There was no definitive way to ascertain to what extent the unexplained variance in state writing scores may be a function of (a) restriction of range of assigned scores; (b) unreliability of assessment scores; (c) other systematic aspects (e.g., scorer effect); or (d) some combination of these factors (Swain, et al., 2011).

After the analysis, the authors continued to look deeply into the student writing and the prominent features. We observed that all the features were either positive or negative; there were no neutral features. From this, we hypothesized the presence of a still point between the positive and the negative, to which we attributed the value "0." Then in each paper we gave a value of +1 for each positive feature and −1 for each negative feature. We summed the values of the features in each paper, resulting in what we called the Prominent Feature Score.

In order to express all scores in positive numbers, we reset the value of the still point from "0" to 10, thus giving each paper an additional 10 points. This resulted in an observed range of scores from 3 to 21, shown in Figure 1.

Interestingly, the mean score of the 464 papers is 10.3, which corresponds to the still point of 10.

Prominent feature analysis provided the kind of information we were seeking originally, the characteristics of seventh grade writing along a continuum of quality. Clearly the prominent feature score discriminates more powerfully among the 464 pieces of writing than does the state holistic score. Important here is that the prominent feature score is *derived* from specific characteristics of student writing, whereas the state score is merely *assigned,* using external criteria. Behind each prominent feature score exists a list of the features from which the score is derived, providing the vital link between the assessment of writing and instruction of writing. The study yielded much more than we had anticipated, a rich lode of information about seventh grade writing as well as a method of analysis and scoring that may prove useful in a range of educational contexts.

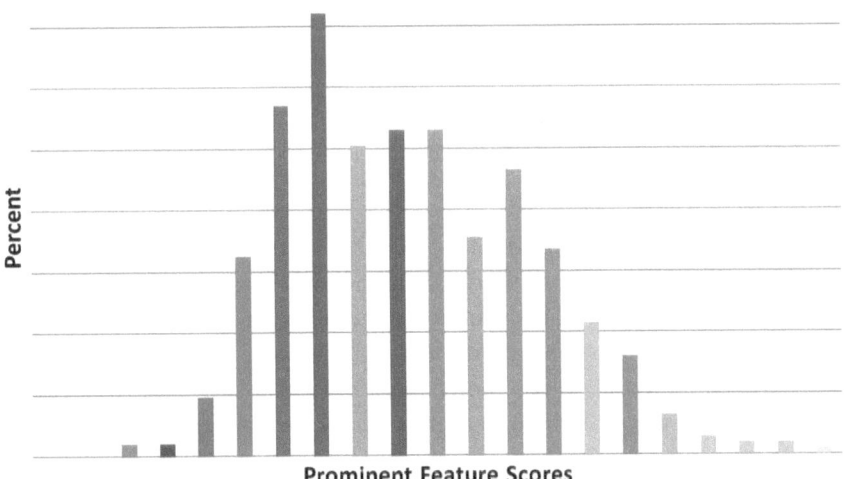

Figure 1. Percent ... Scorepoint

APPLYING PROMINENT FEATURE ANALYSIS

The opportunity to apply prominent feature analysis in a school presented itself when the principal of Pineville Elementary School (fictitious name) contracted with a local National Writing Project site[1] to conduct a yearlong inservice program for her faculty (Swain, Graves, & Morse, 2007). Though the school, nestled in a rural area about 20 miles north of the Gulf Coast, was considered high performing, student writing scores were low, and the teachers there had not participated in professional development focused on writing. Twenty-six faculty members served the 450 students in grades 3, 4, and 5, who were primarily Caucasian, with slightly over half participating in the free- and reduced-price lunch program.

THE PINEVILLE PROJECT

The project involved two teams. A professional development team led workshops, conducted classroom demonstrations, and modeled response to student writing. A research team coordinated a quasi-experimental study that included pre and post assessments for Pineville School and a comparison school, classroom practice data, and prominent feature analysis of student writing.

Students wrote to one of two counterbalanced informative prompts under controlled conditions in the fall and again in the spring. This time a research team of five exemplary English language arts teachers performed the prominent feature analysis of student writing. The fall analysis revealed the strengths and weaknesses of the young Pineville writers and served as a needs assessment to inform content for the professional development program.

PROMINENT FEATURE ANALYSIS OF PINEVILLE STUDENT WRITING

For the prominent feature analysis, team members noted the prominent features of each paper, relying on their professional expertise to distinguish and identify prominent features and calling on other members for clarification. The process included partnered analysis during the early stages, with consensus for papers considered difficult. Preparation and training for the prominent feature analysis cycled through four decision-making processes:
1. Reading from sets of common papers, team members came to consensus on the features observed in each paper. For example, some team members questioned whether a cumulative sentence should also be classified as striking sentence. The decision in such cases was to note every appli-

cable category of prominence. Thus an initial list of features and definitions emerged.
2. Noting newly observed features required periodic pauses for determining whether features should be added to the list or whether the definition of a previously identified feature should be broadened to include it.
3. Distinguishing between the ordinary and prominent for elementary writing also fueled discussions. For example, "white as snow" would not rise to the level of prominence in a high school paper and would not be noted as metaphor at that level. However, in a paper written by a third grader, "white as snow" was considered prominent.
4. Second readings for consistency led to discussions with the first reader and principal investigators. Fifteen percent of the papers were randomly selected for second readings. As in the seventh grade study, the degree of consistency proved to be high.

The complete list of prominent features for the Pineville study turned out to be very similar to that of the seventh grade study.

Immediately following the fall prominent feature analysis, the research team discussed overall impressions of the papers. What do we notice about this set of papers? What are the strengths of these young writers? In what areas should their teachers focus instruction? The group suggested prominent feature content and teaching strategies for the professional development program. The prominent features were to be introduced as content, using strategies for teaching in the context of student writing rather than in isolation. All this was shared with the professional development team and incorporated into the program described below. In this way, prominent features first influenced the needs assessment, then influenced the program, and then made their way into the Pineville classrooms as part of the writing curriculum.

THE PROFESSIONAL DEVELOPMENT PROGRAM

The professional development team, working with the school principal, then designed a program to include both content topics and teaching strategies, among others. Content topics included the following: dialogue; cumulative sentences; adverbial leads; precise nouns; vivid verbs; elaborated detail; voice; and organization, including lead sentences and unifying conclusions. Teaching strategies included the following: student choice, reading-writing connections, idea generation and prewriting, mini-lessons, modeling, analysis of first draft writing, teacher/student conferences, revision strategies, editing, publishing, and student/teacher reflection.

Each teacher participated in 34 hours of professional development, including workshops and demonstration lessons, plus between-session support. In each setting, prominent features were introduced as stylistic or rhetorical elements along with strategies appropriate for teaching them in context rather than in isolation. Table 1 summarizes the on-site program components.

In addition to the activities that took place at the school site, staff developers provided continuing support in two forms. First, they wrote detailed plans from the demonstration lessons and encouraged teachers to adapt these for their classrooms. Plans included suggestions for whole class, small group, and individual instruction, guidelines for moving through the process of the lesson, and a rationale for each lesson.

Second, because the teachers needed models for responding to the sometimes intricate aspects of student writing, the professional development team

Table 1. On-site staff development activities

Activity	Description	Number of Sessions	Length of Session (hours)	Number of Hours per Teacher
Half-day workshops	Interactive sessions; teachers experienced student-centered theories and practices and reflected on how those can be implemented in their classrooms.	7	3	21
Preparation for classroom demonstrations	Teachers prepared to observe and participate in classroom demonstration lessons, including the rationale and processes for the lesson	7	1	7
Classroom demonstrations[a]	Small groups of teachers participated in each demonstration, writing with the students, assisting small groups, reflecting afterward on their insights about the lesson.	40[b]	1	6[c]
Totals		54	5	35

[a] *Each classroom hosted a classroom demonstration at least one time so that all students had the opportunity to be "taught" for one class by staff developer and a small group of teachers from other classrooms.*

[b] *Classroom demonstrations occurred on 12 separate days, three to four demonstrations per day.*

[c] *Each individual teacher attended six demonstration sessions.*

modeled appropriate response to student writing, as shown in Appendix B. Staff developers asked that students work on a single piece over time, taking that piece through multiple drafts. The drafts were sent to writing project staff, who then wrote a response to each student, thus providing a scaffold to support the teachers as they learned to give feedback.

IMPLEMENTATION OF PROGRAM STRATEGIES

One of the chief indicators of the success of a professional development program is the extent to which classroom teachers incorporate program strategies into their practice. Toward the end of the school year, 11 Pineville teachers participated in an extensive interview process to determine which, if any, of the program strategies they had regularly incorporated into their classrooms: (1) student choice, (2) reading-writing connections, (3) prewriting, (4) peer response, (5) teacher/student conferences, (6) mini-lessons on specific rhetorical strategies, (7) revision strategies, (8) editing, (9) publishing, and (10) modeling. An implementation of strategies score was generated for each teacher as follows: 2 points for full implementation, 1 point for partial implementation, and 0 for no implementation. The possible range of scores was 0–20; the observed range of scores was 6–19, with a mean score of 12.7. The use of strategies by Pineville teachers was judged to be very good.

The research team also evaluated the 11 interviews using the 4-point scale of A Descriptive Continuum of Teaching Practice (Graves & Swain, 2004). Level 4 of the continuum describes a completely process-oriented, student-centered practice; Level 3, a partially process-oriented practice; Level 2, a partially traditional, skills-focused practice; and Level 1, a completely traditional and skills-focused practice. Of the 11 teachers interviewed in Pineville, two were rated at Level 4; five at level 3; three at Level 2; and one at Level 1. Following only one year of professional development, these results were considered very good.

The following excerpts from the interviews reveal some of the ways teachers applied strategies to teach prominent features in their classrooms. One teacher described a strategy for making reading-writing connections to teach the value of dialogue:

> What they had written wasn't in dialogue form. After reading a text rich with dialogue, I asked, "How could you use dialogue in your paper"? They changed to dialogue.

Another described using the model lesson on the prominent feature of cumulative sentences to describe a favorite place. In this lesson, she also used the strategies of student choice and modeling.

> I told the children we were going to write magic sentences using doing words. We gathered in a circle, and I started by modeling for them. I asked them to think about a favorite place… I told them mine was the beach…. We went around probably four times. I told them to think of something they might be doing at the beach. I gave some examples: "watching children bury themselves in the sand." My assistant modeled as well. We ran out of time. The next day I modeled what another student had said and made a sentence on the board. I did the whole lesson they gave us.

Yet another described her use of a peer response strategy to focus on the features of description and vivid verbs.

> When they wrote their papers, they skipped lines to make it easier to revise. After they wrote their rough drafts, they got into small groups, four or five in a group, and read to each other. After they read in their groups and got ideas, they went back over their papers, and tried to add descriptive words and vivid verbs.

The detailed accounts in the interviews confirmed that Pineville teachers were using the strategies to teach prominent features in the context of student writing.

Pineville Student Writing Performance, Holistic and Analytic

Following the yearlong program at Pineville School, the fall and spring writing assessments from Pineville and the comparison school were scored independently at a National Writing Project scoring conference (National Writing Project, 2010). Papers were scored analytically and holistically, yielding a total of seven scores per occasion, each on a scale from 1 to 6. The analytic scores included content, structure, stance, sentence fluency, diction, and conventions. An independent summary judgment yielded a holistic seventh score (Swain & LeMahieu, in press). Table 2 shows that over the course of the year, Pineville students, though scoring slightly lower than the comparison students in the fall, showed remarkable gains, both in overall holistic growth and in each of the analytic attributes. Third grade comparison students did improve, though not nearly to the degree that Pineville third graders did.

Table 2. Summary statistics for scores by group

SCORE	PROGRAM			COMPARISON		
	Pre Assessment	Post Assessment	Difference (Post-Pre)	Pre Assessment	Post Assessment	Difference (Post – Pre)
Holistic	2.5 (1.1)	3.2 (1.1)	.7	2.6 (1.0)	2.6 (1.0)	0
Content	2.6 (1.1)	3.2 (1.1)	.6	2.6 (1.0)	2.6 (1.0)	0
Structure	2.3 (1.0)	2.9 (1.2)	.6	2.4 (1.0)	2.4 (1.0)	0
Stance	2.6 (1.2)	3.3 (1.2)	.7	2.6 (1.1)	2.6 (1.1)	0
Sentence Fluency	2.5 (1.1)	3.1 (1.2)	.6	2.6 (1.0)	2.6 (1.0)	0
Diction	2.5 (1.1)	3.2 (1.1)	.7	2.5 (1.0)	2.6 (1.0)	.1
Conventions	2.4 (1.0)	3.0 (1.1)	.6	2.5 (1.0)	2.6 (1.0)	.1

Note: Mean values are given; values in parentheses are standard deviations. N = 435 for program, 217 for comparison group.

Table 3 summarizes the results of a repeated-measures ANOVA of the pre and post writing assessments for program and comparison groups for each attribute of writing as well as for the holistic assessment.

Pineville students showed statistically significant improvement in the overall set of scores (and on each individual score) from pre to post writing assessments in relation to the comparison students' scores, which were essentially unchanged and were statistically indistinguishable across occasions.

For each set of scores, there was a significant difference at the .001 level for occasion, interaction, and six of the seven measures for group. The other measure of significance for group was $p = .008$ for conventions. There was also a significant difference in Pineville students' own scores between pre and post assessments. The significant difference in the interaction between the occasion (pre or post) and the group (program or comparison) indicates that the difference is due to group. Table 3 indicates that the significant differences in all areas of writing that were assessed were due to the program. The main effect of group comparisons and the group-by-occasion interactions are essentially telling the same story here—that the difference between groups is principally due to the fact that only the Pineville students showed a change in performance, improving from pre to post assessment, whereas the comparison students showed no consistent change. In brief, growth in all areas of writing was significantly

Table 3. Repeated-measures ANOVA results for all matched cases on holistic and analytic scores

Score	Variance Component	Df	Mean Square	F Ratio	Significance P (F)	Effect Size
Holistic	Between subjects Program group (pre/post)	1	19.857	13.742	<.001	.021
	Error (between)	650	1.445			
	Within subjects Occasion (pre, post)	1	29.565	33.053	<.001	.048
	Group x Occasion	1	30.565	33.053	<.001	.048
	Error (within)	650	0.894			
Content	Between subjects Program group (pre/post)	1	22.822	15.660	<.001	.024
	Error (between)	650	1.457			
	Within subjects Occasion (pre, post)	1	21.205	24.358	<.001	.036
	Group x Occasion	1	32.969	37.872	<.001	.055
	Error (within)	650	0.871			
Structure	Between subjects Program group (pre/post)	1	15.794	11.369	<.001	.017
	Error (between)	650	1.389			
	Within subjects Occasion (pre, post)	1	25.659	28.291	<.001	.042
	Group x Occasion	1	28.515	31.440	<.001	.046
	Error (within)	650	0.907			
Stance	Between subjects Program group (pre/post)	1	25.804	16.029	<.001	.024
	Error (between)	650	1.610			
	Within subjects Occasion (pre, post)	1	31.294	31.458	<.001	.046
	Group x Occasion	1	28.718	28.868	<.001	.043
	Error (within)	650	0.995			
Sentence Fluency	Between subjects Program group (pre/post)	1	8.986	5.571	<.001	.008
	Error (between)	650	1.613			
	Within subjects Occasion (pre, post)	1	30.109	33.706	<.001	.049
	Group x Occasion	1	22.119	24.761	,.001	.037
	Error (within)	650	0.893			

Table 3. Continued

Diction	Between subjects Program group (pre/post)	1	31.824	22.004	<.001	.033
	Error (between)	650	1.446			
	Within subjects Occasion (pre, post)	1	41.806	50.402	<.001	.072
	Group x Occasion	1	26.748	32.248	<.001	.047
	Error (within)	650	0.829			
Conventions	Between subjects Program group (pre/post)	1	9.907	6.392	.008	.010
	Error (between)	650	1.550			
	Within subjects Occasion (pre, post)	1	35.146	51.731	<.001	.074
	Group x Occasion	1	17.015	25.043	<.001	.037
	Error (within)	650	0.679			

Note: ES is partial eta-squared. Program n = 435; comparison n = 217.

higher for the Pineville group between the pre and post writing assessments, and significantly higher than that of the comparison group.

These results confirmed our hypothesis that prominent feature analysis could be a valid link between assessment and instruction, but our original question still remained: What features or characteristics of student writing are linked most closely with higher (and perhaps, lower) scoring papers? Since NWP's Analytic Writing Continuum Assessment System provides scores, on a six-point scale, for six attributes of writing plus a holistic score, correlations between these scores and prominent features could now be ascertained. (Swain & LeMahieu, in press). A summary of the patterns that emerged from the study follows.

First, statistically significant correlations were observed between 24 of the 33 individual prominent features and the seven scores (holistic and six analytic). There were some exceptions to this. Chief among these was the tendency for correlations of prominent features to be slightly lower with conventions scores than with any other of the analytic scoring categories. It is important to note, however, that such differences were not statistically tested.

Second, prominent feature elements considered to be positive attributes in an essay (e.g., balance/parallelism, voice) generally yielded positive correlations with the analytic and holistic scores, whereas negative prominent feature elements (e.g., weak structural core, poor spelling, unfocused) generally had negative or essentially zero correlations with the scores.

Third, the prominent features that showed the stronger relationships—used here in a relative sense, as none of the correlations observed was moderate or large—with the analytic and holistic scores were: (a) elaborated details, (b) dialogue, (c) sentence variety, (d) effective ending, (e) well-organized, (f) supporting details, and (g) voice. The overall prominent feature scores correlated in the .40s with the holistic score. Clearly, these prominent features (mostly positive) do appear as valid contributors to the scoring judgments on both the analytic and holistic measurements (Swain et al., 2007).

CONCLUSION

Some years back our research focused on ways to help teachers make instructional sense of a state writing assessment. In many ways prominent feature analysis accomplishes this, providing the means for both assessment and instruction. Now, though we cannot claim prominent feature analysis as the single cause for the growth in writing of the Pineville students, we suggest that the interaction between the prominent features and the teaching strategies (along with the cooperation and goodwill of the teachers) was paramount. We now understand prominent feature analysis as a valid link between assessment and instruction. The evidence for this understanding is three-fold:

The Pineville study demonstrates the validity of prominent feature analysis as a needs-assessment tool that is grounded in student writing ability.

Results of the Pineville study confirm that students whose teachers participated in professional development that focused on prominent features significantly outperformed students whose teachers did not participate.

Correlations between prominent features and the AWC assessment validate the link between prominent features and the quality of writing.

As mentioned earlier, between prominent feature analysis and other kinds of writing assessments lies a crucial distinction. Prominent feature analysis *derives* numerical values from specific rhetorical features whereas other forms of assessment *assign* numerical values to student writing based on externally described characteristics. The major task of prominent feature analysis is to determine whether or not a specific rhetorical concept has risen to the level of prominence. The major task of other kinds of writing assessment is to determine whether a piece of writing is a B- or a C+, for example, or a 3 or a 4. While holistic assessments provide comparative data across large sets of papers, and analytic scoring provides comparative data that describes quality in the various attributes of writing, prominent feature analysis adds another dimension to the assessment of writing, one that is grounded in writing itself and that brings into play the possibilities for well-informed writing instruction.

Prominent feature analysis is new, and it is only natural that questions should arise about its efficacy. Already we are exploring how the list of features might be refined, especially the prominent features of genre or content. Further lines of inquiry include the developmental aspects of prominent features, the possibility of ranking features, and a deepening understanding of the interrelationships among features. It seems clear that prominent feature analysis has a vital role to play in the universe of writing assessment.

NOTE

1. The National Writing Project is a network of over 200 university-based sites dedicated to improving writing and teaching in the nation's schools.

REFERENCES

Becker A. L. (1965). A tagmemic approach to paragraph analysis. *College Composition and Communication, 16,* 237–242.

Cazden, C. B. (1993). Vygotsky, Hymes, and Bakhtin. In E. A. Forman, N. Minick, & C. A. Stone (Eds.), *Contexts for learning: Sociocultural dynamics in children's development* (pp. 197–212). New York: Oxford University Press.

Christensen, F. (1963). A generative rhetoric of the sentence. *College Composition and Communication, 14,* 155–161.

Christensen, F. (1965). A generative rhetoric of the paragraph. *College Composition and Communication, 16,* 144–156.

Corbett, E. J. (1991). *Classical rhetoric for the modern student* (3rd ed.). New York: Oxford University Press.

Elbow, P. (1994). Writing first! *Educational Leadership, 62*(2), 8–13.

Faigley, L. (1979). The influence of generative rhetoric on the syntactic maturity and writing effectiveness of college freshmen. *Research in the Teaching of English, 13,* 197–206.

Faigley, L. (1980). Names in search of a concept: Maturity, fluency, complexity, and growth in written syntax. *College Composition and Communication, 31,* 291–300.

Graves, R. L., & Swain, S. S., (2004). A descriptive continuum of teaching practice (Unpublished manuscript). Mississippi Writing/Thinking Institute. Mississippi State University, Mississippi State, MS.

Graves, R. L., Swain, S. S., & Morse. D. T. (2011). The final free modifier—once more. *Journal of Teaching Writing, 26*(1), 85–105.

Krishna, V. (1975). The syntax of error. *The Journal of Basic Writing, 1,* 43–49.

National Writing Project (2010). *Writing project professional development continues to yield gains in student writing achievement* (Research Brief, 2. 2010). Retrieved from http://www.nwp.org/cs/public/print/resource/3208

Palacas, A. L. (1989). Parentheticals and personal voice. *Written Communication, 6*(4), 506–527.

Sperling, M. (1995). Uncovering the role of role in writing and learning to write: One day in an inner-city classroom. *Written Communication, 12*(1), 93–133.

Sperling, M. (1998). Teachers as readers of student writing. In N. Nelson & R. Calfee (Eds.), *The reading-writing connection: Yearbook of the National Society for the Study of Education* (pp. 131–152). Chicago: University of Chicago Press.

Sperling, M., & Freedman, S. W. (2001). Research on writing. In V. Richardson (Ed.), *Handbook of Research on Teaching (4th* ed., pp. 370–389). Washington, DC: American Educational Research Association.

Swain, S., Graves, R. L., & Morse, D. T. (2007). *Effects of NWP teaching strategies on elementary students' writing (Study)*. National Writing Project. Retrieved from http://www.nwp.org/cs/public/print/resource/2784

Swain, S., Graves, R. L., & Morse, D. T. (2010). Prominent feature analysis: What it means for the classroom. *English Journal, 99*(4), 84–89.

Swain, S., Graves, R. L., & Morse, D. T. (2011). A prominent feature analysis of seventh-grade writing. *Journal of Writing Assessment, 4*(1). Retrieved from http://www.journalofwritingassessment.org

Swain, S. S., & LeMahieu, P. (in press). Assessment in a culture of inquiry: The story of the National Writing Project's analytic writing continuum. In L. Perelman & N. Elliott (Eds.), *Writing assessment in the 21st century: Essays in honor of Edward M. White*. Cresskill, NJ: Hampton Press.

Witte, J. A., & Faigley, L. (1981). Coherence, cohesion, and writing quality. *College Composition and Communication, 32,* 189–204.

APPENDIXES

Appendix A. Positive and Negative Prominent Features from the Seventh Grade Study

Positive Features	Negative Features
Elaborated details	Weak structural core
Sensory language	Garbles
Metaphor	Weak organization
Alliteration	Redundancy
Vivid verb/noun	List technique
Hyperbole	Usage problems
Striking words	Faulty punctuation
Cumulative sentences	Faulty spelling
Verb clusters	Shifting point of view
Noun clusters	Illegible handwriting
Absolutes	
Adverbial leads	
Balance/parallelism	
Repetition	
Sentence variety	
Effective organization	
Subordinate sequence	
Transitions	
Coherence/cohesion	
Voice	
Addresses reader	
Narrative storytelling	

Appendix B. Student Draft and Model Response from Professional Development Consultant

I remember the time me and my dad went fishing. We had caught 5 bass 3 brim and 12 grinals. My dad cast his line and I cast mine. We both hook something. I brought in a bass and my dad finally brought in an alligator. I got so scared if I didn't see him stay in the water I probably would have jumped off the boat. Later on that day we go back to that spot after the water goes down some and we find some alligator eggs. I got one and broke it. Then we see the mama coming back. Me and my dad turn the boat around and leave. That is the story about my encounter with a mama alligator.

Dear Adventurous Fisherman,

You really had an exciting day. I can't imagine seeing an alligator close up like you did. Where did you go fishing? Was it a lake or river?

You really built suspense with these sentences:

My dad cast his line and I cast mine. We both hook something.

I was really wondering what it would be.

I want to know more about your dad's hard work trying to reel in that alligator.

I loved your sentence that told me how scared you were. It gave your story voice—made it fun to real out loud and made me feel like I know you a little better.

When you saw that mama alligator coming back to her eggs did you say anything? Did your dad say anything? When you said you and your dad turned the boat around and left, I thought you were going to say something about how fast you got out of there. Can you think of a way to make your reader feel some excitement about getting away from that alligator?

CHAPTER 10.

"A MATTER OF PERSONAL TASTE": TEACHERS' CONSTRUCTS OF WRITING QUALITY IN THE SECONDARY SCHOOL ENGLISH CLASSROOM

Helen Lines
University Of Exeter

In the UK, as in many other Anglophone countries, standards of children's writing remain a public cause for concern. A recent summary report from Government inspectors concluded that, despite improvements in teaching writing, "'many secondary-age students, especially boys, find writing hard, do not enjoy it, and make limited progress" (Ofsted, 2008). At the same time, the complexity of writing as a social and cultural act makes it difficult to specify the gold standard being aimed for or to clarify the nature of progression. It is hard to delineate the features of good writing generically (Marshall, 2007) but in any case simply providing students with criteria for a good piece of writing or performance is insufficient to help them progress: the interrelationship between the components is always too complex to be itemised meaningfully and the potential outcomes are too diverse (Sadler, 1989). Progression in writing is fuzzy, characterised by a broad horizon rather than clearly-defined goals (Marshall, 2004). The complex and less than tangible nature of writing is an issue for pedagogy and for assessment, affecting decisions about "what precisely is to be taught and what and how it is to be evaluated" (Parr, 2011, p. 51). As a consequence, the "non-trivial problem" for the classroom is "how to draw the concept of excellence out of the heads of teachers, give it some external formulation, and make it available to the learner" (Sadler, 1989:127).

Past research into teachers' judgments of writing quality reveals a picture of variation and discrepancy (Huot 1990), "evaluative ambiguity and conflict" (Broad, 2000, p. 214) and subjectivity (Beck, 2006). This seems particularly true of judgments made in the context of summative, "high-stakes" testing;

indeed, in England, national tests of writing at age 14 were abandoned in 2008 after a decade of appeals against results. Research from Australia shows that the introduction of state-wide standardised assessment criteria does not necessarily lead to standardised evaluations. Wyatt-Smith and Castleton (2004; 2005) report variation of judgment between teachers, and by the same teacher from one time period to another, as well as an expectation that the standard would vary from year to year. Teachers' "global" judgments of writing quality, drawing on published criteria, often conflicted with their "local" judgments, based on classroom experience and knowledge of individual students, confirming that evaluation is an emotional practice for teachers (Edgington, 2005; Steinberg, 2008) influenced by classroom interactions and relationships. Huot (2002) and Huot and Perry (2009) call for a re-focusing of research into writing assessment, to take better account of the discourse community of the classroom and to emphasise its instructional value.

FOCUS OF THE PRESENT STUDY

In light of the cited research, the study reported here focuses on the context of the secondary school writing classroom in which teachers make day-to-day judgments of writing quality as they read and respond to students' texts. It assumes writing to be a social and cultural activity, where the writer is a member of "a community of practice" (Sharples, 1999, p. 5), the conventions and emphases of which will play an important part in influencing the criteria used to evaluate writing. It views evaluation as a deeply social act, enmeshed in talk and other classroom interactions, with students and teachers working together as a "community of interpreters" (Wiliam, 1998, p. 6) to define writing quality, in order to improve writing performance. The study aims to shed light on such classroom interactions, examining teachers' judgments of writing by asking the following questions:
- How, and how consistently, do teachers conceptualise quality in writing?
- What is the match between teachers' constructs of quality in writing and national criteria for high-grade writing?

DEFINING THE STANDARD: NATIONAL ASSESSMENT CRITERIA

Currently in England, attainment at age 14 is assessed by teachers and reported to parents with reference to Level-related descriptors for speaking and listening, reading and writing. The statutory criteria for "exceptional performance" in writing are:

> Pupils' writing is original, has shape and impact, shows control of a range of styles and maintains the interest of the reader throughout. Narratives use structure as well as vocabulary for a range of imaginative effects, and non-fiction is coherent, reasoned and persuasive, conveying complex perspectives. A variety of grammatical constructions and punctuation is used accurately, appropriately and with sensitivity. Paragraphs are well constructed and linked in order to clarify the organisation of the writing as a whole. (National Curriculum Attainment Target for Writing: Exceptional Performance: Qualifications and Curriculum Development Agency, 2007)

The difficulty of describing high-grade writing is immediately obvious. Quality in writing (both here and in public examinations at age 16) is characterised by terms such as *original, imaginative, sensitive, creative, confident*- features which are difficult to quantify and, some would argue, impossible to teach. Qualitative measures, such as impact and interest, are clearly dependent on the reader's personal tastes, but also beg questions about the audience and purpose for classroom and examination writing, much of which is produced for an imagined reader of an imaginary text. Compared with other sets of analytic criteria, such as those recently developed in New Zealand[1] (which provide descriptors for both "deep" and "surface" features in each of seven genres), the descriptor is thin, and the lack of specific terms weakens it as an instructional tool.

An additional difficulty for teachers is that the gold standard is not fixed. Constructs of writing quality change over time and are culturally contested (Purves, 1992). In England, past decades have seen changes to "the writing paradigms in which pupils, teachers and policy-makers operate" (DCSF, 2008, p. 6). Broadly speaking, educators have moved from valuing formal rhetorical grammar and correctness, to personal "voice" and expressiveness, to mastery of a range of written genres and multiplicity of voices, with a concomitant shift of emphasis from product to process, as seen in the conceptualization of writing as a series of "creative design" choices (Myhill, 2008; Sharples, 1999). Thus within an average English department, it is likely that teachers of different ages and backgrounds will hold different perspectives on writing quality, shaped by the writing paradigms that have been dominant during their training and practical experience. Moreover, revised versions of the National Curriculum bring subtle

GCSE Criteria for Grade A, 2000	GCSE Criteria for Grade A, 2010
Candidates' writing has shape and assured control of a range of styles. Narratives use structure as well as vocabulary for a range of effects and non-fiction is coherent, logical and persuasive. A wide range of grammatical constructions is used accurately. Punctuation and spelling are correct; paragraphs are well constructed and linked to clarify the organisation of the writing as a whole.	Candidates' writing shows confident, assured control of a range of forms and styles appropriate to task and purpose. Texts engage and hold the reader's interest through logical argument, persuasive force or creative delight. Linguistic and structural features are used skilfully to sequence texts and achieve coherence. A wide range of accurate sentence structures ensures clarity; choices of vocabulary, punctuation and spelling are ambitious, imaginative and correct.

Figure 1. Statutory assessment criteria for high-grade writing at GCSE (General Certificate of Secondary Education) examination at age 16, published by the Office of the Qualifications and Examinations Regulator

changes to assessment criteria describing quality in writing, as shown in Figure 1. Recent criteria stress reader engagement, matching of form to purpose, and variety and accuracy of sentence constructions. Such changes reflect evolving views of text composition as well as political intent: the new government in the UK is currently reviewing the writing curriculum and has already signalled an emphasis on grammatical and technical accuracy from 2012.

METHOD

The study utilises a subset of qualitative data drawn from a three-year (2008-11) large-scale mixed-methods research project investigating the impact of contextualised grammar teaching on students' writing. Participants were one teacher and his or her Y8 class (12-13 year olds) in 31 mixed comprehensive schools in the south west of England and the West Midlands (32 schools were originally recruited but data from one was excluded due to low fidelity to the intervention). Over the course of an academic year, the intervention group taught schemes of work especially written by the research team, contextualising grammar instruction in detailed lesson plans and resources for three different writing genres: narrative fiction; argument and poetry. Teachers in the comparison group taught the same genres but from broad plans that allowed their own pedagogical decisions. For each school, the qualitative component involved three classroom observations; three post-observation interviews with each teacher; three post-observation interviews with one teacher-selected student from each class, and collation of writing samples arising from the schemes of work.

The semi-structured teacher interview schedules probed for pedagogical thinking about planning, learning and assessment, and for beliefs about writing and grammar teaching. Specific questions relating to writing quality and assessment were included in each of the three schedules. These were:

- Term 1: What do you think makes "good" writing? What do you think makes a good teacher of writing?
- Term 2: What criteria would you use to describe good writing? Do the assessment criteria for Key Stage 3 and Key Stage 4 effectively capture good writing?[2]
- Term 3: What are you looking for as indicators of quality in writing? Do you think assessment at each Key Stage rewards those qualities?

The close similarity of these questions was deliberate, in order to compare consistency of individual responses over time, while the subtle differences in emphasis allowed for broader, more nuanced responses.

Data were analysed using NVIVO software, with themes built through repeated sorting, codings and comparisons that characterise the grounded theory approach. To avoid fragmentation and decontextualisation, interview transcripts were read in their entirety several times before and during coding. Some a priori codes were used, derived from the research questions (e.g., *writing quality*) or from labels used in the interview schedules to prompt for pedagogical beliefs (e.g., *testing*). Other categories emerged during analysis, and in vivo coding (where participants' own words and phrases provide labels for categories) was used to capture the imagery employed by teachers when characterising good writing, and to locate patterns and themes within larger categories (see Appendix 1).

FINDINGS

Research Question 1: Teachers' Conceptualisations of Quality in Writing

Three main aspects of the findings are reported here, offering insights into the way that teachers respond to students' texts, the influence on judgment of non-textual features, and significant differences in teachers' conceptualisations of writing quality.

Reading as an Evaluative Act

Phelps argues that responding to students' writing is essentially about the ways in which we read student writing, or "the teacher's receptivity to the student text (and what lies beyond it)" (2000, p. 93). Huot and Perry (2009, p. 431) refer to reading as "an evaluative act," based on the premise that students' writing has intrinsic worth. Teachers in the study clearly positioned themselves as receptive readers of students' texts, as indicated by the following comments:

> Writing isn't there to go in a cupboard; it's there to be read.

> I'm always still surprised by some of the things kids write about and how creative they can be and do new things that you don't expect, and that's fantastic.

Responding to students' writing was evidently a central, valued classroom activity. Several referred to the "privilege" of reading students' work and used images of nurture, growth and empowerment to characterise teaching goals, for example: "Good writing is a piece of clay that you can mould and sculpt," "If they can write well, it gives them an extra bow and arrow when everyone else is still running around in a bearskin," "words are actually magic and have so much power and if you can convey that in your writing then you've won the world, haven't you?"

Descriptions and definitions of good writing were most frequently and strikingly related to the impact of the text on the reader, which was described in physical, affective and intellectual terms. For example, good writing "gets the heart racing," "makes you go weak at the knees," "strikes a chord," "speaks to the reader," "makes you think," "makes you look at the world in a different way." In this respect, students' texts were seen as entirely authentic: teachers often applied the same criteria for quality as they would for published authors.

Evaluation as a Contextual Act

Edgington (2005, p. 141) reports evaluation as a contextual more than a textual act, shaped by personal values and classroom relationships. Teachers' descriptions of good writing and good teaching of writing echoed national assessment criteria (as one would expect, given their statutory nature), for example in use of the terms "interesting," "engaging," "imaginative," "confident." However, teachers added a large number of their own criteria which were frequently couched in affective rather than linguistic terms and related to classroom contexts—"the cultural and social part of the group" as one teacher put it. Thus good writing was seen as "enjoyable," "memorable," "believable," and more prosaically, "something that doesn't give me a headache;" "makes me forget I'm marking;" "doesn't have too many funny errors in it." Several teachers related quality to the "conscious thought," "effort" and "enthusiasm" students had shown, which allowed them to personalise the standard, as this teacher explained:

> My expectations are different for every child, so a delightful piece from Joe who's a four minus is obviously completely different from what I would consider a delightful piece of work from Ellie who's a Level 7.

Criteria were also personalised to teachers' own tastes. One teacher rendered the GCSE criterion "creative delight" as "control and delight," to better reflect her view of quality. Another repeatedly defined good writing as "justified." She valued students' deliberate design choices and their ability to explain them, considering these as "life skills," of greater importance than the quality of the finished product.

Beyond general references to the use of "sentence variety" and "techniques" "for effect," few teachers cited specific linguistic skills or textual features as hallmarks of quality in writing. One defined a good teacher as:

> a person who teaches things explicitly and they don't assume that person knows what a complex sentence is but they show those and they show the effects that they have.

More typically, qualities of a good teacher of writing were cited as "enthusiasm," "inspiration," "encouragement," "motivation," and the ability to provide a safe environment in which students could "take risks and experiment" to counter the fact that "writing is traumatic for some children." There were many references to the teacher's emotional responsibility as evaluator, for instance:

> You have to really believe in their ability and that they know you're there for them.

> They need to see that I'm impressed with their writing and sort of create a sense that it's worthwhile, what you're doing.

> Something really fundamental to me is that whatever a student says you have to give it credibility and worth in a classroom.

Variation Between Teachers

The coding of teacher interviews (93 in total) revealed a wide range of responses to the question of what constitutes good writing, as indicated in Appendix 1. Teachers themselves expected this, with one commenting: "You're going to see thirty-two teachers and everyone is going to be completely different," and several referencing the subjective nature of judgment, for example:

> Some people would be blown away by one piece of writing and some people would hate the same piece of writing, so I think it is subjective and I think it depends on what you're writing and who you're writing for.

Even when concepts drew general agreement, responses were marked by difference in interpretation. "Creativity" was one of the labels used to investigate pedagogical beliefs, which may well have skewed its apparent importance for teachers: almost half the sample claimed that good writing was "all about creativity." (Interestingly, the term was not mentioned at all by students when they were asked to define good writing). Nonetheless, the concept was understood in markedly different ways.

For some, creativity, alongside "originality" and "effective word choices" were allied to self-expression and personal growth, so that these teachers defined good writing in terms of the student's individual, authentic voice. Others viewed creativity in terms of precision and control, judging writing quality by its clarity of communication and clever use of techniques. Teachers disagreed over the relationship between creativity and technical accuracy, some seeing them as divorced: "the one time when we can throw neatness out of the window and spelling and we can fix it later," others expressly yoking them together: "there are two 'goods' there, creativity and competence, by which I mean accuracy, accuracy."

Teachers' conceptualisations of writing quality were marked by individual consistency over the course of an academic year; there was only one instance of contradiction, over the relative importance of spelling. Even though teachers' internal standards varied little, variation between teachers was very much in evidence. To explore this further, individual profiles were created, detailing statistical information and including all interview statements pertaining to writing quality and assessment. Analysis of these profiles revealed patterns to the variation which were strong enough to allow for the formation of six different constructs (shown in Table 1) labelled by the researcher according to their dominant features. Four teachers have been "counted twice" because there was a definite overlap—for two of them between "self-expression" and "technical accuracy" and for another two between "conscious crafting" and "fit for purpose," which are in any case the closest categories.

These constructs helped to give shape to the observed variation in teachers' judgments of quality. Whether they can also help to explain that variation is another matter. A clear limitation of the study is that teachers were asked only to describe good writing; they were not asked to say where their ideas came from, so that the findings have not revealed a great deal about factors that influence teachers' subject philosophies or about the "somewhat indeterminate" process by which teachers make judgments (Lumley, 2002, p. 10). Details of gender, length of service and first degree subject were compared for teachers grouped within each of the six constructs but it was difficult to deduce any significant patterns, beyond the fact that a slightly higher proportion of teachers with a literature-based degree related writing quality to self-expression and emotional engagement or considered it to be instinctive. Moreover, six of the eight teachers in the whole sample who were in their first year of teaching; two of these thought that high-grade writing depended on flair and originality and doubted whether these could be taught. However, this view might be a reflection of a lack of confidence and experience in assessing writing more than an expression of philosophy.

One evident variation between teachers included how much they had to say on the subject of writing quality, as well as how they said it. Some teachers, during interview, and in social exchanges with the researcher, expressed

Table 1. Teachers' personal constructs of quality in writing

Researcher's label for construct *Good writing is…*	Number of teachers	Dominant features of the construct	Verbatim statements typical of the construct
Emotionally engaging	7	These teachers primarily judge writing by its impact on the reader and the reaction it provokes.	Excites and moves you Engages and delights If it pleases you then it's good Makes the hairs on the back of your neck stand up
Self-expressive	7	These teachers primarily value writing that expresses the child's personal and distinctive individual voice, often drawn from the child's own experience.	They've put their own spin on it Personal voice coming through Imaginative writing that's a bit different Not just parroting what they've been taught
Consciously crafted	7	These teachers reward writing that has been deliberately designed and that shows conscious thought and effort.	They've thought about it and have taken pride in it Has thought and deliberation behind it Can justify and explain choices
Fit for purpose	6	These teachers reward writing that is well matched to its audience and purpose and which clearly fulfils its stated function.	It's about clarity of communication and whether or not it hits the purpose Varied techniques appropriate to task Meets the targets set for it
Technically accurate	4	These teachers think accuracy, or "the mechanics" are an essential aspect of good writing.	It's got to be really accurate to enhance the meaning Students can do incredibly creative, original work but if they're technically not there, they're never going to achieve A and A*
Instinctive	4	These teachers either think that quality in writing is too subjective or difficult to define, or that flair and originality are impossible to teach.	It depends on what you're writing and who you're writing for It's a matter of personal taste It's just an instinct How can you say one person's poem is better than another's?

Table 2. Teachers' personal constructs of quality in writing matched to responses to national assessment criteria in use at Key Stages 3 and 4

Personal construct of writing quality: *Good writing is …*	Typical responses to assessment criteria
Emotionally engaging (7) These teachers primarily judge writing by its impact on the reader and the reaction it provokes.	Criteria are too "restrictive," "prescriptive," "narrow," and "reductive." There is too much emphasis on accuracy and formulaic structures, "ticking boxes," "writing by rote," "following a recipe.". Individuality and creativity are insufficiently rewarded.
Self-expressive (7) These teachers primarily value writing that expresses the child's personal and distinctive individual voice, often drawn from the child's own experience.	Judgment is subjective, a "matter of personal taste;" "teachers will judge each child's writing differently." Teachers should be able to reward individual effort and tailor criteria to the child. It's difficult to make the language of assessment criteria accessible for students.
Fit for purpose (6) These teachers reward writing that is well matched to its audience and purpose and which clearly fulfils its stated function.	Criteria adequately describe good writing. They are flexible enough to encourage creative responses. Criteria offer structure that may not have been there in the past. They rightly stress audience and purpose.
Instinctive (4) These teachers either think that quality in writing is too subjective or difficult to define, or that flair and originality are impossible to teach.	There will always be examples of unusual writing that don't fit the criteria. "Really good creative writing can't be taught." "What is wrong with gut instinct? It's usually pretty accurate"

their views about good writing so strongly and in such detail that it amounted to a personal manifesto; others found the questions difficult to answer. This qualitative difference is difficult to show in a limited space but the following snippets from one teacher's profile will hopefully illustrate how, for some teachers at least, personal constructs of writing are central to their personality in the classroom:

> Good writing is something that stimulates you, something you can relate to … for me, good writing needs to jump out of a page … good writing needs to be a little bit more imaginative, it needs to be a little bit more, the voice of a person isn't it, it's like you, it needs to be passionate … it's a person isn't it, it's like a person, good writing is you, and how much you enjoy words and putting them together… .

Research Question 2: Match Between Teachers' Constructs and National Criteria

Emerging from the analysis of individual profiles was a clear finding that many teachers experience tensions between their personal construct of writing quality and the construct of quality referenced by statutory criteria.

Only three teachers reported a close match between their own criteria and national criteria for high-grade writing. Fourteen reported a definite mismatch, while another 14 felt genuinely ambivalent, for a variety of reasons, summarised here:

- Criteria describe essential skills and qualities but are too narrow and prescriptive (5)
- It depends on the Key Stage and the exam board followed (4)
- Criteria guide judgments but there should be more room for professional instinct (2)
- Teachers felt too inexperienced to trust their judgments (2)
- There was uncertainty over how far accuracy should count (1)

The personal construct that most closely matched national criteria was "fit for purpose;" the constructs causing the most conflict with national criteria were "emotionally engaging," "self-expressive," and "instinctive." Table 2 presents this finding in more detail.

Teachers who felt a mismatch expressed it in vehement terms, for example:

> It's tick boxes and even in the creative writing bit they can write a fantastic piece of writing but unless they've got, you know, the range of sentences, the this, that and the other, they can't get the grade, and it's, it's horrible.

> I shouldn't be having to cheat my way round the criteria in order to get them recognition for very original, passionate, Catch-22-esque writing.

Steinberg (2008) suggests that summative and formative assessment are governed by different emotional rules, leading to teachers' conflicted reactions to use of the same criteria for different purposes. There was certainly evidence of this, especially for teachers whose personal constructs of quality did not fit well with official criteria. These teachers viewed summative assessment as "askew with," "diametrically opposed to," "totally at odds with" their view of good writing. They felt that assessment narrowed and distorted the writing curriculum, creating "hurdles that we make them jump over," "a formula for writing," "tick box thinkers" and "a fear of going outside the box." Teachers' antipathy was to testing and examination tasks more than to actual criteria: as one teacher pointed out, "It's ridiculous to ask people to write about their day at the beach if they never go to a beach." However, it did indicate that some teachers think about writing assessment and writing instruction in different ways and that the two might not be compatible.

Teachers were also in conflict with each other about the usefulness of analytic criteria in describing writing quality and guiding the teaching of good writing, as the following opposing examples show:

Do we really need to be so specific? We should be looking at how to inspire them through topics and ideas and feelings, little anecdotes about stuff or books about real experiences, not bloody "organising and presenting a whole text effectively."	If you follow the mark scheme then it's going to inform your teaching because you know exactly what you are looking for and unless you know what you're looking for you can't teach the kids what the examiner is looking for or what good writing is all about.
I think you could argue for a piece of writing to be an A* or an A grade and that's what I don't like about it, that it's so open to that interpretation.	The fact that there was so little to describe what A* was, actually that pleased me more than anything else, that there's something sort of almost intangible.

One can imagine some lively department meetings if these four teachers worked in the same school! Viewing pedagogical differences from the perspective of the match between teachers' personal constructs of quality and published criteria may help to explain such polarised views.

SUMMARY CONCLUSIONS

This study found that teachers' conceptualisations of writing quality were internally consistent but that variation between teachers was marked. Teachers not only valued different qualities in writing, but experienced differing degrees of conflict and ambiguity when relating their personal construct of quality to the official, public construct. The findings support earlier views of teacher judgment as richly textured and complex, "a dynamic, process of drawing on and variously combining available indexes" (Wyatt-Smith & Castleton, 2005, p. 151) The model proposed by Wyatt-Smith, Castleton, Freebody & Cooksey (2003, p. 27) shows statutory criteria as one such index, but not necessarily the most influential; criteria may be over-ridden by contextual factors such as the knowledge of individual children and production history of the writing. It could be useful to see teachers' personal constructs of quality as an addition to this model.

A limitation of the present study is that teachers' stated beliefs have been analysed, rather than classroom enactments of these beliefs. The personal constructs derived from interview transcripts have not been taken back to participants for validity checking and are theoretical only. Nevertheless, in the classroom context where evaluation has a formative, instructional purpose, how students receive and take up teachers' judgments is of obvious importance in developing evaluative expertise (Sadler 2009). Parr (2011, p. 1) stresses the role of "shared repertoires" in a community of practice. These include tools and routines, "as a resource to create meaning in the joint pursuit of an enterprise." Teachers' own constructs of quality have the potential to be shared with students as an "external formulation" of the concept of quality, an expression of "local" knowledge perhaps more accessible than the "global" view of quality embodied in national criteria.

The fact that teachers in the study saw writing quality in subjective terms, as "a matter of personal taste" is not necessarily a problem. Teachers are not automata, and it could be argued that those with a strongly-felt, personal construct of quality in writing, and the ability to share it with students, are likely to be effective teachers of writing, at the very least conveying the message that writing matters. Thus a future direction of this research is to investigate how teachers share conceptualisations of writing quality with their students, framed by the question: Are pedagogical practices and classroom discourse affected by personal constructs? Initial analysis of lesson observation data (Appendix 2) suggests that they may be.

NOTES

1. Ministry of Education and the University of Auckland (2004). Assessment tools for teaching and learning: Project asTTle

2. Key Stage 3 covers ages 11-14 and Key Stage 4 ages 14-16

REFERENCES

Beck, S. W. (2006). Subjectivity and intersubjectivity in the teaching and learning of writing. *Research in the Teaching of English, 40,* 48-460

Black, P., & Wiliam, D. (1998). *Inside the black box: Raising standards through classroom assessment.* London: King's College

Broad, B. (2000). Pulling your hair out: Crises of standardisation in communal writing assessment. *Research in the Teaching of English, 35*(2), 213-260

Department for Children, Schools and Families (2008). *Getting going: Generating, shaping and developing ideas in writing.* London: DCSF.

Edgington, A. (2005). What were you thinking? Understanding teacher reader and response through a protocol analysis study. *Journal of Writing Assessment, 2*(2), 125-148.

Huot, B. (1990). The literature of direct writing assessment: Major concerns and prevailing trends. *Review of Educational Research, 60*(2), 237-263.

Huot, B. (2002). *(Re)articulating writing assessment for teaching and learning.* Logan, UT: Utah State University Press.

Huot, B., & Perry, J. (2009). Toward a new understanding for classroom writing assessment. In R. Beard, D. Myhill, J. Riley, & M. Nystrand (Eds.), *The Sage handbook of writing development* (pp. 423-435). Thousand Oaks, CA: Sage.

Lumley, T. (2002). Assessment criteria in a large-scale writing test: What do they really mean to the raters? *Language Testing, 19,* 246-276.

Marshall, B. (2004). Goals or horizons: The conundrum of progression in English: Or a possible way of understanding formative assessment in English. *The Curriculum Journal, 15,* 101–113.

Marshall, B. (2007). Assessment in English. In T. Cremin, & H. Dombey (Eds.), *Handbook of Primary English in Initial Teacher Education.* London: UK Literacy Association.

Ministry of Education and the University of Auckland (2004). *Assessment tools for teaching and learning: Project asTTle*. Wellington, New Zealand: Learning Media.

Myhill, D. (2008). Towards a linguistic model of sentence development in writing. *Language and Education, 22*(5), 271-288.

Office for Standards in Education, Children's Services and Skills (2008). *English at the crossroads: An evaluation of English in primary and secondary schools, 2005-08* (Report reference: 080247). London: Ofsted.

Parr, J. (2011). Repertoires to scaffold teacher learning and practice in the teaching of writing. *Assessing Writing, 16,* 32-48

Phelps, L. (2003). Cyrano's nose: Variations on the theme of response. *Assessing Writing, 7,* 91-110

Purves, A. (1992). Reflections on research and assessment in written composition. *Research in the Teaching of English, 26*(1), 108-122.

Sadler, D. R. (1989). Formative assessment and the design of instructional systems. *Instructional Science, 18*(2), 119-144.

Sadler, D. R. (2009). Transforming Holistic Assessment and Grading into a Vehicle for Complex Learning. In G. Joughin (Ed.), *Assessment, Learning and Judgement in Higher Education* (pp. 45-63). Dordrecht, Netherlands: Springer.

Sharples, M. (1999). *How we write: Writing as creative design*. London: Routledge.

Steinberg, C. (2008). Assessment as an "emotional practice." *English Teaching Practice and Critique, 7*(3), 42-64.

Wiliam, D. (1998). The validity of teachers' assessments. Paper presented to the 22nd annual conference of the international group for the psychology of mathematics education, Stellenbosch, South Africa.

Wyatt-Smith, C., Castleton, G., Freebody, P., & Cooksey, R. (2003). The nature of teachers' qualitative judgements: A matter of context and salience. *Australian Journal of Language and Literacy, 26*(2), 11-32

Wyatt-Smith, C., & Castleton, G. (2004). Factors affecting writing achievement: Mapping teacher beliefs. *English in Education, 38*(1), 39-63.

Wyatt-Smith, C., & Castleton, G. (2005). Examining how teachers judge student writing: An Australian case study. *Journal of Curriculum Studies, 37*(2), 131–154.

APPENDIX 1: TEACHER INTERVIEW CODING FRAMES

Themes	Definition	Number of Responses
Writing quality	Generic definitions and descriptions of good writing	135
Good fiction writing	Comments specific to quality in fiction writing	21
Good argument writing	Comments specific to quality in argument writing	13
Good poetry writing	Comments specific to quality in poetry writing	13
Good teacher of writing	Comments about the skills and qualities required in order to teach writing effectively	45
Assessing writing	General comments about the nature and use of assessment criteria to judge quality of writing	64
Key Stage 3 criteria	Comments specific to the nature and use of Key Stage 3 assessment criteria	28
Key Stage 4 criteria	Comments specific to the nature and use of Key Stage 4 (GCSE examination) criteria	32
Testing	Comments expressing opinions about formal summative testing of writing	39
Difficulties in making judgments	Comments relating to difficulties or tensions in evaluating the quality of students' writing	21
Using criteria with students	Comments relating to formative use of assessment criteria, including how well students understand them	15

In Vivo Coding (using participants' direct words)		Number of Responses
Images of good writing	Definitions and descriptions of good writing in the form of simile, metaphor or analogy	36
Gets the blood pumping		
Gets the heart racing		
Just catches you		
Holds attention		
Speaks to the reader		
Needs to jump out of the page		
Knocked my socks off		
Touches your insides		
Makes me forget I'm marking		
Doesn't give me a headache		

Images of good writing, continued	Definitions and descriptions of good writing in the form of simile, metaphor or analogy
Something that would prize eight quid out of my purse to buy a book	
Makes you think	
Strikes a chord in you	
Hooks you in from the beginning	
Draws the reader into its world	
Pulls the reader into your world	
Has the X factor	
Has some sort of journey within it	
Has to be nurtured	
Makes the hairs at the back of your neck stand up	
Makes you go weak at the knees	
When they've put their own spin on it	
When you've got the mix just right that you have the reader licking their fingers to turn the page	
Where you can almost touch the reader's enthusiasm	
Drives towards its conclusion right the way through	
Uses all the tools in their armoury	
Gives them an extra bow and arrow when everyone else is still running around in a bearskin	
Arms them for the future	
Hits the purpose	
Needs to have a personality	
Has a voice	
Is like a person	
A piece of clay that you can mould and sculpt	
It's about you stamping your mark	
Makes you look at the world in a different way	
Provokes a reaction	
Provokes a response	

Teachers' Constructs of Writing Quality

In Vivo coding used to sort broad theme of Writing Quality (generic definitions and descriptions of good writing) into more specific categories		Number of Responses
Impact on reader	Effective word choices	24
	Affects the reader	20
	Engaging	18
	Interesting	14
	Grabs your attention	9
	Shows writer's enthusiasm	7
	Enjoyable	6
	Memorable	3
	Believable	2
	Convincing	1
	Has immediacy	1
	Inspirational	1
	Exciting	1
	Delightful	1
	Just pleases you	1
Creativity	Original	20
	Experiments	16
	All about creativity	15
	Own voice	8
	Imagination	8
	Flair	7
	Individual	5
	Natural	5
	Spontaneous	2
	Adventurous	1
Variety	Varied sentences	7
	Variety of techniques	6
	Variety of punctuation	3
	Varied vocabulary	3

In Vivo coding used to sort broad theme of Writing Quality (generic definitions and descriptions of good writing) into more specific categories		Number of Responses
Accurate	Technical accuracy	3
	Communicates clearly	10
	Fluent	5
	Competent	4
Controlled	Confident	14
	Consciously crafted	13
	Sense of purpose and audience	11
	Structured	11
	Control of sentence structure	11
	Shows effort	11
	Appropriate conventions	10
	Techniques	7
	Precision and control	4
	(Choices can be) justified	4
	Planned	3
	Done independently	1
Difficult to define	Too personal to say	2
	Just a feeling	2
	Matter of personal taste	1
	Depends on what you're writing	1
	Instinctive	1

APPENDIX 2: ANALYSIS OF LESSON OBSERVATION DATA

The data was drawn for two schools, investigating match between personal construct of writing quality and classroom practice.

Teacher 9: Dominant construct: Good writing is Emotionally Engaging

Teacher values:	In the writing classroom:
Writing that provokes a strong emotional reaction in the reader	Expects all students' active participation—emphasis is on trying things out
Personal creativity (writes herself)	Motivates through own enthusiasm, especially about vocabulary choices
Powerful choice of words and ideas that move and excite the reader	Shares own writing as models and gives personal examples e.g., how she gathers ideas and plans her own poems and short stories
Responses to assessment criteria:	
Recognises subjectivity of different readers' responses	Adapts project lesson plans by building in more time for discussion of students' writing
Thinks too much weighting given to accuracy over creativity (real writers have editors and proofreaders)	Encourages students to be "critical friends"
	Strong emphasis on evaluating effects of word choices on the reader
Explicitly teaches to exam criteria (e.g., sentence variety) but is ambivalent about providing a formula	Actively promotes thinking about choices and meaning; probes for responses using questioning e.g. in the plenary

Teacher 21: Dominant construct: Good writing is Fit for Purpose

Teacher values:	In the writing classroom:
Writing that communicates clearly to the reader	Explicitly positions students as real readers of texts, both published and their own:
Clever use of techniques	"what matters is how you respond to the writing" "I'm interested in your reactions to these charity adverts"
How well the writing matches the conventions of the text type	
The extent to which writing fulfils its stated purpose	Gives very clear explanations of the purpose of reading and writing tasks:
Responses to assessment criteria:	"to help you see what persuasive techniques are used to get you to part with your money"
They reward the right things	
They encourage students to focus on audience and purpose and what makes a good piece of writing	"to make a judgment about which viewpoint is most effective"
	Doesn't over-direct students' responses—they often feed back to each other as pairs or in small groups and redraft in light of peer response
There is strong continuity between the Key Stages in terms of what is valued	
Assessment tasks can be too narrow	Introduces linguistic terminology (e.g., through games and quizzes) and encourages students to use it when evaluating techniques

SECTION 3.
WRITING AT THE BORDERS OF SCHOOL AND THE WORLD

For many years, writing researchers around the world have sought to understand the ways that social and cultural influences outside of school influence writing development in school. With a variety of methodological approaches, research questions, units of analysis, and theoretical frameworks these researchers have helped us understand in much greater depth the important ways the social, cultural, and symbolic environments in which people live shape writing development and academic performance. This work has extended our understandings of a number of facets of educational practice, including the importance of effective teachers, the limitations of school systems, the many elements that contribute to writing development, the dynamic trajectories along which writers develop, and the rich interplay between text and experience.

The five chapters in this section continue this inquiry into the relationship of literacy development and lived experience beyond schooling. In Daiute's ethnographic study of a writing-based educational intervention in the circumstances of children's lives influenced by war and trauma, the author shows how engaging in different genres of writing extends pupils' engagement with the world. In particular, she highlights the ways in which writing fictional narratives compares with the writing of autobiographical narratives in illuminating student's conceptions of the complex system of relationships surrounding them, and demonstrates that educational interventions in school offer children different possibilities for engaging in life beyond school.

Romain and Robaud use a linguistic approach in investigating writing development and its relationship to students' socio-cultural backgrounds. Their study of naming practices in children's writing supports a view of writing development that includes greater diversification in grammatical and lexical choice making. Students from disadvantaged socio-cultural backgrounds, however, tend to progress along slower trajectories, with the textual markers for this kind of writing development appearing less frequently and later. Their work points to the critical ways literacy development and educational experience are intertwined with the student's lives outside of school.

Extending studies into how students writing outside of class might be relevant in designing effective learning environments for writing, Skaar's interview-based study of college writers investigates differences in student's beliefs, values, and attitudes towards the writing they do on the Internet and their academic writing. Although he finds a significant divide exists between students perceptions of these two writing contexts, he identifies clear overlaps between the two and pedagogical possibilities for linking the two more closely in productive ways.

The next chapter provides a look into the relatively unexplored territory of writing contests, used in many regions. Based on textual and rhetorical analysis of an essay contest sponsored by the World Bank, Porter's study suggests ways that the elements of contest writing, such as the call for papers and the prompt itself, create an environment rich in intertextuality and ideology, encouraging shifts in identity and thinking.

Using interviews and textual analysis, Jones and Milson Whyte take another approach in looking at the ways cultures influences writing development. Using the lens of metaphors as an entry point, their work posits a chain of connection between the cultural practices shaping the identities of Jamaican male students and the influence of those beliefs on their academic writing performance.

—PR

CHAPTER 11.

THE REALITY OF FICTION-WRITING IN SITUATIONS OF POLITICAL VIOLENCE

Colette Daiute
City University of New York

Verbal arts are integral to the mutual development of individuals and society during and after political violence. Although scholars have examined how the powerful use language to provoke political violence, young people's uses of oral and written communication for interacting in unstable environments are relatively unexplored. Researchers and practitioners working with youth in the aftermath of political violence sometimes elicit personal experience narratives for psychological treatment or, less often, for testimony. We now understand, however, that narrating is a dynamic process for making sense of life, rather than primarily a vehicle for reporting feelings or facts. Just as nations in conflict and transition exert pressure on their people to tell stories justifying conflict or guiding the country in a new direction, individuals' stories connect their experiences and ideologies to extant circumstances. From the perspective of socio-cultural theory, we understand that people use symbolic tools to understand and influence their environments (Vygotsky, 1978). On this view, cultural tools like narrating are malleable for interacting with requirements and sanctions in troubled times. We must, thus, acknowledge the social nature of narrating by considering the narrator-audience-context relationship as embedded in knowledge, especially in dramatically changing contexts but also in apparently banal ones.

Although writing does not typically enter into research or practice with youth in political emergencies, we have found that even relatively uneducated and multi-lingual youth seize cultural imaginaries to engage with their environments (Daiute, 2010). In this chapter, I explain how young people growing up across a landscape of political violence and transition in the 1990s former Yugoslavia used fictional genres, in particular, to consider political issues. Inquiry in such contexts where political ideologies are in flux then offers implications for broader inquiry and practice.

This discussion of the politics of fiction writing draws on analyses of a rich database of narratives from a larger study on the mutual development of individuals and society (Daiute, 2010). Aida, 13 year-old participant in that study, used autobiographical and fictional narrative genres strategically, albeit probably implicitly, to express different kinds of conflict in different realms of life. Aida, like her peers, may use personal experience narrating to relieve emotional stress, but she also employs the creative realm of fiction to deal with what is confusing, frightening, or taboo in her environment. When invited to a story-telling workshop at a local Bosnian bakery in a small US city, Aida[1] recounts a rupture in her family.

> My cousin got into a fight with my parents because we we're going to visit Bosnia and my cousin's son was going to Hawaii because he's in the military and we didn't know that and we got mad because they didn't come to wish us luck with our flight. After we came back from Bosnia they still don't come over and we haven't seen them in three years.

In that brief narrative, Aida embeds international events in family history, attendant feelings, and an unresolved estrangement. As a child who lived through war in Bosnia and was then displaced from her homeland, Aida values connection, a quality expressed in relation to life in the United States, in her story entitled "Nina and Elma."

> The news was that the mayor canceled the event. Everyone was so sad. They cancelled it because they didn't like everybody in the community. Everyone went up against the mayor and they won and the mayor went to prison for discrimination.

This brief story recounts power relations among characters in political categories ("the mayor," "everyone in the community"), the exertion of political power ("the mayor cancelled the event"), solidarity with push-back ("Everyone went up against the mayor"), resulting circumstances ("they won," "the mayor went to prison"), and exclusionary intentions ("They cancelled it because they didn't like everybody in the community" "… for discrimination"). Differences across these narratives indicate the context-sensitive nature of narrating, an idea explored in genre theory.

DEVELOPMENTAL GENRES

Genre is a concept linking language, people, and contexts (Bakhtin, 1986; Christie, 2007; Cope & Kalatzis, 1993; Gee, 1993). Genres are texts that "do different things" (Cope & Kalatzis, 1993, p. 7). Defined as responsive activities in chains of communication (Bakhtin, 1986), genres imply a range of interlocutors involved physically and symbolically in relevant events that become interwoven in the content of any text. People experiencing collisions of power and perspectives like those during armed conflict and political revolution use discursive activities to pay close attention to what is going on around them. Understanding this dynamic meaning-making function of written language is critical to teaching and research in the twenty-first century (Smagorinsky, 2001).

Composition researchers have explained that genres develop in communities of practice, yielding, for example, different styles of narrating personal experience in African-American and European-American families (Heath, 1983), in families of different socio-economic means (Nelson, 2003), in home and school (Cazden, 2001), and in gender groups (Bamberg, 2004). Some researchers have applied the concept of genre to examine processes in culturally diverse settings, such as those obscuring or excluding minority people's involvement in mainstream discourses (Gee, 1996). Across time, individuals' experiences with diverse genres increase, as does the complexity and control of their use (Daiute, 2010). Educational contexts can foster young people's increasingly skillful application of diverse genres, as shown in study designs employing African-American Vernacular English (Lee, 1993) and musical genres like hip hop (Fisher, 2007; Mahiri, 1998) to support expository writing skills. Prior research in urban public schools indicated, moreover, that in a violence prevention program, children as young as seven years used features of diverse narrative genres to adjust their personal experience writing *toward* values expressed in the curriculum ("use words, not fists," "conflicts can always be resolved"...), while at the same time adjusting fictional writing *away* from the curriculum values (Daiute, 2004; Daiute et al, 2001; 2003). The present study extends inquiry into such context-sensitive uses of narrating to mediate personal, social, and political relations in situations of political violence.

CONFLICT ACTIVITY ZONES

Millions of young people in over 38 nations and escaping to scores of other nations live in situations of political violence and transition that challenge development. Children and adolescents miss school during acute phases of violence, during escape to safer ground, and often for extended periods of time (http://www.crin.org). Some young people are isolated with their families in shelters or refugee camps, and many are separated from their parents or other adult family, having to care for younger siblings (Hart, 2008). In urban areas of the global south, many young people find refuge with peers on the streets where they are bereft of resources and appropriately mistrustful of formal institutions (Hansen, 2008). One of the most important yet under-explored developmental activities in educational and community organizations in conflict-affected settings is writing. Two major reasons for this gap are the overwhelming focus on psychopathological responses to violent circumstances (Bonanno, 2004; Boyden, 2003) and the assumption that writing is less accessible than other symbolic media.

To many outside the literacy field, writing seems overly challenging, yet, it is in situations of extreme challenge that humans developed symbolic tools for expressing their feelings and thoughts, in part to join forces with others for survival (Donald, 1991). Humanitarian aid workers, anthropologists and others who interact with young people in the field report on their resilient capacities for personal and collective thriving via problem-solving (Hart, 2008; Naidoo, 2011). Such reports implore researchers to study how young people use complex symbol systems like language for coping and development. Long overdue are examinations of whether and how opportunities to communicate in diverse ways increase young people's control over their subjective responses to unstable and dangerous situations. Using a range of genres for relevant purposes may be especially useful for figuring out what is going on, how one fits and, perhaps, how one can make a difference. Given such motivations, even minimal support for narrating can set a developmental process in motion.

THE SOCIO-POLITICAL DIMENSION OF GENRES

An individual guides each communication act in relation to how listeners/readers might judge him/her. Occurring implicitly in everyday life, this metapragmatic process involves monitoring communication acts (Reyes, 2011; Searle, 1970). Research in politically contentious situations replete with inequalities, violence, and societal changes should examine how power relations are embedded in discourse. The dynamic relation of narrator, audience, and context is especially relevant to research and practice in situations where those in power express political positions blatantly (Fairclough, 1992; Foucault, 2001), imposing specific requirements and sanctions on regular folks (Billig, 1995; Bajraktari & Serwer, 2006). Narrating is a means of creating culture (Bruner, 1986), becoming a member of a culture (Nelson, 2003; Tomasello (2005), and influencing the development of culture (Daiute, 2004). For this reason, understanding power dynamics in cultural development is crucial to developmental inquiry and practice. Prior analyses offer insights about how people discursively engage in various kinds of conflict in multicultural urban settings (Labov & Waletzky, 1997), academic settings (Stanley & Billig, 2004), therapeutic settings (Billig, 1999), legal practices (Amsterdam & Bruner, 2000) and everyday interactions between men and women (Tannen, 2001). As in all social relations, but most poignantly in situations of conflict, much is said between the words, some deliberately omitted or repressed (Berman, 1999). Scholars have identified various mechanisms for interweaving explicit statements (referential meaning) and implied meaning (evaluative meaning) (Labov & Waletzky, 1997). Human relations are defined at least in part by the interplay of such referential and evaluative meanings in oral and written communications.

Conversational analysis has shown, for example, that people use linguistic devices, like hedges ("sort of"), negation, repetition, exaggeration, causal connectors, and metaphor to indicate the significance of their communications (Labov & Waletzky, 1997). Beyond enumerating events, Aida, for example, indicates her perspective on events with devices like causal attributions ("because'" "and") and psychological verbs ("didn't know"). Re-reading Aida's narrative with this in mind, we see how a seemingly objective sequence of events expresses her family's blamelessness ("we didn't know"), while cautiously avoiding blaming the cousin's family. In the fictional narrative, Aida does her work more explicitly. In addition to turning the plot on an abuse of power, "the mayor went to prison for discrimination" "because they didn't like everyone in the community," Aida uses evaluative devices, "so," "everybody," "everyone" to heighten the drama of that story of exclusion. With such strategies developed from early in life, Aida deals, at least symbolically, with the dilemma of living in a land of opportunity, while feeling excluded by Americans' animosity toward immigrants and Muslims, two groups with which she identifies. Increasing our understanding of this process is important for research and educational design intending to understand and support human development.

A six-year practice-based research project, *Dynamic Story-telling By Youth*, involved 137 12 to 27 year olds growing up during and after the violent disintegration of the former Yugoslavia in the 1990s (Daiute, 2010). I designed the study to find out whether and how young people across age groups and post-war country locations would orient to past troubles and/or present circumstances. Over several years visiting different ex-Yugoslav countries (2004—2007), I found that community-based organizations would be optimum sites for learning about how young people understand what it means to grow up during and after war. The ethnographic phase of the research indicated that public schools were operating under strong pressures to implement specific histories and reforms, while community centers, although not without their own issues, were more flexible spaces for youth participation and cross-context research.

Community organizations in such contexts provide various kinds resources, like computers and spaces for youth gatherings, supports for thinking critically and creatively about their environments, and guidance toward collective projects like rebuilding damaged bridges. Leaders of participating organizations reviewed a preliminary research workshop curriculum, suggested revisions, offered final approval, reviewed translations, distributed an approved recruitment flyer to young people in their local area, and scheduled workshops as appropriate from April through September 2007.[2] This process yielded 137 participants aged 12 to 27, distributed relatively equally across countries, ages, genders, and extent of participation in a community center.

All participants were exposed to violently changing environments, albeit in different ways based on their locations during and after acute and resolving phases of the war. These young people in Bosnia & Herzegovina, Croatia, Serbia, and a refugee community in the United States faced diverse social, economic, and other challenges and opportunities before and during data collection for this study. Across these contexts, some young people's experiences included direct exposure to violence (bombings, shootings, personal injury, loss of loved ones); displacement (sometimes multiple times); consequences of such violent events (lack of food, water, freedom of movement, schooling); or hearing of losses to others they knew.

Because of strict societal sanctions on what can be said and what should not (Berman, 1999; Billig, 1995; Gagnon, 2004), the workshop curriculum engaged participants in numerous writing activities with diverse author-audience relationships. Applying the concept "addressivity" from literary theory, narrating activities systematically varied author-audience relationships from first person autobiographical conflicts (exposing the author directly to audience judgment) to third person autobiographical conflicts (exposing the author as an observer) and fictional conflicts (allowing the author to remain outside the story or to invent a character position, thus subjecting him/her less to direct exposure), as in the following prompts:

> Write about a time **when you or someone you know** had a conflict or disagreement with someone your age. Tell me what happened. … Who was involved? What happened? Where was it? When was it? How did those involved think and feel about the conflict? How did you handle it? How did it all turn out?
>
> Write about a time when **adults you know (or the "community")** had a conflict or disagreement. Tell me what

happened. ... Who was involved? What happened? Where was it? When was it? How did those involved think and feel about the conflict? How did they(you?) handle it? How did it all turn out?

Using the following story starter, complete your own version of the story.

> ... and (from two groups) met at a ground-breaking of the new town center building. Everyone at the event had the opportunity to break the earth for the foundation and to place a brick for the building. It was an exciting community event and everyone was pleased that the new building would mark a new future. As they were working to begin the foundation, and had a conversation about how they would like to make a difference in their town so their children could live happily together. All of a sudden, someone came with news that changed everything! What was the news? How did everyone involved think and feel? How did it all turn out?

Based on results of prior research, where elementary school children adjusted their autobiographical narratives to conform to classroom values and fictional narratives to express counter-curriculum values, I designed the varying author-audience-context stances to provide the youth in the post-war sites with relationally flexible tools. Given the pressures for discourse to conform to political values, those young people would need some freedom to engage and resist narratives of and beyond war.

As evidence that participants used these narrative genres differently, Table 1 presents the most frequent plot categories accounting for 400 narratives created in the research workshop.[3] The plot analysis summarized in Table 1 indicates the primary literary conflict issue and strategies to resolve that conflict across the genres. To illustrate plot conflict issues, I offer the following brief narrative and subsequent list of continuations to illustrate each category on Table 1:

> It was a chilly day, when the conflict occurred. Events were leading up to it for some time. The girls on the bus approached me whispering ... (narrative continues ...)

The primary plot conflict issues emerging in the analysis include: *Social relations:* then one of them asked why was I saying bad things about their other friend; *Differences of opinion*: then two of them began to argue about who was to blame for the getting in trouble at school; *Physical altercations*: one of the girls pushed me off my seat; *Politics-infrastructure*: then we all turned to commotion in the front of the bus where the bus driver and a parent argue about which politician (all corrupt according to me) would lead the country to a better future; *Character/Emotion*: I went back to reading my book because I didn't want to talk to those hypocrites; *Fate, silly reasons, no conflict*: they were starting to look like their parents making a fuss over nothing.

Subsequent resolution strategy categories include: *Psychological deliberation*: I thought about what they said and realized they had a point; *Other intervention*: after she pushed me off my seat, the bus driver came and made her get off the bus; or *Collective action*: after the corruption touched us personally, we made a workshop to teach other young people about how to recognize corruption as the first step to ending it.

As shown in Table 1, the autobiographical adult conflict narrative and the fictional community narrative elicited more issues of politics-infrastructure than did the autobiographical conflict among peers.

Table 1. Most common plot structures across narrative contexts

	Autobiographical peer conflict narrative	Autobiographical adult conflict narrative	Fictional community conflict narrative
Conflict Issue			
Social relations	X		
Differences of opinion	X	X	
Physical altercations	X		
Politics-infrastructure		X	X
Character/Emotion	X		
Fate or no conflict	X	X	
Resolution strategy			
Psychological	X	X	X
Other intervention		X	
Collective action			X

As shown in Table 1, autobiographical accounts of conflicts among peers revolved around the broadest range of issues, including social relations (altercations about loyalty to friends), differences of opinion (disagreements about whether liking folk-dancing is "yugonostalgic"), character/emotion (she is stubborn), and fate/no reason (fights are inevitable in families). As shown in Aida's narrative about a conflict with a peer, relationship issues and interactions are paramount.

> I used to be friends with Milicia but then she started ignoring me because people liked me better and we started being mean to each other and we aren't friends any more.

Although many educators and researchers emphasize first person writing, genres allowing young narrators some distance are intriguing for further inquiry, as indicated above with the category of "politics-infrastructure" as a narrative focus. A guiding question for this analysis is "How do young people (across political-economic contexts of ex-Yugoslavia) use narrative genres varied for audience-author relationships to enact diverse knowledge of and interactions with socio-political issues?" and "What do those patterns indicate about how these youth were interacting with what was going around them (between the narratives) while crafting their discourses? Ultimately, the question is "How do we use symbolic tools, like narrating, to engage with what is going on in our environments and how we fit?"

ANALYSIS OF POLITICAL ENGAGEMENTS WITH FICTION

Detailed analysis of 154 adult conflict narratives (ACN) and fictional community conflicts (FCN) by 77 young authors (who wrote both) identified differences in plot structures (conflicts and resolutions) revolving around interpersonal relations, social systems, or political relations. Analyses leading to the summary in Table 1 show that the majority of both autobiographical adult conflict narratives (37.2%) and fictional community narratives (54.6%) enact issues of politics-infrastructure. Based on those findings, I delved into that category and found distinctions between plots enacting social systems, defined as conflicts among interlocutors in social or cultural roles (rather than in interpersonal relations) interacting in social situations (such as on buses or in the neighborhood) versus plots enacting institutional relations, defined in terms of political roles (such as mayor, government, or everyone who wanted justice) interacting via power dynamics (such as edicts or protests) and often resolved with collective action. As shown in Table 2, fictional narratives revolve around political relations (45.5%) much more than social systems (11%), while autobiographical adult conflict narratives revolve around social systems (26.6%) compared to a few political plots (9.1%).

Table 2. Percentages of autobiographical and fictional conflict narratives revolving around social systems and political relations

	Interpersonal		Social system		Political relations	
	ACN	FCN	ACN	FCN	ACN	FCN
Bosnia & Herzegovina 18 Pairs* 36 Narrs	0	0	30.6	19.4	0	50
Croatia 32 Pairs 64 Narrs	12.5	1.6	21.9	6.2	12.5	45.3
Serbia 13 Pairs 26 Narrs	3.8	0	26.9	7.7	19.2	42.3
US 14 Pairs 28 Narrs	3.6	3.6	32.1	3.6	14.3	42.9
Totals 77 Pairs 154 Narrs	6.5	1.3	**26.6**	9.1	11.	**45.5**

These young authors used fictional narratives to create plot conflicts around political, economic, or legal issues ("didn't have a permit," "selected a location in the wrong zoning area," "ran out of public funds," "the man who had the money took it and ran from the country and betrayed everyone"); power struggles ("the mayor cancelled the event," "each one blamed the other so nothing got done," "… an ex-cop who still thinks that he has the power … appropriated half the street," "Serbia again under embargo," "everyone goes to their own side to observe the 'foundation'") that threaten collective goals ("the future generation was betrayed," "life in their little town would never again be the same," "the path to the future was destroyed") by at least some characters in institutional roles ("environmentalists versus the Fiat factory," "the left and the right," "mayor," "government," "last century mentality," "Democratic Party and Radical Party"). When resolved, this set of fictional narratives includes protagonists who do so via collective action ("protests," "secured some funds from the people and made the government match the funds," "put the mayor in prison for discrimination," "they will have to work together on the solution of the problem if they want their children to live happily and have better future," "Both sides have formed a unity committee, and figured out that there is no 'higher power' but that they decide, and that the center is after all the most adequate investment"). Literary devices like metaphors sometimes enact such processes, as with the "the Blues and the Greens" who are thinly veiled substitutes for "Serbia and Croatia," "fires" burning houses is the distance across what looked like a "battlefield."

In contrast, social systems involve plots situated in domestic relations, public relations in neighborhoods, in transportation ("people show their frustrations on the bus"), among characters defined in terms of groups ("parents," "employers," "granny," "frustrated people"), around disagreements about values or practices ("argued about how to raise their child"), annoyances in daily life, to be resolved for harmonious daily life (rather than a stated collective goal), and resolved socially without political or legal means. Given the overwhelmingly political nature of the fictional stories, an analysis of what is uniquely expressed in those stories implores us to consider the young authors' explorations between their autobiographical and fictional narratives.

WHAT IS SPOKEN BETWEEN THE NARRATIVES?

Table 3 summarizes differences between social system conflicts and political relations conflicts by authors across settings. Important to note here is that although the story starter depicts a scene, participants inserted characters and plot elaborations, which makes these differences all the more remarkable. Highlighting differences across narrative genres raises questions about what is going on in the life spaces between them.

For example, 18 year-old Nightwish whose family remained in Bosnia & Herzegovina during and after the war sketches a scene of unresolved frustration in her observation of local adults but very differently crafts collective hopeful action in the face of adversity in the subsequent fictional story.

> The most unpleasant are the conflicts in the public transportation when a passenger has an argument with the driver. They usually use bad words and offend each other. … One hot, summer day, I was riding on the bus full of tired, annoyed people who were coming back home from work. Some people were standing in front of the bus because they couldn't get in, which made them very angry. They argued with the driver. Such situations are so uncomfortable. They usually do not get resolved. People who couldn't get in, were left to wait for the next one.

Table 3. Plot-central political relations and social system issues *in* narratives revealing conversations *between* narratives

Common	Bosnia & Herzegovina-specific	Croatia–specific	Serbia-specific	US- specific
Social Systems				
Disturbances, arguments, fights among groups:	Disturbances between retired people/workers, football coach/referee, youth on public transport, shared buildings, neighborhoods, youth clubs; embarrassment about bad behavior in front of peers in school	Similar to Bosnia & Herzegovina, Croatia—also between neighbors over land rights, young/old, employer/employee, youth and police, teachers/students over grades, friends about quality of a film, drunken adults about nothing	Among neighbors over parking spaces, vandalism, trees hanging over yard; among sports fans, ethnic groups (Gypsies), teachers, employer/employee, political official/shoppers in grocery store	When translating for relatives, violence with other ethnic groups in city, local businesses & community
Arguments, fights in family systems:	Over family obligations, over youth rights to go out, among families in a refugee shelter	Similar, over grades, curfew, responsibility to care for elders, parents' affective relationships	Similar to Bosnia & Herzegovina, Croatia	Over participating in family events, violations of religious rules, over going back to Bosnia, music choices
Interventions by non-protagonists:	Donations by generous individuals; Bus driver intervenes:	Often repeats because of human nature	Resolved by participants themselves (Note: unlike other groups)	Cops, Charity donations
Political Relations				
Official rules, practices violated:	No permit, code violations, illegal purchase	No permit, ownership status unresolved, foreign-owned/no Croats allowed, proposal rejected-must reapply	Lack of legal permission, zoning violation, taxes too high, doesn't meet standards, lack of funds, corruption	No license to build, permit not valid, soil not good

Fiction-Writing in Situations of Political Violence

Powers invoked:	Mayor, officials, government, Police, actors not mentioned (use of passive voice)	Same as Bosnia & Herzegovin – add foreign companies, original owner of land (returnees), political groups, "man with briefcase full of papers"	Political parties, companies, external aggressor, unnamed international actors (Serbia in embargo, competitors within)	Mayor, everyone in the community (except Bosnians), immigrants, Professor, extremist groups
Powers-that-be exert control:	Divert funds for "more important purposes", ordered gov't officials to donate $ for the center, failure to do job	Divert funds to build dam destroyed in the war, to build factory that will pollute & hurt people, to build house for mayor himself, to build a park, block progress with belligerence & mistrust, rampant corruption, mayor's second thoughts	Airstrikes by external aggressor interrupt building, insincere approach by companies delays building, delay because Serbia under embargo, Good officials delay funding, require % of salaries	War coming so will have to build center elsewhere
People organize (exert their agency):	To raise funds, to overturn official decisions, apply to foreign organizations for funds, survey people's wishes, protest, debate which group of children killed in war should get monument	Protest, petition, debate, strike, force issue in court, argue in the media (right before elections), call in higher power (Minister from Zagreb)	Funding delays while political parties argue, call in higher power	Protest, everyone goes against mayor causing him to be put in prison, people will be sad waiting while no more immigrants allowed

Illustrating a conflict in a social system, the narrative on the bottom of page 201 circles around people's interactions in public transportation with dynamics among "annoyed people" in roles like "driver" who used a "bad word" to "offend each other." Resolutions developed with feelings like being "uncomfortable" and a status quo of situations that "do not get resolved." In contrast and less predictable, given the political-economic stagnation in Bosnia & Herzegovina at the time, is the sense of hopefulness in this characteristic fictional narrative by Nightwish.

> Adnan and Maja were informed that there were no more funds for the construction of the new youth center. Adnan and Maja were a bit disappointed. They think how the new generations wouldn't have any kind of shelter to go to while they are young; they wouldn't have a place where they could realize their talents and ambitions with people who could direct them and teach them how to make their dreams come true. They knew how disadvantageous it was going to be because they themselves used to have such a place where they spent their youth. They had great memories about that center. Eventually, Adnan and Maja managed to get financial support from a foreign organization and complete the construction of the center, which then served the next generations.

Distinctively, this fictional narrative enacts feelings ("Adnan and Maja were a bit disappointed") and cognitions ("they think," they knew," "they had great memories," "they managed to get financial support," etc.) in the context of political relations, broader than interpersonal or social systems. Those broader domains are invoked with images of "new generations," "shelter," and most poignantly "financial support," and "foreign organizations."

Characteristic of the approach by her local peers, Nightwish reserves resourcefulness and success for a fictional stage, which is not surprising because her country, which suffered major destruction during the war, continued to be dependent on outside economic aid and political forces, like a United Nations protectorate, in the post-war period. While for Aida, being an immigrant and Muslim is an issue to explore in the veil of fiction, her Bosnian Muslim peer Nightwish is more concerned with the economic deprivations of post-war Bosnia & Herzegovina where she lives.

The following texts by 18 year-old Lolita illustrate characteristic concerns audible in the differences between autobiographical adult conflicts and fictional community conflict narratives by young people in Serbia.

> I often have conflicts with my mother, primarily because my parents are divorced and the two of us live together alone. We are both stubborn; out of anger we say things we do not necessarily mean; to offence we respond with offence. I

have a problem with prohibition and she, as a single parent, sometimes worries too much and prohibits a lot of things. I'm trying to understand her fears and she my wishes; we compromise and overcome differences between us.

Lolita's narrative of "conflicts among adults" enacts an issue in a family system, "I often have conflicts with my mother, primarily because my parents are divorced," expressing multiple character perspectives, such as "out of anger we say things we do not necessarily mean" and trying to understand her wishes and she my wishes," with an agreement "to compromise." Enacting a broader relational system, Lolita creates the characters Marija and Marko to embody the responsibilities and hopes of a community to avoid "another failed hope".

They had run out of funds and the construction of the foundations had to be delayed or perhaps cancelled if they did not succeed in finding additional support. Marija and Marko, their neighbors, were disappointed. Another failed hope. Nothing again. ... They decided to talk to the neighbors and to take initiative. They agreed that everybody was going to give 10% of their salary (surprisingly enough, everybody was willing to do it). If somebody couldn't afford it, they might have contributed the amount they could. They raised considerable funds and the municipality agreed to make a contribution to the full amount. The building had been finished. It is now an orphanage. Apart from several people who are employed there, the children are being helped by the neighbors who contribute things they no longer need.

Lolita embodies in Marija and Marko a sense of collective will and strategy in the face of their responsibility, "the foundation had to be … cancelled if they did not succeed in finding additional support," to overcome an overwhelming feeling that the public "were disappointed" because of "Another failed hope. Nothing again … " Mobilizing their neighbors, these characters came up with a plan that "everybody was going to give 10% of their salary" with a provision for those who couldn't afford that to contribute "the amount they could." This effort that "surprisingly enough, everybody was willing to do" succeeded not only by raising "considerable funds" but also because the "municipality agreed to make a contribution to the full amount." Serving the greater good in several ways, this effort to build an orphanage led to employment for several local people and the ongoing participation "by the neighbors who contribute things they no longer need." In the contemporary Serbian context, such an approach might have been scorned as "Yugonostalgic" and, thus, reasonably reserved for a fictional story.

If mediation is the "conductor[s] of human influence on the object of activity" (Vygotsky, 1978, p. 55), we observe mediation in action when we focus between the narratives to examine young people's uses of narratives as symbolic tools to engage with existing and possible worlds. Participants' variations of narrative stances varied for social relations indicate quite strikingly their function as tools "externally oriented ... aimed at mastering and triumphing over nature." If it is, thus, unacceptable to narrate Serbian victimization with a public face, then appropriating the mask of fiction to do so can link shared knowledge and personal feelings to acknowledge that some Serbians suffered in the 1999 NATO bombing of Belgrade. The same process serves youth in Bosnia & Herzegovina where a certain public currency comes from having been victims in the war, while longing for agency. This dilemma emerges in the contrast between young Bosnians' autobiographical narratives where public tensions stagnate in everyday life and their fictional stories enacting collective action and happy endings. We extend the socio-historical meaning of "mediate" to define the functions of narrating and other symbolic tools "to act as a go-between" or "to intercede" in socio-cultural spaces where narrators interact to identify, manage, and change cultural values. Differences between each pair of narratives offer insight into discourses in specific contexts that may have influenced young authors' self-presentations, self-censorings, but also their critical and creative alterations. Because common plots emerged in relation to specific material and symbolic circumstances of places in this study, we have been able reasonably to imagine at least some of the concerns that led to presenting certain issues while reserving others.

SUMMARY AND IMPLICATIONS

This study of youth narrating in situations of political violence indicates the value of using written genres as cultural tools for the interdependent development of individuals and societies. Dangerous situations indicate, moreover, the need for fiction, as an especially fertile companion for autobiography, as it offers young people a protective context for engaging with, reflecting on, and sometimes critiquing circumstances of ongoing conflict. This "between analysis" reveals processes young people use to negotiate the incredibly complex aftermath of war in struggling nations or struggling communities as well as in powerful nations that exclude youth. These results indicate the value of ongoing research and practice with multiple genres as mediations in challenging environments.

This study has implications for writing and psychology studies. In particular, participants' demonstration of *relational complexity,* that is their use of systematically varied narrative genres, indicates their ability to use narrating as a tool rather than as a representation of stable individual meanings or memories. This analysis raising the voices between narrative genres indicates the importance of shifting from valuing autobiographical narrating for singular, authentic, coherent representations of personal self to research and practice allowing narrators to perform their complexity as interlocutors with diverse issues, others, and contexts.

Although many researchers cite socio-cultural theory (cultural-historical theory) as their research foundation, few design research consistent with that theory. One of the major disconnects between that theory and popular method is the emphasis on interviewing about phenomena of interest rather than activities enacting meanings in context per se and/or as the basis for reflecting on issues. A theory positing meaning-making as a socially distributed process must consistently foreground social relational dynamics of the context where, for example, narrating occurs. Comparing narrations varied systematically for their social-relational stances indicates considerations between the narratives, where narrators interact with their broader contexts in relation to an ideological umbrella protecting what is acceptable to state openly and protecting against what is less acceptable or forbidden. With an intervention that varies speaker/author—listener/audience author positions in meaningful activities, we can build studies and interventions to make explicit the reasons and relations motivating why we communicate.

Designing to allow dialogic relations might evoke critique, conflict, and contradiction. When we consider that thought and activity are relational, we must engage complexity, polyphony and even cacophony, given the diverse relationships and circumstances of contemporary life. Uses of symbolic tools develop human capacities but it may be the dialogically strategic uses of those tools to address socio-political issues that in turn develops societies. For these reasons, rather than emphasizing autobiography or defining autobiography as real and fiction as not, our pedagogy should promote relational complexity. In addition to narrating in diverse relational stances, examining deliberations between narratives, as we have done here, can move students' processes a developmental step toward uses of culture to master context.

In summary, this analysis offers theory-based evidence for a new dimension of writing development—relational complexity—a skill to be recognized and supported in writing instruction and writing across the curriculum. Writing development is typically defined hierarchically in terms of incremental complexities of sentence structure and rhetorical structure, processes like planning and revising, and qualities like coherence and voice. These skills are often studied, assessed and taught as though people develop unified rather than context-sensitive capacities. In contrast, relational complexity is the skill to adjust one's communications, including written texts, to audiences (implicit and explicit) and contexts (the specific circumstances present and invoked in the relevant environment). Toward this end, we can create curriculum that involves our students to write about meaningful issues in diverse stances, examining those differences, in part to consider what they are saying between the narratives and how we are making those decisions. Designing multiple activities in terms of diverse purposes, perspectives, and audiences (rather than a single narrative to identify a truth or extended interview with one interlocutor) invites young people to explore issues because those issues are confusing, upsetting, or impressive in some other way. As we see in this study, multiple expressions do not wander aimlessly but provide a participant an opportunity to circle around the contours of a text as well as within the texts for what matters.

NOTES

1. All names are youth-chosen pseudonyms. Transcriptions maintain writers' productions, as do translations from native languages as possible.

2. I and other members of the research team explained the project, observed workshops, and addressed questions.

3. These categories account for the plot central conflict issues and strategies for resolving those conflicts (including no resolution which does not appear in the table) across all the narratives. After generating the categories from several readings through all the narratives, I defined them with examples and applied them to the entire database.

REFERENCES

Amsterdam, A., & Bruner, J. (Eds.). (2000). *Minding the law: How courts rely on story-telling and how their stories change the way we understand the law and ourselves.* Cambridge, MA: Harvard University Press.

Bajraktari, Y., & Serwer, D. (2006). *Explaining the Yugoslav catastrophe: The quest for a common narrative.* USI Peace Briefing. Washington, DC: Center for Postconflict Peace and Stability Operations at the US Institute of Peace.

Bakhtin, M. M. (1986). The problem of speech genres. In C. Emerson & M. Holquist (Eds.), *Speech genres and other late essays* (pp. 60-102). Austin: University of Texas Press.

Bamberg, M. (2006). Stories: Big or small. Why do we care? *Narrative Inquiry, 16*(1), 139–147.

Berman, L. (1999). Positioning in the formation of a 'national' identity. In R. Harre & L. van Langenhove (Eds.), *Positioning theory: Moral contexts of intentional action* (pp. 138–159). Malden, MA: Blackwell.

Billig, M. (1995). *Banal nationalism.* Thousand Oaks, CA: Sage.

Billig, M. (1999). *Freudian Repression: Conversation Creating the Unconscious.* New York: Cambridge University Press.

Bonanno, G. L. (2004). Loss, trauma, and human resilience. *American Psychologist, 59,* 20–28.

Boyden, J. (2003). The moral development of child soldiers: What do adults have to fear? *Peace and Conflict: Journal of Peace Psychology, 9(4), 343-362).*

Bruner, J. S. (1986). *Actual minds, possible worlds.* Cambridge, MA: Harvard University Press.

Cazden, C. B. (2001). Classroom Discourse: The Language of Teaching and Learning. Portsmouth, NH: Heinemann.

Christie, F. (2007). Genres and institutions: Functional perspectives on educational discourse. In N. Hornberger (Ed.), *Encyclopedia of language and education: Vol. 3* (2nd ed., pp. 29–40). New York: Springer.

Cope, B., & Kalantzis, M. (Eds.). (1993). *The powers of literacy: A genre approach to teaching writing.* Pittsburgh, PA: University of Pittsburgh Press.

Daiute, C. (2004). Creative uses of cultural genres. In C. Daiute & C. Lightfoot (Eds.), *Narrative analysis: Studying the development of individuals in society.* (pp. 111–133) Thousand Oaks, CA: Sage.

Daiute, C., Buteau, E., Rawlins, C. (2001). Social relational wisdom: Developmental diversity in children's written narratives about social conflict. *Narrative Inquiry, 11*(2), 1-30.

Daiute, C. (2010). *Human development and political violence.* New York: Cambridge University Press.

Daiute, C., Stern, R., Lelutiu-Weinberger, C. (2003). Negotiating violence prevention. *Journal of Social Issues, 59,* 83-101.

Donald, M. (1991). *Origins of the modern mind: Three stages in the evolution of culture and cognition.* Cambridge, MA: Harvard University Press.

Fairclough, N. (1992). *Discourse and social change. Cambridge, UK: Polity Press.*

Fisher, M. T. (2007). *Writing in rhythm: Spoken word poetry in urban classrooms.* New York: Teachers College Press.

Foucault, M. (2001). *The order of things: Archaeology of the human sciences.* New York: Routledge.

Gagnon, V. P., Jr. (2004). *The myth of ethnic war: Serbia and Croatia in the 1990s.* Ithaca, NY: Cornell University Press.

Gee, J. P. (1996). *Social linguistics and literacies: Ideology in discourse.* New York: Routledge Falmer.

Hansen, K. T. (Ed.). (2008). *Youth and the city in the global south.* Bloomington, IN: Indiana University Press.

Hart, J. (Ed.). (2008). *Years of conflict: Adolescence, political violence, and displacement.* New York: Berghahn Books.

Heath, S. B. (1983). *Ways with words.* New York: Cambridge University Press.

Labov, W., & Waletzky, J. (1997). Narrative analysis: Oral versions of personal experience. *Journal of Narrative and Life History,* 7, 3- 38.

Lee, C. D. (1993). *Signifying as a scaffold for literary interpretation: The pedagogical implications of an African American discourse.* New York: Teachers College Press.

Mahiri, J. (1998). *Shooting for excellence: African American and youth culture in new century schools.* Urbana, IL: National Council of Teachers of English.

Nelson, K. (2003). Narrative and self, myth and memory: Emergence of the cultural self. In R. Fivush & C. Haden (Eds.), *The development of autobiographical memory: Memory and self-understanding* (pp. 3–28). Mahwah, NJ: Lawrence Erlbaum.

Reyes, A. (2011). "Racist!": Metapragmatic regimentation of racist discourse by Asian American youth. *Discourse & Society, 22(4) 458–473.*

Searle, J. R. (1970). *Speech acts: An essay in the philosophy of language.* New York: Cambridge University Press

Smagorinsky, P. (2001). If meaning is constructed, what is it made from?: Toward a cultural theory of reading. *Review of Educational Research,* 71, 133-216.

Stanley, S., & Billig, M. (2004). Dilemmas of storytelling and identity. In C. Daiute & C. Lightfoot (Eds.), *Narrative Analysis: Studying the development of individuals in society* (pp. 159-176). Thousand Oaks, CA: Sage.

Tannen, D. (2001). *You just don't understand: Women and men in conversation.* New York: Harper Paperbacks.

Tomasello, M. (2005). *Constructing a language: A usage-based theory of language acquisition.* Cambridge, MA: Harvard University Press.

Vygotsky, L. S. (1978). *Mind in society: The development of higher order thinking.* Cambridge, MA: Harvard University Press.

CHAPTER 12.
NAMING IN PUPIL WRITINGS (9 TO 14 YEARS OLD)

Christina Romain and Marie-Noëlle Roubaud
Aix-Marseille University

During the analysis of a corpus of interaction, Roubaud and Loufrani (2001, p. 207), in the tradition of Blanche-Benveniste's works (1984), define the term "naming" as follows: *"Ce terme de dénomination nous servira à designer ce qui a trait au fait de nommer, c'est à dire à assigner du lexique."* [The term naming will designate all that concerns the fact of designating, that is to say assigning lexicon]. These naming operations take the two lines of language: the paradigmatic line, which allows the speaker to give or review different properties of the word and the syntagmatic line which gives the opportunity to set syntagms, even approximate, in order to advance in the discourse. These are the naming operations we searched for in 262 papers written by 9- to 14- year-old pupils during writing production. The analysis of the corpus has revealed that the anaphora and the explicitation participate in the naming operation.

Processes such as the anaphora force the reader to return to the reference. The anaphora is a substitution or secondary naming, and it is used to avoid the redundancy effect of repeating the primary naming. Instead, it is a means of repeating by using different forms. In the first example, the syntagm *un homme* [a man] is named *cet homme* [this man], *Il* [He] when used as subject and *le* [him], *D'Artagnan* [D'Artagnan], *lui* [him] when used as object:

> (1) *Un jour ... **un homme** est venu, **cet homme** était ... tout le monde s'arrêta pour **le** regarder. **Il** était grand ... Une balle a touché **D'Artagnan** mais elle n'était pas destinée à **lui** (A, V,10)*[1]

> (1) One day **a man** came, this **man** was ... everybody stopped to look at **him**. **He** was big ... A bullet touched **D'Artagnan** but it was not intended for **him**

As to the explicitation, as an extension of the primary naming, it leads the writer to make a word more precise (ex. 2, the case of the syntagm *trois planètes* [three planets]):

(2) *Tout a commencé avec **trois planètes** : **Jupiter, Mars, Pluton**. (A,II,5)*

(2) It all began with three planets: Jupiter, Mars, Pluto.

That stop on the word, at a precise moment, shows that the pupil is the master of the game. As Steuckardt (2003, p. 5) writes: "Ces moments où le locuteur assure le contrôle des mots qu'il emploie, ces arrêts de jeu, permettent [au lecteur] d'entrevoir sa conception du signe, de saisir sa façon d'en jouer, mais aussi de pénétrer dans son univers lexical propre." [These moments where the speaker has control of the words he uses, these stops, allow the reader to glimpse his conception of the sign, to understand his way of using it but also to enter his own lexical world.] These naming operations clarify a part of the metalinguistic activity of the pupil (Benveniste, 1974; Culioli, 1990; Jakobson, 1963). To enter the lexical world of the pupil was an experience worth attempting, since the corpus allowed a contrastive analysis which takes into account the age of the pupils as well as their socio-cultural background.

THEORETICAL QUESTIONING

The term "naming" covers different realities depending on the linguist's approach. In Kleiber's referential semantic (1984), the naming and the designation are two different ways of representation. However, in the first, the relation between the linguistic expression and the real item corresponds to a lasting referential association, whereas in the designation, this referential association is temporary, and nonconventional. In his discourse analysis, Siblot (2004, 2007), by asking a question about the relation between language and the real, differentiates "nomination" from "naming" as two different designation processes: The first corresponds to the act of naming, designating an object, a reference, while the second corresponds to the lexical word, taken out of context, as it is found in the dictionary. Branca-Rosoff (2007, p. 15) claims that studying nomination means *"étudier la manière dont le locuteur contextualise les unités et la manière dont il exprime sa propre situation dans un interdiscours que l'on peut interpréter socialement"* [studying the way the speaker grounds the units and the way he expresses his own situation in an intercourse which can be socially interpreted]. Is it necessary to see in these naming operations, as the experts of the gloss do, *"reformulations orientées (non réciproques)"* [(non reciprocal) oriented reformulations] (Zoppi-Fontana, 1998: 155)? According to Steuckardt (2003, p. 12), the word and its gloss can be defined as follows: *"toute séquence discursive où le locu-*

teur opère une explication de sens qu'il donne à un mot" [any discourse sequence where the speaker gives an explanation of the meaning he gives to a word]. For clarity reasons, we retained the term "naming" to describe the linguistic processes used to specify a narrative reality.

We considered anaphoric processes as forms of naming since any anaphoric expression corresponds to a previously mentioned referent within the discourse (Kleiber, 1988). Some authors tend to avoid limiting the anaphors to coreferential relations (Corblin 1985, 1987a, 1987b, 1989; Kleiber, 1988, 1991; Milner, 1985). Different classifications appear. Thus, Riegel, Pellat and Rioul (2009) differentiate the anaphoric processes (the coreferential anaphors and those for which the reference is not always made explicit in the text) of the anaphoric expressions. The latter are classified in pronominal anaphors—total or partial, in nominal anaphors—direct, indirect, resumptive (Asher, 1993) or conceptual, associative anaphors (Kleiber, 2003) —in adverbial, verbal and adjectival anaphors. Gardes-Tamine (2008, pp. 199-204) distinguishes the nature of the anaphoric units, the lexical links between the antecedent and the anaphoric process (direct, indirect, resumptive and associative anaphors) and the referential links (total, partial and conceptual anaphors). Adam (2008, pp. 84-93) differentiates the pronominal anaphors, the defined anaphors and the demonstrative anaphors.

Regarding the explicitation processes, we relied on the works of Blanche-Benveniste, Bilger, Rouget and Van den Eynde (1990, p. 125) who use the term *"explicitation lexeme."* In separate publications, Blanche-Benveniste (1986, 1992) shows that nouns (N), both oral and written, such as *"rêve"* (*son rêve c'est d'escalader le Mont-Blanc*), *"chose"* (*une chose m'étonne c'est qu'il a pu rentrer*) or *""résultat"* (*Voici le résultat: ils ne comprennent rien*) fall into explicitation structures. Indeed, the question: *"Quel nom?" (Quel rêve? Quelle chose? Quel résultat?)* can always be asked and be answered using *"c'est"* and choosing an item in a series, in a paradigmatic list. However, as the authors of the français parlé (1990: 125) argue, this explicitation relation may be seen between a lexical item (nominal or verbal) and the nucleus that follows without any linking grammatical item (such as *c'est*); the reader, himself, builds semantic groups between some lexical units (the case of the word chose: *une chose ennuyeuse il est parti*). Nouns are good examples of naming. These are the ones the pupils explicitate first. Bassano's works (1999, 2005) showed that during language acquisition, children speak nouns first. Various factors can explain the late development of verbs compared to nouns: *"Un facteur déterminant est probablement la plus grande complexité cognitive des verbes et de leur emballage conceptuel."* [A decisive factor is probably the higher cognitive complexity of verbs and their conceptual package] (Bassano, 1999, p. 34). David (2000, p. 34) mentions this difference in processing nouns and verbs: *"Le décalage avec la production des verbes ou adjectifs s'expliquerait alors par une difficulté plus grande à établir des relations d'un autre ordre: notionnelles ou conceptuelles, puis grammaticales; toutes relations qui exigent une autonomie sémantique croissante."* [The discrepancy with the verb or adjective production would be thus explained by the greater difficulty to build relations of another nature: notional or conceptual, then grammatical; all the relations which imply an increasing semantic autonomy.] Martinot (2000) showed besides, in his study on the reformulation process among children aged 5 to 11, that verbs are more subject to variation than nouns during oral reproduction. All these observations probably explain why nouns are related to naming activities.

EXPERIMENTATION AND METHODOLOGY

Data Collection

The collected data come from a cross-sectional study carried out in the same year. The experimentation involved six school grades (classes of 9- to 14-year-old pupils) and in each case, the study was conducted under the same conditions in November. The pupils had to produce a narrative text after they were shown the image of a battle scene (a space battle for the primary school pupils and a battle at the time of the French revolution for the secondary school pupils). In order to make all the writing equally readable, before the analysis the texts were computerized and orthographically corrected while keeping the original punctuation (Cappeau & Roubaud, 2005).

These textual constitutive draft productions (Schultz-Romain, 1999, 2000) consist of 91 texts written by the pupils aged 9 (CM1) and 10 (CM2) from primary school and 171 narrative texts written by four secondary school pupils (11 years old-6eme, 12 years old-5eme, 13 years old-4eme and 14 years old-3eme). This data collection allowed us to compare pupils' performance according to their age.

We also selected several schools in different municipalities of the Bouches-du-Rhône (southern department of France) according to the distinction made by the French Ministry of Education between advantaged schools (A) and disadvantaged schools (B). This classification is based upon the socio-economical and cultural background of pupils attending schools in a particular area.

Therefore, we conducted a contrastive analysis which took into account both the age of the pupils and their socio-cultural background.

Methodology

Our study deals with the linguistic analysis of the naming processes among the pupils performing the same task (telling) and focuses on the anaphoric processes and the explicitation processes.

Regarding the anaphoric processes, the corpus analysis led to the following classification: pronominal anaphors and nominal anaphors. The other types of anaphors do not appear significantly: these could be found in only one to three texts. The anaphoric processes formed by ellipsis and repetition were not taken into account. Indeed, we were willing to show and study the use of anaphoric processes which on the one hand are linguistically marked (as opposed to the ellipsis) and on the other hand differentiated from their antecedent (as opposed to the repetition).

Among the pronominal anaphors, we have distinguished the cases where the substitution affected the subject (ex.3) or the object (ex.4):

> (3) *Alors **un petit garçon** pas plus haut que trois pommes arriva à Belleville. **Il** dit ... (A,VI,2)*

> (4) ***Les pirates** tombèrent dans la galaxie et jamais personne ne **les** retrouva. (A,I,17)*

Among the nominal anaphors, we have distinguished the direct anaphors from the indirect ones and have called "anaphoric relation marked by a determiner" the case of the direct nominal anaphora (ex.5) and "nominal anaphora" the case of the indirect nominal anaphora (ex.6):

> (5) ***Une guerre** éclata dans l'espace. ... **Cette guerre** n'était pas comme les autres ... (A,II,8)*

> (6) *Il était une fois un vieux roi. ... Il avait **une fille** ... un cavalier arriva il entra dans le château et alla trouver **la princesse**... (A,VI,15)*

Concerning the explicitation processes, we used the progressive specification notion described by Roubaud (2000). This notion is useful for describing the explicitation since for all the encountered events, the movement is in the direction of a lexicon (*risque, idée, problème*) *that specifies the unspecified noun (in italics in examples (7), (8) and (9))*. We observed the link uniting the explicitation to the noun: Is it directly linked to the noun with the use of the preposition de (ex.7) or as a formula qui consista à (ex.8)? Or does the explicitation appear in a specification structure such as c'est (ex.9)?

(7) Ils prirent le **risque *de*** *se rentrer dedans. (A, I,2)*

(8) Il trouva une idée géniale **qui consista à donner des cadeaux à tous les gens du monde et une petite lettre où il y a écrit: «Nous voulons faire la paix.» (B,V,11)**

(9) Mais il y avait un gros problème c'est *qu'ils avaient mis le feu à un immeuble. (A,IV,13)*

Our study examined also the link between these naming operations and the age of the pupils: Are these used more by the secondary school pupils? Which type are they? The study is also contrastive since the socio-cultural background was taken into consideration. We attempted to compare the means used by the pupils of different backgrounds: Do the pupils from backgrounds A (advantaged group) and B (disadvantaged group) use the same processes? How often?

RESULTS

Analysis of the Anaphoric Processes

We observed the anaphoric processes within the 262 texts. Regarding the antecedents, we noticed that the number of syntagms involved in the anaphoric processes is very similar within both types of schools. Nevertheless, the number decreases by the end of secondary school within the disadvantaged group. In these schools, a significant number of pupils directly use a pronoun as an antecedent, or more exactly, an anaphoric substitute without introducing, previously in the text, an antecedent (10.5% of the pupils aged 11 are involved, 16.6% of the pupils aged 12, 22.2% of the pupils aged 13 and 21% of the pupils aged 14).

The anaphoric processes used were grouped in two parts: the ones corresponding to a non diversified usage (the pupils used one sort of anaphors) and those corresponding to a differentiated usage (usage of several forms).

Non Diversified Use of Anaphors

This group consists of two specific productions using almost exclusively a single form of anaphora:

> a) The use of pronominal anaphors to replace a subject and/or a complement

> (10) *C'était en 1789 … .. Après* **ils** *allèrent à* **la Bastille** *c'était le 14 juillet et* **ils la** *prennent d'assaut … (B,VI,6)*

> b) The use of anaphoric relations marked by the determiner

> (11) *Il était une fois* **un roi** *qui s'appelait Rabzoul… Les gens de la ville n'étaient pas contents car* **le roi** *était méchant …* (A,VI,13)

Diversified Use of Anaphors

We identified another group containing several diverse productions of anaphoric processes, among which we will mention the most significant combinations:

> a) The use of pronominal anaphors as subject and/or complement and of anaphoric relations marked by a determiner.

> (12) *Il était une fois* **un prince** *… mais* **il** *devra affronter* **un dragon** *il faut* **lui** *planter l'épée dans le cœur mais* **le dragon** *était trop fort pour* **lui il** *appelait les habitants de la vallée. … Mélanie et* **le Prince** *se marièrent …* (B,VI,9)

> b) The use of pronominal anaphors to replace a subject and/or a complement and nominal anaphors

> (13) *Dans l'espace il y a* **une bataille entre les extra-terrestres entre les pirates** *dans la voie spatiale, et* **la guerre** *dura des heures et des heures et des années. Mais en fait on savait pas pourquoi* **ils se** *battaient peut-être pour une planète ou l'espace*

*pour **eux** ou un combat parce qu'**ils se** détestent.* (B,II,1)

c) The use of pronominal anaphors to replace a subject and/or a complement, nominal anaphors and anaphoric relations marked by a determiner

(14) *Il était une fois **des pirates** ... Un jour **ils** décidèrent de faire **une bataille** dans l'espace. ... **Des vaisseaux spatiaux** essayèrent d'arrêter **cette guerre** ... mais **les pirates** avec leurs canons **les** ont explosés. **La bataille** continuait ...* (B,I,4)

Assessment

In primary school, the analysis of the results showed that the diversified use of the anaphoric substitution processes increases from one class level (9 years old) to another (10 years old pupils), regardless of the socio-cultural background of the pupils (from 36% to 62.5% for A and from 27% to 48.5% for B).

Nevertheless, at the end of primary school, 48.5% of the pupils from the disadvantaged background use diversified anaphoric processes whereas 62.5% of the pupils from the advantaged background use these processes. Moreover, these results showed that on the one hand, in a disadvantaged background, 4.5% of the 9 years old pupils do not use anaphoric substitution processes; and on the other hand, the nominal substitutions are specific to the advantaged background (4.5% of the 9 years old pupils and 8% of the 10 years old pupils). Indeed, the nominal substitution processes are not part of the processes used by the pupils from the disadvantaged background by the end of primary school.

The results we observed at the starting level of secondary school are similar to those for the elementary school: 60% of the pupils from the advantaged background have recourse to diversified anaphoric processes. Meanwhile the percentage of pupils of the disadvantaged background using diversified processes increases from 48.5% at the end of primary school to 67.5% at the starting level of secondary school.

Throughout secondary school, the anaphoric processes diversify and spread in the textual productions of the various socio-cultural backgrounds. We observed in secondary school as well as in primary school, a primarily quantitative difference between the two groups: at the end of secondary school, 100% of the pupils within the advantaged group have recourse to diversified anaphoric processes while only 79% of pupils from the disadvantaged group do.

Table 1. The anaphoric processes used in advantaged primary schools (A)

	9 years old	10 years old
Non diversified use of anaphors		
Pronominal anaphors (Subject)	32%	4%
Pronominal anaphors (Subject and Object)	27.5%	33.5%
Anaphoric relations marked by a determiner	4.5%	0%
Diversified use of anaphors		
Pronominal anaphors (Subject) + Anaphoric relations marked by a determiner	18%	21%
Pronominal anaphors (Subject and Object) + Anaphoric relations marked by a determiner	13.5%	33.5%
Pronominal anaphors (Subject) + Nominal anaphors	4.5%	0%
Pronominal anaphors (Subject) + Anaphoric relations marked by a determiner + Nominal anaphors	0%	4%
Pronominal anaphors (Subject and Object) + Anaphoric relations marked by a determiner + Nominal anaphors	0%	4%
	36%	62.5%

Table 2. The anaphoric processes used in disadvantaged primary schools (B)

	9 years old	10 years old
Non diversified use of anaphors		
Pronominal anaphors (Subject)	46%	17.5%
Pronominal anaphors (Subject and Object)	18%	35%
Anaphoric relations marked by a determiner	4.5%	0%
No use of anaphors	4.5%	0%
Diversified use of anaphors		
Pronominal anaphors (Subject) + Anaphoric relations marked by a determiner	18%	17.5%
Pronominal anaphors (Subject and Object) + Anaphoric relations marked by a determiner	9%	31%
	27%	48.5%

Nevertheless, we observed a particular use of the nominal substitution. By the end of secondary school, this substitution is used by 52.5% of the pupils from the advantaged background; however, it is used by only 16% of the pupils from the disadvantaged background. In addition, at the beginning of secondary school, the 11- and 12-year-old pupils from the disadvantaged background extensively use nominal substitution processes (42% of the 6th grade pupils and 55.5% of the 5th grade pupils). Finally, the diversity of the anaphoric processes is centralized for these pupils, at the end of secondary school, on the pronominal substitution processes and on the anaphoric relation marked by a determiner, while for the pupils of the advantaged background, the processes extend to nominal substitutions.

We classified these explicitation processes into three groups: ones that have operator nouns, expressions taken from a model, and ones which in 73.8% of the cases take part in progressive specification structures.

Table 3. The anaphoric processes used in advantaged secondary schools (A)

	11 years old	12 years old	13 years old	14 years old
Non diversified use of anaphors				
Pronominal anaphors (Subject)	20%	8%	0%	0%
Pronominal anaphors (Subject and Object)	20%	4%	5%	0%
Diversified use of anaphors				
Pronominal anaphors (Subject) + Anaphoric relations marked by a determiner	0%	15.5%	4.5%	9.5%
Pronominal anaphors (Subject and Object) + Anaphoric relations marked by a determiner	20%	15.5%	33.5%	38%
Pronominal anaphors (Subject) + Nominal anaphors	3.5%	4%	0%	5%
Pronominal anaphors (Subject and Object) + Nominal anaphors	13%	8%	9.5%	14%
Pronominal anaphors (Subject) + Anaphoric relations marked by a determiner + Nominal anaphors	3.5%	0%	0%	5%
Pronominal anaphors (Subject and Object) + Anaphoric relations marked by a determiner + Nominal anaphors	20%	45%	47.5%	28.5%
	60%	88%	95%	100%

Table 4. The anaphoric processes used in disadvantaged secondary schools (B)

	11 years old	12 years old	13 years old	14 years old
Non diversified use of anaphors				
Pronominal anaphors (Subject)	11%	5.5%	5.5%	
Pronominal anaphors (Subject and Object)	11%	11%	22.5%	5%
Anaphoric relations marked by a determiner	0%	0%	0%	11%
No use of anaphors	10.5%	0%	0%	5%
Diversified use of anaphors				
Pronominal anaphors (Subject) + Anaphoric relations marked by a determiner	10%	5.5%	16.5%	5%
Pronominal anaphors (Object) + Anaphoric relations marked by a determiner	0%	0%	5.5%	0%
Pronominal anaphors (Subject and Object) + Anaphoric relations marked by a determiner	15.5%	22.5%	28%	58%
Pronominal anaphors (Subject) + Nominal anaphors	10%	0%	5.5%	0%
Pronominal anaphors (Subject and Object) + Nominal anaphors	0%	0%	5.5%	0%
Pronominal anaphors (Subject) + Anaphoric relations marked by a determiner + Nominal anaphors	5.5%	11%	0%	0%
Pronominal anaphors (Subject and Object) + Anaphoric relations marked by a determiner + Nominal anaphors	26.5%	44.5%	11%	16%
	67.5%	83.5%	72%	79%

ANALYSIS OF THE EXPLICITATION PROCESSES

Operator Nouns

Some nouns, which Gross (1975) named "operator nouns," can directly build a verbal sequence specifying the N by the use of the preposition *de:*

(15) *le duc avait donné **l'ordre** de faire feu sur le peuple* (A,III,4)

(16) *et tous ont eu **l'idée** de faire une guerre* (B,I,16)

> (17) *Mais quand il grandit il lui resta **l'envie** de jouer avec ses copains (A,VI,10)*

These constructions can be seen regardless of the age and the background of the pupils, especially in the cases of some lexemes (such as *ordre* and *idée*). The only difference is that the pupils from the disadvantaged background use the operator nouns less often (10.5% for A versus 4.2% for B).

Formulas

We pointed out six occurrences in both backgrounds where the explicitation relation is marked by a syntagm such as *qui était de* or *qui consistait à,* a formulaic sequence learned as a unit, most probably from literature,[2] which some secondary school pupils have memorized.

> (18) *Le lendemain le conseiller dit son idée **qui était de** faire rentrer un cadeau à Louis XVI (A,IV,17)*

> (19) *Il devait passer l'épreuve du feu **qui consistait à** faire deux guerres pendant trois heures à deux époques différentes. (A,V,25)*

Other formulas with the verb *dire* taken from the discourse represent other ways of marking the explicitation, as early as in CM2 (10- to 11-year-old pupils):

> (20) *En l'an 4 324 les terriens reçoivent un message des martiens **en disant de** se laisser conquérir. (B,II,23)*

Progressive Explicitation Structures

These are the most used explicitation processes by the corpus. We will study its general syntactic frames.

The syntagm containing the N

This (unspecified) noun can appear:

> a) In the valency of the verb as subject (ex.21), non prepositional complement (ex.22) or prepositional complement (ex.23)

(21) **une grande bataille** arriva les riches contre les pauvres (A,VI,23)

(22) Les pirates ont **un projet** ils veulent envahir l'espace. (A,I,10)

(23) les habitants se plaignaient à cause d'une grave maladie : la peste (A,V,8)

b) In the valency of the verb but within a system like "*il y a … qui/que*" which isolates a term of the valency from the others (in this case the non specified N), as well for subjects (ex.24) as for complements (ex.25)

(24) **il y avait** une seule personne **qui** régnait, le roi. (A,IV,2)

(25) *et dans ces jeunes* **il y avait** *un jeune garçon* **que** *je connaissais c'était mon voisin d'en face* (B,IV,10)

c) In a relative clause

(26) *la seule personne* **qui** *est intervenue* **était** *un monsieur* (A,VI,6)

(27) *La raison* **pour laquelle** *ils se battaient* **était que** *les paysans n'avaient pas assez de vivre.* (B,III,15)

d) Within a syntagm without verb

It is generally accompanied by a modifier, an adjective, which specifies it in a series:

(28) *Alors* **la meilleure chose** *le commandant a décidé qu'il faudra se battre contre les pirates.* (B,II,14)

The biggest percentage of explicated Ns can be found in structures where the N is within the valency of a verb (21.7% for A and 18.5% for B) and mainly as a non prepositional object (16.8% for A and 15.1% for B). This verb is usually *il y a* (9 occurrences), *avoir* (9 occurrences) or *faire* (6 occurrences):

(29) *Mais* **il y avait** *un problème, les pirates de l'espace sont*

venus leur prendre leur trésor. (B,1,14)

(30) et le magicien **eut** une idée il jeta un sort (A,I,6)

(31) car Louis XVI **a fait** un privilège à une personne qu'elle n'aurait pas dû avoir : c'est la liberté d'un homme qui aurait du être exécuté pour une trahison du roi. (A,III,1)

If we compare the backgrounds, we can see that all pupils use the explicitation processes but the group A pupils use them more frequently (29.4% for A and 26% for B). We noticed that the pupils from group B use more structures where N appears in a syntagm without a verb than the pupils from group A (5% in B versus 3.5% in A).

Table 5. Student use of explication processes

	A	B
a) N in the valency of the verb	21.7%	18.5%
N subject + V	2.8%	0.8%
V+ N non prepositional complement	16.8%	15.1%
V + N prepositional complement	2.1%	2.6%
b) N in the valency of the verb within a system	1.4%	0.8%
c) N in a relative clause	2.8%	1.7%
d) N within a syntagm without verb	3.5%	5%
	29.4%	26%

Expressing Equivalence

The verb *être* (see Example 9) is the best candidate for establishing an explicitation relation between an unspecified N and a specified lexical item (10.5% for A versus 7.6% for B). However, most commonly, the equivalence expression is not indicated by any morpheme, regardless of the socio-cultural environment (17.5% for A versus 17.7% for B). In most cases, a graphic sign visualizes this link (12.6% for A versus 11.8% for B): The group A pupils use the colon (:) and the group B pupils, the comma (,).

If we link the syntagm containing the N and the marking of the explicitation relation, we can take stock of the explicitation processes among pupils. When the N is in the valency of a verb (without any system), there is a tendency not to mark the explicitation link except by a graphic sign, which is particularly true for the CM1 and CM2 classes (9- to 11-year-old pupils) for the occurrences of the corpus:

(32) ... il y a eu une bataille, les hommes pirates contre les extraterrestres. (B,II,10)

The explicitation morpheme "(c')est" or "il y a" appears at secondary school as early as sixth grade for the advantaged group and the fourth grade for the disadvantaged group. In all the other cases, even though the occurrences are few (system, relative clause and syntagm without verb), the tendency is to mark the explicitation link using a morpheme, regardless of the age and the background.

Table 6. Ways of expressing equivalence

	A	B
With a morpheme		
être	10.5%	7.6%
y avoir	1.4%	0.8%
	11.9%	8.4%
Without any morpheme		
no graphic sign	4.9%	5.9%
graphic sign	12.6%	11.8%
the colon	7%	2.6%
the dot	2.1%	0.8%
the comma	2.1%	8.4%
other	1.4%	0%
	17.5%	17.7%

Syntagm Made Equivalent

The explicitation lexemes are set equivalent whatever the age and the sociocultural environment, within the verbal lexicon (31.5% of the noted examples) and nominal lexicon (68.5% of the examples).

In the cases where the syntagm made equivalent is verbal, there are 20 occurrences of syntagms with a conjugated verb (ex.33) versus 3 occurrences of infinitive syntagms (ex.34):

> (33) *Mais un jour les pirates ont eu une idée,* **ils décidèrent d'aller dans l'espace *(A,I,8)***

> *(34) Mais le 14 juillet 1789 le peuple se décida à faire une action qui restera dans l'histoire :* **se révolter contre la monarchie absolue. (A,III,11)**

In the cases where the syntagm made equivalent is nominal, the unspecified N can relate to a single (ex.35) or several appointed items (ex.36) in a list of possibilities on the paradigmatic axis:

> (35) *La seule passion de la princesse était* **la musique *(B,VI,1)***

> (36) *celui de la moto a eu deux fractures,* **une du tibia et une du crâne *(B,IV,15)***

Assessment

The progressive specification structures serve as explicitation among pupils. They allow them to present information in two stages: once as an N (unspecified) creating an expectant effect and once in a lexical form (specified). Placing the specification in the second stage has two advantages.

The first advantage is that, when the syntactic construction with an unspecified N is placed, the pupil can explain this N in a long rewording (ex.37):

> (37) « *Venez voir, il y a quelque chose de bizarre il y a un monsieur qui vient tous les soirs poser ses poubelles sur mon chat et part en courant.* » *(A,VI,1)*

The second advantage is that the explicit relationship can be taken in its entirety. This applies to the following example, where even though the lexicon is a nominal syntagm, it is the relationship between the name "Mongolians" and the relative clause "qui donnaient l'assaut" that explicates the earthquake. It would be impossible to reduce the explicitation to the noun:

> (38) *Un mois plus tard à une heure du matin ils entendirent* **un tremblement de terre** *c'était les* **Mongoliens qui donnaient l'assaut.** *(A,VI,30)*

> * *Un mois plus tard à une heure du matin ils entendirent* **un**

tremblement de terre c'était **les Mongoliens**

Indeed, "les Mongoliens" forms with the relative clause "qui donnaient l'assaut" a verbo-nominal group, and it is in the link between the two elements that the explicitation of the earthquake should be read.

CONCLUSION

The naming processes, whether they are anaphoric or explicitation, are present in the pupils' writings, regardless of their age and environment. Naming is a fundamental phenomenon found in any language exercise. As already mentioned, the noun is a familiar linguistic reality to young children because it is linked to the activities of naming.

The analysis of the anaphoric processes showed that they diversify progressively throughout schooling, regardless of the type of socio-cultural environment. Nevertheless, the percentage of diversified anaphoric uses by pupils from the disadvantaged background is inferior, although clearly significant for the disadvantaged background

In addition, pupils from the disadvantaged background use significantly less often nominal anaphors relative to other anaphoric processes, except for the sixth and fifth grades (11- to 13-year-old pupils) where the use is clearly significant compared to all other grades studied. The reason for this imbalance between the classes at the beginning of secondary school and the others is likely to be found in school curricula and textbooks which abide by the ministerial decisions. Indeed, the official French curriculum recalls the importance of teaching narrative texts, especially anaphora in the sixth and fifth grades (11- to 13-year-old pupils) in the continuation of the work started on the nominal substitutes in the CM1 and CM2 classes (9- to 11-year-old pupils). This suggests that this focus on alternatives at the beginning of secondary school has an impact on pupils' skills in this area. Since the learning curve of these tools is significantly longer for pupils from disadvantaged socio-cultural background, one can see the interest to revise the anaphors throughout secondary school.

The analysis of the explicitation processes showed that all pupils from the CM1 classes to the third grade (9- to 14-year-old pupils) employ them, but they are used less frequently by pupils in disadvantaged socio-cultural environments, and when used, appear predominantly in progressive specification structures. It is especially in the valency of a verb that the unspecified noun is built, and it is the pupils from the disadvantaged background who produce them more in a syntagm without a verb. The trend is not to mark the explicitation link by a morpheme in primary school but in secondary school; it appears from the sixth for the advantaged pupils (11- to 12-year-old pupils) and only in fourth grade for those in disadvantaged areas (13- to 14-year-old pupils). When this link is not morphologically marked, the disadvantaged pupils tend to use comma while advantaged pupils employ mainly the colon.

It seems that when the disadvantaged environment pupils have the same linguistic means to mark the explicitation, they use it less often, and they use fewer grammatical markers—and when they do use markers, it is later than the pupils of the advantaged environment. What is noteworthy is that in the case of explicitation, no formal teaching is introduced in class; however, pupils use various processes that they draw from both oral and written language. It would be interesting to teach those naming processes, as such literature is a good way to get pupils of all backgrounds to learn naming methods.

Even though we know that these namings are only temporary because they are concomitant to the time of writing, their study leads us to identify formal procedures that seem to structure all the writing in both the advantaged and disadvantaged groups. The differences in the use of naming processes appear in terms of frequency and grammatical or lexical choices. The fact that all pupils use naming operations leads us to reconsider our a priori judgments on the relationship between pupils' writings and their socio-cultural background.

NOTES

1. We coded the texts as follows: The letter specifies whether the pupils belong to an advantaged school (A) or a disadvantaged school (B), the Roman character refers to the level of education: I (CM1), II (CM2), VI (6eme), V (5eme), IV (4eme), III (3eme) and the number corresponds to a pupil, that is to say the number of the copy in the class.

2. For example "Once upon a time" is a well-known literary formula.

REFERENCES

Adam, J.-M. (2008). *La linguistique textuelle. Introduction à l'analyse textuelle des discours.* Paris: Armand Colin.

Asher, N. (1993). *Reference to Abstract Objects in Discourse.* Boston: Kluwer Academic.

Bassano, D. (1999). L'interaction lexique/grammaire et l'acquisition des verbes. *Revue Parole, 9*(10), 29-48.

Bassano, D. (2005). Production naturelle précoce et acquisition du langage: L'exemple du développement des noms. *Lidil, 31,* 61-84.
Benveniste, E. (1966). *Problèmes de linguistique générale (t. 1).* Paris: Gallimard.
Benveniste, E. (1974). *Problèmes de linguistique générale (t. 2).* Paris: Gallimard.
Blanche-Benveniste, C. (1984). La dénomination dans le français parlé: Une interprétation pour les "répétitions" et les "hésitations. " *Recherches sur le Français parlé, 6,* 109-130.
Blanche-Benveniste, C. (1986). Une chose dans la syntaxe verbale. *Recherches sur le Français parlé, 7, 141-168.*
Blanche-Benveniste, C. (1992). Sur un type de nom "évaluatif" portant sur des séquences verbales. Review of Applied Linguistics,*97-98,* 1-25.
Blanche-Benveniste, C., Bilger, M., Rouget, C., & Van den Eynde, K. (1990). *Le français parlé: Etudes grammaticales.* Paris: Editions du CNRS.
Branca-Rosoff, S. (2007). Approche discursive de la nomination / dénomination. In G. Cislara, O. Guérin, K. Morin, E. Née, T. Pagnier, & M. Veniard (Eds.), *L'acte de nommer. Une dynamique entre langue et discours* (pp. 13-24). Paris: Presses Sorbonne Nouvelle.
Brown, G., & Yule, G. (1984). *Discoursive Analysis.* Cambridge, UK: Cambridge University Press.
Cappeau, P., & Roubaud, M.-N. (2005). *Enseigner les outils de la langue avec les productions d'élèves.* Paris: Bordas.
Corblin, F. (1985). Anaphore et interprétation des segments nominaux (Unpublished doctoral dissertation). Université de Paris VII, Paris.
Corblin, F. (1987a). Les chaînes de référence: Analyse linguistique et automatique. *Intellectica, 1*(1), 123-143.
Corblin, F. (1987b). *Indéfinis, définis et démonstratifs.* Genève: Droz.
Corblin, F. (1989). Sur la notion d'anaphore. *Revue Québécoise de linguistique, 15*(1), 173-195.
Culioli, A. (1990). *Pour une linguistique de l'énonciation. Opérations et représentations (t. 1).* Paris: Ophrys.
David, J. (2000). Le lexique et son acquisition: Aspects cognitifs et linguistiques. *Le Français aujourd'hui, 131,* 31-41.
Fayol, M. (1996). La production d'écrits narratifs: Approche de psycholinguistique textuelle chez l'enfant et l'adulte. In J. David & S. Plane (Eds.), *L'apprentissage de l'écriture de l'école au collège (pp. 9-36).* Paris: Presses Universitaires de France.
Fayol, M. (Dir.). (2002). *Production du langage. Traité des sciences cognitives.* Paris: Hermès/Lavoisier.
Gardes-Tamine, J. (2008). *La grammaire (t. 2) Syntaxe.* Paris: Armand Colin.
Gross, M. (1975). *Méthodes en syntaxe.* Paris: Hermann.

Jakobson, R. (1963). *Essais de linguistique générale*. Paris: Editions de Minuit.

Kernan, K. T., (1977). Semantic and expressive elaborations in children's narratives. In S. Ervin-Tripp & C. Mitchell-Kernan (Eds.), *Child discourse* (pp. 91–102), New-York: Academic Press.

Kleiber, G. (1984). Dénomination et relations dénominatives. *Langages, 76,* 77-94.

Kleiber, G. (1988). Peut-on définir une catégorie générale de l'anaphore ? *Vox Romanica, 48,* 1-14.

Kleiber, G. (1991). Anaphore-déixis. Où en sommes-nous ? *L'information grammaticale, 51,* 3-18.

Kleiber, G. (2003). *L'anaphore associative*. Paris: Presses Universitaires de France.

Martinot, C. (2000). Etude comparative des processus de reformulation chez des enfants de 5 à 11 ans. *Langages, 140,* 92-123.

Milner, J.-C. (1985). *Ordre et raisons de langue*. Paris: Seuil.

Ministère de l'Education nationale et Ministère de l'enseignement supérieur et de la recherche. (2008). *B. O. Horaires et programmes d'enseignement de l'école primaire*. Hors série n°3 du 19 juin 2008. Paris: Scéren CNDP.

Ministère de l'Education nationale. (2008). *B. O. spécial. Programmes du collège. Programmes de l'enseignement du français*. N°6 du 28 août 2008. Paris: Scéren CNDP

Riegel, M., Pellat, J.-C., & Rioul, R. (2009). *Grammaire méthodique du français. Paris:* Presses Universitaires de France.

Roubaud, M.-N. (2000). *Les constructions pseudo-clivées en français contemporain*. Paris: Champion.

Roubaud, M.-N., & Loufrani, C. (2001). La dénomination dans le discours perturbé de type aphasique. *Recherches sur le Français parlé, 16,* 207-226.

Schneuwly, B. (1988). *Le langage écrit chez l'enfant*. Neuchâtel, Switzerland: Delachaux et Niestlé.

Schultz-Romain, C. (1999). L'emploi des temps et des organisateurs textuels dans des productions narratives d'élèves du cours moyen issus de milieux socioculturels hétérogènes (Unpublished master's thesis). Université de Provence, Aix-en-Provence, France.

Schultz-Romain, C. (2000). L'emploi des temps et des organisateurs textuels dans des productions narratives d'élèves du collège issus de milieux socioculturels hétérogènes (Unpublished master's thesis). Université de Provence, Aix-en-Provence, France.

Siblot, P. (2004). Préface. In F. Dufour, E. Dutilleul-Guerroudj & B. Laurent (coord.), *La nomination: Quelles problématiques, quelles orientations, quelles applications? Actes des journées d'étude des jeunes chercheurs 16 et 17 janvier 2004* (pp. 13-22), Montpellier, France: Praxiling.

Siblot, P. (2007). La composante déictique des catégorisations lexicales. In G. Cislara, O. Guérin, K. Morin, E. Née, T. Pagnier, & M. Veniard (Eds.), *L'acte de nommer. Une dynamique entre langue et discours* (pp. 25-38). Paris: Presses Sorbonne Nouvelle.

Steuckard, A. (2003). Présentation. In A. Steuckardt & A. Niklas-Salminen (Dir.), *Le mot et sa glose, Langues et langage n°9* (pp. 5-17). Aix-en-Provence, France: Publications de l'Université de Provence.

Zoppi-Fontana, M. (1998). Le mot dans les gloses à usage scolaire. In S. Branca-Rosoff (Ed.), *Le mot: Analyse du discours et sciences sociales, Langues et Langage, 7* (pp. 149-158). Aix-en-Provence, France: Publications de l'Université de Provence.

CHAPTER 13.
DOES THE INTERNET CONNECT WRITING IN AND OUT OF EDUCATIONAL SETTINGS? VIEWS OF NORWEGIAN STUDENTS ON THE THRESHOLD OF HIGHER EDUCATION

Håvard Skaar
Oslo and Akershus University College

What Internet-based writing practice means for the development of writing in young people and how this writing practice should be taken into account by educational institutions is the subject of international debate. In writing-related research there is general agreement that digital technology has led to more writing among young people, but there is less concensus about what significance this has for the development of their writing ability (MacArthur, 2006). A preliminary conclusion in The Stanford Study of Writing, a broad-based American study of several years' standing, claims that students have higher expectations of their own writing practices than they used to: "good writing changes something. It doesn't just sit on the page. It gets up, walks off the page and changes something" (Haven, 2009,p. 1; see also Rogers, 2008). In concurrence, some researchers underline that the writing young people do on the Internet on their own initiative is more engaged and directly aimed at a readership they care about than the writing they are required to produce in their role as school and college students. These researchers argue that this self-initiated online writing should be made as relevant as possible to their classroom writing and learning (situation) (Grabil et al., 2005; Hull & Schultz, 2002; Street, 2005; Yancey, 2006, 2009a).

Sceptics on the other hand assert that the forms of writing now taking shape on the Internet can actually destroy young people's critical awareness of their writing practices (Bauerlein, 2008). This scepticism is commonly voiced in wider criticism of the Internet's cognitive, social or cultural significance (see for example Carr, 2010). A more optimistic view of young people's use of the Internet characterizes these reactions as "moral panic"(Thurlow, 2006). For these proponents, the problem is not that young people's writing is changed through the use of digital media but that educational institutions find difficulty relating to these changes (see for example Tan & Richardson, 2006; Yancey, 2009b).

In the report Writing, Technology and Teens it is pointed out that young Americans do not perceive that the way in which they use e-mail or messaging has any relevance for the development of their written language skills in the school setting. There is, it is claimed, a "disconnection" between young people's overrating of writing skills and their simultaneous underrating of their own writing practices on the Internet."Those who can figure out how to tap into their distinctive, situational communication behaviors and connect them to the process of learning how to write will have taught them an invaluable lesson that will improve their lives"(Lenhart et al., 2008, p. 64). This chapter explores the premises that would enable the creation of such a connection.

Norwegian students here explain how they perceive the relationship between their writing on the Internet in and outside the school setting. The question of the Internet's importance for this connection is just as pertinent in Norway as in the US, Asia and Europe. In Norway, personal computer coverage among young people is close to 100% and netbased communication is now an integral part of the social life of almost all young Norwegians (Torgersen, 2007). In Norwegian schools there has concurrently been a move to integrate both writing (Hertzberg,2011) and digital technology into all subjects in the curriculum. In some upper secondary schools (high schools) over the last three years all pupils have been issued laptop computers, and in higher education it is a prime aim to link students' writing to digital technology, for example by means of online learning management platforms (Krumsvik, 2008; Skaar, 2005;Wilhelmsen et al.,2009).

The present study is based on individual interviews with 19 students in the same class, a preparatory class for pre-engineering students, in a Norwegian university college. In the interviews, the students described the purposes for which they used writing and what part the Internet played in establishing the conditions for their own writing practices. The analysis shows how these particular students experience the relationship between their Internet-based writing in and outside the educational setting (Bazerman & Prior, 2004; Hull & Schultz, 2002; Moss, 2001). Comparisons of their descriptions and evaluations of their writing practices on the Internet reveal the conditions necessary for them to experience their leisuretime writing as relevant to the school setting.

THEORY

The collection and analysis of data are based on three assumptions as to the critical factors in relation to the students' Internet writing.

First, their writing habits can be understood as a social practice (Barton, 2007; Dysthe & Hertzberg, 2007; Hoel, 1999; Kostouli, 2009; Street, 2003). This means that writing is understood and interpreted in the light of the social context in which it takes place. The meaning and function of the writing for the writer always arises from a social basis and this social basis is taken into account in the analysis of how the students choose to express themselves through writing.

Second, digital technology is understood as a new material basis for writing, giving new conditions for the development of writing skills. On the Internet, writing is no longer anchored to the page but becomes part of a multimodal and hypertextual dynamic. The act of writing, the effort it takes to transcribe and compose written text, as well as the act of reading it, is altered (Haas, 2009; Skaar, 2009). At the same time the Internet makes writing socially relevant to life realms where it has normally been absent or of minor importance, and thus contributes to a profound transformation of the social act of writing. Yancey puts it like this:

> Historically, like today, we compose on all the available materials. Whether those materials are rocks or computer screens, composing is a material as well as a social practice; composing is situated within and informed by specific kinds of materials as well as by its location in community (2009a, p. 8).

The material and social basis of writing is bound up in what Bruce calls a "socio-technical practice"(1997), emphasizing that technology and literacy (textual ability) are reciprocal conditions. Digital technology has changed the nature of text and hence also what text means for both writer and reader.

Third, the study is based on an assumption that there is a connection between writing in and outside the educational setting, meaning not only that pupils and students take out with them the writing they learn in this setting but also that they bring their external writing practices into the school.

METHOD

Below, a brief description of these students' relationship to writing is followed by the main findings from their descriptions and assessments of their own practices. The interviews were conducted between February and May 2009 in a class where I was a teacher. In this teacher research (see e.g. Saleh & Khine, 2011) the interviews became material for a "systematic, intentional inquiry" (Lytle & Cochran-Smith, 1989) relevant to my own practice. Each interview lasted 35-75 minutes. In the interviews the students talked about their experience of written texts and writing and also gave a more concrete description and assessment of their own writing practices in and outside the school setting (Kvale, 1996; about the use of interviews in teacher research see also Postholm, 2007, p. 239).

At the time of carrying out my research I had 10 years' experience of teaching this category of student and therefore already had good insight into their writing practices and their out-of-school interests. Although this meant I was not looking at the students and their writing practices from the standpoint of an outsider, I was strongly influenced by the prejudices I had developed over my many years of teaching. The practising teacher's perspective also predisposed me in my role of researcher. My knowledge of the students helped to determine my choice of interview questions and my teaching history was also highly instrumental in forming my critical approach to their writing in and outside the school setting (Kvale, 2005).

My double role as teacher and researcher also entailed the risk that the students might choose to give me the answers that showed them in the best light as scholars. One student answered, for example, when I asked if his laptop was a help in his classroom writing: "I think it helps me ... to take down notes from the lessons ... I write notes from your lessons ... and I don't think there are many others who do that... ." This form of self-depiction was something I experienced to a greater or lesser degree in all the interviews. In other words, it is reasonable to suppose that the students may have presented their writing practices outside the classroom as being more in line with their school writing than they actually were. By far the majority, on the other hand, saw their writing practices outside the confines of their studies as having only minimal relevance for their school-related writing. Even if we allow for an "air-brushed" presentation of their writing practices to me as their Norwegian teacher, this tendency is very clear.

The analytical software Nvivo 8 was used to define categories that differentiated between the writing practices of individual students and the conditions for this (Bazeley, 2007). The main thrust of the analysis was how the students assessed the relationship between their net-based writing in and outside school. The interviews with the students form the primary research data. The texts they had written in both settings were also included in the raw material but were only used to verify their reported writing practices. The students have given written consent to the research results being published in anonymized form.

FINDINGS

STUDENTS' BACKGROUND AND WRITING CAPABILITIES

The students interviewed were with one exception men between the ages of 21 and 29, with a middle-class or lower middle-class background. They described their writing practices both at the time of the interviews and at earlier periods of their life.

Of the students interviewed, five had a general academic education and the other 14 a vocational background. On average, they had two to three years' occupational experience. All of them were taking the preparatory course as a step towards qualifying as engineers. Only two said they had considered courses that would have involved greater emphasis on writing. The sample was therefore taken from a student group who, with a vocational background, tended to have less interest in writing relative to other categories of student.

Three of the interviewees had particular difficulties with writing Norwegian, as a result of dyslexia and/or insufficient mastery of the language. Of the remainder, 11 assessed their writing skills as average and five as above average. However, about half of those who assessed their skills as average were graded as below average on the assignments sent in over the school year.

WRITING PRACTICES *IN* THE EDUCATIONAL SETTING

All the students owned a personal computer and/or laptop and all of them had Internet access both at home and at school. Of the 17 who owned a laptop only four took it with them to school, the others opting to use the personal computers in the school computer room. Twelve of them gave as their reason that using a laptop led to distraction and loss of work concentration.

The students were required to hand in 10 written assignments over the school year before being allowed to take the final examination. When writing these papers all the students, with one exception, elected to use digital tools. In the examination, conversely, longhand was compulsory. The homework assignments took the form of essay-writing in Norwegian, either discursive topics or text analysis. Throughout the year, 2/3 of the students handed in a little less than, and never more than, the minimum length required (typically three to four pages), while four students wrote more than the minimum. The directions for grading examination papers stipulate three main areas for assessment: use of language, structure and content. When a voluntary extra assignment was set at the end of the year, only one student handed in a paper.

WRITING PRACTICES *OUTSIDE* THE EDUCATIONAL SETTING

In their leisure hours, the time the students spent on the Internet varied from 30 minutes to more than seven hours a day. Between one and three hours was typical, with writing taking up 10 to 30 minutes. This writing took place on e-mail, blogs, MSN, Facebook and Twitter. Other arenas for writing were discussion fora and comments columns in online newspapers and in the context of computer games. Writing was primarily a means of pursuing contact and social interaction with friends and acquaintances. One of the students described having set up a blog for this purpose during trips abroad. The following interests were also cultivated in various discussion fora: cycling, computer games, paintball, computer technology, political debate, film and web design.

In addition to digital writing there is longhand writing. Three of the students wrote nothing at all in longhand outside the school context but most said they wrote checklists and Christmas cards. Only one student still wrote letters by hand, while three said they had kept a diary in connection with training, treatment and travel. One student had at some time or other also made an attempt to write fiction.

The texts the students produced on the Internet in their leisure time were consistently brief, most commonly taking the form of comments on MSN or Facebook or in connection with online computer games. These varied from one word to two to three lines, with slightly longer texts occurring in e-mails, discussion fora and on blogs (see Table 1).

ASSESSMENTS OF RELEVANCE

The students' assessment of the relevance out of school writing had for how they wrote in the school context can be categorized in relation to the requirements concerning use of language, structure and content which formed the grading criteria.

Eleven students said that in their view their leisuretime writing was irrelevant or only minimally relevant to use of language, six students said the writing was relevant in terms of use of language, and structure, while two students thought their writing was relevant in relation to all three areas (of use of language, structure and content)(see Appendix 1).

The students justified their online writing with reference to tools, texts and networks/audiences. Tools simplified the coding of words, sentence construc-

Table 1. Student writing

Internet Based Writing		Longhand Writing	
Email	17/19	Notes for memoration	12/19
Facebook	14/19	Postcards	8/19
MSN	11/19	Diary (training, travel or treatment)	3/19
Forum	9/19		
Computer games	3/19	Fictional writing	1/19
Blog	2/19	Letters	1/19

tion and textual disposition on the Internet. Texts linked the use of writing closer to the fostering of their own interests, while networks and audiences made writing functional and meaningful (see Appendix 2).

On the other hand, the same access to tools, texts and networks/audiences was given as a reason for not writing on the Internet. Two of the students stated a preference for longhand over the keyboard, while many more experienced access to texts and networks/audiences as more distracting than stimulating in relation to a writing task (see Appendix 3).

PREREQUISITES FOR RELEVANCE

None of the students in the study were excluded from using the Internet and many of them spent comparatively much time there too. Most were well aware of the continuous development of some websites and communication platforms. Nevertheless, only a few of them used these websites to write in a way relevant to their writing practices in school. The determining factor was not how much they knew about the new forms of digital communication but how they approached the activities of writing, reading and knowledge sharing, whether on the Internet or not.

The students' relationship to writing can be characterized as instrumental or processual. An instrumental relationship meant that writing was chosen because it was the cheapest, simplest, quickest or most effective means of contact in the communicative situation. If it was possible to communicate in a simpler way, writing was not chosen. In contrast, a processual relationship to writing meant that the act of writing was attributed with cognitive and/or social importance beyond that of a purely practical communicative function.

Instrumental relationship to writing	Processual relationship to writing
… I feel I'm living in a world where I really don't have time … or I think I can save so much time at that point … by expressing myself verbally rather than in writing… .	It was something necessary as part of a course of treatment I was undergoing … then I had a very … in a way something of a revelation … you might say … well … I can go around with thoughts in my head … but I don't have any clear idea of what's going on until I write it down and get it on to a sheet of paper I can touch so it becomes something physical … and not just thoughts …

The difficulty for most of these students was to force themselves to accept the time delay writing entailed in relation to speech, and to bear with the frustration and resistance involved in a writing process of the kind they had to tackle when producing written answers to course assignments:

> … I don't like it … I have a struggle getting started… (then) I think well f … it I HAVE to get it over with … and so I sit down at the PC … just staring at the assignment … and then, well, I just seem to make a start . . and the first few lines go f … ing slowly . . and then it gets to be more like a … what shall I call it? A domino effect, that's it. I just begin and then I see, like, that: okay, I can actually do this, how can I put it, build more on it then, change the wording a bit, and maybe flesh it out a bit . . and then suddenly there seems to be . . a lot… .

Only a few of the students in this study chose to write to networks/audiences on the Internet in their leisure time in a way that created this "domino effect." Most of them shied away from it before they got that far.

In terms of their relationship to text, we can distinguish between students who associated their online writing with text-based interests and those who applied it to non-text-based interests. Text-based interests, such as literature, film, political debate or web design, provided more of a platform for writing in line with school-related writing than interests which were not text-based, for example cycling, computer games, paintball or computer technology. An interest in gambling was played out on the website Swiss Casino, while an interest in games was played out through participating in World of Warcraft. These latter interests can in theory also be purely text-based: someone may be interested for example in cycling journalism even if he is a non-cyclist, but for these students the basis for writing was the non-textual activity. Only a minority pursued text-based interests through their Internet writing.

None of the students were active Internet bloggers. A rejection of blogging as "self-digging" was unanimous among these (with one exception) male students, the general opinion being that you needed to have something specific to talk about before joining the ranks of bloggers:

> (Bloggers) ... must be politicians of a sort, actually hold views about different issues ... who are . . where you can get something meaningful out of it.

One student had kept a blog in connection with a journey, while another had tried to blog about societal issues and politics. Both had given up:

> ... I've had (blogs), yes, this summer . . I was at home (sick) for a year, and one of the ways of getting out my frustrations about being (stuck) at home was to write. But it never worked out quite as I'd thought it would, so I gave up and deleted the lot.

Some of the students, however, shared their interests with others in various fora. These students realized that this kind of knowledge-based relationship to networks or audiences fostered school-relevant writing to a greater extent than writing directly about oneself or general social issues. Two students said that they had at various times written texts in online fora that were highly akin to school writing. Both had a relatively good level of writing in the educational setting and they experienced their writing practices in the discussion fora as academically relevant. On the other hand, none of the students who described themselves as writing-shy or had serious writing difficulties in connection with their schoolwork found that they could compensate for, or overcome, these problems through writing on the Internet in their leisure time.

DISCUSSION

The students found that access to tools, texts and networks/audiences on the Internet made it easier to write, to find something to write about and to find someone to write to. This applied to contexts in and outside school. I have described above how the students made use of these opportunities and to what extent they found that the Internet thereby created a connection between their writing in the different settings. Three factors emerged as critical for the creation of such a connection, namely the students' relationship to writing, their relationship to text and their relationship to networks or audiences.

By far the majority of the students had an instrumental relationship to writing. An instrumental writing practice was primarily associated with social interaction and most typically limited to the coding of words and short sentences in contexts where the norms of morphology and syntax were not adhered to. For instrumental users, chatting on MSN, Facebook walls and the comments spaces on webpages gave written expression to verbal discourse but without the typical features of the written genre. Since this instrumental approach meant that they tended to avoid writing if there were less demanding means of communication at their disposal, these students did not find that their leisuretime use of the Internet encouraged a more processual relationship to writing and hence saw it as less academically relevant.

The Internet enabled students to cultivate their interests through writing and the present study provides a basis for differentiating between text-based and non-text-based interests. Text-based interests, much more than non-text-based, were seen to have generated the production of written texts the students saw as relevant to their course-related writing. School assignments are based on textual norms for how discussion and analysis should be practised within the dominant writing culture, and students are examined in their willingness and ability to comply with these norms. An interest in texts obeying the same norms therefore gives the best foundation for writing in accordance with the norms of academic writing, both in and outside the educational setting. A minority of the students in this study had developed an interest in these kinds of text, and had done so independently of their use of the Internet.

Writing outside the school context was seen as educationally relevant by those students who were active in knowledge exchange in different fora or who tried to blog about knowledge-based matters. The problem was that interest in writing about such issues was generally minimal in the group as a whole. Most of the students limited their Internet-based writing outside the school context to personal communication with friends on e-mail, MSN, or Facebook. Knowledge-based writing occurred, but in a textual scope most of the students did not see as relevant to their studies.

The students saw that the Internet lowered the threshold for the practice of writing both in and outside the school context. At the same time, they all recognized that the Internet could also divert their attention, interest and concentration away from writing. In the school context a majority of the interviewees thought it was those interests least calling for writing competence that the Internet served to stimulate. This made it more difficult for them to concentrate on study-related writing, and many of the students therefore chose not to bring their laptops to school. Outside the school context, all the interviewees thought that the Internet had given them a range of new opportunities to write but also to communicate in ways which reduced writing to a kind of verbal hybrid, or rendered it superfluous. The Internet made it easier to write but also easier to reject writing as an option.

EDUCATIONAL IMPLICATIONS

The Internet has created a new textual landscape and given young people new writing possibilities. At the same time, as noted, the majority of students in this study saw their writing on the Internet outside school as little relevant to their studies, at least to the writing required of them on their course. For, even though young people write more than ever on the Internet in their leisure time, the key to educationally-relevant writing is still to be found in the school and other educational institutions. As mentioned in the introduction, it may be claimed that the key question is not how writing outside school can be brought into line with writing in the school context, but how writing requirements in the school context can be brought more into line with students' actual writing practice outside school (See e.g., Yancey, 2008b). The Internet affords new didactic possibilities for also making academic writing relevant outside school, so that students will find that what they write is part of a body of genuine "live" writing, not just an academic exercise. In educational institutions, teachers should naturally seize the opportunities afforded by the Internet to help students realize this. But even if they succeed in doing so, academic studies will inevitably continue to incorporate writing practices most students will not become familiar with in their lives outside the school context and which are not perceived as relevant there either. Educational institutions will also continue to rank student performance in relation to how they satisfy academic requirements, including those tasks in written form. Academic requirements can be made more stringent or less demanding but the challenge of teaching writing will remain how to enable students to engage in academic writing through accepting the need for deeper absorption, concentration and patience this writing requires. In the research study, this appeared to be the factor that caused students the biggest problem.

The study indicates that a connection can be made between writing in and outside school if students using the Internet succeed in moving from instrumental to processual writing, from non-text-based to text-based interests and from the purely social to a knowledge-based relationship to networks/audiences. On the other hand, most of these students had instrumental writing practices linked neither to text-based interests nor to a knowledge-based relationship towards networks/audiences. The minority who perceived that writing was of major or critical relevance all demonstrated good or excellent writing skills in their academic work. Conversely, students with weak or very weak writing skills in the school context found that their writing on the Internet outside school had very limited relevance. This points to the danger that, taken in isolation, tapping into students' out of school writing on the Internet as a strategy for teaching writing will favourize students who already have well-developed writing skills, and hence reinforce the existing imbalance.

According to Baron, the Internet can be held responsible for "flooding the scriptorium" (2008, p. 193). The problem is that when we write so much more we simultaneously become less particular about how we write. At the same time, the Internet has led to a "context collapse" which makes it more difficult to distinguish between the contexts in which writing takes place (Wesch, 2009). An approach to the teaching of writing that pays greater attention to what divides and unites students' writing strategies in different contexts will give all students greater opportunity to develop a critical approach to their own writing. In the school context, the students in this research study used writing to organize a textual totality in line with basic principles not immediately accessible to them. Outside the educational institution, on the other hand, the students described how, in a variety of contexts, they used writing in the simplest ways to communicate with others when and wherever they wanted. In many cases, this writing required no processing other than rudimentary coding, and the writer's relationship to the recipient could be informal, non-committed and undetermined. None of the students believed that this writing practice might apply to the other, but there was nevertheless a connection between their writing ability and their understanding of the similarities and differences between the writing practices they engaged in. Since the Internet has led to a more differentiated use of writing, what is needed now is also a more differentiated awareness of how writing actually functions in different contexts. This understanding is acquired through practical experience but to benefit from experience students must have a reflective relationship to their own practice. This has implications for the teaching of writing. By developing an awareness of the assumptions for their own writing practices in different contexts, it becomes easier for students both to distinguish between their different writing practices and to tie them more closely together. In the school context, this will help them to write better, while outside school it will help them to exploit the opportunities open to them through the Internet of entering into contexts from which they were previously excluded.

As far as possible, students should learn through experience that school-based writing enhances their opportunities for personal development and social interaction. Practical writing assignments must bring them irrefutable proof that writing is truly capable of helping them to overcome difficulties and achieve their goals. Writing teachers who succeed in creating a link between writing in school and the possibilities that mastery of writing opens to students outside school will have won a great victory. The Internet gives teachers novel opportunities to design relevant tasks.

If they succeed, the Internet may play a part in ensuring that more students choose to engage in the painstaking work involved in developing varied and well-functioning writing practices.

REFERENCES

Baron, N. S. (2008). *Always on: Language in an online and mobile world.* New York: Oxford University.

Barton, D. (2007). *Literacy: An introduction to the ecology of written language* (2 ed.). Oxford UK: Blackwell.

Bauerlein, M. (2008). *The dumbest generation: How the digital age stupefies young Americans and jeopardizes our future.* New York: Penguin.

Bazeley, P. (2007). *Qualitative data analysis with NVivo.* London: Sage.

Bazerman, C., & Prior, P. (2004). *What writing does and how it does it: An introduction to analyzing texts and textual practices.* Mahway, NJ & London: Lawrence Erlbaum.

Bruce, B. (1997). Literacy technologies: What stance should we take? *Journal of Literacy Research, 29*(2), 289-309.

Carr, N. G. (2010). *The shallows: What the Internet is doing to our brains.* New York: Norton.

Dysthe, O., & Hertzberg, F. (2007). Kunnskap om skriving i utdanning og yrkesliv: Vor står vi i dag? In S. Matre & T. L. Hoel (Eds.), *Skrive for nåtid og framtid bind I* (pp. 10-28). Trondheim, Norway: Tapir Forlag.

Grabill, J. T., DeVoss, D. N., Cushman, E., Bill, H.-D., & Porter, J. (2005). Why teach digital writing? *Kairos, 10*(1). Retrieved from http://english.ttu.edu/kairos/10.1/binder2.html?coverweb/wide/index.html

Haas, C. (2009). *Writing technology: Studies on the materiality of literacy*. New York: Routledge.

Haven, C. (2009). *The new literacy: Stanford study finds richness and complexity in students' writing*. Stanford University News. Retrieved from http://news.stanford.edu/news/2009/october12/lunsford-writing-research-101209.html

Hertzberg, F. (2011). Skriving i fagene: Viktig, riktig og nødvendig. In K. H. Flyum & F. Hertzberg (Eds.), *Skriv i alle fag!: Argumentasjon og kildebruk i videregående skole* (pp. 9-20). Oslo: Universitetsforlaget.

Hoel, T. L. (1999). Læring som kulturell og sosial praksis: Med eksempel frå elevsamarbeid i skriving. *Norsk pedagogisk tidsskrift, 83*(6), 343-354.

Hull, G. A., & Schultz, K. (Eds.). (2002). *School's out: Bridging out-of-school literacies with classroom practices*. New York: Teachers College Press.

Kostouli, T. (2009). A sociocultural framework:Writing as social practice. In R. Beard, D. Myhill, J. Riley, & M. Nystrand (Eds.), *The Sage Handbook of writing development* (pp. 98-116). London: Sage.

Krumsvik, R. (2008). Educational technology, epistemology and discourses in curricula in Norway. *US-China Education Review, 5*(5), 1-16.

Kvale, S. (1996). *Interviews: An introduction to qualitative research interviewing*. Thousand Oaks, CA: Sage.

Kvale, S. (2005). On interpretation in the qualitative research interview. *NordiskPedagogik, 25*(1), 3-15.

Lenhart, A., Arafeh, S., Smith, A., & Macgill, A. R. (2008). *Writing, technology and teens*. Pew Internet & American Life Project. Retrieved from http://www.pewinternet.org/Reports/2008/Writing-Technology-and-Teens/10-What-Teens-Tell-Us-Encourages-Them-to-Write.aspx?view=all

Lytle, S. L., & Cochran-Smith, M. (1989) Teacher research: Toward clarifying the consept, *National Writing Project Quarterly, 11*(2), 1-3, 22-27. Retrieved from http://www.nwp.org/cs/public/download/nwp_file/11019/Teacher_Research.pdf?x-r=pcfile_d

MacArthur, C. A. (2006). The effects of new technologies on writing and writing processes. In C. A. MacArthur, S. Graham, & J. Fitzgerald (Eds.), *Handbook of writing research* (pp. 248-262). New York: Guilford.

Moss, G. (2001). On literacy and the social organisation of knowledge inside and outside school. *Language and Eduaction, 15*(2&3), 146-161.

Postholm, M. B. (2007). Læreren som forsker eller lærer. *Norsk pedagogisk tidsskrift,* 91(3), 233-244.

Rogers, P. (2008). The Development of Writers and Writing Abilities: A Longitudinal Study Across and Beyond the College-Span (Unpublished doctoral dissertation). University of California, Santa Barbara, CA.

Saleh, I. M., & Khine, M. S. (2011). *Practitioner Research in Teacher Education: Theory and Best Practices.* Frankfurt am Main: Peter Lang.

Skaar, H. (2005). Classfronter, pedagogikk og endring. In O. Talberg (Ed.), *Strategier for læring. Pedagogisk utviklingsarbeid på ingeniørutdanningen* (pp. 37-49). Oslo: HiO-rapport.

Skaar, H. (2009). In defence of writing: A social semiotic perspective on digital media, literacy and learning. *Literacy,* 43(1), 36-42.

Street, B. (2003). What's "new" in new literacy studies? Critical approaches to literacy in theory and practice. *Current Issues in Comparative Education,* 5(2), 77-91.

Street, B. (Ed.). (2005). *Literacies across educational contexts: Mediating learning and teaching.* Philadelphia: Caslon.

Tan, K. E., & Richardson, P. W. (2006). Writing short messages in English: Out-of-school practices of Malaysian high school students. *International Journal of Educational Research,* 45(1), 325-340.

Thurlow, C. (2006). From statistical panic to moral panic: The metadiscursive construction and popular exaggeration of new media language in the print media. *Journal of Computer-Mediated Communication,* 11(3), 667-701.

Torgersen, L.(2007). Kjønnsforskjeller i ungdoms bruk av PC, TV-spill og mobiltelefon. *Tidsskrift for ungdomsforskning,* 7(1),103–112.

Wesch, M.(2009) YouTube and you: Experiences of self-swareness in the context collapse of the recording webcam. *The Journal of the Media Ecology Association,* 8(2), 19-34.

Wilhelmsen, J., Ørnes, H., Kristiansen, T., & Breivik, J. (2009). *Digitale utfordringer i høyere utdanning.* Tromsø, Norway: Norgesuniversitetet.

Yancey, K. B. (2006). Delivering college composition: A vocabulary for discussion. In K. B. Yancey (Ed.), *Delivering college compostition: The fifth canon* (pp.1-16). Portsmouth, NH: Boynton/Cook.

Yancey, K. B. (2009a). *Writing in the 21st century.* Urbana, Illinois: National Council of Teachers of English.

Yancey, K. B. (2009b). By any other name. *Principal Leadership,* 10(1), 26-29.

APPENDIX

Table 1. Assessments of relevance

Not relevant	… it hasn't got anything to do with it, and when I chat the grammar isn't all that good, I suppose… .
Relevant in relation to use of language	Much the same attention to it being correct but perhaps not to content … that the language flows well and so on … I'm not so bothered about that sort of thing … but they are quite like each other.
Relevant in relation to use of language and structure	… I see it as … a kind of basic learning … something you use all the time to … you do get better … or maybe not better … but you keep your basic learning up to scratch, what you once learned.
Relevant in relation to use of language, structure and content	I think I use the same approach to what I write in online fora and school assignments.

Table 2. Why students write on the Internet

Tools	I feel it's easier to keep track of… I feel myself I get better results if I can sit and write on a PC. If I use longhand I think it takes so long … like two steps forward and one back… .
Texts	1. … I play paintball … sports like that … and there's a forum just for that … where I write occasionally to try to influence things, for there's a lot of talk about rules and the like … so I write a few words now and then, but not so often … just to say what I think… . 2. … I had a discussion with a journalist from VG (Norwegian newspaper) by e-mail … not so long ago, and then I wrote about four pages . . on the PC, like, and sent it … (… …) about … the financial crisis.
Networks/ audiences	… You play, you die too, don't you, you get shot … and while you're waiting for the next round you sit and chat … the people you talk to in their ears are usually the same people you're on the team with and such like … maybe friends you have a lot of contact with … but all the other folks that happen to be online you talk to… write … but it's very short in a way, like in an ad … lots of abbreviations… . If you open your inbox and find 10 e-mails you have to answer them all … and then there'a lot of writing … (but) if there's nothing there … and no messages on Facebook … (then) it's not true that I get itchy fingers to send messages on Facebook just so's to get enough answers … then it can be ZERO… . I've written quite a lot on my blog, actually … Yes, I would have written less (if I didn't use the Internet) because I wouldn't have written blogs, for example, last year. No, I guess I wouldn't have done that. I wouldn't have sat down and written … the same … in a book. …

Table 3. Why students don't write on the Internet

Tools	1. I can write, sure, (but) if I could choose I'd rather .. what can I say ... be told what to write ... (rather) than writing it myself ... I don't feel I express myself better in writing than in speaking... . 2. S. Even if I have my PC beside me, I may still choose to write in longhand. Int. Really, how come? S. I don't really know (laughter) depends on my mood, maybe... .
Texts	It's easy to lose concentration when you're using a PC. Because you have so many more choices, don't you? I look at the people round about me with their PCs ... lots of games and websites flying up and down ... and l really feel that when you're at school you should be doing school work and not wasting time with other things.
Networks/ audiences	A problem when you're on the PC is that you have so many other things to, like, distract you, yes ,you could be sitting there with the browser open while you're writing and suddenly there's someone talking to you on MSN, or... something or other, isn't that so ... so there are a lot of like ... distractions ... on the PC. 1. ... I found out that when I spent my evenings chatting on MSN with my schoolmates about this and that ... when I came to school the next day and had half-an-hour to kill ... everything had been said ... there didn't really seem to be much more to talk about ... so I guess it was in my last year at high school that I cut out all those kinds of social media... . 2. ... the worst thing I know ... absolutely the worst I know is those Facebook blogs where people just sit and natter on about their own lives ... and I'm sure it's interesting for friends ... and family and so on, but it's of no interest to me.

CHAPTER 14.

SPONSORING "GREEN" SUBJECTS: THE WORLD BANK'S 2009 YOUTH ESSAY CONTEST

Anne E. Porter
University of Michigan-Ann Arbor

In recent decades, writing scholars have underscored the ways in which writing is facilitated and constrained by social actors. So-called "original" works have been shown to bear the traces of intertextual influence, and an array of rhetorical conventions, including those of genre, have been shown to delimit and enable creativity (Bawarshi, 2003). Every text is necessarily influenced by its context, and, as Brandt (2001) reminds us, sponsors of literacy frequently play a key role in defining the terms by which writers write. In this chapter, I suggest some of the ways in which a powerful literacy sponsor co-constructs specific identifications and forms of discourse.

Brandt (2001) was among the first to foreground the issue of literacy sponsorship among compositionists, suggesting that "it is useful to think about who or what underwrites occasions of literacy learning and use" (p. 19). Brandt defines literacy sponsors as "any agents, local or distant, concrete or abstract, who enable, support, teach, and model, as well as recruit, regulate, suppress, or withhold, literacy—and gain advantage by in in some way" (p. 19). My analysis centers on an essay competition sponsored by the World Bank, a large multilateral lending institution that funds development projects throughout the world. In this study, I focus on a particular literacy event–an international essay competition that each year solicits and receives essays from 18 to 25 year-olds from all over the world. I draw on Heath's (2001) definition of a literacy event as "any occasion in which a piece of writing is integral to the nature of the participants' interactions and their interpretative processes" (p. 445). Using methods of textual and rhetorical analysis, I describe (1) how the contest elicited certain kinds of identification and (2) how the winning essayists responded to the problem/ solution prompt.

THE WORLD BANK AS A LITERACY SPONSOR

In 2009, the World Bank held a Youth Essay Contest, inviting submissions on the topic of "The Next Generation of Green Entrepreneurs." Young people from all over the world—ages 18 to 25—were invited to submit essays over the web in English, French, or Spanish in response to the following questions: "How does climate change affect you?" and "How can you tackle climate change through youth-led solutions?" Nearly 2,500 college age youth from over 150 countries participated in the contest, and 95% of them, according to a report available on the Bank's website, hailed from less industrialized or "developing" countries. The eight winning essayists all present moving testimony about how climate change is affecting their communities and offer ideas for addressing the problem. This chapter considers some of the ways in which their responses were shaped and constrained by the contest "call" and prompt.

The World Bank may at first appear an unlikely literacy sponsor. The Bank is not a Bank in the traditional sense, even though most of the money it lends comes from bonds sold on the financial markets. Instead it is a large, quasi-governmental lending organization, comprised of 184 member nations, the headquarters for which are in Washington, DC. The Bank was initially created after WWII to fund post-war reconstruction efforts, but, today, it has become one of the most important lenders to governments in the Global South. Although the Bank is perhaps best known for large infrastructure projects, it has in recent years become the "largest external (non government) funder of education" (http://www.worldbank.org). Moreover, as Wickens and Sandlin (2007) explain, it has recently "supplanted UNESCO ... as the primary funding agent for international literacy programs" (p. 277).

The Bank held its first essay contest in 2004, and, each year since, has chosen a topic related to social or economic development. In 2009, the contest theme coincided with efforts by the Bank to embrace the rhetoric of environmentalism. In a recent ethnography of the Bank, Goldman (2005) argues that environmental discourse has played an increasingly central role in the Bank's public relations. According to Goldman, the "greening" of the Bank's discourse seems to have assuaged the concerns of many of its most vocal critics. Goldman sees the Bank's "green neoliberalism" as a pragmatic response to the criticisms heaped upon the Bank during the 1980s and 90s, when protestors were denouncing the punitive impact of the Bank's structural adjustment policies on the poor. Within the space of two decades, the Bank's environmental discourse has transformed the public perception of the development project into one that is believed to be compatible with the goals and aims of environmentalism. For Goldman, the Bank's "green neoliberalism" refers to a discursive regime that encompasses not only textual practices but also an entire knowledge-making apparatus. This "green neoliberalism" is apparent in the emphasis on entrepreneurship in the "call" for the contest—the headline for which read, "The Next Generation of Green Entrepreneurs."

THEORETICAL FRAMEWORK

I approached this analysis from the vantage point of constitutive rhetoric—a branch of rhetorical study that deals with the values and assumptions that are tacitly embedded in discourse. Constitutive appeals operate, as Burke (1969) observes, not at the level of logic, but rather via a feeling of "elation wherein the audience feels as though it were not merely receiving, but were itself creatively participating in the poet's or speaker's assertion" (p. 58). Attending to the ways that rhetoric constitutes subjectivities involves highlighting how particular subjects are interpellated by and through social practices (Althusser, 1971) and how the politics of identification are operating in any rhetorical performance (Burke, 1969). Butler calls this the regulation of subjects through regulation of "the domain of the sayable" (p. 133); through rituals, habits, and conventions—including those of genre and narrative—certain kinds of speech are sponsored, while others are dissuaded. It is precisely this tacitness, this repetition, that constitutes the subject. As Charland explains, the power of constitutive rhetoric is "based in its capacity to enthrall an audience, not addressing their reasoning faculty, but poetically transforming their very experience of being" (p. 125). From this perspective, the essayists in this contest were influenced not only by this literacy event, but by this event in relation to other multiple acts of writing, and through their experience of the event as a competition, as well.

Essay contests have received little attention in the scholarly literature, despite the fact that many libraries, schools, newspapers, civic organizations, literary societies and large corporations regularly sponsor such contests. These contests are typically viewed as character-building exercises that encourage writing on issues seen as having civic merit: themes of peace and diplomacy, courage and leadership, or the commemoration of a date or figure in history. Often, these contests explicitly state goals related to the formation of character and are typically targeted at middle-school or high-school age children and young adults. Today, the fact that these contests are conducted via the World Wide Web has dramatically expanded their potential scope and reach.

METHODS

The data set for this study consisted of the essay call and prompt (see Figure 1), as well as the eight winning and finalist essays, which were available online. In this study, I relied on various methods of textual (Bazerman & Prior, 2004) and rhetorical analysis (Selzer, 2004). My analysis of the call and prompt involved examining these texts' linguistic features (e.g., terms like "green," "youth," or "entrepreneurs") to determine how they made their rhetorical appeal. I also examined aspects of the contest that "spoke" to particular audiences, such as the invitation to submit essays in English, Spanish or French. In considering who the audience may have been for these appeals, a World Bank summary report offered demographic information about the actual contest participants. I was also able to access online other needed information about the contest itself.

In narrowing my focus for my analysis of the essays, I relied on contextual information about the Bank's development agenda, along with my earlier analysis of the call and prompt. One of the rhetorical features that became evident as a result of this process was the importance of the two-part narrative structure of the prompt. This led to my examining the arrangement of ideas in the top eight essays to determine whether or not they had adopted this implied format. This involved creating an outline for each essay and recording the page numbers devoted to each section of text. This textual analysis revealed that a two-part, problem/ solution format was indeed evident in all of the winning and finalist essays. Each essay contained a section at or near the beginning which contained elaborate testimony about how climate change was affecting the essayist's community, as well as a section at or near the end in which each essayist offered their proposed solution. These two sections together made up the bulk of each of these papers. All of the papers ranged in length from seven to 16 pages, but in each case, the section on solutions was slightly longer than the section dealing the problem. Common features like these suggest that, despite significant variations in the essays, the influence of the prompt was strong in compelling a problem/ solution format in the essayists' response.

RHETORICAL ANALYSIS OF THE "CALL"

The organizers of the contest solicited essays under the following heading: "WANTED: the Next Generation of 'Green Entrepreneurs.'" This heading, which appeared in bold font on the Bank's website, did constitutive work by collapsing distinctions between youthfulness, environmentalism, and entrepreneurship. As Charland (2001) suggests, "constitutive rhetoric simultaneously presumes and asserts a fundamental collective identity for its audience, offers a narrative that demonstrates that identity, and issues a call to act to affirm that identity" (p. 125). This heading likely captured the attention of college-age readers who may have imagined themselves as fitting some combination of: "next generation," environmentalist, and/or entrepreneurial. The capitalized letters in "WANTED" might have called to mind a job ad or a poster from the American West. This set of associations might have suggested a jobseeker, a "maverick" personality, or both. Responding to this call likely represented an affirmation of this "hailed" identity and—to some degree—as acceptance of the terms within which that identity might be expressed.

The contest invited online submissions in English, Spanish, or French. In doing so, the contest appealed to youth who were able to write in one of the world languages in which the Bank's day-to-day business is conducted. Presumably not "hailed" by the call for submissions would have been those without access to the cultural capital of schooling, not literate in a world language, or on the other side of the digital divide. Also not "hailed"—or hailed with less frequency—seemed to be writers from overdeveloped or industrialized countries, representing only 5% of the submissions and one of the winners. (Incidentally, in 2009, an essayist from Australia won first place.)

The World Bank offers prizes each year for its competition, and the essayists—many of whom are from poor countries—have an especially powerful lure motivating their participation. Incentives like these can be powerful for writers, regardless of their ideological perspective. The finalist from Cameroon, for example, writes movingly about his financial struggles: "It costs a lot to obtain a college education in my country. I have had to struggle with this reality since I obtained my Baccalaureat." This writer explains that, due to his financial situation, he has "taken odd jobs during my free hours to help my family cover a number of expenses. I sell youth magazines to young people, tutor secondary school students, and very often manage a 'call-box' at the university. In November 2007, a relative suggested that I drive his taxi to make some money," this essayist writes. This essayist speaks to some of the lived realities that may have influenced some of these writers' motivation to compete. In this way, the prizes ($3,000 for first place, $2,000 for second place, and $1,000 for third) may have provided a strong incentive for writers, not only for compliance with the essay requirements but also for loyalty to the sponsoring institution. As Brandt (2001) observes "[a]lthough the interests of the sponsor and the sponsored do not have to converge (and in fact, may conflict), sponsors nevertheless set the terms for access to literacy and wield powerful incentives for compliance and loyalty (p. 19).

Aspects of the event itself suggest preferred set of attributes and values for respondents. In conducting this event as a "competition," the Bank implicitly reinforced the value of competitiveness (in contrast to collaboration or cooperation). This value, believed to underlie philosophies of the "free market," is consistent with the Bank's neoliberal agenda, which emphasizes privatization and deregulation. As scholars of critical cultural studies point out, neoliberalism implies not only an economic agenda but also a "a frame of mind, a cultural

> **WANTED: The Next Generation of "Green" Entrepreneurs**
> Climate change has been identified as one of the biggest global threats of our time. Scientists agree that global warming and extreme climate phenomena can be increasingly attributed to human activity—in particular, heavy emission of greenhouse gases, such as carbon dioxide, resulting from industrial processes.
>
> Solutions to those pressing problems could lie in the rapidly growing "green economy": environmentally sustainable enterprises, technological innovations (new sources of clean, renewable energy), energy efficiency measures, economic incentives for low-carbon choices, etc. How can youth contribute?
>
> The Essay Competition 2009 invites youth to share ideas on:
> How does climate change affect you? How can you tackle climate change through youth-led solutions?
> Please answer both questions:
>
> How does climate change affect you, your country, town or local community? How do you think it will affect you in the future? Think about the consequences for employment, health, security and other areas of your life.
>
> 1. What can you do, working together with your peers, to address the problem of climate change in your country, town or local community? Think specifically about the role of youth-led initiatives in the "green economy."
> 2. What can you do, working together with your peers, to address the problem of climate change in your country, town or local community? Think specifically about the role of youth-led initiatives in the "green economy."

Figure 1. Contest call and prompt for the World Bank's 2009 Youth Essay Competition

dynamic, an entrepreneurial personality type, and a rule of law that penetrates the most intimate relations people have with each other, state apparatuses, and their natural environments" (Goldman, 8). Competitive entrepreneurship thus comes to stand for an identity or social orientation that demands that individuals monitor and assess themselves based on values of productivity and self-discipline (Petersen & O'Flynn 2007).

In inviting submissions on the theme of "green entrepreneurship," the Bank was issuing a call to youth who might identify both with the sense of themselves as environmentalists and as entrepreneurs. Additionally, in making this linkage, the Bank encouraged these essayists towards a particular articulation of the issue—one that saw entrepreneurship as not only compatible with environmentalism, but as the preferred solution for climate change. The ordering of the questions, additionally, invited a narrative structure that conformed to this telling—a problem/solution trajectory that culminated in a business model for saving the planet. By structuring the essay task in this way, the Bank issued a powerful incentive for respondents to write the environmental story that it wished to tell.

RHETORICAL ANALYSIS OF THE PROMPT

The prompt for the 2009 World Bank essay contest begins with a brief paragraph that provides some background on the issue of climate change for potential essayists. Many essay prompts contain such a preface, which is typically brief, but provides a backdrop to the question that follows. The first sentence of this statement, which was italicized in the original, read as follows:

> Climate change has been identified as one of the biggest global threats of our time. Scientists agree that global warming and extreme climate phenomena can be increasingly attributed to human activity—in particular, heavy emission of greenhouse gases, such as carbon dioxide, resulting from industrial processes.

Given the debates that still surround the issue, this statement is remarkable for its acknowledgement in 2009 that "scientists agree" not only that climate change is real but also that it has been identified as one of the "biggest global threats of our time." Also remarkable, given the reluctance by some to acknowledge anthropogenic warming, is the explicit acknowledgement by the World Bank that "industrial processes" have played a decisive role. At the same time, the use of the passive voice (*has been identified, can be attributed*) implies that the stance of the author is unclear. Moreover, the problem of attributing causality to "extreme climate phenomena" becomes apparent in the clause qualifying "human activity." Although the sentence ultimately ascribes causality to "heavy emission of greenhouse gases ... resulting from industrial processes" —this chain of qualifiers leaves the relationship between "human activity" and "industrial processes" indeterminate. Additionally, the precise industries, processes, and geographic regions most responsible for greenhouse gas emissions remain unnamed. Such instances of rhetorical indeterminacy leave questions of responsibility unnecessarily vague.

The statement continues, suggesting that

> [s]olutions to those pressing problems could lie in the rapidly growing 'green economy: environmentally sustainable enterprises, technological innovations (new sources of clean, renewable energy), energy efficiency measures, economic incentives for low-carbon choices, etc.

The use of "could" in this sentence suggests a modest recognition that solutions might not lie in the "green economy" at all. It even suggests a certain humility and hopefulness in the face of these "pressing problems." And while it draws on the language of business to posit various examples of possible "solutions" — ranging from "sustainable enterprise" to "technological innovations" to "economic incentives" —their presentation as a kind of brainstorming list suggests the designers of the question were not tied to any particular one of these. At the same time, the requirement that the solution be a "green economy" solution is strongly implied.

The paragraph ends with the question, "How can youth contribute?" This question has the positive tone of consulting young people and encouraging their participation in problem-solving. Like any good essay question, it might be argued, this paragraph ends in a way that makes the question relevant for 18 to 25 year-olds, and engages their motivation to write. This question echoes a theme that has run through all of the contests since 2004 when they began: all of the contests have focused on the initiative of young people and their shared ownership of the difficult problems facing society. In its first contest, for instance, the Bank sought submissions on "Radically Reducing World Poverty." And, in 2011, essayists wrote on the issue of "Youth Migration." On the one hand, this rhetoric of "owning the problems" suggests that college age youth have a responsibility to demonstrate leadership. On the other hand, it may have the unintended effect of blaming of the victim: young people are charged with accepting responsibility for the complex problems that earlier generations have created and been unable or unwilling to solve.

The difficulty of this positioning is apparent in the essay by the finalist from Cameroon. This writer begins with chilling testimony about the unprecedented flooding that is affecting his community, recounting how "[f]looding has become the daily plight of my family and the residents of my neighborhood."

"People have stopped keeping track of cases," he says, recounting the loss of life and increase in water-borne disease resulting from torrential rains and landslides. But the essayist adopts a confessional tone in blaming himself for his contribution to climate change. He explains the harmful health and the environmental effects of "zoa-zoa fuel, a mixture of gas and oil" purchased inexpensively on the black market and used by taxi drivers in his city of Yaounde. This writer describes the strong sense of guilt that he carries about having engaged in this practice. As a taxi driver who has resorted to the use of zoa-zoa, he tells of how he first "came upon the map of global warming on the Internet. … The accompanying testimony sent shivers up my spine. I realized the extent to which I am utterly vulnerable to climate change and the extent to which I bear responsibility for it. … Since that time, I promised myself that if I could acknowledge my culpability, then I could also reverse the trend." The bind in which this essayist finds himself is exacerbated by the use of the second person address and the emphasis in question number two, which might be paraphrased as "What can **you** do to fight global warming?" This essayist may have perceived the prompt's direct address as implying responsibility or singling him out personally for blame.

Problem/ Solution Structure of the Prompt

The prompt reads, "The Essay Competition 2009 invites youth to share ideas on: **How does climate change affect you? How can you tackle climate change through youth-led solutions?**" (bold in original) These questions are briefly elaborated upon in the instructions that follow, which remind the respondent to "Please answer both questions." This brief reminder implicitly introduces a two-part narrative structure that serves as a cue about what will be valued in responses. Essayists are asked to consider: "How does climate change affect you, your country, town or local community?" And "What can you do, working together with your peers, to address the problem of climate change in your country, town or local community?"

This narrative ordering not only serves to structure the responses, but it also primes the respondents to identify with the given framework. As Goldman suggests, the greening of the Bank's reputation requires, to some degree, listening to global constituents who have first-hand knowledge of the realities of environmental devastation. The first question contains an acknowledgment that climate change is real, and accepts this premise as its point of departure. With this move, the Bank is able to disarticulate itself from those who would deny climate change and lay the groundwork for an identification with environmentalism. At the same time, it is the second question that sets certain limits upon that environmentalism. These are limits to which, given the Bank's acquiescence in the first instance, the interpellated group is more likely to be predisposed.

The panel of experts who judged the essays included one representative from the National Autonomous University in Mexico (UNAM), one from the World Bank, and six representatives of international NGO's focused on youth leadership and development issues: Africa Leadership Forum, AIESEC Student Forum, The Glocal Forum, Junior Achievement Worldwide, AIESEC International, and Conciencia Association (from Argentina). When the panel of experts met to select the winners of the contest, they awarded the first prize of $3,000 to a young essayist from Australia who wrote a "Blueprint for Green Schools." The second place essayist, who won $2,000, was from Mexico, and wrote on "The Repercussions of Climate Change on the Rarámuri People." Third place, with a prize of $1,000, went to an essayist from Ghana, who offered green solutions at the Community, National and International Levels. Presumably, each of these winning essays demonstrated successful adherence to the "Selection Criteria" announced by the judges, who evaluated the essays based on "their structure and coherence, originality and creativity and the use of thoughtful and concrete proposals/ examples." But, as is suggested in the following analysis, their narrative framing was additionally in keeping with the order suggested by the prompt.

TEXTUAL ANALYSIS OF THE ESSAYS

Problem/Solution Format of the Essays

Because my rhetorical analysis of the prompt suggested that the two-part structure may have played an important role in framing the essay question, my analysis of the essays looked at the sequential arrangement of ideas. I recorded the page numbers devoted to each section of text and sought to determine whether "climate change" was explicitly identified as the focus of the first (problem) part of each essay. Additionally, I sought to determine whether "solutions" were the explicit focus at the end of the essay. This analysis revealed that all of the essays explicitly identified "climate change" as the problem, along with a number of related environmental issues (deforestation, carbon emissions, pollution, and industrial development, for instance). These sections, in every case, appeared at or near the beginning of each essay. Additionally, all of the essays identified solutions in lengthier sections that came at or near the end. Table 2 provides key citations from each section and page numbers that demonstrate how each problem section appeared sequentially prior to the solution proposed.

Sponsoring "Green" Subjects

Table 1. Problem/solution format of the essays

Title	Problem	Solution
"Blueprint for Green Schools"	"Climate Change in Australia and its Impacts in the Future" pp. 3-5	"Green Schools" Solution pp. 5-10
"The Repercussions of Climate Change on the Indigenous Raramuri People: Local Actions, Global Benefits"	On Impact of Development on the Raramuri and "Effects of Climate Change" pp. 2-3	"How Can We Address Climate Change … ?" (e.g Biointensive Orchards) pp. 6-9
"Greening the Ghanaian Youth"	On Climate Change & "Recent Weather Extremes" pp. 1-3	"The Practical[] Green Solutions" pp. 3-8
"Climate Change is the Defining Issue of Our Time"	Climate Change Impacts to "my city and life" pp. 1-4	"Green Taxi Campaign" pp. 5-9
"Climate Change: A Challenge for Humanity"	"Overview—the current situation with climate change" pp. 4-8	"The Current Economic Model and the Challenge for the Generation of Green Entrepreneurs" including "University for Humanity" pp. 8-15
"Climate Change—An Explosive Long Bill the Earth's Generations Must Pay"	"Deforestation in Indonesia" p. 2 and "Climate Change Does Affect My Country" pp. 3-6	"Youth-the Now Green Generation" —Public Awareness pp. 6-10
"Youth Participation in Green Endeavors" and green initiatives pp. 4-7	"Cebu's Climate Change Crisis" pp. 3-5	"Solutions Offered by Cebuano Youth" and other initiatives pp. 5-9 "STEP UP" initiative pp. 9-12
"Go Green—The New Mantra"	The impact of "Global Warming" on Hindu spirituality p. 1; "The Global Crisis" p. 2; and "The Indian Scenario" p. 3	"Youth Participation in Green Endeavors" and green initiatives pp. 4-7

Although all of the descriptions of climate change as the problem had their own regional or geographical emphases, and some of these descriptions were preceded by a title page, outline, abstract, preface, or summary, all of these essays located their descriptions of climate change as the problem close to or at the beginning of the essay. Each of these descriptions, additionally, ranged

261

from two to four pages in length and appeared sequentially before the author's proposed solutions. In three cases, these sections were separated by brief transitional sections in which the author described the role of youth in green initiatives, generally, or reflected on fieldwork, for instance. But in all of the eight winning and finalist essays, the detailed description of the problem of climate change appeared prior to sections devoted explicitly to solutions. In the solution sections, the degree of elaboration varies, but all of the solutions sections range in length from three to seven pages.

Descriptions of the Problem: Climate Change

Each of the essays begins with detailed and often moving descriptions based on the author's own research into how climate change is affecting their country or locality. The first place winner, for instance, writes of "ferocious bushfires," "flash flooding and king tides" that have destroyed entire townships and made "the northern State of Queensland into an officially declared disaster zone." She explains that her country, Australia, is "the driest inhabited continent on earth and is therefore particularly vulnerable to the negative effects of climate change." The second place winner, too, describes the impact of climate change on his country. He begins by explaining that 60% of families that he visited in the indigenous community of Huiyochi in the Sierra Tarahumara have been affected by an overall increase in temperature, deforestation, drought, and barren farmland. Many of them had to leave ancestral lands and find unskilled jobs, few of which are available. As he puts it, "The effects of climate change are not only the change in the environment, but also the severe social repercussions. Some of the impacts include migration, malnutrition, and drug trafficking."

The third place winner writes of his experience as a volunteer with the relief efforts in Ghana, after a period of severe flooding caused by unusual climatic conditions. He writes of the poor conditions in hospitals, of communities affected by the lack of electricity, food and water shortages, and cholera. This writer conducted interviews and surveys and writes, "One gentleman I interviewed said that before, it was good to be back home in his village but now, the weather conditions do not favor farming... ." Each of the essayists proceed in this way, by offering climate change testimony from his/her unique perspective. Then, each essayist offers a proposal to address the problem, following the sequence implicit in the prompt—which consisted of two consecutive questions and seemed to imply a narrative trajectory culminating in "youth-led," "green," and/or "entrepreneurial" solutions. These solutions, as indicated by the third column in Table 1, ranged from "green schools" to biointensive orchards to public awareness campaigns.

RESULTS

This study suggests that, in the 2009 contest, the influence of the prompt was strong in compelling certain identifications and forms of discourse. As we have seen, the contest call and prompt encouraged "green entrepreneurial" identifications, and, in their responses, all of the essayists took up the implicit problem/solution format of the prompt. At the same time, however, it would be hasty to conclude that the World Bank entirely determined or dictated the essays' ideological content. While I do not have the space here to report on my analysis of the student essays, several did indeed depart from "youth-led," "green" and/or "entrepreneurial" solutions. Thus, while the influence of a literacy sponsor may be strong in compelling particular identifications and generic formats, it would be inaccurate to conclude that this influence was equally decisive in determining content.

DISCUSSION

As this analysis suggests, essay contests comprise a productive site for analyzing the shaping force of genre, literacy sponsorship, and ideological interpellation. Writers both compose and are composed through their literacy practices, and one of the principal ways by which subjects are constituted is via the workings of genre. As Miller (1984) suggests, all genres should be seen in relation to their collectively embedded, social motives. Genres can also be seen, as Berkenkotter and Huckin (1995) suggest, as tools of social or distributed cognition. Genres focus the attention of writers and, in so doing, shape writers' subjectivities and epistemologies. Writers therefore encounter the shaping power of genre in numerous contexts for writing—not only essay contests. As Bawarshi (2003) insists, "[g]enres are defined as much by the actions they help individuals perform as by the desires and subjectivities they help organize" (p. 78). Genres co-constitute the subject, just as they participate in constructing the writer's positionality in relation to the topic at hand. As we have seen, the influence that sponsors may wield in determining these aspects of the writing task can be significant.

One of the remarkable aspects of the 2009 essay contest was that the World Bank provided a necessary forum for an emerging genre: the climate change testimonial. At the same time, this emerging genre was embedded within a broader narrative structure: that of the problem/solution format. While problem/solution formats are not intrinsically a matter for concern, it is worth noting that Li (2009) has pointed to several problems with this format in the practice of writing Environmental Impact Statements—which since 1989 have become "a requirement for all World Bank-financed projects" (p. 222). Here it is worth noting that Carolyn Miller expressed similar hesitations about environmental impact statements in her well-known (1984) article, "Genre as Social Action." One of the consequences of documenting environmental impact has been to keep environmental risk assessment "manageable." (Li, 2009; Goldman 2005). As Li reminds us, "as long as they are "manageable" risks, they are not an impediment to ... development" (p. 228).

Among the issues that complicate the effectiveness of the environmental assessment process, Li finds, are the requirements of the format itself. By definition, Environmental Impact Assessment necessitates that for every risk identified, a solution is articulated. Furthermore, these solutions are limited by the fact that the studies are conducted by the very entities who have a vested interest in seeing these projects go forward. Li's study of the process in the case of a proposed expansion of mining in Peru demonstrates that these conflicts of interest can lead to ignoring long term health and environmental risks. Her description of the potential problems with this problem/solution format suggests that we should be attentive to its limitations. Additionally, the formal similarities between Environmental Impact Statements and the essays generated in the World Bank Contest suggest some of the ways in which writers may be tacitly inducted into ways of knowing endorsed by the Bank.

CONCLUSION

In conclusion, this analysis underscores the need for those who sponsor or design writing tasks to reflect carefully upon the ideological and epistemological assumptions that underpin those tasks. So, too, must writers (and those who rely on the knowledge that they produce) attend critically to the assumptions implicit in a task. Such reflection is necessary because writing tasks influence not only our ways of thinking but also our very identities, our ways of knowing, and our ways of feeling, perceiving, and acting in the world. In the World Bank's 2009 essay contest, respondents were encouraged to identify as the "Next Generation of Green Entrepreneurs" and to tell a story that posited entrepreneurial solutions to the problem of climate change. While any such urging towards a particular identity or narrative deserves our close examination, in the case of an international funder of literacy and development programs, it is especially pressing that we consider the transnational, political and ecological dimensions of this influence.

REFERENCES

Althusser, Louis. (1971). Ideology and ideological state apparatuses (Notes towards an investigation). *Lenin and philosophy and other essays.* New York: Monthly Review Press.

Bawarshi, Anis. (2003). *Genre and the invention of the writer.* Logan, UT: Utah State University Press.

Bazerman, C., & Prior, P. (2004). *What writing does and how it does it: An introduction to analyzing texts and textual practices.* New York: Lawrence Erlbaum.

Berkenkotter, C., & Huckin, T. N. (1995). *Genre knowledge in disciplinary communication: Culture/cognition/ power.* Mahwah, NJ: Lawrence Erlbaum.

Brandt, Deborah. (2001). *Literacy in American lives.* Cambridge, UK: Cambridge University Press.

Burke, K. (1969). *A rhetoric of motives.* Berkeley: University of California Press.

Butler, J. (1997). *Excitable speech.* New York: Routledge.

Charland, M. (2001). Constitutive rhetoric. In T. O. Sloane (Ed.), *Encyclopedia of rhetoric.* Oxford University Press.

Goldman, M. (2005). *Imperial nature: The World Bank and struggles for social justice in the age of globalization.* New Haven, CT: Yale University Press.

Heath, S. B. (2001). Protean shapes in literacy events: Ever-shifting oral and literate traditions. In E. Cushman, E. R. Kintgen, B. M. Kroll, & M. Rose (Eds.), *Literacy: A critical sourcebook* (pp. 443-466). Boston: Bedford/St. Martin's.

Li, Fabiana. (2009). Documenting accountability: Environmental impact assessment in a Peruvian mining project. *Political and Legal Anthropology Review, 32*(2), 218-236.

Miller, Carolyn R. (1984). Genre as social action. *Quarterly Journal of Speech. 70,* 151-167.

Petersen, E. B., & O'Flynn, G. (2007). Neoliberal technologies of subject formation: A case study of the Duke of Edinburgh's award scheme. *Critical Studies in Education, 48*(2), 197- 211.

Selzer, J. (2004). Rhetorical analysis: Understanding how texts persuade readers. In C. Bazerman & P. Prior (Eds.), *What writing does and how it does it: An introduction to analyzing texts and textual practices* (pp. 279-307). New York: Lawrence Erlbaum.

Wickens, C. M., & Sandlin, J. M. (2007). Literacy for what? Literacy for whom? The politics of literacy education and neocolonialism in UNESCO- and World Bank- sponsored literacy programs. *Adult Education Quarterly, 57*(4), 275-292.

World Bank. (2010). *The World Bank 2009 essay competition*. Retrieved from http://www.essaycompetition.org/

World Bank London Office. *Report on the 2009 international essay competition* (Report prepared by Anna Kuznicka, Consultant, External Affairs). Retrieved from http://www.essaycompetition.org/index 2009_1

World Bank Group. (n.d.). *About us*. Retrieved from http://www.worldbank.org

CHAPTER 15.
METAPHORS OF WRITING AND INTERSECTIONS WITH JAMAICAN MALE IDENTITY

Carmeneta Jones and Vivette Milson-Whyte
The University of the West Indies, Jamaica

Over the years, Jamaican male students' achievement in different intellectual activities has been on the decline.[1] Research findings tend to highlight this recurring theme (Bailey, 2003; Bryan & Shaw, 2002; Chevannes, 1999; Evans, 1999; Evans 2001; Miller, 1991), with issues related to Jamaican male students' use of oral and written English in formal settings being an ongoing concern.[28] In her work on gender sensitive education in Jamaica, Bailey (2003) demonstrated that attesting to the problem are the results of local examinations such as the Grade Four Literacy Test and Grade Six Achievement Test for primary school students and the results in the regional Caribbean Secondary Examination Certificate (CSEC). In fact, making reference to the results of the Grade 6 Communication Task (a written examination) results in 1999 and 2000, the Test Unit at the Ministry of Education, Youth and Culture [MOEYC] revealed that the national average percent mark for each year was 60 and 43.25 for females, and 58.75 and 47 for males, respectively. A comparison of these results for the two years for males and females reveals a downward trend in the grade six students' performance in writing. A similar trend was also noted by the MOEYC (2001) for the CSEC English Language results for the year 2000. Of the 16, 830 females and 9, 647 males who sat the exam, 8,221 females and 3,490 males were successful. This means that the overall percentage was 44 and the pass rates for males and females were less than 50%—boys' being 36%.

The dismal results of the Grade 6 Communication Task and the CSEC English language examinations taken by Jamaican students became push factors for the Ministry of Education, the main stakeholder of the country's education system. It responded to the issue by formulating a language policy in which it was noted that, "The unsatisfactory performance of students in language and literacy at all levels of the Jamaican education system, and its accompanying effects on language competence ... the potential for human development in the wider society have potentially been matters of concern" (MOEYC, 2001, para. 1).

Moreover, the poor performance has implications for those students who intend to study at the tertiary level, especially for those who wish to be accepted at the university where the research took place. As in other places such as Nigeria (Fakeye & Ogunsiji, 2009) where English is the language of academe, in Jamaica, English proficiency is a strong predictor and determinant of academic achievement for males and females. Indeed, English is one of the subjects students are required to pass to gain entry to university (Dyche, 1996). Furthermore, having entered university, despite their gender and specified areas of study, all students are expected to demonstrate competence in written communication.

Research and observation suggest that males experience challenges at the university level. Bailey (2003) found that at the higher education level in Jamaica, it has become apparent that males' achievement in literacy-oriented tasks is declining. Bailey also reported that Jamaican males are less represented in tertiary level education and that their academic achievement is lower than that of their female counterparts. As teachers and coordinators in a compulsory university writing course, we observed male students' under-participation and underachievement, with the statistical data from the results of writing courses seeming to accentuate the time-driven issue. For example, in the second semester of the school year 2009-2010, of the 691 students who registered to take a first-year writing course we teach in introduction to academic writing, only 194 (28%) were males. Of the 194 males, 186 (95%) actually started the course and of this number, 55 (30%) were not successful. A reader may say that 30% is not significant; however, their final marks ranged from 27% to 38%. Additionally, a significant percentage of the males scored low grades ranging from a bare pass of 40 to 48.

It can be extrapolated from the research findings and observations in the Jamaican context that one issue concerning the island's males is underachievement in writing (Bailey, 2003; Bryan & Shaw, 2002; Chevannes, 1999; Evans, 1999; Evans 2001; Figueroa, 2000; Miller, 1991; Moey, C., 2001; Parry, 2000). Indeed, writing—considered the "quintessential representation of thought" (Brand, 1987, p. 436) and the principal way in which scholarship is demonstrated—seems to be the most challenging task for some Jamaican males. In response to this problem, researchers have tried to determine the various factors which contribute to the difficulties males experience when they are required to write. The research tells us that the problem may be related to how boys are socialized (Bailey & Brown, 1999; Chevannes, 1999; Figueroa, 2000), to boys' fear of and dislike for writing and the misconception that it is a feminine activity (Jones, 2009), to the eventual marginalization of males (Miller, 1991), to teachers' preferential treatment of boys and girls, teaching methodology and students' interest (Evans, 1999) or to lack of models (Bryan, 2010).

It is clear that, for Jamaica, the issues are multi-layered. However, this problem is not peculiar to Jamaica, given the well-established tradition of research into gender and written literacy elsewhere (Bleach, 1998; Cole, 1997; Graves, 1973; Millard, 1997; Newkirk, 2000; Slavkin; 2001). Some of these researchers have explained the differences in performance based on differences in gender (Slavkin, 2001) and on males and females being "differently literate" (Millard, 1997). Others, such as Newkirk have attempted to explain the "gap in performance" based on male students' perception of "school defined literacy as excluding—or even dismissing—their own narrative preferences" leading them to "conclude early on that proficiency in school-based writing is more 'natural' for girls" (p. 295).

Ultimately, what the statistics and studies from Jamaica and elsewhere did not help us to understand was what accounted for the writing problems male students contend with *in the university setting*—specifically in the courses we teach. In our search, we were not able to locate research that focused on Jamaican male university students' writing. Admittedly, research done by Milson-Whyte (2008a, 2008b) addressed writing instruction for Jamaican university students, but this was not gender-specific. And Bailey's (2003) work did not focus specifically on writing or provide reasons for male university students' underachievement. We therefore remained concerned about males' under-participation and achievement in writing. Based on the mind-boggling issue and the dearth of research, we designed a study to provide a channel through which a selected group of Jamaican male university students from various disciplines could share their perspectives on writing prior to, during, and after their completion of one first-year writing course which introduced them to academic writing requirements.

THEORETICAL FRAMEWORK

WRITING FROM DIFFERENT LENSES

There is no doubt that writing is an important part of university studies (Bazerman, 2007; Hayes, 1996; Haynes, 1996; Kalikokha, 2008; Lavelle & Zuercher, 2001). Writing, like many tasks, entails a step-by-step developmental process (Hayes, 2000; Graves, 1994). For Elbow (1998), this process is dual in that "… writing calls on the ability to create words and ideas out of yourself, but it also calls on the ability to criticize them in order to decide which one to use" (p. 7). Cramer (2001) suggested that writing stimulates one's thought processes. He explained that, "Five characteristics of writing influence thinking. Writing is visible, permanent, active, precise and focusing" (p. 3). It can be deduced from these characteristics that writing requires engagement of the *self: the emotional self, the intellectual self, the critical self*—and these *selves* are linked to identity.

THEORIES OF IDENTITY

To understand male university students as writers, we considered male identities. Making reference to research done on social identity theory in psychology, sociology and communication, Ting-Toomey (1999) stated that "individuals bring their sense of 'self-image' or 'identity' to any type of communicative encounter" (p. 26). She further explained that self-image refers to how people view themselves and that this *self-view* has a strong bearing on "cultural, personal, situational and relational factors" (p. 26). She classified these factors as primary identities and situational identities. These identities which can be viewed through cultural, ethnic, gender, and personal lenses are integral to the construction of the self and the socialization process.

Situational identities which change according to factors such as context, purpose and needs, comprise role identity, relational identity, face work identity and symbolic interactional identity (Ting-Toomey, 1999). It can be deduced that all learners, including male university students are multifaceted, and, ideally, this should be considered in the design and delivery of instructional programmes, including writing courses. However, as noted by Moje and Dillon (2000), research done on aspects of classroom life has not sufficiently represented learners' multiple selves/identities.

Jamaican males' performance in literacy-based subjects such as writing may be linked to gender/identity issues. Figueroa (2000) attested to this when he suggested that when Jamaican males excel in these subjects it may be viewed as gender inappropriateness but he reasoned that this is a stereotype. Jones (2009) also reported that male students who participated in a year-long literacy study perceived writing as a feminine task. Also, there are certain aspects of the socialization process in Jamaica which embrace the idea of *tying the heifer and loosing the bull*. Chevannes (1999) suggested that in some instances, Jamaican males are socialized in the street where they assume control over their lives, including the privilege to choose the activities in which they engage. In this context these Jamaican males pass on knowledge to each other using their own language and preferred mode and style of communication—oral language—*man talk*—governed by rules, values, and meanings which they conceptualize.

While problems related to writing may be considered from a group perspective, individual experiences are also revealing. Wong and Rochlen (2009) make the point that other researchers, including Addis and Mahalik, think that there is the need for "… a shift in research focus from gender differences to within group differences among men" (p. 149). This provocative thought inspired us to search for *below the surface* and *beyond the statistics* answers. Encouraged by works done by Jensen (2006), Levin and Wagner (2006), and Willox, Harper, Bridger, Morton, Orbach and Sarapura (2010), we thought that one way of accomplishing this was to ask the participants to use metaphors to express their writing realities.

METAPHOR THEORY

Lakoff and Johnson (1980) highlighted that metaphors help us to express ideas that literal words do not convey. These scholars proposed metaphors as mappings of knowledge from one conceptual domain to another. They point out that knowledge about one aspect/domain of a metaphorical mapping can help us to understand a less familiar second domain. This is because "[m]appings are not arbitrary, but grounded in the body and in everyday experience and knowledge" (Lakoff, 1993, p. 245).

Importantly, Lakoff and Johnson (1980) asserted that in allowing users to map one area of experience in terms of another that is more complex in order to enable us to understand the latter, metaphors help to convey users' experiences and how they think about those experiences. In other words, in conveying people's conceptual realities, metaphors can indicate users' attitudes to their descriptions and suggest reasons for behavior. In doing metaphor analysis, one tries to identify users' attitudes portrayed in the images by analyzing the tenor (the subject) or the vehicle (the frame or lens). In such analyses, the frequency or intensity of tenors and vehicles provides clues about users' perspectives. In our study, writing was the tenor and the vehicle was the image each participant used to describe writing/experiences.

Unlike Lakoff and Johnson (1980) who focused on how metaphors work, Sheehan (1999) argued that metaphors "serve as a basis for inventing narratives" (p. 48) because the meanings of metaphors are "as much the creation of their interpreters as their authors" (p. 47). For him "metaphors are used to urge us toward further and further invention of meaning as we play with the unexpected connectives to which metaphors draw our attention" (p. 54, emphasis in the original). The narratives that emerged from the students' images of writing provided one way of garnering specific insights into their experiences with this intellectual activity.

RESEARCH QUESTIONS

The research was guided by the following questions:
- What were the male university students' perceptions of writing prior to, during, and after taking their first-year writing course?
- In what ways do the participants' metaphors of writing intersect with their personal and situational identities?
- How can an understanding of the participants' metaphors of writing inform future practice?

METHODOLOGY

RESEARCH APPROACH

The 13-week semester-long study focused on a group of university male students' perceptions of writing. We used a phenomenological approach which "seeks to disclose and elucidate the phenomena of behaviour as they manifest themselves in their perceived immediacy" (van Kaam, as cited in Moustakas, 1994, p. 13). From the outset, we wanted to, as Purcell-Gates (2004) proposed, "understand the world from the participants' perspectives" (p. 96): we wanted to get a sense of what these male university students believed about writing in terms of its role and function in their lives and tertiary level studies. A phenomenological approach helped us "to pay ... attention to qualitative aspects" (Taylor, 2011, p. 1) of the participants' lived reality with writing and what that reality meant to them.

SETTING

The study took place at an urban, public, research-based university situated in eastern Jamaica. It offers pre-university, certificate, diploma, undergraduate, and graduate degree programmes to local, Caribbean, and international students from various socio-economic backgrounds. The university's policy stipulates that, ideally, all first-year students should take a first-year writing course.

The enrolment for the school year when the study took place (2009-2010), was 15,516 students. Of that total, 11,882 were undergraduates and 3,634 were enrolled in graduate programmes. The number of admitted first degree entrants who took first year courses was 3,684. Females account for the majority of the predominantly young student population at the university; 57% of the students in 2009-2010 were 24 years and under. Table 1 shows the population's distribution in terms of age.

Table 1. Age distribution in 2009-2010

Age	2009
Under 20	19%
20-24	38%
25-34	25%
35-49	14%
50 +	4%
Total	100%

PARTICIPANTS

All of the male students who were taught a course in academic writing by the co-researchers during the second semester of the school year 2009-2010 were invited to participate in the study. In the end, eight (8) participants whose age range was 17 to 25 years participated in the study. Five were from the Faculty of Pure and Applied Sciences, two from the Faculty of Social Sciences, and one straddled Pure and Applied Sciences and Education. Principles regarding the confidentiality of participants' responses were adhered to. Table 2 shows each participant's assigned name, discipline, and GPA obtained for the semester when the study was conducted.

Table 2. Participants' profiles

Participant	Major/Programme	GPA
Mr. Vision	Anthropology	2.20
Mr. Explorer	Psychology	1.50
Mr. Dual	Chemistry with Education	2.89
Mr. Work in Progress	Chemistry	3.23
Mr. See What I See	Alternative Energy and General Chemistry	3.23
Mr. Serenade	Mathematics/Computer Science	0.43
Mr. Amphibian	Occupational/Environmental Safety and Health	1.71
Mr. Reader-Writer	Food Chemistry	1.00

DATA COLLECTION

A variety of sources was used for the data collection. Initially, personal data were garnered when each participant completed a questionnaire called Participants' Information Preview (PIP). This source has been used successfully in

Jamaican-based research which focused on males' literacy education (Henry, 2010; Jones, 2009; Solomon, 2010). In our study participants provided data on their disciplines, emotions they associate with writing, and how they perceived writing in general and in relation to their studies prior to their engagement in a first-year writing course. Some of the questions were:

- When you think of writing or when you have to engage in a writing exercise, what kind of emotion(s) do you experience? Please explain.
- What role (s) do you believe that writing plays in the successful pursuit of your degree?
- What role does writing play in other aspects of your life?

The participants also wrote weekly reflections in which they commented on their writing experiences during the course. Some of the prompts were:

- Write down what you thought about academic writing prior to starting [the course].
- Write down what you thought you were going to do in the course regarding academic writing. /What were your expectations?
- Write down your thoughts about what you are learning or unlearning about academic writing.

Data were also gathered from individual interviews and a joint hour-long conversation/group discussion. In the interviews participants elaborated on information presented in the PIP or commented on information in their reflections. In the conversation, participants reflected on their experiences in learning about academic writing. The interviews and conversation were audio taped. It was in the conversation that participants formulated and shared their metaphors about writing. During the semester, the researchers also observed the participants in and out of classes and took anecdotal notes (see Table 3 for the timeline for data collection).

Table 3. Timeline for data collection

Data source	Date	Duration
PIP	February 2010	N/A
Interviews	March 2010	20-30 mins
Reflections	February-April 2010	N/A
Conversation	April 2010	1 hour

DATA ANALYSIS

Analyses of the participants' perceptions were done on a gradual basis, and were guided by work done by Lakoff and Johnson (1980) and Sheehan (1999).

We began this process by cross checking and interpreting information from the PIP, reflections, and audio tapes. We also met on a weekly basis to discuss what we observed in our classroom interactions with the participants and the patterns and themes which emerged from the data. In the final stages of our analyses, as we identified connections between the students' identities and their vivid descriptions of their writing experiences, the narratives surrounding each participant's metaphor of writing provided clues about the participants' varied relationships with writing and connections to their individual identities. In extrapolating meaning from the participants' perspectives, like Lakoff and Johnson (1980), we were able to discover that metaphors are multidimensional and that they can be used as tools to critically analyze human experiences—including students' individual experiences with writing.

FINDINGS

Participants' Views about Writing Prior to Taking the Course

Prior to taking their course in writing for academic purposes, the participants shared their views about writing in the PIP and expanded on these views during interviews. The following are summaries of the sentiments they expressed about writing.

- Writing is an enabler for a university degree and communicative competence (Mr. Vision)

- The writing of English, though challenging, allows you to communicate locally and internationally (Mr. Explorer).

- Manipulating objects is preferable to writing (Mr. Dual).

- Starting to write is difficult; writing is not like tackling a mathematical task (Mr. Work in Progress).

- The thought of writing produces anxiety because of ignorance about what to write and the feeling of violation experienced after completing a writing task (Mr. See What I See).

- Experiences with writing change over time. It is difficult to write outside of a comfort zone (Mr. Serenade).

- Although writing well is the key to success, it is difficult to do it and do it well. Writing is associated with pressure (Mr. Amphibian).

- Writing is a bitter/sweet experience (Mr. Reader-Writer).

Mr. Reader-Writer's description of writing as *bitter-sweet* seems to encapsulate the perceptions of the others. In numerous ways, these findings mirror the thoughts postulated by Cramer (2001) and Elbow (1998) as well as other experts that writing is a demanding cognitive task.

Prior to taking the course, the male students also declared their preferred genres of writing, and these and the emotions they experience when they are required to write are presented in Table 4.

Table 4. Participants' preferred mode of writing and emotions they feel when they write

Participant	Preferred mode of writing	Emotion(s)
Mr. Vision	Persuasion	Elation
Mr. Explorer	Persuasion	Ease
Mr. Dual	Exposition	Excitement/Frustration
Mr. Work in Progress	Exposition	No Enthusiasm
Mr. Reflector	Not sure	Anxiety
Mr. Serenade	Argument	Stress
Mr. Amphibian	Persuasion	Frustration
Mr. Reader-Writer	Narration	Dejection

The different responses are reminders that these male university students, like all human beings, are complex (Ting-Toomey, 1999) because they are unique and have different preferences and idiosyncrasies and that their emotional responses to situations and circumstances are dissimilar. The male students also shared other views about writing prior to taking their writing course. Some of these views were positive while others were negative.

Participants' Reflections on Writing During the Research Process

Findings from the participants' weekly reflections on their writing experiences during the research process are presented in the following summaries:

- Over time one can develop a positive attitude to academic writing and the writing process (Mr. Vision).

- Writing requires practice and is important for success at school and work, but it is difficult if one does not like to read (Mr. Explorer).

- Writing is a means of recording and sharing ideas. (Mr. Dual).

- Writing is a strong determinant of success (Mr. Work in Progress)

- Writing, which is linked to critical reading, is important to university education (Mr. Reflector).

- University writing is more discipline specific; it is different from that which is done in high school (Mr. Serenade).

- Writing and critical thinking are inextricably connected (Mr. Amphibian).

- Writing, like reading, is about problem solving (Mr. Reader-Writer).

These sentiments show that, as the semester progressed, the participants acknowledged the importance of writing—whether it demanded critical thinking or extensive research or prepared them for jobs, or whether they viewed it as a means of sharing knowledge and discoveries or solving problems, among others.

Students' Views of Writing after Taking the Course

After taking the course in academic writing and lauding its benefits in terms of fostering their holistic development, the participants used metaphors to describe writing in ways which seemed consistent with their perceptions of it prior to the course. A metaphorical image provides a vivid picture of participants' individual and collective, *real* realities as expressed in the conversation at the end of the study (see Figure 1).

Figure 1. Image of the participants' writing realities at the university

This graphic representation is explained in a more detailed manner in the following vignette which is a composite of findings from the focus group discussion:

> The group of first year male students attending a Jamaican university desired to arrive at Success in Academic Writing. They soon discovered that they were in a maze—a complicated set of paths, of situations and ideas, of pre-formulated requirements, rudiments, and conventions that would challenge their long-established cultural practice of controlling and practicing their style of communication (liberal man talk). This context was the opposite of their main "socializing site, the street, their comfort zone ... a male domain" (Chevannes, 1999, p. 4). In order to arrive at their final destination, these male students had to figure the best way out of the maze. Table 5 shows the participants' metaphors and additional perspectives on writing.

Table 5. Participants' metaphors of, and additional perspectives on, writing

Participant	Metaphor of writing	Additional Perspectives (s)
Mr. Vision	Journey	The writing process is a never ending journey with only room for improvement.
Mr. Explorer	A walk in the park	I don't think you can go throughout the restof your life ... without writing a proper essay ... whether for a job application or further down the line.
Mr. Dual	Double-edged sword	I think writing is basically the means by which humans become immortals. ... It's important now and it's going to be very important ... in the future.
Mr. Work in Progress	Imperfect man	Improving in writing may even lead to improvements as an individual
Mr. Reflector	Mirror	I've come a long way ... getting over my own inhibitions to writing.
Mr. Serenade	Singing	I'm seeing an improvement where my geography essay is concerned because I'm a little better equipped in terms of structuring my stuff and the whole citation thing.
Mr. Amphibian	Swimming through rough waters	I still don't have a good vibes when it comes to writing but the thought of doing it in Patois really interest me
Mr. Reader-Writer	----	--- (missed conversation)

DISCUSSION

The participants' images of writing suggest that these male students perceive writing as a complex task which causes them to experience different feelings ranging from some struggling for survival amidst the challenges and trepidation they face with writing in the academy to pleasurable encounters they enjoy when they successfully engage in the different stages of the writing process. The metaphors that the participants used to describe writing and their experiences with writing reflect a complex layering of the male students' realities, desire to control their worlds, and transformative experiences with writing.

Although the participants' metaphors are different, it is apparent that in terms of their writing realities, the male university students had something in common. Using the words of Ivanic (1998), these male students were apprentices in the academic writing class. They were in the midst of transitioning from their known territories to the unknown; from their personal/cultural identities to situational identities (Ting-Toomey, 1999). They were at the intersection of different worlds (Murphy, 2002). With new and unfamiliar contours to navigate in the writing class, these male university students had to learn new dynamics and figure strategies to succeed. These Jamaican male university students strongly made the point that although writing poses a variety of challenges for them, it is one of a number of tools that they all need to figure their way out of the *academic maze*. Whether participants began with a love for writing and confidence in their ability to write as Mr. Pathfinder did or preferred to pursue studies that require them to apply mostly numeracy-mathematical and scientific ideas and formulae as did Mr. Dual and Mr. Work in Progress, they grew to believe that this skill is vital to success in the academy.

Indeed, since like their female counterparts they are expected to write English for academic and other purposes, males need to transform their power to talk into proficiency in writing in the structured classroom setting. Although Jamaican males seem to be more comfortable in familiar settings which are driven by orality—the power, economy and buoyancy of the spoken word, the participants realized that their ability to adapt could aid their communicative competencies. When male students have developed the art of adaptability, they should be equipped to transform their way of thinking.

IMPLICATIONS, LIMITATIONS, AND FUTURE RESEARCH

As the Jamaican male students tried to reposition themselves, they were charting a course for self-transformation. Their perceptions of writing indicate a) a need to critically analyze Jamaican male students' desire to conquer and control writing in order to excel in it, b) that students' metaphors profoundly distinguish their identities as well as their views of writing, and c) that students' reflections on writing can be self-transforming. With regard to the latter, the implication of this study is that change in the way of thinking should begin with the selves of the university male students. It is incumbent on male students to accept their realities concerning writing and develop the will and the right attitude to transform those realities in such a way that they are empowered. In this age, when versatility gives university students the competitive edge, male students should transcend cultural and discipline-specific boundaries as well as interrogate and reconstruct any belief, practice, or custom which emphasizes the ideas that writing is an effeminate activity.

The findings also indicate the need for transformation in relation to instructional practices including task-type. They confirm assertions made by local researchers that some Jamaican males may wrestle with written literacy development because of the conventional and traditional modes of delivery (Chevannes, 1999; Evans 1999, 2001; Jones, 2009). The metaphors used by the participants suggest that educators need to evaluate male students' desire to conquer and dominate what they need to master for success.

Since, prior to this study, local related works focused on a mixture of Jamaican male and female students or on quantitative measures, this study, though limited in terms of time and participants, achieved its purpose of discovering insights about the qualitative aspects of the male students' writing experiences. There is no doubt that investigation of a greater magnitude, done over a longer period, would have yielded more comprehensive findings. However, considering the paucity of research on such an important educational issue, this study may be viewed as a step in the right direction to get the within group perceptions as suggested by Addis and Mahalik (as cited in Wong & Rochlen, 2009).

Finally, since the study suggests that students' metaphors of writing can provide facilitators of university writing courses with deep understanding of the multiple realities/selves which male students bring to the classroom, university educators, particularly those who teach writing, could consider combining metaphor analysis with other analytic procedures to discover more about the underlying factors which contribute to the difficulties which some male students face with writing and to help those students transition to university level writing and experience writing's transformative potential.

NOTE

1. We would like to express profound thanks to our institution for partial funding of the research on which this chapter is based and to the reviewers for their insightful comments.

REFERENCES

Bailey, B. (2003). *Gender sensitive educational policy and practice: The case of Jamaica.* Retrieved from http://unesdoc.unesco.org/images/0014/001467/146747e.pdf

Bailey, B., & Brown, M. (1999). Schooling and masculinity: Boys' perceptions of the school experience. *Caribbean Journal of Education 21*(1-2), 42-57.

Bazerman, C. (2007). Introduction. In C. Bazerman (Ed.), *Handbook of research on writing: History, society, school, individual, text* (pp. 1-4.). New York: Lawrence Erlbaum and Associates.

Bleach, K. (1998). Why the likely lads lag behind. In K. Bleach (Ed.), *Raising boys' achievement in schools* (pp.1-20). Staffordshire, UK: Trentham Books Limited.

Brand, A. G. (1987). The why of cognition: Emotion and the writing process. *College Composition and Communication, 38*(4), 436-442.

Bryan, B. (2010). *Between two grammars: Research and practice for language learning and teaching in a Creole-speaking environment.* Kingston, Jamaica: Ian Randle

Bryan, B., & Shaw, G. (2002). Gender, literacy and language learning in Jamaica: Considerations from the literature. *Caribbean Journal of Education, 24*(1), 23-40).

Chevannes, B. (1999). What you sow is what you reap: Violence and the construction of male identity in Jamaica. *Current Issues in Comparative Education, 2*(1), 1-9.

Cramer, R. (2001). *Creative power: The nature and nurture of children's writing.* New York: Longman.

Cole, N. (1997). *The ETS gender study: How females and males perform in educational settings.* Princeton, NJ: Educational Testing Service.

Dyche, C. (1996). Writing proficiency in English and academic performance: The University of the West Indies, Mona. In P. Christie (Ed.), *Caribbean language issues: Old and new* (pp.143-148). Kingston, Jamaica: The University of the West Indies Press.

Elbow, P. (1998). *Writing with power: Techniques for mastering the writing process.* New York: Oxford University Press.

Evans, H. (1999). *Gender and achievement in secondary education in Jamaica.* (WorkingPaper No. 2). Kingston, Jamaica:Policy Development Unit Planning Institute of Jamaica.

Evans, H. (2001). *Inside Jamaican schools.* Kingston, Jamaica: University of the West Indies Press.

Fakeye, D. O., & Ogunsiji, Y. (2009). English language proficiency as predictor of academic achievement among EFL students in Nigeria. *Journal of Scientific Research, 30*(3), 490-495.

Figueroa, M. (2000). Making sense of male experience: The case of academic underachievement in the English-speaking Caribbean. *IDS Bulletin, 31*(2). United Kingdom: University of Angila.

Graves, D. (1973). Sex differences in children's writing. *Elementary English, 50*(7), 1101-1106.

Graves, D. (1994). *A fresh look at writing*. Portsmouth, NH: Heinemann.

Hayes, J. R. (2000). A new framework for understanding cognition and affect in writing. In R. Indrisano & J. R. Squire (Eds.), *Perspectives on writing: Research, theory, and practice* (pp. 6-44). Newark, DE: Guilford.

Haynes, C. (1996). *Interdiscilinary writing and the undergraduate experience: A four- year- writing plan proposal.* Retrieved from http://www.units.muohio.edu/aisorg/pubs/issues/14_haynes.pdf

Henry, J. (2010). An investigation into the responses of boys to arts-based literacy instruction (Unpublished master's thesis), University of the West Indies, Kingston. Jamaica.

Ivanic, R. (1998). *Writing and identity: The discoursal construction of identity in academic writing*. Amsterdam: John Benjamin's.

Jensen, D. F. N. (2006). Metaphors as bridge to understanding educational and social contexts. *International Journal of Qualitative Methods, 5*(1). Retrieved from http://www.ualberta.ca/~iiqm/backissues/5_1/PDF/JENSEN.PDF

Jones, C. (2009). The unfolding: Phenomenological perspectives of a group of grade four inner-city primary school boys engaged in a Jamaican Arts-based Multi-method Instructional Network [JAMIN] (Unpublished doctoral dissertation). University of the West Indies, Kingston, Jamaica

Kalikokha, C. (2008). *The perceptions of a group of first year undergraduate Malawian students of the essay writing process*. Retrieved from http://aut.researchgateway.ac.nz/bitstream/10292/396/1/KalikokhaC.pdf

Lakoff, G. (1993). The contemporary theory of metaphor. In A. Ortony (Ed.), *Metaphor and thought* (pp. 202-251). Cambridge, UK: Cambridge University Press.

Lakoff, G., & Johnson, M. (1980). *Metaphors we live by*. Chicago: University of Chicago Press.

Lavelle, E., & Zuercher, N. (2001). *The writing approaches of university students*. Retrieved from http://www.physics.emory.edu/~weeks/journal/lavelle-he01.pdf

Leeuwen, T & Kress, G. (2011). Discourse semiotics. In T. A. van Dijk (Ed.), *Discourse studies: A multidisciplinary introduction* (pp. 107-125). Los Angeles: Sage.

Levin, T., & Wagner, T. (2006). In their own words: Understanding student conceptions of writing through their spontaneous metaphors in science classroom. *Instructional Science, 34*, 227-278.

Millard, E. (1997). *Differently literate: Boys, girls and the schooling of literacy*. London: Falmer Press.

Miller, E. (1991). *Men at risk*. Kingston, Jamaica: Jamaica Publishing House.

Milson-Whyte, V. (2008a). A history of writing instruction for Jamaican university students: A case for moving beyond the rhetoric of transparent disciplinarity at the University of the West Indies (Unpublished doctoral dissertation). University of Arizona, Tucson, AZ.

Milson-Whyte, V. (2008b). How changed attitudes to academic writing and its instruction may enhance writing across the curriculum. *Caribbean Journal of Education, 30*(2), 399-423.

Ministry of Education, Youth & Culture. (2001). *Language policy.* Retrieved from http://www.moec.gov.jm/policies/languagepolicy.pdf

Moje, E. B., & Dillon, D. B. (2000). Reexamining roles of learner, text and context of secondary literacy. *Educational Research, 93*(3), 165-180.

Moustakas, C. (1994). *Phenomenological research methods.* London: Sage.

Murphy, N. (2002). At the intersection of several possible worlds. In G. Yancy (Ed.), *The philosophical I: Personal reflections on life in philosophy* (pp. 219-235). Lanham: Rowman & Littlefield.

Newkirk, T. (2000) Misreading masculinity: Speculations on the great gender gap in writing. *Language Arts, 77*(4), 294-300.

Parry, O. (2000). *Male underachievement in high school education in Jamaica, Barbados and St. Vincent and the Grenadines.* Kingston, Jamaica: Canoe Press.

Purcell-Gates, V. (1995). *Other people's words: The cycle of low literacy.* Cambridge, MA: Harvard University Press.

Sheehan, R. D. J. (1999). Metaphor as hermeneutic. *Rhetoric Society Quarterly, 29*(2), 47-64.

Slavkin, M. (2001). How can awareness of gender identity improve the performance of students? *Journal of College Reading and Learning, 32*(1), 32-40. Retrieved from http://findarticles.com/p/articles/mi_hb3247/is_1_32/ai_n28876965/

Solomon, J. (2010). Responding to the needs of a group of boys who marginally passed the grade four literacy test: Specialized iteracy project [SLP] (Unpublished master's thesis). University of the West Indies, Kingston, Jamaica.

Taylor, M. (2011). *Connecting the dots: An anatomy of verbal interaction in Jamaican English language classroom.* Kingston, Jamaica: Arawak.

Ting-Toomey, S. (1999). *Communicating across cultures.* New York: The Guildford Press.

Willox, A. C., Harper, S. L., Bridger, D., Morton, S., Orbach, A., & Sarapura, S. (2010). Co-creating metaphor in the classroom for deeper learning: Graduate student reflections. *International Journal of Teaching and Learning in Higher Education, 22*(1), 71-79.

Wong, Y. J., & Rochlen, A. B. (2009). Potential benefits of expressive writing for male college students with varying degrees of restrictive emotionality. *Psychology of Men and Masculinity, 10*(2), 149-159.

SECTION 4.
WRITING THE BORDERS OF SCHOOL AND PROFESSIONAL PRACTICE

Writing researchers tend to be invested in understanding the writing practices within professional cultures because they are invested in helping students learn how to take up those practices. But what are the relationships between school activities and other professional activities? Are these sets of activities, as some scholars (Dias, Freedman, Medway, & Paré, 1999) have claimed, "worlds apart"? If so, then where are the boundary lines between these worlds, and how do learners and instructors negotiate the different roles they inhabit? If not, then how might we distinguish the different enculturation processes, and how might these processes vary from region to region? And what about students who are entering the academic professions?

The jury is still out about how to describe and research the relationships among schools, professions, and academic careers. The authors of the following chapters have taken different stances and approaches. Stephens examines how news reporters respond to comments on their articles made by news editors, comparing especially the reporters' uptake (or not) of indirect and direct comments. Also interested in news reporting, Kohnen considers to what extent a science news editor's tasks and commenting practices are similar to the practices of secondary school teachers. In a comparative study of how Brazilian and Anglo-American graduate students understand the genre(s) of book reviews, Araújo focuses on how the two groups express criticism. Finally, Carrasco et al. introduce the concept of a "learning career" to identify different aspects of enculturation as graduate students work in a Mexican physiology laboratory.

--KL

CHAPTER 16.
TRANSCENDING THE BORDER BETWEEN CLASSROOM AND NEWSROOM: AN INQUIRY INTO THE EFFICACY OF NEWSPAPER EDITING PRACTICES

Yvonne Stephens
Kent State University

Research on workplace literacies is a burgeoning sub-field in the writing studies discipline. Moving research sites beyond the classroom can allow for a broader understanding of how language and texts function in the world, and how writing processes work and can be improved. At newspapers across the country, editors help reporters improve their writing so that novices efficiently create quality texts that, in turn, produce strong newspapers. The interaction between editors and reporters is not unlike the interaction between writing teachers and students; drafts are traded, comments are made, and (hopefully) better quality texts are produced. Because of this similarity, the wealth of research that has explored varied approaches to commenting in the writing classroom (Bardine, Schmitz Bardine, & Deegan, 2000; Ferris, 1997; Huot, 2002a; Sommers, 1982; Straub, 2000; Sugita, 2006; Treglia, 2006) can be compared with and applied to commenting practices in the workplace.

With an interest in assessing the efficacy of editing practices, I ask, How do reporters respond to editors' comments of different syntactical types? What types of comments do reporters incorporate in revision, and what types do they ignore? To begin to answer this question, I study the "conversation" between editors and reporters in the text production process as they create stories for a newspaper (Huot, 2002a, p. 135). This analysis allows me to identify in what ways editors' comments are more or less efficient in prompting reporters to respond in the ways they want. I also compare and contrast the methods of response to writing in the newsroom with response to writing in the classroom to see how both editors and teachers might learn from one another.

Response to writing research explores the ways teachers' comments are understood, used, or ignored by students. Sommers' seminal 1982 work, "Response to Student Writing," notes that teacher commentary can redirect the focus of a student text to the teacher's goals and away from the student writer's goals. Other scholars follow up on this concern, noting that teachers should allow students to maintain authority over the text so that they learn: "Give [students] responsibility for making their own choices as writers—and allow them to learn from those choices" (Straub, 2000, p. 31). In order to avoid taking over control of a student's writing, some teacher-scholars avoid using directive comments that demand that students make certain changes. Instead, they recommend using "hedged" commentary such as suggestions and questions to allow students to maintain a sense of authority (Bardine et al., 2000, pp. 99-100). Comments with hedges such as "You might ... " or "Perhaps try ... " come across to the student as polite suggestions and allow the student to maintain authorial control (Bardine et al., 2000; Treglia, 2006).

Research on teacher commentary focuses on how teachers can best communicate with students in a specific context to help them move their drafts to the next stage (Huot, 2002a). It is focused less on getting students to comply with the teacher's comments and more on getting students to think about their rhetorical choices (Straub, 2000). However, some research finds that comments of certain syntactical types are more effective than others in getting students to make the changes that the teacher requests. Some studies find that directives are the most effective comments in getting students to make substantial revisions. Imperative statements may provide a second-language student with more specific advice that is easier to understand (Sugita, 2006). Imperatives also show teacher authority, and while that has been frowned upon as limiting student authorial control, it does prompt the student to revise in an effort to meet the teacher's demand (Sugita, 2006). While students typically respond to a teacher's request for more information no matter the linguistic form (question, imperative, or observation), the imperative statements are more successful than other linguistic forms (Ferris, 1997). Not all studies have the same conclusions, however. Bardine, Schmitz Bardine, and Deegan (2000) say that direct commands are not received well by students, and Deegan writes that "if it sounds like I am ordering them to do something differently, then I might not get a motivated response" (p. 100).

Questions and observations are less effective in getting students to make changes. Second-language students may be confused by questions or may not understand the questions, which limits their ability to respond (Sugita, 2006; Ferris 1997). Similarly, observation statements also do not prompt much response from students (Ferris, 1997).

Comments with hedges may be more effective in prompting students to make changes than comments without hedges. Ferris (1997) finds in her often-cited, large-scale study on teacher commentary that students are less likely to ignore comments with hedges than those without hedges. This may refute the above assertions that suggestion-styled comments are less likely to prompt the student to make changes than directives or other comments. But Ferris also notes that her research doesn't fully support this conclusion. In her study, the teacher uses relatively few suggestions, making findings less reliable. She also comments that students are typically savvy enough to know that teachers use hedges to avoid poaching authorial control, and that teacher comments still should be taken seriously. This may limit the impact the hedge has on whether or not a student makes the change the teacher suggests.

In sum, the research is inconclusive regarding comments of differing syntactical types and their effectiveness in getting students to make changes.

Research on commentary in the classroom has moved away from looking at the "effectiveness" of getting students to make changes in their drafts, yet this research approach in the newsroom may still be appropriate because classroom and newsroom goals are different. While the goals in the university are for students to learn through revision, the goals in the workplace are for novices to produce texts that function well in the workplace. In the university, students are accustomed to "guided participation" learning, in which the purpose of the activities in which students engage is student learning. Conversely, novices in the workplace engage in activities in order to accomplish certain tasks. While they may learn by doing these tasks, the tasks are not created solely for their learning (Dias et al., 1999). Workplace leaders may recognize that, "over the long haul" (Ferris, 2009, p. 6), learning will help novices to become better and more efficient at generating the necessary texts, yet teaching novices is not necessarily workplace leaders' primary goals.

While there is extensive research relating to workplace literacy and the transition from the university to the workplace in writing studies (Adam, 2000; Beaufort, 1999; Dias et al., 1999; Katz, 1998; MacKinnon, 1993), there appears to be less research looking at the specific types of expert writers' commentary on novice writers' workplace texts. Bisaillon (2006) acknowledges that little attention has been paid to professional editing processes and approaches. Her article seeks to rectify this problem by looking at six professional editors of texts written in French and identifying the approaches more or less experienced editors have to editing these texts. She finds that editors with more experience can fix errors automatically much of the time, while editors with less experience must resort to problem-solving approaches such as reflection. Her work differs from my study in that she studies editors who make changes directly to the texts, whereas I study editors who respond to texts to prompt writers to make changes.

Lanier (2004) explores author-editor interactions, arguing that these are important because editor comments have the capacity to appropriate the author's text. He argues that while some studies have explored editors' attitudes toward electronic editing processes, authors' attitudes toward these processes have been ignored in the literature. He studies authors' attitudes toward electronic versus written editing practices by surveying five authors in a government laboratory. He finds that authors are more receptive to electronic editing practices because the comment function in Microsoft Word allows editors not only to indicate the need for changes but also to explain the need for changes. This mitigates authors' concerns that editors make unnecessary changes. Electronic comments also limit confusion about the changes editors request, limit writers' perceptions that editors make excessive changes, and limit the time authors spend on revision.

Many studies on newspaper editing practices focus on copyediting. Russial (2009) surveys more than 150 newspapers in the United States and finds that 15 percent of newspapers do not copy edit stories before posting them to their Web sites. With a concern for why newspaper errors appear frequently, Wharton-Michael (2008) compares the relative success rates of undergraduate students' proofreading on computer screens versus on paper, finding that it is more difficult to proofread in the former medium.

It appears that research on editing in professional communication does not study editors' comments on writers' texts in the ways composition scholars have studied teachers' comments on students' texts. Composition researchers have found that a variety of teachers' comments function in different ways to appropriate authorial control, prompt student revisions, or facilitate learning. How might comments function in similar or different ways in the newsroom?

Because workplace goals are foremost to complete stories for publication, and only secondly to facilitate reporter learning (Dias et al., 1999), it is necessary to study how editors' comments get the job done (or not). This study first asks, what syntactical types of comments do editors use? Secondly, what syntactical types are most effective in getting reporters to make requested changes? Finally, how do comments and responses in the newsroom compare with comments and responses in the classroom?

METHODS

THE SITE

My data collection site is a business newspaper that is based in a medium-sized Midwestern city and that has a circulation of about 6,000.[1] Part of a large publishing company, the newspaper is printed weekly and includes between six and ten stories (the majority of the editorial content in the paper) that are produced by the local branch. Two editors and three reporters work together each week to write and revise stories for the newspaper. Drafts of stories are traded back and forth between reporters and editors on an electronic server, allowing editors to make electronic comments embedded in the text, and allowing reporters to respond to those comments. I collected printouts of each stage of the story development process for nine stories that were published in one of the paper's weekly editions. Out of the nine stories I collected, five were from one reporter and four were from a second.

Typically, a reporter submits what she considers a finalized version of a story on the server to allow the editor to comment on it. Using text-editing software, one or both editors make comments that show up in the story within the text but with a bordered box surrounding the comments so that the reader can differentiate between the original text and the comment. The editor may italicize parts of the original text, his own comments, or both. I collected printouts of drafts of stories with editors' initial comments as well as printouts of stories after reporters revised in response to editors' comments.

DATA SELECTION AND ORGANIZATION

After collecting the data, I first organized it into a table to compare editors' comments and reporters' revisions based on those comments. The first column of the table contains the reporters' original version; the second column contains the original version with editors' comments, and the third column contains the reporters' revised versions.[2] I decided to use eight of the nine stories I collected; I left out one story that included very few edits, and the remaining eight were split evenly between two reporters. Because writing and editing styles differ greatly from person to person, the even split may help to balance quirks unique to a single reporter. After cutting away unnecessary data, I had a corpus of ninety-nine editing comments with respective reporter responses.

DATA CODING

Because my overarching research question looks to determine what types of edits prompt reporters to make editors' desired changes, I first coded the data to determine whether or not reporters made the changes that editors requested. There were clear instances where reporters made necessary changes and where they did not, but there also were several changes that fell between the two poles.

After sifting through reporters' varied changes, I pinned down a detailed coding scheme that categorized reporters' changes into one of the descriptions found in Table 1.

Table 1. Detailed coding key

√	Reporter made changes
X	Reporter did not make changes
√+	Reporter made changes, plus additional unprompted changes
√-	Reporter did not fully make changes
√+-	Reporter did not fully make changes, but made unprompted, additional changes
X+	Reporter did not make changes, but made unprompted, additional changes

Because many of the edits did not fit into a black-and-white pattern of either "changes made" or "changes not made," it was necessary to create additional categories that allowed for reporters' variations on revisions. To judge where a reporter's revision fell in this categorization scheme, I looked closely at what the editor asked the reporter to change, and I compared that with the reporter's revision. As evidenced by the coding key above, reporters interestingly riffed on the changes editors requested. At times, reporters ignored editors' comments but changed something else; other times, reporters complied with editors' suggestions, and went beyond the suggestions to make additional changes. Many times, reporters appeared to attempt the changes the editor wanted, but they seemed to fall short of the mark. Finally, sometimes reporters fell short of the requested changes, but then made additional changes that were not requested. These diverse revision activities required the detailed coding key found in Table 1.

Even though I filed reporters' changes into one of six categories, I still was able to more generally categorize changes into one of two categories: complying with editors' changes or not complying with changes. Reporters were considered to have complied with editors' requests if they made changes (√) or if they made changes, plus additional unprompted changes (√+). These two categories considered the changes "successful" because reporters did what they were asked to do (√), even if they also did more than they were asked (√+). On the other hand, revisions that fell into one of the other four categories were not complying with editors' demands. This more general categorization allowed me to address the overall efficacy of specific editing practices.

After determining the extent to which reporters made requested changes, I then developed a coding scheme for the types of edits that editors make. To allow for comparison between this data and response-to-writing research, I began to categorize the data into a general coding scheme that included suggestions, questions, observations, directives and re-writes, as these are the commonly used categories in writing research and are general enough to be applicable to my data. Using these categories as a beginning framework, I added or split categories when I uncovered additional types of edits. I ended up with six main categories and an additional six categories that constituted various combinations of the first six. The main categories are as follows.

- **Question:** Asks question to request more information
- **Suggestion for rewrite:** Rewrites text and adds a question mark to indicate a suggestion (e.g., relatives?)
- **Suggestion for change:** Suggests change (indicated by editor's use of "I would," "Maybe," or "You might")
- **Directive:** Demands change be made
- **Rewrite:** Rewrites text (no question mark)
- **Observation:** Indicates reader response

Table 2 includes additional categories that accommodated comments that did not fit into one of the six main categories. These are descriptions of comments that were combinations of two of the original categories identified above.

Categories such as suggested rewrites and suggestions, directives and rewrites, or suggested rewrites and rewrites seem as if they could be combined, respectively, but I kept them separate for specific reasons. First, suggested rewrites and suggestions are separate because the former may be easier to accommodate than the latter. While a suggested rewrite offers new text, a suggestion leaves that up to the reporter, making the latter potentially more difficult to accommodate, which may affect reporters' compliance rates. Directives and rewrites were kept separate for the same reason; the latter may be easier to accommodate because the rewritten text is provided, and this could impact reporters' likelihood of complying with the editor's comment. Finally, suggested rewrites and rewrites were kept separate because the former is a suggestion while the latter is a directive, and, as composition research has indicated, that may affect reporter compliance.

After generating the coding schemes and coding the data, I counted the frequencies with which the types of editing comments and the types of changes appeared in the data and charted these numbers in Table 2.

Table 2. Frequencies of types of editing comments and typs of changes

	Question	Directive	Rewrite	Suggested rewrite	Observation/Directive	Question/Directive	Suggestion	Observation	Directive/Sugg. Rewrite	Observation/ Sugg. Rewrite	Observation/ Question	Question/Suggestion
√	18	16	9	9	5	1	2	3		1		1
√+		1	3	1					1			
X	9			1		1						
√-	1	1	1		1	2			2		1	
√+-		2					1					
X+	2	1			1	1						
Total	30	21	13	12	7	4	3	3	3	1	1	1
Compliance Rate %	60	81	92	83	71	25	67	100	33	100	0	100

Key: √ = made changes; √+ made changes plus additional changes; X = did not make changes; √- = did not fully make changes; √+- = did not fully make changes, but made unprompted, additional changes; X+ = did not make changes, but made unprompted, additional changes

RESULTS

As shown in Table 2, the most commonly made editing comments were questions, with editors writing 30 questions out of the total 99 editing comments made.[3] Reporters supplied answers to editors' questions 60% of the time, indicating a 60% compliance rate. Reporters ignored nine, or 30%, of editors' questions. In the following example, the editor asks two questions which are only partially answered (editors' comments are in bold, my formatting):

Editor Comment: Question	Reporter Response: Reporter did not fully make changes (√-)
Johnstone said the company invites clients in for tours, giving a few each week, and then explains what Johnstone & Sons[4] can do to fix some of the major concerns they have with current suppliers. **(how many competitors does it have? who are some of the?** [sic]	Johnstone said the company invites clients in for tours, giving a few each week, and then explains what Johnstone & Sons can do to fix some of the major concerns they have with current suppliers, including the company the four partners used to work at.

The reporter did answer the second question, "who are some of the [competitors]?" by noting that the company competes with the owners' former employer. However, the reporter did not supply the answer to the first question, "how many competitors does it have?" This reporter response was thus categorized as making some changes, but not all requested changes.

The second-most common editing comment was a directive, which reporters complied with 17 out of 21 times, or 81% of the time. None of the directives were fully ignored, and small but insufficient changes were made in response to the remaining four directives. In the following example, the editor directed the reporter to make a change, and the reporter fully complied:

Editor Comment: Directive	Reporter Response: Reporter made changes (√)
Smith said the new building offers ABC Corp. more efficient space, with *easy access* **(rephrase as it repeats quote)** to Interstate 55.	Smith said the new building offers ABC Corp. more efficient space, with proximity to Interstate 55.

In the above example, the reporter fully complied with the editor's demand by changing the portion of the text the editor had italicized.

Reporters frequently complied with editors' rewrites and suggested rewrites. Of the 13 editor rewrites observed, 12 of them were complied with; of the 12 editor suggested rewrites, 10 were complied with:

Editor Comment: Rewrite	**Reporter Response: Reporter made changes (√)**
Stein said the building was (**originally**) built with student labor *originally* and by restoring it ...	Stein said the building was originally built with student labor and by restoring it ...
Editor Comment: Suggested Rewrite	**Reporter Response: Reporter made changes (√)**
Managing debt, even in a year where many businesses saw revenue decline, is (**stronger verb ... remains?.**) a key part of running a successful business. [sic]	Managing debt, even in a year where many businesses saw revenue decline, remains a key part of running a successful business.

These excerpts show that reporters made changes to the editor's rewrite in the first example and the editor's suggested rewrite (indexed by the question mark) in the second example. Compliance rates and specific compliance types are listed in Table 2.

DISCUSSION

It appears as if the more direct comments—directives and rewrites—are better at getting reporters to make necessary revisions while indirect comments—suggestions, questions, suggested rewrites, and observations—are less successful.

Questions and directives are the two most prevalent types of editing comments (editors made 30 of the former and 21 of the latter), which provides a point of comparison. If editors measure success by how well reporters comply with their comments, then directives appear to be more successful than questions. Reporters fail to answer questions editors ask them 40 percent of the time, and they fail to respond to directives 20 percent of the time. In addition to questions' being less effective in prompting changes than directives, questions also are the most commonly ignored syntactical type of editing comment. A total of 11 comments are fully ignored (simply deleted without additional, unprompted changes), and nine of those 11 ignored comments are questions. The relative failure of questions seems significant, since asking questions is the most commonly used editing comment, representing almost one-third of the total edits in the corpus.

The syntactical construction of the directive may make the editors' directives more difficult to ignore than the syntactical construction of the question, as a directive is a demand to do something, and ignoring this demand would be an overtly subversive act. In the following example, the editor's second comment (in bold, my formatting) is a directive: "Managing debt, even in a year where many businesses saw revenue decline, is **(stronger verb … remains?.)** a key part of running a successful business. **put a another graph in on why**" [sic]. The editor directs the reporter to discuss why managing debt is important to running a business, which addresses the main focus of the story. The reporter responds to the directive edit by adding the following sentence: "By getting their books in order, businesses should be ready to go once the recovery kicks into gear." In this example, the editing comment posed as a directive prompts the reporter to make the required change.

On the other hand, editing comments that prompt the reporter to provide similar information but that are posed as questions may be less likely to produce results, as in the following example:

> Four years ago, four friends and former co-workers decided to leave **(departed/left)** steady jobs at major Camden-area technology companies to form their own firm. **(why? what did they see/recognize in the market? and what kind of company did they create?)**

In the second bolded portion of the excerpt, the first two questions, "why? what did they see/recognize in the market?" go unanswered in the second draft of the article. It is possible that a question is easier to ignore than a directive because a directive demands that the subordinate complete a task, and ignoring that demand may be perceived as a subversive act. Additionally, a reporter may feel more comfortable ignoring a question because it may appear to be a request for information as opposed to a demand for information. Finally, questions can be confusing or ambiguous, as compared with directives, which can give a reporter clearer direction for revision.

Just as reporters more frequently ignore questions, they also ignore other comments that may be perceived as undemanding, such as suggested rewrites, suggestions, and observations. Of the 51 comments that fall into these categories, reporters fully address (√) or fully address with additional changes (√+) 33 of the comments. The remaining 18 comments fall into one of the four non-complicit categories: ignored (X), ignored with additional changes (X+), changes not fully made (√-), and changes not fully made yet additional changes made (√-+). This indicates a 35 percent fail rate for these types of "innocuous" comments.

On the other hand, just as reporters dutifully follow the demands of a directive, they also typically adhere to the directed rewrites. When the two categories of rewrites and directives are taken together, the result is a total of 34 comments. Reporters respond favorably to 29 of the comments and unfavorably to five of them, resulting in a 15 percent fail rate. This suggests that reporters comply with comments more frequently if the comments are of a demanding nature. Conversely, if the comments appear to be options, reporters are less likely to make the required changes.

While demanding comments more frequently prompt changes than subtler comments such as questions and observations, a closer look at some of the categories complicates this conclusion. For instance, one would assume that in a comparison of rewrites and suggested rewrites, reporters would be more likely to make changes for the former instead of the latter because the former is a directive and the latter a question. The numbers do not support this assertion. There are a total of 12 suggested rewrites, and reporters comply with 10 of the 12 changes. Editors make 13 directed rewrites, and reporters comply with 12 of the 13 changes. These numbers imply that reporters are likely to make the changes whether an editor suggests *or* directs the rewrite.

Applying Classroom Findings to Newsroom Data

The comments that writing teachers advocate—those that allow the writer to maintain authorial control—are also the ones that writers in the workplace are less likely to consider in revision. On the other hand, the comments that allow the teacher or editor to appropriate control of the work—directives—are more effective in getting the writer to complete a desired revision. This makes logical sense because the comments that allow for authorial control also allow the author the authority to ignore the comments. Teachers should employ these types of syntactical forms in their comments because, in the classroom, the main goal is student learning (Straub, 2000). However, because the goal in the workplace is get reporters to complete a task (Dias et al., 1999), these types of comments—shown here to be less effective in producing the desired result—may not be the best choices for editors. Paradoxically, in order to get reporters to make changes, editors should use directives; but in order to allow reporters to *learn* to write better, according to writing scholars, editors should use other syntactical forms that allow reporters authorial control.

Implications for the Newsroom

Editors, therefore, seem to be caught in a double bind. Neither commenting strategy seems appropriate. But since this study tells us that reporters respond differently to comments of different types, we might ask, "How can commentary facilitate both reporter compliance *and* learning?" Perhaps commentary that includes combinations of syntactical types (e.g., directives and questions) would both encourage compliance but also allow for the maintenance of authorial control.

Classroom research also may shed light on the trend that reporters tend to comply with both suggestive and directive rewrites, a trend that seems to contradict the general pattern that reporters comply with suggestions more often than directives. Classroom research has found that students shy away from comments that ask them to make difficult changes; we might also assume that students—and possibly reporters—would be more willing to comply with easy requests. Maria Treglia, the researcher who conducted a linguistic study on students' revisions based on instructor comments, found that no matter the linguistic makeup of the comment, if the content is asking students to conduct "challenging analytical tasks—rethinking and connecting ideas, and providing information that wasn't readily available," then students had trouble responding (Treglia, 2006, n.p.). Perhaps the opposite also is true: if the revision requested is easy, writers will make those changes without protest. Rewrites and suggested rewrites are equally easy, since they require only that the reporter copy down the editor's rewritten text. Reporters therefore may be equally likely to make these changes, which might explain the similar numbers in these categories. Editors may take this phenomenon into consideration when working with reporters. Perhaps when editors request difficult revisions, they can provide more guidance or time when asking reporters to make these changes.

While this study sheds light on reporters' responses to comments of differing syntactical types, we might conduct additional research that gets at professional editor and writer interactions in other ways. We could study conference-style mentoring, an alternative approach that may satisfy both editors' and reporters' needs (Wiist, 1997). In short, we might continue this inquiry by asking, "How do novice workplace writers learn *and* get work done?"

IMPLICATIONS FOR THE CLASSROOM

This chapter has been written under the assumption that questions, observations, and suggestions—"soft" comments—allow the writer more authorial control and therefore promote student learning (Bardine et al., 2000; Straub, 2000). As emphasized above, reporters comply with these comments less frequently than with directives. Could the problem lie not with authorial control, but with specificity? Perhaps the ambiguity of questions and suggestions leave the writer unsure of how to proceed. If, in this hypothetical scenario, professional writers are unsure about what to do with these types of comments, what can we expect from students? One conclusion is to resort to appropriating students' work and issuing only directives, going against much research that has told us to do otherwise. The paradox that faces editors seems as if it faces teachers as well.

This dilemma prompts me to return to this question: What are our goals as teachers, and do they differ from those of editors? If we make comments on students' texts, don't we expect students to make changes? Not necessarily. Certain types of assessment, such as using portfolios as a way to focus students on the act of revising and to assess their own work throughout the term, prompt students to take control of their writing and make choices about what and how to revise (Huot, 2002b). What is important to us is not that they make changes but that they make decisions (Straub, 2000) about their writing. This thinking, whether it ultimately produces the best possible draft upon completion or not (Huot, 2002a), facilitates student learning and prepares them for future writing endeavors.

This study, then, in its comparison of teacher and editor response practices, calls us to reflect on our own response processes, an exercise that scholars remind us is crucial to aligning our commentary with our goals (Bardine et al., 2000) and to communicating with students (Huot, 2002a). We must ask ourselves, What *are* our goals when we respond to student writing? Do we want them to make changes? Do we want them to think about alternatives? Do we want them to consider readers' positioned responses (Kynard, 2006)? This self-reflection might prompt us to hone our commenting techniques to better allow us to accomplish carefully defined goals within our individual classrooms (Bardine et al., 2000), and perhaps this same type of reflection might help editors to align their goals and their practices in newsrooms.

ACKNOWLEDGEMENTS

I would like to thank the newspaper editors who supplied me with data for this study. Their efforts to provide me with accurate stages of the revision process took place on busy deadline days, and without those efforts, this study would not have been possible. I also would like to thank Dr. Courtney L. Werner, Assistant Professor, Hope College, and Dr. Suzanne Null, Professor, Fort Lewis College, for providing insightful feedback during my own revision process; my work was strengthened significantly as a result of their careful readings.

NOTES

1. Institutional Review Board approval was obtained for this study.

2. Two additional columns were added to the right of these to provide room for stories that were edited twice. Only one story out of the nine I collected fell into this category, and I decided not to use these second-version edits in my analysis. I felt that including these edits in the corpus might skew the data because the reporter appeared to have ignored almost all of the comments in the second round of revisions. It is possible that the trouble of a second round of edits may have resulted in frustration in the reporter and, thus, the reporter's decision to delete the editors' comments.

3. The results do not pretend to be statistically significant. Instead, this small-scale study provides a snapshot of what commenting practices and subsequent responses look like, and these initial findings can serve as exploratory research on which future work can be based.

4. Names of people, companies, and geographic markers have been changed to protect the identity of the newspaper and its sources.

REFERENCES

Adam, C. (2000). What do we learn from the readers? Factors in determining successful transitions between academic and workplace writing. In P. Dias & A. Paré (Eds.), *Transitions: Writing in academic and workplace settings* (pp. 167-182). Cresskill, NJ: Hampton.

Bardine, B. A., Schmitz Bardine, M., & Deegan, E. F. (2000, September). Beyond the red pen: Clarifying our role in the response process. *English Journal, 90*(1), 94-101.

Beaufort, A. (1999). Creating a fit: Socializing writers into the community. In *Writing in the real world: Making the transition from school to work* (pp. 62-102). New York: Teachers College.

Bisaillon, J. (2007). Professional editing strategies used by six editors. *Written Communication, 24*(4), 295-322.

Dias, P., Freedman, A., Medway, P., & Paré, A. (1999). Students and workers learning. In *Worlds apart: Acting and writing in academic and workplace contexts* (pp. 185-200). Mahwah, NJ: Lawrence Erlbaum.

Ferris, D. R. (1997). The influence of teacher commentary on student revision. *TESOL Quarterly, 31*(2), 315-339.

Ferris, D. R. (2009). Theory, research, & practice in written corrective feedback: Bridging the gap, or crossing the chasm? *New Zealand Studies in Applied Linguistics, 15*(1), 1-12.

Huot, B. (2002a). (Re)Articulating writing assessment for teaching and learning. Logan, UT: Utah State University Press.

Huot, B. (2002b). Toward a new discourse of assessment for the college writing classroom. *College English, 65*(2), 163-180.

Katz, S. (1998). An opportunity for socialization. In *The dynamics of writing review: Opportunities for growth and change in the workplace* (pp. 55-71). Stamford, CT: Ablex.

Kynard, C. (2006, May). "Y'all are killin' me up in here": Response theory from a Newjack composition instructor/SistahGurl meeting her students on the page. *Teaching English in the Two-Year College, 33*(4), 361-387.

Lanier, C. R. (2004). Electronic editing and the author. *Technical Communication, 51*(4), 526-536.

MacKinnon, J. (1993). Becoming a rhetor: Developing writing ability in a mature, writing-intensive organization. In R. Spilka (Ed.), *Writing in the workplace: New research perspectives* (pp. 41-55). Carbondale, IL: Southern Illinois University.

Russial, J. (2009). Copy editing not great priority for online stories. *Newspaper Research Journal 2*, 6-15.

Sommers, N. (1982). Responding to student writing. *College Composition and Communication, 33*(2), 148-156.

Straub, R. (2000). The student, the text, and the classroom context: A case study of teacher response. *Assessing Writing, 7*, 23-55.

Sugita, Y. (2006, January). The impact of teachers' comment types on students' revision. *ELT Journal, 60(1), 34-41.*

Treglia, M. (2006). A study of teacher-written commentary in relation to student revisions and perceptions in college writing classes (Unpublished doctoral dissertation). New York University.

Wharton-Michael, P. (2008). Print vs. computer screen: Effects of medium on proofreading accuracy. *Journalism & Mass Communication Educator, 63*(1), 28-41.

Wiist, W. M. (1997). Seeking a coaching style of teaching news writing. *Journalism and Mass Communication Educator, 51*(4), 68-74.

CHAPTER 17.
TEACHERS AS EDITORS, EDITORS AS TEACHERS

Angela M. Kohnen
University of Missouri-St. Louis

The Writing Across the Curriculum movement has always envisioned two complementary uses of writing in all subjects: "writing to learn" and "learning to write in the disciplines" (McLeod & Maimon, 2000). However, the role of the teacher in each case is quite different. McLeod and Maimon (2000) describe it this way: in writing to learn assignments, which are often ungraded, the teacher can respond as a "facilitator rather than a judge" (p. 579). Yet when responding to student writing designed for communication, they say that content area teachers should "act as the professional already involved in the conversation of that [discourse] community, helping the novice, the student, enter the conversation" (p. 579). Their advice is aimed at professors of higher education, those for whom writing is often an integral part of their own professional obligations and identity. But what about high school content area teachers who may not be part of the conversation themselves? How do they respond to student writing when the writing may be as foreign to them as it is to their students?[1]

These questions framed our work with high school science teachers who sought to incorporate the genre of science news into their courses. In this study, we examine how a professional science news editor and high school teachers respond to student writing in order to understand the values and priorities each bring to bear on student work. These questions guided our work:

- How do teachers respond to authentic genres in content-area classes?
- How does teacher response compare to the responses of a professional editor?

THEORETICAL FRAME

A survey of the field reveals three areas of research that inform this study: writing across the curriculum, genre study, and authentic writing. The past several decades have seen an explosion of research into the uses of genre study as a teaching and learning tool (Bawarshi & Reiff, 2010; Fleischer & Andrew-Vaughan, 2009; Herrington & Moran, 2005; Soliday, 2005).

This work has expanded the notion of what kinds of writing are appropriate in content-area classes to include genres beyond disciplinary articles (Herrington & Moran, 2005). While much of this work has focused on higher education, research in K-12 settings has suggested that writing in authentic genres—i.e., those which have meaning outside of school contexts—increases student learning and motivation (e.g., Lindblom, 2004; Parsons & Ward, 2011; Purcell-Gates, Duke, & Martineau, 2007). In addition, some previous research has looked at how content-area teachers respond to student writing, particularly "writing in the disciplines," i.e., writing in academic genres (Bazerman et al., 2005).

Drawing together the concepts of writing to learn, writing in the disciplines, and genre theory, Bazerman (2009) articulates a "view of how genre might interact with both learning and development, using a Vygotskian lens, considering genres as tools of cognition" (p. 130). Based on Vygotsky's theory that learning precedes development, Bazerman (2009) argues that new genres are first learned—often with difficulty—and only later, with repeated use, do the genres transform a person's way of thinking and seeing the world:

> we then learn not just to talk but to learn the forms of attention and reasoning which the language points us toward. The words of the field become associated with practices and perceptions, changing our systems of operating within the world (p. 135).

Bazerman's (2009) theory offers a reason for choosing particular genres in the classroom and for requiring students to grapple with these genres repeatedly. Within this framework, teacher comments on student writing can serve to focus student attention on certain aspects of the genre while downplaying others. Although decades of research have repeatedly found that student writing ability does not rapidly improve due to written comments (e.g., Gee, 1972; Knoblauch & Brannon, 2006; Sperling & Freedman, 1987), researchers and theorists have considered teacher comments one avenue for understanding the relationships teachers construct with students and the priorities they set for student work (Bazerman, 1990, 1994; Connors & Lunsford, 1993; Lunsford & Straub, 2006; Sperling, 1994). Some research has shown that college professors view student writing from a disciplinary perspective, especially when compared to English teachers (Faigley & Hansen, 1985), yet few studies have looked the comments of high school content-area teachers or at those of teachers using genres with which they do not have personal expertise.

Bazerman (2009) posits that the "practices and perceptions" of a field can be learned and then internalized by writing in genres of the field. For the purposes of this study, the editing and comments on student papers are considered "boundary objects" (Wenger, 1998) designed to facilitate this process by connecting one community of practice (that of students) with another (that of professionals in the field). Novice student writers do not initially belong to the community of practice that produced and continues to reinvent the genre the students are attempting; "brokers" (Wenger, 1998) provide feedback which could help students understand and participate in the new community of practice. The articles produced by these novice writers evidence more problems than any reviewer could reasonably address. Examining how a professional editor and teachers respond to papers—what they attend to and how, as well as what they do not address—can help us understand the kind of brokers these reviewers are trying to be, the issues they are prioritizing, and the kinds of connections they seek to emphasize.

CONTEXT OF THE STUDY

Data for this study were collected through the Science Literacy through Science Journalism (SciJourn) program, a National Science Foundation-funded project which introduces students and teachers to the concepts of science journalism in order to improve student science literacy. As part of the project, students propose, research, and write science news articles and then submit these articles for possible publication in a newsmagazine for teens (*SciJourner* and scijourner.org). Articles are reviewed by science editor Alan Newman, a PhD chemist with 20 years of professional journalism experience. Since 2008, the SciJourn grant has included over 3,600 high school students in urban, suburban, and rural schools.

As we introduced the SciJourn idea to students and teachers, standards for assessing writing became necessary. We first looked to popular writing standards already in use, specifically the Six Traits Writing Model (Spandel & Stiggins, 1997); however only one of the six traits specifically addressed content, and we sought to build a discipline- and genre-specific set of standards. We turned to experts, in this case practicing scientists, science journalists, science journalism editors, and classroom science teachers—all of whom would be considered scientifically literate. What did these experts attend to as they read both professional and student science journalism articles? Table 1 lists the standards developed at the time of this study.[2] The SciJourn standards make clear the parallels between the qualities of a scientifically literate individual[3] and the qualities of a successful science news article. The genre of science news was deliberately chosen as a vehicle for improving student science literacy because of these parallels. In other content areas, other authentic genres could be identified for use.

Table 1. SciJourn standards

A scientifically literate person is able to ...	A high-quality science news article ...
... find and assess the credibility of information about a scientific topic from a variety of perspectives.	... includes multiple, credible, attributed sources from a variety of stakeholders.
... judge the implications and importance of new technologies and scientific discoveries.	... contextualizes information by distinguishing between embryonic and well-established science and noting the political/ethical/economic implications of a story.
... understand how science affects him/her personally.	... makes science information relevant to readers.
... fact check both big ideas and scientific details.	... is factually accurate and forefronts important information.

The SciJourn standards were created not only to represent the way experts think about science news articles, but also as a tool to help non-experts improve their reading and writing of science news. We distributed these standards to teachers who participated in our professional development training and made them publically available on our teacher resource site (http://teach4scijourn.org). Our hunch was that teachers, like the non-expert writers studied in the 1980's, tend to overlook writing problems that experts recognize (Hayes, Flower, Shriver, Stratman, & Carey, 1987) and define revision as fixing problems at the word or sentence level (e.g., Bridwell, 1980; Faigley & Witte, 1981; Sommers, 1980).

METHODS

Professional Science Editing

We began by analyzing a sample of Newman's edits on 50 first-draft student papers written in 2009-2010. The authors were in high school, taught by five different science teachers during the pilot year of the project. The classes varied in difficulty from basic to honors courses. The sample was designed to represent the variety of students, courses, and teachers involved in the project at that time.

We initially worked with a pilot sample of nine student papers. We used a qualitative coding process (Merriam, 2009), first marking all edits[4] with a descriptor. Next, these descriptors were grouped together and refined into codes. We then compared the codes which emerged from the data to the SciJourn standards; many of our codes were encompassed by these standards, but a significant number were not. We grouped together the codes which fell under the SciJourn standards into a category called "content;" these were edits about *what* was being said (or what was omitted), not *how* it was being said. The remaining codes were grouped into two categories, (1) form and (2) coaching. Any edit that addressed the writing itself, including edits about the structure of a news article, were coded as "form" edits; often these were insertions, deletions, or direct rewrites of the text. The third category, "coaching," was made up of all edits that seemed more characteristic of a teacher rather than a professional editor and included comments such as compliments and explanations; if a coaching edit had to do with a specific content or form feature, we double-coded. We developed our initial codebook and then two researchers jointly coded a set of papers to establish clear definitions of terms (see Appendix for a list of codes and examples). Once the categories and codes were established, two researchers coded a set of identical papers to establish inter-rater reliability and then divided the remaining papers between the two researchers. Interpretations and findings were discussed with Newman; these discussions created a check on the researchers' interpretations and served as a means of triangulating data.

Initial Teacher Tendencies

We next wanted to know how teachers who were not trained in science journalism respond to student science news stories. We used three student sample papers and asked twenty-two teachers to edit two of them as a pre-test on the first day of the SciJourn professional development workshop. Each teacher received one paper that had been judged by Newman to have publication potential and one that had not. Once we collected their responses, we analyzed their edits using the same codebook we had developed for Newman's editing. A comparison of average edits made by Newman and the teachers can be found in Figure 1. As part of our analysis, we also looked at observational field notes we had taken during the professional development workshop; these notes included the teachers' comments and reactions to the editing assignment as well as the length of time they took.

307

FINDINGS

THE SCIENCE EDITOR

Early on in our analysis of Newman's editing we noticed that he responded to papers he saw as potentially "publishable" in *SciJourner* differently than he edited papers where he saw no such possibility. To determine whether or not an article was publishable, we relied on Newman's explicit reference to publication, always found in a holistic comment at the beginning of the article (we did not attempt to compare or judge the quality of the articles ourselves). Out of the 50 paper data set, 17 included a specific reference to the possibility of publication; the remaining 33 we categorized as "non-publishable."

The main difference evident in Newman's edits related to issues of form. Publishable and non-publishable papers both received a similar number of content edits (on average 21 and 19, respectively), but in potentially publishable papers Newman made twice as many form edits as he made on the remaining papers (19 compared to nine). For articles with potential to publish, Newman made nearly as many edits on form issues as he did on content (see Figures 2 and 3). On publishable articles, he also made nearly twice as many coaching edits (nine compared with five), offering compliments (four) and explanations of his changes (four).

The fact that all of the papers received nearly the same number of content edits suggests that Newman considered content key. However, the content edits themselves were different in the two types of papers. For example, papers in

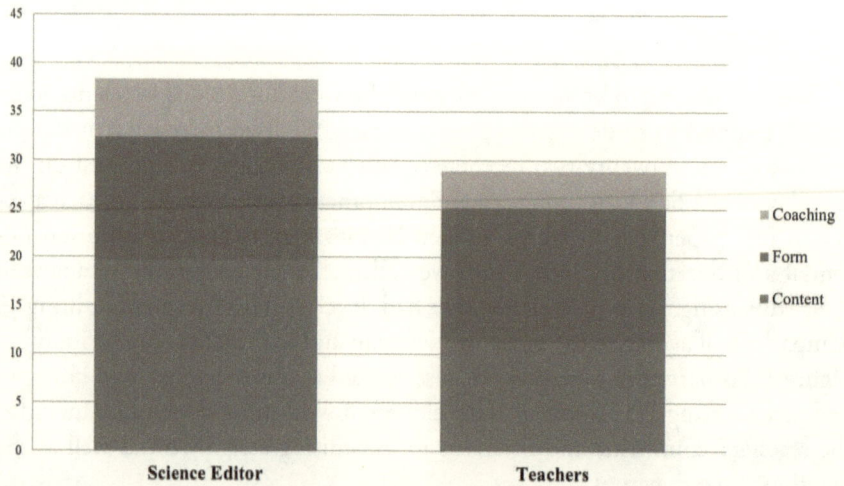

Figure 1. Average number of edits, science editor versus teachers

both groups had similar edits about sources of information, e.g., "according to who?" or "says who?", but non-publishable papers also had edits that often questioned the credibility of unattributed information (e.g., "where did you get this information?" and "where did you read this?"). Perhaps more importantly, both groups had edits about factual accuracy, but in potentially publishable papers these edits were more likely to be specific questions or suggestions (e.g., "did you look for any up to date numbers on how many have died?") while in non-publishable papers these edits often pointed out errors (e.g., "they don't use chromatography for fingerprints").

If we view these edits as boundary objects, Newman appeared to be trying to introduce *all* students to a community of practice where content is critical, but the emphasis was clearly different. Publishable articles elicited content edits

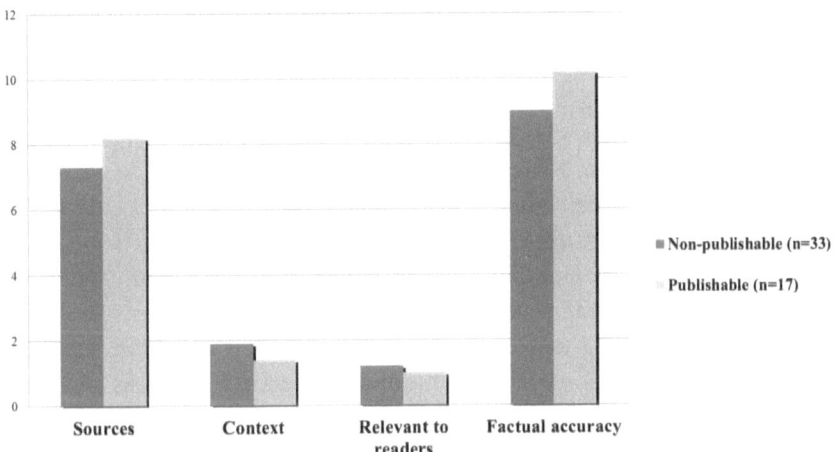

Figure 2. Average number of content edits by a science editor

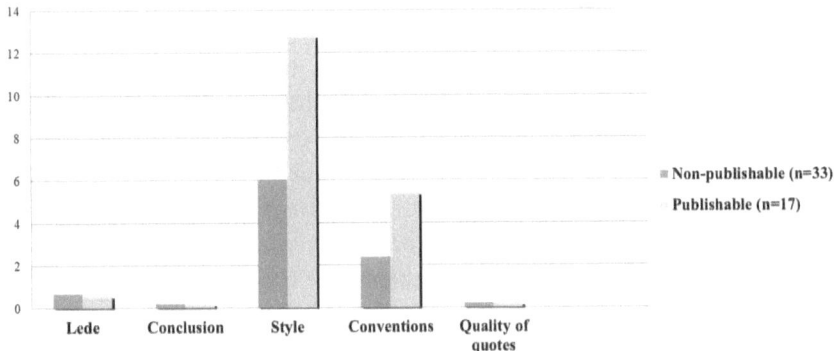

Figure 3. Average number of form edits by a science editor

that were "fixable" with additional legwork whereas content edits in non-publishable articles tended to point to larger problems that could only be addressed by changing topics or starting over. Writers of both kinds of papers could potentially learn something about the values of science journalism (the goal of the boundary object), but it seems writers of publishable articles were recognized for understanding issues germane to science literacy such as credibility or context—they just needed to dig deeper—whereas the authors of non-publishable articles were asked to re-frame their thinking.

In addition to content, a publishable article also must meet criteria of form. Perhaps unsurprisingly then, publishable articles received additional form edits, many of them deletions or direct rewrites of text. However, for students just learning the genre of science news, Newman seemed to consider form far less important than content.

HIGH SCHOOL SCIENCE TEACHERS

Prior to participating in the SciJourn professional development, the teachers responded to student articles very differently than Newman. Despite offering fewer overall edits than Newman (29 to 38), the teachers made more edits about form (14 to 12, see Figure 1). The teachers also made fewer kinds of edits, particularly within the categories of content and form (see Figures 4 and 5). For teachers, "content" was typically equated with factual correctness. The science editor, on the other hand, commented on a wider variety of content issues, particularly issues regarding sources; questions about sources of information rarely appeared in teacher responses. We also found the teachers' emphasis on form to be of interest. When Newman addressed form, his focus was more often on issues related to journalistic style, not on mechanical correctness. In contrast, the teachers tended to correct typographical and grammatical errors that the science editor either ignored or only marked once.

The number of times a recurring error was marked was also notable. For both mechanical and factual errors, the teachers were more likely to mark the same issue again and again (e.g., whether or not the name of an element should be capitalized), while the editor was more likely to edit the error only once or twice. When the teachers made a form edit about the article as a whole, they tended to fall back on terminology from the five-paragraph essay popularly taught in schools (e.g., asking for a thesis or a concluding paragraph), despite the fact that they had been told these were news articles. Finally, teachers' coaching edits tended to be nonspecific and complimentary (e.g., "Good start.").

As boundary objects designed to help students affiliate more directly with a community of practice, the teacher edits did not seem to highlight issues related to science literacy in the same way that Newman's did. Their emphasis on correctness—whether correctness of mechanics or facts—seemed designed to connect students to a community of practice specific to high school classrooms, particularly those operating in an assessment-dominated climate. One researcher noted that some of the pre-test articles seemed to be edited as if they were problem sets or test questions with a single correct answer. Whatever their reasoning, the teachers marked "mistakes" in a way that the editor did not.

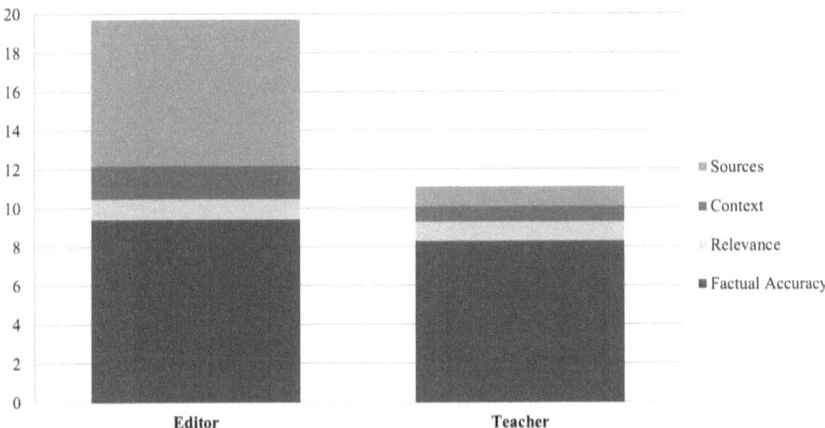

Figure 4. Average number of content edits by code, science editor v. teachers

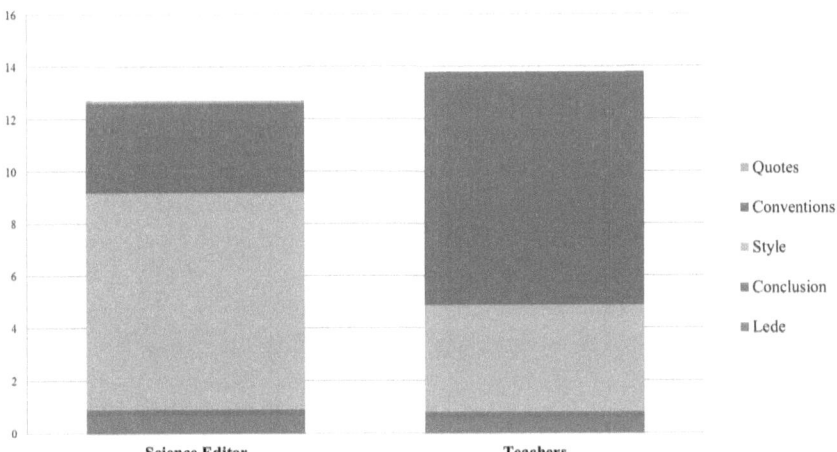

Figure 5. Average number of form edits by code, science editor versus teachers

311

DISCUSSION

Theory suggests that students can learn disciplinary values and ways of thinking by writing in particular genres. Previous research has shown that, when responding to student academic writing, content-area professors emphasize disciplinary characteristics of the academic genre that someone outside the field might not notice. What this study indicates is that high school science teachers, most of whom have not thought about genre, do not naturally prioritize concerns in this same way. Instead, if their editing is viewed as a boundary object, the connections they emphasize are to community of practice that values isolated correctness and five-paragraph essay form, characteristics of high school rather than of the wider world.

Prior to his involvement in this project, Newman had no previous experience working with high school students. Faced with student writing, he had to prioritize the problems he saw in order to move all students forward and find enough articles to publish the newsmagazine. His focus on "big picture" content was consistent, no matter the publishing potential of an article. To him, content was never about isolated factual errors. His concerns—from issues related to credible sources to explanations of the science—seem to recognize the story (and its relationship to the wider world) in a way that the teachers' fact-checking did not. His form concerns also had to do with a holistic view of the article as a piece of journalism and an expert understanding of genre.

The teachers also found themselves perplexed by student writing. Field notes indicate that they seemed nervous as they began editing the papers for our pre-test. Their eyebrows were raised; they eyed one another with skepticism. We also noted that they took much longer to complete the task than we anticipated; they took the assignment seriously—as if they were being graded on a first quiz.

And how did they respond? They seemed to fall back on a general principle, "It is my job to correct errors." Most began to mark the pre-test papers immediately, before reading the entire piece. Their holistic comments tended to be general, e.g., "interesting information," and their comments to promote improvement were drawn from their knowledge of the five-paragraph essay, e.g., "No conclusion" or "Need thesis statement at the end of the first paragraph." They appeared to be uncomfortable with or unaware of genre and had little sense that we had chosen the news article to help them and their students forefront the science.

In a professional newsroom or publishing house, holistic editing comes first. Fact-checking and copyediting wait until articles are closer to final form. However, without training, our teachers immediately moved toward these lower-level skills. Our findings indicate that novice editors are similar to novice writers in their focus on word- and sentence-level concerns rather than more global issues. As teachers respond to student writing, their editing could be misleading, emphasizing problems that professionals may not deem as important. The power of a genre to lead to learning and development could be compromised as a result.

Yet we do not suggest that teachers seek to *become* editors. An editor's primary purpose is to produce a publication; for an editor, a piece of writing must stand alone, independent from the writer, and say something understandable and complete. On the other hand, a teacher cannot see a piece of writing without seeing the writer; the two are intertwined. The teacher's goal is to prepare students for the next step, be it the next assignment, the next year of high school, college courses, or adult life. A news article (or any writing assignment) is just one piece of evidence in how well any given student is progressing toward this goal. As they approach student writing, teachers are armed with additional information about students, their own teaching, and future classroom plans; their feedback is deeply contextualized and rooted in the classroom in a way the outside editor's feedback is not.

CONCLUSION

This study demonstrates that a professional science news editor approaches student writing very differently from high school science teachers. This difference seems to stem from a deep understanding of the values and priorities embedded in the genre of science news; these values and priorities are made manifest in the editing of the professional while a very different set of values can be inferred from teacher feedback. As teachers look to expand the genres they use in their classroom in order to achieve specific learning goals, we recommend that they proceed thoughtfully. By working toward a professional awareness of genre, we suspect teachers could learn to prioritize feedback in a way that would help students in the struggle to learn and grow through genre writing. We also suspect that an understanding of genre would affect not only a teacher's written comments but also classroom discussions, private conversations, and related assessments.

NOTES

1. This material is based upon work supported by the National Science Foundation under Grant No. DRL--0822354. All statements are the responsibility of the author.

2. The SciJourn standards are a work in progress and are regularly revised; the most up-to-date standards are posted at http://www.scijourn.org.

3. Although there are many definitions of scientific/science literacy (see Bybee, 1997; DeBoer, 2000; NRC, 1996; Roberts, 2007; Roth & Barton, 2004), the SciJourn research group is primarily interested in what we can teach today about science that may have utility fifteen years after high school graduation (Polman, Newman, Farrar, & Saul, in press).

4. For the purposes of this study, the term "edit" describes any comment, deletion, or insertion by the responder in the writer's paper. All professional edits and some teacher edits were made using the Track Changes and Comment features of Microsoft Word. Other teacher edits were handwritten.

5. This is the spelling of "lead" in the sense of "lead paragraph" that many journalists have adopted.

REFERENCES

Bawarshi, A. S., & Reiff, M. J. (2010). *Genre: An introduction to history, theory, research, and pedagogy.* Fort Collins, CO: The WAC Clearinghouse and Parlor Press.

Bazerman, C. (1994). Reading student papers: Proteus grabbing Proteus. In *Constructing experience.* Carbondale, IL: Southern Illinois University Press. (Reprinted from: B. Lawson, S. S. Ryan, & W. R. Winterwood (Eds.), *Encountering student texts: Interpretive issues in reading student writing.* Urbana, IL: NCTE, 1990.).

Bazerman, C. (2009). Genre and cognitive development: Beyond writing to learn. *Pratiques N, 143/144,* 127-138.

Bazerman, C., Little, J., Bethel, L., Chavkin, T., Fouquette, D., & Garufis, J. (2005). *Reference guide to writing across the curriculum.* West Lafayette, IN: Parlor Press and the WAC Clearinghouse.

Bridwell, L. S. (1980). Revising strategies in twelfth grade students: Transactional writing. *Research in the Teaching of English, 14*(3), 107-122.

Bybee, R. W. (1997). *Achieving scientific literacy.* Portsmouth, NH: Heinemann.

Conners, R. J., & Lunsford, A. A. (1993). Teachers' rhetorical comments on student papers. *College Composition and Communication, 44*(2), 200-223.

Faigley, L., & Hansen, K. (1985). Learning to write in the social sciences. *College Composition and Communication, 36*(2), 140-149.

Fleischer, C., & Andrew-Vaughan, S. (2009). *Writing outside your comfort zone: Helping students navigate unfamiliar genres.* Portsmouth, NH: Heinemann.

Hayes, J. R., Flower, L. S., Schriver, K. A., Stratman, J., & Carey, L. (1987). Cognitive processes in revision. In S. Rosenberg (Ed.), *Advances in applied psycholinguistics, Volume II: Reading, writing, and language processing* (pp. 176-240). Cambridge, UK: Cambridge University Press.

Herrington, A., & Moran, C. (Eds.). (2005). *Genre across the curriculum.* Logan, UT: Utah State University Press.

Knoblauch, C., & Brannon, L. (2006). The emperor (still) has no clothes: Revisiting the myth of improvement. In R. Straub (Ed.), *Key works on teacher response* (pp. 1-16). Portsmouth, NH: Boynton/Cook.

Lindblom, K. (2004). Teaching English in the world: Writing for real. *The English Journal, 94*(1), 104-108.

Lunsford, R. F., & Straub, R. (2006). Twelve readers reading: A survey of contemporary teachers' commenting strategies. In R. Straub (Ed.), *Key works on teacher response* (pp. 159-189). Portsmouth, NH: Boynton/Cook. (Reprinted from: *Twelve readers reading: Responding to college student writing,* by R. Straub and R. Lunsford, 1995, Cresskill, NJ: Hampton Press).

McLeod, S., & Maimon, E. (2000). Clearing the air: WAC myths and realities. *College English, 62*(5), 573-583.

Merriam, S. B. (2009). Qualitative research: A guide to design and implementation. San Francisco, CA: Jossey-Bass.

Parsons, S. A., & Ward, A. E. (2011). The case for authentic tasks in content literacy. *The Reading Teacher, 64*(6), 462-465.

Polman, J. L., Newman, A., Farrar, C., & Saul, E. W. (in press). Envisioning scientifically literate students fifteen years after graduation: The promise of educative science journalism. *The Science Teacher.*

Purcell-Gates, V., Duke, N. K., & Martineau, J. A. (2007). Learning to read and write genre-specific text: Roles of authentic experience and explicit teaching. *Reading Research Quarterly, 41*(1), 8-45.

Roth, W.-M., & Barton, A. C. (2004). *Rethinking scientific literacy.* New York: Routledge.

Soliday, M. (2005). Mapping genres in a science in society course. In A. Herington & C. Moran (Eds.), *Genre across the curriculum* (pp. 65-82). Logan, UT: Utah State University Press.

Sommers, N. (1980). Revision strategies of student writers and experienced adult writers. *College Composition and Communication, 31,* 378-388.

Spandel, V., & Stiggins, R. J. (1997). *Creating writers: Linking assessment and instruction* (2nd ed.). White Plains, New York: Longman.

Sperling, M. (1994). Constructing the perspective of teacher-as-reader: A framework for studying response to student writing. *Research in the Teaching of English, 28*(2), 175-207.

Sperling, M., & Freedman, S. W. (1987). A good girl writes like a good girl: Written responses to student writing. *Written Communication, 4*(4), 343-369. doi: 10.1177/0741088387004004002

Wenger, E. (1998). *Communities of practice*. New York: Cambridge University Press.

APPENDIX. EDITING CODEBOOK

Category: Content (what is being said, not how it is being said)	
Code:	**Example:**
Sources of information: edits about credibility of sources, lack of attribution to sources, and the number of viewpoints represented by the sources	"Says who?" "Where did you get this percentage?"
Information put into context: edits about the implications of the article topic, including controversies and political/economic/ethical ramifications	"show why this is important" "how much will it cost?"
Information made relevant: edits that point out the article should be accessible to a teenage audience or that topics should be local and/or unusual	"I think you assume the reader knows too much"
Information factually accurate: edits about the necessity for information that is clear, fully explained, up-to-date, and includes quantitative measures.	"I tend to doubt that this statement is true." "I don't understand this"
Category: Form (writing, including edits about the structure of a news article; often insertions/deletions/rewrites).	
Code:	**Example:**
Lede[5]: edits that have to do with catching the readers' attention; often involves moving, shortening or rewriting the opening	Deletion of several sentences to shorten the opening paragraph.
Conclusion: journalism articles do not have conclusions	Deletion of a concluding paragraph
Style (simplification and fluency): edits that put writing into a journalistic style without changing content. Often shortening of sentences but sometimes combining sentences or adding transitions.	Original: "Young people may think that they will never get this type of influenza due to their age or good health, but they are wrong." Edit: "Even healthy young people are at risk."

Conventions: edits that have to do with spelling, grammar, and punctuation	Original: "ballay" Edit: "ballet"
Quality of quotes: edits about the nature of a direct quote; quotes are not factually inaccurate but are unhelpful to the story (boring or wordy)	"Didn't one of you say anything like 'I'm really excited about this opportunity'? This quote makes it sound like a trip to the dentist—it will hurt but it is better than a cavity. Aren't you thrilled to have this really cool trip?"

Category: Coaching (more characteristic of a teacher than an editor. Mostly comments rather than direct changes to the text)

Code:	**Example:**
Compliments: positive comments about what has been done; if it has to do with a feature of form or content, double code	"I like this topic" "You have a lot of information here, which suggests you worked hard"
References to the assignment: direct references to the fact that this was created in a classroom, for a teacher (not a "real" journalism article)	"the assignment was to write a credible news story"
Encouragement: positive comments about what should be done next	"I hope you will take the time to revise"
Explanation of change/clarifying comment: edits that explain other edits; usually they come right after an insertion/deletion/rewrite	"say it simply"

CHAPTER 18.
ACADEMIC GENRES IN UNIVERSITY CONTEXTS: AN INVESTIGATION OF STUDENTS' BOOK REVIEWS WRITING AS CLASSROOM ASSIGNMENTS

Antonia Dilamar Araújo
Universidade Estadual do Ceará

Previous studies on genre awareness have stressed its importance in the production of a piece of discourse that is appropriate to the situation or context of use (Askehave and Swales, 2001, Bazerman, 1994, 2004, 2005a, 2005b; Hyland, 2000; Kress, 1999; Swales, 1990, 2004). These authors assert that knowing what is involved in genre writing may empower students to communicate effectively in society and participate in academic disciplines. This implies that when writing in any genre, one should take into account the target audience, the communicative purpose of the genre, the conventions socially constructed by the discourse community that will influence linguistic choices and their effect on the reader. As studies of genres produced in academic settings in response to assignments are still few (Belcher, 1995; Herrington, 1994), this study aims to report on the results of an investigation that compared the book reviews written by Brazilian and Anglo-American graduate students in the linguistics and education areas.

Based on the notion of genre as social action manifested in specific text structures and linguistic patterns, in this chapter, I address the following questions:
- How does writing of academic book reviews in response to a class assignment reveal students' expertise and knowledge of the conventions of the genre?
- What evaluative strategies do Brazilian and American students use when writing academic book reviews? Are they similar or not?

In attempting to answer these questions, I have analyzed both students' written assignments and responses to a survey on students' perceptions and knowledge of genre conventions within the university context by examining two categories: text structure and evaluative comments.

THEORETICAL BASES

CONCEPT OF GENRE

Several rhetoricians have highlighted the notion of genres as recurrent social actions, practices of everyday life for particular rhetorical purposes in work (Bazerman, 1988, 1994, 2004, 2005a, 2005b; Bhatia, 1993, 2002; Miller, 1984; Russell, 1997; Swales, 1990, 1993, 2004). The concept of genre adopted in this work is aligned with Bazerman's thoughts that genres are "forms of life, ways of being, and frames for social action," (Bazerman, 1994) and they should be considered "what people, as groups and individuals, recognize them to be ... " (2005a, p. 92). This view implies looking at genre as a process that organizes individuals and groups around their interests, behaviors, thoughts, reasons, and that genre use also typifies their actions when shaping interactions. In participating in school activity systems, students "appropriate" knowledge on how genres are elaborated and then use them through practice until they become members of the academic community. Given that my interest in this study is to compare how graduate Brazilian and Anglo-American students reshape book and article reviews written in different contexts to convey meanings and position themselves in their disciplines, I investigate their particular textual practices seen as authorized and valued by the social groups, institutional sites (universities, classrooms), or discourse communities (students and teachers) used by student-writers in interactions as their understanding of writing book reviews.

BOOK REVIEW AS A GENRE

The studies regarding book reviews as genres are few in number. Among them are those that focus on students' assignments (Belcher, 1995; Bezerra, 2001) and on scholars' characterization of textual features and strategies of appraisal to convey interpersonal features (Araújo, 1996, 2009; Hyland, 2000, Motta-Roth, 1995). Araújo's (1996) study on book reviews in the area of linguistics based on Swales's (1990) perspective revealed that scholarly book reviews have a typical and consistent pattern of information and organization displaying different rhetorical moves and that those exemplars of the genre varied as a response for meeting the expectations of a disciplinary community. One of central and recognizable features of book reviews as a persuasive kind of text is evaluation that means "both a statement of personal judgment and an appeal to shared norms and values which are influenced by cultural considerations, socialization, and philosophical background" (Hunston, 2004, p. 193). Hyland (2000, p. 41) claims that book reviews are "crucial sites of disciplinary engagement, demand writers' awareness of how to understand interpersonal relations when conveying meanings and addressing evaluative comments to a specific author and disciplinary community." By interacting with a particular audience through their texts, the reviewer is not only assessing merit and an author's reputation, but he/she is also publicly exposing the writer's views of the text and of its author. Thus, the force of evaluation in this context of interaction is devastating, and writers must be cautioned to avoid friction with a specific author. In this particular study, I am comparatively examining how graduate students interact in different ways through their evaluative strategies in considering their purposes (for a class assignment), audience (teacher), situation (university classroom), and genre conventions.

THE STUDY

This study used a combination of text analyses and closed-and open-ended survey to investigate the writing of reviews by a group of 14 Brazilian and eight Anglo-American graduate students in the humanities as assignments for one of the courses taken in the first/second year of their degree, as well as their perceptions of the purposes, roles and structure for writing critical reviews. We looked at their compositions to see how these written texts reveal their understanding of discursive practices, social purpose, audience, and roles as participants of an academic community constituted by teachers and students in the university settings.

Setting, Participants and Data Collection

The first group of participants was 14 Brazilian graduate students enrolled in a one-semester compulsory course on Applied Linguistics Research Methodology required for all students in their first year in the graduate program at the State University of Ceará (UECE), Brazil, in 2006. Research Methodology is thus an important subject to help them acquire the necessary tools to improve their initial research proposals when entering the master program. All of the volunteers were required to write an article review after having discussed in class as part of the course assignment.

The second group consisted of eight American graduate students from the University of California, Santa Barbara (UCSB). Three of them were PhD candidate students affiliated to the Education Department who wrote their book reviews between 2005 and 2006 for different courses and professors. The remaining students (five) were first year PhD students enrolled in Sociolinguistics 203 in the Linguistics Department, in the fall of 2006.

The corpus analyzed was thus 22 reviews as one of the assignments for courses students were taking in their respective graduate departments. For Brazilian students, the assignment had the aim of having students reflect on the literature about research methods in applied linguistics, develop their analytical and critical thinking skills, and learn how to express the standards of evaluative comments. Students were asked to read research articles selected from international scholarly journals in the area of Applied Linguistics, to present and discuss the selected articles orally in the classroom and, finally, to write a two to three page critical review intended only for grades.

For American students, the assignment had the aim of having students reflect on the literature of recent developments in Sociolinguistics (Department of Linguistics) and Media Studies (Department of Education) as well as demonstrate their critical thinking skills. The students were oriented towards completing the assignment after reading and analyzing book reviews written by scholars and were guided by a three-page handout containing essential information on book review writing. American students were given the option to write their reviews for a class assignment or for publication. Most of them, especially students from the Linguistics Department, preferred to write them for a class assignment, considering that this was their first experience in writing critical reviews.

QUALITATIVE AND QUANTITATIVE ANALYSES

Ten closed- and open-ended written questions on the students' perceptions of their reviews writing were completed in a survey by all participants after they had written the critical review. Their answers as representing writers' voices were used in the analyses to examine their expertise shown in the compositions. For the purposes of this chapter, only the questions 4, 6, 9 and 10 were analyzed.

Q1: The frequency students read book/article reviews
Q2: The frequency students write book/article reviews
Q3: The way students learned how to write book reviews
Q4: The social purpose for writing book/article reviews
Q5: The length of reviews and who determines the length

Q6: The purposes for writing book/article reviews for classrooms
Q7: The teacher's expectations for the written book/article reviews
Q8: The purpose for writing book/article reviews for other situations
Q9: The way information is organized in academic reviews
Q10: The degree of politeness devices in the writing of book/article reviews

Two categories of analysis are considered. The first, *text structure,* examined how students convey meanings and organize information of academic reviews through rhetorical strategies (Araújo, 1996). The quantitative and qualitative analysis of the data consisted of a detailed investigation of the 22 selected reviews comparing the regularity and relatedness of pieces of information in the texts conveyed. The second, *evaluative comments,* focused on evaluative strategies based on Hyland's (2000) study on praise and criticism. Some examples from the corpus are used to illustrate and support the points discussed in the analyses. Codes are included to identify students such that BS1 means Brazilian student while AS1 means American student. Their compositions are referred to BSR1, which means Brazilian Student Review 1 while ASR1 stands for American Student Review 1. Questions from the survey are numbered as in Figure 1, and they are referred according to their number Q1, Q2, Q3 and so forth.

CATEGORY 1: CONVENTIONAL TEXT STRUCTURE OF CRITICAL REVIEWS

The students' critical reviews displayed similarities and differences for rhetorical moves of text structure, showing how they consistently appropriated certain conventions. The majority (18 out of 22, 81.8%) of graduate students used a consistent and typical pattern, as shown in Table 1, when they employed three rhetorical moves to realize the social function of genre and respond to the teacher's assignment; an exception to the pattern were two Brazilian students whose reviews (BSR5 and BSR7) displayed no Move 1 (Introduction) and two other reviews (BSR9 and BSR13) that displayed no Move 3 (Conclusion). It is worth highlighting that four students 5, 7, 9 and 13 at the moment of the research had completed their undergraduate language teaching courses, but they had not had systematic courses on academic writing to learn book reviews. Their responses indicated when they had to accomplish the assignment, they had to learn from other sources accessible to them: reading and analyzing book reviews in periodicals at the university library.

Table 1 shows how students' reviews are similar to those of scholars in the area of linguistics by situating the reader within a theoretical or methodological context in the opening paragraphs when talking about the topic, author, aims, intended audience, previous studies, and a brief book evaluation (Move 1).

Table 1. Frequency of moves in students' critical reviews

	Brazilian Students		American Students	
Moves	Frequency = 14	%	Frequency = 8	%
I - Introducing the book	12*	86	8	100
II - Summarizing the content	14	100	8	100
III - Providing general evaluation	12**	86	8	100

*Students 5 and 7   **Students 9 and 13

Move 2 tends to describe the book organization, to report on its content, make comments on strengths and weaknesses, and sometimes offer suggestions for the author to improve the book. Move 3, the concluding paragraph(s), serves the purpose of evaluating the book as a whole by recommending or (dis)qualifying it for readership by a particular audience. These three parts represent the functions they play in the genre, and may be accomplished by one or more strategies to convey meanings in their texts.

Their written reviews demonstrate how they attempted to meet the audience's expectations (the teacher) by showing their knowledge of genre conventions, despite their limited experiences in writing reviews. Interestingly, nine students, as a group, responded that they were writing a review for the first time (Q2 in the survey, see Figure 1). However, they also responded that they were aware of how to do it, when responding to Q4 on their perceptions for the communicative purpose of the genre and Q9 on the sequence of information in the reviews.

The two Brazilian students (BS5 and BS7) whose articles had no introduction, and the two (BS9 and BS13) whose reviews had neither conclusion nor global evaluation at the end seem to demonstrate a mismatch between their responses and written texts. In answering how information is organized in reviews (Q9), BS5 appeared to reveal a lack of knowledge or even misunderstanding of what was required in this question, given that her answer focused on linguistic features. However, although BS7's comments on Q9 showed knowledge of the genre concept and recognized that introductions are part of the text structure in reviews, this student preferred not to write them. Thus, the fulfillment of the genre purpose for BS5 and BS7 is realized in Moves 2 and 3 only. Although student BS9 recognized that "reviews have a canonical fixed structure" and BS13 only gave a vague response to Q9, these two students seemed to display a lack of knowledge of genre conventions and awareness of importance in expressing an evaluation at the end as a means of consolidating positive views introduced in Move 2. The lack of an introduction and a conclusion in their reviews may signal the students' lack of ability in establishing an interpersonal stake when interacting with their audience: the teacher.

Although the strategies varied, the most preferred ones Brazilian and American students used for reviewing the book and article were: *making topic generalizations* for introducing the book and article in Move 1, summarizing the content of the book/article by *describing its organization, reporting/discussing the content,* and *evaluating parts of the book* in Move 2, and *a general evaluation* of the book/article at the end in Move 3. Indeed, making topic generalizations seems to be one of the main features of scientific discourse as a means of creating a context for the reader to follow their reporting of content and their evaluation of parts of the book/article. As discussed previously, the data revealed that not all students are aware of the generic conventions of critical reviews, as inferred from their responses in the survey. For some of them (four Brazilian students), reviews are similar to a synopsis in that they do not need to situate the reader or evaluate the book in the conclusion, especially when writing for the teacher. To a certain extent, the use of these rhetorical strategies for most students is similar to the ones used in scholars' reviews (Araújo, 1996, 2009) addressed to disciplinary community.

Category 2: Evaluative Comments of Critical Reviews

Given that book reviews are essentially evaluative and persuasive, the second category of analysis regards the students' personal comments in their reviews to examine the structural pattern of evaluation, focus of evaluation, evaluative strategies, amount of appraisal, and politeness devices when expressing praise and criticism. When these aspects are examined in their reviews, their writing practices show both similarities and differences. We discuss similarities first. Taken together, the first similarity between Anglo-American and Brazilian students was noticed in the use of a *structural pattern of evaluation.* Both groups of students expressed an evaluation in the three moves, as mentioned earlier, and tended to offer praise for global features of the book/article: content generalizations; contributions; and recommendations (Moves 1 and 3). Criticisms were addressed mainly to specific content and textual features (Move 2) (see Table 2). These findings may evince two things: students' knowledge and their understanding of the purpose for writing book reviews, and the way conventional reviews should be written in response to class assignments.

As shown in Table 2, only 42.8% of Brazilian students provided global evaluation (positive) in Move 1 and 85% evaluated content and textual features by expressing praise and criticism in Moves 2 and 3. One hundred percent of American students expressed praise and criticism in all three Moves. The major-

Table 2. Frequency of pattern of evaluation

Moves/focus	Brazilian students		American students	
	Frequency=14	%	Frequency=8	%
I—global features	6	43	8	100
II—content and textual features	12	85	8	100
III—global features	12	85	8	100

ity of students (20) presented a structural pattern of evaluation that fulfilled the purpose of genre: praising global features and criticizing specific aspects. This pattern seems to contribute to the dual purpose of book reviews, as Hyland (2000, p. 48) claims: "to provide an overview of the text for readers while raising particular problematic aspects for the field." Thus, for students who praised beyond the introduction, this pattern may reveal both their concern with conveying an assessment of reviewed work and carrying affective meanings.

The second similarity concerns *a preferred method of evaluation* in their texts. Half of the Brazilian students (seven, 50%) and three-quarters of the Anglo-American students (six, 75%) preferred to mix content reporting with expressions of appraisal of specific issues rather than devoting separate paragraphs for praise and criticism, especially when evaluating Move 2. Maybe, this preference may be due to the need to interact with the audience while reporting the content in the texts.

The third similarity regards the *focus of evaluation* in the reviews (what aspects or issues were evaluated). Students addressed their positive comments mainly on practical and theoretical aspects of the book or contributions of the book to the field in their Introductions. Most of the signs of positive evaluation in Move 2 are addressed to particular aspects of theories that ground the reviewed book/article. Thus, most of occurrences (22) of praising comments in Brazilian students' reviews emphasize the validity, reliability, and seriousness of research being reported in the article. Anglo-American students' reviews (12 occurrences, despite only eight students in the study) focus their comments on application of theories and data analyses. These occurrences reveal students' concerns with both content and methodological aspects of the research in an attempt to fulfill the purpose of the genre and to show their understanding and appreciation of particular issues of the book for the teacher.

Move 3 in the reviews are signaled by a concluding expression such as *em suma* (in sum), *concluindo* (concluding), *finalmente* (finally) in Portuguese, and *overall, in short, a final word, all in all*, and *the essays in this volume* in English. Reviewers tended to offer positive comments on the book/ article's contributions to the disciplines, or to recommend the book/article to readers, especially

Table 3. Frequency of occurrences of expression of praise/criticism

Participants	Praise		Criticism	
Students=22	Frequency	%	Frequency	%
Brazilian=14	61	31.28	53	75.71
American=8	134	68.71	17	24.28
Total	195	99.99	70	99.99

students and professionals, followed by a statement justifying the praise comment. The praise expressions in the conclusions are evidence of how students offer "a stronger endorsement" of the texts being evaluated, and create "a socially appropriate solidarity framework" (Hyland, 2000, p. 54).

These results confirm *the amount of appraisal* in graduate students' reviews (Table 3). We perceived that Brazilian and American students taken together tend to praise (195 occurrences) rather than criticizing (70 occurrences). By expressing appraisal, students, as novice genre writers, display an awareness of genre conventions and the need to negotiate personal judgments in their texts.

Table 3 shows that Anglo-American reviews praised more (134 occurrences, 68.71%) than Brazilian ones (61 occurrences, 31.28%). These data reveal that American students are more aware of being polite, and they demonstrated it in their texts. For them, writers should be polite and overall positive but not afraid to offer constructive criticism. However, by analyzing criticism occurrences, Brazilian students were more negatively critical in their evaluative comments (75.71%) than American ones, who expressed negative comments only in 24.28% of statements. These findings were compared and no correlation between most Brazilian written reviews and their responses on politeness devices in the survey (Q10) was found. Thus eight Brazilian students who recognized the use of politeness devices when evaluating the text also made negative comments with no concern with saving the author's face or showing solidarity. On the other hand, the remaining students (6) who did not answer the Q10 or just commented on formal linguistic aspects wrote texts that seemed to be neutral descriptions of aims, organization, content, and a brief and global evaluation at the end. For these students, academic reviews written for grades seem to be only a way to show content knowledge.

With respect to the use of *evaluative strategies* in the reviews in order to persuade the disciplinary community to accept the reviewers' personal viewpoints, the most preferred ones by Brazilian and Anglo-American students were *personal attributions* (for praise), *praise-criticisms pairs, hedging* (for mitigating criticism), *metadiscursive statements,* and *straight negative criticisms.* Personal attributions occurred 28% in Brazilian reviews and 50.8% in American reviews, and this relates to the author's individual judgments to introduce praise by showing how the reviewer is aligned with the author's thoughts. In general, the statements signaling praise were introduced by first person personal pronouns in English or by a verb in the first person in Portuguese that suggests the reviewer's involvement and commitment to an idea and encouraging its acceptance by the readers. Examples of personal attributions in the reviews may be seen in the use of verbs *gostei* (liked) and *recomendo* (recommend), in which the first person is marked in the verbal forms in Portuguese and the use of personal pronouns *I* or *me* followed by a mental verb like *think, believe,* or *find* in English reviews, signaling the reviewer's personal interest, engagement, besides bringing "the writer into his text as a thinker" (Crismore, 1989, p. 85).

The second most frequent evaluative strategy used by both groups (B=18.6% and A=12.1%) regards *praise-criticism pairs* (Hyland, 2000), which are equivalent to "matching relation of contrast" (Hoey, 1983, 2001). This strategy is realized by means of a positive evaluative expression or statement followed by a negative evaluation. Here, expression of praise is syntactically subordinated to a criticism, introduced by conjunctions such as *but, however, although, despite,* and *in spite of* in English, and their equivalents *mas, entretanto, no entanto,* and *embora* in Portuguese that signal a change in the plane of evaluation is to be expected, from positive to negative or vice-versa. Reviewers employ such devices as a way of mitigating his/her negative opinion of aspects that are not significantly important in the book/article.

Hedging is another strategy used by both groups of students (B=9.33%, A=25.8%), in the reviews to mitigate criticism, especially when evaluating book content. Even American students who had no experience with review writing showed awareness of softening criticism through the use of hedges. Such strategy is introduced by a modal or epistemic verb as a device to justify the problem raised in the review. By mitigating, they were invoking a wider audience to share the understandings and views, and to be accepted as members of the community. The use of this strategy was coherent to their answers to Q10 about the importance of being polite in the reviews. All American students were unanimous in acknowledging that reviewers should be polite and respectful, even when they have to point out problematic issues in the reviewed book. Swales (1990) states that the appropriateness of using hedges depends on the norms of a particular discourse community and the context of writing. Perhaps this may justify the fact that Brazilian students' reviews displayed few instances of hedges, thus differing substantially from Anglo-American students' reviews. Their texts may have been influenced by the context of writing in the university setting, whose instruction on hedging as a strategy to decrease the writer's responsibility and to project politeness had not been highlighted.

The students' use of *metadiscoursal statements* (B=5.33%, A=5.17%) helps to predict positive and negative evaluation. Their function is to organize reviewers' discourse, in addition to show how they soften criticism by rhetorically announcing their presence in the text. According to Hyland (2000), "because metadiscourse draws attention to the intentions and activities of the writer, it serves in these texts to refocus the reader on the act of evaluating, rather than the evaluation itself" (p. 58). Lexical items such as *weaknesses, shortcoming, problems* and *drawbacks* signaled a negative evaluative comment and *strength, highlights,* and *merit* introduced positive comments in the students' reviews.

The most remarkable difference between Brazilian and Anglo-American students is related to strategies expressing criticism (only B=24%). Brazilian learners' reviews presented 18 occurrences of "straight negative criticism," a device that is not present in English reviews. This strategy consists of introducing a criticism without toning down or softening his/her evaluation in the reviews. Typical instances of straight criticism in Brazilian reviews are, especially, the author's lack of knowledge of the article topic and the lack of theoretical framework to make the research consistent. More importantly, these criticisms are always supported by evidence, which means that an evaluative comment is followed by a clause or stretch of text functioning as "basis" for the evaluation (Hoey, 1983, 2001), justifying, therefore, the reviewer's claims and his/her position assumed in the text. *Basis* means an expression of evidence that supports the reviewer's viewpoint and is usually introduced by *due to, for this reason, because* (in English), *porque, dado que,* and *pois* (in Portuguese), especially when the comment conveys a negative evaluation. Most Brazilian students' reviews (78.8%, 11 texts) provided basis for their evaluative statements against 21.6% (3 texts) which did not. In justifying their claims, the writers are adopting a position of authority based on knowledge learned in the course and representing themselves as qualified persons to speak for the disciplinary community.

As "straight criticism" is not an integral feature of academic reviews, Brazilian students seem to signal that their purpose is to show their knowledge of the topic learned about research methods for the teacher. This assumption is confirmed by their responses to questions 4 and 6 in the survey (see Appendix) in that eight Brazilian students (57.1%) commented that their purpose for writing reviews was to show their understanding of articles they had read for the course, and six (42.8%) reported that their purpose was to persuade readers to read the review. Their responses suggest that both the purpose in doing the task and having an audience in mind may have enormously influenced their strategy to express straight criticism. In addition, when talking about the degree of politeness in the writing of book reviews, 50% of them commented that reviewers should be polite in spite of pointing out shortcomings.

The students who expressed straight negative criticism (BS 5, 9, 11, 13) revealed that academic reviews, even when written for the teacher, besides content knowledge must also show their critical skills. For those who intermingled praising and criticism (BS 1, 2, 3, 6, 12, and 14), their work showed much more consciousness of the genre's social purpose, even when responding to a class assignment. This difference may indicate that although they acknowledge that academic reviews are typifications of actions, there is still a lack of ability and awareness of highlighting important aspects of the article in their texts. The answers given to the survey questions, when compared to their writing practices, appear to reveal that they struggle between fulfilling genre expectations and showing their linguistic knowledge and expertise for the teacher. In adopting a critique position in their texts, they show their learned and accumulated knowledge of the specific subject matter for the teacher, but forget that reviews, even written for class should not constitute a threat for authors' reputation in their disciplinary community.

Although most of the students acknowledged that evaluation is a central aspect of the reviews writing, when responding to a class assignment, they seemed to figure out that the most important thing is to show content knowledge on specific topics for their primary audience, the teacher. Their concern in demonstrating summarizing skills rather than critical skills is evidence of students' trouble in transforming knowledge in their texts. For these students, reviews are not only a discursive space in which they can summarize content, but also a site in which they may interact with readers by showing their existing knowledge on the topic and by sharing their positions and affective meanings to a specific audience interested in them.

The differences between Brazilian and Anglo-American students can also be attributed to the contexts of learning. Both groups of students reported that they have learned to write reviews through systematic instruction in the classroom and by reading and analyzing reviews in journals. As the classroom context was not examined in this study, maybe other factors may be at play here: lack of opportunities for writing reviews addressed to a real audience; the pedagogical orientation for students to work throughout the assignment; materials provided; and previous experiences. An ethnographic and longitudinal study might reveal which factor(s) most strongly influenced the writing practices of these students.

CONCLUSION

Due to the nature of this investigation, the results cannot be generalized to other students and classrooms. By comparing the writing practices between

Brazilian and Anglo-American students, I did not intend to show cross-cultural differences but rather the students' preferred rhetorical strategies and linguistics choices in their texts. In this respect, the study suggests that, in general, most students appropriated basic features of how to structure and evaluate their texts to accomplish the genre purpose for classroom, in spite of the fact that some students have few experiences with review writing. The results also revealed that the students' responses in the survey did not always correlate with their writing practices, meaning that they may have demonstrated an awareness of genre conventions theoretically, but did not know how to transform their knowledge into effective practice.

Perhaps the most significant contribution of this study was to show how students write critical responses for the classroom. By providing students with enough opportunities to develop their writing skills, they can gradually change from knowledge-telling students to knowledge-transforming, mature writers. Writing instruction in university contexts should also endow graduate students with the knowledge about how they may represent themselves so as to convey their judgments, opinions and commitments and establish a disciplinary voice in their texts. Through practice in varied tasks, they may gain communicative competence. Such knowledge may help students to develop awareness that reviews as genres are one of the forms in which writers may negotiate meanings, share views with readers, and construct knowledge.

Finally, this study opens doors for further research that examines how graduate students in different university contexts get initiated into disciplinary communities by investigating not only formal and rhetorical knowledge, but also processes and procedural knowledge used when writing critically. I believe that such studies may illuminate our understanding of how students elaborate and shape their texts as responses to the socio-cognitive needs of the communities they are engaged in and how academic writing tasks can facilitate students' development of writing genres to communicate effectively in dynamic and situated interactions.

ACKNOWLEDGMENTS

I wish to thank CAPES, a sector of the Brazilian Ministry of Education, FUNCAP, Ceará research agency, and the State University of Ceará which supported this research by grants. I am deeply grateful to Charles Bazerman, my supervisor, for his contributions and valuable feedback to successive versions of this text and wish to acknowledge my gratitude to him and to the Department of Education, University of California, Santa Barbara, for having provided me support for carrying out the research project reported in this chapter during the academic year 2006-2007. Thanks also to my colleague Andrew Heidemann, from UCSB, Department of Education, for his dedicated time and attention in reviewing early draft of this chapter.

REFERENCES

Araújo, Antonia D. (1996). *Lexical signaling: A study of unspecific nouns in book reviews (*Unpublished doctoral dissertation). Universidade Federal de Santa Catarina, Florianópolis, Brazil.

Araújo, Antonia D. (2009). O gênero resenha acadêmica: Organização retórica e sinalização lexical. In B. Biasi-Rodrigues, J. C. Araújo, & S. C. Tavares de Sousa (Eds.), *Gêneros textuais e comunidades discursivas: Um diálogo com John Swales* (pp. 77-94). Belo Horizonte, Brazil: Editora Autêntica.

Askehave, I., & Swales, J. M. (2001) Genre identification and communicative purpose: A problem and a possible solution. *Applied Linguistics, 22*(2), 195-212.

Bazerman, C.(1988). *Shaping written knowledge.* Madison, WI: The University of Wisconsin Press.

Bazerman, C. (1994). Systems of genres and the enactment of social intentions. In A. Freedman & P. Medway (Eds.), *Genre and the new rhetoric* (pp. 79-101). London: Taylor & Francis.

Bazerman, C. (2004). Speech acts, genres and activity systems: How texts organize activity and people. In C. Bazerman & P. Prior (Eds.),*What writing does and how it does it: An introduction to analyzing texts and textual practices* (pp. 309-339). Mahwah, NJ: Erlbaum.

Bazerman, C. (2005a) *Gêneros textuais, tipificação e interação.* Trad e organização de Ângela P. Dionísio & Judith C. Hoffnagel. São Paulo: Cortez Editora.

Bazerman, C et al. (2005b). *Reference guide to writing across the curriculum.* West Lafayette, IN: Parlor Press & The WAC Clearinghouse.

Belcher, D. (1995). Writing critically across the curriculum. In D. Belcher & G. Braine (Eds.), *Academic writing in a second language: Essays on research and pedagogy* (pp. 135-154). Norwood, NJ: Ablex.

Bezerra, B. G (2001). *A distribuição das informações em resenhas acadêmicas* (Dissertação de Mestrado em Lingüística). Fortaleza, Universidade Federal do Ceará.

Bhatia, V. K (1993). *Analysing Genre: Language use in professional settings.* London: Longman.

Bhatia, V. K.(2002). A generic view of academic discourse. In John Flowerdew (Ed.), *Academic discourse* (pp. 21-39). Longman, Pearson Education.

Crismore, A. (1989). *Talking with readers: Metadiscourse as Rhetorical Act.* (Vol. 17. American University Studies). New York: Peter Lang.

Herrington, A. J. (1994). Writing in academic settings: A study of the contexts for writing in two college chemical engineering courses. In C. Bazerman & D. Russell (Eds.), *Landmark essays on writing across the curriculum* (pp. 97-124). Davis, CA: Hermagoras Press.

Hoey, M. (1983). *On the surface of discourse.* London: George Allen & Unwin.

Hoey, M. (2001). *Textual interaction: An introduction to written discourse analysis.* London: Routledge.

Hyland, K.(2000). *Disciplinary discourses: Social interactions in academic writing*, Harlow: Longman.

Hunston, S. (1994). Evaluation and organization in a sample of written academic discourse. In M. Coulthard (Ed.), *Advances in written discourse analysis* (pp. 191-218). London: Routledge.

Kress, G. (1999). Genre and the changing contexts for English language arts. *Language Arts, 76,* 461-469.

Miller, C. R. (1984). Genre as social action. *Quarterly Journal of Speech, 70,* 151-167.

Motta-Roth, D. (1995). Rhetorical features and disciplinary cultures: A genre-based study of academic book reviews in linguistics, chemistry and economics (Unpublished doctoral dissertation). Universidade Federal de Santa Catarina, Florianópolis, Brazil.

Russell, D. R.(1997). Rethinking genre in school and society: An activity theory analysis. *Written Communication, 14*(4), 504-554.

Swales, J. M. (1990). *Genre analysis: English in academic and research settings.* Cambridge, UK: Cambridge University Press.

Swales, J. M. (1993). Genre and engagement. *Revue Belge dePhilology et d'Histoire, 71,* 687-698.

Swales, J. M. (2004). *Research genres: Explorations and applications.* Cambridge, UK: Cambridge University Press.

CHAPTER 19.
LEARNING CAREERS AND ENCULTURATION: PRODUCTION OF SCIENTIFIC PAPERS BY PHD STUDENTS IN A MEXICAN PHYSIOLOGY LABORATORY: AN EXPLORATORY CASE STUDY

Alma Carrasco, Rollin Kent, and Nancy Keranen
Benemérita Universidad Autónoma de Puebla (BUAP)

This institutional case study[1] presents evidence on dimensions of the *learning careers* and *professional enculturation* of Spanish speaking physiology PhD students in a public research university in Mexico from the perspective of professional communication and genre learning in English.[2] Study data sources were interviews with students, heads of laboratories and thesis advisors. The study reported here is part of a larger research project (Kent, Carrasco, & Velázquez, 2009) ongoing since January 2010 in several additional disciplines: astrophysics, biotechnology, agriculture, oceanography, materials science and nanotechnology carried out in several Mexican research institutions. As explained in more detail below the study seeks to fill a gap in the literature on career enculturation processes in L2 contexts through the theoretical lens of *learning career*.

STUDY BACKGROUND

The scientific PhD is a recent development in the Mexican academic system. Historically scientists were trained in some disciplines in the National University but mostly abroad. In 2008 there were 7,000 students enrolled in 348 PhD programs in the natural sciences, health, technology & agriculture. Between 1995 and 2006, the number of yearly graduates in these disciplines grew from 520 to 2,650 (SIICYT, 2008). This growth has occurred in the context of a greater number and diversification of research and training institutions. National policy on science and technology has focused strongly on supporting and evaluating the scientific PhD. There are scholarship funds for accredited PhD programs as well as a developed evaluation system for these programs. Excellence and internationalization of the scientific PhD are vital policy objectives.

The endogenous expansion and disciplinary variation of the scientific doctorate are evidence of a self-sustaining dynamic of the Mexican science and technology system, and the PhD is its main instrument for generational reproduction as well as an important site for new knowledge production, through the research-teaching-learning nexus (Clark, 1993). Doctoral programs are, thus, part of a complex institutional and cultural web of expectations, funding, reputational competition and regulations.

This chapter reports on fieldwork in a physiology laboratory in a large public university in Mexico in May 2010. In our ongoing research on various dimensions of training experiences of Mexican doctoral students in the sciences (Kent et al., 2009), one focus of interest is the analysis of their production of academic texts. Following on the idea that "communication is the life-blood of academia," Becher and Trowler (2001, p. 104) point out that "knowledge production (the principal cognitive question) and the establishment of reputations (the key social consideration) necessarily depend on it." Gaining recognition is a major motivation behind scientific publications, and high impact journals are especially sought out by researchers in their struggle for authorship (Carrasco & Kent, 2011). Overington (1977) states that a scientist is recognized as to the extent that he or she becomes an author, a basic fact of scientific life that was clearly pointed out to us in interviews with research physiologists:

> Our doctoral students understand that if they don't publish, they won't graduate. And later on in their career, if they don't continue publishing they will end up teaching biology in high school (P1).

On the basis of Prior's (1998; 2006) perspective of writing for scientific recognition as a literate activity whereby participants co-produce texts and construct their disciplinary identities, we explore practices of Mexican, Spanish speaking researchers and PhD students in their efforts to express experimental results in written form and to submit them in English to specialized journals.

Central to our study are the theoretical concepts of *learning careers* (Bloomer & Hodkinson, 2000, p. 591) and *enculturation and apprenticeship* (Delamont & Atkinson, 2001, p. 96) and how these theories are seen in terms of *professional communication* and *argument formation* in writing for scientific publication (inter alia, Bazerman, 2006; Newell, et al., 2011; Prior, 2006). These three areas are presented below to form the theoretical framework for the study methods and interpretation presented later on in the chapter.

LEARNING CAREERS AND TRANSFORMATIONS

From the perspective of *situated learning,* i.e., learning as a social practice bound within social contexts, Bloomer and Hodkinson (2000, p. 591) offer the concept of a *learning career.* The term *learning career* refers to the development of dispositions toward learning over time. It takes many forms in different contexts. In their carefully constructed theoretical framework, Bloomer and Hodkinson (2000) review studies that include theories of learning which position learning as situated in a context in which the learner, the activity and the context work as a synergistic triad of elements leading to learning and therefore transformation. As they explain, this perspective regards learning from a constructivist worldview, represented by flexible dispositions influenced by the context-dependent or social construction of personally held schemata. The authors give prominence to social interaction as the generating force of the schemata or meanings learners give to their experiences. Further social interaction generates and refines the schemata in an ongoing, ever changing process (Bloomer & Hodkinson, 2000, p. 589).

This argument is compatible with Blakeslee's point (1997, p. 126) that a student's training trajectory as a future scientist involves learning as a situated construction. The learner-apprentice is guided by an expert in engaging in activities considered typical by the discipline. He/she learns, develops and uses specialized knowledge through his/her participation in specific disciplinary activities, contexts and cultures.

Such intense engagement implies commitment and even passion on the part of the novice. In the absence of strong emotional attachment, it is hard to see how deep absorption in everyday activities in a laboratory may be sustained during the period of four years, required minimally for doctoral completion. Such absorption may lead to *transformation.* Bloomer and Hodkinson (2007) use the term *transformation* rather than change or transition because of the notion of career and the construction of the career identity of the person. It is the learning career as a situated social act that leads to the transformation (p. 590).

If knowledge is co-produced through intense activity in a specific institutional context and disciplinary culture, it is because students are progressively transformed from inexperienced newcomers or "novices," to apprentices and finally to independent researchers (Laudel & Gläser, 2008; Parry, 2007). This change in identity involves the development of autonomy in each PhD student, which is an expected, although often implicit, result of the whole process and is the result of a complex rite of passage (Laudel & Gläser, 2008). This progression is the subject of the following section, which presents another axis of our theoretical framework for understanding the professionalization processes of the PhD students in our study.

Enculturation, Apprenticeship and Tacit Knowledge in Laboratory Science

Thus, a PhD student goes through a process of enculturation in pedagogical forms and interactions that occur in a laboratory context (Delamont & Atkinson, 2001). Bazerman (2006, p. 223) reminds us that the

> ability to understand the genres of academic disciplines—including the kinds of roles and stances one adopts, interpretive procedures, forms of contention, and uses to be made of the texts—is the result of substantial enculturation and apprenticeship that makes these odd and particular forms of communication familiar, meaningful and intelligible in detail and nuance.

The micro-social setting of laboratory science constitutes a special type of intellectual and material working environment for scientific apprenticeship and enculturation (Knorr-Cetina, 1999; Latour & Woolgar, 1986). In their study of graduate students in biochemistry and geology, Delamont and Atkinson (2001, p. 96) report that

> PhD students describe the research group as a mutually supportive environment in which ideas and materials are shared on an everyday basis. Even where members of the group work on different research problems, there are overlaps in the materials, equipment and techniques, which they use ... The research laboratory operates upon the principle of reciprocity whereby members take an active interest in the activities of their colleagues. ... Doctoral supervision is therefore understood by team members to be a shared responsibility (p. 98).

Other scholars, however, stress the hierarchical nature of traditional apprenticing relationships between supervisors and students (Blakeslee 1997, p. 126), since the transmission of authority implicitly accompanies the co-production of knowledge. It seems sensible to suggest that, in laboratory settings, both norms of hierarchy and reciprocity are present.

This type of continuous interaction is the significant context for the appropriation of the tacit skills crucial to laboratory science, skills that are not seen as "teachable" or even particularly "learnable." They cannot be translated into standard formulae but must be grasped in practice and are even talked about as a "gift" (Delamont & Atkinson, 2001, p. 100). Thus, enculturation is built on the practical experiences of apprenticeship. Tacit knowledge is taken up through the apprenticeship mechanism, i.e., membership in the socio-cultural context of, in this case, the science laboratory. This kind of learning is characterized as being "*caught* rather than *taught*, transmitted through personal experience rather than by systematic instruction. ... It travels best where there is personal contact with an accomplished practitioner and where it is already tried and tested" (Delamont & Atkinson, p. 100, emphasis in original).

Analogously, the appropriation of literate practices in science by students may occur obliquely. Prior (2006, p. 64) declares that, as sociocultural research on writing has revealed, "much of literate activity is implicit and learned implicitly." This is the focus of the final axis of our theoretical framework explained in the following section.

THE ROLE OF COMMUNICATION AND GENRES IN CAREER LEARNING

An important aspect of specialized literate activity is the construction of arguments following institutionally established rules. Here, argumentative reading and writing do not refer exclusively to logical reasoning and "winning an argument" but to relationships built on social practices. These practices not only establish group solidarity but form the "material structure, space, and organization of a particular literacy event" (Newell et al., 2011, p. 288).

We understand this research to be informed by two complementary perspectives on academic literacy as a social process and situated cognition: *New Rhetoric Theory* and *Social Genre Theory.* Going beyond traditional rhetoric theory, which presents argumentation as a resource for persuasion or engaging in debate (cf. Bazerman, 2006), new rhetoric theory emphasizes one's relationships with an audience on the basis of shared beliefs or attitudes (cf. Newell et al., 2011). The audience provides a motivational context for writing but also legitimates types of arguments around and through which students must find their way in their literate development.

A related aspect of specialized literate activity, from the perspective *of Social Genre Theory*, is students' grappling with appropriate genres that disciplinary communities recognize as valid for specialized communication (and mutual identification). Bazerman (2006, p. 222) provides a point of departure for understanding genre as "complex signaling of mutual intelligibility" because "most texts sit in among other texts or with few external orientation clues. The reader and writer need the genre to create a communicative meeting place legible from the very form and context of the text." PhD students in the sciences must learn to read, write and speak *disciplinarity* (Prior, 1998) within established genres, such as journal articles, conference presentations, letters, and reviews, among others.

It is within these actions that we examine a cohort of laboratory members—experts and apprentices as they negotiate learning careers and enculturation processes in initiating and being initiated into their professional communities. Specifically the study looked at i) writing production as *learning career, ii)* processes of enculturation, apprenticeship and tacit knowledge in laboratory science, and iii) communication and argument formation in career learning in the research location as described in the following section.

METHOD

Study Context

The research site, a physiology institute of a large state university in central Mexico, was established in 1983. It was one of the first research institutes created on a separate footing from teaching departments in this bureaucratically and politically complex university. In this context, it is no small feat that the institute has been able to establish autonomy in its local management and an integrated cosmopolitan research culture with a collegial ethos. The institute operates with 16 full-time researchers who work in six labs. The work carried out by researchers at the institute, in neuroscience, cardiovascular, and cell biochemistry, is recognized by their publications in specialized journals and their participation in national and international networks. The faculty has one master's and one PhD program. We interviewed professors and students in four labs as described below.

Participants

The interviews were carried out by one researcher and two master's students associated with our project in May 2010. For this study, we interviewed five physiology researchers, including two women and three men. Three of them were founders of the institute, and two were graduates of the institute's doctoral program. All researchers who were interviewed were at the time of the study in charge of their own labs.

Table 1. Academic staff participants (*n*=5)

I	Description	Career level	Gender
P1	Vestibular studies LAB 1	Founder of the institute	Male
P2	Vestibular studies LAB 1	Founder of the institute	Female
P3	Central nervous System LAB 2	Graduate of the institute	Male
P4	Cardiac studies LAB 3	Founder of the institute	Male
P5	Neurobiology LAB 4	Graduate of the institute	Female

Six PhD students associated with these labs also participated. Semi-structured interviews were used as the principal data collection method.

Table 2. Doctoral student participants (*n*=6)

ID	Description	PhD program level	Gender
S1	LAB 1	Advanced student	Female
S2	LAB 3	Early career	Male
S3	LAB 2	Early career	Female
S4	LAB 2	Advanced student	Male
S5	LAB 1	Advances student	Female
S6	LAB 3	Advanced student	Male

Taped interviews were transcribed and later codified and analyzed using Atlas.ti (ver. 5.2).

RESULTS AND DISCUSSION

This section reports the findings of the study interpreted within the framework set out above particularly within the concept of *learning career*. The findings are presented around the three theoretical areas put forward above:
1. Writing production as *learning career*
2. Processes of enculturation, apprenticeship and tacit knowledge in laboratory science
3. Communication and argument formation in career learning

Excerpts are presented exemplifying the comments from participants identified as either professors/researchers (P1, P2, P3 ...) or as PhD students identified as (S1, S2, S3 ...) (see Tables 1 and 2 above). The excerpts were translated from the original transcripts in Spanish.

Writing Production as *Learning Career*

Situated learning takes on several forms in different contexts. In a physiology lab, according to P4.

> Students live here, so tutoring happens constantly on a daily basis, for at least one or two hours. Students spend their lives in here. They get totally involved with the experiment. I'm not on top of them all the time, but if they have questions they come to me. Sometimes I tour the lab and ask them how things are going. This is what we do every day.

In addition to preparing and defending a thesis, to obtain a PhD in physiology the student must publish two journal articles. The principal author of a paper is the person with primary responsibility for developing an experiment and reporting findings, although this often occurs in collaboration with other researchers. A student must learn to initiate, manage and conclude this process successfully.

A professor talks about the responsibility this entails:

> All experimental results, all the data, are the responsibility of the student. I hold her responsible for delivering all processed findings. She delivers them to me, in tables and graphs or figures, and then we initiate a discussion. This is a conversation. I collaborate with the student in generating her results. (P2)

Students also refer to these interactions as conversations:

> Well, I feel that in the informal chats with my advisor we get interesting ideas ... he thinks of something, tells me about it, asks me to get more data. And then I come out with a hypothesis, the articles I've been reading. It all happens in the lab, in small groups ... (S1).

If a thesis advisor is able to state clearly what is required from a student, he is in a position to provide valuable guidance. This guidance has different focuses. One is requiring students to have a good grasp of the state of the art of their research topics, pointing out the important names and journals. This is not only a question of managing content but also of familiarization with typical models of publications or genres. When, further down the line, the student begins writing, these models play an important part.

From the perspective of a student, it is not different:

> My advisor is present in all things ... in an experiment, he says "look, I suggest you do it this way" ... in writing stuff, he'll even show you how to write ... "you'd better correct this." ... He's really attentive to our results ... he'll suggest "Try this kind of analysis" ... or if things didn't work out, he'll suggest another way of going about it. (S2).

COLLABORATIVE PRACTICES IN DEVELOPING GENRES RECOGNIZED BY THE DISCIPLINE: ENCULTURATION AND APPRENTICESHIP

Working in the lab and learning to produce texts go together. Initially, students work on professors' manuscripts, but this occurs in a collaborative environment in the lab where advanced students help newcomers as well. One apparently significant transformation is the student's transition from individual work to collaborative work in the lab:

> Teamwork is very important for us, a student must be able to work with others, with three or four other students with whom he/she must coordinate to carry out experiments. (P3).

Living in the lab, working intensively and writing with others constitute key learning experiences for doctoral students, and, as Delamont and Atkinson (2001) point out, this context is crucial for developing tacit competencies through observing others and learning vicariously from them.

Similarly, a student compared his lonely experience as a masters student in a physiology lab in the United Kingdom with his current experience, now as a PhD candidate, in the Mexican lab:

> Here we've been told from the beginning that we're a team, we have to help each other, we have to work for the benefit of the lab. This is really different from my masters studies in the UK, where everything was more private, everybody working on his own . . it was actually weird for somebody

> to help out another student ... OK, it's a very large lab with students from all over the world, so you didn't get the feeling of belonging [to a larger endeavor] ... Here, although we each have our own projects, we're a team following common goals. (S2).

Helping others and receiving guidance from them are accepted as natural practices in this lab, as one PhD student expressed it:

> Sometimes you get an undergraduate student coming to the lab, sitting down with you to see what you're doing. So you explain, this is how you do this and that. ... We all get to be observers in others' experiments. ... So, at the beginning you're just a spectator but then you learn stuff that you pass on to others. It's really important to have somebody watching you, questioning stuff you probably didn't observe on your own. (S3).

Another student emphasized that a collaborative working environment was very important for her initial induction to the PhD program, becoming a member of the team.

Clearly, collaboration is not only a common practice that has evolved "naturally" as a normal form of social interaction in this lab culture. Teamwork is a crucial practice for carrying out complex tasks in the lab, as pointed out by one student:

> Collaboration is important, like when I have to perform a surgical procedure, I can't do it alone. Some experimental procedures require working together with someone else. (S4)

Collaboration is an objective necessity in lab work in physiology, where instruments, procedures and analysis necessitate several hands and eyes (Latour & Woolgar 1986; Knorr-Cetina 1999).

In addition to working collaboratively on experimentation, researchers also write in collaboration. Most texts are authored collectively, with five or six coauthors.

> If a student appears as first author, it is because he was in charge of the research. Other students may appear in the author list or else as collaborators, depending on the importance of their collaboration, whether substantive or procedural. (P4)

This statement by a professor is confirmed by a student:

> All or most publications are collaborative. In our lab, the research director may appear as the last author and the student as first author. We may even include collaborators from other labs. (S5)

Co-authorship is a standard practice that students assimilate from the beginning of their masters and doctoral studies.[3] Journals accept unlimited numbers of authors and allow the authors' list to be changed in the course of revisions.

Importantly, researchers early on become accustomed to the various genres required by journals.[4] Students initially become aware of established genres and forms of argumentation when they carry out literature reviews. Later on, when they prepare texts for publication, they pay attention to instructions usually provided by journals for prospective authors. "We make sure our students look at these instructions and have them try to follow them," says one professor (P4).

The Perception of Audience and its Relationships with Writing: Communication and Genre Learning

A crucial decision in the doctoral experience is defining a research problem within a specialized area of the discipline. Students spend significant amounts of time studying the relevant literature on their respective research problems. One professor states:

> I give each student a list of articles related to their topics, which they must read and discuss with me. ... They must also produce written reports on these reading ... like reviews. Once this literature is well known by the student, we can proceed to define specific research questions for experimental procedures. (P5)

The student is made to understand that her research must add to existing knowledge. This fund of knowledge must therefore be read, reviewed and understood.

The literature review serves other purposes. In the course of the effort of becoming familiar with the names, the methodologies and the findings that are relevant to their specializations, students not only explore established genres but also develop an identification with "invisible networks" of scientists whose articles they are reading (Fortes & Lomnitz, 1991). Initially, this is one-way identification: the student begins to express herself using the specialized terminology and naming the authors she deems important (or those deemed important by her advisor).

Interacting with a scientific audience, however, starts out concretely within the lab at the beginning of doctoral studies. The student's initial audience is represented by their direct advisors and other qualified researchers in the lab. One student says:

> I'm about to make a presentation of my thesis proposal to the researchers in the institute. It must be a three-year project, with clear objectives. I have to convince them that I've read enough to understand what I'm doing. ... (S2)

A second student pointed out that he first worked on his proposal with two thesis advisors, before making a presentation to the institute's research committee. It is interesting to note that he uses the first person plural:

> We [his two tutors and himself] have to defend this proposal before the committee ... whether it's interesting for the lab ... we get comments on method, timing. .... (S6)

Further on in their work, students travel to conferences to make their first presentations before a wider audience:

> Well, I guess we all want to attend conferences ... I mean, what's the point of working so hard in the lab if nobody's going to find out what you're doing. (S3)

At this point, it would seem that, beyond merely complying with an academic requirement of the doctoral program, conference presentations emerge as a necessity for the student, who begins to feel the need to communicate with a wider audience to justify his work in the lab. Communication of results emerges as an existential necessity for a budding scientist.

A professor points out that conference presentations may be papers or posters. She feels that student newcomers are more comfortable initially with poster presentations.

She states that conferences are means by which students become familiarized with academic models of communication and evaluation:

> We're very focused on conference presentations, both locally

and internationally. Every year we send papers to the International Conference of Neuroscience and the National Conference of Physiological Sciences. This allows us to see whether our work measures up. (S5)

Before travelling to a conference, students and professors have seminar sessions where papers are presented and discussed.

Writing for an international public means writing in English (Buckingham, 2008; Englander, 2011). One head of a lab stated that it is desirable at the very least

> for students to read English and write well in Spanish. Our students come to us with deficits in reading and writing [in their native Spanish]. (P4)

Research directors monitor their students' writing of first drafts in Spanish, which are also read and commented on by student peers. A student said

> My advisor supervises all our publications and in fact we publish through him. We sort of write up the introduction, the materials, the methods and the discussion. Then he reads it and makes a lot of corrections.(S3)

At that point the Spanish version must be translated to English. Some established researchers do this work themselves. They then reach out for assistance in improving their written English. For example, says one student:,

> Some investigators rely on external consultants. My advisor knows somebody who works for *Scientific American* in style and grammar correction. He sends his papers to this guy before submitting it to a journal. (S4)

Students must learn written and spoken English, but they also learn that not all scientific language is textual. A professor points out that

> when our students go to conferences they find people from all over speaking in English ... at first students only understand half of what's going on ... but then they see presenters using images ... and this helps a lot. (P2)

Standardization seems to be an aid in L2 writing. Learning to write specialized English is in a way facilitated by the standardized genres, structures, styles and specialized vocabulary employed by scientific journals.

CONCLUSION

> Transformations in learning careers take many forms. They are not predetermined, although they are oriented by the habitus of the individual and by the material and cultural contexts within which the habitus has developed and the person is located.(Bloomer and Hodkinson, 2000, p. 591)

From the findings two aspects stand out: i) learning to produce texts by working initially on professors' manuscripts, and ii) a collaborative environment in the lab. Although the responsibility for carrying out an experiment and preparing a paper fall to one student, this is done collaboratively, following several moments that we were able to glean from the interviews:

1. The literature review: searching bibliographic databases available online from the university library.
2. The production of experimental data.[5]
3. The analysis of the discursive models required by journals. Preparing a draft for discussion among researchers and fellow students in the lab.
4. Preparing and making presentations at conferences.
5. Further drafts are prepared by the author-student with the assistance of corrections and suggestions made by her student peers who make annotations using Microsoft Word's tracking control function.
6. Translating the text to English.
7. Submitting the text to a journal and rewriting it when necessary.

These moments are reported by students and professors as the standard steps toward publication and, hence, a successful PhD. The changing dispositions toward learning that underly this process are perceived as a *normalized* (Starke-Meyerring, 2011) series of stages to be followed. A student pointed out that this kind of work helped her to understand the *steps she must follow* to do written reports: where to start, where to search for data, and how to carry out analysis. However, this progression actually involves complex processes of induction, interaction, teamwork, genre learning, co-production and presentation to specialized publics. Identifying and learning to use specialized genres are central this development. It is interesting to note how the perceptions of its practitioners translate this manifold experience of transformation from a newcomer-apprentice to an autonomous scientist, i.e., a validated professional, into a straightforward trajectory. Standardization, in genres and in self-perceptions, seems to cover complex and multifaceted scientific practices with a "cloak of normalcy" (Starke-Meyerring, 2011) that contributes to stabilize and legitimate the research enterprise. But, seen from the perspective of the learning career, a PhD student in physiology brings into play multiple dispositions that develop in the working context of the lab.

NOTES

1. This research was supported by grants from the office of the Vice Rector for Research and Graduate Studies at the Autonomous University of Puebla and the Program for Academic Development (PROMEP) of the Federal Secretary of Education, Mexico. PROMEP Project IDCA-8850/BUAP-CA-249.

2. We want to express our gratitude to Paul Rogers and other readers for their comments and support in revising previous drafts of this text.

3. This lab has both master's and PhD students working together and often includes students from the schools of medicine and biology.

4. The most highly valued genres by our interviewees are research articles, brief communications and reviews. Simple and direct writing is valued by editors and reviewers, a fact that is not often grasped initially by students and which they must learn.

5. This expression is too facile, glossing over extremely complex and time-consuming activities in a lab: preparing an experiment, executing it, and collecting data.

REFERENCES

Bazerman, C. (2006). The writing of social organization and the literate situating of cognition: Extending Goody's social implications of writing. In D. Olson & M. Cole (Eds.), *Technology, literacy and the evolution of society: Implications of the work of Jack Goody* (pp. 215-240). Mawah, NJ: Erlbaum.

Becher, T., & Trowler, P. (2001). *Academic tribes and territories. intellectual enquiry and the culture of disciplines* (2nd ed.). Buckingham, UK: The Society for Research into Higher Education & Open University Press.

Blakeslee, A. M. (1997). Activity, context, interaction and authority: Learning to write scientific papers in situ. *Journal of Business and Technical Communication, 11*(2), 125.

Bloomer, M., & Hodkinson, P. (2000). Learning Careers: Continuity and change in young people's dispositions to learning. *British Educational Research Journal, 26*(5), 583-597.

Buckingham, L. (2008). Development of English academic writing competence by Turkish scholars. *International Journal of Doctoral Studies, 3,* 1-18.

Carrasco, A., & Kent, R. (2011). Leer y escribir en el doctorado o el reto de formarse como autor de ciencias. *Revista Mexicana de Investigación Educativa, 16*(51), 679-686.

Clark, B. (1993). *The research foundations of graduate education: Germany, Britain, France, United States and Japan.* Berkeley, CA: University of California Press.

Delamont, S., & Atkinson, P. (2001). Doctoring uncertainty: Mastering craft knowledge. *Social Studies of Science, 31*(1), 87-107.

Englander, K. (2011). The globalized world of English scientific publishing: An analytical proposal that situates a multilingual scholar. In G. López-Bonilla & K. Englander (Eds.), *Discourses and identities in contexts of educational change. Contributions from the United States and México* (pp. 209-228). Pieterlen, Switzerland: Peter Lang, 209-228.

Fortes, J., & Lomnitz, L. A. (1990). Becoming a scientist in Mexico: The challenge of creating a scientific community in an underdeveloped country, University Park, PA: Penn State University Press.

Kent, R., Carrasco, A., & Velázquez, I. (2009). *Trayectorias de formación de jóvenes científicos. Proyecto de Investigación del Programa Institucional de Fomento a la Investigación y a la Consolidación de Cuerpos Académicos, Vicerrectoría de Investigación y Estudios de Posgrado.* Benemérita Universidad Autónoma de Puebla.

Knorr-Cetina, K. (1999). *Epistemic cultures: The cultures of knowledge societies.* Cambridge, MA: Harvard University Press.

Latour, B., & Woolgar, S. (1986). *Laboratory life. The construction of scientific facts.* Princeton, NJ: Princeton University Press.

Laudel, G., & Gläser, J. (2008). From apprentice to colleague: The metamorphosis of early career researchers. *Higher Education, 55,* 387-406.

Newell, G. E., Beach, R., Smith, J., & Van Der Heide, J. (2011). Teaching and learning argumentative reading and writing: A review of research. *Reading Research Quarterly, 46(3), 273-304.*

Overington, M. (1977). The scientific community as audience: Toward a rhetorical analysis of science. *Philosophy and Rhetoric, 10*(3), 143-164.

Parry, Sharon (2007). *Disciplines and Doctorates.* Dordrecht, Netherlands: Springer.

Prior, P. (1998). *Writing/disciplinarity: A sociohistoric account of literate activity in the academy.* Mawah, NJ: Erlbaum.

Prior, P. (2006). A sociocultural theory of writing. In C. A. MacArthur, S. Graham, & J. Fitzgerald (Eds.), *Handbook of Writing Research* (pp. 54-66). New York: Guilford.

SIICYT (2008). *Sistema de información sobre investigación científica y tecnológica).* Benito Juarez, México: Consejo Nacional de Ciencia y Tecnología.

Starke-Meyerring, D. (2011). The paradox of writing in doctoral education: Students experience. In L. McAlpine & C. Amundsen (Eds.), *Doctoral Education: Research-Based Strategies for Doctoral Students, Supervisors and Administradorsi* (pp. 75-95). New York: Springer.

SECTION 5.
SCIENTIFIC AND ACADEMIC PRACTICE

Writing in science has long been a concern of writing studies in part because it gets so visibly to the issue of the role of writing in the formation of knowledge and contests so directly the idea that science eschews language to go directly to facts of nature, untainted by the colors of rhetoric. But of course modern science could not exist without the publication system of science, and that would not exist without the journals and books that must be written to represent and contest knowledge. On the other hand, those writings would not reach toward scientific knowledge if they did not accountably attempt to represent our experience of the world through methodically collected evidence, theoretically careful argument, and communal comparison and aggregation of findings across the wide intertexts of fields of inquiry.

Yet it is the practical importance of science and the practical difficulties scientists face in writing science that keep it at the forefront of writing studies, for these motives challenge us in our role as writing educators to understand the struggles of scientific writers and provide support for writing development in scientists' degree and post-degree careers. It is to these struggles to write successfully for publication and to meet communal standards that all seven of the chapters in this section speak—by studying the practices and orientations of either erstwhile writers seeking publication (Mur-Duenas; and Boch et al.) or experts with substantial publication records (Emerson; Watson; Keranen et al.; Iñesta & Castelló; and Riazi). The struggles are even greater for non-native English speaking scientists who seek international publication in English language journals, and to that particular problem three of the articles are addressed (Watson; Keranen et al.; and Riazi).

Yet, while the problems of scientists writing may seem specialized and particular, they highlight phenomena of importance to all writers, often with a striking clarity because of the visible specialization of the writing. In the past, scientific writing was one of the key research sites for exploring genre, intertextuality, nominalization and lexis, register, and specific purposes. The articles here find in scientific writing windows into a new range of issues of more general concern: the processes and practices of advanced writers, their cognitive and affective orientations, their development over careers, and the role of evaluation. This research is leading us beyond the typical school-based models earlier

research proposed for writing processes and development to see the complexity and subtlety gained by writers engaged in advanced intellectual endeavors.
—CB

CHAPTER 20.
THE LIFE CYCLE OF THE SCIENTIFIC WRITER: AN INVESTIGATION OF THE SENIOR ACADEMIC SCIENTIST AS WRITER IN AUSTRALASIAN UNIVERSITIES

Lisa Emerson
Massey University

> [T]here has been a great deal of research on writing; however, there has been less consideration of ... the transition from novice to expert science writer. (Yore, Hand, & Florence, 2004, p. 673).

Despite extensive interest in teaching writing in the sciences and the rhetoric of science in recent years, the beliefs, attitudes and practices of the senior scientific writer remain largely unexplored. While many resources on how to write scientific documents are available,[1] Morrs and Murray (2001) and Bishop and Ostrum (1997), both commenting on the scarcity of research exploring the writing process of academics more generally, suggest that there is a gap between the writing processes described in such texts and "the real contexts and practices of [academic] writers" (Morrs & Murray 2001, p. 3), and that empirical research on the writing practices of academic writers is needed. Recent empirical research on academic scientists as writers by Larry Yore and his associates between 2002 and 2008 explored the practices and beliefs of scientific writers post-PhD. The present study focuses on a smaller section of the academic scientific community, the senior scientific writer, hypothesising that this subset of the scientific community, in line with Dreyfus and Dreyfus's model of expertise, will exhibit specific attitudes and beliefs and engage with a wider audience than that identified in the studies of Yore and his associates.

EXPERTISE AND THE CHARACTERISTICS OF THE EXPERT SCIENCE WRITER

Traditionally, experts have been characterised, in contrast to the novice, by the extent of their knowledge and complexity of their skills (see, for example, Berliner, 1994; Carter et al., 1988; Livingston & Borko, 1989).

Advances in the field have challenged both a simple expert/novice dichotomy and the notion of expertise as skills and knowledge accumulation. Dreyfus' five stage model (Dreyfus, 2004; Dreyfus & Dreyfus, 1986, 2005), an influential model of expertise development, characterises expertise as developing through five stages (novice, advanced beginner, competent, proficient and expert) which outline a progression from explicit rule-following and detached, analytical engagement at novice level to advanced, intuitive "know-how" based on experience and engagement at the expert level.

Experts, according to Dreyfus' model, exhibit a number of characteristics. First, their expertise is *context-specific* and achieved by situational experience acquired over extensive periods (Dall'Alba & Sandberg, 2006). Second, they exhibit specific *attitudes* to their work: they are engaged and emotionally invested in working to a standard of excellence based on internal discipline rather than external supervision (Benner, 1984, 2004). Third, their *practice* is based on tacit understanding of context, practice and discipline which they have built up over an extensive period (Dreyfus, 2004); and finally, experts have a holistic view of complex situations within the context of practice, and are able to engage both analytical and intuitive understandings of a situation dependent on their understanding and experience of context (Dreyfus, 2004). Benner (2004, p.189), following Aristotle, characterises this as exhibiting skills of both *techne* (standardised routines in practice) and "*phronesis* (situated actions based on skill, judgment, character, and wisdom)."

Dall'Alba and Sandberg (2006), in their critique of this model, argue that "understanding of and in practice" is another vital component in the development of professional capability and that an individual's *beliefs* about the nature and purpose of their practice may define an individual's ability to attain expertise.

The literature on expert science writing has tended to focus primarily on the novice-expert distinction, and is largely informed by older models of expertise based on skills and knowledge. For example, Fahnestock and Secor (1986) focus on the expert writer's ability to engage with the needs of a scientific audience, Holyoak (1991) on expert writers' writing strategies, and Carter (1990) and Geisler (1994) on expert science writers' knowledge of both general writing and discipline-specific writing skills.

Florence and Yore (2004), however, suggest that expertise involves more than "stacking additional skills and knowledge on pre-existing competencies" (p. 640). They observe that expertise in science writing involves "a complex interplay of cognitive abilities, emotional dispositions, strategies, metacognitive awareness, executive control, domain knowledge, and discourse knowledge" (p. 640).

Attitudes of Expert Science Writers

Although Dreyfus (2004) sees attitudes as a critical factor of expertise, research into senior scientists' attitudes to writing, ie the extent to which they enjoy or feel confident about writing, has been very limited. James Hartley and Alan Branthwaite (1989)in a study of academic psychologists, noted that the most productive writers in psychology had positive attitudes to academic writing, and felt that their writing was important to them (see also, Hartley & Knapper, 1984). They identify attitudinal distinctions amongst writing-active psychologists, that of "anxious" and "enthusiastic" writer, noting that those who enjoyed writing were less anxious and most productive: writing anxiety decreased with experience and productivity.

A more recent study, Florence and Yore (2004), following Daley (1999) identifies specific emotional characteristics of expert science writers, seeing them as driven individuals, continually dissatisfied with present understandings (Bereiter & Scardamalia, 1993), passionate about disciplinary investigation, and compelled to write by their passion to contribute to a continuing disciplinary debate.

A somewhat broader literature has gauged academics' attitudes towards professional writing. Rodgers and Rodgers (1999), for example, show that prolific academic writers are likely to enjoy writing, be energised by writing, and respond constructively to reviewer criticism. A sense of personal accomplishment and dedication (Fox & Faver, 1985; Jones & Preusz, 1993), resilience (Boice, 1994), and confidence (Morrs & Murray, 2001; Shah, J., Shah, A., & Pietrobon, 2009) have also been identified as key characteristics of successful academic writers.

Beliefs

Dall'Alba and Sandberg (2006) suggest that a practitioner's initial beliefs about the nature of a particular practice are an important determinant of the path to expertise. Florence and Yore (2004), Bereiter and Scardamalia (1987) and Keys (1999), by contrast, see beliefs as shifting over time, suggesting that while novices see scientific writing as knowledge reporting, experts see the purpose of writing as being the construction or transformation of knowledge.

However, the latter construction of expert beliefs about scientific writing was not supported by Yore et al. (2002), Yore, Hand, & Prain (2004), and only tentatively supported by Yore, Florence, Pearson, & Weaver (2006). Yore et al. (2004) conclude:

> the [beliefs of the] prototypical science writer ... did not match the literature-based image [that expert writers see writing as knowledge building[2]]. These scientists perceived writing as knowledge telling not knowledge building (p. 346).

Not only did the beliefs of Yore et al.'s participants not conform to the literature on writing expertise, they also didn't conform with the scientists' stated understanding of the nature of science. Yore et al. observe (2004) that participants in their studies described writing in language associated with a traditional positivist view of science, even when they held a more modernist view of the nature of science. However, they do note that "the metacognition [of these scientists' views] of written discourse was tacit" (p. 346), observing that the scientists did recognise that drafting enabled them to construct a clearer story, but without conscious awareness of clarification as construction.

Related to this connection between beliefs concerning the nature of science and the purpose of writing is the question of whether scientific writing is persuasive, Yore et al. (2002, 2004) suggest that although scientists are unlikely to believe their writing is persuasive, nevertheless, they do use writing for persuasive purposes.

According to Dreyfus' model (2004), one of the difficulties of identifying the beliefs of expert practitioners is that their understanding of their purpose and practice is intuitive. As Benner (2004) observes of expert nurses: "situated practical innovations or sensible variations in practice may seem intuitively obvious to the [expert] practitioner and might not be easily captured in a narrative description of the situation" (p. 196). Such observations might equally be applied to academic science writers, most of whom learn scientific writing not by instruction but by observation and engagement with senior practitioners followed by extensive practice (Florence & Yore, 2004; Jacoby & Gozales, 1991), and whose beliefs about writing may indeed be tacit. Observation or close analysis of writers' descriptions of their writing process may yield a more useful understanding of scientists' beliefs about writing than direct questioning.

WRITING TASKS AND AUDIENCE

Yore at al. (2004) comment that novice scientists most commonly begin their professional life by writing for the disciplinary community related to their doctoral research, "but some scientists belong to several discourse communities and cross borders among these communities, dealing with the public awareness of science, professional education of scientists, and multiple research interests" (p. 344). Similarly, Bazerman (1998) suggests that science communication begins with communication within a narrowly defined disciplinary community and then spreads into the public arena. Bazerman (1988) further suggests, more generally, that competent writers tend to cross disciplinary boundaries and conventions rather than writing focusing narrowly on the requirements of a single discourse community—which may lead to the expectation that senior scientific writers would engage with a range of audiences, both peers and public.

However, the findings of Yore et al. (2002, 2004, 2006) in relation to writing tasks suggest that expert science writers are not broadly but narrowly focused in terms of audience and task. Their conclusions are somewhat contradictory, but four clear findings emerge from the composite data: most scientists write primarily for teaching purposes; they write secondarily for the small number of journals that they read within their discipline; scientists are unlikely to write across disciplinary boundaries or for a general audience; and they do not see communicating with non-scientific audiences (other than students) as a necessary role of a scientist.

Within these narrow constraints, Yore et al.'s findings (2002, 2004, 2006) suggest science writers are highly cognisant of audience and skilled in writing in a way that suits their disciplinary discourse community (see Fahnestock & Secor, 1986; Ferrari, Bouffand, & Rainville, 1998). However, the extent to which expert scientists can articulate their rhetorical choices remains largely unexamined.

In relation to task and audience, there are some weaknesses in the studies of Yore and his colleagues. In particular, the range of tasks examined did not include some common activities that might be expected of senior academic scientists, e.g., rewriting or editing for co-authors, or reviewing for journals. Furthermore, only two non-scientific genres beyond lecture notes were investigated: letters to the editor and essays/short articles (conflating science and non-science publications). This study addresses this problem by investigating a greater range of publication types.

METHOD

This study investigates a subset of the scientific community in Australasian universities, the senior academic science writer, using the Dreyfus and Dreyfus' (1986) model of practitioner expertise in the context of research into academic scientific writers. The participants for this study comprised 20 university scientists (thirteen male and seven female) who had achieved the status of associate professor or professor[3] from seven universities in Australia and New Zealand. The sample included theoretical (e.g., physicists) and applied scientists (e.g., researchers in human and animal nutrition, and environmental economics), with an aim of sampling as wide a range of scientific disciplines as possible. The sample was collected using a snowballing effect, asking participants to identify colleagues in related (but not identical) disciplines who were senior scientists, with a high publication rate, who might be interested in participating. The sample's median experience as research scientists was 25 years (dating from the completion of the PhD). All were prolific writers: several participants had published over 200 peer reviewed scientific papers as well as text books, book chapters and industry reports.

Data collection methods used were a questionnaire and a semi-structured individual interview. The questionnaire collected demographic and quantitative data for comparative purposes and identified common writing activities. Participants were asked to identify writing tasks they had engaged with in the last six months out of a list of 22 items including pre-writing activities (such as brainstorming and note-taking), writing tasks in a range of genres (such as writing a journal article, industry report, web-page, popular science article or piece of fiction), post-writing activities (e.g., reviewing the writing of a colleague or co-author), and quality assurance tasks (e.g., peer reviewing for a journal or editing a journal). Participants were then asked to identify up to five items which had taken up most of their professional time in the last six months. Nineteen out of 20 participants returned a useable questionnaire.

The interview was semi-structured, including questions covering writing process and environment, attitudes to science writing, issues of audience and persuasion, and how participants had gained skills as writers of science. These were followed by specific questions which arose from the questionnaire. Interviews ranged in duration from one to three hours. All 20 participants completed the interview. Interviews were transcribed and coded by hand.

RESULTS

The results have been analysed by addressing the sample as a whole: because the sample size is not large, and there was very little disciplinary overlap, analysing the senior scientists by discipline was not appropriate in this study.

Attitudes

Benner's (2004) and Dreyfus' (2004) suggestion that experts tend to be emotionally engaged with their practice was strongly supported by this study. The overall attitude of the senior scientists to writing was strongly positive. Given that this group of participants were highly productive writers, this supports the findings of Hartley and Branthwaite (1989) that highly productive writers were likely to be more positive and less anxious about writing. Eighteen participants said they enjoyed writing, and most spoke with passion about, not just their science, but also their science writing:

> I love writing. It's probably the part of the job that I love the most.

> I love to write—and to convey the passion I feel for my work.

> If I had the option, I would sit in my office all day and write.

When asked to rate themselves on a scale of one to ten, where 10 is an excellent writer, 17 rated themselves as seven or above, indicating a high level of confidence.

Most (16) participants were confident enough as writers and scientists to engage robustly with peers and reviewers rather than simply accepting critique:

> So eventually, after about eight or nine papers where he had done this I wrote to him and said "I know you're trying to be helpful; I really appreciate the effort you're putting in; but to be perfectly honest, I think you're going over the top, because I believe you are now trying to convert my writing into your style. I'm very happy to accept the things that really do make it clearer, but I frankly want to retain my style" … He got back and he said "yeah yeah fine. No problems. Take or leave what I say as you see fit."

Although most of the group classified themselves as confident writers, all, at some stage in the interview, discussed situations where they became anxious about writing. Generally this related to writing to an unfamiliar audience or in an unaccustomed genre, or writing for a high sakes journal with a specific and tightly controlled style such as *Nature*. However, many participants discussed this anxiety in positive terms:

> I do quite a lot of outreach type of activities and sometimes that involves writing things that are very non-specialist and I try to write them in ways that people who don't have scientific backgrounds can understand. It's challenging, but I enjoy doing it.

Only three participants could have been classified as anxious writers (Hartley & Branthwaite, 1989). However, these writers had developed strategies for overcoming their difficulties, mainly through collaboration with colleagues who were more confident or proficient writers.

Generally, participants wrote because they were compelled to do so by their passion for their discipline and not by external pressures. Without exception their attitudes to external systems designed to compel a certain level of productivity[4] were negative, with many of the participants suggesting such external controls were not conducive to high-quality science research, which was their primary concern.

Attitudes to popular scientific writing varied. All participants commented on the importance of communicating with the public about science, but they were divided on whether they enjoyed or felt confident writing in these genres. Several spoke of the pleasure of writing to groups who would be actively using their work (e.g., growers), or of enjoying the challenge of writing science for lay people (e.g., a newspaper column or a school text) while others saw writing for the public as their biggest and most fear-inducing challenge.

BELIEFS

All participants believed writing is not simply reporting science but part of science, both in relation to writing for peers and writing for the public, and their beliefs about writing were consistent with their modernist beliefs about the nature of science, i.e., they saw writing as being about knowledge construction rather than simply knowledge reporting.

> Writing is an incredibly important part of science. ... the next great advance in science is always based on ... half a dozen little tiny advances in science, and these are written

in journals. And it takes somebody clever to put those little threads together and do the next best thing. So it's an absolutely critical part of the process.

Writing was seen as being part of idea generation, both in relation to the immediate study participants were engaged with and the larger debate. Only one participant said he wrote an outline prior to writing; the rest generated ideas through the writing:

> You don't really know what the main point's going to be until you start telling the story and analysing the data. And what you discover in that process definitely drives the next set of experiments. So I teach my students not to try to understand the whole problem they're working on first and then start writing because we could have missed something fundamental that we're not going to see until we start writing about it and thinking what the story is.

The concept of "telling a story" or "creating a picture" in the reader's mind were recurring themes for all participants, again supporting the notion of scientific writing as knowledge construction. Several participants reflected on the complexity of results and evidence, and the role of the scientific writer in sifting through the evidence to construct the story:

> You are telling a story and in truth you've done all these experiments and this didn't work and this didn't work, but this did and ... we've got to somehow sift out of all this complexity, what we've learned, and throw the extraneous stuff away, and tell a story.

The more experienced participants suggested that their mastery of their field meant that, when they designed a project, they simultaneously anticipated the outcome, and for this reason, generated ideas at a higher level than simply interpreting the data when writing:

> you get to the stage where you've worked it out what it means , , , you've got an idea of where you you're heading before you start... . That isn't to say that in the process of writing, and then pulling in the references to give the embellishments and the support or the caveats, that you don't suddenly have

a fresher idea than you've had. It might take a different direction. But it's not from the very beginning working out your ideas.

Several participants believed the purpose of producing writing, evidence, results, and communicating about science to the public was an ethical dimension of science:

> This is how much money I've had in research grants over the years. That's 600 hip replacements or 120 septum treatments for one year of breast cancer. That's what my scientific research has cost the tax payer. How do I justify that? Who pays for what we do? It's people who clean the buildings at three o'clock in the morning ... how do we say to these people that that was money well spent? ... We have to communicate the beauty and the passion around the subject and get people excited. So they see that science is ... a wonderful thing.

However, the question of whether scientific writing (beyond grant applications) was persuasive caused most of the participants in this study some difficulty. Most participants (18), after considerable discussion, decided that scientific writing was persuasive, but with over half expressing reluctance or reservation, particularly in relation to speculation or "rhetorical language." These anxieties seemed to relate mainly to the importance of not biasing results, and of, in the language of creative writing, "showing not telling," i.e., letting the evidence speak to the reader. Generally the key to persuasion was seen as shaping and presenting enough evidence to convince the reader of its significance or relevance. While they acknowledged that authorial construction of the evidence was part of writing, they felt that the implications of the evidence should, to come extent, be shaped by the reader. This sits somewhat uneasily with beliefs of scientific writing as "story," which implies theme as well as plot, and would bear further investigation.

TASKS

Contrary to Yore et al.'s (2002) findings, the participants in this study were not narrowly focused in terms of audience and task, and saw the role of science as being to communicate on a wider stage.

Classroom-based students were not a primary audience for the participants in this study: only three participants identified writing teaching materials for a class as a key recent activity. Instead, participants engaged primarily with scientific peers, both within their discipline and more widely within the scientific community. The most common recent activities were brainstorming or making notes for a new project and drafting a scientific paper (19 participants), editing a research proposal, redrafting or editing a co-authored paper (18 participants), drafting a research proposal and peer reviewing for a journal (17 participants). Interviews showed that participants had not only engaged with these tasks in the last six months, but saw these activities as amongst their most regular writing tasks. With the exception of brainstorming or taking notes, these activities were also identified as the writing tasks that had taken up most of the participants' time in the last six months. All participants wrote not only in their own discipline but also for cross-disciplinary or broad-based journals.

A majority (14), while primarily writing for peers, also wrote for a broader public. In the previous six months, five participants had written for a popular journal, five for a science-related website and three had engaged in some form of creative writing. During their professional lives, participants had published creative writing (four), popular science (12), and documents for specific non-scientific audience (eight). Furthermore, rather than showing scepticism about popular forms of scientific writing, over half of the participants (12) expressed strong interest in having more opportunity to write popular science or creative non-fiction.

In terms of audience, all but one participant said they were continually making rhetorical decisions based on audience. Several participants commented that there were very few people in their field, most of whom they knew personally, and so when they wrote for this small disciplinary group they could target their writing to the knowledge and interests of this group. But generally participants were engaged in writing for larger cross-disciplinary scientific (and sometimes non-scientific) audiences, and so were conscious of the need to consider to engage their audience:

> the ... common thread from an 8 year old to an 80 year old professor is to try and think well what would be their experience and perspective? ... To help people assimilate information you've got to think, well what hanging hook have they already got in their brain? Most hanging hooks are shaped by experience and knowledge at that time. So [for]an 8 year old ... their world is small, ... this is me and there's my mum and dad and there's my dog and there's my school and that's about it. ... So I'm trying to link in to their level of experience. ... Whereas when I'm writing for a scientific audi-

ence—and undergraduates is different from postgraduates is different to a research colleague—I'm going to assume a level of knowledge.

All participants articulated ways in which they managed some aspects of style, particularly in relation to various audience:

> [with scientists in the discipline] I'm going to assume that they're busy people, and I'm going to assume that they will want clarity, and they will want to be able to skim it. So I will tend to use a style of writing, which is: I'm going to tell you in my first sentence or my first couple of words what this paragraph is going to be about. If I'm writing for somewhere in-between. like an undergraduate who's got a degree of knowledge—I'm going to keep the terminology from overwhelming the concept and I'm going to be trying to pull out the concept ... that's number one I want them to get, the terminology is number two. So I have a priority of how I want you to pick up this information.

As well as considering audience, all participants engaged analytically with issues of sentence length, active and passive voice, and use of personal pronouns. Beyond this, however, they were likely to work more intuitively, using broad terms such as conciseness, clarity, story, creativity and beauty, without explaining what constituted these essential qualities of scientific writing in relation to audience. This more intuitive approach to writing style they saw as based on immersion in the discourse:

> fundamentally the ability to write comes from the fact we've read. There's a resonance to the language ... we write almost instinctively because there's a register of voice that we're used to and we've picked it up, you know, from our reading. Things unconsciously become part of the means in our brain and they end up on the page.

Even when working with PhD students, all but one participant worked intuitively, rewriting sections of student writing rather than using the language of writing instruction. Direct questions about style, such as questions about the use of metaphor or paragraph structure, usually elicited long discussion where the participant worked their way towards a tentative answer.

DISCUSSION

The findings of this study provide support for the hypothesis that senior academic scientists would conform with Dreyfus and Dreyfus' model of expertise as demonstrating particular attitudes, beliefs and practices concerning writing which differ from those of academic scientists more generally.

Yore and his colleagues, investigating scientists post-PhD, develop a portrait of the scientist as narrowly focused in practice and demonstrating an understanding of the purpose of scientific writing which is both limited and inconsistent with their beliefs about the nature of science. Such observations contrast with Bazerman (1988), who perceives expert writers more generally as working across boundaries, and science itself as moving from a narrow to a broader focus (Bazerman, 1998) and with the literature on expert writers (Yore et al., 2002, 2004).

The findings of this study support Bazerman's observations and contrast with those of Yore and associates. The participants in this study were broadly focused in practice and showed a sophisticated understanding of the purpose of scientific writing which was consistent with both research into the writing of experts and their understanding of the nature of science. While they were all engaged in narrowly-focused writing in their discipline (though often by reviewing/revising the work of others), participants were also engaged with broader cross-disciplinary audiences and saw writing for non-scientists as an important aspect of science.

Senior academic scientists in this study perceived writing to be an intrinsic aspect of the science itself, and implicitly perceived the function of writing as being knowledge construction. Their focus on developing and shaping new knowledge through writing, creating a story or picture for the reader, and through consciously excluding information in the interests of crafting a story, suggests they have a sophisticated understanding of the integration of writing, science and meaning, which is developed largely through immersion in practice. While the issue of persuasion was contentious, these senior academic scientists were aware of the importance of crafting their work for an audience, and writing in a way that would enable the reader to make meaning from the evidence presented.

Furthermore, in line with Hartley and Branthwaite (1989), Boice (1994), Morrs and Murray (2001), and Shah et al. (2009), most participants in this group were strongly engaged by writing: most relished the challenges of writing in new genres to new audiences, showed an ability to engage both analytical and intuitive understandings of scientific writing, and exhibited both confidence and resilience.

Some of the differences between this study and those of Yore and associates may, in part, be attributed to methodology: for example, this study investigated a wider range of writing tasks, and extrapolated beliefs from detailed analysis of scientists' description of their writing processes in relation to a particular project.

However, another explanation lies in the group investigated in this study and the model of expertise employed. Yore et al. construct the expert science writer as a scientist who is post-PhD. This study, following Dreyfus and Dreyfus (1986), Benner (1984, 2004) and Dall'Alba and Sandberg (2006), started from the premise that expertise is developed more slowly, and that the expert science writer is not simply a research scientist who has completed a PhD, but one who is acknowledged as a disciplinary leader through extensive publication and situational experience acquired over extensive periods. Such an individual is likely, according to Dreyfus and Dreyfus, to have developed an emotionally engaged, intuitive, broad view of both practice and context, and this is supported in this study.

One of the participants in this study, in a discussion of the wide range of genres and audiences he engaged with, proposed the idea of the "lifecycle" of scientific writers, postulating that scientific writers go through several stages in the types of writing they engage with post-PhD and that the final stage involves a more expansive view of science which leads to a perceived need to bring science into a broader arena for various publics. Subsequent discussion of this cycle with other participants led to acknowledgement that this was a general model that applied in the scientific community and lively debate about whether such a model was ideal. Such a model supports Dreyfus and Dreyfus' model and would bear further investigation.

One of the questions that might be asked of this study is whether the findings are generalisable beyond the Australasian context. This is not easy to answer without conducting empirical investigation beyond the Australasian context, but several factors suggest the findings may apply more broadly across Western nations. First, a little over a third of participants were born and educated (schooling and/or undergraduate studies) outside of Australasia. Two-thirds had conducted their PhD or post-doctoral education in a university in another (most commonly Western) country. And finally, all participants saw themselves as part of an international community of scholars, within their own discipline and, often, more broadly; all had co-authored work with international colleagues, and most travelled regularly to international conferences. Nevertheless, it would be useful to test the generalisability of the findings by investigating the beliefs, attitudes and experiences of senior scientists as writers in other countries. It would be particularly interesting to investigate these issues in countries where English was not a first language and where scientists, in order to join their disciplinary communities, were compelled to work in a second language.

This study suggests further directions for future research. Given the limited empirical research into the beliefs and practices of the expert science writer, and the conflicting findings of this study and those of Yore et al., it is clear that more research is needed on both the writing and development of academic scientists. In particular, it would be useful to investigate the concept of the "lifecycle" of the scientific writer, perhaps in the context of Dreyfus and Dreyfus's five-stage model of expertise, by researching the attitudes, beliefs and writing practices of academic scientists at various stages in their academic careers. An investigation of whether academic scientists' beliefs about science and writing change over time on the basis of situational experience would be particularly useful given the conflicting observations of Dall'Alba and Sandberg (2006), and Florence and Yore (2004). Academic scientists, it seems, are an almost "forgotten tribe" of writers, and yet they have much to tell us about writing in practice, especially in the context of the teaching of science writing; it is surely timely that their voices are heard.

NOTES

1. See, for example Penrose and Katz (2004), Blum, Knudson and Henig (2006), and Day & Gastel (2006).

2. See Bereiter and Scardamalia, 1987.

3. Australia and New Zealand follow the British system of academic ranking: associate professor and professor status is reserved for faculty who have achieved academic leadership in their field.

4. E.g., New Zealand's Performance based research fund.

REFERENCES

Bazerman, C. (1988). *Shaping written knowledge.* Madison, WI: University of Wisconsin Press.
Bazerman, C. (1998). The production of technology and the production of human meaning, *Journal of Business and Technical communication, 12,* 381-187.
Benner, P. (1984). *From novice to expert: Excellence and power in clinical nursing practice.* Reading, MA: Addison-Wesley.

Benner, P. (2004). Using the Dreyfus model of skill acquisition to describe and interpret skill acquisition and clinical judgement in nursing practice and education. *Bulletin of Science, Technology and Society, 24*(3), 189-199.

Bereiter, C., & Scardamalia, M. (1987). *The psychology of written composition.* Hillsdale, NJ: Erlbaum.

Bereiter, C., & Scardamalia, M. (1993). *Surpassing ourselves.* Peru, IL: Open Court.

Berliner, D. (1994). Expertise: The wonder of exemplary performances. In J. Mangieri & C. Block (Eds.), *Creating powerful thinking in teachers and students: Diverse perspectives* (pp.161-186). Fort Worth, TX: Harcourt Brace College.

Bishop, W., & Ostrom, H. (1997), *Genre and writing: Issues, arguments and alternatives.* Portsmouth, NH: Boynton/Cook.

Blum, D., Knudson, M., & Henig, R. M. (2006). *A field guide for scientific writers (2nd ed.).* New York: OUP.

Boice, R. (1994). *How writers journey to comfort and fluency: A psychological adventure.* Westport, CT: Praeger, Greenwood.

Carter, M. (1990). The idea of expertise: An exploration of cognitive and social dimensions of writing, *College Composition and Communication, 41,* 265-286.

Carter, K., Cushing, K., Sabers, D., Stein, P., & Berliner, D. (1988). Expert-novice differences in perceiving and processing visual classroom information. *Journal of Teacher Education, 39,* 25-31.

Dall'Alba, G., & Sandberg, J. (2006). Unveiling professional development: A critical review of the stages models, *Review of Educational Research, 76,* 383-412.

Daley, B. J. (1999). Novice to expert: An exploration of how experts learn, *Adult Education Quarterly, 49,* 133-148.

Day, R. A., & Gastel, B. (2006). *How to write and publish a scientific paper.* Westport, CT: Greenwood.

Dreyfus, H. L., & Dreyfus, S. E. (1986). Mind over machine: The power of human intuition and expertise in the era of the computer. New York: Free Press.

Dreyfus, H. L. (2004). The five-stage model of adult skill acquisition, *Bulletin of Science, Technology and Society, 24*(3), 177-181.

Dreyfus, H. L., & Dreyfus, S. E. (2005). Peripheral vision: Expertise in real world contexts. *Organisation Studies, 26*(5), 779-792.

Fahnestock, J., & Secor, M. (1986). Accommodating science: The rhetorical life of science facts. *Written Communication, 3,* 275-296.

Ferrari, M., Bouffard, T., & Rainvile, L. (1998). What makes a good writer ? Differences in good and poor writers' self-regulation of writing. *Instructional Science, 26,* 473-488.

Florence, M. K., & Yore, L. D. (2004). Learning to write like a scientist, *Journal of Research in Science Teaching, 41,* 637-668.

Fox, M. F., & Faver, C. A. (1985). Men, women, and publication productivity: Patterns among social work academics, *The Sociological Quarterly, 26,* 537-49.

Geisler, C. (1994). *Academic literacy and the nature of expertise: Reading, writing, and knowing in academic philosophy.* Hillsdale, NJ: Erlbaum.

Hartley, J., & Branthwaite, A.(1989). The psychologist as wordsmith: A questionnaire study of the writing strategies of productive British psychologists, *Higher Education, 18,* 423-452.

Hartley, J., & Knapper, C. K. (1984). Academics and their writing, *Studies in Higher Education, 9,* 151-167.

Holyoak, K. (1991). Symbolic connectionism: Towards third-generation theories of expertise. In K. A. Ericsson, & J. Smith (Eds.), *Toward a general theory of expertise: Prospects and limits* (pp. 301-336). Cambridge, UK: Cambridge University Press.

Jacoby, S., & Gonzales, P. (1991). The constitution of expert-novice in scientific discourse. *Issues in Applied Linguistics, 2,* 149-181.

Jones, J. E., & Preusz, G. C. (1993). Attitudinal factors associated with individual factor research productivity, *Perceptual and Motor Skills, 76,* 1191-1198.

Keys, C. W. (1999). Revitalizing instruction in scientific genres: Connecting knowledge production in the writing to learn in science, *Science Education, 83,* 115-130.

Livingstone, C., & Borko, H. (1989). Expert-novice differences in teaching: A cognitive analysis and implications for teacher education. *Journal of Teacher Education, 40,* 36-42.

Morss, K., & Murray, R. (2001). Researching academic writing within a structured programme: Insights and outcomes, *Studies in Higher Education, 26(1),* 35- 52.

Penrose, A. M., & Katz, S. B. (2004). *Writing in the sciences: Exploring conventions of scientific discourse.* New York: Pearson Longman.

Rodgers, R., & Rodgers, N. (1999). The sacred spark of academic research, *Journal of Public Administration Research & Theory, 9*(3), 473-492.

Shah, J., Shah, A., & Pietrobon, R. (2009), Scientific writing of novice researchers: What difficulties and encouragements do they encounter?, *Academic Medicine, 84,* 511-516.

Yore. L. D., Hand, B. M., & Prain, V. (2002). Scientists as writers, *Science Education, 86,* 672-692.

Yore, L. D., Hand, B. M., & Florence, M. K. (2004). Scientists' views of science, models of writing, and science writing practices, *Journal of Research in Science Teaching, 41,* 338-369.

Yore, L. D., Florence, M. K., Pearson, T. W., & Weaver, A. J. (2006). Written discourse in scientific communities: A conversation with two scientists about their views of science, use of language, role of writing in doing science, and compatibility between their epistemic views and language, *International Journal of Science Education, 28*(2-3), 109-141.

CHAPTER 21.

PUBLICATION PRACTICES AND MULTILINGUAL PROFESSIONALS IN US UNIVERSITIES: TOWARDS CRITICAL PERSPECTIVES ON ADMINISTRATION AND PEDAGOGY

Missy Watson
Syracuse University

The stakes for publishing in English are high for scholars seeking advanced degrees, academic positions, tenure, promotion, or research funding within and beyond US borders.[1] The demands facing multilingual scholars[2] whose first language is other than English are no doubt comparable to those of native English speaking scholars. Multilingual writers, however, often negotiate cultural and linguistic divides in addition to navigating—as all publishing scholars must—the rhetorics of the text, topic, genre conventions, writing processes, and communication with gatekeepers. The literature that investigates publication practices and other high stakes writing processes of multilingual graduate students and faculty at US colleges and universities has been prolific, especially in the last ten years. Scholars, for example, have worked to demystify the manuscript writing and review process of publication for multilingual writers, noting the sociopolitical interactions that take place and the authorial identities formed (Burrough-Boenisch, 2003; Casanave & Vandrick, 2003; Flowerdew, 2000, 2001; Li, 2006). Others have inspected the numerous "literacy brokers" involved during the composing and submission processes—the various readers, editors, and reviewers that participate in the composing and revision processes (Curry & Lillis, 2004; Lillis & Curry, 2006). Further, the cultural, linguistic, and geopolitical challenges multilingual researchers face, reflections they provide, and coping strategies they use have also been studied (Belcher, 2007; Belcher & Connor, 2001; Canagarajah, 2002; Cho, 2004; Gosden, 1992, 1995).

This investigation extends conversations surrounding the sociopolitical networks occurring as multilingual professionals pursue academic publication in English-medium journals. I interview multilingual faculty about their experiences and reflections about their journey to published research-writer. While these participants' insights are many, my purpose in this chapter is to interpret their testimonies in hopes of imagining new systems of support to be initiated in US universities. Given the influx of international students and teachers, I argue, a new paradigm for literacy and rhetorical education in US universities for multilingual research-writers is long overdue. Thus, I begin with the following broad research questions:

> What insights might be gleaned from exploring the educational histories and reflections of multilingual scholars schooled outside of the US who have made the transition to published research-writer? How might such an analysis be useful for educators and administrators seeking innovative solutions for implementing literacy and rhetorical training for multilingual graduate students and faculty?

RESEARCH METHODS

This study is informed by theories that view learning and writing as socially constructed ideological events where individuals rhetorically negotiate their entrance into discourse communities (see, among many others, Berkenkotter & Huckin, 1995; Casanave & Vandrick, 2003; Johns, 1997; Lave & Wenger, 1991; Ramanathan, 2002; Swales, 1988, 1990; Wenger, 2000). Results are based on interviews with multilingual faculty teaching at US universities who have experienced the transition from being an unpublished, novice researcher to a published research-writer. Data collected consists of semi-structured audio-recorded interviews, copies of email correspondence with journal reviewers, participants' curriculum vitae, and email communications with participants. I explore these interview-based case studies for salient trends in participants' literacy practices in order to reveal insights based on participants' ongoing experiences with academic writing and publication in English.

Of the six participants, three were chosen for this chapter because they offered unique perspectives while sharing the same field of research. All three are currently working as international faculty at large public universities in the US and are employed in linguistics departments as tenured or tenure-track professors.[3] The participants have each published at least six articles in international journals and each received her undergraduate degree at a university located in her native country. However, participants come from varying native countries, have different native languages, and have had very different experiences learning and practicing academic English writing. The participants' linguistic and educational background, together with a limited summary of their academic writing background, can be viewed in Table 1.

Table 1. Participant backgrounds

	Dr. Huszár	Dr. Nakajima	Dr. Sanchez
Native Language	Hungarian	Japanese	Spanish
Country of origin	Hungary	Japan	Argentina
Grade School			
Location	Hungary	Japan	Argentina
Language	Hungarian	Japanese	Spanish
Undergraduate Studies			
Location	Hungary	Japan	Argentina
Language of instruction	English	Japanese	English
Explicit writing instruction	None	None	None
Course writing assignments	Some short answer essays in English	Some essays written in Japanese	Some short answer essays in English
Major writing assignments in English	Undergrad thesis in English	Undergrad thesis in English	None
Graduate Studies			
Location	England and United States	Japan and United States	United States
Language	English	English	English
Explicit writing instruction	None	None	None
Seminar writing assignments	Term papers	Term papers	Term papers
Major writing projects	1 M.A. thesis in English, 1 Ph.D. dissertation in English	2 M.A. theses in English, 1 Ph.D. dissertation in English	No M.A. thesis, 1 Ph.D. dissertation in English

CASE PROFILES AND ANALYSIS

Cultural, Educational, and Linguistic Backgrounds

Dr. Huszár,[4] the first participant, grew up in Budapest, Hungary, and it was there that she received her early education through her bachelor's degree—all of which was taught in Hungarian. When she attended a Budapest university as an English Language and Literature major, she was taught entirely in English. Although she had received biweekly English language training from her mother, an English as a Foreign Language teacher, when looking back she wonders how she was able to survive undergraduate courses, since she recalls not understanding a single word spoken by the professor in her very first lecture. Today it is quite clear that she communicates in English with ease—both in conversation and in writing.

Dr. Nakajima, the second participant, grew up in Japan and is a native speaker of Japanese. Like many students learning English as a foreign language in their native countries, Dr. Nakajima studied English in high school and college through courses taught by non-native English speaking instructors. Dr. Nakajima completed her schooling up until her first masters degree in Japan. Although instructed solely in Japanese through her first MA, she received both of her first degrees in American literature. Therefore, most of the texts she read were written in English, but class discussions and coursework were completed in Japanese. In fact, her coursework mostly consisted of translating and interpreting English texts into Japanese. Similar to Dr. Huszár, Dr. Nakajima was not given explicit instruction in writing in English. Essentially, the only writing in English she did before her PhD program was during the writing of her theses for her BA and first MA degrees.

The third participant, Dr. Sanchez, was born and raised in Buenos Aires, where she communicated in her native language of Spanish. She was instructed completely in Spanish all through her early education until college. Besides learning Spanish verbs by heart in high school, she did not receive any explicit instruction in writing in her native language. She went on to receive her BA as a Professor of English and Technical English also in Argentina, where her courses were primarily taught in English. Dr. Sanchez was not required to take any formal writing courses during her college years, although one class from her undergraduate studies included discussions of materials and methods for teaching English reading and writing as a foreign language.

On Major Influences towards the Transition to Emerging Scholar

Despite their scholarly interests falling under the broad discipline of linguistics, one of the most notable variations between participants are their graduate experiences. Dr. Huszár explained that the culture at her graduate institution encouraged students to join writing circles, and she received support and feedback on writing from faculty. It was common knowledge in Dr. Huszár's graduate department that doctoral students should be striving to publish their work in academic journals. Some of her seminars included assignments where students were charged with writing with publication in mind, and faculty would then respond to seminar papers in similar ways as do reviewers of journals. Dr. Nakajima, on the other hand, reported that her graduate institutions did not prepare her for academic research and publication; the importance of publishing was never acknowledged or discussed, she explained, by any of her professors or fellow graduate students. Instead of introducing her to research, her degrees prepared her to teach language at various competency levels. In fact, it wasn't until she applied for a tenure-track position that she learned of the need to publish research studies in her field in order to advance professionally within her department.

In Dr. Sanchez's case, she was able to get some explicit support on advanced academic writing during her graduate career, but this came out of her own discoveries, not from her graduate program. Dr. Sanchez explained how puzzled she was when she discovered (accidentally) the explicit analyses of the conventions for academic writing (such as Swales, 1990; Swales and Feak, 1994). She could not understand, for example, why her program did not explicitly address conventions of academic discourse or why they did not refer students to the vast literature investigating academic discourse communities. When rereading her old papers now, she notices strong research questions in her studies, but feels like the "moves" (Swales and Feak, 1994) of her texts were not in line with the academic writing conventions of her discipline. Her case illuminates a different kind of instruction, since writing mentorship for her happened textually, not socially. Unlike the previous cases where social mentorship either occurred or didn't in graduate studies, Dr. Sanchez succeeded through explicit instruction, but the instruction was happenstance and self-sponsored.

Participants also pointed to the transition from graduate student to faculty member as greatly impacting their development as writers. Drs. Nakajima and Sanchez both regret not having been more practiced in academic writing and publication during their graduate studies and are still wanting support in writing as faculty. Even Dr. Huszár, who received the most intense mentorship, struggles as a faculty member seeking publication. There are no networks in place within her department, and she worries about overburdening her already busy colleagues by asking them to discuss or review her manuscripts. She now relies solely on feedback from journal reviewers and editors. According to Dr. Huszár, writing without the support of mentors and peers often results in her publishing fewer manuscripts or doing so at the expense of her administration and teaching duties.

On the Use of Rhetorically-Informed Coping Strategies

In addition to the practices occurring in graduate studies and as new faculty, another theme that emerged from the participants' experiences and reflections are the coping strategies often called upon by multilingual writers when seeking scholarly publication in English. That Dr. Sanchez found explicit examination of academic genre conventions the most useful in her transition from novice researcher to published research-writer, for instance, is representative of the kinds of coping strategies each of the participants drew on, especially as they became more experienced writers. That is, participants relied on text-based rhetorical analysis and imitation practices. Besides receiving mentorship from her faculty advisor, Dr. Huszár recalls in graduate school how she relied on articles she read as models, and she noticed with the help of her instructor some characteristics of the IMRD format (Introduction, Methods, Results, Discussion). While her work now often varies from the IMRD format, it has been a significant organizational strategy for her throughout her academic career. Like the other two participants, upon determining her topic, literature review, and argument, Dr. Nakajima will similarly seek out models written in her research area for organizing and presenting her studies, usually articles addressing similar topics within the journal in which she seeks publication.

The use of models, however, was not found to be limited to structural features. To explain how her writing processes have altered and advanced as she entered the professoriate, Dr. Sanchez divulged that before her first publication her only use of models was for *external organization,* while today she looks to models as guides to *internal moves* in addition to external structure. For example, when writing her dissertation, she referenced a previously published dissertation as a model for format and chapter organization, but today when she refers to models she will look more closely at an article's organization scheme for the moves within each section. Thus, for Dr. Sanchez, when attempting to gain a more critical understanding of the rhetorical organization and moves of research writing in one's discipline, it is crucial to analyze the more nuanced rhetorical features than the overarching placement and order of sections. Similar to Dr. Sanchez, Dr. Huszár finds importance in building this kind of rhetorical knowledge.

Using previously published articles as models for argumentative tone and style is also a practice of Dr. Nakajima. Dr. Nakajima recalled being uncomfortable when she first started writing for publication when reviewers suggested that she adopt a more assertive tone and pushed her to criticize previous scholarship. Dr. Nakajima named this particular quality of English academic writing as conflicting with how she might write arguments in Japanese. Because she experienced some difficulty revising her tone to meet reviewers' demands, she began analyzing models closely for the kinds of writerly moves that accomplish this goal. She looked at the tones and grammatical structures of claims and also paid attention to where in research articles claims were being made. Her experiences, as well as those of the other participants, demonstrate how important models can be for scholars transitioning as published academics in their disciplines, especially when writers do not prefer to adopt an assertive tone or are not familiar with claim-making strategies in their fields. More than merely noting the overall structures, the kind of analysis participants were engaging in had to do with observing and imitating the rhetorical qualities of argument-making.

The Prospect of Explicit Rhetorical Training

The case profiles of Drs. Huszár, Nakajima, and Sanchez suggest a number of trends in the literacy practices occurring in graduate education, including the use of coping strategies and the kinds of "literacy brokers" and brokering available to multilingual international graduate students. First, the differences in graduate education among the three participants indicate the benefits of fostering a culture of publication where students are informed about the social, political, and cultural aspects of publishing in their discipline, encouraged to write towards publication, provided support and feedback for publication, and are explicitly instructed on the rhetorical features and genre conventions of scholarly articles in English. Second, a coping strategy often utilized among this group of scholars suggests the desire for explicit instruction in recognizing and applying the rhetorical genre features recurring and privileged in research writing in their field. That is, participants' testimonies make clear the importance of looking closely at how arguments and evidence are rhetorically presented. For participants, it is not only mentorship and instruction on the politics of publishing or feedback on their writing that worked for them; it was explicit instruction on and analysis of the nuanced rhetorical features occurring in the kinds of genres in which they would be required to perform mastery.

It is important to recognize that while some of the interview questions asked participants to reflect on the kinds of writing completed at the graduate level, each participant was drawn towards discussing the *quality* of her graduate education. It is not surprising that graduate studies act as a major contributor when analyzing individuals' early experiences engaging in the research writing practices of their discipline. Still, the fact that each participant honed in on this context as having such a significant effect on their future practices for publication indicates the need for graduate education and administration to further recognize and investigate the teaching of advanced research-writing.

Of course, many researchers have acknowledged the powers of graduate programs, especially the politics of professors mentoring native English speaking and non-native English speaking students during dissertation and manuscript writing (Belcher & Braine, 1995; Belcher & Connor, 2001; Blakeslee, 1997; Cho, 2004; Li, 2006; Ramanathan, 2002; Reid, 1994; Spack, 1988). Li (2006), for example, argues that professors should bring more conversation within graduate classrooms regarding the sociopolitical interactions facing them as novices, such as when they work on research projects or manuscripts with mentors, professors, and journal gatekeepers in their discipline. What is noteworthy is that Dr. Huszár's effective professionalization experiences in her graduate studies suggest that some US university graduate departments are ensuring their students gain critical awareness about publishing practices in their discipline. Colleges and universities which are currently providing support to multilingual graduate writers ought to be investigated and assessed in hopes of making public innovative solutions for acquiring literacy and rhetorical strategies.

While the current study did not investigate such model programs, the case profiles provide insight into future directions that writing teachers, graduate directors, and university officials might consider when designing educational programs that address literacy brokering. One such issue to consider is the approach to teaching academic genres. Whether or not it is more effective to gain genre awareness *explicitly* through the teaching of genres, or by learning *implicitly* through the ongoing practice of academic writing, has been debated in genre studies (Freedman, 1993; Williams & Colomb, 1993). Questioning whether explicit or implicit genre-based teaching should be enacted in literacy education, Freedman (1993) argues individuals acquire genre knowledge implicitly, and so explicit instruction is not necessary or effective in transferring genre knowledge. For Freedman, explicit teaching is no more transferable to new contexts than implicit learning of genre conventions. However, while the participants of the current study did not receive explicit *instruction,* they did go on to learn genres explicitly *on their own.* Since they studied the rhetorical features of genres and sought reading material which addresses explicit strategies for analyzing genres, their experiences support the argument for the explicit teaching of academic genre conventions, a process whereby writers work to identify, analyze, and practice recurring communicative moves. It was precisely the participants' experiences with analyzing texts explicitly for their features and their review of books which suggest explicit strategies for rhetorical reading and writing in academia are most useful. Their testimonies, furthermore, reveal that multilingual writers are eager to receive explicit instruction at the graduate level.

Approaches to remediating the lack of explicit teaching have been documented by many. Belcher (1995) suggests we teach critical reading so that graduate students can begin to recognize features in articles within disciplines across the curriculum. She believes that if students learn about these features, they will in turn begin to use them in their own writing. Ramanathan (2002) comments that university departments should genre-sensitize students and teachers so that they can develop metaknowledge about the socialization processes in disciplines, including academic publication. She adds that part of this sensitization should include making students aware of the relative power associated with mastery of these genres. Similarly, Canagarajah and Jerskey (2009) conclude that

> We [as educators] should help students demystify the dominant conventions behind a specific genre of writing, relate their writing activity to the social context in which it takes place, and shape writing to achieve a favourable voice and representation of themselves (483).

Using textual models is a coping strategy that has been cited before by multilingual writers (Belcher & Connor, 2001), so it is also not surprising that each of the participants promotes the practice of drawing on models as a significant strategy for writing for publication. It is surprising, however, that studies in this specific area of inquiry have not investigated the ways that models help to shape the language and structure of a multilingual writer's text. Most of these studies aim at analyzing how individuals—such as multilingual and native-English-speaking colleagues, language experts and journal reviewers and editors—shape multilingual writers' texts (Belcher & Connor, 2001; Burrough-Boenisch, 2003; Curry & Lillis, 2004; Flowerdew, 2001; Lillis & Curry, 2006). The contributions of "literacy brokers" (Curry & Lillis, 2004; Lillis & Curry, 2006) have been rhetorically analyzed in order to assess how significant these changes are to a multilingual writer's draft. Still, studies that investigate the ways texts and the modeling of texts help to shape scholars' manuscripts during the writing process may provide significant insight concerning the extent to which these models influence the intertextuality of research writing—the textual interactions between content, structure, or language found within and between these texts and their contexts.

More than pedagogical strategies, however, teachers and administrators would need to think critically about how to institutionalize literacy and rhetorical instruction for multilingual graduate students and junior faculty. Flowerdew (2000) asserts that in addition to more formal training in graduate studies, graduate programs should create centers where students meet to reflect and share resources or information about publishing in their disciplines. Braine (2005) suggests that Hong Kong universities should have departmental mentoring services across disciplines, similar to those existing in engineering. He also suggests that Hong Kong journals "establish a mentoring service between the author and a more experienced writer" (p. 714). Again, Dr. Huszár indicated that she relies on reviewers as her only source of feedback since she does not feel comfortable seeking help from her already busy colleagues when drafting and revising manuscripts. She lamented not having alternative outlets for reviewing her texts, and ultimately concluded that she would be very interested in participating in other forums dedicated to manuscript review. These types of programs mentioned by Flowerdew and Braine where colleagues get together to share experiences and review works in progress are precisely what Dr. Huszár would be interested in participating in. Research assessing the need or apparent positive results of programs like these for university faculty in the US might lead to more university departments considering the inclusion of such programs. Studies like Kwan's (2010)—where a Hong Kong graduate program is investigated for its instruction of academic publication—could be replicated in and outside of the US to determine the practices and outcomes of departmental attempts to implement explicit instruction to graduate students on publication conventions in English.

CONCLUSION

Becoming "fluent" in the subtle discourse practices of one's discipline may very well mean garnering a better conceptualization of the more intricate communicative moves in research writing. Such a nuanced understanding of discourse practices fits well within the theories and practices that inform the advancing field of Rhetorical Genre Studies. Bawarshi and Reiff (2010), in their review of the growing field of genre studies, explain that

> The emphasis within RGS [Rhetorical Genre Studies] has been to show that genres are not only communicative tools. Genres are also socially derived, typified ways of knowing and acting; they embody and help us enact social motives, which we negotiate in relation to our individual motives; they are dynamically tied to the situations of their use; and they help

> coordinate the performance of social realities, interactions and identities. To study and teach genres in the context of this socio-rhetorical understanding requires both a knowledge of a genre's structural and lexico-grammatical features as well as a knowledge of the social action(s) a genre produces and the social typifications that inform that action: the social motives, relations, values, and assumptions embodied within a genre that frame how, why, and when to act. (77)

The conceptualization of genres as social actions in RGS provides a helpful framework for understanding and interpreting the stories and strategies shared by participants of this study. Participants pointed to the benefit of explicit genre-based instruction, especially on the social, rhetorical, and lexico-grammatical levels. It was not efficient for participants to merely understand the structural features of the genres they were expected to engage in; instead, they remarked on the importance of recognizing the nuanced rhetorical features occurring and communicative tasks achieved when writing in their disciplines. Understanding how one crafts effective claims in one's field, for example, suggests an understanding of the social motives behind a given topic of inquiry. Analyzing and practicing the nuanced rhetorical moves in research writing that are privileged in certain scholarly circles suggests an understanding of the kinds of assumptions and values held by the intended audience. Seeing genres as typified responses utilized for socially engaging a discourse community may permit writers and educators to treat the learning of genre conventions in ways that more effectively initiate individuals as research-writers. It is crucial, in other words, that the explicit teaching of genres be accomplished critically—so that the varying and nuanced rhetorical contexts that guide research writing are considered—rather than being taught mechanically as if learning genre conventions could successfully be treated as a stagnant checklist of moves to complete.

Furthermore, that none of the participants received formal training or were given any referrals to the literature on this topic, suggests an existing discrepancy between the knowledge produced in academia and the knowledge and resources that are actually passed on to graduate students. Even graduate students in language-based disciplines such as Dr. Huszár, Dr. Nakajima, and Dr. Sanchez are apparently not engaged in this literature, at least at the time they were enrolled. Studies exploring the information gap between research and practice in graduate writing education could potentially illuminate the possible resources geared toward demystifying disciplinary writing conventions which administrators might implement in their programs and curricula. Based on the trends illuminated by this limited set of examples, it may serve them well to begin questioning how we might better translate our knowledge about literacy practices and the learning of advanced genres into more effective pedagogical, institutional, and administrative practices aimed at better preparing multilingual graduate students and junior faculty for academic publication.

As a final note, while the scope of the current study was to explore graduate experiences and administration within US borders, it is crucial to acknowledge that despite participants questioning the effectiveness of their graduate programs in preparing them for writing for publication, each case presented here is representative of practices in the English-dominant center. Being schooled in English-medium institutions within the US provided participants with access to technology, published work, and writing resources including centers, editors, and native-English-speaking colleagues. Further, participants of the current study were in language programs where issues like sociolinguisitics, discourse conventions, and English grammar are fundamental to the curriculum. Some have even gone on to teach writing for publication courses and have reflected on the politics of their writing processes and of publication practices. Despite all these advantages, the participants still reported facing numerous challenges in learning the conventions for publishing in their field and ultimately pointed to the need for additional support. Research is far from complete which investigates institutions both inside and outside US borders for the writing resources available (or not available) to multilingual graduate students and faculty. The exigence for more research on (and more implementation of) these resources has perhaps never been more apparent as it is now, especially considering the influx of international students and faculty in the US and the continued dominance of English in academia. The extent to which new resources are informed by research findings in rhetoric, linguistics, and composition studies—especially regarding the specific needs and experiences of multilingual graduate students and faculty—will play a significant role the effectiveness of such institutional implementations.

NOTES

1. The research presented in this chapter comes out of the study completed for my master's thesis published in 2010. I'd like to thank Ann M. Johns, my Thesis Chair, for her feedback on the early stages of this research.

2. The terms "multilingual writers" or "multilingual scholars/researchers" will be used in this chapter to refer to those writers in US contexts whose first language is other than English.

3. Prior to the interview, each participant signed or verbally agreed to the informed consent form as part of the Human Subjects research approval process through the Institutional Review Board (IRB) in 2009 at my previous institution.

4. According to IRB policy, the names used in this study are pseudonyms and measures were taken to protect the identities of the participants involved, including not disclosing their current universities, the universities they have previously attended, and the titles of the articles they have published.

REFERENCES

Bawarshi, A. S., & Reiff, M. J. (2010). *Genre: Introduction to history, theory, research, and pedagogy.* West Lafayette, IN: Parlor Press and the WAC Clearinghouse.

Belcher, D. (2007). Seeking acceptance in an English-only research world. *Journal of Second Language Writing, 16*(1), 1-22.

Belcher, D., & Braine, G. (Eds.). (1995). *Academic writing in a second language: Essays on research and pedagogy.* Norwood, NJ: Ablex.

Belcher, D., & Connor, U. (Eds.). (2001). *Reflections on multiliterate Lives.* Clevedon, England: Multilingual Matters LTD.

Berkenkotter, C., & Huckin, T. (1995). *Genre knowledge in disciplinary communication: Cognition/culture/power.* Hillsdale, NJ: Lawrence Erlbaum.

Blakeslee, A. M. (1997). Activity, context, interaction, and authority: Learning to write scientific papers in situ. *Journal of Business and Technical Communication, 11*(2), 125-169.

Braine, G. (2005). The challenge of academic publishing: A Hong Kong perspective. *TESOL Quarterly, 39*(4), 707-716.

Burrough-Boenisch, J. (2003). Shapers of published NNS research articles. *Journal of Second Language Writing, 12,* 223-243.

Canagarajah, A. S. (2002). *A geopolitics of academic writing.* Pittsburgh, PA: University of Pittsburgh Press.

Canagarajah, A. S., & Jerskey, M. (2009). Meeting the needs of advanced multilingual writers. In R. Beard et al. (Eds.), *The SAGE handbook of writing development.* (pp. 472-488). London: Sage.

Casanave, C. P., & Vandrick, S. (Eds.). (2003). *Writing for scholarly publication: Behind the scenes in language education.* New Jersey: Lawrence Erlbaum.

Cho, S. (2004). Challenges of entering discourse communities through publishing in English: Perspectives of non-native-speaking doctoral students in the United States of America. *Journal of Language, Identity, and Education, 3*(1), 47-72.

Curry, M. J., & Lillis, T. (2004). Multilingual scholars and the imperative to publish in English: Negotiating interests, demands, and rewards. *TESOL Quarterly, 38*(4), 663-688.

Gosden, H. (1992). Research writing and NNSs: From the editors. *Journal of Second Language Writing, 1,* 123-139.

Gosden, H. (1995). Success in research article writing and revision: A social-constructionist perspective. *English for Specific Purposes, 14*(1), 37-57.

Flowerdew, J. (2000). Discourse community, legitimate peripheral participation, and the non-native English-speaking scholar. *TESOL Quarterly, 34*(1), 127-150.

Flowerdew, J. (2001). Attitudes of journal editors to non-native speaker contributions. *TESOL Quarterly, 35*(1), 121-150.

Freedman, A. (1993). Show and tell? The role of explicit teaching in the learning of new genres. *Research in the Teaching of English, 27*(3), 222-51.

Johns, A. M. (1997). *Text, role and context: Developing academic literacies.* Cambridge, UK: Cambridge University Press.

Kwan, M. S. C. (2010). An investigation of instruction in research publishing offered in doctoral programs: The Hong Kong case. *Higher Education, 50*(1), 55-68.

Lave, J., & Wenger, E. (1991). *Situated learning: Legitimate peripheral participation.* Cambridge, UK: Cambridge University Press.

Li, Y. (2006). A doctoral student of physics writing for publication: A sociopolitically-oriented case study. *English for Specific Purposes, 25,* 456-478.

Lillis, T., & Curry, M. J. (2006). Professional academic writing by multilingual scholars: Interactions with literacy brokers in the production of English-medium texts. *Written Communication, 23*(1), 3-35.

Ramanathan, V. (2002). *The politics of TESOL education: Writing, knowledge, critical pedagogy.* New York: Routledge Falmer.

Reid, J. (1994). Responding to ESL students' texts: The myths of appropriation. *TESOL Quarterly, 28,* 273-292.

Spack, R. (1988). Initiating ESL students into the academic discourse community: How far should we go? *TESOL Quarterly, 22,* 28-51.

Swales, J. (1988). Discourse communities, genres and English as an international language. *World Englishes, 7*(2), 211-220.

Swales, J. (1990). *Genre analysis: English in academic and research settings.* Cambridge, UK: Cambridge University Press.

Swales, J., & Feak, C. (1994). *Academic writing for graduate students: Essential tasks and skills: A course for non-native speakers of English.* Ann Arbor, MI: The University of Michigan Press.

Wenger, E. (2000). *Communities of practice: Learning, meaning, and identity.* Cambridge, UK: Cambridge University Press.

Williams, J., & Colomb, G. (1993). The case for explicit teaching: Why what you don't know won't help you. *Research in the Teaching of English, 27*(3), 252-64.

CHAPTER 22.
IMMERSED IN THE GAME OF SCIENCE: BELIEFS, EMOTIONS, AND STRATEGIES OF NNES SCIENTISTS WHO REGULARLY PUBLISH IN ENGLISH

Nancy Keranen, Fatima Encinas, and Charles Bazerman
Benemérita Universidad Autónoma de Puebla and University of California, Santa Barbara

Not all scientists or researchers need to communicate their research in English. However, those who do face a complexity of challenges as we discussed in an earlier publication where we examined the struggles of non-native English Speakers (NNES) to become engaged in international scientific fields conducted in English (Bazerman, Keranen, & Encinas, in press). There we argue that lack of experience and fluency in English impede their immersion in cutting edge science, but lack of immersion in cutting-edge science limits their experience in scientific English, impeding growth of fluency to support more complete, immersive participation. Thus, scientific success breeds linguistic success and linguistic success supports scientific success, in a version of the "Matthew Effect" by which the rich get richer and the poor get marginalized (Merton, 1968).

Applied linguistics studies of the experience of NNES scientists writing in English for international publication have focused on novice scientists at the periphery of their fields who have not yet achieved success or fluency (reviewed in Bazerman, Keranen, & Encinas, in press). However, there is very little available research on NNES scientists who have managed, in spite of the well-documented problems, to succeed.

In this current chapter, we explore more fully what it means for an NNES scientist to overcome linguistic and scientific challenges to become a successful published researcher in an English-dominant discipline. In particular, we study the psychological orientation that a group of successful NNES physicists and mathematicians working in Mexico have developed in the course of their careers. We find that they are deeply immersed and invested in the work of science. They strongly identify with their scientific careers, played out within an international community to which they contribute by their publications.

We find that their self-reported confidence in their expertise is matched by a set of dispositions and orientations similar to those of immersed players of computer games. Karl Popper (1959) conceived of science a game—an activity, like games, subject to a set of rules structuring a competition between theories. Zamora-Bonilla (2010) further proposed that the "competition" is between the *scientists* rather than their theories. Our interview study indicates that this game metaphor can tell us much about how successful NNES scientists orient towards and participate in writing for their international community.

STUDY PARTICIPANTS

The participants were NNES scientists working in a faculty of physics and mathematics in a large public research university located in central Mexico. We used purposive sampling to select the experts with the highest levels of institutional recognition of expertise, i.e., those recognized by membership and rating (with rating 3 the highest) within the *Sociedad Naciónal de Investigadores* (SNI) (the National Society of Researchers). SNI membership and rating are based on triennial evaluations of academic production, including funded research projects and publication in international high impact journals. Their professional profiles generally conform to international definitions of successful scientists working in academic settings (Keranen, 2008).

The participants represented a number of specialties, came from a variety of national and linguistic backgrounds, and ranged from mid-career to late career as indicated in Table 1.

METHODS

We used three methods to interview these subjects. First, we used narrative life story interviews to understand the dispositions and orientations that lie behind the expert performances and to understand how they currently defined themselves in terms of professional development and to bring out antecedent factors which might have contributed to their levels of development (Lieblich, Tuval-Mashiach, & Zilber, 1998). To elicit the data, we provided each interviewee with a sheet of paper listing numbers to indicate the years of their life, but otherwise blank. They were then asked to either fill in information related to anything that seemed important to them or just to use the format to orient their narrative to the years. The scientists talked about the periods of their lives, important people, their personalities and reactions to events. We asked follow-up questions when necessary to prompt details and to encourage them to think about their lives and experiences as those events related to their career development.

The second interview protocol, based on Gordon and Dawes (2005), elicited the subjects' experiences associated with their ability to write publishable scientific articles in English. This protocol used a framework or "array" for arranging the interview data (see Figure 1).

The elements elicited in the interview were from four principal categories: beliefs—a central belief criterion, cause and effect—and equivalencies beliefs; emotions—sustaining (i.e., those held all the time regarding the activity) and feedback emotions (those that give information about the activity when engaged in it); strategies—primary and secondary (used when primary strategies fail); and external behaviors—any other behaviors when engaged in the activity.

During the interview the interviewer acted as a mediator or guide to help the participant access his (all the participants were males) subjective experience through guided questioning (cf. Varela & Shear, 1999). The process adopts a second-person subjective perspective rather than a third-person objective view (as, for example, in a standardized questionnaire) or a first-person subjective account (as in the open-ended reflective narrative). The array (see Figure 1) is filled out by the interviewer in the course of the interview, but open to visual inspection by the interviewee, so that it can serve as an explicit framework for conducting the interview, allowing the interviewer and interviewee spontaneously and associatively to co-construct the recorded responses and make sure all items are covered. While this protocol does not purport to provide a complete representation of the individual engaged in the activity, it does elicit and map a number of elements of the interviewee's orientations to the activity and competence explored. Further, while the array factors are separated for the purposes of elicitation and analysis, they are likely enacted in practice as an integrated ensemble within the ability.

Finally, to clarify certain issues found in the narrative and array data, semi-structured interviews (eight open-ended items) were sent to the participants via email, with one further face to face follow-up interview. Trustworthiness of the data was established based on member checking of the interview data at the close of the interviews (Creswell, 2003).

Ten of the narrative and array interviews were carried out in Spanish; the rest, in English. These interviews were then transcribed, and the Spanish ones translated into English. The follow-up semi-structured interviews were in English or Spanish depending on the primary language used in the other interviews.

Table 1. Study participants' research areas, career levels, SNI levels and nationalities

ID	Research Area	Career level	SNI Level	Nationality
R14	Particles, fields and general relativity	Mid-career	3	Mexican
R9	Particles, fields and general relativity	Mid-career	1	Mexican
R6	Particles, fields and general relativity	Mid-career	2	Mexican
R3	Particles, fields and general relativity	Late-career	Unknown	Mexican
R7	Optics	Mid-career	1	Mexican
R12	Optics	Late-career	2	Mexican
R11	Mathematical analysis	Late-career	2	Cuban
R15	Mathematical analysis	Mid-career	2	Mexican
R10	Differential equations and mathematical modeling	Late-career	2	Cuban
R13	Differential equations and mathematical modeling	Late-career	2	Russian
R5	Quantum optics	Mid-career	1	Salvadoran
R1	Quantum optics	Mid-career	1	Mexican
R2	Optoelectronics and photonics	Mid-career	1	Mexican

Each participant's interview data were entered in Atlas.ti (ver. 5.7.1) as primary documents. The narrative and elicitation data were then coded and analyzed independently by two of the study researchers. The two analyses were then brought together and discussed and further refined by all three researchers.

RESULTS

Self-Reported Characteristics of Expert Status

In the narrative interviews all our successful NNES scientists define their expert status as writers of publishable scientific papers in English based on international recognition, a strong network of connections with other researchers on international and national levels; international publication; and citations. Several also mentioned their role in forming researchers and directing master's and doctoral theses; two also mentioned the importance of engaging in more popular forms of science dissemination. They all feel pride and accomplishment in their work that they perceive as important to themselves, their institutions, and the wider world (Keranen, 2008).

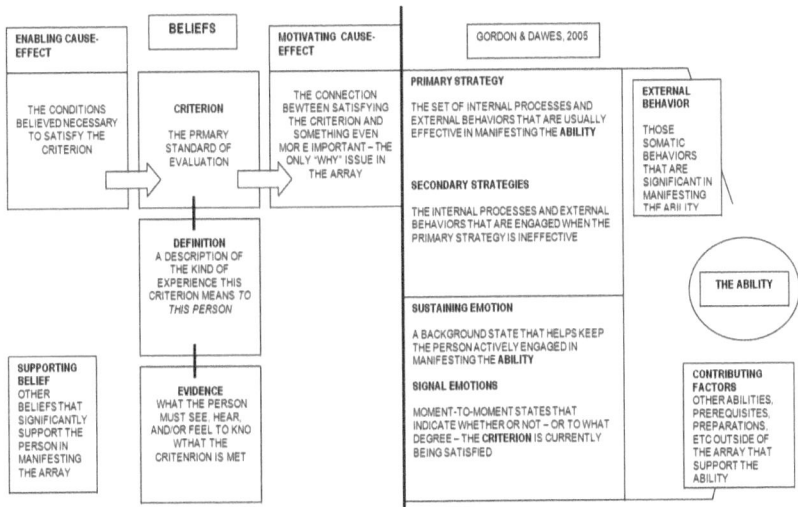

Figure 1. Blank Array (taken from Gordon & Dawes, 2005, pp. 192-193)

Reports of Subjective Orientations

The second interview protocol incorporated elicited subjective reports of the beliefs, emotions, and strategies associated with producing publishable articles in English. We present the results in each area in separate sections.

Beliefs

For Gordon and Dawes (2005) the center of the beliefs is the criterion. For all of the participants the criterion of success was whether they contributed new results to the international scientific community, which they also believed conformed to the expectations of that international community. R5 comments:

> Well, I think we always want to present, to highlight the physics results that we have on hand. So that's always the main, the main thing that I try to keep in mind when I write. … So this is something that we always have in mind, to put in perspective the physics results, eh to write some paragraphs saying "previous to this work, people did this and that, now I'm going to describe my eh, recent results" and mm, always in a thesis very important for physics you have to publish this because if you don't do that the world stops

revolving! (R5—original English).

The evidence indicating whether their criterion is being met is based on a model they have of how scientific articles should be written. To construct this model (enabling cause and effect beliefs), they all emphasized the importance of extensive reading in their fields, and some (R1, R2, R6, R12) mentioned the importance of reading literature and other types of genres in English to acquire a kind of ear for the language and of the target discourse. Six mentioned the importance of speaking in English. They noted a connection between their spoken and written English, as R6 explains.

> I would like to say something which comes from my experience. If I speak better, I write better. I found that eh, that procedure, at the beginning my speaking expression was not good, so my writing was not good. So I found it's good to practice English conversation, speaking English conversation, then writing is easier. I don't know how, I don't know, I'm sure you have found this relation, if you speak well, you write well (R6—original English).

Immersion into the profession and their work was also reported within their cause and effect beliefs, both as an enabler and as a motivator. For these scientists the motivation is to be able to participate in the wider international community. "Puedo decir cosas" [I can say things] (R9). One of the most dominant motivating factors is whether they can write in English at a level that conforms to the community's expectations—reporting research that is valued by the community, they will be cited, one benchmark in their development, one piece of evidence that says they have arrived.

> I don't publish only for the SNI. I want to establish relationships with other members of the physics community. ...
> When you publish in the sciences you feel proud when other people quote your work. This is probably the most important step. Now after 10 years, I received 12 references for a more theoretical article I wrote in 1998 ... The truth is it is very exciting (R5—original English).

Several researchers express being motivated by their being able to participate in and contribute to the professional community and the pride from doing so.

Emotions

Most of the scientists like to write in L1 and L2. They feel challenged and rewarded, both internally and externally for their efforts, so they continue to do it in spite of the negative emotions sometimes encountered:

> Ah, well always is a challenge to write. It's always a challenge to write something and I eh, I have to, like yesterday I was finishing a report from last year, and I knew that I have to write at the end, I have to write an acknowledgment to the eh, financial organization who gave us the support to do this and I was trying to say "Thank you" in a very formal way and I was very stressed, trying to say, well, not saying thank you very much, it was crucial, not but trying to be, to have an official document saying that the help was good but not only they helped us, only my Mexican agencies helped us so. My problem was to give the correct portion of credits to everybody. That was the difficult part (R6—original English).

Their feedback emotions range from pride, happiness and satisfaction, to frustration, anxiety and "torture," as R5 expresses when referring to his secondary strategies engaged when experiencing a type of "writer's block."

Strategies

Many of their writing strategies are specific to the individual, but in general they all use writing models. They are aware of genre conventions in their fields and use published articles as templates for their writing. They perceive the value of extensive knowledge and experience in writing new research:

> Because yes it is easier, because one has a more experience, it is easier to choose a good research topic and choose especially when I am going to choose something. The first thing one thinks, is in what journal am I going to publish this before I see if I'm going to do it or not (R11—translated from Spanish).

They have certain established ways of going about the writing as well. Almost all of them say they write the introduction sections and the abstract last because the most important elements are the results and the conclusions of the work, the elements that are going to be evaluated by the international scientific community (R1, R2, R5, R6, R9, R11, R14). Most stated that they find the introductions much more difficult to write than other sections. None write a paper alone. They all rely on a variety of help from colleagues, some L1 English speakers and some L2 English colleagues who have a greater command of the language:

> First I did everything like intuitively, and a few years ago I met a colleague from Colima, his English is much better that mine. I compare many songs of Pink Floyd. I don't understand the lyrics and then he explains them to me. So what he does is that from the very beginning that we start a project he starts to write notes in English, and then making that a paper is easier and that's something that I'm starting to do. I would write but many small pieces, very disorganized and now I'm trying from the very beginning to write and it's easier to make a paper from that. There are also some things, some information from previous papers that one repeats. It's not very creative but, then the papers look flat and I like the papers from this friend of mine. They are better. I would like to improve that (R14—original English).

Planning before writing is also something that comes up.

> I, before, when I learnt eh, some years ago, was to, not to start writing or to sit in front of the computer. I, I like to think what I want to express what I want to communicate and, in my mind I just to, to construct the paper and then I sit and I start writing. Sometimes I found that I get stuck in my mind I cannot follow, I cannot follow the idea I cannot develop the idea, then I start writing eh, staying there for minutes, hours and then I start writing my documents (R5—original English).

The language used to write initial drafts also varies. Many will start in Spanish and then work with co-authors, graduate students, and even family members to change the language to English (R2, R3, R7, R13, R15). Some use a combination of languages:

> A champurrado as we say in Mexico, that is, some parts in

> English and others in Spanish and the last because it is more or less uniform. Because sometimes you write ideas and concepts that are already previously made of course, then one has to be more or less consistent with oneself, one then grabs pieces of other authors or one who has written in English, and then one pulls them. The copy, it reformulates them. This writes it in English and others are original ideas which are written, that is the rule, if they are written then already are not original, this one writes and translates them. But it is a question I already learned in English; my son is also a researcher. He is in chemical engineering and originally writes articles in English directly. He had the chance to take English from a very young age and I did not (R12—translated from Spanish).

R1, R5, R6, R14 write in English only.

In terms of more external actions when writing, seven explicitly mention the need to eliminate all distractions and to remove themselves from the physical world (R1, R5, R6, R9, R14, R11, R15):

> You are forgetting about your family, about students, about paperwork, about everything. And you want to report the results in these graphs, in only these two graphs ... I'm here in the office I lock the door, close the curtains. ... Not showing the face of the enemies, not talking to anyone in the university, showing that you are not for no one, exchange no word, not saying hello to anyone, not drinking water so you don't have to go to the bathroom. I'm even disconnecting the internet connection because it is time to be down in the hole, to take yourself in your hands, I need to focus ... I need to focus myself ... the best way for me to write is when I'm at home alone there is no one there. I'm just there with my coffee ... I'm there just for writing, nothing more (R5—original English).

When their primary strategies fail, all of the scientists report secondary strategies that they mobilize to help them write. These involved things like starting over again, using organizers—adhesive notes which could be moved around and rearranged, going back to articles and reading for ideas, and when all else fails all said they remove themselves physically from the task and come back later. What might differentiate these experts from novices, as substantiated in the expertise literature, is their ability to know what secondary strategies they can set in motion to keep writing and to have enough self-awareness to know when they need to physically remove themselves from the writing situation and come back to it later.

UNDERSTANDING IMMERSIVE ENGAGEMENT

The researchers in this study have all managed to participate in international science at a high level by publishing results that meet the current research interests and standards of their fields. In doing so they have developed psychological orientations toward their work revealed in their beliefs, emotions, and strategies that show themselves immersed in the world and work of their specialties. In this sense we can see their writing as enabled by a set of dispositions towards their perceived situation (Russell & Harms, 2010, drawing on Bereiter, 1995).

Their criteria for success internalize the criteria of their fields, and the evidence of their success is in produced work that meets these standards and becomes published and recognized as contributing to their fields. They find the work enabled by increasing their own engagement and participation by reading, immersing oneself in the language and culture, taking writing courses, writing drafts, and increasing social connections. They are motivated by their participation in the field, and their increasing levels of access, participation, and opportunities as their recognition in the field advances. They enjoy the work and challenge, although they find it exhausting and at times frustrating.

The engagement these authors have shown with scientific writing bears strong psychological similarities to the kind of engagement found among players of computer games, particularly Massively Multiplayer Online Role-playing Games (MMORPGs). Four elements of similarity stand out: 1) the "virtual worlds" with their 2) characteristics of worldwide collaboration, participation, and advancement, enhanced and motivated by 3) occurrences of "flow" from immersive states and involving 4) complex cognitive functions necessary for these levels of participation. For each of these interconnected features we bring in corresponding evidence from the gaming literature and link it to evidence from our data.

Virtual Worlds

A "virtual world" in the MMORPG is a simulated environment or community, society or culture accessed by members, characters, or players through remotely located computers. Typically, players engage in activities that lead to forms of progression—from novices to those of higher status based on experience in the game. This comes about through their social interactions and actions in the community. Immersion into the game is seen as critical to success and enjoyment and motivation to stay in the game (Jennett, Cox, & Cairns, 2009). Such immersion involves "perceiving oneself to be enveloped by, included in, and interacting with an environment that provides a continuous stream of stimuli and experiences" (Witmer & Singer, 1998, p. 227).

The similarities with the scientific worlds of our researchers are clear. Their research, articles, and presentations are their vehicles for participation. When asked what percentage of the time the researchers were thinking of their work—in their virtual worlds—most replied around 70-80%. R15 stated:

> I have a feeling that all the time I am thinking what I'm doing and what should I do. However, in reality it can't be so. If I feel that I spend in the university an average nine or 10 hours a day, counting that also I take my backpack home to continue writing or resolving a problem, then they are like 10 or 12 hours a day. I think that in these last five or four years I've obsessed with work, more than in previous years. Work is thought and when not specifically working anyway there is thought about work. In addition, at night, I sleep thinking about some problem. I sleep but soon after I wake up and am still thinking about the problem. I believe that I have had some success with this method (R15—translated from Spanish).

When reflecting on his processes of becoming a high-level member of his field, R11 mentions his time spent immersed in mathematics:

> … I think I studied around 15 or 16 hours a day. Now I do it less, I study around 14 hours, but the whole day, from Monday to Sunday I dedicate it to mathematics. You can imagine the way my wife fights with me over that; she says that I'm working all the time on mathematics (R11—translated from Spanish).

Yee's (2006) study of MMORPG players found that time investment was a strong characteristic of major players. According to his sample of over 30,000 players, among the most successful players 8% claim to spend at least 40 hours per week in their virtual worlds. An astonishing 70% spend at least 10 continuous hours in a sitting in their virtual worlds. His study also found that 18% of users reported that their high use caused academic, health, financial or relationship problems, with the amount of game time correlated with the amount of problems reported.

Worldwide Collaboration, Participation, and Advancement

As in MMORPGs, science is comprised of vast communities of characters cooperating and working together from all over the world, as a number of our subjects commented on. For examples,

> I want to establish relationships with other members of the physics community. ... When you publish in the sciences you feel proud when other people quote your work. This is probably the most important step. Now after 10 years, I received 12 references for a more theoretical article I wrote in 1998... The truth is it is very exciting (R5—original English).

> Yes, this is, um let me explain to you. Ok ... I think that we are part of a community, a scientific community, and this community wants to work to increase knowledge, in this case for physics, and the best way to increase knowledge, is to, publish your ideas. And this community is going to do a criticism of this idea, so it's a fundamental part for increasing knowledge, so I think that the, the need for publication is this process. So we can say *"granito de arena,"* how do you say? (R1—translated from Spanish).

In MMORPGs the means to progress or advance require increasing cooperation or dependency on other users (Yee, 2006), which matches closely the comments of our interviewees.

> So I started working here as a research professor and from here I continued working as a professor. And the things involved, I think that back then when I had an idea of the type of research I wanted to do, I think it was clearly defined, but I lacked two things, I didn't have the experience nor the detailed technical information of what I had to do. ... But at that moment it was clear to me, that is the reason why I do

> this type of research.... at that moment I had what is called a master's in science, and one is able then to be a research assistant. ... But we can say that from there came two or three other stages that in my academic life ... [etc.] ... I was chief director of the faculty, I've been coordinator of everything you can think of, of the postgraduates here in the faculty, and so on, I have done everything that is needed to be done ... (R12—translated from Spanish).

Talking about his most recent article associated with an experiment in CERN, R5 comments:

> And ... these collaborations ... if your name is on these lists, it means you did something ... good for this ... job. But ... this is the first paper ... we are ... planning on having ... hundreds of them, like these. And ... this first one is the result of more than ten years of ... work, many many people collaborated in it, so this is it, this is it, it is fifteen pages long, the first ... four are just names and institutions ... here we have the place where our experiment is. ... That's ... ALICE and ATLAS and CMS. ATLAS has three thousand four hundred collaborators. ... I'm also very proud, see? We are the institution number 83, 83 out of 113 institutions. Russia, Rumania, China, Germany, the States, Poland, Netherlands, Italy, France, South Korea, Spain (R5—original English).

Being in the Game: "Flow" from Advanced Immersive States

The isolation from immediate demands the scientists reported as facilitative for high level engagement appears to be setting the conditions for flow experiences (Csikzsentmihalyi, 1988) that occur within the state of total immersion. It is characterized by momentary or fleeting suspensions of time and physical reality. "Flow ... is an extreme experience where goals, challenge and skill converge. As such flow is an all or nothing experience" (Sanders & Cairn, 2010, p. 1—pdf version). Flow is also easily lost when interruptions or distractions occur (Brown & Cairns, 2004).

When asked whether they have experienced such moments when working, the scientists all responded in the affirmative, but also acknowledge the temporality and the dependence on certain conditions to sustain the experience.

> Of course but that only happens if things are going well, otherwise the time passes slowly. ... Sometimes because I'm normal only once in a while I get that ecstasy ... [and when it does happen], I am sorry when I have to stop and return home (R12—translated from Spanish).

The ability to work at these levels and attain flow is associated with extreme pleasure and levels of concentration so intense that time and reality are suspended, but when it is over and reality resumes, feelings of disorientation and physical exhaustion can result. However, the euphoric feelings of flow are sirens' calls to return again and again.

Complex Cognitive Processes

Players with high levels of expertise can experience flow in situations that call for higher levels of challenge which engage increasingly complex cognitive processes (Prensky, 2003).

Writing likewise engages complex, multiple and simultaneous actions (Torrance & Galbraith, 2005). R6 expressed this well:

> Oh, I, I think that happens also in Spanish. I hold a lot of emotion when I write, I get tired, exhausted when I write, in English and in Spanish. Because I think a lot, and sometimes because, one of your questions ... I cannot find the correct words to express something and I say, how can I do it? How can I express this? And I think it's not because of the writing, it's because of what I want to express, to say better and better. Yes, I feel a lot of emotion when I write ... It's always a challenge to write ... like yesterday I was finishing a report from last year, and I knew that I have to write ... an acknowledgment to the ... financial organization who gave us the support to do this and I was trying to say "Thank you" in a very formal way and I was very stressed, trying to say, well, not saying thank you very much ... My problem was to give the correct portion of credits to everybody. That was the difficult part.
>
> Q: That's quite a challenge, isn't it? Do you generally like challenges?
>
> R6: Yes.

FINAL COMMENT

Ultimately the game of science is played on the game board of publication, and entering more deeply into the publication system draws one more deeply into the game and the dispositions of the game-player. Communication is the center of the game: "what you want is that others write that what you wrote was right" (Zamora-Bonilla, 2010, p. 9). How these scientists reached this point of engagement and overcame the obstacles that language created for their total immersion in the international game of science—and what this might mean for helping early career researchers get caught up in the game—is the subject of a future publication.

REFERENCES

Bazerman, C., Keranen, N., & Encinas, F. (in press). Facilitated immersion at a distance in second language scientific writing. In M. Castello & C. Donahue (Eds.), *University writing: Selves and texts in academic societies.* Bradford, UK: Emerald.

Bereiter, C. (1995). A dispositional view of transfer. In A. McKeough, J. Lupert, & A. Marini (Eds.), *Teaching for transfer: Fostering generalization in learning* (pp. 21-34). Mahwah, NJ: Erlbaum.

Brown, E., & Cairns, P. (2004, April). A grounded investigation of game immersion. Paper presented at CHI 2004, Vienna, Austria.

Creswell, J. W. (2003). *Research design: Qualitative, quantitative, and mixed methods approaches.* London: Sage.

Csikszentmihalyi, M. (1988). The flow experience and its significance of human psychology. In M. Csikszentmihalyi & I. S. Csikszentmihalyi (Eds.), *Optimal experience: Psychological studies of flow in consciousness* (pp. 15-35). Cambridge, UK: Cambridge University Press.

Gordon, D., & Dawes, G. (2005). *Expanding your world: Modeling the structure of experience.* Tucson, AZ: Desert Rain.

Jennett, C., Cox, A. L., & Cairns, P. (2009, April). Investigating computer game immersion and the component real world disassociation. Conference paper presented at CHI 2009, Boston, MA.

Keranen, N. (2008). A multi-theoretical mixed-methods approach to investigating research engagement by university ELT staff (Unpublished doctoral dissertation). Lancaster University: United Kingdom.

Lieblich, A., Tuval-Mashiach, R., & Zilber, T. (1998). *Narrative research: Reading, analysis, and interpretation.* London: Sage.

Merton, R. K. (1968). The Matthew effect in science. *Science, 159*(3810), 56-63. DOI: 10.1126/science.159.3810.56

Popper, K. R. (1959). *The logic of scientific discovery.* New York: Basic Books.

Prensky, M. (2003). Digital game-based learning. *ACM Computers in Entertainment, 1*(1), 1-4.

Russell, D., & Harms, P. (2010). Genre, media, and communicating to learn in the disciplines: Vygotskian developmental theory and North American genre theory, *Revista Signos, 43,* 227-248.

Sanders, T., & Cairn, P. (2010, September). *Time perception, immersion and music in videogames.* Conference paper presented at HCI 2010, Dundee, Scotland.

Torrance, M., & Galbraith, D. (2005). The processing demands of writing. In C. MacArthur, S. Graham, & J. Fitzgerald (Eds.), *Handbook of writing research.* New York: Guilford.

Varela, F. J., & Shear, J. (1999). First person methodologies: What, why, how? *Journal of Consciousness Studies, 6*(2-3), 1-14.

Witmer, B. G., & Singer, M. J. (1998). Measuring presence in virtual environments: A presence questionnaire. *Presence, 7*(3), 225-240.

Yee, N. (2006). The psychology of MMORPGs: Emotional investment, motivations, relationship formation, and problematic usage. In R. Schroder & A. Axelsson (Eds.), *Avatars at work and play: Collaboration and interaction in shared virtual environments* (pp. 187-207). London: Springer-Verlag. Retrieved from http://vhil.stanford.edu/pubs/2006/yee-psychology-mmorpg.pdf.

Zamora-Bonilla, J. (2010). Science : The rules of the game. *Logic Journal of the IGPL, 18*(2), 294-307.

CHAPTER 23.

CRITICAL ACTS IN PUBLISHED AND UNPUBLISHED RESEARCH ARTICLE INTRODUCTIONS IN ENGLISH: A LOOK INTO THE WRITING FOR PUBLICATION PROCESS

Pilar Mur-Dueñas
Universidad de Zaragoza

It is now well attested that academics worldwide are concerned—to varying degrees depending on their field—with getting the results of their research accepted for publication in high impact journals generally published in English.[1] Spanish academics are no exception, and having their papers published in indexed journals is key to their academic promotion and achieving institutional rewards (Moreno, 2010). In the last decades there has been an upsurge in scholarly writing, a steadily increasing number of publication sites, and English has become the predominant language for the dissemination of new academic knowledge.

This pressure to write and publish in English has generated a great deal of cross-cultural analyses (Connor, 2004) within English for Academic Purposes (EAP), and more specifically, within English for Research Publication Purposes (ERPP). This research has been extremely prolific in the Spanish context, where text-based analyses have shown remarkable differences in the rhetorical structure and style of several academic genres written and read in the Spanish local context and in the English international context. More specifically, research has focused on the contrastive analysis of rhetorical and lexico-grammatical features in English and Spanish research article abstracts (e.g., Lorés-Sanz, 2006, 2009a; Martín Martín, 2003, 2005; Martín Martín & Burgess, 2004), book reviews (Lorés-Sanz 2009b; Moreno & Suárez, 2008a, 2008b, 2009) and research articles (e.g., Fagan & Martín Martín, 2004; Moreno, 2004; Mur-Dueñas, 2007, 2010; Salager Meyer et al., 2003; Sheldon, 2009).

Less research has focused on the analysis of L2 English academic texts written by (Spanish) scholars and the potential discursive difficulties that non-native scholars may encounter when seeking publication in English-medium international journals. That is, less attention has been paid to the writing process, especially by L2 academics, in the course of knowledge production, in general, and in article drafting and publication in particular. A notable exception is the work by Lillis & Curry (2006, 2010) on the publishing practices of 50 scholars in education and psychology across four non-Anglophone contexts: Slovakia, Hungary, Spain and Portugal.

This chapter aims to analyse evaluation—defined by Hunston and Thompson (2000) as the expression of writers' attitudes or stance, their viewpoints or feelings towards particular entities—in one of the sections of the RA where both native and, especially non-native, scholars state they have more difficulty in writing, namely, the introduction. The choice of this particular pragmatic function of language is highly relevant firstly because evaluation, which entails judging relevant entities such as one's research and findings and the research and findings of other scholars, is considered essential in order to "market" the academics' research. Such evaluation can contribute to persuading "gatekeepers," first, and readers, later, of the validity of the research, and can therefore affect the chances of having an article published and read. In addition, evaluation, and more specifically, academic conflict and criticism have been shown to be subject to intercultural variation (Lorés-Sanz, 2009a; Moreno & Suárez, 2008a, 2008b; Salager-Meyer et al., 2003), which may imply that scholars from different linguistic and cultural backgrounds may be used to employing different academic conventions when expressing their attitude towards their own and other colleagues' research.

The aim of this chapter is two-fold: (1) to explore how positive and negative evaluation is framed in the introductions of published papers in three highly prestigious journals in the field of finance, and (2) to unveil the potential difficulties a group of Spanish informants may have in framing their research within these conventions and the possible effect this may have on decisions about their manuscripts. As a result, the findings obtained from the analysis of evaluation in the introductory sections of the manuscripts submitted for publication drafted by a team of Spanish finance scholars will be compared to the results obtained from the analysis of a corpus consisting of successful RA introductions published in the journals where the Spanish academics aim to have their research published.

CORPUS AND METHOD

The corpus consists of 21 RA introductions (28,778 words) published in three high impact journals in the field of finance: *Journal of Business Finance and Accounting, JBFA*, (0.832 impact factor), *European Financial Management, EFM*, (0.892 impact factor) and *Journal of Banking and Finance, JBF* (1.908 impact factor). The choice of these particular journals was motivated by the informants' difficulties and their desire to have their research published on these sites. The articles were randomly chosen; in the case of the first and third journals the first and fifth articles in the three last issues and the first article in the fourth last issue at the time of compiling the corpus were retrieved; in the case of the second journal all the articles in the single free access issue were retrieved. The most relevant details of the corpus are summarised in Table 1.

Two of the Spanish scholars' manuscripts, which had been submitted to these journals, were selected for analysis. The first manuscript was submitted to and rejected by JBFA, then submitted to and rejected by EFM, and subsequently submitted to and rejected by JBF. Although the manuscript was rejected by two journals with a lower impact factor, the authors believed it merited publication in one of the most important journals in their field and decided to scale jump (Lillis & Curry, 2010). However, they were not successful and, after receiving a third rejection report from a high impact factor journal, they decided to address a much lower ranking journal as the fourth possible site of publication for their study. The second manuscript was submitted to JBF and received a major revision report. The authors revised the manuscript in line with the suggestions of the referee and it was finally accepted for publication.

For the analysis I will draw upon two important methodological proposals. The first one is that of the Text History (Lillis & Curry 2006, 2010), defined as "a key unit of data collection and analysis for exploring the trajectories of texts toward publication, including the impact of literacy brokers"[2] (2006, p. 7). Thus, two Text Histories (THs) are analysed in depth in this chapter. In order

Table 1. Description of the corpus of published material

	Journal of Business Finance & Accounting (JBFA)	European Financial Management (EFM)	Journal of Banking & Finance (JBF)
2009 impact factor	0.832	0.892	1.908
Ranking position	28th	27th	6th
No. of introductions	7	7	7
Average length	1,417	1,302	1,391
Total No. of words	9,921	9,116	9,741

to build those THs I have collected documents and information surrounding the abovementioned manuscripts, which are summarised in Table 2.

Second, the analysis of evaluation is based on the concept of "critical act" proposed by Moreno and Suárez (2008a, 2008b), which they define as "positive or negative remarks on a given aspect or sub-aspect of the book under review in relation to a criterion of evaluation with a higher or lower degree of generality" (2008b, p. 18). The concept has only been applied to the analysis of critical attitude in book reviews. It is considered, nevertheless, valid as a starting point for the analysis of evaluation in other academic texts, or sub-texts, as in this case. The critical act is a functional, not a grammatical unit, and, therefore, several critical acts may appear in the same sentence. Likewise, a critical act may span several clauses or sentences. This functional analysis requires a manual analysis of the texts, as identifying critical acts can only be achieved through careful reading.

Table 2. Description of the Spanish academics' text histories

Text History 1	Manuscript 1a (JBFA)
	Rejection report 1a (JBFA)
	Manuscript 1b (EFM)
	Rejection report 1b (EFM)
	Manuscript 1c (JBF)
	Rejection report 1c (JBF)
	Author's email to editor + editor's response (JBF)
	Manuscript 1d (a low impact factor journal)
	Notes on discussions
Text History 2	Manuscript 2a (JBF)
	Proofread manuscript 2a
	Editor's decision letter + Major revision report 2a (JBF)
	Manuscript 2b (JBF)
	Author's response to report 2a
	Editor's decision letter + Reviewer's response 2b (JBF)
	Manuscript 2c (JBF)
	Author's response to report 2b
	Editor's decision letter
	Publication of paper
	Notes on discussions

Both the published RA introductions in the corpus and the introductions of the Spanish scholars' manuscripts were carefully examined in search of positive and negative critical acts. These critical acts were analysed in terms of: 1) value—i.e., positive or negative attitudes being expressed; 2) target—i.e., the scholars' own research, the critical act therefore being self-referential, or previous research by other scholars; 3) (im)personality (Fagan & Martín Martín, 2004) —i.e., whether the target of the negative evaluation is made explicit (Example 1), or whether it is addressed to the disciplinary community as a whole (Examples 2), impersonality can also be achieved by reporting criticism made by others (Example 3), 4) directness (Fagan & Martín Martín, 2004) —i.e., whether the evaluation is hedged (indirect) (Example 4) or bold-on-record (direct) (Example 5), and 5) writer mediation (Fagan & Martín Martín, 2004) —i.e., whether the evaluative act is phrased in personal terms through first person pronouns or adjectives.

> (1) Koski (1996) uses a location metric … . <u>However, she does not distinguish the trading activities of different types of investors… (-).</u> Koski and Scruggs (1998), using the TORQ database, distinguish buy and sell trades for various types of investors. <u>However, they cover only 70 ex-dividend observations … (-)</u>. (JBFA-2)

> (2) Although specification errors can potentially have significant effects on tests of market misreaction (e.g., Heynen et al., 1994), <u>the existing literature has not addressed the issue of how model misspecification may lead to conflicting findings on market misreaction (-)</u>. (JBF-4)

> <u>Most prior research explores the issues of multiple directorships and M&As separately (-)</u>. (JBF-5)

> (3) However, <u>a number of other papers cast doubt on (-)</u> the interpretation that the diversification discount reflects value destruction (JBF-3)

> (4) <u>My large sample study of trade directions and trader identities *potentially* furthers our understanding of the ex-day pricing of dividends and investor trading behavior. (+)</u> (JBFA-2)

> (5) Our analysis is most closely related to that of Coval et

al.(2009) who show that it is possible to exploit investors who rely on default probability based ratings for pricing securities, by selling bonds whose default losses occur in high marginal utility states. <u>However, their theory has no explicit role for debt tranching (-) as ours does (+)</u>. (JBF-7)

Finally, a note was also made regarding the particular rhetorical function of the negative critical acts in the introductions: identifying a gap in the literature or signalling flaws in past research, and of the positive critical acts: specifying the contribution of the scholars' research, highlighting the centrality and/or novelty of the topic of their research, justifying their research in the light of previous work and emphasising the motivation of their own research by establishing links with past literature.

The extent of inclusion of critical acts and their particular characteristics in the published RA introductions will be compared with the encoding of evaluation through critical acts in the manuscripts of the Spanish scholars. Such comparison will allow us to determine the extent to which the Spanish L2 scholars match or differ from this rhetorical convention as featured in successfully published RAs and to gain an insight into the possible role of critical acts in the writing for publication process.

RESULTS AND DISCUSSION

ANALYSIS OF CRITICAL ACTS IN PUBLISHED RA INTRODUCTION

As shown in Table 3, a total of 175 critical acts, i.e., attitudinal comments on their own research or on other academics' research, were found in the corpus of published RA introductions. Critical acts were further analysed in terms of value, target and function, (im)personality, directness and writer-mediation.

Positive critical acts are far more common than negative critical acts in the RA introductions in the three publications. More than 90% of positive critical acts are self-referential, whereas none of the negative critical acts refer to the author's own research. Negative evaluation tends to be coded through impersonal critical acts (65%), that is, criticism is aimed at the community as a whole, rather than through personal ones (35%), in which criticism is aimed at the work of particular academics. It can be concluded from these results that it is more necessary to promote one's own research than to criticise previous research. That is, according to Swales' (1990, 2004) CARS (Create a Research Space) model, more emphasis is to be discursively placed on occupying the niche than on creating it. Especially important for scholars when marketing their own research in the introduction of their RAs is first, to be explicit about the particular contribution made by the research presented, as the following rather extreme example illustrates:

> (6) <u>Our study makes a number of important contributions to the existing literature</u> (+). <u>First, while controlling for the home bias phenomenon we examine the role ...</u> (+). <u>Second, unlike previous studies on international portfolio allocations</u> (-), we control for market microstructure effects by ... (+). Existing research ignores the role of ... (-). In this study, instead of using a bilateral effective exchange rate, <u>we use ... which is a much better measure of exchange rate risk</u>. (+) (JFB2)

It is also important to emphasise the research's topic centrality (as illustrated by the first positive critical act in Example 7) and to highlight the motivation of the authors' research and its relation to already existing research (as illustrated by the second positive critical act in Example 7):

> (7) <u>Our study is timely in the wake of recent financial accounting scandals</u> (+) and subsequent concerns that discretion in GAAP can be a vehicle for management to opportunistically manage earnings to achieve certain targets (e.g., Dhaliwal et al., 2004). <u>It also answers calls to develop a better understanding of the consequences for listed firms from countries that have adopted International Financial Accounting Standards (IFRS) issued by the International Accounting Standards Board</u> (e.g., Gordon & Joos, 2004; Jubb, 2005). (+) (JBFA1)

It is also important to note that it is the journal with the highest impact factor that accrues most critical acts, both positive and negative ones. It becomes apparent that academics need to fully master praise and criticism in the introduction of their RAs to convince "gatekeepers" of the validity of their research.

Evaluation tends to be expressed in a direct way; very few critical acts, whether positive or negative, have been hedged. Only a few positive critical acts (see Example 4 above) and a few negative ones (as in Example 8 below) include a hedging device:

Table 3. Corpus-based analysis of critical acts in published RA introductions

	JBFA	EFM	JBF	TOTAL
Positive critical acts	45	34	50	129
Negative critical acts	14	10	22	46
Total	59	44	72	175

(8) *Much* prior research has failed to provide conclusive evidence of earnings management using deferred tax accruals.(-). (JBF1)

Hedging, therefore, does not seem to be a salient rhetorical strategy in framing one's own research in the light of previous literature.

Finally, lack of writer mediation characterises positive and negative critical acts regarding others' research. Personal references are only included in self-referential positive critical acts. Almost 50% of the latter are expressed in a personal way through an inclusive we or our form.

(9) Instead, *we* contribute to the extant literature by proposing an ex ante benchmark portfolio approach to estimate … . (EFM6)

The novelty of *our approach* lies in the focus on insider trading decisions ahead of … (+) as opposed to other studies that analyze earnings announcement only (-). This allows us to better explore insiders' incentives and disincentives … (+). (JBFA6)

Academics, therefore, highlight their role as researchers undertaking worthwhile, original, relevant studies.

ANALYSIS OF CRITICAL ACTS IN THE SPANISH ACADEMICS' MANUSCRIPTS

The second step of the research was to compare the results from the analysis of the corpus of published introductions with the introductions of the papers that the Spanish informants had submitted for publication to the same sites.

Text History 1

This TH revolves around a manuscript which was submitted to and rejected firstly by JBFA, secondly by EFM, and finally by JBF (see Table 2). Therefore,

Table 4. Comparison of critical acts in published articles and informants' TH1 manuscript

	Positive critical acts (average per article)	Negative critical acts (average per article)
JBFA	6.4	2
EFM	4.8	1.4
JBF	7.1	3.1
manuscript 1a	11	2
manuscript 1b	13	2
manuscript 1c	13	2

three referee rejection reports were received from the three journals. These were analysed together with the extent of use of positive and negative critical acts made by the informants in the subsequent versions of their manuscript.

Two main criticisms were made by the JBFA referee report: the first concerned the literature review: "the paper needs to include more comprehensive literature review on … if it is the topic the authors argue as one of the main contributions", and the second one concerned their contribution "the authors need to do a better job at convincing their contribution to the readers," which the referee stressed again at the end of the report "The authors also need to better convince the readers with what they think the main contribution of the paper is." Similar comments were included in the EFM referee's report: "I have several concerns about the motivation, method, and contribution of the paper," "the authors fail to go deep enough to motivate their analysis." In the third report from JBF the referee was more straightforward by stating that "the paper makes only a minor contribution to the literature. … . I doubt that considering … provides us with deep insights."

Having read these criticisms and knowing from previous intercultural analyses (Spanish-English) that Spanish academics do not as frequently follow the CARS model (Swales 1990, 2004) in the introduction when drafting their RAs in Spanish or in English (Burgess 2002; Mur Dueñas 2010), especially regarding the creation and filling of a research space, it was expected that few critical acts would be found. However, that was not the case. As can be seen in Table 4, Spanish scholars have included even more positive critical acts than the corpus average.

All the positive critical acts in the Spanish manuscript but one are self-referential, fulfilling the function of "marketing" their own research. Some of these positive critical acts specifically tackle the issue of their contribution (Examples

10). Nevertheless, the JBFA referee, first, and then the EFM and JBF referees after two such acts had been added (Examples 11) still considered them to be lacking in detail or unconvincing.

> (10) For this reason, <u>this paper firstly investigates herding behaviour in the strategic style allocations of UK personal pension plans in the period 2000-2007.</u> (+) (manuscript 1a, 1b and 1c)
>
> <u>*We* thus contribute to financial literature by means of our attempt to improve the traditional method of detecting herding behaviour.</u> (+) (manuscript 1a, 1b and 1c)
>
> <u>Consequently, *we* add to the financial literature, as *we* study herding phenomenon from different perspectives</u>. (+)(manuscript 1a, 1b and 1c)
>
> (11) By moving beyond examining herding at the individual security level, <u>*our* study contributes to the growing "style investing" literature (see, e.g., Teo and Woo, 2004; Barberis et al., 2005 and Choi and Sias, 2009)</u>. (+) (manuscript 1b and 1c)
>
> Previous studies within this growing literature on ... focus on ... <u>whereas this paper pays attention to strategic style allocations and therefore includes the bond and cash style, which adds to the literature</u>. (+) (manuscript 1b and 1c)

It follows from this that, contrary to expectations, Spanish scholars have at least partially complied with what seems to be customary in the RA introductions in these journals in terms of the inclusion of positive and negative critical acts and have even boosted the positive evaluation of their own research beyond the average.

Not only the value and target of the critical acts in the Spanish manuscripts but also their specific features (e.g., (in)directness, writer mediation and (im)personality) are similar to the findings in the published RA introductions. As in the case of the published RA introductions, critical acts tend to be direct in the manuscript introductions. Also in line with the critical acts in the corpus of published introductions, self-references are only included in positive critical acts in the manuscripts (see Examples 9 and 10 above), whereas the writer's presence is avoided in negative critical acts, which also tend to be impersonal, that is, addressed to the whole community.

In general, then, the use of critical acts in the introductions of the Spanish academics' manuscripts is similar to that in the published RA introductions. That is, the Spanish scholars follow to a large extent the evaluative conventions prevailing in the published RAs to "market" their own research. Thus, the referees' rejection may be interpreted as based not on the academics' failure to comply with the conventions to rhetorically encode evaluation to promote their own research, but rather on the referees' belief that the scholars' research did not present a worthy enough contribution to deserve publication. This is only clearly stated in the third report.

Text History 2

The second TH concerns an article which the informants submitted to JBF. This journal has the highest impact factor (1.908) of the three journals constituting the corpus and it is a great challenge for any scholar—and especially for these Spanish informants— to have their research published on this site. They received a major revision report, which was very good news as the rejection rate is around 70% in this journal. They worked on their manuscript following the referee's suggestions and provided a long response to the reviewer's comments. The reviewer acknowledged their effort, asked for a few minor changes and finally recommended its publication, which was granted by the editor (see Table 2 for a summary of texts in this TH).

As in the TH1 manuscript, the total number of critical acts included by the Spanish academics in their manuscript was even higher than in any of the published articles and higher than the average (see Table 5).

Negative critical acts in the Spanish scholars' manuscript were introduced (and even accrued) in order to define the niche, by identifying gaps or flaws in

Table 5. Comparison of critical acts in published articles and informants' TH2 manuscript

	Positive critical acts (average per article)	Negative critical acts (average per article)
JBF	7.1	3.1
manuscript 2a[3]	11	13
manuscript 2b	12	11

previous research. As in the case of published RA introductions, these negative attitudinal comments were not writer-mediated, that is, no self-references were included, and they were impersonal, that is, addressed to the whole community, rather than to the work of specific scholars:

> (13) Most of the studies on window dressing examine its influence on return anomalies, but <u>little attention has been paid to the existence and motivations of this institutional practice</u> (-). <u>The scarce literature on this topic</u> (-) finds <u>important limitations to test window dressing</u> (-), which *may* bias the conclusions found in *most* of the literature (-). <u>A major problem/concern is the unavailability of high-frequency data that would allow a direct comparison between disclosed and undisclosed information.</u> (-) (manuscript 2a)

The first report they received contained two major concerns or criticisms, one related to the method applied and especially regarding the data provided in tables and their discussion, and a second one about the "missing clear motivation and positioning of the paper." This report, unlike those in TH1, included a suggestion for improvement in relation to each of the points raised. In this particular case, the reviewer stated "I would suggest to more clearly explain and structure what the author(s) hypotheses is and how it relates to existing literature." Although, as can be seen in Example 13 above, a gap was identified in the first version of the manuscript, the referee seemed to expect the authors to draw links between that presumed faulty research and their own, establishing stronger connections between the author's research and past research in the field and making the differences, extensions or deviations from the latter explicit. This is something found in many of the published articles:

> (14) Second, unlike previous studies on international portfolio allocations, <u>we control for</u> (+) … (JBF2)
>
> In contrast to previous studies, <u>we do not make any specific assumptions about</u> … .(+) (JBF4)
>
> unlike existing studies, <u>we further utilize alternative measures of</u> … .(+) (JBF5)
>
> <u>A second feature that distinguishes our paper from most existing literature is that we explicitly model a</u> … .(+) (JBF5)

> In comparison to … —which also incorporate estimation noise in measures of portfolio tail risk—<u>this paper conducts the analysis in a more transparent framework</u> … .(+) (JBF6)

In the Spanish authors' attempt to highlight what is different in their research and worth pursuing, as suggested by the referee, they included the following positive critical acts:

> (15) *Our* approach is quite similar to that of Musto (1999) and Morey and O'Neal (2006), <u>but we detect different window dressing patterns</u>. (manuscript 2b)

> (16) *We* also focus on the intensity of this cosmetic practice according to institutional features of our fund database, such as size, fees, age, portfolio duration and recent performance. <u>These analyses expand on the potential factors initially tested by Musto (1999) and Morey and O'Neal (2006)</u> (+) and <u>offer results that help us to better understand the main factors driving this management behaviour</u> (+). (manuscript 2b)

In line with the results from the corpus of published articles, these self-referential positive critical acts that highlighted the motivation of their research were writer-mediated.

The authors also responded to a comment made by the reviewer in relation to their insistence on the creation of a research gap "… seems a little bit exaggerated considering the amount of literature available." As a result, they deleted two negative critical acts which emphasized "the scarce literature on this topic" and "the practically non-existent background on this cosmetic practice in bond funds." Therefore, the revision Spanish authors undertook entailed some differences in the inclusion of critical acts, aimed at evaluating their own research and that of others.

Besides addressing the criticism by the reviewer in the new version of their manuscript, the Spanish authors clarified their revision regarding this negative comment (as well as to the rest of comments referring to the method and data) in their response to their report: "we explain more clearly what our paper adds to the literature, which analyses window dressing in this straightforward manner, that is, … . Our contributions are the following: … ." In the second report the reviewer seemed to be satisfied with the motivation and positioning of their paper in the literature, which had been the first and one of the most salient objections, as no further references were made in this respect.

FINAL REMARKS

The aim of this chapter has been to analyse evaluation through the concept of "critical acts" in the introductions of RAs published in three high impact journals in the field of finance and to compare the findings with those obtained from a parallel analysis of two introductions of RAs drafted by Spanish academics, submitted for publication to those top journals, and rejected, or recommended to undergo a major revision (although finally accepted). The encoding of evaluation in the Spanish academics' manuscripts has also been analysed in the light of the referee reports received. The ultimate purpose of this research into the writing and research publication process is to gain an insight into possible rhetorical factors potentially affecting the decisions made on submitted papers, and ultimately helping (non-native) academics to get their research published in English-medium international high impact journals. This is currently a pressing need, as academic promotion, credentials and prestige are based on the publication of research papers on these sites.

The results found indicate that published RA introductions feature a similar pattern of use of positive and negative critical acts across the three journals. Positive critical acts outnumber negative ones. It is, therefore, highly relevant to stress the author's own contribution to the discipline, to justify it in the light of previous research, to stress its motivation and the originality of the topic their research is based upon. Positive critical acts are self-referential to a large extent and authors tend to express their own voice through first person pronouns and possessive adjectives. Negative critical acts only refer to previous research, frequently in an impersonal way through references to the whole community rather than indicating specific pieces of work, and the authors' voice tends to be unveiled. Both positive and negative critical acts are most frequently unhedged.

The analysis of the Spanish academics' manuscripts has revealed, contrary to expectations, a high number of critical acts. In the case of the unsuccessful TH1, although the referee's comments in the first two reports indicated the scholars' unconvincing reference to the contribution and motivation of their research, the results show that those functions were actually discursively addressed by means of positive critical acts. The criticism seemed to be addressed more to the contribution itself, rather than to the authors' rhetorical encoding of it, as becomes clear in the third rejection report. Therefore, it is not enough to include positive critical acts to highlight the value of one's research; "gatekeepers" need to judge that such positive attitudinal comments actually match the research reported in the paper.

In TH2 it was found that Spanish scholars included a great deal of negative critical acts, emphasising gaps or flaws in previous research so that an appropriate niche was created for their research. However, such negative evaluation did not prompt the appropriate contextualization of their research, according to the referee. In this particular case, a recommendation or course of action accompanied the referee's criticism. Indeed, the academics in the second version of the manuscript established further links between their own research and previous literature through positive critical acts, and softened the creation of the niche by deleting two negative critical acts. They seem to have responded satisfactorily to this criticism, and also to further criticisms regarding their methods and some discussions of their data, which granted them publication in one of the most prestigious journals in the field.

It is of great importance that scholars correctly interpret referee comments in their reports. In the case of TH1 analysed in this chapter, Spanish scholars may have in some way underestimated the criticisms received by the reviewers, since despite them, they then attempted to submit their papers with minor rhetorical (or research) changes to a journal with a higher impact factor each time, which turned out not to be a good approach. On the other hand, the specific response in their manuscripts to all issues raised by the reviewer convinced "gatekeepers" of the value of their research in TH2. This task was facilitated by the reviewer as each concern was accompanied by a suggestion on how to deal with it. It seems that the reviewer was at least partially convinced of the merit of their research and therefore decided to help them in the process. No suggestions were offered in the rejection reports in TH1, so it seems that the (non) inclusion of recommendations on how to improve the manuscript may be a hint to better interpret the referee's more or less veiled criticisms. In any case, both the rejection and the major revision reports addressed the issue of evaluation of the Spanish scholars' research and its interpretation in the light of previous research, that is, as regards motivation and contribution. This indicates that it is necessary—though not sufficient—for scholars to discursively address these evaluative aspects in their papers. The Spanish academics were aware of this requirement, as shown by their inclusion of numerous critical acts and as confirmed in discussions with them.

The analysis has focused on the introduction of the RAs, since, although critical acts may also be found elsewhere in the article, it is in this section that academics most clearly need to position their research in the field and to evaluate it so that it is convincingly "marketed." In fact, most of the referees' rhetorical concerns need to be addressed in this section of the article. Nonetheless, the contrastive analysis of critical acts could be expanded to include the whole article in order to determine possible areas of differences in terms of the realization of attitudinal comments between published RAs and (un)successful manuscripts.

The analysis of evaluation through "critical acts" in academic writing had previously only been applied to book reviews. It has shown to be an appropriate analytical tool in this analysis of RA introductions. Although many other issues may be at stake when deciding (not) to publish a manuscript, this research has highlighted the importance of the rhetorical interpersonal component of discourse to negotiate new academic knowledge within the research publication context. Further large scale analyses including a higher number of journals in this and other fields covering more authors and texts would help us learn more about the writing for publication process that academics undergo and, in particular, the problems faced, especially, by non-native scholars in getting their research accepted for publication. The results from the present and future, more extensive studies will allow us to offer scholars guidelines which will help them attain their goal of publishing their research in international English-medium publications.

NOTES

1. This research has been carried out within the framework of a research project financed by the Spanish Ministry of Science and Innovation, Plan Nacional de I+D+i (2008-2011), Ref: FFI2009-08336

2. Literacy brokers encompass friends, academic colleagues, editors, translators, proofreaders, that is, any agents, besides the authors, who contribute to the shaping of their article (Lillis & Curry, 2010).

3. It is interesting to note that no changes in the inclusion of critical acts were found between the authors' manuscript and its proofread version.

REFERENCES

Burgess, S. (2002). Packed houses and intimate gatherings: Audience and rhetorical strategies. In J. Flowerdew (Ed.), *Academic discourse* (pp. 196-225). London: Longman.

Connor, U. (2004). Intercultural rhetoric research: Beyond texts. *Journal of English for Academic Purposes, 3*, 291-304.

Fagan, A., & Martín Martín, P. (2004). The use of critical speech acts in psychology and chemistry research papers. *Ibérica, 8*, 125-137.

Hunston, S., & Thompson, G. (2000). Evaluation: An introduction. In S. Hunston & G. Thompson (Eds.), *Evaluation in text: Authorial stance and the construction of discourse* (pp. 1-27). Oxford, UK: Oxford University Press.

Lillis, T., & Curry, M. J. (2006). Professional academic writing by multilingual scholars: Interactions with literacy brokers in the production of English-medium texts. *Written Communication, 23,* 3-35.

Lillis, T., & Curry, M. J. (2010). *Academic writing in a global context: The politics and practices of publishing in English.* London and New York: Routledge.

Lorés-Sanz, R. (2006). "I will argue that": First person pronouns as metadiscoursal devices in research article abstracts in English and Spanish. *ESP Across Cultures, 3,* 23-40.

Lorés-Sanz, R. (2009a). Different worlds, different audiences: A contrastive analysis of research article abstracts. In E. Suomela Salmi & F. Drevin (Eds.), *Cross-linguistic and cross-cultural perspectives on academic discourse* (pp. 187-197). Amsterdam/Philadelphia: John Benjamins.

Lorés-Sanz, R. (2009b). (Non-) critical voices in the reviewing of history discourse: A cross-cultural study of evaluation. In K. Hyland & G. Diani (Eds.), *Academic evaluation: Review genres in university settings* (pp. 143-160). Basingstoke, Hampshire, UK: Palgrave MacMillan.

Martín Martín, P. (2003). A genre analysis of English and Spanish research paper abstracts in experimental social sciences. *English for Specific Purposes, 22,* 25-43.

Martín Martín, P. (2005). *The rhetoric of the abstract in English and Spanish scientific discourse: A cross-cultural genre-analytic approach.* Bern: Peter Lang.

Martín Martín, P., & Burgess, S. (2004). The rhetorical management of academic criticism in research article abstracts. *Text, 24,* 171-195.

Moreno, A. I. (2004). Retrospective labelling in premise-conclusion metatext: An English-Spanish contrastive study of research articles on business and economics. *Journal of English for Academic Purposes, 3,* 321-339.

Moreno, A. I. (2010). Researching into English for research publication purposes from an applied intercultural perspective. In M. F. Ruiz-Garrido, J. C. Palmer-Silveira, & I. Fortanet-Gómez (Eds.), *English for professional and academic purposes* (pp. 57-71). Amsterdam: Rodopi.

Moreno, A. I., & Suárez, L. (2008a). A framework for comparing evaluation resources across academic texts. *Text & Talk, 28,* 749-769.

Moreno, A. I., & Suárez, L. (2008b). A study of critical attitude across English and Spanish academic book reviews. *Journal of English for Academic Purposes, 7,* 15-26.

Moreno, A. I., & Suárez, L. (2009). Academic book reviews in English and Spanish: Critical comments and rhetorical structure. In K. Hyland & G. Diani (Eds.), *Academic evaluation: Review genres in university settings* (pp. 161-178). Basingstoke, Hampshire, UK: Palgrave MacMillan.

Mur Dueñas, P. (2007). "I/we focus on ... ": A cross-cultural analysis of self-mentions in business management research articles. *Journal of English for Academic Purposes, 6,* 143-162.

Mur Dueñas, P. (2010). A contrastive analysis of research article introductions in English and Spanish. *Revista Canaria de Estudios Ingleses, 61,* 119-133.

Salager-Meyer, F., Alcaraz Ariza, M.A., & Zambrano, N. (2003). The scimitar, the dagger and the glove: Intercultural differences in the rhetoric of criticism in Spanish, French and English medical discourse (1930-1995). *English for Specific Purposes, 22*(3), 223-247.

Sheldon, E. (2009). From one I to another: Discursive construction of self-representation in English and Castilian Spanish research articles. *English for Specific Purposes, 28*(4), 251-265.

Swales, J. (1990). *Genre analysis: English in academic and research settings.* Cambridge, UK: Cambridge University Press.

Swales, J. (2004). *Research genres: Exploration and applications.* Cambridge, UK: Cambridge University Press.

CHAPTER 24.
TOWARDS AN INTEGRATIVE UNIT OF ANALYSIS: REGULATION EPISODES IN EXPERT RESEARCH ARTICLE WRITING

Anna Iñesta and Montserrat Castelló
Ramon Llull University

Since the early nineties, the field of academic writing has increasingly captured researchers' attention, partially due to the increasing relevance of writing and publishing for academics' careers. Research has mostly aimed at characterizing the writing process in either experimental writing tasks (Breetvelt, van den Bergh, & Rijlaarsdam, 1994; Chenoweth, & Hayes, 2003; Galbraith & Torrance, 2004; Galbraith, Ford, Walker, & Ford, 2005; Kellogg, Olive, & Piolat, 2007; Nottbusch, Weingarten, & Sahel, 2007; Pajares & Johnson, 1994; Van den Bergh & Rijlaarsdam, 2007) or in tasks proposed in the context of the classroom (Alamargot, Dansac, Chesnet, & Fayol, 2007; Boscolo, Arfé, & Quarisa, 2004; Braaksma, Rijlaarsdam, van den Bergh, & van Hout-Wolters, 2004; Castelló & Monereo, 2000; Dysthe, Samara, & Westrheim, 2006; Ivanic, 1998; Mateos, Cuevas, Martin, & Luna, 2008; Segev-Miller, 2007 Yore, Florence, Pearson, & Weaver, 2006).

Regarding the discourse genre studied, the argumentative essay has tended to be the focus of the researchers' attention (Breetvelt et al, 1994; Castelló, & Monereo, 2000; Galbraith et al., 2005; Galbraith & Torrance, 2004; Ivanic, 1998; Kamberelis & Scott, 1992; Mateos et al., 2008; Van den Bergh & Rijlaarsdam, 2007), while the sample has most frequently been composed of secondary (Braaksma et al., 2004; Breetvelt et al., 1994; Pajares & Cheong, 2004) or undergraduate students (Boscolo et al., 2004; Castelló, 1999; Castelló, Iñesta, Pardo, Liesa & Martínez-Fernández, 2011; Galbraith et al, 2005; Galbraith & Torrance, 2004; Ivanic, 1998; Kellogg et al., 2007; Mateos et al., 2008; Nottbusch et al., 2007; Segev-Miller, 2007).

Most of the studies specifically devoted to clarifying how writers manage, control and regulate writing have been concerned with identifying the strategies that appear to be most useful at different moments of the writing process. The results obtained in these studies have frequently ended up with lists of categories which make it difficult to portray writing regulation as a dynamic activity, especially if we understand it as a socially and culturally situated activity (Camps & Castelló, 1996; Candlin & Hyland, 1999; Castelló, Gonzalez, & Iñesta, 2010; Flowerdew & Peacock, 2001; Iñesta, 2009; Johns, 2002; Lea & Stierer, 2000). Indeed, current approaches to the study of self-regulation suggest the need to go beyond the analysis of isolated actions, identifying those patterns in which actions are organized and given a situated meaning (Järvelä, Volet, Summers, & Thurman, 2006). In this chapter, we present a study attempting to assess a new unit of analysis, the Regulation Episode (RE) (Castelló & Iñesta, 2007; Castelló, Iñesta, & Monereo, 2009; Zanotto, Monereo & Castelló, 2011), as a means to approach the regulation of a challenging task such as research article writing (RA) in a comprehensive way and to find meaningful writing strategy patterns in ecological conditions.

THE WRITING REGULATION AND COMPOSITION PROCESSES

Research conducted on writing regulation has allowed us to learn quite a lot about the specificities of the writing process. One of the main results obtained in early cognitive studies revealed the relevance and the different role of three subprocesses: planning, formulating, and revising (Bereiter & Scardamalia, 1987; Flower & Hayes, 1980), with planning appearing key to obtain a high quality text (e.g., Galbraith, 1999; Galbraith & Torrance, 2004). Idea generation appears as one of the key strategies taking place during the planning stage (Flower & Hayes, 1980), while revising tends to occur at a micro (sentence- and paragraph-level) and a macro (or structural) level (Fitzgerald, 1987; Graham & Harris, 2000; Roussey & Piolat, 2005; van Waes & Schellens, 2002). And finally, we also know that working memory plays a major role in the writers' capacity to orchestrate the different dimensions involved in text production (Alamargot et al., 2007; Galbraith, Ford, Walker, & Ford 2005; Hayes & Chennoweth, 2006; Kellogg, 1999, 2001; Olive & Piolat, 2003).

Recent research has also revealed that the moment and frequency of occurrence of certain strategies have a differential impact on final text quality, which suggests a dynamically changing relation between writing process and text quality (Beauvais, Olive, & Passerault, 2011; Breetvelt et al., 1994; Van den Bergh & Rijlaarsdam, 2007). In fact, this has led Rijlaarsdam and van den Bergh (2006, p. 46) to claim that "combinations rather than single activities should be considered as the unit of analysis." On the other hand, studies such as those by Page-Voth & Graham (1999), or Pajares & Cheong (2004) have shown that the intentional and conscious use of writing strategies in accordance with specific writing objectives translates into increased final text quality.

Those studies conducted from cognitive and sociocognitive approaches have signaled the importance of certain factors in the participants' writing experience and, in turn, in final text quality. Firstly, the perception of self-efficacy has a clear positive effect on final text quality (Pajares & Johnson, 1994). Secondly, an increase in the knowledge of the writing process and of the writing strategies results in more complex conceptualizations of the writing process (Boscolo et al., 2004; Castelló & Monereo, 2000; Englert, Raphael, & Anderson, 1992; Englert, Mariage, & Dunsmore, 2006; Graham & Harris, 2000;).

TOWARDS AN INTEGRATIVE AND SOCIALLY SITUATED APPROACH TO WRITING REGULATION RESEARCH: THE REGULATION EPISODE AS A NEW UNIT OF ANALYSIS

Despite the relevance of previous studies' results, the possibility to comprehensively explain the complexities that current conceptualizations of self-regulation emphasize (e.g., Fitzsimons & Finkel, 2011; Koole, van Dillen & Sheppes, 2011; Papies & Aarts, 2011) when applied to writing tasks still remains an open question. The importance of such complexities lies in that they result from in-depth situated analysis of the "self-generated thoughts, feelings and actions that individuals plan and cyclically adapt while solving a specific task to the attainment of personal goals" (Zimmerman, 2000, p. 14). We will claim that this kind of situated analysis is also necessary if we aim to gain a complex perspective on self-regulation of the academic writing activity learning. In the following lines we will briefly present what we consider to be the five main complexities that writing regulation research should address.

The first complexity stems from the consideration that the thoughts and actions implemented by the individual during task resolution can no longer be simply categorized as "correct" or "incorrect." Rather, a more careful analysis is required so as to consider them more or less strategic or adjusted to the established goals (Boekaerts, 2002; Boekaerts & Cascallar, 2006; Castelló & Monereo, 2000; Monereo, 2007; Pozo, Monereo, & Castelló, 2001).

The second complexity has to do with the establishment and maintenance of goals, two processes which are considered the key that allows the transition from thought—knowing which strategies are best suited to solve a given task— to action—their actual implementation. Different approaches are currently interested in the nature and implications of goal establishment and maintenance in self-regulation (Carver & Scheier, 2000; Shah & Kruglanski, 2000). Among these, the need to study of the "whole-person-in-context" (Boekaerts, 2002) as well as the dynamics of task- and context-specific conflicting goals stands out as those which can dialogue with the situated approach to writing regulation research this chapter advocates.

The third complexity also derives from a situated approach to self-regulation. Indeed, in the last few years, context has come to be considered a constituting element that configures regulation, which is considered to be a socially shared activity (Jackson, Mackenzie, & Hobfoll, 2000; Järvelä, Järvenoja, & Veermans, 2008), even when sharing takes place intra-subjectively (Monereo, Badia, Bilbao, Cerrato, & Weise, 2008). This intrasubjectivity refers to those occasions in which the individual recreates the voices of significant others during a task-resolution process, and tailors his/her activity accordingly.

The fourth complexity relates to one of the most important emerging concepts in the reflection on self-regulation, that of identity (Farmer, 1995; Ivanic, 1998; Walker, 2007), which in fact may be even considered to function as an articulating construct, with the potential to integrate coherent thought-emotion-and-action scripts, socially and culturally situated, according to what the individual may perceive as more suitable to the given learning situation (Castelló & Iñesta, 2012; Monereo, 2007).

The complexities outlined so far may be related to the situated approach of current research on writing regulation. The fifth and final complexity we would like to refer to relates to the debate regarding the degree of explicitness involved in the implementation of self-regulation activities. While classical approaches tend to consider that self-regulation is possible when individuals exercise explicit control or monitoring over the task resolution process (e.g., Flavell, 1981; Zimmerman, 1989, 1990, 2000), some authors have proposed that intentional decisions may also take place implicitly (Beauvais, Olive, & Passerault, 2011; Boekaerts & Cascallar, 2006; Kuhl, 2000; Liesa, 2004; Shapiro & Schwartz, 2000). In this respect, for instance, Efklides' model of self-regulation (e.g., 2001, 2006), with the constructs of Metacognitive Experiences and Metacognitive Feelings, portrays self-regulation as a highly dynamic activity depending on cognitive as well as emotional processes which take place at a conscious and unconscious level.

As we have seen, current views on self-regulation present it as a complex activity of a highly situated and social nature (Hurme, Palonen, & Järvelä, 2006; Järvelä & Järvenoja, 2007; Järvelä et al., 2008; Veermans & Järvelä, 2003), involving cyclical thought-action-emotion dynamics, and the individual's capacity to monitor his/her self-regulation activity at varying levels of explicitness. However, this dynamic approach to self-regulation has not been applied to writing. On the other hand, those studies addressing the situated dimension of writing have focused on issues other than writing regulation.

Our study attempted to apply a dynamic approach to the study of writing regulation in authentic task-resolution processes in ecological conditions. We have done so by accessing and characterizing the writing regulation activities implemented by two experienced researchers while writing a RA in Spanish as their academic writing L1.[1] More specifically, our study aimed at answering the following research questions:

When, how and for what purpose do expert writers regulate their writing activity when confronted with a complex task such as research article writing?

Can the regulation activities implemented be related so as to be said to constitute a meaningful and dynamic unit of analysis? In other words, is it possible to identify Regulation Episodes which help us catch the complexity of writing regulation?

METHOD

SAMPLE

Two experienced researchers in the field of psychology participated in the study (Writer 1 and Writer 2). The researchers were members of the same research group, so they had an expert and shared knowledge of the topic they were writing about (strategic reading in Spanish secondary education). Moreover, they were considered to be expert writers given the number of RA articles published (W1: 15; W2: 14) and their experience as reviewers for other journals in the field (W1 collaborated as a reviewer of five journals, while W2 did so with four journals).

These researchers had decided to write in co-authorship conditions a RA, an earlier version of which had been previously rejected by a national journal. The writing of this earlier version had been led by another member of their research group, and only one of the writers (Writer 2) had participated in this process as coauthor. Therefore, the writing regulation analyzed in this study does not correspond to the mere revision of that earlier version. Partly for the purpose of research and partly with the objective of approaching the writing process without the limitations of the previous version of the article, Writer 1 and Writer 2 agreed to work separately on the whole article and then to compare their versions and negotiate a joined final text for submission to another national journal. This final negotiation and the response of the target journal editors were not taken into account in this chapter.

Procedure

Participants wrote their paper as they usually did, having freedom to work at any time they wanted, with no time limit or space restrictions. They worked on their RA for approximately one month and a half. Specifically, Writer 1 devoted a total of 660 hours (distributed in 11 sessions) to write the RA, while Writer 2 devoted 1,016 hours (distributed in 12 writing sessions). In order to portray the researchers' writing process with as much fidelity as possible, we asked them to follow a series of steps every time they sat to work on their RA.

First, participants completed a writing diary for every writing session, where they had to respond to prompts such as "My objectives for today's session are … ", "I have found no/little/some/serious difficulties related with … ", "I believe that such difficulties are due to … ", "I have solved the difficulties by … ", "I am not at all/a little / very satisfied with the solutions found because … ".

Second, writers were asked to save every newly produced draft of their RA, which would allow for the identification of changes among them.

Third, they were asked to activate the Camtasia screen-capture software to record their writing activity in every session. This software was installed in their personal computers to ensure their writing in natural conditions. The video-recordings obtained were transcribed so as to facilitate the analysis of the writers' activity.

Fourth, short interviews were conducted on a weekly basis in order to capture the writers' impressions during the writing process. Finally, a retrospective recall interview was conducted at the end of the process where writers commented on the writing process.

Therefore, analyzed data involved the writing diaries, the different drafts that each researcher produced of the RA, the transcripts of the participants' writing activity as captured in their word-processor video-recordings in each of the sessions that the participants devoted to writing a RA, and the transcripts of the interviews conducted during and at the end of the writing process.

Analysis of the Data

With all the collected information, two kinds of analyses were conducted: the macro- and the micro-analysis of regulation. On the one hand, the *macro-analysis of regulation* combined declarative information (content analysis from writing diaries and interviews) and procedural information (draft analysis and Camtasia screen-recordings).

Content analysis of the writing diaries and interviews (conducted with Atlas.ti) allowed us to identify the challenges or difficulties explicitly identified by the writers as well as the solutions they had introduced (that same session) or would introduce (in ensuing sessions) to overcome them.

Once writers' perceptions about challenges and solutions had been identified, we moved on to find traces of action that would constitute evidence of writing regulation activity. In order to do this, we first analyzed the different drafts produced by the writers to identify the changes (e.g., from draft 3 to draft 4). Then we related such traces with the solutions that writers declared they would implement or had already implemented to solve the challenges they had explicitly identified.

Following this, we aimed to learn about the specificities of the writing regulation activity that had resulted in the changes present in the drafts. In other words, we wanted to know which steps had lead to the solutions present in the text. In order to do that, we conducted a *micro-analysis* of the transcripts of each of the researchers' video-recorded writing sessions to see which actions had been implemented from one draft to the following one.

This analysis was conducted from a bottom-up approach involving the in-context analysis of all the actions implemented by the writers in every writing session. In these transcripts, the writers' actions were segmented into bursts,[2] that is, sequences of action framed either by changes in the activity, by more than five second-long pauses, or by actions categorized as "other" (i.e., scroll up or down in the document, open another document, check e-mail inbox ...).

With all this information we constructed an *integrated view template* with the aim to gain an integrated representation of information. This template allowed us to see when a challenge appeared and when solutions to this challenge had been implemented. Therefore, a Regulation Episode may be defined as a *sequence of actions that writers strategically implement with the objective of solving a difficulty or challenge identified during the writing process* (Castelló & Iñesta, 2007; Castelló, Iñesta & Monereo, 2009; Zanotto et al., 2011). Also, in order to obtain a global picture of RE occurrence/distribution throughout the different sessions each participant had devoted to RA writing, a *table of RE distribution* was elaborated for each writing process.

Inter-Judge Reliability

Data from both writing processes were used to establish the reliability of the coding systems. Two independent judges participated in the categorization of the data both at the macro- and micro-levels of analysis.

Once the individual decisions had been compared, the doubtful cases were also agreed upon by consensus. Finally, two other independent judges analyzed 30% of the data, registering a degree of agreement of 96.33%. Lack of agreement led to reviewing and discussing the cases until consensus was reached on the assignment of categories. Once this done, the rest of the data were analyzed by both judges.

RESULTS

Explicit and Implicit Regulation Episodes: The Dynamics of Writing Regulation Activity

Results obtained show that regulation happens by means of two kinds of Regulation Episodes: explicit and implicit.

Explicit Regulation Episodes

Explicit Regulation Episodes (RE) were those characterized by an explicit challenge that writers had identified and evidence of actions that the writer had implemented to solve that particular challenge. Data show that the experienced researchers of our sample implemented Explicit Regulation Episodes all along the RA writing process. To illustrate this, Table 1 shows the distribution of Explicit Regulation Episodes in the RA writing process of Writer 1.

The combination of macro- and micro-analyses allowed us to portray writing regulation as it takes place in Explicit Regulation Episodes, as a two-layered system. This is illustrated in the integrated view template for Writer 1's Regulation Episode 3, shown in Table 2. This RE was selected as an example of a regulation episode developing along practically all the writing process, addressing the challenge regarding the *need to reorganize information.*

As we can see, this shows:
- The identified *challenge* and the *section* in the RA where Writer 1 was working when identified
- The *writing sessions* during which the writer worked on the challenge
- The *result or outcome* of each of the sessions (either handwritten notes or new drafts of the articles together with video-recorded activity)
- The *writing objectives* expressed before initiating each of the writing sessions
- The *challenge as formulated by the writer* for each of the writing sessions
- The *cited solution* for each of the writing sessions
- The *implemented solution* for each of the writing sessions
- The *micro-level changes introduced in the text*, as revealed by the micro analysis of the writing activity video recordings

Implicit Regulation Episodes

The analysis of the video-recorded actions revealed evidence of sequences of actions of at least 10 bursts, some of which were aimed at reformulating or adjusting various elements of the sentence, showing an intention to address a challenge, despite not having made any explicit reference to it during the writing process. Such sequences of actions were considered Implicit Regulation Episodes (IREs).

Table 3. Translation from Spanish of Implicit Regulation Episode 9, Writer 2 W2.IRE7.A

Burst	Time code	Transcript
1	0:35:45	New sentence: "It is necessary to have more data but
2	0:36:00	Correcting: "It **is** would be necessary to have more data but
3	0:36:05	Correcting: "It would be necessary to have more **data** research but
4	0:36:14	Continuing: "It would be necessary to have more research but (1) this could (2) the mechanisms through which own action is decided could
		Pause
5	0:37:40	Continuing: "It would be necessary to have more research but the mechanisms through which own action is decided could **move along different paths to those which explain the acquisition of conceptual knowledge (authors cited).**

Later in the same session:

Burst	Time code	Transcript
6	0:41:02	Correcting: "It would be necessary to have more research **in order to try to validate the hypothesis** but the mechanisms through which own action is decided could move along different paths to those which explain the acquisition of conceptual knowledge (authors cited)."
7	0:42:05	Correcting: "It would be necessary to have more research in order to try to validate **the** a hypothesis **but** that the mechanisms through which own action is decided could move along different paths to those which explain the acquisition of conceptual knowledge (authors cited)."
8	0:42:35	Correcting: " It would be necessary to have more research in order to try to validate a the hypothesis that the mechanisms through which own action is decided could move along different paths to those which explain the acquisition of conceptual knowledge (authors cited)."

Table 1. Distribution of Regulation Episodes in the RA writing process of Writer 1

Writing session	1	2	3a	3b
Date	30.09.07	01.10.07	06.10.07	06.10.07
Draft		1	2a	2b
Section		Method Results	Method / Results	
Challenges cited in the writing diary of the session		P.ER2	P.ER1 P.ER3	
Cited and implemented solutions		S.ER2	S.ER1 S.ER3	
Implemented actions		S.ER2: presentation of variables	S.ER3: paragraphs are reorganized / S.ER1: S.2.2.: the Results section is reorganized	S.ER3: the position of two paragraphs is modified

Writing session	4	5a	5b	6
Date	08.10.07	09.10.07	09.10.07	10.10.07
Draft	3	4a	4b	5
Section	Discussion	Discussion / Results		
Challenges cited in the writing diary	P.ER4	P.ER4		
Cited and implemented solutions	S.ER4.A			
Implemented actions	S.ER4.A: the writing of the Discussion begins		S.ER4A: modifications are introduced in the Discussion	

Table 1. Continued

Writing session	7	8	9a	9b
Date	12.10.07	28.10.07	01.11.07	01.11.07
Draft	6	7	8a	8b
Section	Results	Introduction	Introduction	
Challenges cited in the writing diary	P.ER4		P.ER3	
Cited and implemented solutions	S.ER4.B S.ER4.C		S.ER3	S.ER3
Implemented actions	S.ER1 Results are developed S.ER4.B: the simple-complex / explicit-implicit table is included S.ER4.C: the target journal requirements are noted in the writing diary	S.ER1: the Introduction starts to be developed once the Results and Discussion sections are ready	S.ER3: information from the source text is included and reorganized	S.ER3: the Introduction is reorganized around 2 theme units

Writing session	10a	10b	11
Date	02.11.07		03.11.07
Draft	9a	9b	10
Section	Introduction		Method Results Discussion
Challenges cited in the writing diary			P.ER3
Cited and implemented solutions			S.ER3
Implemented actions			S.ER3: 2 paragraphs in the Method section are reorganized

Table 1. Continued

Cited challenges	Cited and implemented solutions
P.ER1: Difficulty is to construct a representation of the Introduction	S.ER1: To work on the Results section first
P.ER2: Lack of clarity in the presentation of the study variables	S.ER2: To explicitly distinguish between dependent and independent variables
P.ER3: Need to reorganize information	S.ER3: To reorganize information
	S.ER4.A: To use the Discussion section as a reference point
	S.ER4.B: To elaborate tables
P.ER4: Difficulty is to select information from the source text	S.ER4.C: To revise the requirements set by the target journal

Table 2. Integrated view template for W1's RE3

W1.RE3	Challenge addressed: Need to reorganize information Article scope: Method, Results, Discussion		
		Objectives	Challenges
RE3.A Session 3a (of a total of 11) 06.10.07	drafts & activity	"Today I have decided to start directly with the study and skip the theoretical framework, to which I'll go back later. I've done this because, given that in the source text there is a lot of interesting information, but it needs to be synthesized and adjusted to the article, the best was start directly with the study, and thus the work on selecting the theoretical basis would be easier and more adjusted." (Same objectives because these two writing sessions take place on the same day and W1 produces just one writing diary.)	The expression of the action implemented includes the expression of the challenge
RE3.B Session 3b 06.10.07	drafts & activity		
RE3.C Session 9a 01.11.07	drafts & activity	"Tots Sants[National holiday]. I'm about to devote this holiday to progress in the development of the theoretical framework of the article."	The expression of the action implemented includes the expression of the challenge
RE3.D Session 9b 01.11.07	drafts & activity	(Same objectives because these two writing sessions take place on the same day and W1 produces just one writing diary.)	The expression of the action implemented includes the expression of the challenge

Table 2. Continued

RE3.E Session 11 03.11.07	drafts & activity	None are cited		"I've found a problem of disorder in two sections of the Method"

	Cited solution	Implemented solution	Micro-level changes in the text
RE3.A Session 3a 06.10.07	"I have filled in the empirical section in both sessions and I have found some sections which, in my opinion, should be relocated (e.g., I've moved the paragraph on independent judges)."	Information from the source text is included and reorganized	Discursive Style: 8.33% Precision-Clarity: 91.66%
RE3.B Session 3b 06.10.07		The position of two paragraphs is changed	Relationship with Reader: 10% Precision-Clarity: 80%
RE3.C Session 9a 01.11.07	"In the first part I have filled in the set sections, first with ideas expressed in sentences and later with a development, connection and relocation of different subsections."	Information from the source text is included and reorganized	Discursive Style: 12.5% Positioning: 6.81% Questioning: 5.68% Relationship with Reader: 5.68% Precision-Clarity: 63.63% Cohesion-Coherence: 5.68%
RE3.D Session 9b 01.11.07	"In the second part I have worked on the coherence and consistency of the text, reducing the initial topics to two: studying to learn in secondary school and the study of expository texts. I haven't found any special difficulty. What I've found hardest is to decide what to eliminate and how to integrate the selected information around these two topics."	The Introduction is reorganized around two theme units: 1. Studying to learn at the secondary school and 2. The study of expository texts	Relationship with Reader: 20% Precision-Clarity: 20% Cohesion-Coherence: 60%
RE3.E Session 11 (of a total of 11) 03.11.07	"Basically I've copied what I had corrected on paper"	One of the paragraphs in the Method is reorganized	Precision: 100%

		Pause
9	0:43:29	Correcting: " It would be necessary to have more research in order to try to ~~validate~~ analyze the hypothesis that the mechanisms through which own action is decided could move along different paths to those which explain the acquisition of conceptual knowledge (authors cited)."
10	0:43:33	Correcting: " It would be necessary to have more research in order to try to ~~analyze~~ explore the hypothesis that the mechanisms through which own action is decided could move along different paths to those which explain the acquisition of conceptual knowledge (authors cited)."
11	0:43:40	Correcting: " It would be necessary to have more research in order to try to explore the hypothesis **regarding the possibility** that the mechanisms through which own action is decided could move along different paths to those which explain the acquisition of conceptual knowledge (authors cited)."
		Pause
12	0:44:03	Correcting: " It would be necessary to have more research **but** ~~in order to try to explore~~ the hypothesis regarding the possibility that the mechanisms through which own action is decided could move along different paths to those which explain the acquisition of conceptual knowledge (authors cited)."
		Pause
13	0:44:57	Correcting: " It would be necessary to have more research but the **working** hypothesis **appears to be clear; it could** regarding the possibility that the mechanisms through which own action is decided could move along different paths to those which explain the acquisition of conceptual knowledge (authors cited)."
14	0:45:07	Correcting: " It would be necessary to have more research but the working hypothesis appears to be clear; it could ~~regarding the possibility~~ **be possible** that the mechanisms through which own action is decided could move along different paths to those which explain the acquisition of conceptual knowledge (authors cited)."
		Long pause
	0:53:42	Stops video-recording
15	0:54:41	Correcting, marking in yellow a fragment of the sentence here marked in bold: "**It would be necessary to have more research but the working hypothesis appears to be clear; it could be possible** that the mechanisms through which own action is decided could move along different paths to those which explain the acquisition of conceptual knowledge (authors cited)."

Later in the same session:

Burst	Time code	Transcript
16	1:16:21	Correcting: "It would be necessary to have more ~~research~~ information to validate some ~~but the~~ working hypothesis ~~appears to be clear~~ that results point towards; it could be possible that the mechanisms through which own action is decided could move along different paths to those which explain the acquisition of conceptual knowledge (authors cited)."
17	1:16:56	Correcting: "It would be necessary to have more information to validate some working hypothesis that results point towards; **firstly**, it could be possible that the mechanisms through which own action is decided could move along different paths to those which explain the acquisition of conceptual knowledge (authors cited)."

Table 3 shows the translation of Writer 2's IRE 9 video-recorded transcript, originally elaborated in Spanish. We have chosen this episode because it provides clear evidence of intentional writing regulation as well as of the socially situated dimension of this activity. More specifically, the writer's awareness of the conceptually challenging nature of the sentence is revealed in the intrasession discontinuity of the IRE and in the amount and kind of adjustments he introduces until he reaches a satisfactory version. In this respect, this transcript reveals the history of actions involved in the writer's establishing his authorial positioning and making his voice and identity visible.

In this sense, though, Writer 2 addresses the complexity of softening the reader's possible disagreement with the hypothesis that procedural decision-making may be a highly complex matter, tied to implicit conceptions regarding the task, the learning situation and to one's own previous experiences and interpretations. As we can see, burst 2 corrects burst 1, changing "It is necessary to have more data … " for "It would be necessary to have more data." Also, bursts 6 to 11 illustrate how Writer 2 moves from saying "It would be necessary to have more research in order to validate the hypothesis … " to saying "It would be necessary to have more research in order to try to explore the hypothesis regarding the possibility that … ", thus adding more tentativeness to the claim. Burst 13, however, shows a move towards a more emphatic expression of the claim: "It would be necessary to have more research but the working hypothesis appears to be clear; it could … ". However, the inclusion of the adjective "working" shows Writer 2's awareness of the need to balance the assertiveness of the expression "appears to be clear." Finally, this expression disappears from the last version of the sentence, which is connected to the results obtained in the study conducted: "It would be necessary to have more information to validate some working hypothesis that results point towards." All in all, it seems the Writer is aware that these results could be questionable and tries to avoid or minimize some possible readers'—or reviewers'— critiques. However, the Writer does not renounce highlighting the interest of the results obtained, thus is positioned as someone who anticipates readers' voices but at the same time is able to dialogue with them to maintain a personal stance.

We believe that this example fully illustrates the complexity of RA writing regulation, suggesting that key aspects of this regulation (such as voice/identity and the social) are addressed by expert writers in an implicit mode.

Table 4. Implicit RE distribution in the RA writing process of Writer 2

Writing Session	Initial negotiation	1a	1b	2	3
Date	19.03.2007	01.04.2007	01.04.2007	02.04.2007	05.04.2007
Sections		Introduction	Introduction	Introduction	Introduction
IRE				ERI3	
Inferred Challenge				Need to enhance clarity	

Writing Session	4	5a	5b		6a
Date	08.04.2007	21.04.2007	21.04.2007		22.04.2007
Sections	Introduction	Introduction	Introduction		Method
IRE			ERI1	ERI4	
Inferred Challenge			Need to avoid questioning + enhance clarity + self-directed signals	Need to enhance clarity	

Writing Session	6b	7	8	9	10
Date	22.04.2007	01.05.2007	02.05.2007	03.05.2007	05.05.2007
Sections	Method	Results	Results	Results	Introduction Method Results
IRE		ERI2			

Inferred Challenge		Need to enhance clarity + need to avoid questioning			
Writing Session	11		12		
Date	17.05.2007		19.05.2007		
Sections	Discussion		Whole article		
IRE	ERI5	ERI6	ERI7	ERI8	ERI9
Inferred Challenge	Need to enhance clarity	Need to enhance clarity	Need to enhance clarity	Need to avoid questioning	Need to enhance clarity

Table 4 shows the distribution of Implicit REs along the writing sessions devoted by Writer 2 to the elaboration of the RA. As we can see, most of the Implicit REs concentrate at the end of the writing process, in sessions 11 and 12, where five of the Implicit REs are implemented, while in the rest of the sessions only 4 IREs are implemented.

The Division of Labor between Implicit and Explicit Regulation Episodes

When writing the Introduction of the RA, participants identified challenges related to constructing a representation of the RA section (RE1.W1), reorganizing information (RE3.W1; RE4.W2), justifying the approach taken to the study of the topic (RE1.W2), selecting information from the source text (RE2.W2), and ensuring the argumentative progression of the text (RE3.W2). On the other hand, when elaborating the Method section, the writers encountered challenges related to presenting the variables clearly (RE2.W1), justifying the comparability of the texts used in the study (RE0a.W2), and organizing information (RE3.W1; RE4.W2). Finally, the challenges identified while working on the Results section had to do with selecting information from the source text (RE4.W1) and with justifying the use of a certain categorization of procedures (RE0b.W2). W2 also declared the need to edit the expression and the format of the tables in all the sections of the RA (RE6.W2).

Regarding the challenges in IREs, here too, certain challenges appear to be addressed more frequently while working in certain sections of the RA, with the particularity that Implicit Regulation Episodes address more than one challenge in an integrated way. The IREs identified in the video-recorded writing activity happening while writing the Introduction addressed the challenge of enhancing clarity (IRE7.W1; IRE8.W1; IRE9.W1; IRE2.W2), adjusting phrasing to academic discursive style (IRE7.W1; IRE9.W1), directing the reader's interpretation (IRE8.W1), establishing authorial positioning (IRE9.W1), and obtaining an adequate formulation of a word or expression (IRE1.W1).

The IREs identified in the writers' activity while working on the Method section, on the other hand, focus on enhancing clarity (IRE2.W1; IRE1.W2; IRE2.W2; IRE4.W2), obtaining an adequate formulation of a word or expression (IRE3.W1), avoiding questioning (IRE1.W2; IRE2.W2), and regulating the writing process through the inclusion of self-directed signals (IRE1.W2).

When the writers worked on the Results sections, their IREs focused on enhancing clarity (IRE4.W1; IRE6.W1; IRE5.W2) and on obtaining an adequate formulation of the word or expression (IRE5.W1). Finally, while no IREs were identified in W1's elaboration of the Discussion section, W2's process focused on enhancing clarity (IRE6.W2; IRE7.W2; IRE8.W2; IRE9.W2) and on avoiding questioning (IRE8.W2).

The analysis of the challenges addressed in RE shows that Explicit RE tend to address more molar issues while Implicit RE address more local challenges.

CONTINUOUS AND DISCONTINUOUS REGULATION EPISODES: THE TIME DIMENSION IN THE DYNAMICS OF WRITING REGULATION ACTIVITY

Results revealed a morphological difference in both Implicit and Explicit REs: the existence of continuous REs (where the challenge and the solutions are cited and implemented in the same writing session) and discontinuous REs (where the challenge and the solutions are cited and implemented in the course of various writing sessions). In addition, two kinds of discontinuity were distinguished: inter-session discontinuity (indicating that the writer works on the

Table 5. Continuous and discontinuous Implicit and Explicit Regulation Episodes identified in participants' writing processes:

		Writer 1		Writing 2	
		Explicit	Implicit	Explicit	Implicit
Continuous		1	7	4	3
Discontinuous	Inter-session	3	0	4	0
	Intra-session	0	2	0	3
	Inter- & intra-session	0	0	0	2
Total		4	9	8	8

same challenge or RE in different writing sessions) and intra-session discontinuity (the writer does so at different moments of one writing session).

Table 5 shows the continuous and discontinuous Explicit and Implicit REs identified in the participants' writing processes. As we can see, no clear pattern can be distinguished. Interestingly, Writer 2's writing process shows a peculiarity: the existence of an Implicit RE showing both an inter- and intra-session discontinuity.

These results constitute empirical evidence of the recursive nature of writing regulation because even in the case of continuous Regulation Episodes, writers appear to implement actions associated with a particular intentionality at different times of the same writing session.

DISCUSSION

With the objective of going beyond the analysis of isolated actions and the intention of approaching regulation activities in an integrative way (Järvelä, Volet, & Järvenoja, 2010; Rijlaarsdam & van den Bergh, 2006; Volet, Summers, & Thurman, 2009), this chapter has presented a study aimed at assessing the Regulation Episode as a meaningful unit of analysis of research article writing regulation. Results showed this unit to be useful for identifying meaningful and orchestrated patterns in the writing activity of the two experienced researchers which formed part of the sample. One possible limitation of this study is that although the RA was written from the start, it had a previous history. Nevertheless, since each RA writing situation has its own previous history and it is situated in a different constellation of contextual conditions, we consider that the current analysis is useful for knowing how the regulation activity develops in those complex and specific writing situations. Precisely, we consider that writing regulation research should aim to transcend the unavoidable specificity of these writing situations while, at the same time, understanding that such specificity must be taken into consideration so as to approach writing regulation as it truly develops.

As for the first research question, results show that the when, the how and for what purpose of expert writers' activity regulation during research article writing have to do with the complexity of the writing patterns or Regulation Episodes. More specifically, regarding when writers implement regulation activities, such complexity is revealed in the fact that they can take place all along the writing process, their implementation spreading along different writing sessions. On the other hand, regarding how writers regulate their writing activity when working on a research article, the Regulation Episodes' complexity has to do with what we could call dynamics of writing regulation.

Regarding the regulation dynamics, it seems that expert writers are able to perform a kind of complex regulation oriented by goals aimed at solving molar challenges and involving a myriad of micro decision-making processes which finally bring the "rehearsed text" (Camps, 1994) to a strategically-adjusted final version. In this sense, regulation appears as a two-layered system involving both Implicit and Explicit Regulation Episodes in a dialogue aimed at solving specific challenges. More research would be necessary to know whether the observed "division of labor" between Implicit and Explicit Regulation Episodes is common in experts' writing regulation. In any case, these results show the complexity of academic writing regulation, a complexity that novice writers have had trouble addressing at the beginning of their research careers (e.g.,Castelló & Iñesta, 2012; Castelló, Iñesta, & Monereo, 2007; Castelló, González, & Iñesta, 2010; Castelló, Iñesta, Pardo, Liesa, & Martinez-Fernández, 2011; Maher, Seaton, Mullen, Fitzgerald, Otsuji, & Lee, 2008; Rinck, 2006), probably because they are unable to master this two-layered system and its division of labor that our writers have displayed all along the writing process. The complexity of mastering this system is paramount especially if we take into account that some of the implicit actions involved in IRE have to do with social concerns about how readers will interpret the author's positioning, as we have discussed in our results displaying the nature of Implicit Regulation Episodes.

In addition, regarding the time dimension in the regulation dynamics, the unit of analysis of the Regulation Episode has allowed us to obtain evidence of the theoretically agreed-upon recursivity of the writing process, also when focusing on writing regulation. In this respect, our results suggest that writers work on the challenges identified (either implicitly or explicitly) in intra- and inter-session recursive dynamics whereby increasingly adjusted or strategic thoughts and actions are implemented until the text reaches a satisfactory version which fulfills the established writing objectives.

Moreover, the discontinuity of RE has shown that expert writers are capable of setting and maintaining their goals all along the writing process. Our results also seem to suggest that the kind of goals expert writers use as signposts during writing self-regulation are molar and task and socially dependent. The kinds of challenges that writers address and which we consider to be the focus of the writers' goals may be considered evidence of this. The social dimension of such goals can be seen, on the one hand, in that generally the challenges addressed are aimed at fulfilling the conventions of academic texts and, thus, the readers' expectations (e.g., need to reorganize information [RE3.W1; RE4.W2], the need to ensure the argumentative progression of the text [RE3.W2], and the lack of adjustment between the introduction and the discussion sections [RE5.W2]). On the other hand, some of the challenges addressed are aimed at avoiding the journal editors' and ultimately the readers' problematization of the study conducted (e.g., lack of clarity in the presentation of the variables [RE2. W1], need to justify the comparability of the texts used in the study [RE0a. W2], need to justify the use of a specific categorization of procedures [RE0b. W2]), which adds to the socially dependent nature of the challenges addressed and thus of the writers' goals. More research would be necessary on the study of the "whole-person-in-context" (Boekaerts, 2002) to deepen our understanding of the dynamics of task- and context-specific goal setting and maintenance in writing regulation in ecological conditions.

Results obtained in this study complement those found in recent research on regulation (Efklides, 2001; Papies & Aarts, 2011) and which point towards the existence of an implicit mode of regulation. Although regulation has been generally considered to take place consciously (Boekaerts, 2001; Monereo, 2007; Zimmerman, 2001) our results indicate that another kind of regulation may take place in an implicit and yet intentional level. Despite the very incipient nature of these results, the data seem to suggest that this kind of regulation is very much imprinted in the writing process, even automatized. In this sense, then, the results obtained invite us revisit the conceptualization of regulation in complex tasks such as RA writing.

In relation to this, it seems also necessary to consider whether implicit regulation is a characteristic of expert RA writing, and whether the kind of regulation these writers implement takes place mostly implicitly. In fact, having to complete the writing diary may have brought to the writers' awareness certain issues that may otherwise have remained at the same level of unconsciousness as the challenges addressed in the Implicit Regulation Episodes.

On the other hand, the characteristics of Implicit REs add other dimensions to our understanding of RA writing regulation, which refer to the interrelation of the when, how and for what purpose dimensions of writing regulation implied in our first research question. Among this is the fact that key aspects of this regulation may be addressed by expert writers in an implicit mode while affecting text production both at the macro (structural) and micro (local) levels. In this respect, the results obtained present authorial voice and the social dimension as central both in the kind of micro-changes visible in Implicit Regulation Episodes and in the macro-changes visible in Explicit Regulation Episodes. This would provide evidence to the consideration of identity as an articulating construct with the potential to explain socially and culturally situated thought-emotion-and-action scripts (Castelló & Iñesta, 2012; Ivanic, 1998; Prior, 2001) such as those presented in the Regulation Episodes.

This suggests that a huge amount of craftsmanship is involved in strategic text tailoring, and that such craftsmanship has remained invisible to the eyes of those who, like student researchers, would very much benefit from accessing and learning from it. This would again point towards the need to conduct further studies involving the micro-analysis of regulation, that is, the in-content analysis of the actions implemented during writing sessions conducted in ecological conditions in order to learn more about the process whereby expert but also other profiles of writers construct their discursive identity as researchers (Walker, 2007).

We are conscious that our study is limited in scope firstly because we have worked only with two writers. Moreover they were experienced writers in a very particular condition: writing their paper separately. Our intention was to develop a new unit of analysis and to find out if this allowed us to explain regulation activities all along an extended process such as RA writing. Different writing situations should be analyzed with the same unit to find out if the different types of Regulation Episodes can be maintained.

REFERENCES

Alamargot, D., Dansac, C., Chesnet, D., & Fayol, M. (2007). Parallel processing before and after pauses: A combined analysis of graphomotor and eye movements during procedural text production. In A. M. Torrance, L. van Waes, & D. Galbraith (Eds.), *Writing and cognition: Research and applications. Studies in writing, 20* (pp. 13-29). Amsterdam: Elsevier.

Beare, S., & Bourdages, J. S. (2007). Skilled writers' generating strategies in L1 and L2: An exploratory study. In A. M. Torrance, L.van Waes, & D. Galbraith (Eds.), *Writing and cognition: Research and applications. Studies in writing, 20* (pp. 151-161). Amsterdam: Elsevier.

Beauvais, C., Olive, T., & Passerault, J-M. (2011). Why are some texts good and others not? Relationship between text quality and management of the writing processes *Journal of Educational Psychology, 103,* 415-428.

Bereiter, C., & Scardamalia, M. (1987). *The psychology of written composition.* Hillsdale, NJ: Lawrence Erlbaum.

Boekaerts, M. (2002). Bringing about change in the classroom: Strengths and weaknesses of the self-regulated learning approach: EARLI Presidential Address, 2001. *Learning and Instruction, 12,* 589-604.

Boekaerts, M., & Cascallar, E. (2006). How far have we moved toward the integration of theory and practice in self-regulation? *Educational Psychology Review, 18,* 199-210.

Boscolo, P., Arfé, B., & Quarisa, M. (2007). Improving the quality of students' academic writing: An intervention study. *Studies in Higher Education, 32*(4), 419-438.

Braaksma, M. A. H., Rijlaarsdam, G., van den Bergh, H., & van Hout-Wolters, B. H. A. M. (2004). Observational learning and its effects on the orchestration of writing processes. *Cognition and Instruction, 22*(1), 1-36.

Breetvelt, I., van den Bergh, H., & Rijlaarsdam, G. (1994). Relations between writing processes and text quality: When and how? *Cognition and Instruction, 12*(2), 103-123.

Camps, A., & Castelló, M. (1996). Las estrategias de enseñanza-aprendizaje en la escritura. In C. Monereo & I. Solé (coords.) *El asesoramiento psicopedagógico: Una perspectiva profesional y constructivista.* Madrid: Alianza.

Camps, A., & Milian, M. (2000). Metalinguistic activity in learning to write: An introduction. In A. Camps & M. Milian (Eds.), *Metalinguistic activity in learning to write* (pp. 49-78). Amsterdam: Amsterdam University Press.

Candlin, C. N., & Hyland, K. (1999). *Writing: Texts, processes and practices.* London: Pearson.

Carver, C. S., & Scheier, M. F. (2000). On the structure of behavioral self-regulation. In M. Boekaerts; P. R. Pintrich; & M. Zeidner (Eds.), *Handbook of self-regulation.* London & New York: Academic Press.

Castelló, M., & Iñesta, A. (2007). The writing process: Methodological strategies to access the cognitive and emotional dimensions of the writing process. Seminar Reading and Writing to Learn in Secondary and Higher Education, September 27, 2007, Barcelona.

Castelló, M., & Iñesta, A. (2012). Texts as artifacts-in activity: Developing authorial identity and academic voice in writing academic research papers. In M. Castelló & C. Donahue (2011). (Eds.), *University writing: Selves and Texts in Academic Societies.* London: Emerald Group.

Castelló, M., Gonzalez, L., & Iñesta, A. (2010). La regulación de la escritura académica en el doctorado: El impacto de la revision colaborativa en los textos. [The regulation of academic writing. The impact of collaborative revision on texts] *Revista Española de Pedagogía, 7*(3), 1107-1130.

Castelló, M., Iñesta, A., Pardo, M., Liesa, E., & Martinez-Fernández, R. (2011). Tutoring the end-of-studies dissertation: Helping psychology students find their academic voice. *Higher Education, 63*(1), 97-115.

Castelló, M., & Monereo, C. (2000). Students' conceptions on academic writing. In A. Camps & M. Milian (Eds.), *Metalinguistic activity in learning to write* (pp. 49-78). Amsterdam: Amsterdam University Press.

Chennoweth, N. A., & Hayes, J. R. (2001). Fluency in writing. Generating text in L1 and L2. *Written Communication, 18*(1), 80-98.

Chenoweth, N. A., & Hayes, J. R. (2003). The inner voice in writing. *Written Communication, 20*(1), 99-118.

Dysthe, O., Samara, A., & Westrheim, K. (2006). Multivoiced supervision of master's students: A case study of alternative supervision strategies in higher education. *Studies in Higher Education, 31*(3), 299-319.

Efklides, A. (2001). Metacognitive experiences in problem solving: Metacognition, motivation and self-regulation. In A. Efklides, J. Khul, & M. Sorrentino (Eds.), *Trends and prospects in motivation research*. Dordrecht, Netherlands: Kluwer.

Efklides, A. (2006). Metacognition and affect: What can metacognitive experiences tell us about the learning process? *Educational Research Review, 1,* 3-14.

Englert, C. S., Raphael, T. E., & Anderson, L. M. (1992). Socially mediated instruction: Improving students' knowledge and talk about writing. *The Elementary School Journal, 92*(4), 411-449.

Englert, C. S., Mariage, T. V., & Dunsmore, K. (2006). Tenets of sociocultural theory in writing instruction research. In C. A. MacArthur, S. Graham & J. Fitzgerald (Eds.), *Handbook of writing research* (pp. 208-221). New York & London: Guilford.

Farmer, F. (1995). Voice reprised: Three etudes for a dialogic understanding. *Rhetoric Review, 13*(2), 304-320.

Fitzgerald, J. (1987). Revision in writing. *Review of Educational Research, 57*(4), 481-506.

Fitzsimons, G. M., & Finkel, E. J. (2011). The effects of self-regulation on social relationships. In K. D. Vohs & R. F. Baumeister (Eds.), *Handbook of self-regulation. Research, theory and applications* (2nd ed., pp. 407-421). New York & London: Guilford.

Flavell, J. H. (1981). Cognitive monitoring. In W. P. Dickson (Ed.), *Children's oral communication skills* (pp. 35-60). New York: Academic Press.

Flower, L., & Hayes, J. R. (1980). The dynamics of composing: Making plans and juggling constraints. In L. W. Gregg & E. R. Steinberg (Eds.), *Cognitive processes in writing* (pp. 3-30). Hillsdale, New Jersey: Lawrence Erlbaum.

Flowerdew, J., & Peacock, M (2001). *Research perspectives on English for academic purposes*. Cambridge, UK: Cambridge University Press.

Galbraith, D. (1999). Writing as a knowledge-constituting process. In M. Torrance & D. Galbraith (Eds.), *Knowing what to write: Conceptual processes in text production* (pp. 139-160). Amsterdam: Amsterdam University Press.

Galbraith, D., & Torrance, M. (2004). Revision in the context of different drafting strategies. In L. K. Allal, L. Chanquoy, & P. Largi (Eds.), *Revision. Cognitive and instructional processes* (pp. 63-86). Amsterdam: Springer.

Galbraith, D., Ford, S., Walker, G., & Ford, J. (2005). *The contribution of different components of working memory to knowledge transformation during writing*

L1: Educational Studies in Language and Literature. Amsterdam: Amsterdam University Press.

Graham, S., & Harris, K. R. (2000). The role of self-regulation and transcription skills in writing and writing development. *Educational Psychologist, 35*(1), 3-12.

Hayes, J. R., & Chennoweth, A. (2006). Is working memory involved in the transcribing and editing of texts? *Written Communication, 23*(2), 135-149.

Hurme, T-R., Palonen, T., & Järvelä, S. (2006). Metacognition in joint discussions: An analysis of the patterns of interaction and the metacognitive content of the networked discussions in mathematics. *Metacognition and Learning, 1*(1), 181-200.

Iñesta, A. (2009). The regulation of research article writing. Strategies of expert writers in Spanish as their first language (L1) and in English as an international language (EIL) (Unpublished doctoral dissertation). Ramon Llull University, Barcelona, Spain.

Ivanic, R. (1998). *Writing and identity. The discoursal construction of identity in academic writing.* Amsterdam & Philadelphia: John Benjamins.

Jackson, T., Mackenzie, J., & Hobfoll, S. E. (2000). Communal aspects of self-regulation. In M. Boekaerts, P. R. Pintrich, & M. Zeidner (Eds.), *Handbook of self-regulation* (pp. 275-299). New York & London: Academic Press.

Järvelä, S., & Järvenoja, H. (2007, August-September). Socially constructed self-regulated learning in collaborative learning groups. Paper presented at the Socially constructed self-regulated learning: Strategic regulation of learning and motivation in social learning context, EARLI Conference, Budapest, Hungary.

Järvelä, S., Järvenoja, H., & Veermans, M. (2008). Understanding the dynamics of motivation in socially shared learning. *International Journal of Educational Research, 47*(1), 122-135.

Järvelä, S., Volet, S. E., & Järvenoja, H. (2010). Research on motivation in collaborative learning: Moving beyond the cognitive-situative divide and combining individual and social processes. *Educational Psychologist, 45*(1), 15-27.

Johns, A. (2002). *Genre in the classroom: Multiple perspectives.* Mahwah, NJ: Lawrence Erlbaum.

Kamberelis, G., & Scott, K. D. (1992). Other people's voices: The coarticulation of texts and subjectivities. *Linguistics and Education, 4,* 359-403.

Kellogg, R. T. (1999). Multiple systems of working memory in writing. In M. F. Crété & E. Espéret (Eds.), *Writing and learning to write at the dawn of the 21st century: Proceedings of the 1998 Writing Conference* (pp. IX-XXX-VI). Poitiers, France: LaCo-CNRS, University of Poitiers.

Kellogg, R. T. (2001). The psychology of the writing process. In N. J. Smelser & P. B. Baltes (Eds.), *International encyclopedia of the social and behavioral sciences,* W. Kintsch (Section Ed.). Cognitive Psychology and Cognitive Science. Amsterdam: Elsevier Science.

Kellogg, R. T., Olive, T., & Piolat, A. (2007). Verbal and visual working memory in written sentence production. In M. Torrance, L. van Waes, & D. Galbraith (Eds.), *Writing and cognition: Research and applications* (Studies in Writing, Vol. 20) (pp. 97-108). Bingley, UK, Emerald Group.

Koole, S. L., van Dillen, L. F., & Sheppes, G. (2011). The self-regulation of emotion. In K. D. Vohs & R. F. Baumeister (Eds.), *Handbook of self-regulation: Research, theory and applications* (pp. 101-112). New York & London: Guilford.

Kuhl, J. (2000). A functional-design approach to motivation and self-regulation: The dynamics of personality systems and interactions. In M. Boekaerts, P. R. Pintrich, & M. Zeidner (Eds.), *Handbook of self-regulation: Research, theory and applications* (pp. 111-169). New York & London: Academic Press.

Lea, M. R., & Stierer, B. (2000). *Student writing in higher education: New contexts.* Buckingham, UK: SRHE & Open University Press.

Liesa, E. (2004). *Els procediments d'estudi de textos a l'ESO: Concepcions i pràctiques [Procedures to study from texts in secondary education: Conceptions and practices]* (Unpublished doctoral dissertation). Ramon Llull University, Barcelona, Spain.

Maher, D., Seaton, L., Mc Mullen, C., Fitzgerald, T., Otsuji, E., & Lee, A. (2008). "Becoming and being writers": The experiences of doctoral students in writing groups. *Studies in Continuing Education, 30*(3), 263-275.

Mateos, M., Cuevas, I., Martín, E., Martín, A., & Luna, M. (2008). Concepciones de los estudiantes de psicología sobre la lectura y la escritura y su papel en el aprendizaje [Psychology students' conceptions about reading and writing and their role in learning]. Seminari Intern de Recerca Castell-Ona, UOC-IN3, 25 i 26 de juny de 2008.

Monereo, C. (2007). Hacia un paradigma del aprendizaje estratégico: El papel de la mediación social, del self, y de las emociones [Towards a strategic learning paradigm: The role of social mediation, self and emotions]. *Revista Electrónica de Investigación Psicoeducativa, 5*(3), 497-534.

Monereo, C., Badia, A., Bilbao, G., Cerrato, M., & Weise, C. (2009). Ser un docente estratégico: Cuando cambiar la estrategia no basta [Being a strategic teacher: When strategy change does not work] *Cultura y Educación, 21*(3), 237-256.

Nottbusch, G., Weingarten, R., & Sahel, S. (2007). From written word to written sentence production. In A. M. Torrance, L.van Waes, & D. Galbraith

(Eds.), *Writing and cognition: Research and applications (Studies in writing, Vol. 20)* (pp. 31-53). Bingley, UK: Emerald Group.

Olive, T., & Piolat, A. (2003). Activation des processus redactionnels et qualite' des textes [Writing processes activation and texts' quality]. *Le Langage et L'Homme, 38*(2), 191–206.

Pajares, F., & Johnson, M. J. (1994). Confidence and competence in writing: The role of self-efficacy, outcome expectancy and apprehension. *Research in the Teaching of English, 28*(3), 313-331.

Papies, E. K., & Aarts, H. (2011). Non-conscious self-regulation or the automatic pilot of human behavior. In K. D. Vohs & R. F. Baumeister (Eds.), *Handbook of self-regulation. Research, theory and applications* (pp. 125-142). New York & London: Guilford.

Prior, P. (2001) Voices in text, mind, and society. Sociohistoric accounts of discourse acquisition and use. *Journal of Second Language Writing, 10,* 55-81.

Pozo, J. I., Monereo, C., & Castelló, M. (2001). El uso estratégico del conocimimento [The strategic use of knowledge]. In C. Coll, J. Palacios, & A. Marchesi (Eds.), *Desarrollo psicológico y educación 2. Psicología de la educación escolar* (pp. 211-234). Madrid: Alianza.

Rinck, F. (2006). Gestion de la polyphonie et figure de l'auteur dans les parties théoriques des Rapports de stage. Revue de linguistique et didactique des langues *Lidil, 34*. Retrieved from http://lidil.revues.org/index23.html

Roussey, J. Y., & Piolat, A. (2005). La révision du texte: Une activité de contrôle et de réflexion [Text revision: A control and reflection activity]. *Psychologie française, 50,* 351-372.

Shah, J. Y., & Kruglanski, A. W. (2000). Aspects of goal networks: Implications for self-regulation. In M. Boekaerts, P. R. Pintrich, & M. Zeidner (Eds.), *Handbook of self-regulation* (pp. 86-110). New York & London: Academic Press.

Shapiro, S. L., & Schwartz, G. E. (2000). The role of intention in self-regulation: Toward intentional systemic mindfulness. In M. Boekaerts, P. R. Pintrich, & M. Zeidner (Eds.), *Handbook of self-regulation* (pp. 253-274). New York & London: Academic Press.

Segev-Miller, R. (2007). Cognitive processes in discourse synthesis: The case of intertextual processing strategies. In M. Torrance, L.van Waes, & D. Galbraith (Eds.), *Writing and Cognition: Research and Applications. (Studies in Writing, Vol. 20)* (pp. 1-10). Bingley, UK: Emerald Group.

Van den Bergh, H.; & Rijlaarsdam, G. (2007). The dynamics of idea generation during writing: An online study. In M. Torrance, L. van Waes, & D. Galbraith (Eds.), *Writing and Cognition: Research and Applications. (Studies in Writing, Vol. 20)* (pp. 125-150). Bingley, UK: Emerald Group.

Van Waes, L., & Schellens, P. J. (2003). Writing profiles: The effect of the writing mode on pausing and revision patterns of experienced writers. *Journal of Pragmatics, 35*(6), 829-853.

Veermans, M., & Järvelä, S. (2003). Generalized achievement goals and situational coping in inquiry learning. *Instructional Science, 32*(4), 1-23.

Volet, S. E., Summers, M., & Thurman, J. (2009). High-level co-regulation in collaborative learning: How does it emerge and how is it sustained? *Learning and Instruction, 19*(2), 128-143.

Walker, R. (2007, August-September). Sociocultural perspectives on academic regulation and identity: Theoretical issues. Paper presented at the Twelfth Biennial Conference for Research on Learning and Instruction. Budapest, Hungary.

Yore, L. D., Florence, M. K., Pearson, T. W., & Weaver, A. J. (2006). Written discourse in scientific communities: A conversation with two scientists about their views on science, use of language, role of writing in doing science, and comparability between their epistemic views and language. *International Journal of Science Education, 28*(2-3), 109-141.

Zanotto, M.; Monereo, C., & Castelló, M. (2011). Estrategias de lectura y producción de textos académicos: Leer para evaluar un texto científico. [Reading strategies and the production of academic texts: Reading to evaluate a scientific text.] *Perfiles Educativos,v. XXXIII, 133,* 10-29 Retrieved from http://www.iisue.unam.mx/seccion/perfiles/

Zimmerman, B. J. (1989). A social cognitive view of self-regulated academic learning. *Journal of Educational Psychology, 81,* 329-339.

Zimmerman, B. J. (1990). self-regulated learning and academic achievement: An overview. *Educational Psychologist, 25*(1), 3-17.

Zimmerman, B. J. (2000). Attaining self-regulation: A social-cognitive perspective. In M. Boekaerts, P. R. Pintrich, & M. Zeidner (Eds.), *Handbook of self-regulation* (pp. 13-85). New York & London: Academic Press.

CHAPTER 25.
PRODUCING SCHOLARLY TEXTS: WRITING IN ENGLISH IN A POLITICALLY STIGMATIZED COUNTRY

Mehdi Riazi
Macquarie University

With English increasingly acquiring the academic lingua franca (Flowerdew, 1999a , 1999b) status in the scholarly text production arena and the implication this will have for researchers in non-Anglophone countries to publish in English, research on multilingual scholars writing in their L2 (English) has received considerable attention from academic writing researchers over the last couple of decades. These studies have addressed a range of issues related to scholarly writing in L2 and have contributed to our understanding of how personal, textual, and contextual factors foster or constrain text production in English. Leki, Cumming, and Silva (2008, p. 57) have summarized research studies on professional L2 writing in English over the last 25 years into the categories of text analysis, writing processes and strategies of novice and successful L2 authors, first person accounts by L2 scholarly authors writing in English, case studies of bilingual authors, and the variety of communities that these scholars envision as their audience. The contexts represented in the studies reported in Leki et al. (2008) include Spanish (St. John, 1987), Scandinavian (Jernudd & Baldauf, 1987), Hungarian (Medgyes & Kaplan, 1992), Hong Kong (Flowerdew, 1999a, 1999b, 2000), Danish (Phillipson & Skutnabb-Kangas, 2000), Hungarian, Slovakian, Spanish, Portuguese (Curry & Lillis, 2004; Lillis & Curry, 2006, Lillis & Curry, 2010), Chinese (Liu, 2004), Japanese (Casanave, 1998; Okamura, 2006), Armenian (Sahakyan, 2006), Polish (Duszak & Lewkowicz, 2008), and Turkish (Buckingham, 2008). These studies are all from contexts and countries where no vivid and formally articulated political agony defines the political relation between English speaking countries and the countries in which the participants of studies were living and working. No sanctions are leveled against these countries, and scholars in these countries do not experience any restrictions accessing resources, networking with their colleagues in Anglophone countries, nor do they have any visa restrictions when travelling to Anglophone countries. Even when it comes to socio-political and ideological issues related to L2 text production mostly represented in the works of Canagarajah (1996, 2001, 2002, 2005), Pennycook (1997, 1999, 2001), and Benesch (1996, 2001), the peripheral participants or contexts studied are not politically in conflict with the Anglophone center.

It is therefore important to study the pattern of scholarly text production in English in countries like Iran in which political relations with Anglophone countries have been dramatically and diametrically changed over the past decades. There is now a high wall of distrust between Iran and the West, particularly English speaking countries, which has escalated over the last three decades after the 1979 Islamic revolution in Iran. On the one hand, the West considers Iran as an outlier and as a threat in a presumably defined world order so that the US and the UK have not been reluctant in hiding their desire of collapsing the Islamic regime even through a military attack. Such a position on the part of the US and the UK has been accounted for by different reasons; the most salient has been the debate on nuclear energy and the possibility of Iran's access to nuclear weapons. The recent UN sanctions on Iran mobilized by the US and the UK and endorsed by other members of the UN Security Council have been meant to force the regime to change its position before giving more impetus to those who support a military attack. On the other hand, based on historical events and documents, Iran accuses the West and particularly the US and the UK for a pervasive hegemony over the country for many years. This hostility between the two sides has been realized in the formulation of socio-cultural and economic policies at all levels within each camp, resulting in Iran being ostracized in the world's political scene. The term "stigmatized" in the title of the chapter is meant to convey this situation. Stigma as defined by Goffman (1967) is a study of situations where normal and abnormal meets, and of the ways in which a stigmatized person, in this case country, can develop a more positive social and personal identity.

This study, therefore, set out to investigate how scholarly text production in English is perceived by Iranian scholars in such a conflicted context and how it is represented in the global knowledge production and dissemination. The study seeks to explore the following two research questions:

1. What has been the share of post-revolution Iranian scholars in the global knowledge production and dissemination as realized in the academic English publications indexed in the Web of Science (WOS)?
2. How do Iranian scholars perceive their participation in global knowledge production and dissemination through publishing papers in international English-medium journals?

The chapter is organized in three sections. First, the pattern of post-revolution knowledge production and dissemination in Iran is presented. Second, Iranian scholars' perceptions of publishing papers in international English-medium journals will be discussed. Finally, the chapter ends with discussion and concluding remarks.

KNOWLEDGE PRODUCTION AND DISSEMINATION IN POST-REVOLUTION IRAN

Nouruzi, Hassanzadeh, and Nourmouhammadi (2008) have gathered and analyzed the share of Iranian scholars in the world's production and dissemination of knowledge over a period of 15 years (1993-2007). They have stated the following reason for choosing this 15-year time period:

1. 1993 marks the end of the first 5-year development plan (1989-1993) after the revolution. The next 5-year development plans (the 2nd, 3rd, & 4th) continued after the first one, with the fourth one completed in 2007.
2. 1990 marks the end of the Iraq-Iran war and so any change and growth in the country's scientific position is expected to show up in subsequent years.
3. Though there were some developments in the scientific publications before 1993, they were unstable.

Table 1 (Nourouzi et al., 2008, p. 38) presents the number of Iranian scholars' publications as indexed in Web of Science (WOS) over the 15 years (1993-2007).

As Table 1 indicates there has been an exponential rise in Iran's scientific publications over the 15 years as presented in Figure 1. The rate of publications as indexed in WOS increased thirty times from 310 in 1993 to 9061 in 2007.

Table 1. Iran's share of scientific publications over 15 years (Source: WOS)

Year	1993	1994	1995	1996	1997	1998	1999	2000
No. of docs	310	377	470	598	682	1036	1204	1387
Growth (%)	--	21.61	24.93	26.96	14.04	51.91	16.22	15.2

Year	2001	2002	2003	2004	2005	2006	2007
No. of docs	1735	2224	3283	3855	5582	6750	9061
Growth (%)	25.09	28.18	47.62	17.42	44.8	20.92	34.24

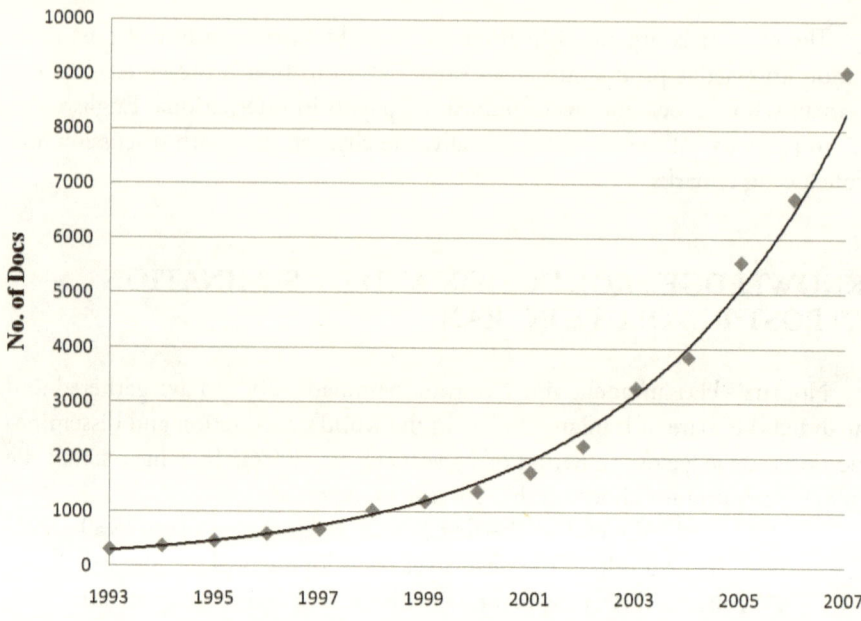

Figure 1. Number of documents over 15 years

These publications are extracted from three data bases of Science Citation Index Expanded (SCIE), Social Science Citation Index (SSCI), and Art and Human Citation Index (AHCI). Twenty fields of study including sciences (different areas of chemistry, physics, plant sciences, and mathematics), medicine and engineering accounted for 70.72 percent of the total indexed documents over five years (1998-2002). The other two general disciplines (social sciences, art and humanities) accounted for 29.28 percent of the indexed documents in WOS in this period. One hundred universities and institutions of higher education were involved in the trend of knowledge production over the 15 years. However, five pioneer universities in this list were the University of Tehran, University of Shiraz, University of Sharif, Tehran University of Medical Sciences, and Tarbiate Modaress University. This trend has more or less continued over the subsequent periods presented in Table 2.

Table 2. Iran's share of scientific publications over its three development plans

Period	1993-1997 (2nd development plan)	1998-2002 (3rd development plan)	2003-2007 (4th development plan)
No. of docs	2437	7585	28531
Growth (%)	--	211.12	276.15

Table 2 summarizes the information in Table 1 for the three five-year development plans. As can be seen in Table 2, the highest growth belongs to the 2003-2007, or the fourth development plan.

These publications comprise a variety of documents including full articles, conference abstracts, review papers, editorials, letters to the editor, book reviews, and some other genres. Among these, the highest rate belongs to the articles and conference abstracts respectively (Nourouzi et al., 2008) which together account for more than 90% of the total share. Table 3 presents the share of articles and conference abstracts in each period.

Table 3. Iran's share of published articles and conference abstracts over three periods

Period	1993-1997 (2nd development plan)	1998-2002 (3rd development plan)	2003-2007 (4th development plan)
No. of docs	2437	7585	28531
Articles	2124 (87.15%)	6804 (89.70%)	24469 (85.76%)
Conf. Abstracts	113 (4.63%)	563 (7.42%)	2962 (10.38%)

Web of Science indexes scientific publications published in 49 languages (Thomson Scientific, 2007). The scientific publications of Iran in WOS over the 15 years were published in five languages (1993-2002) and eight languages (2003-2007); among them, publications in English language had the highest percentage (over 99%). This is, of course, in line with the global trend of publishing in English (see, e.g., Curry & Lillis, 2010). A surprising point is that none of the Iranian publications in the WOS over the 15 years was in Persian. The journal articles were published in 30 journals, and only seven of them were Iranian journals indexed in WOS. The share of indexed Iranian journals in publishing Iranian scholars' articles was 3.2 percent. These journals, which publish articles only in English, all belong to sciences and engineering and none from social sciences or humanities. The following points could be highlighted from the pattern of scholarly text production in Iran over the 15 years:

1. There has been an exponential increase in the rate of knowledge production and dissemination in Iran over the 15 years (1993-2007)
2. Almost all scholarly publications have been in English (over 99%) and published in English-medium journals and conferences
3. 90% of the scholarly texts indexed in WOS included journal articles and conference abstracts

4. Of the three general disciplines of sciences, social sciences, and art and humanities, sciences had the highest contribution (almost 71%) and the other two disciplines had a share of almost 29%
5. All seven Iranian journals of science and technology indexed in WOS publish papers in English, and none of the Persian or bilingual journals of humanities or social sciences is indexed in WOS

With this general pattern of knowledge production in Iran, the next part of the chapter presents a study to shed more light on this trend. The study investigated how Iranian scholars perceived publishing papers in English in international, indexed journals.

IRANIAN SCHOLARS' ATTITUDES, PROBLEMS AND STRATEGIES TOWARD PUBLISHING IN INTERNATIONAL ENGLISH-MEDIUM JOURNALS

In response to an invitation letter, 72 faculty members (63 males and 9 females) of one of the five top universities of Iran with 550 academic staff agreed to participate in the study. All participants spoke Persian as their native language and used English as the language of their publications and paper presentations in international conferences. Their age ranged from mid-forties to late seventies and they were from various fields as presented in Table 4 within three general disciplines.[1] Sciences (39 participants), Social Sciences (15 participants), and Art and Humanities (18 participants) and with different ranks (31 assistant professors, 24 associate professors, and 17 full professors). Twenty-two participants (30.6%) had completed and obtained their PhDs from Iranian universities and fifty (69.4%) had completed their PhDs in other countries, mostly English speaking countries.

In terms of teaching experience, seven participants had five years' or less teaching experience; sixty had between six and 30 years' experience; and five had more than 30 years' experience. With regard to participants' experience of publishing in English language journals, 76.4% had already published several articles in these journals.

Interviews were conducted in Persian (participants' native language) to prevent any language barrier. The interviews were conducted in the participants' offices on their university campus. An attempt was made to create a friendly atmosphere and encourage the interviewees to freely express their experiences of publishing their research articles in English. The interviews lasted from nine to 82 minutes and all were recorded with participants' consent except in two cases where notes were taken. The interviews were then transcribed for codification

Table 4. Three major disciplines and their related fields based on ISI categorization

Sciences	Social Sciences	Art and Humanities
Agricultural Engineering	Economics	Architecture
Biology	Law[2]	History
Chemistry	Management	Language Teaching and Linguistics
Engineering, Chemical	Political Science	
Engineering, Civil	Psychology	Literature, English
Engineering, Computer	Sociology	Literature, Persian
Engineering, Electronic		Theology
Engineering, Mechanical		
Engineering, Metallurgical		
Geology		
Mathematics		
Physics		
Veterinary Sciences		

and content analysis. The codification and analysis of the interviews were done on the Persian transcripts; however, the selected quotes in the results section are the author's translation, which was checked with another colleague proficient in Persian and English languages for accuracy and consistency. Except for some minor discrepancies which were resolved through discussion, the whole translations proved to be accurate.

RESULTS

Coded segments of the interview transcripts were extracted and organized around the three themes of attitudes, problems, and strategies.

ATTITUDES

The category of attitudes had two subcategories: research publication and evaluation of research activities.

The majority of the participants (68, 94.4 %) viewed conducting and publishing research as knowledge production and dissemination in so far as the findings of their research could contribute to disciplinary knowledge. However, while they had a positive attitude towards research and publishing research reports, two distinct positions of whether they should publish in international or local journals were observed. The positions were advocated by sciences and humanities scholars respectively. The following quotes represent the positions.

> The publication of articles in foreign journals has different aspects. First you make your achievements accessible to the international community. A greater number of readers will read the journal and use the article. Publishing in international journals also represents the country's research activities and puts you in the international research showcase. In my opinion science and research is something international; therefore, different thoughts and ideas should be communicated between internal and external scientists. One of the best ways for this communication to happen is publishing articles in international journals (senior scholar from sciences).

> I think one of the responsibilities of a university professor is to develop and disseminate science[3] and to contribute new knowledge to the field. While it is important to publish articles in English to achieve this goal, I do not believe, as some colleagues do, that we should only publish in English and in international journals; we should also pay attention to our own language and our internal journals. One way of developing a language is to have scientific publications in that language, and one way of improving the quality of local journals is to submit to and publish high quality articles in these journals. The role and position of our local Persian journals should not be downplayed. Too much emphasis on publishing articles in English and ISI journals will damage our self-esteem (senior scholar from humanities).

Participants from some fields of social sciences and humanities, including those from law and political sciences, sociology (women studies), history, theology, and Persian literature, believed that the evaluation of their research activities should not be done by the same criteria and the same committees as it is done for sciences or engineering, especially with regard to publications in English-medium journals as a criterion. These participants believed publishing in English-medium journals is not as easy for them as it is for their colleagues in sciences and engineering. The following two quotes are illuminative.

> Based on the correspondence I have had with some of the international journals, I have come to the understanding that they show some bias against my country and affiliation. As soon as they see the word "Iran" in my affiliation, they develop prejudgments which certainly affect their decision. Of course, I have been able to publish in some English-medium international journals, but they are sometimes not interested in the topics we work on and we cannot easily publish research on our local and national problems in those journals (early career scholar in social sciences).

> While papers from scholars in other countries get accepted and published, when we send an article we do not know what their judgement would be. Will they read it? Will they be inclined to publish it? Sometimes, there is no answer, and in some cases it takes a long time to get a feedback. That is why we have problems with these foreign journals and I am not clear why there is a push on the part of the university on us to publish in international journals. Of course, part of this problem might be due to language problems. This is why I always try to edit my paper before sending it out. If the English of my article is not fluent or there are some language problems, it will surely influence the editor's decision. However, the problem is beyond language issues (mid-career scholar in humanities).

Problems

As relates to participants' problems in writing papers in English, again participants from the humanities believed it is more challenging to do research and write papers particularly in English in their discipline than it is in sciences.

> In humanities we deal with different value-laden complexities and problems, but experimental sciences are somehow value-free. Research projects in sciences are mostly done in laboratories and with substances, but this is not the case in humanities. Even our colleagues in other disciplines usually do not have any problem finding topics and doing research. However, in humanities this is not the case as sometimes

the topics and the findings conflict with the cultural norms and values of the society, and it is not easy for the researcher to conduct and publish research on such topics (mid-career scholar in humanities).

Apart from the above distinctive views, participants referred to problems related to research management, funding, equipment and facilities, materials, teaching load, administrative responsibilities, team-working, freedom of expression, and the overall context of doing research as barriers to their research and publication. The following quotes illustrate some of the problems.

First there are problems with research management policies and the organization of research activities and publications are usually weak. We lack the necessary facilities, and the funding for research projects is low and distributed improperly. There are some journals that we are not subscribed to due to high subscription fees. Therefore one of my problems is the lack of some of the necessary resources on the topic (senior scholar in sciences).

You know in American universities, for example, professors rarely teach more than two courses. They use their time for doing research. But when you are teaching the whole week then you are left with little if any time for research and publication. Moreover, here as a researcher you are alone; there are no research groups formed on the same topic throughout the country (mid-career scholar in social sciences).

In addition to problems faced in the process of research and managing the research process, participants also referred to writing problems, especially when it comes to writing the introduction and discussion sections of their papers.

Based on my own experience, I think the most important and the most difficult part is the introduction. If the reviewers do not recognize your main goal in the research you are reporting, they will not continue reading the rest of your article. Therefore, I spend more time on the introduction section. The way you link your work with others and try to convince your audience about the significance of your research is really important in this part. Sometimes I write three or four drafts of the introduction section to finalize it (mid-career scholar in sciences).

Some participants also mentioned that in academic writing, arguing for and elaborating on points is very important and at the same time challenging, especially for those whose native language is not English. Part of this problem, they believed, was related to their limited English lexicon, restricted knowledge and skill in using appropriate expressions and suitable structures.

> Even if you want to write in Persian, you have problems. Writing is composition and composition is creation. Creating a piece of written material has its own problems. My native language is not English; therefore, in comparison to native speakers of English it takes more time to develop ideas (mid-career scholar in social sciences).

> Sometimes I change my arguments two or three times. I try to look at the issue from different perspectives and to discuss it in a better way. I present the data in the tables, but the explanation and justification of the results is difficult. It is hard to get my points across to the reader (mid-career scholar in sciences).

> My problem is fluency and facility of expression in English. Sometimes I should find the proper words; therefore, I refer to the available resources to find the most appropriate terms. I can easily use the phrases and idioms in my native language, but in English it is difficult for me to use them like a native speaker of English. Certainly I do not have their command of expression. Instead of one short sentence, I use two sentences to get the point across. They express whatever they want easily, but it is difficult for me to express my points (mid-career scholar in humanities).

STRATEGIES

To remedy the problems the participants faced in writing their papers in English, they referred to some strategies they had found useful. Most of them reported their extensive reading of the English texts in their disciplines as a good resource for them to learn about writing styles, sentence structures, vocabulary and expressions besides the topical knowledge. Revising and editing of the articles by themselves and by their colleagues was another main writing strategy they reported. Most of these strategies were, however, reported by participants from sciences.

> I start typing the article as the first draft. Then I continuously do the revisions. For example, yesterday I submitted an article to a journal. I had revised and edited this article at least ten to 12 times (mid-career scholar in sciences).

> I try to give my article to one or two colleagues who have published more than me to comment on its content and language. This type of cooperation is very common in our department (mid-career in sciences).

Some of the participants considered the opportunity of sabbatical leave to embark on new research and to enhance their writing abilities.

> The sabbatical leave helped me a lot to get familiar with the most recent topics in my own field and learn about research methods better. The leave was almost seven or eight years after my Ph.D. I had just five articles at that time. After my sabbatical leave I have been able to write more papers. I learnt a lot during my stay in United States. My collaboration with researchers over there is still continuing. I have email correspondence with my foreign colleagues. We have written four joint articles so far (mid-career in sciences).

DISCUSSION AND CONCLUSION

In light of the two research questions presented in the introduction section of the chapter, conclusions and discussions of the study are presented in this part. As presented in the first part of the chapter, the rate of scholarly publications by Iranian scholars as indexed in WOS has increased considerably from 1993 to 2007. This is during the last 30 years Iran has experienced an unstable relationship with Anglophone countries as a result of its 1979 Islamic revolution and the post-revolution aftermaths. The unstable and even sometimes hostile relation between the two sides has had implications in the academic arena. Western countries have made restrictions and bans on selling and transferring technology and materials including resources necessary for Iranian scholars to conduct research. Such restrictions have even been extended to policies related to admitting Iranian PhD students and issuing visas to Iranian scholars for spending their sabbatical leave in English-speaking countries. Finding themselves in an explicitly articulated soft combat in technological and academic scenes, Iranian policy makers have defined knowledge production and technological development as one of their major strategies, changing a threat into an opportunity. Publishing in international, high ranking journals has been translated into a promotion and merit policy in Iranian universities. Other scholars (see, e.g., Curry & Lillis, 2004; Flowerdew, 1999a; Li, 2006; Lillis & Curry, 2006) have pointed out that institutional policies for promotion and awards should not be underestimated in the participants' desire to publish in international journals.

It is thus not incidental that notwithstanding the serious and tight Western sanctions, Iranian scholars have been able to increase their knowledge production and dissemination 30 times over 15 years, with the majority of such knowledge production in sciences (71%). Moreover, the case was reported that seven out of nine Iranian journals that publish science papers in English are indexed in Web of Science, which is another leap toward increasing Iran's share in knowledge production. These facts were corroborated by Iranian scholars' attitudes toward writing and publishing in English. As Erdbrink (2008) cites Burton Richter, an American Nobel laureate in physics, "Iran wants to join the group of countries that want to know about the biggest things, like space" and that Iranian students are very impressive, and that he expects to hear more from them in the future. Erdbrink goes further and states, "Iranian scientists claim breakthroughs in nanotechnology, biological researchers are pushing the boundaries of stem cell research and the country's car industry produces more cars than anywhere else in the region."

The following main points could be extracted from the scholars' viewpoints:
1. Participants considered knowledge production and dissemination of their research as their main goal.
2. While participants from the sciences advocated (strongly) publishing in international English-medium journals, participants from the social sciences and the humanities were more in favor of publishing in their native language and in local journals.
3. Participants from the social sciences and the humanities expressed some experiences of bias from international English-medium journals which they referred to value-laden issues.

4. All participants agreed they had problems composing in English. The writing problems included a wide variety of issues from lexico-grammatical to elaboration and discussion of ideas in their second language.
5. Participants from the sciences were found to be more strategic in terms of using a variety of strategies to overcome their problems in conducting and writing up their research.

While all the 72 participants in the study considered knowledge production and dissemination as their goal in publishing papers, there were two distinct, but perhaps complementary views on where the outcome of their research should be published. Science scholars defined their role to be more visible in international scenes by publishing in international English-medium journals, while social sciences and humanities scholars found it more plausible disseminating knowledge in local journals. Three reasons could be discerned from these scholars' standpoints on this issue. The first was participants' conception of sciences being value-free and social sciences and humanities being value-laden—an issue which they thought would affect the whole research process and their choice of journals to send their research report to. At a more general level, such a finding is in line with the findings of previous research studies (see, for example, Belcher, 2007; Canagarajah, 1996; Cho, 2004; Flowerdew, 1999a, 2000; Gibbs, 1995; Gosden, 1992; Li, 2006; Swales, 1998; Wood, 1997) in which the participants of the studies contended there is bias against non-native authors who try to publish in international journals. Secondly, these scholars believed one way of promoting native and national language is through academic publication and that they found this as one of their mandates. Thirdly, they believed getting their papers published in international English-medium journals required them to devote more time and effort compared to the time and effort spent on similar tasks by themselves when publishing in their native language and by native English speakers when they publish in English; a finding similar to Flowerdew's (1999a) study in that the Cantonese academics felt they were at a disadvantage when writing for publication in English compared to NSs. This could even be extrapolated to findings on problems in writing for publication in English by both science and social science scholars of the study. This finding corroborates previous findings on the issue (see, for example, Adams-Smith, 1984; Bazerman, 1988; Buckingham, 2008; Dudley-Evans, 1994; Flowerdew 1999b; Johns, 1993; St. John, 1987; Swales, 1990). Such problems ranged from language-oriented lexico-grammatical issues to more writing and rhetorically-oriented problems of writing introduction and discussion sections of the papers and adequately arguing for and interpreting findings.

Regarding the strategies Iranian scholars reported they used to write papers in English, the findings of this study are supportive of the strategies reported by other participants in other studies and contexts. The strategies included, but were not limited to, revising and editing, attending to audience, using a co-author (see, for example, Buckingham, 2008; Flowerdew,1999a), and discipline-specific reading (Buckingham, 2008; Okamura, 2006). Okamura (2006) suggested that reading academic texts in one's field resulted in participants' learning typical writing patterns. In the present study, the scholars not only reported on learning writing patterns but also writing styles, sentence structures, vocabulary, and register through reading extensively in their own field. Some of the Iranian scholars complained about the lack of research networks in the country, and others highlighted the opportunity their sabbatical leaves created to form research networks, which was a key resource for their co-authored papers, a finding in line with Curry and Lillis's (2010) study. While Iranian scholars, like other international scholars, reported using language, writing, and social strategies in their attempt to publish papers in English, they could be considered strategic at a higher level. That is, they contributed to the macro strategy of promoting the country's status in international knowledge production completion and in particular neutralizing Western countries' sanction policies toward Iran, especially in the areas of science and technology.

The general conclusion reached by this study is that despite the turmoil in the political relation between Iran and the West, the rate of scholarly publications by Iranian scholars in international English-medium journals has exponentially increased notwithstanding the constraints these scholars have faced. While scholars from sciences advocated and practiced a more universal pattern of scholarly publication, scholars from social sciences and humanities preferred and practiced a more local trend of academic publication.

ACKNOWLEDGEMENTS

I wish to thank Akram Bahrami for her contribution of interviewing Iranian scholars as reported in this study.

NOTES

1. It is based on the ISI (Institute of Scientific Information) categorization.

2. The faculty of law and political science provides both of the subject categories in this university.

3. The words "science" and "scientific" are used in a generic sense in Persian and refer to scholarly work carried out by academics in all disciplines--sciences, social sciences

and humanities. The words "scientific" and "academic" are also used interchangeably. When used by academics from the social sciences and humanities, as in this quotation, "science" and "scientific" imply a piece of scholarly work that can be empirical (using primary data) or library-based (using secondary data).

REFERENCES

Adams-Smith, D. E. (1984). Medical discourse: Aspects of author's comments. *The ESP Journal 3*, 25–36.

Bazerman, C. (1988). *Shaping written knowledge: The genre and activity of the experimental article in science*. Madison, WI: University of Wisconsin Press.

Belcher, D. (2007). Seeking acceptance in an English-only research world. *Journal of Second Language Writing, 16*(1), 1–22.

Benesch, S. (1996). Needs analysis and curriculum development in EAP: An example of a critical approach. *TESOL Quarterly, 30*(4), 723-738.

Benesch, S. (2001). *Critical English for Academic Purposes: Theory, politics and practice*. Mahwah, NJ: Lawrence Erlbaum.

Buckingham, L. (2008). Development of English academic writing competence by Turkish scholars. *International Journal of Doctoral Studies, 3*, 1-18.

Canagarajah, A. S. (1996). Nondiscursive requirements in academic publishing, material resources of periphery scholars, and the politics of knowledge production. *Written Communication, 13*(4), 435-472.

Canagarajah, A. S. (2001). Addressing issues of power and difference in ESL academic writing. In J. Flowerdew & J. Peacock (Eds.), *Research perspectives on English for academic purposes* (pp. 117-131). Cambridge, UK: Cambridge University Press.

Canagarajah, A. S. (2002). *A geopolitics of academic writing*. Pittsburgh, PA: University of Pittsburgh Press.

Canagarajah, A. S. (2005). Reconstructing local knowledge, reconfiguring language studies. In A. S. Canagarajah (Ed.), *Reclaiming the local in language policy and practice* (pp. 3-24). Mahwah, NJ: Lawrence Erlbaum.

Casanave, C. P. (1998). Transitions: The balancing act of bilingual academics. *Journal of Second Language Writing, 7*(2), 175–203.

Cho, S. (2004). Challenges of entering discourse communities through publishing in English. *Journal of Language, Identity, and Education, 3*, 47-72.

Curry, M. J., & Lillis, Th. (2004). Multilingual scholars and the imperative to publish in English: Negotiating interests, demands, and rewards. *TESOL Quarterly, 38*(4), 663-688.

Curry, M. J., & Lillis, T. M. (2010). Academic research networks: Accessing resources for English-medium publishing. *English for Specific Purposes, 29*, 281-295.

Dudley-Evans, T. (1994). Genre analysis: An approach to text analysis for ESP. In M. Coulthard (Ed.), *Advances in written text analysis* (pp. 219–228). London: Routledge.

Duszak, A., & Lewkowicz, J. (2008). Publishing academic texts in English: A Polish perspective. *Journal of English for Academic Purposes, 7,* 108-120.

Erdbrink, T. (2008, June 6). Iran makes the sciences a part of its revolution. Washington Post Foreign Service.

Flowerdew, J. (1999a). Writing for scholarly publication in English: The case of Hong Kong. *Journal of Second Language Writing, 8*(2), 123-145.

Flowerdew, J. (1999b). Problems in writing for scholarly publication in English: The case of Hong Kong. *Journal of Second language Writing, 8*(3), 243-264.

Flowerdew, J. (2000). Discourse community, legitimate peripheral participation, and the non-native-English speaking scholar. *TESOL Quarterly, 34*(1), 127–150.

Gibbs, W. W. (1995, August). Trends in scientific communication: Lost science in the third world. *Scientific American,* 76-83.

Goffman, E. (1963). *Stigma: Notes on the management of spoiled identity.* New York: Prentice-Hall.

Gosden, H. (1992). Research writing and NNSs: From the editors. *Journal of Second Language Writing, 1*(2), 123-139.

Jernudd, B. H., & Baldauf, R. B., Jr. (1987). Planning science communication for human resource development. In B. K. Das (Ed.), *Language education in human resource development* (pp. 144-189). Singapore: SEAMEO Regional Language Centre.

Johns, A. M. (1993). Written argumentation for real audiences: Suggestions for teacher research and classroom practice. *TESOL quarterly, 27*(1), 75-90.

Leki, I., Cumming, A., & Silva, T. (2008). *A synthesis of research on second language writing in English.* New York: Routledge.

Li, Y. (2006). A doctoral student of physics writing for international publication: A sociopolitically-oriented case study. *English for Specific Purposes, 25,* 456-478.

Lillis, T., & Curry, M. J. (2006). Professional academic writing by multilingual scholars: Interactions with literacy brokers in the production of English-medium texts. *Written Communication, 23*(1), 3-35.

Liu, J. (2004). Co-constructing academic discourse from the periphery: Chinese applied linguists' centripetal participation in scholarly publication. *Asian Journal of English Language Teaching, 14,* 1–22.

Medgyes, P., & Kaplan, R. B. (1992). Discourse in a foreign language: The example of Hungarian scholars. *International Journal of the Sociology of Language, 98, 67-100.*

Nourouzi Chakoli, A. R., Hassanzadeh, M., & Nourmouhammadi, H. A. (2008) (Persian). *An analytical view on the dissemination of Iranian knowledge in the world (1993-2007).* Tehran: National Research Institute.

Okamura, A. (2006). Two types of strategies used by Japanese scientists, when writing research articles in English. *System, 34,* 68-79.

Pennycook, A. (1997). Cultural alternatives and autonomy. In P. Benson & P. Voller (Eds.), *Autonomy and Independence in Language Learning* (pp. 35-53). London: Longman.

Pennycook, A. (1999). Introduction: Critical Approaches to TESOL. *TESOL Quarterly. Special-Topic Issue: Critical Approaches to TESOL, 33*(3), 329-348.

Pennycook, A. (2001). *Critical applied linguistics: A critical introduction.* Mahwah, NJ: Lawrence Erlbaum.

Phillipson, R., & Skutnabb-Kangas, T. (2000). Drepturi si nedreptati lingvistice. *Altera, 14,* 5-21. [Translation into Romanian (1995), Linguistic rights and wrongs.] *Applied Linguistics, 16*(4), 483-504.

St. John, M. J. (1987). Writing processes of Spanish scientists publishing in English. *English for Specific Purposes, 6,* 113-120.

Swales, J. M. (1990). *Genre analysis: English in academic and research sittings.* Cambridge, UK: Cambridge University Press.

Swales, J. (1998). *Other floors, other voices: A textography of a small building.* Mahway, NJ: Lawrence Erlbaum.

Thomson Scientific (2007). *Web of science.* Retrieved from http://thomson-reuters.com/products_services/science/

Wood, A. (1997). International scientific English: Some thoughts on science, language and ownership. *Science Tribune.* Retrieved from http://www.tribunes.com/tribune/art971woodshtm/

CHAPTER 26.

THE EVALUATION OF CONFERENCE PAPER PROPOSALS IN LINGUISTICS

Françoise Boch, Fanny Rinck, and Aurélie Nardy
Université Grenoble, CNRS/Université Paris Ouest Nanterre La Défense, and Université Grenoble

This chapter falls within the scope of work on scientific writing.[1] From the 1980s onwards, many studies have focused upon describing the characteristics of scientific discourse according to genre, discipline or language.[2] Genres studied include articles and PhD dissertations, but also, to a lesser degree, proposals for conference papers. In this chapter, we focus indirectly on the latter, analyzing their evaluation by conference peer review panels. The genre of the proposal evaluation—insofar as it can be labelled a genre—is in fact subject to very little study. However, in our view, it presents features making it a particularly rich type of writing. Indeed, analysing this genre can provide valuable information regarding both the linguistic practices of researchers under evaluation and the criteria retained by those conducting this evaluation.[3]

First, it is interesting to examine the practices of the researchers constituting the community of experts from a linguistic point of view. We are referring here to a strand in discourse analysis that focuses upon the linguistic functions of scientific writing so as to highlight the specificities of the scientific community,[4] or, in other words, its *manières de faire* ("ways of doing" things) (Maingueneau, 1992). We will examine the rhetoric of evaluation in a corpus of evaluations. Strictly speaking, the latter are not scientific writing but they nonetheless reflect researchers' ways of doing things. We will look in particular at how the reviewer addresses the author and whether these forms of address vary according to the verdict pronounced on the proposal.

Second, the study of such a genre can provide information regarding the norms in place within a given discipline. What criteria are retained today in order to deem a proposal acceptable or not? Is there a consensus regarding these criteria within a group of experts or are these criteria heterogeneous and linked to subjective perceptions of what constitutes a "good" or "bad" proposal? We will consider the extent to which the evaluative discourse of evaluations enables us to grasp the institutional requirements and expectations for proposals. Recent studies (cf. in particular Fløttum, 2007) have highlighted substantial differences within the field of the humanities. We shall therefore focus specifically on one discipline—linguistics—whilst also remaining aware of the variations that exist within the different domains of this field (such as psycholinguistics, sociolinguistics or the didactics of language).

METHODOLOGICAL ASPECTS

The corpus studied is composed of 284 evaluations by reviewers in linguistics examining proposals submitted to a conference for "young researchers" (i.e., doctoral students or recent doctors) in language sciences. This conference took place in France in July 2006.

Each proposal (142 in total) was evaluated by two anonymous reviewers who provided both a commentary evaluating the proposal and a verdict: accepted, refused or to be revised.

The breakdown of verdicts was as follows: 60% accepted, 30% to be revised and 10% rejected.[5]

After obtaining the consent of each of the reviewers, the entire corpus was processed and placed on a publicly available online platform (http://scientext.msh-alpes.fr) created for this purpose. The platform included linguistic search functions[6] and these tools allowed us to examine the corpus using, in part, automatic searches (see detail below). The results were then checked manually with a view to disambiguation. Finally, qualitative analysis was carried out based on the observation of phenomenon highlighted by the raw data.

RESULTS

Rhetoric of Evaluative Discourse in Proposal Evaluations

Markers of the Reviewer and Addresses to the Author

The aim of this initial analysis was to identify the markers indicating both the reviewer's presence and their addresses to the author. K. Fløttum & al. (2006) developed a typology of the roles of the author in scientific writing (more specifically, in the research article). This typology was based on a large study of all pronominal markers of the author, and the associated verbs and other lexical items. This Norwegian team thus identified three roles taken on by authors: the writer (in this section, I shall present …), the researcher (the study we conducted) and the arguer (I would defend the idea that). Here we will only focus upon the "I" of the arguer because it refers explicitly to the reviewer and the way in which he positions himself personally in his evaluation of the proposal, thus raising a number of interesting questions. Does the presence of this "I" vary according to the verdict given on the proposal? Does the reviewer assert himself more or, on the contrary, adopt a self-effacing position when giving a negative evaluation? Similarly, how does he address the author of the proposal? Does the reviewer use "you" (the most direct form of address possible) in the same way depending on whether or not he is accepting or rejecting the proposal?

We took the number of texts[7] including reviewer-arguer "I"s and "you"s referring to the author of the proposal and cross-examined them with the verdict given on the latter, distinguishing three possibilities: proposal accepted, to be revised or rejected. Figure 1 provides a synthesis of the results obtained.

As Figure 1 illustrates, the use of personal pronouns remains relatively low in this type of evaluation corpus: "I" appears on average in 8.3% of texts and "you" in 25.4%, all corpora included. In general, the reviewer tends not to draw attention to himself as someone putting forward an argument, and, to a lesser degree, tends to give preference to depersonalized utterances when addressing the author (we find more utterances such as "the methodological aspects should be looked at in more depth" as opposed to "you should develop the methodological aspects further"). In keeping with the canons of usage in place in the scientific community, there is an effort to keep the debate centered upon the object in question—the proposal—rather than upon the people in question.

However, in the evaluations where these pronouns do appear, their use differs depending on the verdict. While the "you"s and the "I"s appear in a balanced fashion throughout the "proposal accepted" corpus, the gap is far greater in the "to be revised" corpus, and becomes quite substantial in the "proposal rejected" corpus, where the "I" tends to disappear (it is present in only 3% of texts). In order to be understood by the author, it would seem that the quite powerful act of refusing a proposal must go hand-in-hand with an objective argument, grounded in facts. And such an argument, it seems, does not allow for the marked linguistic presence of the reviewer, which would give a subjective tone to the evaluation.

However, this progressive disappearance of the "I" in negative decisions gives way to the increasingly marked presence of the "you." This raises the following question: if we accept the hypothesis that researchers wish to make their evaluations objective, should we not expect negative evaluations to be characterized by impersonal utterances regarding both the reviewer and the author? The observation of the contexts in which these pronouns appear will help us refine this hypothesis.

We can indeed note that in the proposals accepted (where the "I" is more present and the "you" the most absent), the reviewer's "I" is used recurrently in language acts of the type "masked advice" (example 1) or indirect criticism (example 2).

> Example 1: *En biblio j'aurais rajouté P. Charaudeau, Grammaire du sens et de l'expression et Riegel, Pellat et Rioul, Grammaire méthodique du français (A169)*
>
> [In the bibliography, I would have added *P. Charaudeau, Grammaire du sens de l'expression and Riégel, Pellat & Rioul, Grammaire méthodique du français*]
>
> Example 2: *Je me demande si le concept de Vion d'histoire interactionnelle est vraiment intéressant dans ce cadre (A155)*
>
> [I wonder whether Vion's concept of interactional history is really interesting in this context]

In these cases, the exchanges do not seem particularly hierarchical. The reviewer is addressing a peer and indicating possible improvements to the proposal in the form of personal suggestions (of the type "this is what I would do in your place, fellow researcher"). On the contrary, in the corpus of rejected proposals (where the "you" is dominant and the "I" disappears) the tone is no longer that of an exchange between peers: the presence of "you" is most often found in correlation with an explicit and barely modalized criticism (example 3) or with the highlighting of shortcomings (example 4).

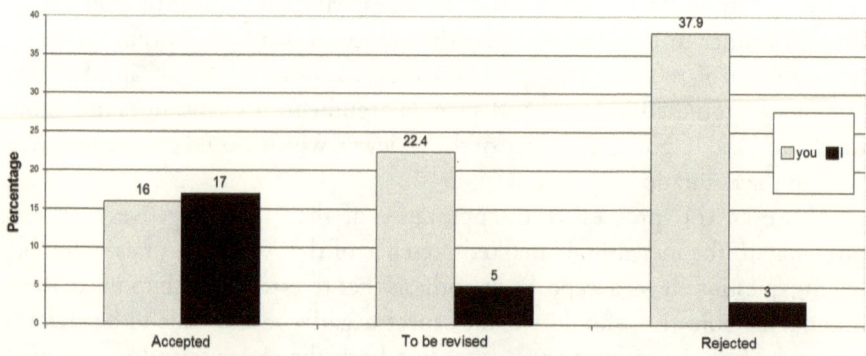

Figure 1. Markers of address

Example 3: *le concept de " faute" que vous semblez utiliser sans distance mériterait d'être précisé (Rj173)*

[the concept of "mistake" that you seem to be using without any distance would be worth clarifying]

Example 4: *vous ne dites pas clairement quelles sont vos données, comment vous les avez recueillies et traitées (Rj123)*

[you don't state clearly what your data are nor how you collected and processed them.*]*

Thus, while most reviewers use few personal forms, when the "you" does appear, it is mainly in the context of negative evaluations. In these cases, it most often serves the purpose of putting the author in the hot seat by highlighting his errors or weaknesses, thus allowing the reviewer—taking on a superior, dominant, position—to auto-justify his verdict.

Yet in most cases, according to our observations, the reviewers' qualitative evaluation is linguistically modalized showing a common desire to allow the author to save face.

Allowing the Author to Save Face

The tendency of reviewers to try to be tactful and not offend the authors is evident in their use of negation and evaluative adjectives.

Use of Negation. Figure 2 shows that the markers expressing negation (ne-pas in French) are gradually more present when the evaluation is mixed (proposals to be revised) or definitive (proposals rejected). In the latter case, negation markers are present in almost three out of four evaluations of the corpus, and yet barely exceed one-third in the positive evaluations (proposals accepted).

In many cases, the negation concerns adjectives, adverbs or positive verbs of evaluation. Examples 5 (rejected proposal) and 6 (proposal to be revised) are representative of this tendency.

Example 5: *Il **n'est pas vrai** (cf. votre point 3) que l'on ne peut pas distinguer deux verbes ... (Rj63)*

[It **is not true** (cf. your point 3) that one cannot distinguish between two verbs ...]

Example 6: *Votre proposition mériterait cependant d'être remaniée car en l'état* **la problématique n'est pas suffisamment claire.** (Rs193)

[However, your proposal would benefit from being reworked as in its current state, **the key research question is not sufficiently clear.**]

Qualitative observation of the utterances that included negations framing adjectives shows that these are characteristic patterns. These, therefore, indicate a ritualized rhetoric: as with examples 5 & 6, criticism is expressed through the negation of a positive term rather than the foregrounding of a weakness. Reviewers prefer to qualify an aspect by saying it *"n'est pas développé"* [is not developed] or it is *"pas clair"* [not clear] rather than stating it is *"flou"* [vague] or *"lacunaire"* [lacking].

In other words, rather than expressing how the proposal is "bad," the reviewers indicate how it is "not good." We could, therefore, hypothesize that this is a way of softening the criticism directed at the author, while still providing ways in which to improve the proposal even in cases where it has been rejected.

Evaluative Adjectives. This hypothesis is strengthened by another result, which could seem somewhat surprising if the presence of negation markers were not taken into account: the analysis of evaluative adjectives in the corpus shows that the five most cited adjectives in all three sub-corpora are positive adjectives—interesting, clear, original, good, relevant.

As we can see, the number of these positive adjectives is subject to relatively little variation depending on sub-corpus. We could have expected a different distribution, with greater use of positive adjectives in the proposals accepted than in those refused. The fact that these adjectives are sometimes framed by negation[8] can explain this tendency in part. Only in part, however, for this tendency towards modalization, and more generally towards softening criticism with a view to allowing the author to save face, can also be observed throughout the corpus through the use of another linguistic process characteristic of argumentative writing: the dynamic of concession/refutation. This consists in granting the value of something in the point of view defended by the author (approval) and then highlighting a weakness (disapproval) with a counter-argument.

Process of Concession/Refutation

This process can be examined through the example of the most used adjective in the corpus, the adjective "interesting." Figure 3 shows that this adjective

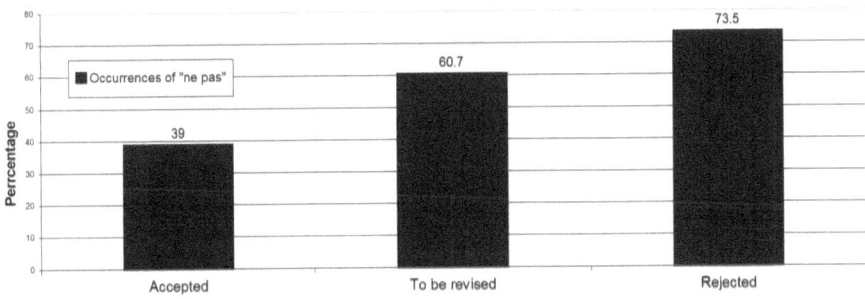

Figure 2. Negation as a tool in allowing the author to save face

is used in relatively similar proportions in all three sub-corpora: approximately 38% for the "accepted proposals" corpus and 28% if we combine the "to be revised" and "proposal rejected" corpora.

The interest of a study is therefore the quality most subject to evaluation in our corpus. Furthermore, a proposal being "interesting" is not incompatible with its rejection. Qualitative analysis of the context in which "interesting" appears shows that it is always used positively: in contrast with all the other evaluative adjectives, there are no occurrences of "not interesting," or "not very interesting," even in the proposals rejected or those subject to a somewhat reticent judgment. It is as if it were impossible to officially indicate to a researcher that his study lacks interest, no doubt because this type of judgment—that is highly subjective—does not fall within the remit of academic judgment. We can suppose, on the contrary, that in the sphere of research, any subject can be considered of potential interest, as Bourdieu (1993, p. 911) states, "Everything is interesting, provided you look at it long enough." So, while it is clear that the absence of interest of a study cannot be highlighted, it is, on the contrary, very common to underscore its interest. In our corpus of proposals rejected or to be revised, while this quality in itself seems to be off limits for criticism, it can nonetheless offer a springboard for the latter. Often preceded by "Certes" —an archetypal concession marker in French (which could best be translated as "admittedly" or "no doubt" depending on the context) and often followed by "but" (example 7)—the interest of the research is sometimes reduced to certain aspects (example 8) or diminished by specifications such as "*de prime abord*" [at first glance] (example 9).

> Example 7: *Ce texte présente un certain nombre de principes pédagogiques,* **certes** *intéressants* **mais** *qui ne sont ni questionnés ni inscrits dans une recherche de terrain.* [Rj-191]
>
> [This text presents a certain number of pedagogical principles

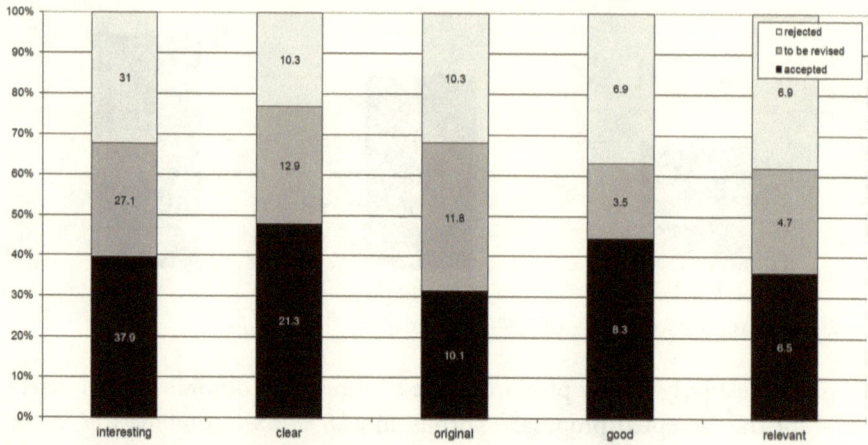

Figure 3. Distribution of most cited adjectives in the three sub-corpora

that are **no doubt** interesting (**certes** intéressants) **but** are not called into question nor situated within any field work.]

Example 8: ***Certains concepts*** *présentés par l'auteur sont intéressants et aptes à apporter une contribution efficace à la recherche en didactique des langues (Rs182)*

[**Certain concepts** presented by the author are interesting and could make an efficient contribution to research in the didactics of language]

Example 9: *Le thème de cette proposition de communication est **de prime abord** intéressant: en effet, on dispose de peu d'informations sur l'intégration du parler de jeunes urbains (Rs126)*

[The topic of this proposal seems **at first glance** to be interesting: indeed, relatively little information is available regarding the integration of the speech of urban youths.]

This dynamic of concession and then refutation, which is very visible through the recurrent use of the "interesting"-"but" [9] pair, is therefore one of the subtle processes put into play in our corpus by the reviewers to express their criticism tactfully to the authors and lead to a negative verdict.[10] But above and beyond this argumentative function, the routine use of this linguistic pattern also seems to play a simple pragmatic role of initiation for the reviewer—along the lines of a verbal tic of argumentative writing—that simply helps him lead into his evaluative discourse, in particular when it is critical. Indeed, the context of certain utterances shows that this adjective can be followed by a very hard comment against the author; is it still possible to speak of "allowing the author to save face" in the following examples, concerning a proposal rejected (example 10) and to be revised (example 11)?

> Example 10: *L'idée d'une telle étude en sémantique est **intéressante mais** le cadre théorique est inexistant et la problématique reste trop vague (Rj-114)*

> [The idea of such a study in semantics is **interesting but** the theoretical framework is nonexistent and the research question remains too vague.]

> Example 11: *Recherche **intéressante mais** qui en l'état n'apporte rien de bien nouveau dans le champ. (Rs-283)*

> [The research is **interesting but** in its current state does not bring anything new to the field.]

In conclusion to this initial part of this paper, we can note that the rhetoric of evaluation does vary depending on the verdict addressed to the author. In our view, the most salient point, which we shall now develop further, concerns the difference between the tone adopted by the reviewer when he accepts or rejects a proposal. In the "proposals accepted" corpus, the reviewers tend to underline the positive points of the proposal and to suggest improvements to the author on the mode of an exchange between peers. In the "rejected proposal" corpus, however, the exchanges are linguistically more hierarchical, and while there is a tendency to try and enable the author to save face—in particular through the use of concession/refutation and through negation—the evaluative discourse often seems to be limited in its pedagogical scope. The following part to this study, focusing on identifying the criteria for success in proposals, will offer some details backing up this observation.

NORMS IN PLACE: THE CRITERIA FOR SUCCESSFUL CONFERENCE PAPER PROPOSALS

In order to approach this question of the criteria for successful proposals, we first calculated the degree of agreement between the two reviewers responsible for evaluating the proposal: Table 1 summarizes the results obtained by cross-matching the verdict of the two reviewers.

Table 1. Distribution of proposals according to each reviewer's verdict

Proposal	Rejected	To be revised	Accepted
Rejected	4,3%		
To be revised	9,2%	4,3%	
Accepted	13,5 %	24,4%	44%

The degree of agreement (the sum of the figures in bold) barely exceeds half of all cases (52.6% in total) and mainly concerns the proposals accepted. At the same time, a not insignificant number of proposals (13.5%, or 19 proposals, and 38 evaluations) were accepted by one reviewer and rejected by the other. The degree of homogeneity between evaluations is therefore relatively weak and the subjective nature of the evaluation is clearly apparent. In order to back up this observation, we carried out a more detailed analysis of these cases where the evaluations differed greatly (proposal accepted VS rejected) by questioning the type of qualitative criteria called upon by each reviewer. Two possible explanations appear, concerning, on the one hand, the low level of convergence between the criteria retained, and, on the other hand, the different weighting given to common criteria.

Low level of convergence between criteria retained. The analysis of the corpus of 38 highly divergent evaluations consisted in identifying the qualitative criteria highlighted by each of the 19 pairs of reviewers in order to determine what differed between the two evaluations (we could imagine, for example, that one might consider the proposal to be original and the other not). However, there are very few cases in which this analysis is possible. More often than not, the two reviewers do not base their verdict on common criteria. In other words, each reviewer foregrounds different criteria to justify their verdict. The following two examples concerning the same proposal offer an illustration of this:

> Example 12: *une problématique claire et bien circonscrite (prop. accepted)*
>
> [a clear and well defined research question]
>
> Example 13: *l'exposé ne dit rien de l'arrière plan théorique de ce travail (prop. rejected)*

[the presentation says nothing of the theoretical background of this work*]*

In the first evaluation, no reference is made to the theoretical background identified as lacking by the second reviewer. Similarly, this second reviewer does not mention the research question, which was underscored as being "clear and well defined" by the first reviewer. This type of focus on different criteria in each evaluation can no doubt be explained in many ways. In this case, as the research question is essentially the product of an in-depth knowledge of the theoretical background, it could be imagined that reviewer 1 (who gave a very positive evaluation of the proposal) is familiar with this background, the implicit nature of which could, on the contrary, pose a problem for reviewer 2, who is perhaps not a specialist in the author's domain. However, whatever the reasons for the discrepancy, one might wonder how the young researcher is likely to interpret these differing views of his work and how they will be of use to him in progressing. Perhaps it is necessary to question the sacrosanct practice of "blind" reviewing, which is so widespread (at least in the context of humanities in France). Could we not imagine that each reviewer, after having written an initial version of his evaluation, should then be made aware of the evaluation written by his counterpart? He would then have the option of rethinking his own selection filter and altering his evaluation (or even his verdict) if necessary before it is sent to the author. This additional stage in the process could well benefit both the homogeneity of the two evaluations and the conscious awareness of practices.

It should be noted, however, that one criterion is evaluated in opposing terms by both reviewers: clarity. Thus, in examples 14 and 15, the clarity of the proposal is considered to be one of its strengths by the first reviewer whose verdict is positive (*"exposé clair quoiqu'un peu abstrait"* [the outline is clear, if somewhat abstract]) whereas it is called into question by the second (*"propos confus"* [argument unclear.]

> Example 14: *L'outil que vous décrivez répond à un besoin réel … . L'exposé de l'architecture globale de la plateforme est clair quoiqu'un peu abstrait* (prop. accepted).
>
> [The tool that you describe corresponds to a real need … . The outline of the overall architecture of the platform is clear, if somewhat abstract.]
>
> Example 15: *Cette proposition est difficile à lire. Elle comporte trop de faiblesses aussi bien du point de vue du fond que du*

> *point de vue de la forme. Le propos est confus dans son organisation générale* .... (prop. rejected)

> [This proposal is difficult to read. It has too many weaknesses both in terms of content and form. The argument is unclear in its general organization.]

Three other pairs of evaluations reveal contradictory points of view concerning this criterion. And yet clarity is an omnipresent requirement in French pedagogical discourse whether it be in the words of teachers or in those of writing manuals, where the instruction "be clear!" abounds. Are we sure that we actually know what the "clarity" of a text means? Does this notion correspond to the same reality for everyone, whether reviewer or author? Our observations lead us to doubt that this is the case. Analysis of our corpus highlights the relative nature of the discernment at work when we evaluate our peers' scientific production. We would thus argue in favour of multiple or cross-referenced evaluations of work, produced in such a way as to call into question—and thus reduce—the bias introduced by our individual filters of judgement.

Different Weighting Given to the Same Criteria. Qualitative analysis of the corpus of differing evaluations highlighted a criterion for which there was a consensus amongst the reviewers who mention it. However, it does not seem to carry the same weight for each of them. The criterion in question is that of methodological aspects. In our corpus, methodology is always brought up in terms of being lacking, whether the proposal is accepted or refused, as in examples 16 and 17.

> Example 16: *il reste à apporter des précisions de nature méthodologique (qu'est ce qui caractérise les deux versions du récit, comment les gestes sont-ils caractérisés, y a-t-il un traitement quantitatif des données)* (prop. accepted)

> [methodological details remain to be given (what characterizes the two versions of the narrative; how are gestures characterized, is there quantitative processing of data)]

> Example 17: *des précisions seraient nécessaires concernant la méthodologie. Quels sont les facteurs situationnels considérés ? Les analyses ont-elles porté sur deux récits différents ou sur un même conte dans deux situations différentes ? Comment le récit a-t-il été analysé ? Comment les facteurs situationnels et internes ont-*

ils été intégrés dans l'analyse de la gestualité ? S'agit-il d'analyses qualitatives ou quantitatives ? ... (prop. rejected)

[further details would be necessary concerning the methodology. What are the situational factors considered? Did the analyses focus upon two different narratives or upon the same tale in two different situations? How was the narrative analyzed? ... Are these analyses quantitative or qualitative? ...]

The importance given to one criterion is therefore different depending on the reviewer, whose position (in terms of verdict) has a clear influence on the way the questions are formulated. The first questions (example 16) are intended to allow the young researcher to progress and are clearly pedagogical: there is an impression that the reviewer believes in the proposal's potential for improvement. The second questions, on the other hand (example 17), fall more within the scope of auto-justification than pedagogy—and one could suppose that their length and number would produce a fairly discouraging effect for their reader. In sum, this type of evaluation seems to be directed more towards the organizing committee than towards the author.

These brief analyses raise the question of the didactic scope of the evaluative commentary, which can sometimes appear limited for a young researcher who is still unfamiliar with the workings of scientific writing and only just discovering the institutional expectations of the domain. It should be noted that, given the specificity of the group of authors in question, the organizing committee had explicitly requested that reviewers provide constructive comments to help the young researchers improve their practice. When the proposal was accepted, in particular, there was a tendency to respect this instruction: as we have seen here, the reviewer expressed praise and made suggestions to the author for improvements. Conversely, when the proposal was rejected, this request was not always enacted: in other words, it is when the proposals show the most weaknesses and when the young researchers would most benefit from constructive comments that they are least likely to receive them. It is true that proposals are sometimes very far from meeting expectations, which could serve to discourage the reviewer in his intention to comment helpfully and lead him to simply justify his decision to reject the proposal with a comment expressing a definitive and irrevocable judgment. This raises the question of the doctoral student's supervision. Indeed, it seems important to us to provide support for doctoral students not only in the writing of their PhD dissertation but equally in the necessary dissemination of their work; in other words, through the submission of articles and conference papers. More generally, we need to make the effort (which would take time but no doubt be highly beneficial to young researchers' training) to produce precise and constructive comments when we find ourselves in the position of evaluating young researchers' proposals for conference papers or articles

CONCLUSION AND FURTHER PERSPECTIVES

As mentioned in the introduction, studies focusing on the evaluation of conference paper proposals are only just beginning. This chapter can thus be considered as an initial foray in the field, with a view to opening up avenues for further analyses. The first conclusion to be drawn from this study is methodological: a larger corpus would enable more interesting observations to be carried out. The corpus in question here is too limited to allow some of our hypotheses to be validated or to provide sufficient evidence for certain comparisons, which nonetheless seem promising. In particular, our analysis of evaluative adjectives warrants further development. The adjective "clair" (clear) seems to be used far more with negation than "original" or "interesting"; it would be useful to carry out a similar analysis for the other three most prevalent adjectives in our corpus i.e., "pertinent" (relevant), "important" (important), and "bon" (good).

Similarly, in terms of the linguistic routines used by researchers, it would be interesting to examine further the differences according to the verdict given on the proposal. The number of cases here is too limited to allow any reliable tendencies to be observed.

We have seen that the use of the personal pronouns "I" and "you" depended greatly upon the viewpoint of the reviewer on the proposal in question. A high number of "you"s addressed to the author seemed to correlate with a negative evaluation of the proposal, allowing the reviewer to justify his rejection by highlighting the author's weaknesses and shortcomings. Conversely, a high number of "I"s seems to correlate with positive evaluations: it appears that the reviewer wants to offer advice to the author from a personal standpoint. However, given that personal pronouns were absent from the majority of texts in our corpus, this hypothesis would need to be refined and tested upon a larger corpus. This would enable greater analysis of the differences between the "to be revised" and "rejected" sub-corpora, from the point of view of indicators of didactic intention. It could be thought that the most advice and constructive criticism would be found in the sub-corpus regarding proposals "to be revised" with a view to enabling the author to go on to achieve a positive evaluation. This hypothesis could be tested by counting the number of conditional verbs leading into a suggestion present in both corpora (eg., "il faudrait développer … "/"… should be developed;" "il vaudrait mieux préciser … "/"it would be better to specify … "; "il serait judicieux de … "/"it would be wise to … "). Another possibility would be to analyze in more detail the types of questions asked by reviewers. Indeed, some are in fact of an advisory nature (of the type "pourquoi ne pas … "/"why don't you … ") while others are in fact simply critical (of the type "où sont les données?" "where are the data?"). In either case, statistical analysis alone would obviously not suffice and would need to be supplemented by qualitative analysis.

We would argue in favour of the pooling of resources of a large variety of evaluation corpora. This would pave the way for further, more ambitious, studies looking at comparisons between disciplines or languages in the same way as existing studies on other types of scientific writing. Studies could also consider differences depending upon the status of the author of the text being evaluated (young or experienced researcher) and upon the institutional context of the evaluation (evaluation of a conference paper, an article or a funding proposal).

The comparison between languages strikes us as a particularly promising avenue. The researcher's native linguistic culture has been shown to be of limited influence in the case of research articles (cf. Fløttum et al., 2006), but is this also the case for evaluations? More specifically, it would be interesting to determine the extent to which the phenomena in question are specifically French. Can similar observations be made concerning English, for example? To take this even further, it is worth considering the possible variations linked to non-native use of English given that this is now the dominant language for the dissemination of scientific research. Do non-native speakers of English bring to bear their own cultural specificities upon their language use, or does the language itself shape usage in this field?

In sum, although this study remains merely exploratory, in our view it opens up a vast number of possible avenues for further analysis. The methodological tools offered by the Scientext platform (which is freely accessible to all), adapted for the purposes of this study to the type of corpus in question, can enable linguistic analysis of substantial corpora.[11] These future studies, of which we hope there will be many, will allow us to better understand our own habitus in terms of evaluation. They may also allow us to become more aware of the linguistic routines specific to our scientific communities and to take a more critical view of the (more or less explicit) criteria that we bring to bear upon our evaluations of our peers.

NOTES

1. By the term "scientific writing," we refer to the pieces of writing produced by researchers (doctoral students or professional researchers) that have as their aim the building and dissemination of scientific knowledge. In the Francophone context, contrary to the Anglophone one, the label "scientific writing" does not only cover the physical and natural sciences, but equally social sciences and the humanities.

2. For two overviews of the state of the art in this field, see Hyland & Bondi (2006) in English, and Rinck (2010) in French.

3. This contribution is part of a research project entitled Écrits Universitaires: Inventaires, Pratiques, Modèles (2007-2010), and funded by the Agence Nationale de la Recherche in France.

4. These studies (cf. for example Hyland, 2002; Harwood, 2005; Grossmann & Rink, 2004; Boch & Rink, 2010) have shown that far from being neutral and objective, scientific writing includes a form of subjectivity and a persuasive aim, and that this dimension varies according to the context: by studying research articles in medicine, linguistics and economics in three languages (English, French and Norwegian), Fløttum (2007) demonstrated that the disciplinary parameter was in fact more decisive than the national culture (the language) of the researcher.

5. This breakdown refers to the verdict given by the reviewers and not the final decision, which came down to the organizing committee when there was disagreement between the reviewers.

6. This platform was created as part of Scientext, another project in the laboratoire LIDILEM (address: http://scientext.msh-alpes.fr, directed by F. Grossmann and A. Tutin), which includes three large corpora that can be consulted online:

- A pluridisciplinary corpus of scientific writing in French representing a variety of genres and containing just under five million words.
- A corpus of learners' English including long pieces of work by students studying English as a foreign language (1.1 million words).
- An English corpus of scientific writing, taken from the BMC corpus, mainly in the fields of biology and medicine, that comes close to 13 million words and is the subject of lexicological study (Williams & Million, in press).

7. All our calculations take into account the number of texts in which the term studied appears and not the number of occurrences of the term. This allows us to neutralize any bias caused by the personal style of the reviewer, who might use "you" or "I" excessively and thus skew the averages.

8. Due to a lack of occurrences of adjectives preceded by negations (none for "interesting" and 11 for "clear") it was not possible to carry out a comparative analysis of the three sub-corpora.

9. This analysis also applies to the adjective "original," more present in the "to be revised" and "rejected" corpora than in the "proposal accepted" corpus (cf. Figure 3). While utterances of the type "le sujet est peu original" [the subject is not very original] can be found, this adjective is often used in a positive manner in the form of a concession followed by a "but" introducing an element that requires further work ("thématique originale mais aspects théoriques insuffisamment développés" [the topic is original but the theoretical aspects are insufficiently developed]). For a detailed analysis of evaluative adjectives in scientific discourse, see Tutin (2010).

10. On this subject, it should be noted that in the "proposals accepted" corpus, "interesting" is never followed by "but" or any other marker of refutation. It would seem that the adjective takes on its full meaning again, moving away from the recurrent argumentative role that it plays in the case of proposals refused/to be revised.

11. Given that nowadays conference paper proposals are more often than not evaluated using online electronic tools, collecting evaluations seems far more feasible than before. The greatest difficulty lies in obtaining permission from the reviewers to use these evaluations.

REFERENCES

Boch, F., & Rinck, F. (Eds.). (2010). Enonciation et rhétorique dans l'écrit scientifique. *Lidil, 41*. Retrieved from http://lidil.revues.org/index3001.html

Bourdieu, P. (1993). *La misère du monde*. Paris: Seuil.

Fløttum, K. (2007). *Language and discipline perspectives on academic discourse*. Cambridge, UK: Cambridge Scholars.

Fløttum, K., Dahl, T., & Kinn, T. (Eds.). (2006). *Academic voices. Across languages and disciplines*. Amsterdam/Philadelphia: John Benjamins.

Grossmann, F., & Rinck, F. (2004). La surénonciation comme norme du genre: L'exemple de l'article de recherche et du dictionnaire en linguistique. *Langages. 156*, 34-50.

Harwood, N. (2005). We do not seem to have a theory. ... The theory I present here attempts to fill this gap: Inclusive and exclusive pronouns in academic writing. *Applied Linguistics, 26*(3), 343-375.

Hyland, K. (2002). Authority and invisibility: Authorial identity in academic writing, *Journal of Pragmatics. 34*, 1091-1112.

Hyland, K., & Bondi, M. (Eds.). (2006). *Academic discourse across disciplines. Linguistic Insights, 42*. Bern: Peter Lang.

Maingueneau, D. (1992). Le tour ethnolinguistique de l'analyse du discours. *Langages, 26*(105), 114-125.

Rinck, F. (2010). L'analyse linguistique des enjeux de connaissance dans le discours scientifique: Un état des lieux. *Revue d'anthropologie des connaissances,*

3(4), 427-450. Retrieved from http://www.cairn.info/revue-anthropologie-des-connaissances-2010-3-page-427.htm

Tutin, A. (2010). Evaluative adjectives in academic writing in the humanities and social sciences. In R. Lores-Sanz, P. Mur-Duenas, & E. Lafuente-Millan (Eds.), *Constructing interpersonality: Multiple perspectives on written academic genres* (pp. 219-240). Cambridge, UK: Cambridge Scholars.

Williams, G., & Million, C. (2009). The general and the specific: Collocational resonance of scientific language. In M. Mahlberg, V. Conzalez-Diaz, & C. Smith (Eds.), *Proceedings Corpus Linguistics 2009*. Liverpool: University of Liverpool. Retrieved from http://ucrel.lancs.ac.uk/publications/CL2009/129_FullPaper.doc.

SECTION 6.
CULTURES OF WRITING IN THE WORKPLACE

Whenever writing researchers seek to define and analyze our topic, "writing," we are confronted with an array of elements that might be included within our purview: people, technologies, media, social conventions, institutions, and so on. In the classical, rhetorical perspective, this array of elements was narrowed to foreground the people involved in a communicative act, a rhetor attempting to persuade an audience. In contrast, recent theories have broadened the approach to include a fuller array, variously referring to "system," "context," "situation," or, as here, "culture." These theories foreground the complexity and interconnectedness of the elements, and they emphasize that the elements are co-constructed. A relevant metaphor comes from chaos theory: the "butterfly effect," where a small change in initial conditions (the flapping of a butterfly's wings) cascades into later system-changing consequences (altering the pathway of a storm).

How, though, might writing researchers study the impact of small changes within cultures, as well as the concomitant impact that distinct elements in the cultures have on the writers who inhabit them? What frameworks might we apply? How might we manage and track the data collection and analysis? How, in short, might we best deal with the complexity of cultures?

The authors in this section have provided different responses to these questions, as they provide examples of situated studies. Focusing on the impact that automated systems for scribing information have had in the culture of search engine optimization (SEO), Spinuzzi draws upon Manuel Castells's labor theory to provide a framework for analyzing rapidly changing genres. Nikolaidou and Karlsson examine how care providers wrestle with an institutional requirement that they keep journals about the care given to residents of retirement homes—and thus, the researchers develop a technique for analyzing how the care providers' work identities are co-constructed with their word choices. Laquintano addresses issues of how credibility is generated within a specific community, as he examines how writers and reviewers of advice books for playing online poker interact with each other, and in the process, alter the traditional purposes for the book review genre. Finally, Perrin offers a method for capturing and tracing complex interactions within dynamic systems, and models this method by tracing the impact that small word revisions within news stories have within the context of a newsroom.

--KL

CHAPTER 27.
GENRE AND GENERIC LABOR

Clay Spinuzzi
University of Texas at Austin

Those of us who have worked for a while in what Russell calls writing, activity, and genre research (WAGR; see Russell 2009) tend to draw a certain distinction between genres. Schryer and Spoel (2005) summarize this distinction quite well:

> Regulated resources refer to knowledge, skills, and language behaviors that are recognized and required by a field or profession. Regularized resources, on the other hand, refer to strategies that emerge from practice situations and are more tacit (p. 250).

WAGR scholars use different terms for shades of this distinction, such as official/unofficial (Spinuzzi, 2003; cf. Bakhtin, 1981), authoritative/internally persuasive (Dias et al., 1999), stability/change (Berkenkotter & Huckin, 1995; Devitt, 1991; Starke-Meyerring, 2010), and explicit/tacit (Schryer & Spoel, 2005; see Table 2). But in all these cases, scholars have tried to distinguish between (a) genres that are more formally or authoritatively constrained by the activity and (b) genres that represent more grounded, less authoritative, and frequently more individual or local solutions. That is, we have focused on *authorial discretion:* the degree to which the author has the freedom to exercise her or his own voice (in the Bakhtinian sense, entailing beliefs, logics, traditions, and ideologies; see Bakhtin, 1981).

This distinction turns out to be quite useful for understanding genre development, particularly in genre assemblages (e.g., genre sets, systems, ecologies, repertoires; see Spinuzzi, 2004). As an activity develops over time, actors within that activity tend to develop unofficial genres—or import genres from other activities—some of which over time become more integrated into the activity and more officially sanctioned. That is, some of these more unofficial, regularized resources develop into more official, regularized resources. Examples include letters that evolved into the genre of the experimental article (Bazerman, 1988) and prose that became tables and forms (Yates, 1989). Over time, some genres develop to become more regulated. Indeed, some become templated to a degree that authorial voice is exercised almost solely in selecting parts to reuse (Swarts, 2009). Such genres have become more prevalent with the increase in automated genres such as content management systems (e.g., Clark, 2008; Hart-Davidson et al., 2008).

As Schryer, Lingard, and Spafford (2007) argue, genre includes not only replicable structures but also "regularized improvisations" (p. 26). They argue that "Genres are constellations of regulated and regularized improvisational strategies triggered by the interaction between individual socialization, or habitus, and an organization or field" (p. 31; cf. Gygi & Zachry, 2010; Teston, 2009; Winsor, 2007). Regulated genres explicitly enforce an orientation; regularized genres tend to implicitly support it (although they can also introduce very different orientations, often inherited from other activities from which they are drawn).

This official/unofficial distinction is quite useful for understanding how genres develop. However, I have begun to wonder whether it adequately analyzes the relationships among genres or genre development. I especially began to question the distinction after conducting a study of rapid genre development in a highly contingent and unstable activity, *search engine optimization* (SEO; see Spinuzzi, 2010).

SEO involves bringing more or better quality traffic to a website via search engines. Essentially, SEO specialists identify search queries that potential customers might use to find a client's website, then improve the website's ranking in those queries so that the website shows up in the first few pages of search results. They use various techniques for achieving this goal, including defining the most advantageous queries for which to optimize results; restructuring the client's website itself; suggesting content that clients might add to their websites (such as press releases, videos, and PDFs); and building links to the website. They also monitor traffic to sites via these queries. Site rankings are constantly in flux due to frequent changes in search algorithms, competition from other websites, and news stories that affect search rankings. Because of this constant flux, and because new SEO tools are constantly in development, specialists are continually changing and improving their tools and practices.

The most visible product of their work is their customized monthly report to the client; although SEO specialists do not see themselves as writers, each SEO specialist writes 10-12 complex 20-page monthly reports in the first ten business days of each month. The reports are structurally and rhetorically complex.

In my three-month field study of Semoptco, I interviewed the director of product services twice; observed three of the six SEO specialists and one of the three account managers twice each; conducted one pre-observational interview and two post-observational interviews for each observed participant; and collected artifacts from each observed participant's workspace, including photos, printed collateral, and electronic documents. (See methodological details in Spinuzzi, 2010.) These methods allowed me to observe, examine, and interview participants about various genres in use at Semoptco.

Let's examine four such genres from that study, summarized below:

> **Competitors table.** One of the SEO specialists, Luis, was faced with the problem of customizing a standard report to address the particular contingencies of his client. The client had identified competitors against which it wanted its SEO metrics compared. But Luis determined that they should actually compare themselves against others who were more direct competitors in the SEO space. To make the case, he took the initiative of developing a comparison table, which had no direct precedent. Luis's table could serve as such a precedent, since his current report will serve as a template for future reports.
>
> **Social bookmarks.** On the other hand, Seoptco's SEO specialists all used social bookmarking services such as delicious.com or StumbleUpon to create bookmarks pointing to their clients' sites. Interestingly, specialists could decide which bookmarking service(s) they wanted to use, how to write and tag bookmark descriptions, and they could even individually try out various tools that post bookmarks to several services at once. But that freedom was waning: Carl, one of the specialists, noted excitedly that Semoptco developers were developing such a tool for all SEO specialists at Semoptco. "The interns will love this!" he exclaimed. After all, social bookmarking is relatively low-skill work, so specialists farmed it out to interns whenever possible.
>
> **Action items in monthly reports.** The SEO specialists had to rapidly pull together detailed monthly reports for each client. Parts of the report, such as the Action Items section, were based on the judgment of the individual specialist handling the account (although they were also vetted by the account manager before being sent to the customer). These Action Items set the course for future SEO action, and played a large

part in retaining customer business. They followed a regular format and contained specific types of information, but only a trained SEO specialist could put them together.

"Report cards." But the monthly reports also contained sections that weren't written by human beings at all. Perhaps the most critical section was the "report card," a table that provided a measurable, verifiable, reliable summary of how well SEO was performing relative to targets set during the launch process. These "report cards" were essentially database tables, generated by an internal system without any human intervention.

As these summaries show, we can categorize these texts using the official/unofficial distinction.

Table 1. Examples of official and unofficial genres

Unofficial (regularized, tacit)	Competitors table	Social bookmarks
Official (regulated, explicit)	Action Items in Semoptco's monthly reports	"Report cards"

All of these texts can be considered genres in the tradition of WAGR: they are types of texts, responses to recurrent situations, and they are recognizable by their readers and writers. Yet some of these genres are obviously different from others.

Unofficial genres. For instance, in the top row of Table 1, the competitors table and social bookmarks are "unofficial" genres, genres that may have become somewhat regularized but are still highly idiosyncratic: selected, developed and applied by individuals, not centrally mandated, and consequently both flexible and subject to drift. These genres do not (initially, at least) speak for the organization; they operate in the spaces between the official requirements of the organization. For instance, SEO specialists could choose which social bookmarking tools they personally wanted to use—or they could choose not to use them at all. Similarly, Luis personally developed the table to compare different competitors' performances; no table quite like this had appeared in a Semoptco report before, although the notion of comparing things with a table was of course familiar to all the SEO specialists.

Official genres. On the other hand, in the bottom row of Table 1, the Action Items section and the "report cards" are "official" genres, genres that are not just regularized but *regulated* (Schryer & Spoel, 2005). They represent the organization as a whole, and outside entities understand them this way. So their format is centrally mandated and largely fixed, not idiosyncratic; their composition and use must meet certain guidelines; and they are officially required by the organization. They officially represent an authoritative voice, an organizational voice (cf. Coney & Chatfield, 1996). Both genres are taken to represent Semoptco's official stance, not just the thoughts of an individual analyst.

This continuum between official and unofficial genres provides what I call "a dimension of stability" (Spinuzzi, 2010, p. 398). In WAGR, many have examined texts in terms of this continuum between the unofficial and official (or if you prefer, the regularized and the regulated). Yet as we examine the four examples above, we may perceive other groupings.

Specifically, notice that in the right column of Table 1, the social bookmarks and "report cards" are both *automated:* an operator runs a command or query, and a computer performs the actions. Tasks such as posting social bookmarks and summarizing keyword statistics are repetitive; they're complex enough that human beings tend to do them imperfectly; and they involve enough operations that it takes human beings a long time to perform them. Social bookmarks are unofficial, the "report card" is official, but both are formalized so that they can be offloaded to a machine.

On the other hand, in the left column of Table 1, the comparison table and the Action Items section both require a human being to create and use them; in their current configuration, they require too much operational discretion to automate. They require human judgment that can't be offloaded to a machine, judgment that is reliant on the individual who uses or composes them.

This second distinction—the continuum between automation and discretion, or in Manuel Castells' terminology, between generic labor and self-programmable labor—is quite different from the first. Whereas the official-unofficial distinction focuses on authorial discretion, this one focuses on *operational discretion:* the degree to which the author exercises discretion over the execution of processes. This second distinction has been underexplored in WAGR, although we see a bit of it in design-oriented work drawing from distributed cognition and related approaches (Freedman & Smart, 1997; Dias et al., 1999). Perhaps this distinction has been underexplored because automation has been a rather limited part of writing research until recently. Yes, we have automated texts, but they have seemed out of reach of most authors. Not long ago, end-user programming (Nardi, 1993) was relatively rare and work was harder for most people to automate. Now it is more common: more and more texts are automated or automatable, such as macros, templates, scripts, and HTML forms.

And we need to theorize such examples of automation in WAGR, as I fretted recently: "What does it mean for rhetorical genre theory that so many genres are becoming automated and customized for specific problems?" (Spinuzzi, 2010, p. 394). I argue that this second distinction can be productively discussed in terms of Castells' distinction of generic and self-programmable labor, which was developed to address such changes.

We might gloss these two distinctions, these two types of discretion, as being about authoritative *voice* and operational *choice*. Authorial discretion involves the freedom of actors to exercise their authoritative voice, bringing in beliefs, logics, traditions, and ideologies to operate in a given activity; low-freedom activities are monologic, while high-freedom activities are dialogic. Operational discretion involves the freedom of actors to exercise their operational choice, the extent of their discretion over task execution and problem-solving.

These two distinctions can certainly be related: for instance, someone who is given choices can choose to bring in different voices. Nevertheless, these distinctions are quite different, as I attempt to demonstrate in this chapter.

Below, I first explore the official/unofficial distinction in WAGR, particularly how it describes the black-boxing of authoritative voices. Next, I introduce Castells' distinction between generic and self-programmable labor, particularly how it describes the black-boxing of operational choices: procedures, decisions, judgments. I then apply the two distinctions to the examples above in order to discuss a two-dimensional analysis of genres and genre development. Finally, I conclude with a discussion of implications for WAGR, particularly for understanding how genres develop.

AUTHORITATIVE VOICE: THE OFFICIAL/ UNOFFICIAL DISTINCTION IN WAGR

As we've seen, the official/unofficial distinction (authorial discretion) has been widely used to discuss and differentiate genres in WAGR. Table 1 characterizes our four examples in these terms. Below, I discuss the analytical work that the official/unofficial distinction does for us, focusing on what it is, what it black-boxes or analytically encapsulates, and the dynamic that characterizes interrelations between unofficial and official genres.

Definition and Characteristics

As we've seen, the official/unofficial distinction assumes an authority to which the genre is oriented. For instance, Luis' comparison table is an innovation that is oriented to discovering the needs of his client. So is the "report card," which represents what Semoptco the organization officially knows about how its clients' keywords are performing.

The unofficial is just as oriented to authority as the official, but its relationship is characterized by difference and dialogue with that authority (see especially Dias et al., 1999, in which they discuss the cultural imperatives, epistemologies, and values that are embedded in genres; cf. Bazerman, 1994, p. 82; Miller, 1984). Table 2 lays out some of the differences between official and unofficial genres.

Table 2. Contrasting official and unofficial genres

Official	Unofficial	Source
Monologic (one logic or voice)	Dialogic (Many logics or voices)	Bakhtin, 1981
Authoritative (cultural imperative)	Internally persuasive (private intentions)	Dias et al., 1999
Regulated	Regularized	Schryer & Spoel, 2005; Schryer, Lindgard & Spafford, 2007
Stability/Regularity	Change/Flexibility	Berkenkotter & Huckin, 1995; Devitt, 1991; Spinuzzi, 2003; Starke-Meyerring, 2010
Explicit	Tacit	Schryer & Spoel, 2005

As the above suggests, this official/unofficial continuum is oriented toward voice. Below, I discuss how the continuum relates to black-boxing.

BLACK-BOXING: VOICE

As a genre develops, it tends to become more official, incorporating more regulated moves that instantiate the assumptions of the activity. The many unofficial voices are black-boxed (Latour, 1987) into a single official, authoritative voice.

For example, Bazerman shows that in its long development, the genre of the experimental article became more regulated, instantiating the developing assumptions of the scientific community (Bazerman, 1988). Yates similarly demonstrates that the business memo became more regulated over time in response to assumptions about its purpose and storage (Yates, 1989). And in the examples at the beginning of this chapter, Semoptco's action items and "report cards" similarly became regulated, drawing on and yielding specific types of information tailored to specific activities, while omitting others. Sometimes this regulation occurs through genre conventions and oversight, as in Semoptco's action items and the experimental article; sometimes it occurs through restricted format, as in forms (see Yates for examples); and sometimes it occurs through automation (as in the "report cards").

These increasingly regulated moves ensure that authoritative assumptions are built into the genres that they regulate. That is, *official genres black-box voices/ dialogue*. The discussions, disagreements, logics, worldviews, and assumptions that are present in dialogue become "flattened" in official genres.

Dynamic

Of course, heavily regulated genres lose a considerable degree of flexibility. When genres in a given activity become more heavily regulated, people in the activity tend to develop unofficial, less regularized genres to reinject flexibility. For instance, in a previous study (2003), I described how conflicting official genres with different logics caused systemic disruptions. Individuals developed idiosyncratic genres to reinject flexibility into the system. Similarly, Luis' comparison table was an idiosyncratic response that helped him to address the particular needs of a particular client. Genres decay (Dias et al., 1999, p. 23); they change in response to "their users' sociocognitive needs" (Berkenkotter & Huckin, 1995, p. 4).

We can think of this dynamic in terms of *agency*. As unofficial genres become more widely used, they become more regularized, and eventually tend to be absorbed into official genres; the tacit expectations and moves become explicit. In the process, the unofficial genres, which were idiosyncratic and represented individuals' tools, become more generalized and more broadly applicable, more representative of the voice of the organization.

But the more regulated official genres are, they more inflexible they tend to become. To address unique, infrequent, or contradictory situations, people in the activity tend to supplement these official genres with new unofficial genres. See Figure 1.

As intimated earlier, however, the official/unofficial distinction is a fairly limited way to characterize genres and genre development. That's especially true as digital texts yield a broader range and broader circulation of genres.

Recall Table 1. We can see that the left column represents genres that involve considerable operational discretion during execution. The right column doesn't: in fact, both examples are automated functions, with really no operational discretion after the setup! Different parameters and different data yield different texts—e.g., each month the contents of the "report card" will change—but unless someone reformulates it, the database query that yields the "report card" will not change. Given predictable inputs, it will yield predictable outputs.

Such automated genres have been around for a while, of course (Mirel, 1996), but have become far more prevalent recently due to various factors. These factors include the spread of digital tools and the digitization of texts (Andersen, 2008; Clark, 2007, 2008; Hart-Davidson et al., 2008); the rise of knowledge work, which mainly takes information as its work object (Spinuzzi, 2007); and end user programming, in which "non-programmers" learn the basics of automation (think in terms of spreadsheet functions, social networking filters, and customized searches; see Nardi, 1993). To properly account for them, we must examine another distinction of genre development.

OPERATIONAL CHOICE: THE DISTINCTION BETWEEN GENERIC AND SELF-PROGRAMMABLE LABOR

To account for the role of automation in genre development and its impact on operational discretion, I turn to sociologist Manuel Castells' distinction between generic and self-programmable labor. Castells is in some quarters a controversial figure, but his generic/self-programmable labor distinction shows potential in terms of more fully accounting for developments—particularly developments at which I have hinted in Table 1. In fact, this distinction leads us to recategorize those genres as shown in Table 3.(Again, this distinction is binary for the purposes of the discussion. In practice, distinctions become much more vexed.)

I see this discussion as speaking to an aspect of genre that has sometimes been lumped in with the official/unofficial distinction (Spinuzzi, 2003) or addressed in other ways (Dias et al., 1999; Freedman & Smart, 1997).

Definition and Characteristics

Castells describes the distinction between generic and self-programmable labor in various works, but summarizes it well in *Communication Power:*

> *Self-programmable labor* has the autonomous capacity to focus on the goal assigned to it in the process of production, find the relevant information, recombine it into knowledge, using the available knowledge stock, and apply it in the form of tasks oriented toward the goals of the process. The more our information systems are complex, and interactively connected

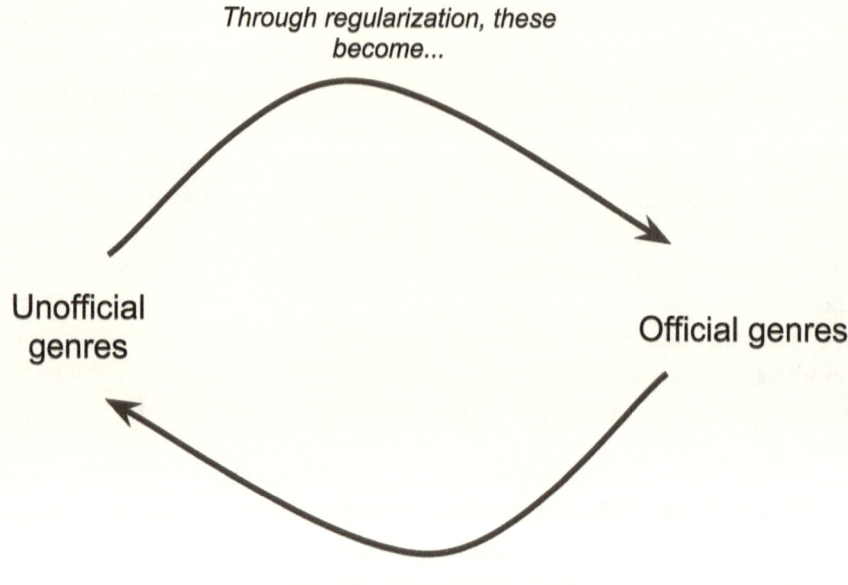

Figure 1. The dynamic between official and unofficial genres.

to databases and information sources via computer networks, the more what is required from labor is the capacity to search and recombine information. This demands appropriate education and training, not in terms of skills, but in terms of creative capacity, as well as in terms of the ability to co-evolve with changes in organization, in technology, and in knowledge. By contrast, tasks that are little valued, yet necessary, are assigned to *generic labor*, eventually replaced by machines, or shifted to lower-cost production sites, depending on a dynamic, cost-benefit analysis (Castells, 2009, p. 30).

The distinction is not necessarily[1] in terms of automation: generic labor can include any labor that involves predictably transforming defined inputs into defined outputs (Castells, 1998, p. 361). "Generic labor is assigned a given task, with no reprogramming capability, and it does not presuppose the embodiment of information and knowledge beyond the ability to receive and execute signals" (Castells, 1998, p. 361). Such tasks can easily be automated—or outsourced (just as some SEO specialists had given the task of social bookmarking to their interns). As Castells argues elsewhere,

> Generic labor is embodied in workers who do not have special skills, or special ability to acquire skills in the production process, other than those necessary to execute instructions from management. Generic labor can be replaced with machines, or by generic labor anywhere else in the world, and the precise mix between machines, on-site labor, and distant labor depends on *ad hoc* business calculation. (Castells, 2003, p. 94)

Castells emphatically doesn't endorse the rise of generic labor, and he believes that much labor that is treated as generic, such as the work of security guards, is really self-programmable, involving considerable discretion and autonomy (2003, p. 94; cf. Blomberg, Suchman & Trigg, 1994). However, he argues that understanding the split between generic and self-programmable labor is critical for understanding how work is done and value is created in the knowledge society. See Table 4.

As the table suggests, the distinction between generic and self-programmable labor is about operational discretion, i.e., discretion over the execution of

Table 3. Generic and self-programmable genres

Self-programmable (high operational discretion)	Generic (low operational discretion)
Competitors table	Social bookmarks
Action Items in Semoptco's monthly reports	"Report cards"

Table 4. Contrasting generic and self-programmable labor

Generic	Self-Programmable	Source
Low-skilled	Multiskilled	Castells, 1998, p. 361
Automated or low cost	Specialists	Castells, 2003, p. 94
Focus on tasks; receive and execute signals	Focus on goal; generate own tasks to achieve; autonomous	Castells, 2006, p. 10
Routine, repetitive tasks	Problem-solving, creating knowledge	Castells, 1996, p. 242
Predictably transform inputs to outputs (low discretion)	Coevolve (high discretion)	Castells, 1998, p. 361, 2003, pp. 90-91, 2009, p. 30
Formalizable (explicit)	Unformalizable (tacit)	Castells, 1996, p. 242
Low value	High value	Castells, 1996, p. 243
Terminal learning	Lifelong learning	Castells, 1998, p. 361, 2003, pp. 90-91

processes. To gloss, self-programmable labor involves a high level of operational discretion in order to solve problems. Generic labor involves a low level of operational discretion; in generic labor, the problems have been solved and routinized, leaving only the execution. Self-programmable labor involves responding to contingencies; generic labor doesn't.

The distinction is not the same as the official/unofficial distinction, but it shares one characteristic: the distinction between explicit and tacit. Self-programmable labor involves the operationally tacit, as self-programmable laborers work in contingency-laden environments to solve problems. Once problems are solved, they can make the problem-solving explicit in routines that involve defined inputs, outputs, and processes.

For instance, look at the top right corner of Table 3. At Semoptco, SEO specialists chose their own tools to automate the bookmarking that they had to do repeatedly. These tools were not shared or mandated, they were selected personally and idiosyncratically, but they still represented automated solutions—solutions that the SEO specialists had chosen to execute through automated processes. That is, they were authorally tacit, but operationally explicit.

Self-programmable labor involves generating a customized solution to a problem; generic labor involves using a formalized solution that was once generated and made repeatable. This distinction sheds some light on genre development in knowledge work environments.

BLACK-BOXING: CHOICE

Generic labor black-boxes discretion, processes, decisions, and judgments, formalizing and flattening them. Once someone solves a problem and formalizes it, that formalization can be made generic; the tacit operations become explicit instructions, either programmed or set out for generic laborers. It becomes a routine, one that takes defined inputs and generates defined outputs. Procedures and decisions are *programmed* into the genre (or to put it another way, artifacts crystallize intentions (Bødker, 1991; cf. Hutchins, 1995; Latour 1999).

That's not to say that even generic labor is completely inflexible. Jobs that are taken as generic have tacit, self-programmable aspects (Blomberg, Suchman, & Trigg, 1994); programmed texts have bugs and undefined cases (Adler, 2007; Suchman, 1987).

DYNAMIC

In the generic/self-programmable distinction, we see another dynamic: continual black-boxing as problems are solved and formalized, forming the base for further problem-solving. This dynamic has arguably accelerated with the spread of automation.

For instance, in one study (Spinuzzi, 2003), I demonstrated that the Iowa DOT and related organizations began gathering traffic accident data by hand well before 1974, compiling them into basic descriptive statistics bound into annual reports. But once the Iowa DOT automated accident queries in 1974, more sophisticated queries became possible, and users began to submit more detailed, complex queries. This demand drove the Iowa DOT to develop further automated tools and to generate hybrid genres that crossed traditional genres with interface elements. My more recent study of Semoptco (2010) shows similar, but more rapid, automation (and genre) changes in the world of search engine optimization. In this dynamic, self-programmable labor becomes generic labor, which in turn becomes a base on which to layer more self-programmable labor. See Figure 2.

The dynamic is different from that of the official/unofficial distinction in Figure 1. That authorial dynamic was characterized by black-boxing authorial voice—making genres more regulated—and then reintroducing flexibility via additional, unofficial texts. But the dynamic in Figure 2 involves formalizing processes to make them solid enough to build other processes on top of them. Processes become explicit, stepwise, and predictable operations.

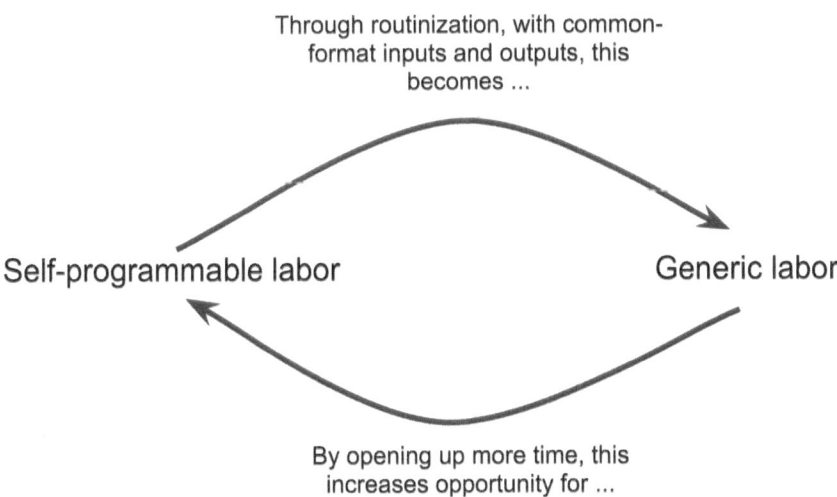

Figure 2. The dynamic between generic and self-programmable labor.

APPLYING THE TWO DISTINCTIONS: TOWARD A RICHER MODEL OF GENRE DEVELOPMENT

The two distinctions here can deepen and enrich each other. Here, let's apply to the example from the beginning.

Table 5. Two dimensions of genre analysis

	Self-programmable	Generic
Unofficial (regularized)	Competitors table	Social bookmarks
Official (regulated)	Action Items in Semoptco's monthly reports	"Report cards"

Here, we begin to see how the two distinctions might interact. Informating (Zuboff, 1988) involves not just applying knowledge, but also finding ways to offload the repetitive labor involved (cf. Nardi, 1993).

Using both distinctions, it could be possible to examine dynamics/ecology development in genre assemblages. And here, I'll stop apologizing for the binary distinctions I've been making. One could map these in Sullivan and Porter's (1997) postmodern mapping. But let's not. Instead, let's trace genre development in both distinctions simultaneously, observing their transits across the quadrants (Table 6).

Table 6. Genre development across quadrants

	Self-programmable	Generic
Unofficial (regularized)	Competitors table ↓	Social bookmarks ↓
Official (regulated)	Action Items in Semoptco's monthly reports	"Report cards"

As my initial descriptions of these genres suggested, some of the genres are undergoing development (signified by the arrows). That development tends to pull toward the bottom right quadrant, toward generic, official solutions.

For instance, Luis' comparison table was an idiosyncratic solution, but in this contingent, rapidly changing environment, idiosyncratic solutions become part of the archive of reports that SEO specialists use as templates for subsequent reports. If the table is successful, it becomes more stabilized and official, just as previous report elements had begun as innovations but quickly became part of the template.

Similarly, as Carl mentioned, Semoptco had seen how successful social bookmarking tools were, and its developers were working on a single official tool to replace the ones that specialists had selected ad hoc. This trend echoed the developers' previous work, which had automated the collection of most SEO statistics and the "report card." My second interview with Stan, the director of product services, confirmed a year later that Semoptco had continued to develop and seek automated tools to replace the ad hoc tools that SEO specialists had adopted.

In both cases, the trend is toward stabilizing existing genres along both dimensions: toward more official (regulated) forms and toward more automated generation. More unofficial and self-programmable genres become incorporated into official, generic genres, making them easier and faster to generate because participants need to exert less effort and engage in less decision-making. In turn, specialists use the time that has been freed up via regulation and automation to scout and develop additional self-programmable and official genres, genres that allow the participants to quickly react to new contingencies.

Table 6 suggests directions in which these genres might develop; a longitudinal study might produce a series of such tables, showing where genres emerge and how they are stabilized across the quadrants.

IMPLICATIONS

WAGR has focused on the development of genres, but has had trouble distinguishing authorial discretion from operational discretion. The latter distinction is increasingly important as we examine how people work automation (in a more informated, automated world) and outsourcing (in a more interlinked, more specialized world) into their activities.

Clearly, these are not the only two distinctions along which we can examine genre development. Yet these two distinctions seem particularly relevant as we examine professional writing in increasingly automated environments. Further longitudinal studies might illuminate their relationship more clearly.

ACKNOWLEDGEMENTS

My thanks to Dave Clark for his critical comments on a previous draft, which helped me to think through and clarify the distinction between authorial and operational discretion. Thanks also to the editors of this volume for their perceptive comments and suggestions.

NOTE

1. One might even object that in the above quote, Castells seems to draw a distinction between generic labor and automation. Castells is not terribly clear on the question. Here, I treat automation as a case of generic labor since it seems to fit the characteristics in Table 4.

REFERENCES

Adler, P. S. (2007). Beyond hacker idiocy: The changing nature of software community and identity. In C. Heckscher & P. S. Adler (Eds.), *The firm as a collaborative community: Reconstructing trust in the knowledge economy* (pp. 198-258). New York: Oxford University Press.

Andersen, R. (2008). The rhetoric of Enterprise Content Management (ECM): Confronting the assumptions driving ECM adoption and transforming technical communication. *Technical Communication Quarterly, 17,* 61-87.

Bakhtin, M. M. (1981). *The dialogic imagination: Four essays.* Austin, TX: University of Texas Press.

Bazerman, C. (1988). *Shaping written knowledge: The genre and activity of the experimental article in science.* Madison, WI: University of Wisconsin Press.

Bazerman, C. (1994). *Constructing experience.* Carbondale, IL: Southern Illinois University Press.

Berkenkotter, C., & Huckin, T. N. (1995). *Genre knowledge in disciplinary communication: Cognition/culture/power.* Hillsdale, NJ: Lawrence Erlbaum.

Blomberg, J., Suchman, L., & Trigg, R. (1994). Reflections on a work-oriented design project. In R. Trigg, S. I. Anderson, & E. Dykstra-Erickson (Eds.), *PDC '94: Participatory Design Conference* (pp. 99-109). Palo Alto, CA: Computer Professionals for Social Responsibility.

Bødker, S. (1991). *Through the interface: A human activity approach to user interface design*. Hillsdale, NJ: L. Erlbaum.
Castells, M. (1996). *The rise of the network society*. Malden, MA: Blackwell.
Castells, M. (1998). *End of millennium*. Malden, MA: Blackwell.
Castells, M. (2003). *The Internet galaxy: Reflections on the Internet, business, and society*. New York: Oxford University Press.
Castells, M. (2006). The network society: From knowledge to policy. In G. Cardoso & M. Castells (Eds.), *The network society: From knowledge to policy* (pp. 3-21). Baltimore, MD: Johns Hopkins University Press; Center for Transatlantic Relations, Jhu-Sais.
Castells, M. (2009). *Communication power*. New York: Oxford University Press.
Clark, D. (2007). Content management and the production of genres. In D. Novick & C. Spinuzzi (Eds.), *SIGDOC '07: Proceedings of the 25th annual ACM international conference on design of communication* (pp. 9-13). New York: ACM Press.
Clark, D. (2008). Content management and the separation of presentation and content. *Technical Communication Quarterly, 17*(1), 35-60.
Coney, M. B., & Chatfield, C. S. (1996). Rethinking the author-reader relationship in computer documentation. *Journal of Computer Documentation, 20*(2), 23-29.
Devitt, A. J. (1991). Intertextuality in tax accounting: Generic, referential, and functional. In C. Bazerman & J. Paradis (Eds.), *Textual dynamics of the professions: Historical and contemporary studies of writing in professional communities* (pp. 336-357). Madison, WI: University of Wisconsin Press.
Dias, P., Freedman, A., Medway, P., & Paré, A. (1999). *Worlds apart: Acting and writing in academic and workplace contexts*. Mahwah, NJ: Lawrence Erlbaum.
Freedman, A., & Smart, G. (1997). Navigating the current of economic policy: Written genres and the distribution of cognitive work at a financial institution. *Mind, Culture, and Activity, 4*(4), 238-255.
Gygi, K., & Zachry, M. (2010). Productive tensions and the regulatory work of genres in the development of an engineering communication workshop in a transnational corporation. *Journal of Business and Technical Communication, 24*(3), 358-381.
Hart-Davidson, W., Bernhardt, G., McLeod, M., Rife, M., & Grabill, J. (2008). Coming to content management: Inventing infrastructure for organizational knowledge work. *Technical Communication Quarterly, 17*(1), 10-34.
Hutchins, E. (1995). *Cognition in the wild*. Cambridge, MA: MIT Press.
Latour, B. (1987). *Science in action: How to follow scientists and engineers through society*. Philadelphia: Open University Press.

Latour, B. (1999). *Pandora's hope: Essays on the reality of science studies.* Cambridge, MA: Harvard University Press.

Miller, C. R. (1984). Genre as social action. *Quarterly Journal of Speech, 70*(2), 151-167.

Mirel, B. (1996). Writing and database technology: Extending the definition of writing in the workplace. In P. Sullivan & J. Dautermann (Eds.), *Electronic literacies in the workplace: Technologies of writing* (pp. 91-112). Urbana, IL: National Council of Teachers of English.

Nardi, B. A. (1993). *A small matter of programming: Perspectives on end user computing.* Cambridge, MA: MIT Press.

Russell, D. R. (2009). Uses of activity theory in written communication research. In A. Sannino, H. Daniels, & K. D. Gutierrez (Eds.), *Learning and expanding with activity theory* (pp. 40-52). New York: Cambridge University Press.

Schryer, C. F., Lingard, L., & Spafford, M. (2007). Regularized practices: Genres, improvisation, and identity formation in health-care professions. In M. Zachry & C. Thralls (Eds.), *Communicative practices in workplaces and the professions: Cultural perspectives on the regulation of discourse and organizations* (pp. 21-44). Farmingdale, New York: Baywood.

Schryer, C. F., & Spoel, P. (2005). Genre theory, health-care discourse, and professional identity formation. *Journal of Business and Technical Communication, 19*(3), 249-278.

Spinuzzi, C. (2003). *Tracing genres through organizations: A sociocultural approach to information design.* Cambridge, MA: MIT Press.

Spinuzzi, C. (2004). Four ways to investigate assemblages of texts: Genre sets, systems, repertoires, and ecologies. *SIGDOC '04: Proceedings of the 22nd annual international conference on design of communication* (pp. 110-116). New York: ACM Press.

Spinuzzi, C. (2007). Guest editor's introduction: Technical communication in the age of distributed work. *Technical Communication Quarterly, 16*(3), 265-277.

Spinuzzi, C. (2010). Secret sauce and snake oil: Writing monthly reports in a highly contingent environment. *Written Communication, 27*(4), 363-409.

Starke-Meyerring, D. (2010). Between peer review and peer production: Genres, wikis, and the politics of digital code in academe. In C. Bazerman, R. Krut, K. Lunsford, S. McLeod, S. Null, P. Rogers, et al. (Eds.), *Traditions of writing research* (pp. 339-350). New York: Routledge.

Suchman, L. A. (1987). *Plans and situated actions: The problem of human-machine communication.* New York: Cambridge University Press.

Sullivan, P., & Porter, J. E. (1997). *Opening spaces: Writing technologies and critical research practices.* Greenwich, CT: Ablex.

Swarts, J. (2009). Recycled writing: Assembling actor networks from reusable content. *Journal of Business and Technical Communication, 24*(2), 127-163.

Teston, C. B. (2009). A grounded investigation of genred guidelines in cancer care deliberations. *Written Communication, 26*(3), 320-348.

Winsor, D. A. (2007). Using texts to manage continuity and change in an activity system. In M. Zachry & C. Thralls (Eds.), *Communicative practices in workplaces and the professions* (pp. 3-20). Amityville, NY: Baywood.

Yates, J. (1989). *Control through communication: The rise of system in American management.* Baltimore, MD: Johns Hopkins University Press.

Zuboff, S. (1988). *In the age of the smart machine: The future of work and power.* New York: Basic Books.

CHAPTER 28.
CONSTRUCTION OF CARING IDENTITIES IN THE NEW WORK ORDER

Zoe Nikolaidou and Anna-Malin Karlsson
Södertörn University

In the last ten years, the elder care sector in Sweden has undergone significant changes. Following a general pattern in the market, nursing and retirement homes have changed from being administered by local authorities to becoming private institutions. In private care facilities, the elderly and their relatives have become customers selecting a care provider from a large number of competitors. As a result, elder care has become a marketable product and new practices have been introduced to assist this transformation.

Documentation has emerged as a useful tool for ensuring the quality of services and is given a dominant role within care facilities. In line with the social welfare law (SoL) in Sweden, caregivers and assistant nurses document the elders' lives, focusing on the social aspects of their lives. The digitalization of documentation has raised concerns about issues of computer literacy, staff education and allocation of time. Whether documenting electronically or on paper, documentation is often experienced as external and imposed. According to a report from the Stockholm Gerontology Research Center, documentation is considered time-consuming and unrelated to the practice and ideals of caring (Norrman & Hedberg, 2010, p. 44).

We understand these practices as a result of socio-economic changes, new technologies, and new workplace ideologies, which form part of the "new work order." In this article we examine, first, how new institutional documentation practices influence the care-workers' identity construction and, second, how the care-workers negotiate these new practices. Relevant for this study is the new role given to workers as individuals with great responsibility at work and the dominant role of texts. Extended workplace documentation and its impact on workers' social practices and identities has been an ongoing issue in a number of workplace ethnographies (e.g. Iedema & Scheeres, 2003; Karlsson, 2009; Searle, 2002). A number of these ethnographies are concerned with literacy practices within medical care (Alexander, 2000) and elder care (Cuban, 2009; Wyse & Casarotto, 2004). Such studies have shown that documentation demands have partly resulted in genres such as checklists. However, the directive from the social welfare law to document "actual circumstances and meaningful events" calls for additional genres, where a less patterned kind of writing is required. In this article, we focus on one such genre: the resident's journal. By discussing the care-workers' attitudes to the content and language of the journal, we show how the different kinds of knowledge and work-identities are handled and formed in connection with documentation practices.

The project participants[1] are caregivers and assistant nurses in a retirement home and a nursing home. The retirement home is run by the local authorities and is organised in two large wards. In total, it hosts 94 apartments, with staff offices on the ground floor. The care-workers visit each resident daily, providing care according to the resident's care-plan. The nursing home is a privately owned institution with a total of 96 rooms divided into ten smaller wards. In each ward, there are seven to nine residents and approximately seven staff members working in shifts. Most care-workers work in the same ward and with the same residents for many years.

In this ethnographic study of the care-workers' literacy practices, data collection methods include participant observation and individual and group interviews. The research participants were chosen randomly, based on their availability and interest in the project. Out of the total 24 research participants, 20 were born outside of Sweden and Swedish is their second or third language. This selection is representative of the working population in Swedish nursing homes. Similarly, the majority of the participants were women, with only two men participating in the study. The gender distribution of the population reflects older views of the care profession as a traditionally female one and a development from earlier phases when women were doing similar unpaid work at home (Törnquist, 2004). All care-workers started working as caregivers, a work role that until recently demanded no special training. Some of them later registered in vocational courses and advanced to assistant nurse, a more demanding role that calls for specialized knowledge. However, in both research sites, caregivers and assistant nurses shared the same work roles and tasks.

THE INDIVIDUAL, THE PROFESSIONAL AND THE INSTITUTIONAL

Research has shown that the care-workers' professional knowledge can be divided into education-based knowledge and experience-based competence (Törnquist, 2004). A significant part of the skills within care-work are associated with what might be called everyday knowledge. This could also be the reason why care-work has historically not been sufficiently valued as a profession (Törnquist, 2004, pp. 14-15). Experienced-based knowledge within care-work is, to a large extent, not verbally expressed. For example, in home care the care-workers work in solitude and have built up their knowledge without communicating it to someone else (Törnquist, 2004, p. 41). In the past, research on nurses' work knowledge tended to use terms such as "tacit knowledge" or "language absence," implying that a distinct, precise and scientifically-based register does not exist within the field (e.g., Josefsson, 1991, pp. 34-37). Today, being a nurse is an academic profession and nursing is an established scientific field. We believe, though, that the difficulties with creating and establishing a scientific language have moved downwards in the hierarchy and are now relevant to the work performed by care-workers. We choose not to talk about "language absence" in absolute terms. Instead, we suggest that care-work consists of various kinds of knowledge, discourses, and identities. Törnquist (2004) makes a distinction between three aspects of care-workers' professional competence: the first is related to formal education, the second to professional skills and the third to individual competence. The three aspects represent different reference frameworks of knowledge, the most obvious being the one related to formal education. Professional skills are defined as the skills and knowledge considered necessary by the care-workers in order to accomplish their tasks (Törnquist, 2004, p. 208). Individual competence refers to the care-workers' character and personal experiences (Törnquist, 2004, pp. 211–212). These categories can be compared to the institutional, professional and personal discourses, which are identified based on interactional grounds by Roberts and Sarangi (1999, 2003).

THEORY, METHOD AND CENTRAL CONCEPTS

The project's theoretical and methodological framework originates from the field of New Literacy Studies (Barton, 2007; Gee, 1996; Street, 1993), where reading and writing is considered as situated in specific contexts: in events and in practices. As a result, the focus is not placed upon individual competence, but on the frameworks, norms, roles and traditions of a literacy practice. The most important analytical tool when analyzing data from observations is the literacy event (Barton, 2007; Heath, 1983). Literacy events instantiate cultural conventions associated with the use of reading and writing or they instantiate literacy practices. These practices should be understood as abstract patterns that also include norms and evaluations.

The situated nature of literacy practices associates them with identity construction. This is particularly true when looking at identity as situated and manifested in our interaction with other people and social practices (Gee, 2001). In this chapter, parallel to institutional, professional and personal discourses, we are going to talk about institutional, professional and individual work-identities. The institutional identity is the one we adopt through our position in an institution. It can also be manifested discursively, for example, when expressing oneself according to institutional rules. A professional identity is constructed together with colleagues in the same workgroup. This identity can also be manifested discursively, through referencing the group's norms and routines. The professional identity is, to a larger extent than the institutional identity, based on belonging and participation in a common practice. Finally, the individual identity is based upon personal experience, for example, on the manifestation of one's individual qualities.

There is reason to believe that there is a differentiation between the institutional, the professional, and the individual identities of care-workers. The difference between the two latter is more obscure, since a part of the care-worker's professional skills are based on individual experience. When analyzing the employees' texts and interviews, we take into consideration the extent to which they refer to the group or to colleagues, as well as to their personal experiences and life outside the workplace. We consider those occasions when the individual and the professional are merged as an interesting result of our analysis.

THE PROBLEMATIC JOURNAL

The resident journal is indeed one of the most problematic texts in the elder care facilities. The employees are asked to free-write about significant events in the resident's life (though not on a daily basis). The care-workers do not often have a clear understanding of who will read these journals. Some of them believe that the journals are read only by staff, while others, like the employee in the following interview extract,[2] believe that the resident's relatives, the supervisor, and the nurses can also read the journal:

> Z: But it's just your colleagues that read it, right?
>
> Employee: No, the supervisor can read this, the relatives and then the nurse, they can read it, so it's not just my colleagues, a lot of people are involved.

We will examine here how the journal as a genre offers possibilities for identity construction. The focus will be on the way the employees navigate between institutional, professional and individual discourses. We discuss the care-workers' understanding of what should be written in the journal, and then continue to examine different ways of writing.

DECIDING ON WHAT SHOULD BE DOCUMENTED

A first step in documentation is to distinguish between what is relevant and useful to be included in the journal. In a group interview, the care-workers discussed what it means to document only significant incidents. They argued that "significant" refers to events that deviate from the norm. This means that when reading the following entry, "She ate lunch with everyone else in the kitchen … she was in a good mood today," the reader would assume that the resident usually eats food in her room and that she is often not in a good mood. For the same reason, the employees agree that they should not include in their writing routine events, such as showering—but they should write if someone refuses to have a shower. At the same time, they believe that there is value in writing down positive experiences, for example when a resident plays bingo. As one of the participants said: "it is about quality in their lives …, it's not just eating, sitting, they also do activities."

The decision of what information to include in the journal is an overarching dilemma. Resistance to documenting the routine events can be connected to an institutional discourse where the focus lies on communicating information effectively and avoiding documenting unnecessary data. At the same time, the care-workers express a wish to document activities related to the quality of the residents' lives. This can be connected to a more individual discourse, but it can also be interpreted as a part of the employees' professional conduct.

In the group interview, it was stated that care-workers are not responsible for writing down medical information. The sentence "coughs a lot and sounds wheezy," found in a resident's journal, is considered by an interviewee to be an acceptable comment, since it deals with what the care-workers can see and hear and is not a medical interpretation. Interestingly, some care-workers do include medical details in their journal entries. We interpret this as the result of a new or extended professional identity construction, mainly from the assistant nurses, who possess medical knowledge and find it unprofessional to omit writing significant medical observations.

Not making interpretations is in line with a restrictive stance that is often expressed by the care-workers. They talk about "not writing what one thinks" and "not painting a picture" of what they can only guess. An example discussed in the group interview was a resident who had a fight with his son. The participants agreed that such events should not be included in documentation. "I know nothing about their situation," says one of the care-workers. Any problems between the residents and their families lie outside of the care-workers' responsibilities and any concerns should be discussed with the nurse.

In the above examples, the care-workers assume an institutional identity. They place themselves in a hierarchical position where they have limited responsibilities and authority. When in doubt, it is better not to write at all. In the interviews, this is explicitly mentioned as a problem more than once. One of the assistant nurses says: "Honestly, it is stupid not to be able to write what has really happened."

What should be included in documentation is also connected to a division of functions between oral and written form. Information that cannot be written can be orally reported in a report meeting or in the corridor between colleagues. In the case of oral reporting, the institutional restrictions are fewer and, therefore, this type of communication is experienced as more effective. It can be argued that in the report meetings, the care-workers construct mainly their professional identity. For instance, during a report meeting, a caregiver describes an encounter with the resident's angry daughter and the negative impact of this encounter on the resident. This kind of information is not included in the resident's journal. Even though it would be useful information for all the care-workers to know, including it would violate the restrictions around written documentation.

In some instances, the care-workers choose to discursively construct their professional identity in the journal. They write entries where they relate to their colleagues and document what they consider as important information, regardless of the institutional guidelines. The following extracts are taken from journals and they include information of what, according to some participants, should not be included in official documentation:

> She fights a lot when given care.
>
> He was very disagreeable, threatening and screamed really loud.
>
> He spread poo all over the place on the bed, toilet, clothes, on the body.

This contradiction suggests that the institutional and the professional work-identities are, in a way, opposing each other. It is also clear that the individual identity is rarely manifested in written documentation. Writing about feelings and individual experiences with the residents is unthinkable. In one of our observations, a caregiver comes back from a resident and is very upset because of a racist comment. The caregiver chooses not to document the incident and does not report it in any other way. In similar cases, the employees claim that they should not be insulted by the residents' behavior, since it can be justified by their health circumstances. The employees' individual needs are repudiated in favor of their decision to maintain a professional stance, and the choice not to write, based on their professionalism, overlaps with the institutional instructions.

When the residents' feelings are in focus, the individual and the professional identity of the care-workers overlap. In the group interview, the participants discussed whether they should write down a resident's weight. One resident had privately asked the care-worker, after being weighed, not to include her weight gain on the documentation form. The care-worker followed the resident's wish, but she orally informed her colleagues and the nurse. The choice not to write is based upon her individual aspect of identity, in an effort to show solidarity with the resident. The fact that the care-worker later informed her colleagues is related partly to the professional and partly to the institutional aspect of her identity. One of the interviewees confirmed the professional aspect by saying that they need to report completion of each task so that their colleagues will not have to repeat it. The institutional aspect is expressed by reporting back to the nurse.

Different understandings of the journals' potential readers play an important role in the employees' choices of what to document. The idea that the relatives may read the journal is often a reason for restrictions in writing. One assistant nurse believes that the journals do not depict reality. She argues: "If they want us to lie, then we will lie." With "they," she refers to the institution; the employee here shows how she adjusts to the institutional demands. The word "lie" indicates what she really believes about the situation. Another care-worker says that they often choose not to document some incidents because it is difficult to abide by the institutional demands, that is, to write with "fine words."

THE CORRECT WAY OF WRITING

"Sometimes it is difficult to find fine words in order to describe a situation. We don't know what we should write." This is how a care-worker describes the problem of correct writing. In the interviews, the employees argue repeatedly that they must document with respect for the residents. Using "fine words" can be linked to the social welfare law (SoL), which clearly states that documentation should protect the individual's integrity. Respect and integrity are also emphasized during documentation training, as well as in language courses for staff in Swedish as a second language. Thus, the main problems faced when writing journal entries have to do with finding the correct language and perspective. The care-workers discuss in the interviews, as well as amongst themselves, the balance between the individual and the professional experience, between the human truth and the respectful distance:

> Employee: It is not possible to write how as stupidly as one wants. "Poo" or I don't know what, there should also be some finesse and this is the hardest part. We should write but it should not be derogatory, it should be a nice documentation.
>
> Z.: So when you say finesse do you mean which words you should use?
>
> Employee: Yes, that we cannot just write, like I said, "very angry" or those unnecessary, strange, I don't know how to say it … as I said finesse … it will not be derogatory for the resident, it is them we work for so it's difficult when it comes to language because it is important to describe events exactly as they happened.

In another interview, an assistant nurse talks about the struggle to find a professional language that is relevant to his job. He looks for this professional language in the medical world, where it is possible to use specialized vocabulary:

> Z.: I have heard from other colleagues … that you cannot use everyday words. Is that also a problem?
>
> Employee: Yes, exactly. Because each work area has its own language. I've seen how they document at the hospital. They don't need to write like a story, it should be short and concise and then comes the next person who will read it and they understand exactly what it's about. But here it's very mixed. People who have had a bit more education, others who haven't, so it can be difficult. For example, if someone wants to write "blood pressure," they can write BP and an upwards arrow and this means high blood pressure. There are people who have difficulties understanding this.

The same person discusses the issue of correct language in relation to time and effectiveness. He does not refer to the institutional frameworks, but to himself as a professional and the way he wants to see documentation develop according to the work needs. Brevity and conciseness are ideals related to collegiality and, by talking about them, the care-worker expresses the professional aspect of his identity:

> Z.: Does it take a lot of time?
>
> Employee: Sometimes. Not much time but it can be good to think that it's not just me reading this, so I should formulate it as good as I can. To try, you know, to find words that are easy to understand and then try to limit my documentation as much as possible, because if it's long then it can be boring, so you need to be short and concise.

A clear pattern here is that some assistant nurses (as opposed to the caregivers) instantiate discursively a professional identity that leans towards the medical direction. One assistant nurse continuously writes down medical details in the journal:

> I discovered that she had two plasters of 25mg matrifen on the right shoulder and one on the left side of the upper back.
>
> She is given penicillin Kåvepenin …

These assistant nurses anchor their professional skills to their formal education, both in their (discursive) practices and in the interviews. The opposite happens when a caregiver discusses her professional skills as based on her individual experience. Here, she answers a question about her previous education:

> Employee: The usual education and I had, how can I say, classes at school, on needlework, women's manual work, painting.
>
> Z.: For how long?
>
> Employee: All my life, we are a big family and we work together and we learn from each other and then pass it on to the children.
>
> Z.: So it's more experience than education?

> Employee: Yes, yes, exactly.

The same caregiver has different ideas regarding writing in a short and concise manner. She would rather write longer and more complete journal entries, but language restricts her:

> It is very important for me to write exactly as it is, not just short words, cohesive stories I can't do that, I cannot write many stories because they are very wrong. It just doesn't work.

The caregivers and the assistant nurses belong to the same staff group and have similar tasks, while at the same time they orientate towards somewhat different identities. This indicates the complex nature of care-work and shows that a professional care identity can be related to both formal education and everyday experience. In both cases the care-workers' feelings and integrity do not play a central role when the professional identity is manifested in writing. We witnessed no journal entry describing a resident's cruelty or a care-worker's degradation. This may explain why it is not allowed to include expressions like "aggressive" in social documentation, since the word describes the employee's experience and interpretation and is therefore not an objective comment.

FINAL DISCUSSION

The overarching question in this chapter has been how a traditionally practical profession, based, to a large extent, on experience-based skills, is influenced by the introduction of new work practices and by the increasing role of literacy. A question related to this is how different aspects of nursing knowledge are shaped and reshaped through the employees' writing practices. We have set out to answer these questions by studying the care-workers' everyday work and literacy practices. This has given us ground to talk about different work-identities that are related to different uses of writing.

Based on earlier research on care work (Törnquist, 2004) and on discourses in medical care (Roberts & Sarangi, 1999, 2003), we have introduced three aspects of work-identity: institutional, professional and individual. The demand to document at the workplace has promoted an institutional expression of identity. At the same time, the journal as a genre has a free form and allows for a possible inscription of other identity aspects.

The institutional aspect is dominant, mainly in relation to the individual. Writing personal reflections is not allowed, and it should be noted that there is no genre in the social documentation system where the care-workers' experiences can be included. Thus the institutional aspect appears to dominate over the professional. This leads employees to turn to oral communication when passing on collegial knowledge.

In our understanding, this inherent conflict explains many of the difficulties that the care-workers in this study experience: the social in the care sector appears to have elements of the "language absence" discussed by Josefson (1991). We argue, therefore, that it is difficult to write the social within the framework of documentation. This is tied up with institutional literacy's demand for objectivity, neutrality and (relative) context-independence. There are many possible readers and many possible interpretations. The need for writing in a "fine," respectful way is, in the worst case, restrictive. The fact that the care-workers avoid writing, or choose to "lie," points to a constraint in developing a functional professional literacy, a literacy that would actually serve to facilitate their colleagues' work.

In the new work order, even traditionally public services are exposed to competition and various types of evaluation and comparison. The minor role of the individual aspect of writing can be interpreted as an attempt to standardize the employees' language and the content of their documentation. By restricting social documentation by restricting the use of certain words and phrases and by not permitting any input of a personal nature, it is possible to ensure that all entries in the logbook are similar to each other and do not deviate from the norm. Indeed, a large number of the entries in the texts we have analyzed are repetitive and sometimes even identical. This is in contrast to the more general philosophy behind social documentation, which asks for personalized documentation.

Such standardization processes are in line with quality assurance measures, found today in the private sector, which demand documenting compliance and standard operating processes (e.g., Defoe, 2004; Jackson, 2000). The fact that the eldercare sector follows such a policy line is not a surprise, since one of the two nursing homes in our research has recently been privatized. In this facility, the future aim of social documentation is that the residents' relatives will have online access to their relatives' journals. It is possible, therefore, that the nursing home's management must make sure that all documentation entries are standardized and more importantly, that all entries testify to the elder's well-being and quality of life in the specific home, just as initially advertised. It is important, therefore, that the care-workers document efficiently, present a positive image of life in the nursing home, and place emphasis upon the resident rather than upon themselves and their own experiences.

Taking all this into consideration, one must ask whether it is possible to marry the social care ideal with the ambition to be marketable. It becomes obvious that one of the two factors needs to be sacrificed for the sake of the other. The impact that such a sacrifice has had for the development of workplace literacy practices is significant. In the past, literacy was a useful tool in the hands of care-workers; they could effectively communicate and construct a common professional identity through it. Now, however, literacy events are of an institutional nature and are often restricting the employees' work practices. Whereas workplace texts had an internal and temporary character, and were generally disregarded by institutional regulations, they are now put in the service of marketing and are therefore given a dominant role. The texts are no longer written in the intimate professional or personal discourse, but are underpinned by an imposed language of an institutional nature. The care-workers are forced to change their old practices and follow the new discourse, making sacrifices with regard to the content and the quality of the services they provide. What remains to be seen is whether the new private sector will detect the possible inefficiency of the documentation system and therefore introduce new practices, or whether the care-workers will adjust their work practices even more to meet the existing demands.

NOTES

1. The study described here is part of a larger project under the name "Care work as language work: Affordances and restrictions with Swedish as a second language in the new work order." The project is formed by two parts, one focusing upon oral interaction and the other upon written communication within the elder care sector. This chapter reports on the initial phase within the written communication study.

2. All interview extracts and examples have been translated from Swedish.

REFERENCES

Alexander, K. (2000). Writing up/writing down: Literate practices in a mental health boarding home. *Literacy and Numeracy Studies, 10*(1&2), 23-38.
Barton, D. (2007). *Literacy: An Introduction to the ecology of written language* (2nd ed.). Oxford: Blackwell.
Cuban, S. (2009). Skilled immigrant women carers in rural England and their downward mobility. *Migration letters, 6*(2), 177-184.
Defoe, T. (2004). Literacies at work in a culture of documentation. In M.-E. Belfiore, T. Defoe, S. Folinsbee, J. Huner, & N. Jackson (Eds.), *Reading work: Literacies in the new workplace* (pp. 151-190). New York: Routledge.

Gee, J. (1996). *Social linguistics and literacies: Ideology in discourses*. London: Falmer Press.

Gee, J. (2001). Identity as an analytic lens for research in education. *Review of Research in Education, 25*, 99-125.

Heath, S. B. (1983). *Ways with words*. Cambridge, UK: Cambridge University Press.

Iedema, R., & Scheeres, H. (2003). From doing work to talking work: Renegotiating knowing, doing, and identity. *Applied Linguistics, 24*(3), 316-337.

Jackson, N. (2000). Writing-up people at work: Investigations of workplace literacy. *Literacy and Numeracy Studies, 10*(1&2), 5-22.

Josefsson, I. (1991). *Kunskapens former: Det reflekterande yrkeskunnandet*. Stockholm: Carlssons.

Karlsson, A.-M. (2009). Positioned by reading and writing: Literacy practices, roles, and genres in common occupations. *Written Communication, 26*(1), 53-76.

Norrman, E., & Hedberg, R.-M. (2010). *Dokumentera eller ge vård och omsorg? Utvärdering av projektet "Social dokumentation på Kungsholmen."* Stockholm: Stiftensen Stockholms läns Äldrecentrum.

Roberts, C., & Sarangi, S. (1999). Hybridity in gatekeeping discourse: Issues of practical relevance for practitioners. In S. Sarangi & C. Roberts (Eds.), *Talk, work and institutional order* (pp. 473–503). Berlin: Mouton de Gruyter.

Roberts, C., & Sarangi, S. (2003). Uptake of discourse research in interprofessional settings: Reporting from medical consultancy. *Applied Linguistics, 24*(3), 338-359.

Searle, J. (2002). Situated literacies at work. *International Journal of Educational Research, 37*, 17-28.

Street, B. (1993). *Cross-cultural approaches to literacy*. Cambridge, UK: Cambridge University Press.

Törnquist, A. (2004). *Vad man ska kunna och hur man ska vara: En studie om enhetschefers och vårdbiträdens yrkeskompetens inom äldrevårdens olika boendeformer*. Stockholm: HLS Förlag.

Wyse, L., & Casarotto, N. (2004). Literacy in the world of the aged care worker. *Literacy and Numeracy Studies, 13*(1), 19-30.

CHAPTER 29.
ONLINE BOOK REVIEWS AND EMERGING GENERIC CONVENTIONS: A SITUATED STUDY OF AUTHORSHIP, PUBLISHING, AND PEER REVIEW

Tim Laquintano
Lafayette College

In his extensive study of the book in early modern Europe, Johns (1998) argued that print's status as a reliable and credible communication medium did not derive from an intrinsic property of the technology. Rather, it was achieved through enormously challenging work—through trial and error, material processes, dialogue, review, and debate. Enacted in local contexts, such work happened amid plural constellations of authorship, publishing, printing, and gifting. For Johns, this enabled the presumptions of accuracy and fixity that Western readers often ascribe to the book, even as these characteristics are highly contingent, happening through processes that have been largely effaced by print technologies and hidden from the reader. The current move to the digital has unsettled the arrangements that helped print achieve credibility. The transition to the digital has demanded extensive reorganization of literate activity as stakeholders work to achieve similar presumptions of reliability that were naturalized into systems of print (also see Baron, 2009).

This ethnographic study conducted in an online community of professional poker players who have self-published e-books of poker theory examines how online authors use dialogue, debate, and review processes to legitimize digital writing. I document how participants manipulated the generic features of online book reviews to help self-published books achieve credibility, and I consider how the changing publishing procedures of writing can alter the review's rhetorical function. Such book reviews are recent iterations of a genre that has helped books achieve status for more than three hundred years.

THE BOOK REVIEW AS A CHANGING GENRE

This study aims to understand how literate people are learning—or failing to learn—to use reviews to negotiate shifting (or disappearing) relationships among authors, publishers, booksellers, and readers. Whereas brick and mortar booksellers once helped mediate these relations through decisions of which books to carry and how to arrange them in the space of the bookstore (Miller, L., 2009), and through explicit recommendations (Radway, 1984), book buying can now be mediated by algorithms, user-generated book reviews, and online communities. These discursive arrangements foster common problems of reviewing, problems inflected by easy self-publication that pressures the generic features of the review, as writers and readers must negotiate varying expertise, status differentials among authors and reviewers, and complexities introduced by anonymity. Digital systems also create different opportunities for manipulation and fraud than the opportunities that existed in systems of print. A now ubiquitous and easily published genre, book reviews challenge digital readers and writers to reckon with deep social issues instigated by technological shifts in systems of literate activity.

I approach the analysis through genre studies that conceptualizes genres as texts that mediate recurring social situations and, in the process, acquire fluid and flexible yet regularized formal features, typified characteristics that help people achieve social tasks (Miller, C. R., 1984). With over 300 years of history (See Roper, 1978, for the early history of the book review), the book review has acquired a consistent pattern often talked about as a hardened genre of evaluation with predictable conventions. The longevity of the book review means that is true to an extent. Although Motta-Roth (1998) found variation in discourse patterns when she studied academic book reviews, she also found that reviews have a number of consistent rhetorical moves across diverse disciplines, even though the disciplines had significantly differing epistemologies. However, as genre theory suggests, even if a successful genre has stabilized into seemingly static features, it still exists in a dynamic social situation subject to variation and change (Bazerman, 1988, p. 63). The generic dynamics of the book review often fluctuate according to rhetorical contingencies: the nature of the book reviewed, the length of the review, the status of the reviewer and her relationship to the author, and whether a book is reviewed anonymously. In one of the only articles to address the dynamics of writing in online consumer reviews, Mackiewicz (2010) found, for example, that consumer reviewers often asserted expertise online in multiple ways to establish ethos while publishing reviews about digital cameras (see also Chevalier & Mayzlin, 2006). Because of variations in reviewing strategies and the flexibility of genres, and because generic formation and change can "reveal the forces to which textual features respond" (Bazerman, 1988, p. 62), e-book reviews can disclose how writers and readers adapt to shifting conditions of writing and the properties of digital texts, and how those adaptations are becoming regularized as nascent generic conventions.

The economy of online poker instruction offers a strategic site to investigate issues of genre and textual reliability because dynamics common to digital writing spaces deeply inflect the practices in it. The writing of amateurs and professionals bleeds together in public discussions about the texts. Writing often traverses multiple media and information technologies, and the production of texts has been widely distributed across space and time in highly collaborative environments.

THE CULTURE AND ECONOMY OF ONLINE PUBLICATION

The writers in this study author texts in a digital niche market against a background of participatory web culture. Henry Jenkins (2006) has used the term participatory culture to explain how people use web platforms to both create and consume cultural goods. Online niche markets enable users to congregate on the basis of shared and sometimes obscure interests, and they are poised to be of collective importance to digital economies (Byrnjolfsson, Hu, & Smith, 2006). In the poker niche, e-books contain rivalrous information that readers try to protect because the value of the information decreases as it spreads, many e-books are prohibitively expensive, and the advanced poker theory built on statistics and probability is of limited interest to the wider public. These dynamics give this study characteristics of a negative case compared to research of web writing that investigates participants writing in open systems and circulating their writing for free to acquire audiences (e.g., Alexander, 2006; Black, 2008). The value of this case, though, is to show how deeply the nature of information can influence the dynamics of writing and publishing in digital contexts.

While participatory culture helps frame e-book authorship, so too do the economics of digital texts. Networked computers, e-readers, and print on demand technologies drive down e-book reproduction and distribution costs, characteristics of digital texts that Porter (2009) has theorized as changes in rhetorical delivery. These technologies contribute to an ongoing reconfiguration of authorship, publishing, and reading. Bradley, Fulton, Helm, and Pittner (2011) have reported on how new distribution mechanisms have influenced the book trade: in 2010, "nontraditional" publishing happening through digital channels accounted for eight times the output of traditional publishing. Reprints of public domain material and even spam comprise much of this output, but it also includes copious amounts of original content, including self-published books that likely number in the hundreds of thousands of titles produced yearly, though as Bradley et al. note (2011), accurate estimates are impossible.

Situated amid this output, my project focuses on the work of self-publishing authors. I'm pursuing the research question of how writers learn to become authors, publishers, and booksellers without the mediation of print institutions. Elsewhere I have argued that under these conditions, the work of publishing can be distributed through online networks in diverse configurations as literate activity (Laquintano, 2010). Prior (1998) defines literate activity as dialogic processes oriented toward specific goals that are situated, mediated and dispersed across diverse spheres of social practices (pp. 25-32). To the extent afforded by my methodology, then, I aim to theorize the kinds of literate activity that support the processes of self-publishers as they produce and distribute e-books using the internet.

METHODOLOGY

This study is part of a larger one that concentrated on the production, circulation, and reception of thirteen poker e-books distributed through the internet without formal publishers (see Laquintano, 2010). As a result of the rapid global spread of poker and the sharp rise in popularity of online gambling, a class of professional and semi-professional online poker players emerged in the past decade. Looking to increase earnings, or looking for more meaning in their lives, players began instruction businesses to satisfy demand for pedagogical materials. Some began subscription-based instructional websites that functioned as mass education, while others offered individual coaching programs. Self-published poker e-books emerged from these programs, either because a coach could not satisfy demand for his time, or because he had amassed coaching materials that could be marshaled into an instructional text. Aimed at a tightly defined niche of advanced players, the e-books were often several hundred dollars, priced to reflect the coaching rates of the players and their hourly playing rates. The e-books were produced, circulated, and advertised through blogs, discussion boards, and backchannels, and these writing spaces constitute the setting of the study.

I used theoretical sampling (Strauss, 1987) to locate and conduct multiple interviews with thirty-five participants who were writers, editors, or readers of the e-books. I also studied the writing of countless others who contributed comments about the e-books in public writing spaces, which became part of the analysis. Of those I interviewed, most of the participants were males between the ages of 20 and 30, and the majority lived in the United States, although I interviewed participants from several European countries, too. I could not always determine the identity of the countless players who contributed public writing about the e-books. Some of these writers had long-established reputations on the discussion boards and public personas, and I could pinpoint their basic demographic information with reasonable certainty. However, anonymous participants contributed too, and although mostly unknowable, I analyzed their writing as well because it often mattered to the reception of the e-books.

As coaches developed their programs and began publishing their e-books, I began tracking the public writing of all of the authors and to the extent possible, their readers. I followed the work of 13 authors and their e-books and the reception of their texts for three years. I archived discussions about the books on forums and blogs, including 42 book reviews with discussions that followed. I conducted interviews, and I occasionally asked clarifying questions through instant messaging programs. Between 2007 and 2010, trustworthy self-published poker texts were quite rare, and this sample represented most reputable self-published poker e-books written in English, although the numbers of these books have grown significantly since the time of data collection.

My analysis and coding procedures have been grounded in the data (Strauss, 1987). In the larger project, I established a series of provisional categories through initial coding of interview and web data. One of the provisional categories was peer review, and as I fleshed out the concept I noticed that authors imagined book reviews as important to the public image of their work. That insight drove another round of data collection, where I archived all of the book reviews I could find and the discussion threads attached to the review. As described above, this amounted to forty-two primary book reviews and several thousand discussion comments that followed them.

I analyzed the data for indications that peer review was occurring through the assessment and valuation of different characteristics of e-books. I found three common conventional patterns that recurred in most of the reviews particular to the technological conditions and in which writers came to terms with issues of credibility and the circumstances of publication. These conventions made rhetorical moves, by which I mean a "stretch of discourse that realizes a specific communicative function and that represents a stage in the development of an overall structure of information that is commonly associated with the genre" (Motta-Roth, 1998, p. 33). As a communicative function, the three patterns enabled reviewers to: 1) situate the value of the book amid other online learning options; 2) anticipate interaction with their audience; and 3) assess the digital affordances of the e-book. I then coded all of the review data again for these three specific patterns and their characteristics. Not all of the reviews shared all of these three conventions, but they appeared in a pattern robust enough to suggest they were emerging formal features of the book review in this context. As online writing evolves, some of these conventions may yield to others, while some may become more widespread and durable. In the following section, I situate the book reviews in the larger systems of trust that I found helped establish the credibility of authors. I then delineate the three generic features that appeared as common patterns in reviews.

FINDINGS

Situated in larger systems of peer review and reputation, the reviews of poker e-books worked as spaces for interaction and functioned as nodes of attention that channeled awareness to an author's work and shaped its status. In this context, where publishing technologies have become radically distributed, reviews have helped mediate relationships among authors and their audience in the absence of formal publishers. My analysis shows that nascent generic conventions have emerged in response to these conditions, and these conventions illustrate how writers are coming to terms with credibility voids and the changing materiality of the text. Absent publisher, absent printed object, these reviews work to establish what counts as a book.

The larger infrastructure of reputation helped authors commercialize their work. Authors have acquired reputations from published results of websites that track the outcomes of the games, word of mouth, media exposure, and public writing. In a posting about the value of e-books, Mason Malmuth, owner of the industry-leading print publishing company TwoPlusTwo, summarized how the value of e-books was partially achieved through public forum contributions:

> The best way to tell if this stuff is worth the money is through peer review. And specifically what I mean by this are his strategy posts on our forums and the reaction to them by our posters, particularly those who are considered the better players (Malmuth, 2009, Re: PLO book, post 167; All web data is left in its original, unedited version.)

While public response to an author's discussion posts shaped reputation, another form of review came through underground peer-to-peer file sharing of e-books. Not easily traced through ethnographic data, and often an act that infringed on copyright, peer-to-peer file sharing surfaced in interview data as a de facto method of review, a digital equivalent of word-of-mouth recommending. The book reviews examined in this chapter, then, were a single element in a networked system that contributed to the formation of an author's reputation as a player and, importantly, as a teacher too.

The audience's response to the reviews suggested pluralism in their uptake. To potential readers, the reviews marked an attempt to assess the credibility of the book. To skeptical onlookers, reviews inflated the value of e-books they considered "snake oil." To owners of the websites where they were posted, the reviews channeled attention to their websites. My analysis concentrates mostly on earnest attempts to assess the knowledge contained in the books, but I draw some implications for this diversity of this uptake as well. The reviews consistently contained dominant features that have been established conventions of book reviews of information-rich texts. Motta-Roth (1998) identified four rhetorical moves ubiquitous in academic book reviews that included introducing the book, outlining the work, highlighting sections, and providing a closing analysis of the work (p. 49). These conventions appeared in most poker reviews, although in cases they were clearly absent, in part because some writers obligated to the authors published hastily written reviews. Perhaps the most prominent function, though, consisted of reviewers situating the e-books in relation to previously published material, as they addressed the same question used to justify the value of many print books: To what extent did the book advance new concepts, or to what extent did it present old concepts in a new or lucid manner? E-book reviews attempted to locate the book in a field of common texts, building imagined annals in which to situate a book's contribution. Reviewers made no distinction between print book and e-books; e-books were evaluated as much against each other as they were the history of print poker books that emerged in the 1970s and the 1980s.

Situating E-books in the Digital Economy of Instruction

Reviewers went beyond intertextual evaluation to situate the e-books not simply against competing books, but also among competing modes of learning online. Reviewers assessed how the time and money needed to extract value from writing compared to subscription video resources, highly interactive personal coaching, free articles, forum posts, blog posts, and printed material. This rhetorical move, then, appraised the value of the book not just for its novelty of contribution, but also relationally against various multimedia.

The move to evaluate a book against existing multimedia appears in the following discussion posted in a thread of Ed Miller, Matt Flynn, and Sunny

Mehta's e-book on small stakes poker. This reviewer criticizes the laudatory tone of previous reviews before offering his own assessment:

> I've finally finished the book and I found it to be pretty good, but I do think some of the hyperbole in this thread is a little overboard. The information in this book isn't anything new or groundbreaking, and if you are subscribing to any of the video training sites then most of this information should be familiar to you. What the book does well is driving those points home with a ton of well thought out examples. ("Spaceball," 2009, Re: review of SSNLHE, post 56)

In this estimation the value of the book does not derive from new knowledge, but rather from carefully planned examples that reinforce preexisting concepts. Although not homogenous, the video instruction to which the book is compared often tends to be more extemporaneously produced, with more loosely defined patterns of organization than the e-books. This reviewer has identified those differences, registering the book's value insofar as it organizes and illustrates existing knowledge in more extensive ways than could be found elsewhere in different media.

When reviewers measured the book's value against competing media, they recommended that potential readers consider their learning styles carefully before they bought a book, or that the book be purchased in conjunction with other modalities of learning. The assessment of a book became inseparable from the imagined learning styles of the potential buyers:

> The book is good for people that are self-learners, or are already doing well at say 2/4 or above. ... The book was good for my situation, since I could read it faster than going through his 13 lesson coaching program. It is also much cheaper. Coaching would be better for someone needing a complete overhaul and confidence boost in their game (Edirisinghe, 2008, Bobbos Book, post 48).

> Beyond just putting in time which is required of everyone to grasp the material, you should also consider how you learn. This book is very math heavy and reminds me of my engineering days (Townsend, 2010).

If you buy the book, you have to learn from it and be good at thinking on your own. ... You have to be a receptive individual who is capable of self-critique and highlighting one's strengths and weaknesses ... You should combine the book purchase with hiring a top-level coach (Newman, 2009).

These recommendations consider the relationship among book learning and the emotional state of the learners, their ability for reflection, and the time it would take for them to extract information from the materials. The reviews show some consistency in their attitude toward the function of the book when it is compared to other media; the book enables, for example, self-paced learning in solitude in ways coaching does not. But this function is always contingent upon the personal history and learning style of the reader. To extract value readers must have certain characteristics as learners: formal education, dispositions, and preferences. These contingencies frustrate the possibility of imagining the writing's general trajectory in multimodal systems of online learning: it competes with and complements other media only ever in relation to personal learning preferences and styles.

Anticipating Interaction

Like the e-books whose value they colored, book reviews were also self-published: they suffered from the same crisis of credibility as the e-books. In a click-to-publish environment, the credibility of any single review had limitations, and their status as self-published texts led potential readers and recreational onlookers to scrutinize reviews on public discussion boards. The publication of a book review thus functioned less as an end point to the evaluation of a book and more as an opening point of discussion. Two genre conventions emerged from this constellation. The first convention was a disclaimer disclosing reasons why the reviewer was not an objective evaluator. The disclaimer worked as a mechanism that facilitated productive discussion and steered the written interaction away from ad hominem attacks on the reviewer, lest s/he be accused of posting inflated reviews to increase artificially the value of the book. The following disclaimer came during an emotionally charged review thread: "DISCLAIMER: I am a personal friend of all three authors; however, I'm also fair, and a goddamn genius to boot" ("Cer0_z," 2009, "Re: review of small stakes," post 20). Taken in context, the playful comment of "Cer0_z" is a rhetorical attempt to defuse the tone of the heated review thread in which it was posted. Because third parties would usually expose personal relationships between author and reviewer, he documents his relationship to the authors before providing a positive review of the book. This disclaimer surfaces as a response to the freedom of self-publishing, and its rhetorical effect seeks to prevent the discussion thread from devolving into simplistic critiques of the reviewer's ethos. It focused discussion on the merits of the book, not the allegiances or credibility of the reviewer. Disclaimers came attached to reviews if the reviewer knew the author, if the reviewer was a student of the author, or if the reviewer received a free copy of the book in exchange for reviewing it. Although these relationships have often existed among reviewers and authors in print culture, without the ethos of a print venue endowing a review with credibility, they become a necessary point of articulation to sustain productive discussion in an emotionally charged writing environment.

When reviewers treated the review as a site of interaction, the second rhetorical move that emerged anticipated the author as an active audience member of the review. Although only a small part of establishing reputation, e-book authors understood reviews directed attention to their work, and they read reviews, monitored discussions of them, and intervened when asked to. Authors engaged in these discussion threads with rhetorical dexterity to avoid the appearance of "shilling" their own work. This constellation of activity regularized as a generic feature that anticipated interaction with the author's future literate activity. Here we see the alleged potential of the e-book's affordances—easy revision and redistribution—appear as a recurring feature in e-book reviews:

> So on an overall scale of 1 to 10 …, I would give this book an 8.8. Keep in mind that Tri gave me this book before it was completely finished, and my review may encourage him to add a section or two, at which point I would probably edit this review (Haynie, 2009).

In this section the reviewer exerts agency on the book's reception and the book's production. The reviewer writes to both reader and author, noting both the book and his review are contingent upon future literate activity he attempts to shape. This recurring relationship between reviewer, author, and revisable text created a synergy that surfaced in reviews as "wish lists" of potential improvements that ranged from global additions to local corrections, including the request for additional chapters, better editing, and layout improvement. These lists exposed weaknesses in the quality of the books, suggesting the author make revisions before distribution or in subsequent versions. Feedback helped reviewers negotiate status differentials between themselves and authors, providing space for the language of critique to be cloaked in the language of revision. In other words, suggestions for revision often softened critiques of the books, providing a qualifier that diffident reviewers used to hedge the harshness of their review. Reviewers seemingly used this convention as a social lubricant in a niche where many people knew each other and shared a sense of community.

The addition of author as audience member showed reviewers often expected—and evaluated—interaction with the author that moved beyond the point of sale. Reviewers expected authorship to bleed into private exchanges:

> I think a private forum would add tremendous value to the book, and since most people are going to have questions after reading it, many of which will be the same questions, the best way to answer them would be posting responses in one location available to everyone that bought the book ("Irishman07," 2008, Re: Bobbos book, post 257).

> I would like to add that after buying the book I have IMd Rob a few times and hes answered some of my questions, which was probably worth nearly as much as the book itself ("Squizzel," 2008, Re: Bobbos book, post 260).

In these reviews interaction that happens via literate exchange surrounds the texts and contributes to their value. This extended engagement results partly from the ease of an author interacting with his audience online, but also because of textual distribution patterns. Given the ease with which copies of their book could be shared freely among readers, writers provided incentive to potential purchasers by answering questions through private forums and "office hours." The reviewers thus reflected on an author's availability and willingness to help, a point that emerged as a consistent evaluative feature of the book reviews.

DIGITAL AFFORDANCES

When book reviewers anticipated author revisions, they were working in a larger trend to address the material characteristics and digital affordances of electronic books in book reviews. E-books represent the changing conditions of materiality of technologies of reading and writing, a condition whereby even the definition of what constitutes a book becomes socially negotiated and contingent, and writers exploit or ignore various affordances of the digital text. Reviewers thought through this fluidity and the changing form of the book, as we can see in Andrew "Foucault" Brokos's review of Tri Nguyen's book about Pot-Limit Omaha. The review at large and this passage in particular address how the quick publication of an e-book can make it responsive to current game conditions:

The text provides plenty of examples and in-depth analysis of advanced concepts like blockers, backdoor draws, and floating. It just makes me realize what a tall mountain there is to climb. Thankfully, Nguyen also emphasizes how many players in today's PLO games don't have an inkling about any of this stuff, which is reassuring. It does beg the question of the book's longevity, though. There's a mix of tactics that seem fundamental to playing the game well in any context and those designed to exploit mistakes and tendencies common in contemporary PLO games. It will be interesting to see how long the latter remain viable. Since Transitioning is an e-book, Nguyen could theoretically update it, though to my knowledge he hasn't promised anything like this (Brokos, 2010).

In this portion of the review, an assessment of poker content mingles with an assessment of the technological potential of the e-book, which produces ambivalence in the reader: on the one hand praise for the book's immediate responsiveness to the dynamics of contemporary poker trends, on the other hand questions over the permanence of the material. The book form as a medium of communication does not come under question; rather the concern derives from the temporal relationship between the expertise of the book and its relevance for future players. The expectations—and anxieties over—temporal stability has less to do with the technology itself, and more to do with how the book's legacy induces the reviewer to conceptualize the relationship between time and stability. The legacy of the book as a slow medium provokes uncertainty toward a text's value whose relevance might fade quickly.

Hesse (1996) has addressed the relationship between books and time in ways that anticipate Brokos's ambivalence. Using work on the history of the book in eighteenth-century France, Hesse argues that the book's mode of temporality enabled it to become a revered medium of communication. Perceived to be an "unhurried form of mediation" (Hesse, 1996, p. 27), the book was censored less because it less often responded to unfolding events the way incendiary— and quickly produced—political pamphlets. For Hesse, the potential change in the book's mode of temporality becomes a pivotal difference when moving from print to digital form. Hesse's modes of temporality are an elegant way of expressing the umbrella concept of Shirky's (2008) well-known formulation of new information technologies: "faster is different" (p. 161). Torn between the unhurried legacy of the book coloring his expectations for durability, and the affordance of the e-book's quick responsiveness, Brokos confronts these temporalities with both ambivalence toward the object's stability, and as an opportunity to observe the unfolding of the history of a specific book. The outcome becomes a curiosity for the reviewer, an "interesting" point of observation and an opportunity to bear witness to the consequences of technological change.

The relationship among book, time, and value extends beyond the durability of content to ruminations on rapid dissemination and the consequences to the buyer. In this example, a reviewer reflects on the book's materiality, worrying that a substantial investment will diminish through rapid dissemination:

> Before I talk about some of the details of the book, I want to talk about its "packaging." First of all, you aren't getting a hard copy, so you are essentially paying for an "e-book." I think most people knows this. Before purchasing, you are to agree to not distribute his book to anybody period. I kind of want to talk briefly about that concept. Surely, in a perfect world, all buyers are honest and won't break their agreement. But we don't live in a perfect world. People lie and do a lot of shady things. It's very easy for the book to get distributed, especially being in the digital age and there is almost no way to track who distributed. As a consumer, you SHOULD be a little worried that something you paid $750 today might be worth $0 tomorrow because anyone can obtain it from a one-click download ("SirNeb," 2008, Re: Bobbos book, post 35).

Addressing the liabilities of the e-book's affordances becomes a preliminary move to discussing the e-book's content. The perceived value hinges on a readership willing to protect it because poker strategy decreases in value as more people have it. Eschewing the notion that a book's value derives from widespread distribution, the reviewer weighs potential value as a risky investment contingent upon the possibility that readers will respect copyright. Its worth depends on limited circulation. The evidence I have collected suggests the authors' books sustained commercial viability for between six to eighteen months before they lost their monetary value, either because sales slowed, or because widespread sharing of free copies on the internet, in their original form or in unauthorized translations, diminished their value.

DISCUSSION

Book reviews help answer the question of how writers learn to produce books and become authors without the mediation of publishers. Reviews represent not only assessment of books, but also spaces for opening sustained discussion that provides back and forth interaction. This interaction acts as a surrogate for the presumed authority that marked print publications. At times unruly, the discussions channeled attention to the book and lent it partial credibility; the discussion joined backchannel recommendations and file sharing as ad hoc measures readers took to assess the text's value. Writers participating in the discussions participated in processes of sustained authorship: the immediate relationship among authors and readers fostered exchange that produced effects similar to those of formal print publishers: publicity, credibility, and peer review.

Johns (1998) identified processes that worked to establish the legitimacy of print work; and the processes that work to establish the credibility of digital text are similar insofar as they are situated and localized processes of debate and negotiation. The processes I have detailed in this section represent a deeply contextual instance where the characteristics of the book and the interaction that surrounded them surfaced as genre conventions. They provide evidence of how the destandardization of traditional publishing procedures occurring via digital environments enables the nature of information found in texts to exert intense pressure on writing practices. Although it's possible these conventions will not surface in other contexts—and indeed they might collapse with the poker economy—documenting them provides evidence of the measures participants will take to exploit properties of new writing technologies in the service of achieving value for their work. As I will note in the following section that draws implications from the study, though, the greatest value of the findings for genre studies may be that I derived many of them from publicly available data: digital technologies leave traces of the processes writers use to legitimize them, traces that were not as accessible in print culture.

IMPLICATIONS FOR GENRE STUDIES IN DIGITAL ENVIRONMENTS: TRACES OF UPTAKE

Reflecting on the methodological challenges of reconstructing the contingencies on which the perceived stability of print rests, Johns (1998) notes processes of print cultures were often dedicated to their own effacement, a necessary erasure in order for the book to be seen as an inherently reliable, stand-alone technology. In a similar matter, Bazerman (2004) highlights how the challenges of reconstructing generic uptake limit our understanding of the concept. Bazerman suggests this challenge has partly prevented writing scholars from moving beyond an understanding of genre that too often focuses on uptake by "naturalized" users of it. In other words, only understanding genre from the perspective of the intended audience can limit our understanding of generic reception. In the age of print, different readers could understand genres in different ways, and that understanding was often hidden from the view of researchers in invisible acts of reading separated from the writer in space and time. For Bazerman this presents an obstacle to more "carefully researched, observed, and analyzed knowledge" in writing research (p. 321).

With these limitations in mind, I want to suggest that because contemporary writing technologies begin to help reconfigure boundaries of space and time that underpinned Bazerman's print-based assumptions of generic study, and because contemporary writing technologies offer readers unprecedented access to respond to reading through public writing, the data inscribed on digital writing spaces can contribute to a multifaceted and plural understanding of generic uptake. To the serendipity of scholars studying contemporary writing and knowledge production, the social processes through which web writing achieves credibility are often rendered visible through archival processes inscribed on the very writing technologies that enable participation (e.g., revision histories on wikis and comment sections on blogs). Online writing technologies register uptake, not in a holistic manner, but through trace data left on social reading and writing technologies as writers respond to each other and the genre systems in which they write; this affordance enables us to observe some of the difficult work of digital cultures in the making.

The data showed diversity of uptake when participants responded to the changing conventions of book reviews. As I have suggested, only some participants read book reviews as an attempt at publicly peer reviewing knowledge. While poker insiders read them as a legitimate effort to evaluate new e-books, extreme skeptics read them as poker professionals trading endorsements with each other in an effort to swindle "suckers" of their money; authors read them as feedback that could inform revisions on a text; and website owners read them as nodes of attention that either concentrated—or diverted—literate activity and thus money from their website. Each of these groups registered their uptake through online discussion boards, and each had vastly different stakes in the success of the genre and its characteristics. Genres and the responses to them as they register on web technologies can show us how readers respond differently to similar texts, and to how the shifting roles of authorship amid changing technological conditions work their way into the fabric of a long-established genre. Online book reviews reveal how peer review systems operate that help legitimize born-digital knowledge. They also provide new data for writing inquiry, traces of processes that disclose the tangled work of writing and knowledge production as authors and readers negotiate shifting relationships in digital environments.

REFERENCES

Alexander, J. (2006). *Digital youth: Emerging literacies on the World Wide Web.* Cresskill, NJ: Hampton Press.

Baron, D. E. (2009). *A better pencil: Readers, writers, and the digital revolution.* New York: Oxford University Press.

Bazerman, C. (1988). *Shaping written knowledge: The genre and activity of the experimental article in science.* Madison, WI: University of Wisconsin Press.

Bazerman, C. (2004). Speech acts, genres, and activity systems: How texts organize activity and people. In C. Bazerman & P. Prior (Eds.), *What writing does and how it does it: An introduction to analyzing texts and textual practices* (pp. 309-339). New York: Erlbaum.

Black, R. W. (2008). *Adolescents and online fan fiction.* New York: Peter Lang.

Bradley, J., Fulton, B., Helm, M., & Pittner, K. (2011). Non-traditional book publishing. *First Monday, 16*(8). Retrieved from http://firstmonday.org/htbin/cgiwrap/bin/ojs/index.php/fm/article/view/3353/3030

Brokos, A. (2010). *Book review: Transitioning from NLHE to PLO* [Blog post]. Retrieved from http://www.thinkingpoker.net/poker-book-reviews/transitioning-from-nlhe-to-plo/

Byrnjolfsson, E., Hu, Y., & Smith, M. (2006). From niches to riches: The anatomy of the long tail. *Sloan Management Review, 47*(4), 67-71.

CerO_zz. (2009, August 5). Re: review of small stakes no limit hold'em by Ed Miller, Sunny Mehta, and Matt Flynn [Online forum comment]. Retrieved from http://forumserver.twoplustwo.com/33/books-publications/review-small-stakes-no-limit-hold-em-ed-miller-sunny-mehta-matt-flynn-551065/index2.html

Chevalier, J., & Mayzlin, D. (2006). The effect of word of mouth on sales: Online book reviews. *Journal of Marketing Research. 43*(3), 345-354.

Edirisinghe, I. (2008, March 6). Re: Bobbos Book … ? [Online forum comment]. Retrieved from http://www.leggopoker.com/forums/poker-discussion/bobbos-book-149-page5.html

Haynie, D. (2009, March, 28). *SlowHabit's unreleased PLO book review* [Blog post]. Retrieved from http://www.cardrunners.com/blog/SixPeppers/slow-habits-unreleased-plo-book-review

Hesse, C. (1996) Books in time. In Nunberg, G. (Ed.), *The future of the book* (pp. 21-36). Berkeley, CA: University of California Press.

Irishman07. (2008, December 9). Re: Bobbos book … ? [Online forum comment]. Retrieved from http://www.leggopoker.com/forums/poker-discussion/bobbos-book-149-page26.html

Jenkins, H. (2006). *Convergence culture: Where old and new media collide.* New York: New York University Press.

Johns, A. (1998). *The nature of the book: Print and knowledge in the making.* Chicago: University of Chicago Press.

Laquintano, T. (2010). Sustained authorship: Digital writing, self-publishing, and the e-book. *Written Communication, 27*(4), 469-493.

Mackiewicz, J. (2010). Assertions of expertise in online reviews. *Journal of Business and Technical Communication, 24,* 3-28.

Malmuth, M. (2009, December 14). Re: PLO book for 2500$ (LearnedfromTV's Advanced PLO Theory)?? [Online forum comment]. Retrieved from http://forumserver.twoplustwo.com/33/books-publications/plo-book-2500-learnedfromtvs-advanced-plo-theory-543219/index12.html

Miller, C. R. 1984. Genre as social action. *Quarterly Journal of Speech, 70,* 151-167.

Miller, L. (2009). Selling the Product. In D. P. Nord, J. S. Rubin, & M. Schudson (Eds.), *A history of the book in America: The enduring book: Print culture in postwar America* (pp. 91-106). Chapel Hill, NC: University of North Carolina Press.

Motta-Roth, D. (1998). Discourse analysis and academic book reviews: A study of text and disciplinary cultures. In I. Foranet, S. Posteguillo, J. C Palmer, & J. F. Coll (Eds.), *Genre studies in English for academic purposes* (pp. 29-58). Castello de la plana, Spain: Universitat Jaume.

Newman, C. (2009, January, 16). Review: CTS E-Book "Let There Be Range" [Blog post]. Retrieved from http://www.leggopoker.com/blogs/clayton/review-cts-e-book-let-there-range-2926.html

Porter, J. E. (2009). Recovering delivery for digital rhetoric. *Computers and Composition. 26,* 207-224.

Prior, P. (1998). *Writing disciplinarity: A sociohistoric account of literate activity in the academy.* Mahwah, NJ: Lawrence Erlbaum.

Radway, J. A. (1984). *Reading the romance: Women, patriarchy, and popular literature.* Chapel Hill, NC: University of North Carolina Press.

Roper, D. (1978). *Reviewing before the Edinburgh:1788-1802.* Newark, NJ: University of Delaware Press.

Shirky, C (2008). *Here comes everybody.* New York: The Penguin Press.

Spaceball. (2009, June 19). Re: review of SSNLHE [Online forum comment]. Retrieved from http://forumserver.twoplustwo.com/33/books-publications/review-ssnlhe-510735/index4.html

SirNeb. (2008, March 1). Re: Bobbos book ... ? [Online forum comment]. http://www.leggopoker.com/forums/poker-discussion/bobbos-book-149-page4.html

Squizzel. (2008, December 14). Re: Bobbos book ... ? [Online forum comment]. Retrieved from http://www.leggopoker.com/forums/poker-discussion/bobbos-book-149-page26.html

Strauss, A. L. (1987). *Qualitative analysis for social scientists.* New York: Cambridge University Press.

Townsend, B. (2010, April, 25). *Advanced PLO Theory Volume One* [Blog post]. Retrieved from http://www.cardrunners.com/blog/Brian/advanced-plo-theory-volume-one

CHAPTER 30.
COMING TO GRIPS WITH COMPLEXITY: DYNAMIC SYSTEMS THEORY IN THE RESEARCH OF NEWSWRITING

Daniel Perrin
Institute of Applied Media Studies, Zurich University of Applied Sciences

Systems such as languages are dynamic: they change continually as their elements and contexts interact. In the context of newswriting for example, if journalists invent new words and these words become part of the general vocabulary over time, then language is changed through language use—with impacts upon further language use. DST is a research framework focusing on principles of change.[1]

Depending on the system, change can be discrete, linear and completely predictable, such as when the flow of traffic is controlled by stoplights. In contrast, language change as well as conversations and text production are complex dynamic processes; they are not entirely predictable. Explaining them needs to take into account processes and interrelations from individual to global levels and from short to long-term timeframes. Therefore, DST treats the complexity and dynamics of its object as integrally as possible.

DST originated in biology, mathematics, and physics. Later, it was applied to mental and social processes. Today, DST deals with systems as varied as evolution, weather, business organizations—and language. In their position paper, Beckner, et al., 2009 propose a DST approach to explain how language is acquired and used, and how it changes. Cameron & Deignan (2006), Ellis & Larsen-Freeman (2006), Lantolf (2006), Larsen-Freeman (2006), MacWhinney(2006), and Verspoor, de Bot, & Lowie (2011) focus on emergence in the development, acquisition, and use of language.

As Larsen-Freeman and Cameron (2008, pp. 18-19) argue in the introduction of their book *Complex Systems and Applied Linguistics*, sociocultural, interactionist, systemic, integrationist, and ecological approaches to language (e.g., Halliday, 1973; Harris, 1993; Sealey & Carter, 2004; Vygotski, 1978) overlap with DST in their basic assumption that language use, and mental, linguistic, and societal structures are interconnected. In the chapter about "complex systems in discourse" Larsen-Freeman and Cameron broach the issue of "the dynamics of written discourse" (pp. 185-188) —a reasonable starting point for combining DST and linguistics of newswriting.

In this chapter, I focus on DST's potential for explaining the dynamics and complexity of writing processes in real-world contexts. A newswriting process by an experienced journalist about demonstrations in Lebanon is referred to throughout the chapter, as a case of such real-world writing. The case is selected from the Idée Suisse research project, where newswriting practices were investigated in the context of conflicting media policies and market demands.[2] Drawing on data from the Lebanon case, interactions between micro and macro dynamics of newswriting can be explained within the limited space of this chapter. For example, it can be shown that the apparent detail of changing one single word at the beginning of the writing process means reframing both the process and the resulting text product dramatically. By making an example of this Lebanon case, I outline key concepts of DST from five relevant perspectives.

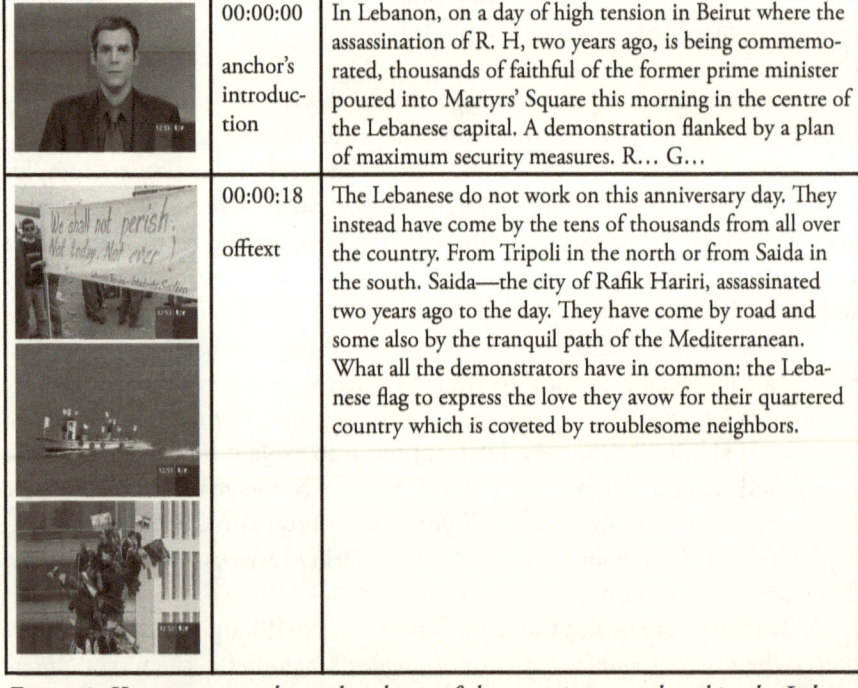

	00:00:00 anchor's introduction	In Lebanon, on a day of high tension in Beirut where the assassination of R. H, two years ago, is being commemorated, thousands of faithful of the former prime minister poured into Martyrs' Square this morning in the centre of the Lebanese capital. A demonstration flanked by a plan of maximum security measures. R... G...
	00:00:18 offtext	The Lebanese do not work on this anniversary day. They instead have come by the tens of thousands from all over the country. From Tripoli in the north or from Saida in the south. Saida—the city of Rafik Hariri, assassinated two years ago to the day. They have come by road and some also by the tranquil path of the Mediterranean. What all the demonstrators have in common: the Lebanese flag to express the love they avow for their quartered country which is coveted by troublesome neighbors.

Figure 1. Key pictures and translated text of the news item produced in the Lebanon case. The context: In Lebanon, ethnic and religious diversity as well as expansion plans of neighboring countries are threats to national unity. In 2005 the

Investigating text production processes as dynamic systems means reconstructing their structure and dynamics, that is, their elements and relations (part 1) as well as their processes, their stability and change (part 2). Beyond explaining what systems actually consist of and do, DST then evaluates dynamic alternatives: what a system, at any state, could do and why (part 3). Finally, explanation is needed on how the dynamic system maintains its identity despite change (part 4). Such research produces outcomes mapping micro-development and macro perspectives: for example situated knowledge about emergence in collaborative text production, or empirically-grounded models of writing phases (part 5).

STRUCTURES: ZOOMING THROUGH LEVELS AND TIMESCALES

One of the key questions for DST is what a dynamic system consists of at a given point in time. When DST focuses on structure, it describes the *elements*

	00:00:47 quote man	We are here for Rafik Hariri and all the martyrs. And to truly say: I protest against Syria.
	00:00:57 quote woman	We want culture, education, public transportation, not arms. We wish to learn, make progress, and live a normal life like everyone else.
	00:01:07 offtext	The demonstration is orchestrated by the anti-Syrian majority, currently in power but whose legitimacy is contested by the opposition forces, led by the Shiites of Hezbollah. Where the fear of new violence today, is again resounding in people's heads so much, the two explosions that went off yesterday morning on the Christian mountain very close by. Two unattributed attacks but double the warning to the Lebanese army, the only guarantee of the country's unity at the moment.

Figure 1, continued. … Lebanese Prime Minister, Rafic Hariri, was killed in a bomb attack. While European media often report on politically motivated violence in Lebanon, this item foregrounds peaceful demonstrations on the second anniversary of Hariri's assassination.

and *relations* of the system under investigation, its nested *levels* and *timescales*, the *openness* for interaction with other systems, and the *context*.

In DST, a written text can be seen as the frozen state of the dynamic system of newswriting. Different kinds of semiotic elements, such as letters, words, sentences, paragraphs, and pictures, are interrelated in a way that the news item can evoke complex mental representations in the dynamic system of reading or listening to and understanding news. In the Lebanon case, the journalist R. G. produced the following text about demonstrations in Saida (Figure 1). It was broadcast on the 14th of February 2007, in the French news program *Journal* of the Swiss public broadcaster SRG SSR. Just like the written text or a writing process, every system consists of interacting *elements* and *relations* producing a certain overall behavior at a given time. In a DST view, elements can be dynamic systems themselves. A newsroom, for example, can then be seen as a dynamic system consisting of other dynamic systems such as individuals, peer groups, organizations, roles, rules, expectations, tasks, products, processes, money, time allocations, and so on. This dynamic system is embedded in contexts such as audience, sources, public sphere, and competitors in media markets. In a TV newsroom, this interplay results in overall activities such as broadcasting at airtimes and conferencing, newsgathering, and newswriting in between (Figure 2).

However, behavior in such a system happens on various nested and interconnected levels and timescales: from the milliseconds of neural processing to the minutes of newswriting, hours of daily production cycles, years of organizational restructuring, decades of professional careers, centuries of language

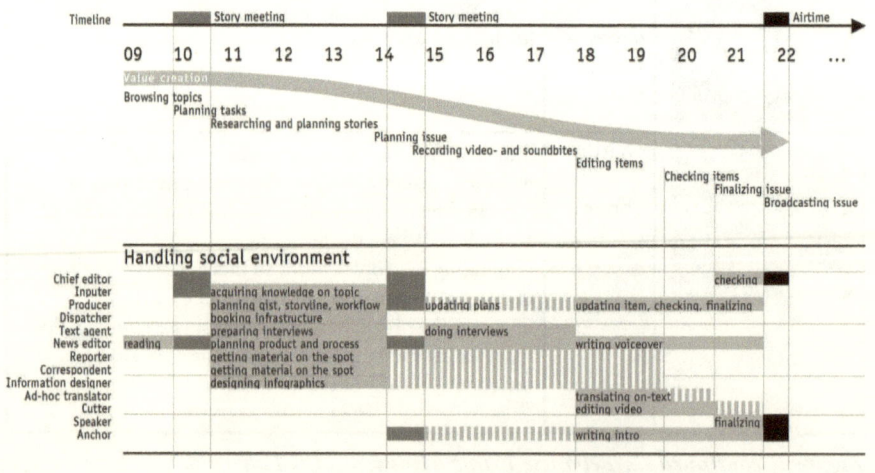

Figure 2. Roles, tasks, and time allocations as key elements of the workflow structure in a newsroom

change, and eons of evolution. On some levels such as newswriting or daily production cycles, the agents are mostly aware of their activity, on others, the system behaves beyond the agents' awareness.

Open systems allow and need particular in- and output to maintain their stability: Resources such as source texts enter the dynamic system of newswriting from outside, products such as news items leave it. The dynamic system of writing a single news item ends when the deadline is reached or the item is submitted to be broadcast.

Ignoring the deadline when writing a single news item could affect the *context* of this system, namely the overall system that produces news continuously. Conversely, the unpleasant experience of lack of content at airtimes could trigger a stricter management of deadlines and thus change the contextual constraints for the next newswriting processes. Thus, dynamic system and contexts are mutually and inseparably connected. A dynamic system can initiate changes in its contexts and it can also adapt to changes in its contexts. This is why DST treats context as a part of the complexity and dynamics of a system under investigation.

DYNAMICS: TRACKING CHANGE IN CONTEXT

What happens with the dynamic system over time? When DST focuses on dynamics instead of structure, it describes how systems *change*, why this often takes place in a *non-linear* way, and how *stability* and *variability* of the system are balanced as *stability in motion*. Change in the system of writing a single news item for example can take the system from smooth writing-down phases (Figure 3, phases A and B) to jumpy phases where the emerging text is restructured (D and E).

In a DST view, systems are always open to *change*. Elements, relations, and contexts change in their specific timescales as they interact. In this multilevel flow of change, the future states of a dynamic system continuously depend on the respective present states. In the dynamic system of collaborative newswriting, even highly routinized and standardized procedures such as writing a newsflash or embedding a quote are adapted to context each time they are performed. Moreover, revising a peer's text under time pressure can end in rewriting the item and offhand comments about the peer's writing style; the comments can initiate changes in procedures and policies—which in turn will affect future collaboration in newswriting. Returning to the Lebanon case, a linear flow of words into stretches of language on the screen can suddenly be interrupted, for example in order to delete and replace a previously written word (Figure 4).

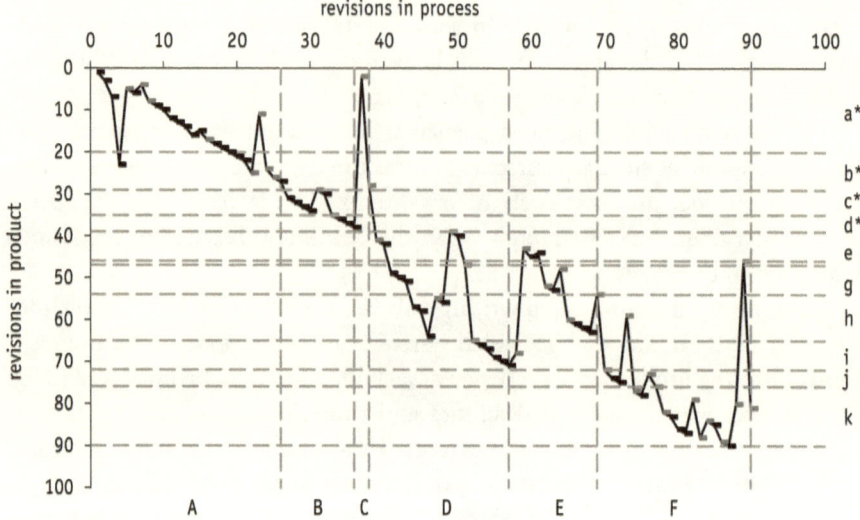

Figure 3. Progression graph of the Lebanon writing process. Progression graphs indicate how the writer moved the cursor through the developing text. These cursor movements are interpreted as the writer's shifts in focus. The temporal sequence of revisions in the writing process is represented on the ordinal scale of the x-axis; the spatial sequence of revisions in the text product shows on the y-axis, also ordinal. For further discussions of progression graphs in particular and progression analysis in general see Perrin (2003, 2006) or Perrin & Ehrensberger-Dow (2008).

Such complex changes are not random, but neither are they completely predictable. New system properties may emerge when a dynamic system adapts to context. As these new properties can change the way a dynamic system behaves, they also can alter the way the system changes. Therefore, change can be *non-linear:* sudden, radical, dramatic, turbulent, and chaotic instead of smooth, continuous, and steady. New words on the screen can trigger new ideas in the mind of the writer and thus set a story off in an unpredictable direction.

Another example of the unpredictability of complex processes: in the Idée Suisse research project that the Lebanon case was part of, coping with overbooked cutting rooms proved to be an important success factor on the logistic level of newswriting. However, from a DST view, this does not mean that providing additional cutting rooms would augment wellbeing, efficiency or text quality. If a newsroom were a simple system, behaving linearly, then adding more workplaces for cutters would proportionally shorten the waiting line of journalists wanting to cut their videos. In a non-linear DST scenario, however, easier access to video workplaces can discourage planning and eventually extend the wait. In an alternative non-linear scenario, easier access motivates experimentation; new, more effective strategies of cutting might emerge, the cutting time per news item would decrease, and many of the new workplaces would remain under-utilized.

The emergence of new strategies in the non-linear scenarios can start by varying the cutting procedures or lexical choices and end in different fundamental changes in the overall behavior of the dynamic system. *Variability* being the seed of change, capturing local variation around stabilized ways of activity is crucial for DST. In contrast to top-down research, DST thus considers variability as data, not as noise. Smoothing away seemingly senseless details and variability, for instance by statistical averaging, would mean losing crucial information for detecting emergence and explaining change. Thus, the lexical change in the example above from "voie express" to "voie tranquille" could be crucial and deserves attention, as discussed below.

EVALUATION: IDENTIFYING THE CONTROL PARAMETERS OF CHANGE

Of all the various possibilities, what does a dynamic system do at a particular moment in time? When DST focuses on evaluation, it outlines the *state space* as the landscape of the potential *trajectories* the dynamic system under investigation could follow on its way from *state* to *state* through *shifts*. *Attractors* in this state space stabilize the system, and *control parameters* determine its trajectory.

---

^{19}{Ils sont venus p}$^{19}|_{20}$ar la route et même pour certains par la voie ^{20}[express]$^{20}|_{21}$^{21}{tranquille}^{21} de la Médit^4[e|$_4$]^{4}érannée … |$_5$

^{19}{They have come b}$^{19}|_{20}$y the road and some even by the path ^{20}[express]$^{20}|_{21}$^{21}{tranquil}^{21} of the Medit^4[e|$_4$]^{4}erranean … |$_5$

Figure 4. Excerpt and translation of S-notation, showing deletions in n[square brackets]n and insertions in n{ curly braces }n. Wherever the writing is interrupted to delete or add something, S-notation inserts the break-character |n. The subscript and superscript numbers indicate the order of the steps: Right after having inserted "Ils sont venus," the author jumps forward to delete "express" and insert "tranquille." For further discussions of S-notation see Kollberg & Severinson-Eklundh (2002) and Severinson-Eklundh & Kollberg (2003).

The overall behavior of a system at a given time is called a *state*. A *shift* is the dramatic change between very different states of a system. At a particular moment, a system is in a particular state, performing a particular pattern of behavior. The synopsis of all possible states of the system is its *state space*. In the example of the newsroom, the state space includes three typical states: conferencing, newswriting, and broadcasting. The simplified system of the newsroom shifts cyclically from one state to the next on its *trajectory* through the state space. A very different state shift can be observed in the Lebanon case: After R. G. had written the first two paragraphs and translated the selected quotes himself from a written English translation received from the news service, the computer crashed. The translations were not saved, so R. G. had to do them again before writing the last three paragraphs. This crash and other computer problems increased the time pressure, in particular for the cutter who, as R. G. says, then had to rely on R. G. for the story instead of asking critical questions.

The more finely graded an analysis of a dynamic system is, the greater the number of states in the state space. In the newsroom, the state of *newswriting* then might expand to three states: *defining the task, writing the text,* and *implementing the product.* The state of *writing the text* can further expand to *setting the goal, planning the text, controlling the writing flow,* and *revising the text.* No matter how fine the gradation, change will happen smoothly within the preferred states and dramatically in the shifts between them.

The states into which a dynamic system preferably moves are called *attractors.* The simplified system of the newsroom moves cyclically among the three attractors *conferencing, newswriting,* and *broadcasting.* Such attractors are called *cyclic attractors.* In addition to this type, there are two others. The *fixed point attractor* is where a dynamic system prefers to settle down. In a dynamic system of writing a single news item, a fixed point attractor is reached when the final version of the text is ready for publication. On a more general level, reaching expertise is a fixed point attractor in the dynamic system of a professional's trajectory. In the Lebanon case, the journalist R. G. can be considered close to this attractor:

> R. G. (born 1959) was awarded a degree in modern languages, took a six-month trip around the world to "20 or 30 countries" in between, wrote four suitcases full of travel diaries that he still reads, and produced short films ("three to four minutes long") for a TV travel show ("*Trip around the World*").[3] He completed a two-year program in journalism and was a journalist at Radio Suisse Romande, the French-speaking public service radio station in Switzerland, for 20

years. In the first 10 years, he worked on the local desk and
after that in foreign affairs, which involved a lot of travel.[4]
On the side, he helped set up an agency for which he produced foreign television reportages. R. G. still travels a lot; in
the previous year for instance, he was in Lebanon.

In contrast to the fixed point attractor, the *strange attractor* is where a system shows high responsiveness and unstable behavior; a minute change in input can produce a dramatic change in behavior. Looking for good pictures among masses of uninteresting ones is such a strange attractor in the trajectory of the dynamic system of newswriting: the system remains in this highly unstable, critical state until the pictures are found and the system moves on:

Three hours before airtime, the journalist R. G. received the
assignment to prepare an item about demonstrations in Lebanon. Since R. G. knows his way around Lebanon and had
been there recently, he said he felt familiar with the topic. He
read an ample amount of text too and received lots of visual
material—two hours of images from Lebanese TV, mostly
crowds of people with placards. In addition he obtained
video recordings of two interviews with demonstrators. Although he found two passages in them with relevant quotes,
he said he found it an effort to make the material vibrant.

An attractor thus draws the dynamic system like a magnet. It is easy for the system to move into a strong attractor, but once it is there, a push is needed to overcome stability and send the system out again. In the newsroom example, it takes such a push to get people ready for the newsroom conference in time. Towards the end of the conference, it can be hard to finish on time and then start researching. The same goes for the transitions between activities of text production: once in research mode, writers might find it hard to stop gathering information and start writing. In text production mode, some feel more attracted to revising the text they have written so far than to composing new text. Finally, close to the deadline, they might have problems to stop revising and post their items for publication. In the Lebanon case, reproducing the well-known stories of violence was such a strong attractor the journalist had to overcome:

R. G. limited himself to the main topic, "a photograph"
of the demonstrations starting on the martyrs' square.[5] He
consciously abstained from biographical background infor-

mation and spectacular pictures of the assassination of the former prime minister of Lebanon that the demonstrators were commemorating, since the assassination had already been shown many times. Moreover he decided not to start with pictures of the demonstration itself. Instead, he first showed the people arriving in masses to demonstrate.

The pushes to overcome attractors come from *drivers* in the dynamic system. The drivers help the system move around the state space, avoid certain attractors, meet others, and leave them again. Motivation is an example of such a driver, helping a dynamic system of reflexive newswriting to switch between the attractors of routinized activity and purposeful learning. This means alternating between newswriting routines and breaking out of these routines, trying out new procedures, and enhancing repertoires of writing strategies and techniques. As the drivers control the trajectory of the dynamic system in its state space, they are also called *control parameters*. Knowing what they are facilitates interventions to the system, for instance in coaching sessions. In the Lebanon case, the journalist's experience and, at the same time, his openness to the unexpected worked as drivers:

In an early, linear phase in the writing process [revisions 1-25, see Figure 3], R. G. wrote the voice-over for the introductory scene. The scene shows how people traveled en masse to the demonstration in boats. Finding these boats in the video material surprised him, he says.[6] In his very first sentence, R. G. refers to another fact new to him: as he just learns from the news service, the Lebanese had that day off. So the beginning of the product was shaped by details that were new to the experienced journalist.

After a closer look at the pictures that were new to him, he then adjusted a word that turned out to be a key word for the whole writing process. R. G. had first talked about an expressway to describe the direct route over the Mediterranean Sea ("la voie express de la méditerrannée"). While interweaving the text with the images he realized that a tranquil path ("la voie tranquille") would better fit the slow journey of a boat. So he deleted "express" and inserted "tranquille" instead [see Figure 4]. With this revision, cued by new details and R. G.'s language awareness, the design of the item emerged: R.

G. started combining strong symbols.

IDENTITY: EXPLAINING EMERGENCE AND STABILITY IN MOTION

Despite change, a dynamic system must maintain its identity; otherwise, there would be no reason to conceptualize it as an entity in space and time.[7] How does the dynamic system persist in the face of change? When DST focuses on identity, it explains *stability in motion, cycles of emergence* in the light of *co-adaptation* and *self-similarity.*

As change never stops, any perceived stability of a dynamic system is *stability in motion,* an equilibrium in continuous adaptation and change—for a certain period, between more dramatic phases of change. Larsen-Freeman & Cameron (2008) illustrate this concept of dynamic stability with the "constant adjustments [that] are required to overcome the force of gravity in order for us to stand erect on two feet" (p. 87) and with swimming: "without the extra input of energy produced by waggling hands or feet, floating would cease. ... the movements of the swimmer are adaptations made in response to the environment—to the need to prevent sinking" (p. 33).

Changes on one level of a dynamic system can lead to categorically new, *emergent* properties on a higher level. Such emergence happens, for example, if revising and criticizing single news reports triggers changes in style policies or if missed deadlines stimulate a media organization to optimize its workflows. The emergent new properties on the higher level of the dynamic system then affect activity on lower levels, for instance stylistic choice or process planning in newswriting. Whereas activities such as qualified criticism or missing deadlines can be identified ex-post as some of the reasons for the emergence, it is hardly predictable which specific activity will cause a shift in state. Thus, emergence produces a new whole which is not reducible to and not explainable by the sum of its parts. Holland (1998, p. 2), describes this phenomenon as "much coming from little." In the Lebanon case, deciding on the formulation of "voie tranquille" provides the journalist with the idea of using strong symbols as leitmotifs.

> With "tranquille" R. G. found the leitmotif of his item. He says that he loves the adjective because it corresponds not only to the image of the boats but also to the tranquility of the demonstration. He expects the "tranquil" to resonate in the minds of the audience.[8] Just as consciously, he talks about

using the term *drapeau libanais* (Lebanese flag) as a symbol of the demonstrators' desire for political independence. The same is true for the term résonnent (resonate): explosions from Syrian terror attacks had not simply happened the previous day, they were reverberating in the minds of the demonstrators.

It is through *cycles* of such emergence that a dynamic system evolves—and may change fundamentally on particular levels over time. In newswriting, new procedures, skills, policies, workflows, and technologies emerge. However, the system maintains its overall identity as long as salient properties change in line with contextual changes. Newswriting is, after centuries of change, still bound to investigation, facts, relevance, recency, and broad impact in a context of public discourse which has also changed in similar ways to newswriting itself. In the Lebanon case, this means mapping traditional expectations of Swiss media politics with new media market demands:

> R. G. overcame the critical situation of using brash stereotypes when under time pressure. Instead of catering to the market and resorting to predictable images that could overshadow publicly relevant developments, he absorbed his source material, listened to what was being said, and discerned what was important in the pictures. By doing so, he was able to discover a gentle access to the topic that allowed him to produce a coherent and fresh story and at the same time managed to reflect the political finesse required by his employer's remit of promoting public understanding.

Changing in line with contexts means changing in mutual response, in *co-adaptation* and, in the long term, *co-evolution*. Elements and relations of a dynamic system perpetually interact with each other, within and beyond the system. Thus, emergence on one particular level of a dynamic system motivates change throughout the system, the connected systems and the context—and feeds back to that level as the co-adapted context fuels future activity. That is what happens if faster technology accelerates newswriting and enables tighter deadlines, which call for even faster technology. The behavior of a dynamic system changes, but since the context likewise changes, the system maintains its identity—dynamically.

Self-similarity is another characteristic of dynamic identity. A textual, static realization of self-similarity is the leitmotif, where some simple concepts represent the gist of an entire text. DST, however, focuses on dynammic self-similarity. It considers change in dynamic systems self-similar on several levels and timescales. A very general pattern is that throughout a dynamic system most changes are minor, whereas major changes are seldom. Specific patterns are formulated in power laws such as Zipf's law, which says that, in a reasonably large corpus of language data, the most frequent word occurs twice as often as the second in the frequency rank, three times as often as the third, and so on (Zipf, 1949). The linguist George K. Zipf found this pattern of word frequency in English, Latin, and Chinese. Moreover, the distribution has remained stable throughout centuries of language change. Zipf summarized that the recurrence of the pattern meant "finding for the acts of speech what physicists have long since found for the acts of inanimate nature: behind all the apparent diversity and complexity of the phenomena lies the sameness of fundamental dynamic principle." (Zipf, 1949, p. 126). It can be assumed that Zipf's law "holds in all languages where it has been tested" (Ferrer i Cancho, 2006, 131).

Clauset, Shalizi, and Newman, (2009) scrutinized and re-analyzed 24 sets of real-world data from studies whose authors assumed that the data structure followed power laws similar to Zipf's law. Clauset et al. found that most of the data sets followed power laws or similar regularities. Examples are "The frequency of occurrence of unique words in the novel Moby Dick" (best fit in the sample), "The number of citations received between publication and June 1997 by scientific papers published in 1981 and listed in the Science Citation Index," and "Sizes of e-mail address books of computer users at a large university" (p. 677). Thus, there are good reasons to search for similar scalable patterns in writing processes in general and newswriting in particular.

In the Lebanon case, the emergent solution makes a case for solutions to similar problems on more general levels. On an institutional level, emergent solutions are needed by R. G.'s employer, the Swiss public service provider SRG SSR, which has to find its way out of increasingly intense conflicts between the traditional public mandate and the pressure of media markets. On a societal level, emergent solutions are urgently needed by journalism in the face of media convergence.

Public service broadcasting companies are among the most important broadcasting companies in Europe. In Switzerland, the public broadcaster, SRG SSR, also has the highest ratings. As a public service institution, SRG SSR has a federal, societal, cultural, and linguistic mandate to fulfil: to promote social integration by promoting public understanding. "In their programs SRG SSR promotes understanding, coherence, and exchange among the parts of the country, linguistic communities, cultures, religions, and social groups …" (Translation of the programming mandate 2007, article 2, paragraph 2).

As a media enterprise, though, SRG SSR is subject to market and competitive forces. Losing audience would mean losing public importance. Therefore, the mandate presupposes that reaching the public will promote public understanding. In the research project in which the Lebanon case was analyzed, the researchers investigated how those working for the broadcaster deal with the following tasks a) fulfilling their public duty by providing programs and items that contribute to the public debate and promote public understanding, while also b) actually reaching the public in an increasingly competitive media market, and finally c) dealing with growing economic pressure and increasingly faster technological change.

The overall findings show that the knowledge of how to bridge the public mandate and market forces cannot be identified in executive suites, but in newsrooms. Whereas the managers usually are frustrated by the expectations of media politics, some experienced journalists find solutions to overcome the conflict between the public mandate and the market. These solutions tend to emerge when the journalists tackle complex and unexpected problems in critical situations within their daily routines, as R. G. did.

The following conclusions could be drawn from these findings: The conditions for emergent solutions in news teams need to be systematically improved top-down by media politics and media management, and the tacit knowledge involved must be systematically identified bottom-up at the workplaces and then made available to the whole organisation. Based on these recommendations, the stakeholders working in media policy, media management, media practice, and media research have set up follow-up activities for knowledge transformation, such as systematic organisational development, consulting, coaching, and training.

OUTCOMES: CONCEPTUALIZING AND MODELING COMPLEX DYNAMICS

Doing research in the framework of DST means exploring behavior within and across very different levels and timescales. As DST considers everything to be connected with everything else, decontexualizing and atemporalizing single phenomena is out of the question. Instead, DST research foregrounds certain aspects, such as the role of emergence in individual writing processes, and investigates them in more detail while remaining open to contextual behavior that might explain change. This calls for multi-method approaches combining in-depth case studies and large corpora as well as analysis and modeling.

Case studies can reveal where, when, how, and why change happens on the micro level of situated activity. As the Lebanon case has shown, a new pattern of process management or product design can emerge in the critical situation of newswriting when a journalist tries to juggle conflicting expectations. If the new pattern succeeds, it might become part of that journalist's repertoire. Understanding such micro processes means shifting from a static view of newswriting (see Section 1, above) to the dynamic perspective of DST (Section 2). An evaluation perspective (Section 3) identifies control parameters of micro change. Finally, an identity perspective (Section 4) allows us to see the micro development as representing a principle that also underlies changes on higher levels and larger timescales.

Thelen and Corbetta (2002) describe the study of micro development as "the study of the processes of change, not only the endpoints." (p. 59). "The goal of microdevelopmental studies is to understand change itself: what are the mechanisms by which people forgo old ways of behaving and adapt new ones" (Thelen & Corbetta, 2002, p. 60). Micro developments are "the motors of change" (Thelen & Corbetta, 2002, p. 59). Because of the self-similarity of dynamic systems, it can be assumed that "the processes that cause change in a matter of minutes or hours are the same as those working over months or years. In other words, the general principles underlying behavioral change work at multiple time scales"(Thelen & Corbetta, 2002, p. 60).

Tracing such micro development as the motor of change needs *dense corpora* with rich procedural data over short periods of time: the activities of collaborative writing and conferencing in the newsroom have to be captured as broadly and in as much detail as possible. In contrast, tracing change on macro levels and timescales of the newsroom, journalism, or even society in general needs *large corpora*. The samples have to be wide enough to allow for generalization; the sampling intervals close enough to infer variability and shifts in state; and the data collection prolonged enough to grasp long-term change. Combining dense and large corpora enables researchers to situate micro development within the context of macro development.

In the research project the Lebanon case study is part of, newswriting was conceptualized as balancing practices in a complex context of conflicting expectations. Newswriting, then, was metaphorically modeled as a helix of 16 interacting fields of situated activity (Figure 5).

The dynamic system of situated text production can be described in terms of fields of relevant activity (Figure 5). It begins when writers understand and accept a production task *(defining the task)* and ends when they send the results of their work along the production chain, such as to colleagues who assemble news programs from individual items *(implementing the product)*. In between, reading processes *(source reading* and *product reading)* interact with writing processes on various time frames and scales (from *grapheme* to *text* version levels). In the

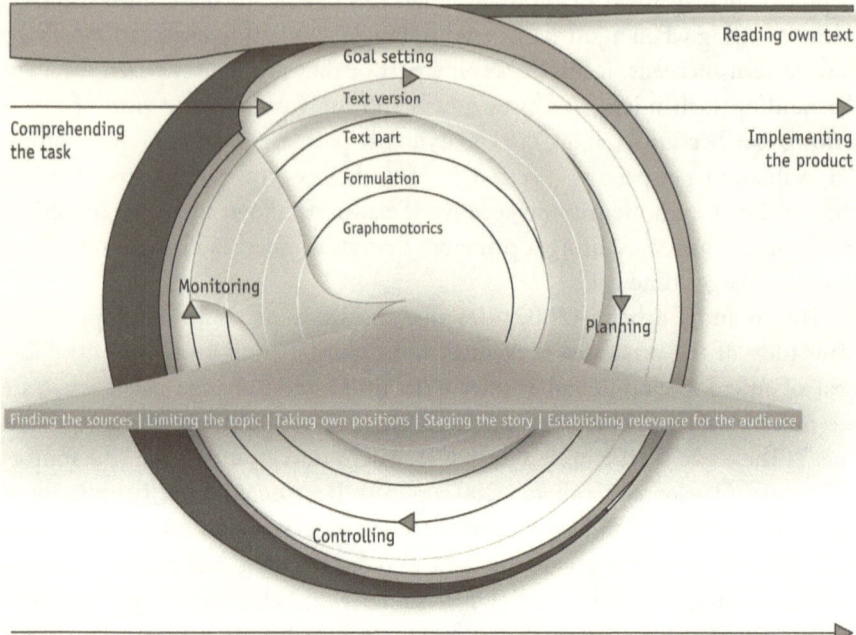

Figure 5. The dynamic system of situated text production

inner circle of the writing process, four phases recur and overlap, each dominated by activities which contribute, on their specific levels, to the incremental production of the text. *Goal setting* typically focuses on the text as a whole, planning on sequences of text parts such as paragraphs, and *controlling* on the formulations under construction. *Monitoring*, in contrast, traces the results of the production process throughout all of the levels.

However, DST can be more than a useful metaphor in scientific approaches to writing processes. Research can also proceed heuristically, starting with assumptions instead of data. In this case, the processes of change in a dynamic system are reconstructed through dynamic models: simulations and analogies which are tested against reality for best fit. The outcome of a computer simulation is compared with observations of the real-world system under investigation. Relations are redesigned and parameters adjusted until the model behaves like the observed reality. The dynamic model simulates change through iteration of algorithms: rules are applied in loops where the output of one loop is the input for the next. Thus, the mechanisms of change in the model are exactly known and can be taken as metaphors for the principles of change in the real world system.

Based on data of hundreds of cases similar to the Lebanon case, models of writing phases have been extracted and are being tested. In Modeling Writing Phases, an interdisciplinary research project subsequent to Idée Suisse,[9] writing phases will be modeled as time periods with predominant activities. These phases are identifiable in the data throughout scales and time frames by more or less homogeneous (predictable) time series dynamics between critical states (with rather unpredictable ends). First findings show, for example, that the two dominant progression types of the Lebanon case, linear writing (Phase A in Figure 3, above) and chiseling (Phase E) support a prediction of successful text production in terms of coherence, whereas chaotic jumping back and forth as dominant phase would allow for predictions of coherence gaps.

Thus, changing one single word, depending on the context, can take the dynamic system of writing to strong symbols and leitmotifs—or to weak cohesion and coherence. It's a tricky, a complex matter, and that's what makes writing research and DST a promising couple.

NOTES

1. As the purpose of writing research is to explain processes and thus dynamics, I prefer the term Dynamic Systems Theory (DST) to other widespread terms which focus on other key properties of such systems, such as complexity, nonlinearity or adaptivity.

2. The research project Idée Suisse: Language Policy, Norms, and Practice as Exemplified by Swiss Radio and Television was funded from 2005 to 2007 with EUR 120,000 by the Swiss National Science Foundation. It is part of the National Research Program 56, Language Diversity and Linguistic Competence in Switzerland, 2005-2010. Outlines and reports of the program and its projects (in German, French, and Italian) can be found on http://www.nfp56.ch. For a discussion of the project see, e.g., Perrin (2011) and Perrin (2012).

3. tsr_tj_070212_1220_guillet_frame, lines 16-18: "c'était déjà pour la télévision, pour une émission qui s'appelait la course autour du monde, c'était pendant mes études de lettres"

4. tsr_tj_070212_1220_guillet_frame, lines 36-39: "et après dix ans à la rubrique internationale où j'ai fait passablement de voyages, de reportages à l'étranger, pendant dix ans ça fait pas mal de séjours et reportages à l'étranger"

5. tsr_tj_070214_1230_guillet_libanon_review, lines 946-954: "moi je fais une photographie de ce qui se passe pendant la matinée, puisque ce premier sujet passe à douze heures quarante cinq. au liban cette manifestation, elle draine une foule immense, comme on le voit sur les images, et je dois montrer que cette foule répond à un certain

nombre d'aspirations, et je dois donner les clés pour la personne qui n'y connaît pas grand chose"

6. tsr_tj_070214_1230_guillet_libanon_review, lines 985-987: "je fais attention vraiment aux images, par exemple je ne m'attendais pas à voir ces bateaux, ça je savais que j'allais le mettre"

7. tsr_tj_070214_1230_guillet_libanon_verbal, lines 180-185: "j'aime bien cet adjectif parce que pour l'instant, les mots ils résonnent dans la tête des gens, tranquille c'est pour l'instant le point de cette manifestation, elle est plutôt bon enfant pour l'instant, parce qu'il n'y a pas eu de heurts, donc je mets la voie tranquille"

8. tsr_tj_070214_1230_guillet_libanon_review, lines 1019-1024: "mais dans toutes les images que j'ai vues pour l'instant, c'est une manifestation qui ne dégénère pas, donc si je peux saupoudrer le texte de mots qui résonnent justes par rapport à ce qui a l'air de se passer sur place, je les garde"

9. The Modeling Writing Phases project, funded from 2011 to 2013 by the Swiss National Science Foundation, is to statistically model and explain writing phases as temporal procedural units. The project attempts to overcome limitations of traditional writing phase concepts that are based on introspection or single case studies. On the methodological level of the project, DST-informed statistical techniques beyond those normally associated with corpus linguistics are developed. For a discussion of initial results see Perrin & Wildi (2010) and Perrin, Fürer, Gantenbein, Sick, and Wildi (2011).

REFERENCES

Beckner, C., Blythe, R., Bybee, J., Christiansen, M. H., Croft, W., Ellis, N. C. et al. (2009). Language is a complex adaptive system. Position paper. *Language Learning, 59*(1), 1–26.

Cameron, L., & Deignan, A. (2006). The emergence of metaphor in discourse. *Applied Linguistics, 27*(4), 671–690.

Clauset, A., Shalizi, C. R. , & Newman, M. E. (2009). Power-law distributions in empirical data. *SIAM Review, 51*(4), 661–703.

Ellis, N. C., & Larsen-Freeman, D. (2006). Language emergence. Implications for applied linguistics. Introduction to the special issue. *Applied Linguistics, 27*(4), 558–589.

Ferrer i Cancho, R. (2006). On the universality of Zipf's law for word frequencies. In P. Grzybek & R. Köhler (Eds.), *Exact methods in the study of language and text. In honor of Gabriel Altmann* (pp. 131–140). Berlin: De Gruyter.

Halliday, M. A. K. (1973). *Explorations in the functions of language.* New York: Elsevier.

Harris, R. A. (1993). *The linguistic wars.* New York: Oxford University Press.

Holland, J. H. (1998). *Emergence. From chaos to order.* Redwood City, CA: Addison-Wesley.

Kollberg, P., & Severinson-Eklundh, K. (2002). Studying writers' revising patterns with S-notation analysis. In C. M. Levy & T. Olive (Eds.), *Contemporary tools and techniques for studying writing* (pp. 89–104). Dordrecht, Netherlands: Kluwer.

Lantolf, J. P. (2006). Language emergence. Implications for applied linguistics. A sociocultural perspective. *Applied Linguistics, 27*(4), 717–728.

Larsen-Freeman, D. (2006). The emergence of complexity, fluency, and accuracy in the oral and written production of five chinese learners of English. *Applied Linguistics, 27*(4), 590–619.

Larsen-Freeman, D., & Cameron, L. (2008). *Complex systems and applied linguistics* (2nd ed.). Oxford, UK: Oxford University Press.

MacWhinney, B. (2006). Emergentism. Use often and with care. *Applied Linguistics, 27*(4), 729–740.

Perrin, D. (2003). Progression analysis (PA). Investigating writing strategies at the workplace. *Journal of Pragmatics, 35*(6), 907–921.

Perrin, D. (2006). Progression analysis. An ethnographic, computer-based multi-method approach to investigate natural writing processes. In L. Van Waes, M. Leijten & C. Neuwirth (Eds.), *Writing and digital media* (pp. 175–181). Amsterdam: Elsevier.

Perrin, D. (2011). "There are two different stories to tell": Collaborative text-picture production strategies of TV journalists. *Journal of Pragmatics, 43*(7), 1865–1875.

Perrin, D. (2012). *The linguistics of newswriting.* Amsterdam: John Benjamins.

Perrin, D., & Ehrensberger-Dow, M. (2008). Progression analysis. Tracing journalistic language awareness. In M. Burger (Ed.), *L' analyse linguistique des discours des médias: Théories, méthodes en enjeux. Entre sciences du langage et sciences de la communication et des médias* (pp. 155–182). Québec: Nota Bene.

Perrin, D., Fürer, M., Gantenbein, T., Sick, B., & Wildi, M. (2011 in press). *From walking to jumping. Statistical modeling of writing processes.*

Perrin, D., & Wildi, M. (2010). Statistical modeling of writing processes. In C. Bazerman (Ed.), *Traditions of writing research* (pp. 378–393). New York: Routledge.

Sealey, A., & Carter, B. (2004). *Applied linguistics as social science.* London: Continuum.

Severinson-Eklundh, K., & Kollberg, P. (2003). Emerging discourse structure: Computer-assisted episode analysis as a window to global revision in university students' writing. *Journal of Pragmatics, 35*(6), 869–891.

Thelen, E., & Corbetta, D. (2002). Microdevelopment and dynamic systems. Applications to infant motor development. In N. Granott & J. Parziale (Eds.), *Microdevelopment. Transition processes in development and learning* (pp. 59–79). Cambridge, UK: Cambridge University Press.

Verspoor, M. H., de Bot, K., & Lowie, W. (2011). *A dynamic approach to second language acquisition.* Amsterdam: Benjamins.

Vygotski, L. S. (1978). *Mind in society. The developments of higher psychological processes.* Cambridge, MA: Harvard University Press.

Zipf, G. K. (1949). *Human behavior and the principle of least effort. An introduction to human ecology.* New York: Hafner.

www.ingramcontent.com/pod-product-compliance
Lightning Source LLC
Chambersburg PA
CBHW030102010526
44116CB00005B/60